D0999962

Poetry and Its Conventions

Poetry

and Its Conventions:
An Anthology
Examining
Poetic Forms and
Themes

Edited by

Frederick R. Lapides
and

John T. Shawcross

The Free Press
New York

The Free Press
A Division of The Macmillan Company
866 Third Avenue, New York, New York 10022

Collier-Macmillan Canada Ltd., Toronto, Ontario

Library of Congress Catalog Card Number: 77–143517

printing number
   2 3 4 5 6 7 8 9 10

Acknowledgments

Permission to reprint from the works of the authors and translators listed below has been given as indicated:

Acconci, Vito Hannibal. "Re" is reprinted from *The Young American Poets* (© 1968) by permission of Follett Publishing Corporation.

Auden, W. H. "In Memory of W. B. Yeats" and "The Unknown Citizen" are reprinted from *Collected Shorter Poems 1927–1957* (copyright 1940, renewed 1968 by W. H. Auden) by permission of Random House, Inc., and Faber and Faber Ltd.

Bacon, Leonard. "Richard Tolman's Universe" is reprinted from *Rhyme and Punishment* (copyright 1936 by Leonard Bacon, renewed 1964 by Martha S. Bacon) by permission of Holt, Rinehart and Winston, Inc.

Barker, George. "Secular Elegies III," "To Any Member of My Generation," and "To My Mother" are reprinted from *Collected Poems 1930 to 1965* (© 1957, 1962, and 1965 by George Granville Barker) by permission of October House, Inc., and Faber and Faber Ltd.

Bell, William. "To a Lady on her Marriage" is reprinted from *Mountains Beneath the Horizon* by permission of Faber and Faber Ltd.

Benet, Stephen Vincent. "Metropolitan Nightmare" is reprinted from *The Selected Works of Stephen Vincent Benet*, published by Holt, Rinehart and Winston, Inc. (copyright 1933 by Stephen Vincent Benet, renewed 1961 by Rosemary Carr Benet) by permission of Brandt and Brandt.

Berryman, John. "Canto Amor" is reprinted from *The Dispossessed* (copyright 1948 by John Berryman) by permission of Farrar, Straus & Giroux, Inc.

Betjeman, John. "Cornish Cliffs," "Harvest Hymn," and "Late-Flowering Lust" are reprinted from *High and Low* (1967) and

Collected Poems (1959) by permission of John Murray Ltd and Houghton Mifflin Company.

Bishop, John Peale. "Epithalamion" is reprinted from *The Collected Poems of John Peale Bishop* (copyright 1948 by Charles Scribner's Sons) by permission of Charles Scribner's Sons.

Bishop, Morris. "Ozymandias Revisited" is reprinted from *Spilt Milk* (copyright 1942, renewed 1969 by Morris Bishop) by permission of G. P. Putnam's Sons.

Blackburn, Paul. "The Watchers" (© 1966 by The New Yorker Magazine, Inc.) is reprinted by permission of The New Yorker Magazine, Inc.

Booth, Philip. "The Tower" is reprinted from *The Islanders* (© 1960 by Philip Booth) by permission of The Viking Press, Inc.

Brooke, Rupert. "The Soldier" is reprinted from *The Collected Poems of Rupert Brooke* (copyright 1915 by Dodd, Mead & Company, Inc., renewed 1943 by Edward Marsh) by permission of Dodd, Mead & Company, Inc., and McClelland and Steward, Limited, Toronto.

Chesterton, G. K. "A Ballad of Suicide" is reprinted from *The Collected Poems of G. K. Chesterton* (copyright 1932 by Dodd, Mead & Company, Inc., renewed 1959 by Oliver Chesterton) by permission of Miss D. E. Collins, Methuen & Company, and Dodd, Mead & Company, Inc.

Crane, Hart. "Black Tambourine," "To Brooklyn Bridge," and "Voyages II" reprinted from *Complete Poems and Selected Letters and Prose of Hart Crane* (copyright 1933, 1958, 1966 by Liveright Publishing Corporation) by permission of Liveright Publishing Corporation.

Crapsey Adelaide. "Three Cinquains" reprinted from *Verse* (copyright 1922 by Algernon S. Crapsey, renewed 1950 by The Adelaide Crapsey Foundation) by permission of Alfred A. Knopf, Inc.

Cummings, E. E. "i sing of Olaf glad and strong" (copyright 1931, renewed 1959 by E. E. Cummings), "Poem, or Beauty Hurts Mr. Vinal" (copyright 1926 by Horace Liveright, renewed 1954 by E. E. Cummings), "anyone lived in a pretty how town" (copyright 1940 by E. E. Cummings, renewed 1968 by Marion Morehouse Cummings), "o sweet spontaneous earth," "all in green went my love riding," and "a wind has blown the rain away" (copyright 1923, renewed 1951 by E. E. Cummings) reprinted from *Poems 1923–1954* by permission of Harcourt Brace Jovanovich, Inc.

D., H. "At Baia" reprinted from *The Collected Poems of H. D.* (copyright renewed 1952 by Hilda Doolittle) by permission of Liveright Publishing Corporation.

Dickey, James. "Between Two Prisoners" and "On the Hill Below the Lighthouse" (© 1960 by James Dickey) reprinted from *Poems 1957–1967* by permission of Wesleyan University Press.

Dickinson, Emily. "He Preached Upon Breadth," "My Life Closed Twice Before Its Close," "The Soul Selects Her Own Society," "This Is My Letter to the World," and "Title Divine Is Mine" are reprinted by permission of the Trustees of Amherst College and the publishers of *The Poems of Emily Dickinson,* Thomas H. Johnson, ed. (Cambridge, Mass.: The Belknap Press of Harvard University Press copyright 1951, 1955 by the President and Fellows of Harvard College).

Dobson, Austin. "The Ballade of Prose and Rhyme," "The Wanderer: Rondel," and "Urceus Exit" from "Rose-Leaves" are reprinted from *The Complete Poetical Works of Austin Dobson,* edited by Alban Dobson, by permission of Oxford University Press, Inc.

Dodson, Owen. "Hymn Written After Jeremiah Preached to Me in a Dream" is reprinted by permission of the author.

Dugan, Alan. "Letter to Eve" and "On Finding the Meaning of

Radiance" are reprinted from *Poems* (© 1961 by Alan Dugan), published by Yale University Press, by permission of the author.

Eberhart, Richard. "Cold Fall" is reprinted from *Great Praises* (© 1957 by Richard Eberhart) by permission of Oxford University Press, Inc.

Eliot, T. S. "The Love Song of J. Alfred Prufrock" and "Sweeney Among the Nightingales" are reprinted from *Collected Poems 1909–1962* (copyright 1936 by Harcourt, Brace and World, Inc., renewed 1963, 1964 by T. S. Eliot) by permission of Harcourt Brace Jovanovich, Inc., and Faber and Faber Ltd.

Empson, William. "Aubade" and "Missing Dates" are reprinted from *Collected Poems of William Empson* (copyright 1949 by William Empson) by permission of the author, Chatto and Windus Ltd., and Harcourt Brace Jovanovich, Inc.

Fearing, Kenneth. "American Rhapsody (4)" is reprinted by permission of the Estate of Kenneth F. Fearing, Ira Koenig, executor.

Ferlinghetti, Lawrence. "Constantly Risking Absurdity" and "In Goya's Greatest Scenes" are reprinted from *A Coney Island of the Mind* (© 1958 by Lawrence Ferlinghetti) by permission of New Directions Publishing Corporation.

Frost, Robert. "Carpe Diem," "The Silken Tent," "The Star-Splitter," "The Witch of Coös," and "West-running Brook" are reprinted from *The Complete Poems of Robert Frost* (copyright 1923, 1928 by Holt, Rinehart & Winston, Inc.; 1936, 1942, 1951, 1956 by Robert Frost; 1964, 1970 by Lesley Frost Ballantine) by permission of Holt, Rinehart & Winston, Inc.

Greene, Richard L. "Ubi Iam Sunt" is reprinted from *Digressions and Indiscretions* (CEA Chap Book, June, 1968) by permission of the author and The College English Association.

Hardy Thomas. "At a Hasty Wedding" and "The Convergence of the Twain" are reprinted from *Collected Poems* (copyright 1925 by The Macmillan Company) by permission of the Hardy Estate; Macmillan & Co. Ltd., London; The Macmillan Company of Canada Ltd.; and The Macmillan Company.

Hayden, Robert. "Middle Passage" is reprinted from *Selected Poems* (© 1966 by Robert Hayden) by permission of October House, Inc.

Hecht, Anthony. "The Dover Bitch" is reprinted from *The Hard Hours* (© 1960, 1967 by Anthony E. Hecht) by permission of Atheneum Publishers. This poem first appeared in the *Transatlantic Review*.

Henderson, David. "Sketches of Harlem" is reprinted from *New Negro Poets: USA* (1964), edited by Langston Hughes, by permission of Indiana University Press.

Hillyer, Robert. "A Letter to a Teacher of English" and "Pastorals, II" are reprinted from *Collected Poems* (copyright 1933, renewed 1961 by Robert Hillyer) by permission of Alfred A. Knopf, Inc.

Hodgson, Ralph. "Eve" is reprinted from *Collected Poems* by permission of the author, St. Martin's Press, Inc., Macmillan & Co., Ltd., and The Macmillan Company of Canada Ltd., and Allen & Unwin, Ltd.

Honig, Edwin. "Walt Whitman" is reprinted by permission of the author.

Hopkins, Gerard Manley. "God's Grandeur," "Pied Beauty," "Spring and Fall," "The Leaden Echo and the Golden Echo," and "The Windhover" are reprinted from *The Complete Poems of Gerard Manley Hopkins,* published by Oxford University Press.

Horne, Frank. "Letters Found Near a Suicide: To James" is reprinted by permission of the author.

Housman, A. E. "Is My Team Ploughing" is reprinted from "A

Shropshire Lad"—Authorized Edition, *The Collected Poems of A. E. Housman* (copyright 1939, 1940, 1959 by Holt, Rinehart & Winston, Inc.; © 167, 1968 by Robert E. Symons) by permission of The Society of Authors as the literary representative of The Estate of A. E. Housman, Jonathan Cape Ltd., and Holt, Rinehart & Winston, Inc.

Hughes, Langston. "Mulatto" (copyright 1927 by Alfred A. Knopf, Inc., renewed 1955 by Langston Hughes) and "Winter Moon" (copyright 1926 by Alfred A. Knopf, Inc., renewed 1954 by Langston Hughes) are reprinted from *Selected Poems* by permission of Alfred A. Knopf, Inc.

Hulme, T. E. "Autumn" is reprinted from *Personae,* by Ezra Pound (copyright 1926 by Ezra Pound) by permission of New Directions Publishing Corporation.

Humphries, Rolfe. "A Sad Song" and "Looking up at Airplanes, Always" are reprinted from *Collected Poems* (1965) by permission of Indiana University Press.

Jeffers, Robinson. "Compensation" is reprinted by permission of Jeffers Literary Properties.

Joans, Ted. "It Is Time" is reprinted from *New Negro Poets: USA* (1964) edited by Langston Hughes, by permission of Indiana University Press.

Johnson, James Weldon. "O Black and Unknown Bards" is reprinted from *Saint Peter Relates an Incident* (copyright 1917, renewed 1935 by James Weldon Johnson) by permission of The Viking Press, Inc.

Jones, LeRoi. "Preface to a Twenty Volume Suicide Note" (© 1961 by LeRoi Jones) is reprinted by permission of Corinth Books.

Kennedy, X. J. "In a Prominent Bar in Secaucus One Day" is reprinted from *Nude Descending a Staircase* by permission of Doubleday & Company, Inc.

Kipling, Rudyard. "Sestina of the Tramp-Royal" is reprinted from *Rudyard Kipling's Verse: Definitive Edition* by permission of Mrs. George Bambridge, Doubleday & Company, Inc., and The Macmillan Co. of Canada.

Kostelanetz, Richard. "Tribute to Henry Ford—1, —2, —3" is reprinted from *The Young American Poets* (© 1969 by Richard Kostelanetz) by permission of Follett Publishing Company.

Kunitz, Stanley. "For Proserpine" is reprinted from *Selected Poems* (1958) by permission of Little, Brown and Company.

Lawrence, D. H. "Letter From Town: The Almond Tree" is reprinted from *The Complete Poems of D. H. Lawrence, Vol. I,* edited by Vivian de Sola Pinto and F. Warren Roberts (copyright by B. W. Huebsch, Inc., renewed 1948 by Frieda Lawrence) by permission of The Viking Press, Inc.

Levertov, Denise. "Obsessions" was first published in *Mademoiselle* and is reprinted from *With Eyes at the Back of Our Heads* (© 1959 by Denise Levertov Goodman) by permission of New Directions Publishing Corporation.

L'Heureux, John. "St. Ignatius Loyola, Founder of the Jesuits" (© 1969 by Rev. John L'Heureux, S.J.) is reprinted by permission of the author.

Lowell, Robert. "After the Surprising Conversions" and "In Memory of Arthur Winslow" are reprinted from *Lord Weary's Castle* (copyright 1944, 1946 by Robert Lowell) by permission of Harcourt Brace Jovanovich, Inc.

Lowry, Malcolm. "Sestina in a Cantina" is reprinted from *Selected Poems* (© 1962 by Marjorie Lowry) by permission of City Lights Books.

MacLeish, Archibald. "Ars Poetica," "Epistle to Be Left in the Earth," "L'an trentiesme de mon age," and "The End of the World" are reprinted from *Collected Poems 1917–1952* (copyright 1952 by Archibald MacLeish) by permission of Houghton Mifflin Company.

MacNeice, Louis. "Aubade" is reprinted from *The Collected Poems of Louis MacNeice,* edited by E. R. Dodds (© 1966 by The Estate of Louis MacNeice) by permission of Oxford University Press.

Malone, Kemp (translator). "Deor" is reprinted from *Ten Old English Poems* (copyright 1941 by The Johns Hopkins Press) by permission of The Johns Hopkins Press.

Mayer, Hansjorg. "Composition" is reprinted from *Anthology of Concretism,* 2nd Edition, edited by Eugene Wildman, Swallow Press: Chicago, 1969.

Merrill, James. "The World and the Child" is reprinted from *Water Street* (© 1960, 1962 by James Merrill) by permission of Atheneum Publishers. This poem originally appeared in *The New Yorker.*

Miles, Josephine. "Opal" is reprinted from *Poems 1930–1960* (1960) by permission of Indiana University Press.

Miller, Vassar. "Song for a Marriage" is reprinted from *Wage War on Silence* (1967) by permission of Wesleyan University Press.

Mitchell, Roger. "Riding with Some North Vietnamese Students in a Polish Elevator, 1966," is reprinted by permission of the author.

Moore, Marianne. "Poetry" (copyright 1935 by Marianne Moore, renewed 1963 by Marianne Moore and T. S. Eliot) and "Spenser's Ireland" (copyright 1941, renewed 1969 by Marianne Moore) are reprinted from *Collected Poems* by permission of The Macmillan Company.

Nash, Ogden. "The Anatomy of Happiness" is reprinted from *I'm a Stranger Here Myself* (copyright 1938 by Ogden Nash) by permission of Little, Brown and Company.

Olson, Charles. "Maximus, to Gloucester, Letter 19" is reprinted from *The Maximus Poems* (© 1960 by Charles Olson) by permission of Corinth Books.

Olson, Elder. "A Valentine for Marianne Moore" is reprinted by permission of the author.

Parker, Dorothy. "One Perfect Rose" is reprinted from *The Portable Dorothy Parker* (copyright 1926, renewed 1954 by Dorothy Parker) by permission of The Viking Press, Inc.

Patchen, Kenneth. "Do the Dead Know What Time It Is?" and "How To Be an Army" are reprinted from *Collected Poems* (copyright 1939 by New Directions Publishing Corporation, copyright 1943 by Kenneth Patchen) by permission of New Directions Publishing Corporation.

Pound, Ezra. "Canto I" is reprinted from *The Cantos* (copyright 1934 by Ezra Pound), "A Pact," "Ballad of the Goodly Fere," "Elegy VII," "Mr. Housman's Message," "The New Cake of Soap," "The River Merchant's Wife: A Letter," and "Villonaud for This Yule" are reprinted from *Personae* (copyright 1926 by Ezra Pound), and "Trahison des Clercs" is reprinted from *The Confucian Odes* (copyright 1954 by the President and Fellows of Harvard College), all by permission of New Directions Publishing Corporation.

Randall, Dudley. "The Southern Road" is reprinted by permission of the author.

Ransom, John Crowe. "Bells for John Whiteside's Daughter" (copyright 1924 by Alfred A. Knopf, Inc., renewed 1952 by John Crowe Random) and "Piazza Piece" (copyright 1927 by Alfred A. Knopf, Inc.; renewed 1955 by John Crowe Ransom) are reprinted from *Selected Poems* by permission of Alfred A. Knopf, Inc.

Rexroth, Kenneth (translator). "Haiku" and "Tanka I and II" are reprinted from "Forty-five More Japanese Poems" in *Collected Shorter Poems* (© 1956 by New Directions Publishing Corporation) by permission of New Directions Publishing Corporation.

Robinson, Edward Arlington. "Mr. Flood's Party" is reprinted from *Collected Poems* (copyright 1921 by Edward Arlington Robinson, renewed 1949 by Ruth Nivison) by permission of The Macmillan Company. "Cliff Klingenhagen," "How Annandale Went Out," and "Richard Cory" were originally published in *The Children of the Night* by Charles Scribner's Sons, 1897.

Roethke, Theodore. "Elegy for Jane" (copyright 1950 by Theodore Roethke) is reprinted from *The Collected Poems of Theodore Roethke* by permission of Doubleday & Company, Inc.

Sandburg, Carl. "Cool Tombs" is reprinted from *Cornhuskers* (copyright 1918 by Holt, Rinehart and Winston, Inc., copyright 1946 by Carl Sandburg) by permission of Holt, Rinehart and Winston, Inc. "Four Preludes on Playthings of the Wind" is reprinted from *Smoke and Steel* (copyright 1920 by Harcourt, Brace & World, Inc., renewed 1948 by Carl Sandburg) by permission of Harcourt Brace Jovanovich, Inc.

Santayana, George. "On the Death of a Metaphysician" is reprinted from *Poems* (copyright 1923, renewed 1951 by Charles Scribner's Sons) by permission of Charles Scribner's Sons.

Schwartz, Delmore. "In the Naked Bed, in Plato's Cave" is reprinted from *Selected Poems* (*Summer Knowledge*) (copyright 1938 by New Directions Publishing Corporation) by permission of New Directions Publishing Corporation.

Simpson, Louis. "The Green Shepherd" (© 1956 by Louis Simpson) is reprinted from *A Dream of Governors* by permission of Wesleyan University Press. This poem was first published in *The New Yorker*.

Snodgrass, W. D. "Vampire's Aubade" is reprinted from *After Experience* (© 1968 by W. D. Snodgrass) by permission of Harper & Row, Publishers.

Starbuck, George. "Making It" is reprinted from *White Paper* (© 1960, 1961, 1962, 1963, 1964, 1965, 1966 by George Starbuck) by permission of Atlantic-Little, Brown & Company.

Stark, Irwin. "Poets of My Epoch" is reprinted by permission of the author.

Stevens, Wallace. "A High-Toned Old Christian Woman," "Peter Quince at the Clavier," "The Emperor of Ice-Cream" (copyright 1923, renewed 1951 by Wallace Stevens) and "Of Modern Poetry" (copyright 1942 by Wallace Stevens, renewed 1970 by Holly Stevens Stephenson) are reprinted from *The Collected Poems of Wallace Stevens* by permission of Alfred A. Knopf, Inc.

Tate, Allen. "Mr. Pope," "Ode to Fear," and "Sonnets at Christmas" are reprinted from *Poems (1960)* (copyright 1932, 1934 by Charles Scribner's Sons, renewed 1960, 1962 by Allen Tate) by permission of Charles Scribner's Sons.

Taylor, Edward. "Meditation Eight" is reprinted from *The Poetical Works of Edward Taylor,* edited by Thomas H. Johnson (Princeton Paperback, 1966, copyright 1939 by Rockland, 1943 by Princeton University Press) by permission of Princeton University Press.

Thomas, Dylan. "Do Not Go Gentle into That Good Night," "In My Craft or Sullen Art," "Light Breaks Where No Sun Shines," "The Force That Through the Green Fuse," and "When All My Five and Country Senses See" are reprinted from *Collected Poems* (copyright 1938, 1939, 1946 by New Directions Publishing Corporation) by permission of the Trustees for the Copyrights of the late Dylan Thomas, J. M. Dent & Sons Ltd., and New Directions Publishing Corporation.

Untermeyer, Louis. "Edna St. Vincent Millay Inflates a Passion for Little Boy Blue" is reprinted from *Selected Poems and Parodies* (copyright 1935 by Harcourt, Brace & World, Inc., renewed 1963 by Louis Untermeyer) by permission of Harcourt Brace Jovanovich, Inc.

Wain, John. "Reason for Not Writing Orthodox Nature Poetry" is reprinted from *A Word Carved on a Sill* (1956) by permission of St. Martin's Press, Inc., Macmillan & Co., Ltd., and Routledge & Kegan Paul Ltd.

Weismiller, Edward. "The Soliloquies" is reprinted by permission of the author.

Wilbur, Richard. "A Late Aubade" (© 1968) is reprinted from *Walking to Sleep* by permission of Harcourt Brace Jovanovich, Inc. This poem was first published in *The New Yorker*.

Williams, William Carlos. "The Dance" is reprinted from *Collected Later Poems* (copyright 1944 by William Carlos Williams) by permission of New Directions Publishing Corporation.

Winters, Yvor. "Sir Gawaine and the Green Knight" is reprinted from *The Giant Weapon* (copyright 1943 by New Directions Publishing Corporation) by permission of New Directions Publishing Corporation.

Woodcock, George. "Windows" is reprinted by permission of the author.

Wright, Jay. "This Morning" is reprinted from *New Negro Poets: USA* (1964), edited by Langston Hughes, by permission of Indiana University Press.

Wylie, Elinor. "Puritan Sonnet" from "Wild Peaches" and "The Eagle and the Mole" are reprinted from *Collected Poems* (copyright 1921 by Alfred A. Knopf, Inc., renewed 1949 by William Rose Benet) by permission of Alfred A. Knopf, Inc.

Xisto, Pedro. "Epithalamium—II" is reprinted from *Anthology of Concretism*, 2nd Edition, edited by Eugene Wildman, Swallow Press: Chicago, 1969.

Yeats, William Butler. "The Ballad of Father Gilligan" (copyright 1906 by the Macmillan Co., renewed 1934 by William Butler Yeats), "A Dialogue of Self and Soul" (copyright 1933 by The Macmillan Co., renewed 1961 by Bertha Georgie Yeats), "Easter, 1916" (copyright 1924 by The Macmillan Co., renewed 1952 by Bertha Georgie Yeats), "Leda and the Swan" and "Sailing to Byzantium" (copyright 1928 by The Macmillan Co., renewed 1956 by Georgie Yeats) are reprinted from *Collected Poems* by permission of The Macmillan Company, A. P. Watt & Son, Mr. M. B. Yeats, and The Macmillan Co. of Canada. "Purgatory" is reprinted from *Collected Plays of W. B. Yeats* (copyright 1934, 1952 by The Macmillan Company) by permission of The Macmillan Company, A. P. Watt & Son, Mr. M. B. Yeats, and The Macmillan Co. of Canada.

Yuasa, Nobuyuki (translator). "Haiku" is reprinted by permission of The Regents of the University of California.

CONTENTS

SPECIFIC VERSE FORMS: THE SONNET   49

Regular   50

SPECIFIC VERSE FORMS: THE ODE   81

The "Pindaric" Ode   83

The "Horatian" Ode   102

The "English" Ode   114

SPECIFIC VERSE FORMS: OTHER FORMS   119

The Ballade   119

The Canzone   123

The Débat   123

The Epigram   133

Haiku   137

The Rondeau   137

The Rondel   138

The Roundelay   140

The Sestina   143

Tanka   145

The Triolet   146

The Villanelle   147

Part III

Poetic Conventions:
The Poem as Narrative   297

THE BALLAD   298

THE NARRATIVE 318

THE EPIC 355

Part IV
Poetic Conventions:
The Poem as Drama 365

THE SOLILOQUY 365

THE DRAMATIC MONOLOGUE 369

DRAMATIC POETRY   391

VERSE DRAMA   409

Part V
Recurrent Strains and Other Occasions   417

THE ALBA AND THE AUBADE   418

CARPE DIEM   421

THE COMPLAINT
AND THE LAMENT   424

POEMS AS SEQUENCE   497

INTRODUCTION

The way to read a poem, Robert Frost observed, is to read it "in the light of all the other poems ever written." "We read the second," Frost says, "the better to read the third, the third the better to read the fourth, the fourth the better to read the fifth, the fifth the better to read the first again, or the second if it so happens." Our experience as teachers of literature at both the graduate and undergraduate level suggests that students seldom read in this manner. We find that students are often aware of theme, irony, paradox, and symbol in the poems they read; they frequently are able to talk in a general way about form in poetry ("This poem has fourteen lines and ends in a couplet and therefore must be a sonnet"). Many students can identify and distinguish among the various meters, can recognize elision, enjambment, alliteration, consonance and other techniques and devices associated with the writing of poetry. But most students have not become familiar with the important poetic traditions; they lack a sense that poetry may be read in light of the poems and traditions that have preceded it. Hence, this anthology.

We have attempted to present the traditional poetic forms and conventions, and we have tried to show how these genres and conventions developed, how they have been used, how they have undergone modifications, and how they are used today in poetry.

To study literary genre and form is to use a method of classifying literature and literary history through an examination of types, organizational principles, and structure. Poets and critics of the seventeenth and eighteenth centuries had a fondness for the classical conceptions of genres, and though they did not slavishly imitate classical precedents, they wrote with some attention to categories established by the Greek and Roman writers. By the nineteenth century, writers were concerned with the uniqueness and individual expression of their poetry, though these Romantic poets also indicate an awareness of the importance of genre; critics of that period, however, paid less attention to genre theory than had their predecessors. By the end of the nineteenth century, there was a return to formalistic poetry. Today, a number of the traditional genres still exist, still challenge a writer's ability to measure himself against his literary heritage.

Not all readers will, or should, agree with our groupings or with our selections. Lord Kames, in his *Elements of Criticism* (1762), pointed to the problem of genre studies: "Literary compositions run into each other, precisely like colors: in their strong tints they are easily distinguished; but are susceptible of so much variety, and so many different forms, that we never can say where one species ends and another begins." We have, therefore, attempted in this book to discuss the strong "tints": What is an ode? Where did it originate and for what purposes? What has been its traditional (in English) form or forms? Its subject matter? Is it still used? If so, how and why is it used today?

To study genre is to study two aspects of a poem. First, there is an outward form—the specific meter or "structure" of the work. Second, there is an inner "form"—an attitude, tone, purpose that is bounded by the shape of its outward form. It is a commonplace of a great deal of current writing that one cannot separate form from content; that one becomes the other, establishes the other. Looked at another way, the substance (inner form) of a sonnet may be shaped by the fact that the poet has selected the English (Shakespearian) sonnet form, but the questions remain: Why has the poet elected to write a sonnet? Why has he selected the English sonnet form? Read against the history of this form, what has he added or done to the form? The study of genre, then, is the attempt to classify poems by the various arrangements of inner and outer forms, to find which poems group together, and by which principles they may be grouped.

Another distinction is useful. Genre studies may be divided into two schools or views. The earlier, or "classical," view of genre is a prescriptive one. According to this view, genres differ each from the other. Each genre has its own aesthetic principles, its own reasons for being, its own rules. By contrast, the later, or "modern," view is descriptive. According to this understanding of genre, there are many possible kinds of genre. Moreover, there are no prescribed rules for authors to follow. Genres, in fact, may be mixed in order to produce new genres. This modern view of genre is not so concerned in distinguishing between genres; instead, it seeks out common denominators; it searches out the uniqueness of an individual work while at the same time it places that work within a literary tradition. Since the poetry in this anthology is largely the work of major poets, the emphasis is upon a descriptive view of genre: yet major poets are seldom bound by rules established by their predecessors.

In collecting poems for this book we have based our selections upon the important traditional forms, genres, and conventions. We believe that the serious student of literature needs a familiarity with his literary past; that he needs a critical tool, a method, that will enable him to discuss a poem that he is examining within the perspective of this literary past.

That the genre approach to an understanding and appreciation of poetry is not the only valid approach is obvious, but in our experience as teachers of literature, we have found that there has been enough exclusive concentration on close textual reading. In compiling this anthology, we intend to encourage a more balanced approach to poetry. Diction, imagery (figurative language), scansion, tone, and other aspects of poetry are discussed in the glossary at the end of this anthology, and those students who feel uncomfortable with these important aspects of poetry are advised to page through that section before beginning their study of genres and conventions.

The poems in our anthology are examples of various types, from early periods as well as from contemporary poetry. Though our emphasis has been upon the heritage of the past, our focus is upon the past as it relates to the present: A literary heritage is constantly being evaluated, added to, built upon by the writers and readers of each generation. If we are to accept and understand our literary heritage, we must familiarize ourselves with it. If we are to understand our literary present, we must familiarize ourselves with the traditions and conventions that have helped to shape our contemporary writing.

Frederick R. Lapides
John T. Shawcross

Poetry and Its Conventions

PART I

Poetic Conventions: The Lyric

The basic poetic form is the lyric. Other forms—the narrative and the drama—combine the poetic convention of theme with that of form, and will be treated in Parts III and IV. A lyric is a brief or relatively brief poem expressing emotion or meditation. Originally it was to be sung, and hence its name. It has come to be a catch-all term for poetry which is not narrative or drama, although it may relate a kind of story and although it may have dramatic qualities about it. Part VI examines such narrative or dramatic lyrics.

The lyric is found in a variety of stanzas, forms, unstructured series of lines, and meters. A stanza—which implies that a pattern of lines is repeated—may range from two lines upward. Sometimes names are attached to specific stanzas: e.g., couplet (two lines); tercet, terza rima, triplet (three lines); Alcaic, Anacreontic, ballad stanza, elegiac stanza, quatrain, sapphic (four lines); rhyme royal (seven lines); ottava rima (eight lines); and Spenserian stanza (nine lines). Often requirements of rhyme, line length, or stress differentiate these specific stanzas from others with the same number of lines. Definitions are given in the *Glossary of Poetical and Critical Terms,* and examples of each are given below. Such stanzas are repeated as often as the poet desires. Some stanzas employ rhyme in repeated patterns or without pattern; some stanzas do not employ rhyme. Some stanzas consist of lines of equivalent lengths; some employ lines of varying lengths both in repeated patterns and without patterns.

Verse forms also have been developed employing stanzas. The differentiation that is being made here between general stanzaic lyrics (e.g., the triplet, repeated often to complete the poem) and a specific lyric form is that the pattern of the latter defines a complete poem (e.g., the villanelle). Certain verse forms, however, like the ode or the virelay, are not quite so precise in length as the sonnet or the sestina. All these verse forms are illustrated below and described in the *Glossary*.

Nonstanzaic lyrics are poems with a varying number of unpatterned lines. At times the unstructured series of lines constitutes the poem itself; at times groups of lines are separated from other groups of lines, but without repetition of any pattern. Line lengths are sometimes equivalent for all lines of such nonstanzaic lyrics; or they may be of any length, occurring randomly. Nonstanzaic lyrics may employ rhyme both with pattern and without pattern or they may be rhymeless, being either a form of blank verse or a form of free verse.

There are a few nonstanzaic lyrics given distinguishing names. A poem of two lines of identical structure is called a distich; one of three lines of identical structure is called a tristich. Irregular short lines with two or three accents per line are called skeltonics, after John Skelton (1460–1529), and the poem consisting of such lines, therefore, a skeltonic. Three types of verse used for humorous effect are doggerel, Hudibrastic verse, and the macaronic. The first is characterized by irregular meter and forced rhyme; the second, a form of doggerel, by its iambic tetrameter lines; and the third, by its use of various languages.

Certain poems create a pattern of some nature as one looks at them or reads them. Such a poem may be shaped to present a picture suggestive of the subject or meaning of the poem; or the "picture-pattern" may be achieved by eye-movement as one reads, such as the fall of a leaf by having the line read downward. Related to the pattern poem is emblematic verse. Here a picture (emblem) usually accompanies the poem (and probably also a quotation usually drawn from the Bible), and the poem attempts to suggest the meaning or idea or circumstance of the picture. It thus interprets the significance of the emblem, usually allegorically. But the more general term "hieroglyphic," which encompasses both shaped verse and emblematic verse, covers also those nonstanzaic poems which are devised out of nonverbal or only partly verbal matter as in verse called Dadaistic or in "concrete poems." The latter category of poems often presents a picture through the placement of letters or signs in certain patterns on the page; the picture, it is expected, will evoke an emotion or an idea in the "reader" (that is, "viewer"). In addition some poems are presented in prose form.

Three additional types of poems which use a device to supplement meaning are the acrostic, a poem whose first letters of each line spell out a name or word having significance for the poem; the echo poem, in which the last word of a preceding line, or part of the word, is repeated as a response to that line; and the pruning poem, whose last words are altered by dropping letters in successive lines. Variations on the acrostic exist, for example, the telestich, a poem whose last letters of each line spell out a name or word; these are not illustrated here.

STANZAIC FORMS: GENERAL

Two-line Stanzas

Alfred, Lord Tennyson   The Higher Pantheism

The sun, the moon, the stars, the seas, the hills and the plains—
Are not these, O Soul, the Vision of Him who reigns?

Is not the Vision He, though He be not that which He seems?
Dreams are true while they last, and do we not live in dreams?

Earth, these solid stars, this weight of body and limb,   5
Are they not sign and symbol of thy division from Him?

Dark is the world to thee: thyself art the reason why,
For is He not all but that which has power to feel "I am I"?

Glory about thee, without thee; and thou fulfillest thy doom
Making Him broken gleams and a stifled splendor and gloom.   10

Speak to Him, thou, for He hears, and Spirit with Spirit can
    meet—
Closer is He than breathing, and nearer than hands and feet.

God is law, say the wise: O soul, and let us rejoice,
For if He thunder by law the thunder is yet His voice.

Law is God, say some; no God at all, says the fool;   15
For all we have power to see is a straight staff bent in a pool;

And the ear of man cannot hear, and the eye of man cannot see;
But if we could see and hear, this Vision—were it not He?

Josephine Miles   Opal

The steamfitter had no notion of buying an opal,
But a stone comes sudden in its meaning often.

He looked for a new watch, that part of his life, there was none,
He had to furnish his own time sense.

But this opal. Fire of time that burned in the antique reaches,   5
Roman omen, power of the sooth.

How comes so much actual straight evil into an opal?
Fix on a streak of bad luck, it goes out.

How comes so much red, then green, into an opal?
There aren't those colors in a glass of milk.   10

His wife didn't want the jewel but he bought it
And took that burden on, which fate forbore.

Three-line Stanzas

John Donne   To Mr. Rowland Woodward

Like one who in her third widowhood doth profess
Herself a nun, tied to retiredness,
So affects my muse now a chaste fallowness;

Since she to few, yet to too many hath shown
How love-song weeds and satiric thorns are grown   5
Where seeds of better arts were early sown.

Though to use and love poetry, to me,
Betrothed to no one art, be no adultery;
Omissions of good, ill, as ill deeds be.

For though to us it seem and be light and thin,   10
Yet, in those faithful scales where God throws in
Men's works, vanity weighs as much as sin.

If our souls have stained their first white, yet we
May cloth them with faith and dear honesty,
Which God imputes as native purity.   15

There is no virtue but religion:
Wise, valiant, sober, just are names which none
Want, which want not vice-covering discretion.

Seek we then ourselves in our selves; for as
Men force the sun with much more force to pass,   20
By gathering his beams with a crystal glass;

So we, if we into ourselves will turn,
Blowing our sparks of virtue, may outburn
The straw which doth about our hearts sojourn.

You know, physicians, when they would infuse   25
Into any oil, the souls of simples, use
Places where they may lie still warm, to choose.

So works retiredness in us. To roam
Giddily and be everywhere but at home,
Such freedom doth a banishment become.   30

We are but farmers of ourselves, yet may,
If we can stock ourselves and thrive, uplay
Much, much dear treasure for the great rent day.

Manure thyself then, to thyself be approved,
And with vain outward things be no more moved,   35
But to know that I love thee and would be loved.

21 *crystal glass*: magnifying glass.   26 *simples*: medicinal herbs.
33 *the great rent day*: Judgment Day.

Ben Jonson   A Fit of Rime Against Rime

Rime the rack of finest wits,
That expresseth but by fits,
        True conceit.
Spoiling senses of their treasure,
Cozening judgment with a measure,   5
        But false weight.
Wresting words from their true calling;
Propping verse for fear of falling
        To the ground.
Jointing syllables, drowning letters,   10
Fastening vowels, as with fetters
        They were bound!
Soon as lazy thou wert known
All good poetry hence was flown
        And art banished.   15
For a thousand years together,
All Parnassus' green did wither
        And wit vanished.
Pegasus did fly away,
At the wells no Muse did stay,   20
        But bewailed,
So to see the fountain dry
And Apollo's music die,
        All light failed!
Starveling rimes did fill the stage,   25
Not a poet in an age
        Worth crowning.
Not a work deserving bays,
Nor a line deserving praise,
        Pallas frowning;   30
Greek was free from rime's infection,
Happy Greek by this protection!
        Was not spoiled.
Whilst the Latin, queen of tongues,
Is not free from rime's wrongs,   35
        But rests foiled.
Scarce the hill again doth flourish,
Scarce the world a wit doth nourish,
        To restore
Phoebus to his crown again;   40
And the Muses to their brain,
        As before.
Vulgar languages that want

Words, and sweetness, and be scant
                  Of true measure,   45
Tyrant rime hath so abused,
That they long since have refused
                  Other ceasure.
He that first invented thee,
May his joints tormented be,   50
                  Cramped forever;
Still may syllables jar with time,
Still may reason war with rime,
                  Resting never.
May his sense when it would meet   55
The cold tumor in his feet
                  Grow unsounder.
And his title be long fool,
That in rearing such a school
                  Was the founder.   60

Fit: canto.   28 *bays*: laurels.   30 *Pallas*: Minerva.   37 *hill*:
Parnassus.   48 *ceasure*: caesura.

George Herbert   Trinity Sunday

Lord, who hast formed me out of mud,
    And hast redeemed me through thy blood,
    And sanctified me to do good;

Purge all my sins done heretofore:
    For I confess my heavy score,   5
    And I will strive to sin no more.

Enrich my heart, mouth, hands in me,
    With faith, with hope, with charity;
    That I may run, rise, rest with thee.

Trinity Sunday: the Sunday after Pentecost.

Robert Herrick   Upon Julia's Clothes

Whenas in silks my Julia goes,
Then, then, methinks, how sweetly flows
The liquefaction of her clothes!

Next, when I cast mine eyes and see
That brave vibration each way free,   5
—O how that glittering taketh me!

Charles Lamb   The Old Familiar Faces

I have had playmates, I have had companions,
In my days of childhood, in my joyful school-days—
All, all are gone, the old familiar faces.

I have been laughing, I have been carousing,
Drinking late, sitting late, with my bosom cronies—   5
All, all are gone, the old familiar faces.

I loved a Love once, fairest among women:
Closed are the doors on me, I must not see her—
All, all are gone, the old familiar faces.

I have a friend, a kinder friend has no man: 10
Like an ingrate, I left my friend abruptly;
Left him, to muse on the old familiar faces.

Ghost-like I paced round the haunts of my childhood,
Earth seemed a desert I was bound to traverse,
Seeking to find the old familiar faces.   15

Friends of my bosom, thou more than a brother,
Why wert not thou born in my father's dwelling?
So might we talk of the old familiar faces—

How some they have died, and some they have left me,
And some are taken from me; all are departed —   20
All, all are gone, the old familiar faces.

Walt Whitman   "Darest Thou Now O Soul"

Darest thou now O soul,
Walk out with me toward the unknown region,
Where neither ground is for the feet nor any path to follow?

No map there, nor guide,
Nor voice sounding, nor touch of human hand,   5
Nor face with blooming flesh, nor lips, nor eyes, are in that land.

I know it not O soul,
Nor dost thou, all is a blank before us,
All waits undreamed of in that region, that inaccessible land.

Till when the ties loosen,   10
All but the ties eternal, Time and Space,
Nor darkness, gravitation, sense, nor bounds bounding us.

Then we burst forth, we float,
In Time and Space O soul, prepared for them,
Equal, equipped at last (O joy, O fruit of all), them to fulfill O
   soul.   15

Thomas Hardy   The Convergence of the Twain

(LINES ON THE LOSS OF THE "TITANIC")

I
    In a solitude of the sea
     Deep from human vanity,
And the Pride of Life that planned her, stilly couches she.

2
    Steel chambers, late the pyres
      Of her salamandrine fires,   5
Cold currents thrid, and turn to rhythmic tidal lyres.

3
    Over the mirrors meant
      To glass the opulent
The sea-worm crawls—grotesque, slimed, dumb, indifferent.

4
    Jewels in joy designed   10
      To ravish the sensuous mind
Lie lightless, all their sparkles bleared and black and blind.

5
    Dim moon-eyed fishes near
      Gaze at the gilded gear
And query: "What does this vaingloriousness down here?"   15

6
    Well: while was fashioning
      This creature of cleaving wing,
The Immanent Will that stirs and urges everything

7
    Prepared a sinister mate
      For her—so gaily great—   20
A Shape of Ice, for the time far and dissociate.

8
    And as the smart ship grew
      In stature, grace, and hue,
In shadowy silent distance grew the Iceberg too.

9
    Alien they seemed to be!   25
      No mortal eye could see
The intimate welding of their later history,

10
    Or sign that they were bent
      By paths coincident
On being anon twin halves of one august event,   30

11
    Till the Spinner of the Years
      Said "Now!" And each one hears
And consummation comes, and jars two hemispheres.

6 *thrid:* thread.

Four-line Stanzas

Sir Thomas Wyatt   The Lover Beseecheth His Mistress
   Not to Forget His Steadfast Faith and True Intent

Forget not yet the tried intent
Of such a truth as I have meant;
My great travail so gladly spent,
  Forget not yet!

Forget not yet when first began   *5*
The weary life ye know, since whan
The suit, the service, none tell can;
  Forget not yet!

Forget not yet the great assays,
The cruel wrong, the scornful ways,   *10*
The painful patience in delays,
  Forget not yet!

Forget not! oh! forget not this,
How long ago hath been, and is
The mind that never meant amiss,   *15*
  Forget not yet!

Forget not then thine own approved,
The which so long hath thee so loved,
Whose steadfast faith yet never moved:
  Forget not this!   *20*

Thomas Campion   "Rose-Cheeked Laura, Come"

 Rose-cheeked Laura, come;
Sing thou smoothly with thy beauty's
Silent music, either other
  Sweetly gracing.

 Lovely forms do flow   *5*
From concent divinely framed:
Heaven is music, and thy beauty's
  Birth is heavenly

 These dull notes we sing
Discords need for helps to grace them;   *10*
Only beauty purely loving
  Knows no discord;

 But still moves delight,
Like clear springs renewed by flowing,
Ever perfect, ever in them-   *15*
  selves eternal.

6 *concent*: harmony; concert.

George Herbert   Discipline

Throw away thy rod,
Throw away thy wrath:
      O my God,
Take the gentle path.

For my heart's desire   5
Unto thine is bent:
      I aspire
To a full consent.

Not a word or look
I affect to own,   10
      But by book,
And thy book alone.

Though I fail, I weep:
Though I halt in pace,
      Yet I creep   15
To the throne of grace.

Then let wrath remove;
Love will do the deed;
      For with love
Stony hearts will bleed.   20

Love is swift of foot;
Love's a man of war,
      And can shoot,
And can hit from far.

Who can scape his bow?   25
That which wrought on thee,
      Brought thee low,
Needs must work on me.

Throw away thy rod;
Though man frailties hath,   30
      Thou art God:
Throw away thy wrath.

George Berkeley   Verses on the Prospect of Planting Arts and Learning in America

The muse, disgusted at an age and clime
  Barren of every glorious theme,
In distant lands now waits a better time,
  Producing subjects worthy fame:

In happy climes where from the genial sun   5
  And virgin earth such scenes ensue,
The force of art by nature seems outdone,
  And fancied beauties by the true:

In happy climes, the seat of innocence,
   Where nature guides and virtue rules,
Where men shall not impose for truth and sense   *10*
   The pedantry of courts and schools:

There shall be sung another golden age,
   The rise of empire and of arts,
The good and great inspiring epic rage,   *15*
   The wisest heads and noblest hearts.

Not such as Europe breeds in her decay;
   Such as she bred when fresh and young,
When heavenly flame did animate her clay,
   By future poets shall be sung.   20

Westward the course of empire takes its way;
   The four first acts already past,
A fifth shall close the drama with the day;
   Time's noblest offspring is the last.

22 *The four first acts:* referring to the civilizations in Babylon, Greece, Rome, and Western Europe.   23 *A fifth:* alluding to the Fifth Monarchy, or Millennium, which would exist just before Judgment Day.

Samuel Johnson   Lines Written in Ridicule of Certain Poems Published in 1777

Wheresoe'er I turn my view,
All is strange, yet nothing new;
Endless labor all along,
Endless labor to be wrong;

Phrase that time has flung away,   5
Uncouth words in disarray,
Tricked in antique ruff and bonnet,
Ode, and elegy, and sonnet.

7 *tricked:* dressed deceptively.

Robert Burns   A Red, Red Rose

O my Luve's like a red, red rose,
   That's newly sprung in June:
O my Luve's like the melody
   That's sweetly play'd in tune!

As fair art thou, my bonnie lass,   5
   So deep in luve am I:
And I will luve thee still, my dear,
   Till a' the seas gang dry:

Till a' the seas gang dry, my dear,
   And the rocks melt wi' the sun;   *10*

And I will luve thee still, my dear,
   While the sands o' life shall run.

And fare thee weel, my only Luve,
   And fare thee weel a while!
And I will come again, my Luve,   15
   Tho' it were ten thousand mile.

William Blake   The Sick Rose

O Rose, thou art sick!
The invisible worm
That flies in the night
In the howling storm

Has found out thy bed   5
Of crimson joy;
And his dark secret love
Does thy life destroy.

William Blake   London

I wander through each chartered street,
Near where the chartered Thames does flow,
And mark in every face I meet
Marks of weakness, marks of woe.

In every cry of every Man,   5
In every Infant's cry of fear,
In every voice, in every ban,
The mind-forged manacles I hear.

How the chimney-sweeper's cry
Every blackening Church appalls;   10
And the hapless soldier's sigh
Runs in blood down palace walls.

But most through midnight streets I hear
How the youthful harlot's curse
Blasts the new-born infant's tear,   15
And blights with plagues the marriage hearse.

William Wordsworth   "A Slumber Did My Spirit Seal"

A slumber did my spirit seal;
   I had no human fears:
She seemed a thing that could not feel
   The touch of earthly years.

No motion has she now, no force;   5
   She neither hears nor sees;
Rolled round in earth's diurnal course,
   With rocks, and stones, and trees.

Ralph Waldo Emerson   Brahma

If the red slayer think he slays,
    Or if the slain think he is slain,
They know not well the subtle ways
    I keep, and pass, and turn again.

Far or forgot to me is near;   5
    Shadow and sunlight are the same;
The vanquished gods to me appear;
    And one to me are shame and fame.

They reckon ill who leave me out;
    When me they fly, I am the wings;   10
I am the doubter and the doubt,
    And I the hymn the Brahmin sings.

The strong gods pine for my abode,
    And pine in vain the sacred Seven;
But thou, meek lover of the good!   15
    Find me, and turn thy back on heaven.

Brahma: the supreme essence of the universe in Hinduism.   *12*
Brahmin: one of the priestly Hindu caste.   *14 the sacred Seven:*
the Maharshis or highest saints.

Emily Dickinson   "My Life Closed Twice Before Its Close"

My life closed twice before its close;
It yet remains to see
If Immortality unveil
A third event to me,

So huge, so hopeless to conceive,   5
As these that twice befell.
Parting is all we know of heaven,
And all we need of hell.

Emily Dickinson   "The Soul Selects Her Own Society"

The soul selects her own society,
Then shuts the door;
On her divine majority
Obtrude no more.

Unmoved, she notes the chariot's pausing   5
At her low gate;
Unmoved, an emperor is kneeling
Upon her mat.

I've known her from an ample nation
Choose one;   10
Then close the valves of her attention
Like stone.

Elinor Wylie   The Eagle and the Mole

Avoid the reeking herd,
Shun the polluted flock,
Live like that stoic bird,
The eagle of the rock.

The huddled warmth of crowds   5
Begets and fosters hate;
He keeps, above the clouds,
His cliff inviolate.

When flocks are folded warm,
And herds to shelter run,   10
He sails above the storm,
He stares into the sun.

If in the eagle's track
Your sinews cannot leap,
Avoid the lathered pack,   15
Turn from the steaming sheep.

If you would keep your soul
From spotted sight or sound,
Live like the velvet mole;
Go burrow under ground.   20

And there hold intercourse
With roots of trees and stones,
With rivers at their source,
And disembodied bones.

Hart Crane   Black Tambourine

The interests of a black man in a cellar
Mark tardy judgment on the world's closed door.
Gnats toss in the shadow of a bottle,
And a roach spans a crevice in the floor.

Aesop, driven to pondering, found   5
Heaven with the tortoise and the hare;
Fox brush and sow ear top his grave
And mingling incantations on the air.

The black man, forlorn in the cellar,
Wanders in some mid-kingdom, dark, that lies   10
Between his tambourine, stuck on the wall,
And, in Africa, a carcass quick with flies.

e. e. cummings   "anyone lived in a pretty how town"

anyone lived in a pretty how town
(with up so floating many bells down)
spring summer autumn winter
he sang his didn't he danced his did.

Women and men(both little and small)   5
cared for anyone not at all
they sowed their isn't they reaped their same
sun moon stars rain

children guessed(but only a few
and down they forgot as up they grew   10
autumn winter spring summer)
that noone loved him more by more

when by now and tree by leaf
she laughed his joy she cried his grief
bird by snow and stir by still   15
anyone's any was all to her

someones married their everyones
laughed their cryings and did their dance
(sleep wake hope and then) they
said their nevers they slept their dream   20

stars rain sun moon
(and only the snow can begin to explain
how children are apt to forget to remember
with up so floating many bells down)

one day anyone died i guess   25
(and noone stooped to kiss his face)
busy folk buried them side by side
little by little and was by was

all by all and deep by deep
and more by more they dream their sleep   30
noone and anyone earth by april
wish by spirit and if by yes.

Women and men(both dong and ding)
summer autumn winter spring
reaped their sowing and went their came   35
sun moon stars rain

Richard Eberhart   Cold Fall

The coldness that falls upon the hours
As the years go by.
    It was the tremolo in a voice said this.
    It was when the voice and music became one.

Quietly from the whole heartbreak of the world   5
Was distilled a single consciousness:
The coldness that falls upon the hours
As the years go by.

Five-line Stanzas

George Herbert   Jordan (I)

Who says that fictions only and false hair
Become a verse? Is there in truth no beauty?
Is all good structure in a winding stair?
May no lines pass, except they do their duty
    Not to a true, but painted chair?   5

Is it no verse, except enchanted groves
And sudden arbors shadow coarse-spun lines?
Must purling streams refresh a lover's loves?
Must all be vailed, while he that reads, divines,
    Catching the sense at two removes?   10

Shepherds are honest people; let them sing:
Riddle who list, for me, and pull for Prime:
I envy no man's nightingale or spring;
Nor let them punish me with loss of rhyme,
    Who plainly say, My God, My King.   15

12 *pull for Prime:* draw the winning card in the card game primero.

Edmund Waller   Song

    Go lovely rose,
Tell her that wastes her time and me,
    That now she knows,
When I resemble her to thee,
    How sweet and fair she seems to be.   5

    Tell her that's young
And shuns to have her graces spied,
    That hadst thou sprung
In deserts where no men abide
    Thou must have uncommended died.   10

    Small is the worth
Of beauty from the light retired;
    Bid her come forth,
Suffer herself to be desired,
    And not blush so to be admired.   15

    Then die, that she
The common fate of all things rare

May read in thee;
How small a part of time they share
    That are so wondrous sweet and fair.   20

Edgar Allan Poe   To Helen

Helen, thy beauty is to me
    Like those Nicean barks of yore,
That gently, o'er a perfumed sea,
    The weary, way-worn wanderer bore
    To his own native shore.   5

On desperate seas long wont to roam,
    Thy hyacinth hair, thy classic face,
Thy Naiad airs have brought me home
    To the glory that was Greece
    And the grandeur that was Rome.   10

Lo, in yon brilliant window-niche
    How statue-like I see thee stand,
The agate lamp within thy hand!
    Ah, Psyche, from the regions which
    Are Holy Land!   15

Robert Browning   Epilogue

At the midnight in the silence of the sleep-time,
    When you set your fancies free,
Will they pass to where—by death, fools think, imprisoned
    Low he lies who once so loved you, whom you loved so,
            —Pity me?   5

Oh to love so, be so loved, yet so mistaken!
    What had I on earth to do
With the slothful, with the mawkish, the unmanly?
    Like the aimless, helpless, hopeless, did I drivel
            —Being—who?   10

One who never turned his back but marched breast forward,
    Never doubted clouds would break,
Never dreamed, though right were worsted, wrong would
        triumph,
    Held we fall to rise, are baffled to fight better,
            Sleep to wake.   15

No, at noonday in the bustle of man's work-time,
    Greet the unseen with a cheer!
Bid him forward, breast and back as either should be,
    "Strive and thrive!" cry "Speed—fight on, fare ever
            There as here!"   20

Hart Crane   Voyages II

—And yet this great wink of eternity,
Of rimless floods, unfettered leewardings,
Samite sheeted and processioned where
Her undinal vast belly moonward bends,
Laughing the wrapt inflections of our love;   5

Take this Sea, whose diapason knells
On scrolls of silver snowy sentences,
The sceptred terror of whose sessions rends
As her demeanors motion well or ill,
All but the pieties of lovers' hands.   10

And onward, as bells off San Salvador
Salute the crocus lustres of the stars,
In these poinsettia meadows of her tides,—
Adagios of islands, O my Prodigal,
Complete the dark confessions her veins spell.   15

Mark how her turning shoulders wind the hours,
And hasten while her penniless rich palms
Pass superscription of bent foam and wave,—
Hasten, while they are true,—sleep, death, desire,
Close round one instant in one floating flower.   20

Bind us in time, O Seasons clear, and awe.
O minstrel galleons of Carib fire,
Bequeath us to no earthly shore until
Is answered in the vortex of our grave
The seal's wide spindrift gaze toward paradise.   25

4 *undinal:* wave-like.

Dylan Thomas   "The Force That Through the Green Fuse Drives the Flower"

The force that through the green fuse drives the flower
Drives my green age; that blasts the roots of trees
Is my destroyer.
And I am dumb to tell the crooked rose
My youth is bent by the same wintry fever.   5

The force that drives the water through the rocks
Drives my red blood; that dries the mouthing streams
Turns mine to wax.
And I am dumb to mouth unto my veins
How at the mountain spring the same mouth sucks.   10

The hand that whirls the water in the pool
Stirs the quicksand; that ropes the blowing wind
Hauls my shroud sail.
And I am dumb to tell the hanging man
How of my clay is made the hangman's lime.   15

The lips of time leech to the fountain head;
Love drips and gathers, but the fallen blood
Shall calm her sores.
And I am dumb to tell a weather's wind
How time has ticked a heaven round the stars.   20

And I am dumb to tell the lover's tomb
How at my sheet goes the same crooked worm.

James Dickey   On the Hill Below the Lighthouse

Now I can be sure of my sleep;
I have lost the blue sea in my eyelids
From a place in the mind too deep
For thought, a light like a wind is beginning.
    Now I can be sure of my sleep.   5

When the moon is held strongly within it,
The eye of the mind opens gladly.
Day changes to dark, and is bright,
And miracles trust to the body,
    When the moon is held strongly within it.   10

A woman comes true when I think her.
Her eyes on the window are closing.
She has dressed the stark wood of a chair.
Her form and my body are facing.
    A woman comes true when I think her.   15

Shade swings, and she lies against me.
The lighthouse has opened its brain.
A browed light travels the sea.
Her clothes on the chair spread their wings.
    Shade swings, and she lies against me.   20

Let us lie in returning light,
As a bright arm sweeps through the moon.
The sun is dead, thinking of night
Swung round like a thing on a chain.
    Let us lie in returning light.   25

Let us lie where your angel is walking
In shadow, from wall unto wall,
Cast forth from your off-cast clothing
To pace the dim room where we fell.
    Let us lie where your angel is walking,   30

Coming back, coming back, going over.
An arm turns the light world around
The dark. Again we are waiting to hover
In a blaze in the mind like a wind
    Coming back, coming back, going over.   35

Now I can be sure of my sleep;
The moon is held strongly within it.

A woman comes true when I think her.
Shade swings, and she lies against me.
Let us lie in returning light;   40
Let us lie where your angel is walking,
Coming back, coming back, going over.

Six-line Stanzas

Chidiock Tichbourne   Written the Night Before His
    Execution

My prime of youth is but a frost of cares;
    My feast of joy is but a dish of pain;
My crop of corn is but a field of tares;
    And all my good is but vain hope of gain;
My life is fled, and yet I saw no sun;   5
And now I live, and now my life is done.

The spring is past, and yet it hath not sprung;
    The fruit is dead, and yet the leaves be green;
My youth is gone, and yet I am but young;
    I saw the world, and yet I was not seen;   10
My thread is cut, and yet it is not spun;
And now I live, and now my life is done.

I sought my death and found it in my womb,
    I looked for life, and saw it was a shade,
I trod the earth and knew it was my tomb,   15
    And now I die, and now I am but made:
The glass is full, and now my glass is run,
And now I live, and now my life is done.

Edmund Waller   Of the Last Verses in the Book

    When we for age could neither read nor write,
The subject made us able to indite.
The soul with nobler resolutions decked,
The body stooping does herself erect:
No mortal parts are requisite to raise   5
Her that unbodied can her maker praise.

    The seas are quiet when the winds give o'er;
So calm are we when passions are no more:
For then we know how vain it was to boast
Of fleeting things, so certain to be lost.   10
Clouds of affection from our younger eyes
Conceal that emptiness which age descries.

    The soul's dark cottage, battered and decayed,
Let's in new light through chinks that time has made

Stronger by weakness, wiser men become   15
As they draw near to their eternal home:
Leaving the old, both worlds at once they view,
That stand upon the threshold of the new.

Robert Burns   To a Mouse

ON TURNING HER UP IN HER NEST WITH THE
PLOW, NOVEMBER 1785

Wee, sleekit, cowrin, tim'rous beastie,
O, what a panic's in thy breastie!
Thou need na start awa sae hasty
                    Wi' bickering brattle!
I wad be laith to rin an' chase thee,   5
                    Wi' murdering pattle!

I'm truly sorry man's dominion
Has broken Nature's social union,
An' justifies that ill opinion
                    Which makes thee startle   10
At me, thy poor, earth-born companion
                    An' fellow mortal!

I doubt na, whyles, but thou may thieve;
What then? poor beastie, thou maun live!
A daimen icker in a thrave   15
                    'S a sma' request;
I'll get a blessin wi' the lave,
                    An' never miss't!

Thy wee-bit housie, too, in ruin!
Its silly wa's the win's are strewin!   20
An' naething, now, to big a new ane,
                    O' foggage green!
An' bleak December's win's ensuin,
                    Baith snell an' keen!

Thou saw the fields laid bare an' waste,   25
An' weary winter comin fast,
An' cozie here, beneath the blast,
                    Thou thought to dwell,
Till crash! the cruel coulter past
                    Out through thy cell.   30

That wee bit heap o' leaves an' stibble,
Has cost thee monie a weary nibble!
Now thou's turned out, for a' thy trouble,
                    But house or hald,
To thole the winter's sleety dribble,   35
                    An' cranreuch cauld!

But, Mousie, thou art no thy lane,
In proving foresight may be vain:

The best-laid schemes o' mice an' men
            Gang aft agley,   40
An' lea'e us nought but grief an' pain,
            For promised joy.

Still thou art blest, compared wi' me!
The present only toucheth thee:
But och! I backward cast my e'e,   45
           On prospects drear!
An' forward, though I canna see,
           I guess an' fear!

1 sleekit: sleek. *4 bickering brattle:* sudden scamper. *5 wad:* would. *laith:* loath. *rin:* run. *6 pattle:* paddle. *13 whyles:* at times. *15 daimen:* occasional. *icker:* ear of corn. *thrave:* bundle (of 24 sheaves). *17 lave:* remainder. *20 wa's:* ways. *win's:* winds. *21 big:* build. *22 foggage:* grass. *24 Baith:* both. *snell:* sharp. *29 coulter:* cutter on a plow. *34 But:* without. *hald:* abode. *35 thole:* endure. *36 cranreuch:* hoar-frost. *37 no thy lane:* not alone. *40 agley:* awry.

Henry Wadsworth Longfellow   Serenade

Stars of the summer night!
    Far in yon azure deeps,
Hide, hide your golden light!
    She sleeps!
My lady sleeps!   5
    Sleeps!

Moon of the summer night!
    Far down yon western steeps,
Sink, sink in silver light!
    She sleeps!   10
My lady sleeps!
    Sleeps!

Wind of the summer night!
    Where yonder woodbine creeps,
Fold, fold thy pinions light!   15
    She sleeps!
My lady sleeps!
    Sleeps!

Dreams of the summer night!
    Tell her, her lover keeps   20
Watch! while in slumbers light
    She sleeps!
My lady sleeps!
    Sleeps!

Dylan Thomas   "Light Breaks Where No Sun Shines"

Light breaks where no sun shines;
Where no sea runs, the waters of the heart

Push in their tides;
And, broken ghosts with glowworms in their heads,
The things of light   5
File through the flesh where no flesh decks the bones.

A candle in the thighs
Warms youth and seed and burns the seeds of age;
Where no seed stirs,
The fruit of man unwrinkles in the stars,   10
Bright as a fig;
Where no wax is, the cradle shows its hairs.

Dawn breaks behind the eyes;
From poles of skull and toe the windy blood
Slides like a sea;   15
Nor fenced, nor staked, the gushers of the sky
Spout to the rod
Divining in a smile the oil of tears.

Night in the sockets rounds,
Like some pitch moon, the limit of the globes;   20
Day lights the bone;
Where no cold is, the skinning gales unpin
The winter's robes;
The film of spring is hanging from the lids.

Light breaks on secret lots,   25
On tips of thought where thoughts smell in the rain;
When logics die,
The secret of the soil grows through the eye,
And blood jumps in the sun;
Above the waste allotments the dawn halts.   30

Stanzas of More Than Six Lines

Edmund Bolton   A Palinode

As withereth the primrose by the river,
As fadeth summer's sun from gliding fountains,
As vanisheth the light-blown bubble ever,
As melteth snow upon the mossy mountains:
So melts, so vanisheth, so fades, so withers   5
The rose, the shine, the bubble, and the snow
Of praise, pomp, glory, joy—which short life gathers—
Fair praise, vain pomp, sweet glory, brittle joy.
The withered primrose by the mourning river,
The faded summer's sun from weeping fountains,   10
The light-blown bubble vanished for ever,
The molten snow upon the naked mountains,
Are emblems that the treasures we up-lay
Soon wither, vanish, fade, and melt away.
For as the snow, whose lawn did overspread   15

The ambitious hills, which giant-like did threat
To pierce the heaven with their aspiring head,
Naked and bare doth leave their craggy seat;
Whenas the bubble, which did empty fly
The dalliance of the undiscerned wind,   20
On whose calm rolling waves it did rely,
Hath shipwreck, where it did dalliance find;
And when the sunshine which dissolved the snow,
Colored the bubble with a pleasant vary,
And made the rathe and timely primrose grow,   25
Swarth clouds withdrawn (which longer time do tarry)—
Oh, what is praise, pomp, glory, joy, but so
As shine by fountains, bubbles, flowers, or snow?

Palinode: retraction.   *25 rathe:* early-blooming.

John Donne   The Good-Morrow

I wonder by my troth, what thou and I
Did till we loved? Were we not weaned till then
But sucked on country pleasures, childishly?
Or snorted we in the seven sleepers' den?
'Twas so. But this, all pleasures fancies be.   5
If ever any beauty I did see
Which I desired and got, 'twas but a dream of thee.

And now good morrow to our waking souls
Which watch not one another out of fear;
For love, all love of other sights controls   10
And makes one little room an everywhere.
Let sea-discoverers to new worlds have gone;
Let maps to other, worlds on worlds have shown;
Let us possess one world, each hath one and is one.

My face in thine eye, thine in mine appears,   15
And true plain hearts do in the faces rest.
Where can we find two better hemispheres
Without sharp North, without declining West?
Whatever dies was not mixed equally;
If our two loves be one, or thou and I   20
Love so alike that none do slacken, none can die.

4 seven sleepers' den: seven Christian youths, to escape Roman
persecution, hid in a cave; they awakened two hundred years later.
17 hemispheres: the lovers who together comprise their world.
19 equally: uniformly. The thought was an alchemical commonplace.

Andrew Marvell   The Garden

How vainly men themselves amaze
To win the palm, the oak, or bays;

And their uncessant labors see
Crowned from some single herb or tree:
Whose short and narrow verged shade   5
Does prudently their toils unbraid;
While all flowers and all trees do close
To weave the garlands of repose.

Fair Quiet, have I found thee here,
And innocence, thy sister dear!   10
Mistaken long, I sought you then
In busy companies of men.
Your sacred plants, if here below,
Only among the plants will grow.
Society is all but rude,   15
To this delicious solitude.

No white nor red was ever seen
So am'rous as this lovely green.
Fond lovers, cruel as their flame,
Cut in these trees their mistress' name.   20
Little, alas, they know, or heed,
How far these beauties hers exceed!
Fair Trees! wheres'e'er your barks I wound,
No name shall but your own be found.

When we have run our passion's heat,   25
Love hither makes his best retreat.
The gods, that mortal beauty chase,
Still in a tree did end their race:
Apollo hunted Daphne so,
Only that she might laurel grow;   30
And Pan did after Syrinx speed,
Not as a nymph, but for a reed.

What wond'rous life in this I lead!
Ripe apples drop about my head;
The luscious clusters of the vine   35
Upon my mouth do crush their wine;
The nectarine, and curious peach,
Into my hands themselves do reach;
Stumbling on melons, as I pass,
Ensnared with flowers, I fall on grass.   40

Meanwhile the mind, from pleasure less,
Withdraws into its happiness:
The mind, that ocean where each kind
Does straight its own resemblance find;
Yet it creates, transcending these,   45
Far other worlds, and other seas;
Annihilating all that's made
To a green thought in a green shade.

Here at the fountain's sliding foot,
Or at some fruit-tree's mossy root,   50
Casting the body's vest aside,
My soul into the boughs does glide:

There like a bird it sits, and sings,
Then whets, and combs its silver wings;
And, till prepared for longer flight,   55
Waves in its plumes the various light.

Such was that happy garden state
While man there walked without a mate:
After a place so pure, and sweet,
What other help could yet be meet!   60
But 'twas beyond a mortal's share
To wander solitary there:
Two paradises 'twere in one
To live in Paradise alone.

How well the skillful gardener drew   65
Of flowers and herbs this dial new;
Where from above the milder sun
Does through a fragrant zodiac run;
And, as it works, th' industrious bee
Computes its time as well as we.   70
How could such sweet and wholesome hours
Be reckoned but with herbs and flowers!

37 *curious*: requiring care.   41 *pleasure less*: lesser pleasure.
51 *body's*: body as.   66 *dial*: sundial made of flowers.

William Blake   The Lamb

   Little Lamb, who made thee?
   Dost thou know who made thee?
Gave thee life, and bid thee feed
By the stream and o'er the mead;
Gave thee clothing of delight,   5
Softest clothing, woolly, bright;
Gave thee such a tender voice,
Making all the vales rejoice?
   Little Lamb, who made thee?
Dost thou know who made thee?   10

   Little Lamb, I'll tell thee,
   Little Lamb, I'll tell thee:
He is called by thy name,
For He calls Himself a Lamb.
He is meek, and He is mild;   15
He became a little child.
I a child, and thou a lamb,
We are called by his name.
   Little Lamb, God bless thee!
   Little Lamb God bless thee!   20

Wallace Stevens   The Emperor of Ice-Cream

Call the roller of big cigars,
The muscular one, and bid him whip

In kitchen cups concupiscent curds.
Let the wenches dawdle in such dress
As they are used to wear, and let the boys   5
Bring flowers in last month's newspapers.
Let be be finale of seem.
The only emperor is the emperor of ice-cream.

Take from the dresser of deal,
Lacking the three glass knobs, that sheet   10
On which she embroidered fantails once
And spread it so as to cover her face.
If her horny feet protrude, they come
To show how cold she is, and dumb.
Let the lamp affix its beam.   15
The only emperor is the emperor of ice-cream.

Dudley Randall   The Southern Road

There the black river, boundary to hell,
And here the iron bridge, the ancient car,
And grim conductor, who with surly yell
Forbids white soldiers where the black ones are.
And I re-live the enforced avatar   5
Of desperate journey to a dark abode
Made by my sires before another war;
And I set forth upon the southern road.

To a land where shadowed songs like flowers swell
And where the earth is scarlet as a scar   10
Friezed by the bleeding lash that fell (O fell!)
Upon my father's flesh. O far, far, far
And deep my blood has drenched it. None can bar
My birthright to the loveliness bestowed
Upon this country haughty as a star.   15
And I set forth upon the southern road.

This darkness and these mountains loom a spell
Of peak-roofed town where yearning steeples soar
And the holy holy chanting of a bell
Shakes human incense on the throbbing air   20
Where bonfires blaze and quivering bodies char.
Whose is the hair that crisped, and fiercely glowed?
I know it; and my entrails melt like tar
And I set forth upon the southern road.

O fertile hillsides where my fathers are,   25
And whence my woes like troubled streams have flowed,
Love you I must, though they may sweep me far.
And I set forth upon the southern road.

5 *avatar*: manifestation, incarnation.

Stanzas of Various Shapes

John Donne   The Message

Send home my long-strayed eyes to me,
Which (Oh) too long have dwelt on thee;
Yet since there they have learned such ill,
    Such forced fashions,
    And false passions,   5
        That they be
        Made by thee
Fit for no good fight, keep them still.

Send home my harmless heart again,
Which no unworthy thought could stain;   10
But if it be taught by thine
    To make jestings
    Of protestings,
        And cross both
        Word and oath,   15
Keep it, for then 'tis none of mine.

Yet send me back my heart and eyes,
That I may know, and see thy lies,
And may laugh and joy, when thou
    Art in anguish   20
    And dost languish
        For someone
        That will none,
Or prove as false as thou art now.

Robert Herrick   To Daffodils

Fair daffodils, we weep to see
    You haste away so soon:
As yet the early-rising sun
    Has not attained his noon.
        Stay, stay,   5
    Until the hasting day
            Has run
    But to the even-song;
And, having prayed together, we
        Will go with you along.   10

We have short time to stay, as you,
    We have as short a spring;
As quick a growth to meet decay,
    As you, or anything.
        We die,   15

          As your hours do, and dry
                    Away,
          Like to the summer's rain;
Or as the pearls of morning's dew
                    Ne'er to be found again.   20

Marianne Moore   Spenser's Ireland

has not altered—
          the kindest place I've never been,
          the greenest place I've never seen.
Every name is a tune.
Denunciations do not affect   5
          the culprit;   nor blows, but it
is torture to him to not be spoken to.
They're natural—
          the coat, like Venus'
mantle lined with stars,   10
buttoned close at the neck—the
          sleeves new from disuse.

If in Ireland
          they play the harp backward at need,
          and gather at midday the seed   15
of the fern, eluding
their 'giants all covered with iron,' might
          there be fern   seed for unlearn-
ing obduracy and for reinstating
the enchantment?   20
          Hindered characters
seldom have mothers—
In Irish stories—
          but they all have grandmothers.

It was Irish;   25
          a match not a mariage was made
          when my great great grandmother'd said
with native genius for
disunion, 'although your suitor be
          perfection,   one objection   30
is enough; he is not
Irish.'   Outwitting
          the fairies, befriending the furies,
whoever again
and again says, 'I'll never   35
          give in,' never sees

that you're not free
          until you've been made captive by
          supreme belief—credulity
you say?   When large dainty   40
fingers tremblingly divide the wings
          of the fly   for mid-July

with a needle and wrap it with peacock-tail,
or tie wool and
        buzzard's wing, their pride,   45
like the enchanter's
is in care, not madness. Con-
        curring hands divide

flax for damask
        that when bleached by Irish weather   50
        has the silvered chamois-leather
water-tightness of a
skin.   Twisted torcs and gold new-moon-shaped
        lunulae   aren't jewelry
like the purple-coral fuchsia-tree's. If Eire—   55
the guillemot
        so neat and the hen
of the heath and the
linnet spinet-sweet—bespeak
        relentlessness, then   60

they are to me
        like enchanted Earl Gerald who
        changed himself into a stag, to
a great green-eyed cat of
the mountain. Discommodity makes   65
        them invis   ible; they've dis-
appeared. The Irish say your trouble is their
trouble and your
        joy their joy? I wish
I could believe it;   70
I am troubled; I'm dissat-
        isfied, I'm Irish.

Spenser's Ireland: Edmund Spenser wrote a history of Ireland and
had been in government services there.   *53 torcs*: necklaces.
54 lunulae: crescent-shaped objects.   *56 guillemot*: an auk.   *57–
58 hen of the heath*: black grouse.

Stanzaic Combinations

John Gay   Fable XLV: The Poet and the Rose

I hate the man who builds his name
On ruins of another's fame.
Thus prudes by characters o'erthrown
Imagine that they raise their own:
Thus scribblers, covetous of praise,   5
Think slander can transplant the bays.
Beauties and bards have equal pride,
With both all rivals are decried.
Who praises Lesbia's eyes and features,

Must call her sister, awkward creature;   10
For the kind flattery's sure to charm,
When we some other nymph disarm.
   As in the cool of early day
A poet sought the sweets of May,
The garden's fragrant breath ascends,   15
And every stalk with odor bends.
A rose he plucked, he gazed, admired,
Thus singing as the Muse inspired.

Go, Rose, my Chloe's bosom grace;
   How happy should I prove,   20
Might I supply that envied place
   With never-fading love!
There, phoenix-like, beneath her eye,
Involved in fragrance, burn and die!

Know, hapless flower, that thou shalt find   25
   More fragrant roses there;
I see thy withering head reclined
   With envy and despair!
One common fate we both must prove;
You die with envy, I with love.   30

   "Spare your comparison," replied
An angry rose, who grew beside;
"Of all mankind you should not flout us;
What can a poet do without us!
In every love-song roses bloom;   35
We lend you color and perfume.
Does it to Chloe's charms conduce,
To found her praise on our abuse?
Must we, to flatter her, be made
To wither, envy, pine and fade?"   40

Trumbull Stickney   Mnemosyne

It's autumn in the country I remember.

How warm a wind blew here about the ways!
And shadows on the hillside lay to slumber
During the long sun-sweetened summer-days.

It's cold abroad the country I remember.   5

The swallows veering skimmed the golden grain
At midday with a wing aslant and limber;
And yellow cattle browsed upon the plain.

It's empty down the country I remember.

I had a sister lovely in my sight: 10
Her hair was dark, her eyes were very somber;
We sang together in the woods at night.

It's lonely in the country I remember.

The babble of our children fills my ears,
And on our hearth I stare the perished ember   15
To flames that show all starry through my tears.

It's dark about the country I remember.

There are the mountains where I lived. The path
Is slushed with cattle-tracks and fallen timber,
The stumps are twisted by the tempests' wrath.   20

But that I knew these places are my own,
I'd ask how came such wretchedness to cumber
The earth, and I to people it alone.

It rains across the country I remember.

Mnemosyne: Memory, mother of the muses.

e. e. cummings   song

All in green went my love riding
on a great horse of gold
into the silver dawn.

four lean hounds crouched low and smiling
the merry deer ran before.   5

Fleeter be they than dappled dreams
the swift sweet deer
the red rare deer.

four red roebuck at a white water
the cruel bugle sang before.   10

Horn at hip went my love riding
riding the echo down
into the silver dawn.

four lean hounds crouched low and smiling
the level meadows ran before.   15

Softer be they than slippered sleep
the lean lithe deer
the fleet flown deer.

Four fleet does at a gold valley
the famished arrow sang before.   20

Bow at belt went my love riding
riding the mountain down
into the silver dawn.

four lean hounds crouched low and smiling
the sheer peaks ran before.   25

Paler be they than daunting death
the sleek slim deer
the tall tense deer.

Four tall stags at a green mountain
the lucky hunter sang before.   30

All in green went my love riding
on a great horse of gold
into the silver dawn.

four lean hounds crouched low and smiling
my heart fell dead before.   35

Stanley Kunitz   For Proserpine

Our purple tongues that testify
The pomegranate has been broken
Are stained, their roots and buds are stained, with the shy
Fruity pleasure of us, met, spoken.

(I shall remember the days   5
Of my youth and your beautiful new ways.)

In fierce decay I'll find a stripe
Of honey sweetening the tart
Old brain. I shall not know again such ripe
Beauty of the burst, dark heart.   10

(I'll think of my absurd,
Impossible, pledged, serious word.)

My undivulged interior world
A country for our souls shall be,
Till I am done with name and number, gnarled   15
and mindless like a babbling tree.

(A heavy bird will brood
On women stagnant in their blood.)

Preserve you from the long farewell
Whose sex is flowers, whose breasts are grain.
Return, return. Into a leafless hell   20
Gradually drops the brain.

(The bulls, the stallions, have tasted
Incredible fruit. Their seed is wasted.)

Proserpine: goddess of the underworld, who returned to earth
periodically and thus symbolized spring and vegetation.

LeRoi Jones   Preface to a Twenty Volume Suicide Note

Lately, I've become accustomed to the way
The ground opens up and envelops me
Each time I go out to walk the dog.
Or the broad edged silly music the wind
Makes when I run for a bus—   5

Things have come to that.

And now, each night I count the stars,
And each night I get the same number.
And when they will not come to be counted
I count the holes they leave.   10

Nobody sings anymore.

And then last night, I tiptoed up
To my daughter's room and heard her
Talking to someone, and when I opened
The door, there was no one there . . .   15
Only she on her knees,
Peeking into her own clasped hands.

STANZAIC FORMS: SPECIFIC*

Terza Rima

Percy Bysshe Shelley   Ode to the West Wind

1

O wild West Wind, thou breath of Autumn's being,
Thou, from whose unseen presence the leaves dead
Are driven, like ghosts from an enchanter fleeing,

Yellow, and black, and pale, and hectic red,
Pestilence-stricken multitudes: O thou,   5
Who chariotest to their dark wintry bed

The winged seeds, where they lie cold and low,
Each like a corpse within its grave, until
Thine azure sister of the Spring shall blow

Her clarion o'er the dreaming earth, and fill   10
(Driving sweet buds like flocks to feed in air)
With living hues and odors plain and hill:

Wild Spirit, which art moving everywhere;
Destroyer and preserver; hear, oh, hear!

2

Thou on whose stream, mid the steep sky's commotion,   15
Loose clouds like earth-decaying leaves are shed,
Shook from the tangled boughs of Heaven and Ocean,

Angels of rain and lightning: there are spread
On the blue surface of thine aery surge,
Like the bright hair uplifted from the head   20

* See the *Glossary of Poetical and Critical Terms* for descriptions
of each specific stanza illustrated on the following pages.

Of some fierce Maenad, even from the dim verge
Of the horizon to the zenith's height,
The locks of the approaching storm. Thou dirge

Of the dying year, to which this closing night
Will be the dome of a vast sepulchre,   25
Vaulted with all thy congregated might

Of vapors, from whose solid atmosphere
Black rain, and fire, and hail will burst: oh, hear!

3

Thou who didst waken from his summer dreams
The blue Mediterranean, where he lay,   30
Lulled by the coil of his crystalline streams,

Beside a pumice isle in Baiae's bay,
And saw in sleep old palaces and towers
Quivering within the wave's intenser day,

All overgrown with azure moss and flowers   35
So sweet, the sense faints picturing them! Thou
For whose path the Atlantic's level powers

Cleave themselves into chasms, while far below
The sea-blooms and the oozy woods which wear
The sapless foliage of the ocean, know   40

Thy voice, and suddenly grow gray with fear,
And tremble and despoil themselves: oh, hear!

4

If I were a dead leaf thou mightest bear;
If I were a swift cloud to fly with thee;
A wave to pant beneath thy power, and share   45

The impulse of thy strength, only less free
Than thou, O uncontrollable! If even
I were as in my boyhood, and could be

The comrade of thy wanderings over Heaven,
As then, when to outstrip thy skiey speed   50
Scarce seemed a vision; I would ne'er have striven

As thus with thee in prayer in my sore need.
Oh, lift me as a wave, a leaf, a cloud!
I fall upon the thorns of life! I bleed!

A heavy weight of hours has chained and bowed   55
One too like thee: tameless, and swift, and proud.

5

Make me thy lyre, even as the forest is;
What if my leaves are falling like its own!
The tumult of thy mighty harmonies

Will take from both a deep, autumnal tone,   60
Sweet though in sadness. Be thou, Spirit fierce,
My spirit! Be thou me, impetuous one!

Drive my dead thoughts over the universe
Like withered leaves to quicken a new birth!
And, by the incantation of this verse,   65

Scatter, as from an unextinguished hearth
Ashes and sparks, my words among mankind!
Be through my lips to unawakened earth

The trumpet of a prophecy! O Wind,
If Winter comes, can Spring be far behind?   70

9 *sister of the Spring*: the south wind.   21 *Maenad*: a votary of
Bacchus, god of wine and orgies.   32 *pumice*: volcanic. *Baiae*:
a village west of Naples.

John Berryman   Canto Amor

Dream in a dream the heavy soul somewhere
struck suddenly & dark down to its knees.
A griffin sighs off in the orphic air.

If (Unknown Majesty) I not confess
praise for the rack the rock the live sailor   5
under the blue sea—yet I may You bless

always for hér, in fear & joy for hér
whose gesture summons ever when I grieve
me back and is my mage and minister.

—Muses, whose worship I may never leave   10
but for this pensive woman, now I dare,
teach me her praise! with her my praise receive.—

Three years already of the round world's war
had rolled by stoned & disappointed eyes
when she and I came where we were made for.   15

Pale as a star lost in returning skies,
more beautiful than midnight stars more frail
she moved towards me like chords, a sacrifice;

entombed in body trembling through the veil
arm upon arm, learning our ancient wound,   20
we see our one soul heal, recovering pale.

Then priestly sanction, then the drop of sound.
Quickly part to the cavern ever warm
deep from the march, body to body bound,

descend (my soul) out of dismantling storm   25
into the darkness where the world is made.
Come back to the bright air. Love is multiform.

Heartmating hesitating unafraid
although incredulous, she seemed to fill
the lilac shadow with light wherein she played,   30

whom sorry childhood had made sit quite still,
an orphan silence, unregarded sheen,
listening for any small soft note, not hopeful:

caricature: as once a maiden Queen,
flowering power comeliness kindness grace,   35
shattered her mirror, wept, would not be seen.

These pities moved. Also above her face
serious or flushed, swayed her fire-gold
not earthly hair, now moonless to unlace,

resistless flame, now in a sun more cold   40
great shells to whorl about each secret ear,
mysterious histories, strange shores, unfold.

New musics! One the music that we hear
this is the music which the masters make
out of their minds, profound solemn & clear.   45

And then the other music, in whose sake
all men perceive a gladness but we are drawn
less for that joy than utterly to take

our trial, naked in the music's vision,
the flowing ceremony of trouble and light,   50
all Loves becoming, none to rest upon.

Such Mozart made—an ear so delicate
he fainted at a trumpet-call, a child
so delicate. So merciful that sight,

so stern, we follow rapt who ran awild.   55
Marriage is the second music, and thereof
we hear what we can bear, faithful & mild.

Therefore the streaming torches in the grove
through dark or bright, swiftly & now more near
cherish a festival of anxious love.   60

Dance for this music, Mistress to music dear,
more, that full storm through the disordered wood
ravens at midnight of my thirtieth year

and only the trial of our music should
still this irresolute air, only your voice   65
spelling the tempest may compel our good:

Sing then beyond my song: whirl & rejoice!

9 *mage:* magician, wise man.

Alcaic

Alfred, Lord Tennyson   Milton

O mighty-mouthed inventor of harmonies,
O skilled to sing of Time or Eternity,
   God-gifted organ-voice of England—
     Milton, a name to resound for ages;
Whose Titan angels, Gabriel, Abdiel,   5
Starred from Jehovah's gorgeous armories,
   Tower, as the deep-domed empyrean
     Rings to the roar of an angel onset—
Me rather all that bowery loneliness,
The brooks of Eden mazily murmuring,   10
   And bloom profuse and cedar arches
     Charm—as a wanderer out on ocean,
Where some refulgent sunset of India
Streams o'er a rich ambrosial ocean isle,
   And crimson-hued the stately palm-woods   15
     Whisper in odorous heights of even.

Anacreontic

Abraham Cowley   Drinking

The thirsty earth soaks up the rain,
And drinks, and gapes for drink again.
The plants suck in the earth and are
With constant drinking fresh and fair.
The sea itself, which one would think   5
Should have but little need of drink,
Drinks ten thousand rivers up,
So filled that they o'erflow the cup.
The busy sun (and one would guess
By's drunken fiery face no less)   10
Drinks up the sea, and when h'as done,
The moon and stars drink up the sun.
They drink and dance by their own light,
They drink and revel all the night.
Nothing in Nature's sober found,   15
But an eternal health goes round.
Fill up the bowl then, fill it high,
Fill all the glasses there, for why
Should every creature drink but I,
Why, man of morals, tell me why?   20

William Oldys The Fly

Busy, curious, thirsty fly,
Gently drink, and drink as I;
Freely welcome to my cup,
Could'st thou sip, and sip it up;
Make the most of life you may,   5
Life is short and wears away.

Just alike, both mine and thine,
Hasten quick to their decline;
Thine's a summer, mine's no more,
Though repeated to threescore;   10
Threescore summers when they're gone,
Will appear as short as one.

Ballad Stanza

Anonymous   Ballad

As you came from the holy land
　　Of Walsinghame,
Met you not with my true love
　　By the way as you came?

How shall I know your true love,   5
　　That have met many a one,
As I went to the holy land,
　　That have come, that have gone?

She is neither white nor brown,
　　But as the heavens fair;   10
There is none hath a form so divine
　　In the earth or the air.

Such a one did I meet, good sir,
　　Such an angelic face,
Who like a queen, like a nymph, did appear,   15
　　By her gait, by her grace.

She hath left me here all alone,
　　All alone, as unknown,
Who sometimes did me lead with herself,
　　And me loved as her own.   20

What's the cause that she leaves you alone,
　　And a new way doth take,
Who loved you once as her own,
　　And her joy did you make?

I have loved her all my youth,   25
    But now old, as you see;
Love likes not the falling fruit
    From the withered tree.

Know that Love is a careless child,
    And forgets promise past;   30
He is blind, he is deaf when he list,
    And in faith never fast.

His desire is a dureless content,
    And a trustless joy;
He is won with a world of despair,   35
    And is lost with a toy.

Of womenkind such indeed is the love,
    Or the word love abused,
Under which many childish desires
    And conceits are excused.   40

But true love is a durable fire,
    In the mind ever burning,
Never sick, never old, never dead,
    From itself never turning.

Elegiac Stanza

Allen Tate   Mr. Pope

When Alexander Pope strolled in the city
Strict was the glint of pearl and gold sedans.
Ladies leaned out, more out of fear than pity;
For Pope's tight back was rather a goat's than man's.

One often thinks the urn should have more bones   5
Than skeletons provide for speedy dust;
The urn gets hollow, cobwebs brittle as stones
Weave to the funeral shell a frivolous rust.

And he who dribbled couplets like the snake
Coiled to a lithe precision in the sun,   10
Is missing. The jar is empty; you may break
It only to find that Mr. Pope is gone.

What requisitions of a verity
Prompted the wit and rage between his teeth
One cannot say: around a crooked tree   15
A mortal climbs whose name should be a wreath.

Sapphic

Isaac Watts   The Day of Judgment

AN ODE ATTEMPTED IN ENGLISH SAPPHIC

When the fierce north wind with his airy forces
Rears up the Baltic to a foaming fury,
And the red lightning with a storm of hail comes
        Rushing amain down,

How the poor sailors stand amazed and tremble,   5
While the hoarse thunder, like a bloody trumpet,
Roars a loud onset to the gaping waters,
        Quick to devour them!

Such shall the noise be and the wild disorder
(If things eternal may be like these earthly),   10
Such the dire terror, when the great Archangel
        Shakes the creation,

Tears the strong pillars of the vault of heaven,
Breaks up old marble, the repose of princes;
See the graves open, and the bones arising,   15
        Flames all around 'em!

Hark, the shrill outcries of the guilty wretches!
Lively bright horror and amazing anguish
Stare through their eyelids, while the living worm lies
        Gnawing within them.   20

Thoughts like old vultures prey upon their heart-strings,
And the smart twinges, when the eye beholds the
Lofty Judge frowning, and a flood of vengeance
        Rolling afore him.

Hopeless immortals! How they scream and shiver,   25
While devils push them to the pit wide-yawning
Hideous and gloomy, to receive them headlong
        Down to the center.

Stop here, my fancy: (all away ye horrid
Doleful ideas); come, arise to Jesus;   30
How He sits God-like! and the saints around him
        Throned, yet adoring!

Oh may I sit there when he comes triumphant
Dooming the nations! then ascend to glory
While our hosannas all along the passage   35
        Shout the Redeemer.

Algernon Charles Swinburne   Sapphics

All the night sleep came not upon my eyelids,
Shed not dew, nor shook nor unclosed a feather
Yet with lips shut close and with eyes of iron
    Stood and beheld me.

Then to me so lying awake a vision   5
Came without sleep over the seas and touched me,
Softly touched mine eyelids and lips; and I, too,
    Full of the vision

Saw the white implacable Aphrodite,
Saw the hair unbound and the feet unsandaled   10
Shine as fire of sunset on western waters;
    Saw the reluctant

Feet, the straining plumes of the doves that drew her,
Looking always, looking with necks reverted,
Back to Lesbos, back to the hills whereunder   15
    Shone Mitylene;

Heard the flying feet of the Loves behind her
Make a sudden thunder upon the waters,
As the thunder flung from the strong unclosing
    Wings of a great wind.   20

So the goddess fled from her place, with awful
Sound of feet and thunder of wings around her;
While behind a clamor of singing women
    Severed the twilight.

Ah, the singing, ah, the delight, the passion!   25
All the Loves wept, listening; sick with anguish,
Stood the crowned nine Muses about Apollo;
    Fear was upon them,

While the tenth sang wonderful things they knew not.
Ah, the tenth, the Lesbian! the nine were silent,   30
None endured the sound of her song for weeping;
    Laurel by laurel,

Faded all their crowns; but about her forehead,
Round her woven tresses and ashen temples
White as dead snow, paler than grass in summer   35
    Ravaged with kisses,

Shone a light of fire as a crown forever.
Yea, almost the implacable Aphrodite
Paused, and almost wept; such a song was that song.
    Yea, by her name, too,   40

Called her, saying, "Turn to me, O my Sappho";
Yet she turned her face from the Loves, she saw not
Tears for laughter darken immortal eyelids,
    Heard not about her

Fearful fitful wings of the doves departing,   45
Saw not how the bosom of Aphrodite
Shook with weeping, saw not her shaken raiment,
  Saw not her hands wrung;

Saw the Lesbians kissing across their smitten
Lutes with lips more sweet than the sound of lute-strings,   50
Mouth to mouth and hand upon hand, her chosen,
  Fairer than all men;

Only saw the beautiful lips and fingers,
Full of songs and kisses and little whispers,
Full of music; only beheld among them   55
  Soar, as a bird soars

Newly fledged, her visible song, a marvel,
Made of perfect sound and exceeding passion,
Sweetly shapen, terrible, full of thunders,
  Clothed with the wind's wings.   60

Then rejoiced she, laughing with love, and scattered
Roses, awful roses of holy blossom;
Then the Loves thronged sadly with hidden faces
  Round Aphrodite,

Then the Muses, stricken at heart, were silent;   65
Yea, the gods waxed pale; such a song was that song.
All reluctant, all with a fresh repulsion,
  Fled from before her.

All withdrew long since, and the land was barren,
Full of fruitless women and music only.
Now perchance, when winds are assuaged at sunset,   70
  Lulled at the dewfall,

By the gray seaside, unassuaged, unheard of,
Unbeloved, unseen in the ebb of twilight,
Ghosts of outcast women return lamenting,
  Purged not in Lethe,   75

Clothed about with flame and with tears, and singing
Songs that move the heart of the shaken heaven,
Songs that break the heart of the earth with pity,
  Hearing, to hear them.   80

Rhyme Royal

Thomas Sackville, Earl of Dorset   "Induction"
  FROM *A Mirror for Magistrates*

The wrathful winter, 'proaching on apace,
With blustering blasts had all ybared the treen,
And old Saturnus, with his frosty face,

With chilling cold had pierced the tender green;
The mantles rent, wherein enwrapped been   5
   The gladsome groves that now lay overthrown,
   The tapets torn, and every bloom down blown.

The soil, that erst so seemly was to seen,
Was all despoiled of her beauty's hue;
And soote fresh flowers, wherewith the summer's queen   10
Had clad the earth, now Boreas' blasts down blew;
And small fowls flocking, in their song did rue
   The winter's wrath, wherewith each thing defaced
   In woeful wise bewailed the summer past.

Hawthorn had lost his motley livery,   15
The naked twigs were shivering all for cold,
And dropping down the tears abundantly;
Each thing, methought, with weeping eye me told
The cruel season, bidding me withhold
   Myself within; for I was gotten out   20
   Into the fields, whereas I walked about.

When lo, the night with misty mantles spread,
Gan dark the day and dim the azure skies;
And Venus in her message Hermes sped
To bloody Mars, to will him not to rise,   25
Which she herself approached in speedy wise;
   And Virgo, hiding her disdainful breast,
   With Thetis now had laid her down to rest.

Whiles Scorpio, dreading Sagittarius' dart,
Whose bow prest bent in fight, the string had slipped,   30
Down slid into the ocean flood apart;
The Bear, that in the Irish seas had dipped
His grisly feet, with speed from thence he whipped;
   For Thetis, hasting from the Virgin's bed,
   Pursued the Bear, that ere she came was fled.   35

And Phaethon now, near reaching to his race
With glistering beams, gold streaming where they bent,
Was prest to enter in his resting place;
Erythius, that in the cart first went,
Had even now attained his journey's stent;   40
   And, fast declining, hid away his head,
   While Titan couched him in his purple bed.

And pale Cynthia, with her borrowed light,
Beginning to supply her brother's place,
Was past the noonstead six degrees in sight,   45
When sparkling stars amid the heaven's face
With twinkling light shone on the earth apace,
   That, while they brought about the nightë's chair,
   The dark had dimmed the day ere I was ware.

And sorrowing I to see the summer flowers,   50
The lively green, the lusty leas forlorn,
The sturdy trees so shattered with the showers,

The fields so fade that flourished so beforn,
It taught me well all earthly things be born
  To die the death, for nought long time may last;   55
  The summer's beauty yields to winter's blast.

2 *ybared*: denuded.   *treen*: trees.   7 *tapets*: tapestries.   8 *erst*:
formerly. *seen*: see.   10 *soote*: sweet.   11 *Boreas*: the North
Wind.   28 *Thetis*: the sea.   39 *Erythius*: relating to a western
isle; here, a star of the west.   40 *stent*: end.   42 *Titan*: the sun.
43 *Cynthia*: the moon, sister of the sun.

William Morris "An Apology"
FROM *The Earthly Paradise*

  Of Heaven or Hell I have no power to sing;
I cannot ease the burden of your fears,
Or make quick-coming death a little thing,
Or bring again the pleasure of past years,
Nor for my words shall ye forget your tears,   5
Or hope again for aught that I can say—
The idle singer of an empty day.

  But rather when, aweary of your mirth,
From full hearts still unsatisfied ye sigh,
And, feeling kindly unto all the earth,   10
Grudge every minute as it passes by,
Made the more mindful that the sweet days die:
Remember me a little then, I pray—
The idle singer of an empty day.

  The heavy trouble, the bewildering care   15
That weighs us down who live and earn our bread,
These idle verses have no power to bear;
So let me sing of names remembered,
Because they, living not, can ne'er be dead,
Or long time take their memory quite away   20
From us poor singers of an empty day.

  Dreamer of dreams, born out of my due time,
Why should I strive to set the crooked straight?
Let it suffice me that my murmuring rhyme
Beats with light wing against the ivory gate—   25
Telling a tale not too importunate
To those who in the sleepy region stay,
Lulled by the singer of an empty day.

  Folk say, a wizard to a northern king
At Christmas-tide such wonderous things did show,   30
That through one window men beheld the spring,
And through another saw the summer glow,
And through a third the fruited vines a-row—
While still, unheard, but on its wonted way,
Piped the drear wind of that December day.   35

So with this Earthly Paradise it is,
If ye will read aright, and pardon me,
Who strive to build a shadowy isle of bliss
Midmost the beating of the steely sea,
Where tossed about all hearts of men must be;   40
Whose ravening monsters mighty men shall slay—
Not the poor singer of an empty day.

Ottava Rima

William Butler Yeats   Sailing to Byzantium

1
That is no country for old men. The young
In one another's arms, birds in the trees,
—Those dying generations—at their song,
The salmon-falls, the mackerel-crowded seas,
Fish, flesh, or fowl, commend all summer long   5
Whatever is begotten, born, and dies.
Caught in that sensual music all neglect
Monuments of unageing intellect.

2
An aged man is but a paltry thing,
A tattered coat upon a stick, unless   10
Soul clap its hands and sing, and louder sing
For every tatter in its mortal dress,
Nor is there singing school but studying
Monuments of its of magnificence;
And therefore I have sailed the seas and come   15
To the holy city of Byzantium.

3
O sages standing in God's holy fire
As in the gold mosaic of a wall,
Come from the holy fire, perne in a gyre,
And be the singing-masters of my soul.   20
Consume my heart away; sick with desire
And fastened to a dying animal
It knows not what it is; and gather me
Into the artifice of eternity.

4
Once out of nature I shall never take   25
My bodily form from any natural thing,
But such a form as Grecian goldsmiths make
Of hammered gold and gold enamelling
To keep a drowsy Emperor awake;
Or set upon a golden bough to sing   30

To lords and ladies of Byzantium
Of what is past, or passing, or to come.

19 *perne:* move, gyrate.   *gyre:* circle described by a spiraling
object.

Spenserian Stanza

Edmund Spenser   "Induction"
    FROM *The Faerie Queene, Book I*

The Induction to the First Booke, Contayning the Legend of
the Red Crosse or of Holinesse

1

Lo! I the man, whose Muse whylome did maske,
As time her taught, in lowly shephards weeds,
Am now enforst, a farre unfitter taske,
For trumpets sterne to chaunge mine oaten reeds,
And sing of knights and ladies gentle deeds;   5
Whose praises having slept in silence long,
Me, all too meane, the sacred Muse areeds
To blazon broade emongst her learned throng:
Fierce warres and faithfull loves shall moralize my song.

2

Helpe then, O holy virgin, chiefe of nyne,   10
Thy weaker novice to performe thy will;
Lay forth out of thine everlasting scryne
The antique rolles, which there lye hidden still,
Of Faerie knights, and fayrest Tanaquill,
Whom that most noble Briton Prince so long   15
Sought through the world, and suffered so much ill,
That I must rue his undeserved wrong:
O helpe thou my weake wit, and sharpen my dull tong.

3

And thou, most dreaded impe of highest Jove,
Faire Venus sonne, that with thy cruell dart   20
At that good knight so cunningly didst rove,
That glorious fire it kindled in his hart,
Lay now thy deadly heben bowe apart,
And with thy mother mylde come to mine ayde:
Come both, and with you bring triumphant Mart,   25
In loves and gentle jollities arraid,
After his murdrous spoyles and bloudie rage allayd.

4

And with them eke, O Goddesse heavenly bright,
Mirrour of grace and majestie divine,

Great Ladie of the greatest Isle, whose light   30
Like Phoebus lampe throughout the world doth shine,
Shed they faire beames into my feeble eyne,
And raise my thoughtes, too humble and too vile,
To thinke of that true glorious type of thine,
The argument of mine afflicted stile: 35
The which to heare vouchsafe, O dearest dread, a while.

1 *whylome*: formerly.   7 *areeds*: declares.   12 *scryne*: a chest
for papers.   23 *heben*: ebony.   25 *Mart*: Mars.   28 *eke*: also.

George Gordon, Lord Byron   FROM *Canto Fourth of*
Childe Harold's Pilgrimage

VENICE AND SUNSET

1

I stood in Venice on the Bridge of Sighs,
A palace and a prison on each hand;
I saw from out the wave her structures rise
As from the stroke of the enchanter's wand:
A thousand years their cloudy wings expand   5
Around me, and a dying Glory smiles
O'er the far times, when many a subject land
Looked to the winged Lion's marble piles,
Where Venice sate in state, throned on her hundred isles!

2

She looks a sea Cybele, fresh from ocean,   10
Rising with her tiara of proud towers
At airy distance, with majestic motion,
A ruler of the waters and their powers.
And such she was: her daughters had their dowers
From spoils of nations, and the exhaustless East   15
Poured in her lap all gems in sparkling showers;
In purple was she robed, and of her feast
Monarchs partook, and deemed their dignity increased.

3

In Venice Tasso's echoes are no more,
And silent rows the songless gondolier;   20
Her palaces are crumbling to the shore,
And music meets not always now the ear.
Those days are gone—but Beauty still is here:
States fall, arts fade—but Nature doth not die,
Nor yet forget how Venice once was dear,   25
The pleasant place of all festivity,
The revel of the earth, the masque of Italy!

4

But unto us she hath a spell beyond
Her name in story, and her long array

Of mighty shadows, whose dim forms despond   *30*
Above the dogeless city's vanished sway:
Ours is a trophy which will not decay
With the Rialto; Shylock and the Moor,
And Pierre, cannot be swept or worn away—
The keystones of the arch!—though all were o'er,   *35*
For us repeopled were the solitary shore.

                    5
The beings of the mind are not of clay;
Essentially immortal, they create
And multiply in us a brighter ray
And more beloved existence. That which Fate   *40*
Prohibits to dull life, in this our state
Of mortal bondage, by these spirits supplied,
First exiles, then replaces what we hate;
Watering the heart whose early flowers have died,
And with a fresh growth replenishing the void.   *45*

10 *Cybele:* a nature goddess.   30 *despond:* become discouraged.
31 *dogeless:* without its former governer, the doge.   33 *Rialto:*
the center of commerce in the city.   *Shylock:* of *The Merchant
of Venice.*   *Moor:* Othello.   34 *Pierre:* a character in Otway's
Venice Preserved.

SPECIFIC VERSE FORMS: THE SONNET

Etymologically the term "sonnet" means a little song. It has
been so used since the Renaissance, and may thus consist of
a varying number of lines in slightly varied meters and rhyme
schemes. However, the term has more usually been applied to
a fourteen-line verse form in iambic pentameter with a definite
rhyme scheme. The Petrarchan or Italian sonnet is divided into
two parts: an octave, setting forth the background or premise,
and a sestet, setting forth the resolution. The distinct change
between the first and second parts occurs with the *volta*
(or turn), and in the Italian sonnet this change or turn in
thought occurs at the beginning of the ninth line. What is
particularly significant is that the sestet is the main concern
of the author; it is that which encompasses his vision or
realization, even though this vision or realization is often fairly
commonplace. Accordingly criticism has frequently stressed the
octave since it is here that the more peculiar set of circumstances
or more individualistic presentation of those circumstances can
be seen. But remembering that it is the sestet that is the author's
main concern forces us to read a different poem from that which
we otherwise might. The rhyme scheme of the Italian sonnet
is abba, abba, cdd, ccd (or cde, cde), with variations possible.
    The Shakespearean or English sonnet follows the Italian
sonnet in setting forth the background or premise in the first

eight lines and the resolution in the next four lines, but differs from it by employing a couplet to complete the poem. This couplet generally summarizes the conclusion epigramatically. Thus what we have in the English sonnet are three quatrains and a couplet; but at times the third quatrain only moves toward resolution, and it is the couplet that sets forth the conclusion. Because of this structure the rhyme scheme is altered: abab (abba), cdcd (cddc), efef (effe), gg. The turn still occurs at the beginning of the ninth line, but it is not always so definite and may more strongly sound at the beginning of the thirteenth line. This latter position of stress is particularly true of the Spenscrian sonnet. At times the turn is displaced to a medial position in line 7, 8, 9, or 10, from Milton onward. The modern sonnet may indeed avoid all breaks in continuity and may also be rhymeless.

Sonnets which employ fewer or more lines than the standard form are illustrated below, as are those in tetrameter lines. A special form—the *sonetto caudato*, or the tailed sonnet—adds six lines: a trimeter, two pentameters, a trimeter, and two pentameters, rhyming each set of pentameter lines and rhyming the trimeters with previous lines, with themselves, or with the added pentameters.

The subject matter of the sonnet once was almost exclusively devoted to love or the brevity of life, and thence, to man's condition, but with Milton the themes became patriotic, moral, or philosophic. Today the modern poet employs the sonnet form for any and all subject matter. Frequently the sonnet has been the vehicle employed to narrate the course of a love affair; the nine sonnets given here from George Meredith's *Modern Love* will suggest the nature of these popular sonnet sequences.

Regular

Sir Thomas Wyatt   The Lover Compareth His State to a Ship in Perilous Storm Tossed on the Sea

My galley charged with forgetfulness
Through sharp seas, in winter nights, doth pass
'Tween rock and rock; and eke my foe, alas,
That is my lord, steereth with cruelness;
And every oar a thought in readiness,   5
As though that death were light in such a case.
An endless wind doth tear the sail apace,
Of forced sighs and trusty fearfulness;
A rain of tears, a cloud of dark disdain,
Have done the wearied cords great hinderance;   10
Wreathed with error and with ignorance,
The stars be hid that led me to this pain;

Drowned is reason, that should be my comfort,
And I remain despairing of the port.

3 *eke*: also.

Sir Thomas Wyatt   Description of the Contrarious
Passions in a Lover

I find no peace, and all my war is done;
I fear and hope; I burn, and freeze like ice;
I fly aloft, yet can I not arise;
And nought I have, and all the world I season.
That locks nor looseth holdeth me in prison,   5
And holds me not, yet can I 'scape no wise;
Nor lets me live, nor die, at my devise,
And yet of death it giveth me occasion.
Without eye, I see; without tongue, I plain;
I wish to perish, yet I ask for health;   10
I love another, and thus I hate myself;
I feed me in sorrow, and laugh in all my pain.
Lo, thus displeaseth me both death and life,
And my delight is causer of this strife.

9 *plain*: complain, lament.

Henry Howard, Earl of Surrey   A Vow to Love Faithfully,
Howsoever He Be Rewarded

Set me whereas the sun doth parch the green
Or where his beams do not dissolve the ice;
In temperate heat, where he is felt and seen;
In presence pressed of people, mad or wise;
Set me in high, or yet in low degree;   5
In longest night, or in the shortest day;
In clearest sky, or where clouds thickest be;
In lusty youth, or when my hairs are grey:
Set me in heaven, in earth, or else in hell,
In hill, or dale, or in the foaming flood;   10
Thrall, or at large, alive whereso I dwell,
Sick, or in health, in evil fame or good,
Hers will I be; and only with this thought
Content myself, although my chance be nought.

Sir Philip Sidney   Two Sonnets
FROM *Astrophil and Stella*

I

With how sad steps, O moon, thou climbest the skies!
How silently, and with how wan a face!

What! may it be that even in heavenly place
That busy archer his sharp arrows tries?
Sure, if that long-with-love-acquainted eyes   5
Can judge of love, thou feelest a lover's case:
I read it in thy looks; thy languished grace
To me, that feel the like, thy state descries.
Then, even of fellowship, O Moon, tell me,
Is constant love deemed there but want of wit?   10
Are beauties there as proud as here they be?
Do they above love to be loved, and yet
Those lovers scorn whom that love doth possess?
Do they call virtue there ungratefulness?

2

Come, Sleep; O Sleep! the certain knot of peace,
The baiting-place of wit, the balm of woe,
The poor man's wealth, the prisoner's release,
The indifferent judge between the high and low;
With shield of proof shield me from out the prease   5
Of those fierce darts Despair at me doth throw:
O make in me those civil wars to cease;
I will good tribute pay, if thou do so.
Take thou of me smooth pillows, sweetest bed,
A chamber deaf to noise and blind of light,   10
A rosy garland and a weary head;
And if these things, as being thine by right,
Move not thy heavy grace, thou shalt in me,
Livelier than elsewhere, Stella's image see.

5 *prease*: throng.

Edmund Spenser   Three Sonnets
FROM *Amoretti*

1

Happy ye leaves! whenas those lily hands,
Which hold my life in their dead doing might,
Shall handle you, and hold in love's soft bands,
Like captives trembling at the victor's sight.
And happy lines! on which, with starry light,   5
Those lamping eyes will deign sometimes to look,
And read the sorrows of my dying spright,
Written with tears in heart's close-bleeding book.
And happy rhymes! bathed in the sacred brook
Of Helicon, whence she derived is,   10
When ye behold that angel's blessed look,
My soul's long-lacked food, my heaven's bliss.
Leaves, lines, and rhymes, seek her to please alone,
Whom if ye please, I care for other none.

2

Unquiet thought, whom at the first I bred
Of th'inward bale of my love-pined heart,

And sithens have with sighs and sorrows fed,
Till greater than my womb thou woxen art:
Break forth at length out of the inner part,   5
In which thou lurkest like to viper's blood,
And seek some succor, both to ease my smart
And also to sustain thyself with food.
But if in presence of that fairest proud
Thou chance to come, fall lowly at her feet;   10
And with meek humbless and afflicted mood
Pardon for thee, and grace for me entreat.
Which if she grant, then live, and my love cherish,
If not, die soon, and I with thee will perish.

3 *sithens:* since that time.   4 *woxen:* grown.

3

The sovereign beauty which I do admire,
Witness the world how worthy to be praised;
The light whereof hath kindled heavenly fire
In my frail spirit, by her from baseness raised:
That being now with her huge brightness dazed,   5
Base thing I can no more endure to view;
But looking still on her, I stand amazed
At wondrous sight of so celestial hue.
So when my tongue would speak her praises due,
It stopped is with thoughts' astonishment;   10
And when my pen would write her titles true,
It ravished is with fancies' wonderment.
Yet in my heart I then both speak and write
The wonder that my wit cannot indite.

William Shakespeare   Five Sonnets

1

Shall I compare thee to a summer's day?
Thou art more lovely and more temperate:
Rough winds do shake the darling buds of May,
And summer's lease hath all too short a date:
Sometimes too hot the eye of heaven shines,   5
And often is his gold complexion dimmed;
And every fair from fair sometime declines,
By chance or nature's changing course untrimmed;
But thy eternal summer shall not fade,
Nor lose possession of that fair thou owest;   10
Nor shall Death brag thou wanderest in his shade
When in eternal lines to time thou growest:
So long as men can breathe, or eyes can see,
So long lives this, and this gives life to thee.

2

When, in disgrace with fortune and men's eyes,
I all alone beweep my outcast state,
And trouble deaf heaven with my bootless cries,

And look upon myself, and curse my fate,
Wishing me like to one more rich in hope,   5
Featured like him, like him with friends possessed,
Desiring this man's art and that man's scope,
With what I most enjoy contented least;
Yet in these thoughts myself almost despising,
Haply I think on thee, and then my state,   10
Like to the lark at break of day arising
From sullen earth, sings hymns at heaven's gate;
For thy sweet love remembered such wealth brings
That then I scorn to change my state with kings.

3 *bootless*: useless.

3

When to the sessions of sweet silent thought
I summon up remembrance of things past,
I sigh the lack of many a thing I sought,
And with old woes new wail my dear time's waste:
Then can I drown an eye, unused to flow,   5
For precious friends hid in death's dateless night,
And weep afresh love's long since cancelled woe,
And moan the expense of many a vanished sight:
Then can I grieve at grievances foregone,
And heavily from woe to woe tell o'er   10
The sad account of fore-bemoaned moan,
Which I new pay as if not paid before.
But if the while I think on thee, dear friend,
All losses are restored and sorrows end.

4

Not marble, nor the gilded monuments
Of princes, shall outlive this powerful rhyme;
But you shall shine more bright in these contents
Than unswept stone, besmeared with sluttish time.
When wasteful war shall statues overturn,   5
And broils root out the work of masonry,
Nor Mars his sword nor war's quick fire shall burn
The living record of your memory.
'Gainst death and all-oblivious enmity
Shall you pace forth; your praise shall still find room   10
Even in the eyes of all posterity
That wear this world out to the ending doom.
So, till the judgment that yourself arise,
You live in this, and dwell in lovers' eyes.

5

When I have seen by Time's fell hand defaced
The rich-proud cost of outworn buried age;
When sometime lofty towers I see down-razed,
And brass eternal slave to mortal rage;
When I have seen the hungry ocean gain   5
Advantage on the kingdom of the shore,

And the firm soil win of the watery main,
Increasing store with loss, and loss with store;
When I have seen such interchange of state,
O state itself confounded to decay;   10
Ruin hath taught me thus to ruminate—
That Time will come and take my love away.
This thought is as a death, which cannot choose
But weep to have that which it fears to lose.

Fulke Greville, Lord Brooke   Two Sonnets
FROM *Caelica*

1

I offer wrong to my beloved saint,
I scorn, I change, I falsify my love,
Absence and time have made my homage faint,
With Cupid I do every where remove.

I sigh, I sorrow, I do play the fool,   5
Mine eyes like weathercocks, on her attend:
Zeal thus on either side she puts to school,
That will needs have inconstancy to friend.

I grudge, she saith, that many should adore her,
Where love doth suffer, and think all things meet,   10
She saith, all selfness must fall down before her:
I say, where is the sauce should make that sweet?
   Change and contempt (you know) ill speakers be,
   Caelica, and such are all your thoughts of me.

2

The nurse-life wheat within his green husk growing,
Flatters our hope and tickles our desire,
Nature's true riches in sweet beauties showing,
Which set all hearts, with labor's love, on fire.

No less fair is the wheat when golden ear   5
Shows unto hope the joys of near enjoying:
Fair and sweet is the bud, more sweet and fair
The rose, which proves that time is not destroying.

Caelica, your youth, the morning of delight,
Enamelled o'er with beauties white and red,   10
All sense and thoughts did to belief invite,
That love and glory there are brought to bed;
   And your ripe years' love-noon (he goes no higher),
   Turns all the spirits of man into desire.

1 *nurse-life:* life-nourishing.

Michael Drayton Two Sonnets
FROM *Idea*

1

Whilst thus my pen strives to eternize thee,
Age rules my lines with wrinkles in my face,
Where in the map of all my misery
Is modelled out the world of my disgrace;
Whilst in despite of tyrannizing times,   5
Medea-like I make thee young again;
Proudly thou scornest my world-outwearing rhymes
And murderest virtue with thy coy disdain.
And though in youth my youth untimely perish
To keep thee from oblivion and the grave,   10
Ensuing ages yet my rhymes shall cherish,
Where I entombed my better part shall save;
And though this earthly body fade and die,
My name shall mount upon eternity.

2

Since there's no help, come, let us kiss and part.
Nay, I have done. You get no more of me.
And I am glad, yea, glad with all my heart,
That thus so cleanly I myself can free.
Shake hands for ever, cancel all our vows;   5
And when we meet at any time again,
Be it not seen in either of our brows
That we one jot of former love retain.
Now at the last gasp of Love's latest breath,
When, his pulse failing, Passion speechless lies,   10
When Faith is kneeling by his bed of death,
And Innocence is closing up his eyes,
Now, if thou wouldst, when all have given him over,
From death to life thou mightest him yet recover.

Samuel Daniel Two Sonnets
FROM *Delia*

1

Beauty, sweet love, is like the morning dew,
Whose short refresh upon the tender green
Cheers for a time, but till the sun doth show,
And straight 'tis gone as it had never been.
Soon doth it fade that makes the fairest flourish   5
Short is the glory of the blushing rose;
The hue which thou so carefully dost nourish,
Yet which at length thou must be forced to lose.
When thou, surcharged with burden of thy years,

Shall bend thy wrinkles homeward to the earth;   10
And that, in beauty's lease expired, appears
The date of age, the calends of our death—
But ah, no more!—this must not be foretold,
For women grieve to think they must be old.

12 *calends*: first day of the month.

2

Care-charmer sleep, son of the sable night,
Brother to death, in silent darkness born,
Relieve my languish and restore the light,
With dark forgetting of my cares return.
And let the day be time enough to mourn   5
The shipwreck of my ill-adventured youth;
Let waking eyes suffice to wail their scorn,
Without the torment of the night's untruth.
Cease, dreams, the images of day desires,
To model forth the passions of the morrow;   10
Never let rising sun approve you liars,
To add more grief to aggravate my sorrow.
Still let me sleep, embracing clouds in vain,
And never wake to feel the day's disdain.

11 *approve*: prove.

Sir John Davies   Two Gulling Sonnets

1

The lover, under burden of his mistress' lo e
Which like to Etna did his heart oppress,
Did give such piteous groans that he did move
The heavens at length to pity his distress.
But for the Fates, in their high court above,   5
Forbade to make the grievous burden less,
The gracious powers did all conspire to prove
If miracle this mischief might redress.
Therefore, regarding that the load was such
As no man might with one man's might sustain,   10
And that mild patience imported much
To him that should endure an endless pain,
By their decree he soon transformed was
Into a patient burden-bearing ass.

2

The sacred muse that first made love divine
Hath made him naked and without attire;
But I will clothe him with this pen of mine,
That all the world his fashion shall admire:
His hat of hope, his band of beauty fine,   5
His cloak of craft, his doublet of desire,

Grief, for a girdle, shall about him twine,
His points of pride, his eyelet-holes of ire,
His hose of hate, his codpiece of conceit,
His stockings of stern strife, his shirt of shame,   10
His garters of vainglory gay and slight,
His pantofles of passions I will frame;
Pumps of presumption shall adorn his feet,
And socks of sullenness exceeding sweet.

9 *codpiece:* flap concealing the opening in men's breeches.   12
pantofles: slippers.

John Donne   Two Holy Sonnets

1

At the round earth's imagined corners, blow
Your trumpets, Angels, and arise, arise
From death, you numberless infinities
Of souls, and to your scattered bodies go,
All whom the flood did, and fire shall o'erthrow,   5
All whom war, dearth, age, agues, tyrannies,
Despair, law, chance, hath slain, and you whose eyes
Shall behold God and never taste death's woe.
But let them sleep, Lord, and me mourn a space,
For if above all these my sins abound,   10
'Tis late to ask abundance of Thy grace,
When we are there; here on this lowly ground,
Teach me how to repent; for that's as good
As if Thou hadst sealed my pardon with Thy blood.

2

Death, be not proud, though some have called thee
Mighty and dreadful, for thou art not so,
For those, whom thou thinkest thou dost overthrow,
Die not, poor death, nor yet canst thou kill me.
From rest and sleep, which but thy pictures be,   5
Much pleasure, then from thee much more must flow,
And soonest our best men with thee do go,
Rest of their bones and soul's delivery.
Thou art slave to fate, chance, kings and desperate men,
And dost with poison, war, and sickness dwell,   10
And poppy or charms can make us sleep as well
And better than thy stroke; why swellest thou then?
One short sleep past, we wake eternally,
And death shall be no more; death, thou shalt die.

Edward Herbert, Lord Cherbury   Sonnet of Black Beauty

Black beauty, which, above that common light,
  Whose power can no colors here renew

But those which darkness can again subdue,
Dost still remain unvaried to the sight,
   And like an object equal to the view,   5
Art neither changed with day, nor hid with night;
When all these colors which the world call bright,
   And which old poetry doth so pursue,
Are with the night so perished and gone
   That of their being there remains no mark,   10
Thou still abidest so entirely one,
   That we may know thy blackness is a spark
Of light inaccessible, and alone
   Our darkness which can make us think it dark.

George Herbert Prayer

Prayer the Church's banquet, Angels' age,
   God's breath in man returning to his birth,
   The soul in paraphrase, heart in pilgrimage,
The Christian plummet sounding heaven and earth;
Engine against the Almighty, sinners' tower,   5
   Reversed thunder, Christ's side-piercing spear,
   The six-days' world transposing in an hour,
A kind of tune, which all things hear and fear;
Softness, and peace, and joy, and love, and bliss,
   Exalted manna, gladness of the best,   10
   Heaven in ordinary, man well dressed,
The milky way, the bird of Paradise,
   Church-bells beyond the stars heard, the soul's blood
   The land of spices; something understood.

4 plummet: a weight.   *11 in ordinary:* in constant service.

John Milton Three Sonnets

I

How soon hath time the subtle thief of youth,
   Stolen on his wing my three and twentieth year!
   My hasting days fly on with full career,
   But my late spring no bud or blossom sheweth,
Perhaps my semblance might deceive the truth   5
   That I to manhood am arrived so near,
   And inward ripeness doth much less appear,
   That some more timely-happy spirits indueth.
Yet be it less or more, or soon or slow,
   It shall be still in strictest measure even   10
   To that same lot, however mean or high,
Toward which time leads me, and the will of Heaven;
   All is, if I have grace to use it so,
   As ever in my great task-master's eye.

3 career: speed.   *8 indueth:* endows.   *9 it:* i.e., the inward ripeness.

2

Captain or Colonel, or Knight in Arms,
   Whose chance on these defenseless doors may seize,
   If ever deed of honor did thee please,
   Guard them, and him within protect from harms.
He can requite thee, for he knows the charms   5
   That call Fame on such gentle acts as these,
   And he can spread thy name o'er lands and seas,
   Whatever clime the sun's bright circle warms.
Lift not thy spear against the Muses' bower:
   The great Emathian conqueror bid spare   10
   The house of Pindarus, when temple and tower
Went to the ground: and the repeated air
   Of sad Electra's poet had the power
   To save the Athenian walls from ruin bare.

2: The occasion was the advance of the Royalist troops on London
in November 1642, during the Civil War with the Parliamen-
tarians.   10 *Emathian conqueror:* Alexander the Great.   11
Pindarus: the Greek lyric poet Pindar.   13 *poet:* Euripides.   14
The first chorus of the play (ll. 167 ff.) turned the Spartans
away from sacking Athens in 404 B.C.

3

When I consider how my light is spent,
   Ere half my days in this dark world and wide,
   And that one talent which is death to hide
   Lodged with me useless, though my soul more bent
To serve therewith my maker, and present   5
   My true account, lest he returning chide,
   Doth God exact day labor, light denied,
   I fondly ask; but patience to prevent
That murmur, soon replies, God doth not need
   Either man's work or his own gifts, who best   10
   Bear his mild yoke, they serve him best; his state
Is kingly. Thousands at his bidding speed
   And post o'er land and ocean without rest:
   They also serve who only stand and wait.

3–6: See Matt. xxv. 14–30.   8 *fondly:* foolishly.

Thomas Gray   Sonnet On the Death of Richard West

In vain to me the smiling mornings shine,
   And redd'ning Phoebus lifts his golden fire:
The birds in vain their amorous descant join;
   Or cheerful fields resume their green attire:
These ears, alas! for other notes repine,   5
   A different object do these eyes require:
My lonely anguish melts no heart but mine;
   And in my breast the imperfect joys expire.
Yet morning smiles the busy race to cheer,
   And new-born pleasure brings to happier men: 10

The fields to all their wonted tribute bear;
  To warm their little loves the birds complain:
I fruitless mourn to him that cannot hear,
  And weep the more because I weep in vain.

Richard West: an intimate friend, who died in 1742.

William Lisle Bowles   The Bells, Ostend

How sweet the tuneful bells' responsive peal!
As when, at opening morn, the fragrant breeze
Breathes on the trembling sense of pale disease,
So piercing to my heart their force I feel!
And hark! with lessening cadence now they fall!   5
And now, along the white and level tide,
They fling their melancholy music wide,
Bidding me many a tender thought recall
Of summer days, and those delightful years
When from an ancient tower, in life's fair prime,   10
The mournful magic of their mingling chime
First waked my wondering childhood into tears!
But seeming now, when all those days are o'er,
The sounds of joy once heard, and heard no more.

Ostend: a seaport in Belgium.

Samuel Taylor Coleridge   Pantisocracy

No more my visionary soul shall dwell
On joys that were; no more endure to weigh
The shame and anguish of the evil day,
Wisely forgetful! O'er the ocean swell
Sublime of hope, I seek the cottaged dell   5
Where virtue calm with careless step may stray,
And dancing to the moonlight roundelay,
The wizard passions weave an holy spell.
Eyes that have ached with sorrow! Ye shall weep
Tears of doubt-mingled joy, like theirs who start   10
From precipices of distempered sleep,
On which the fierce-eyed fiends their revels keep,
And see the rising sun, and feel it dart
New rays of pleasance trembling to the heart.

Pantisocracy: a program for an ideal community to be set up in
America, proposed by Coleridge and Robert Southey in 1794.
14 pleasance: delight.

William Wordsworth   London, 1802

Milton! thou shouldst be living at this hour:
England hath need of thee: she is a fen

Of stagnant waters: altar, sword, and pen,
Fireside, the heroic wealth of hall and bower,
Have forfeited their ancient English dower   5
Of inward happiness. We are selfish men;
Oh! raise us up, return to us again;
And give us manners, virtue, freedom, power.
Thy soul was like a star, and dwelt apart;
Thou hadst a voice whose sound was like the sea: 10
Pure as the naked heavens, majestic, free,
So didst thou travel on life's common way,
In cheerful godliness; and yet thy heart
The lowliest duties on herself did lay.

William Wordsworth   Composed upon Westminster Bridge, September 3, 1802

Earth has not anything to show more fair:
Dull would he be of soul who could pass by
A sight so touching in its majesty;
This city now doth, like a garment, wear
The beauty of the morning; silent, bare,   5
Ships, towers, domes, theaters, and temples lie
Open unto the fields, and to the sky;
All bright and glittering in the smokeless air.
Never did sun more beautifully steep
In his first splendor, valley, rock, or hill;   10
Ne'er saw I, never felt, a calm so deep!
The river glideth at his own sweet will:
Dear God! the very houses seem asleep;
And all that mighty heart is lying still!

William Wordsworth   Two Sonnets

I

The world is too much with us; late and soon,
Getting and spending, we lay waste our powers;
Little we see in nature that is ours;
We have given our hearts away, a sordid boon!
This sea that bares her bosom to the moon,   5
The winds that will be howling at all hours
And are upgathered now like sleeping flowers,
For this, for everything, we are out of tune;
It moves us not. Great God! I'd rather be
A pagan suckled in a creed outworn—   10
So might I, standing on this pleasant lea,
Have glimpses that would make me less forlorn;
Have sight of Proteus rising from the sea;
Or hear old Triton blow his wreathed horn.

13 *Proteus:* a sea god who could assume various shapes.   14
Triton: a sea god, half man, half fish.

2

Nuns fret not at their convent's narrow room;
  And hermits are contented with their cells;
  And students with their pensive citadels;
Maids at the wheel, the weaver at his loom,
Sit blithe and happy; bees that soar for bloom,   5
  High as the highest peak of Furness Fells,
  Will murmur by the hour in foxglove bells:
In truth the prison, unto which we doom
Ourselves, no prison is: and hence for me,
  In sundry moods, 'twas pastime to be bound   10
  Within the sonnet's scanty plot of ground;
Pleased if some souls (for such there needs must be)
Who have felt the weight of too much liberty,
  Should find brief solace there, as I have found.

6 *Furness Fells*: in northwestern Lancashire, on the Irish Sea.

George Gordon, Lord Byron   Sonnet on Chillon

Eternal Spirit of the chainless mind!
  Brightest in dungeons, liberty! thou art,
  For there thy habitation is the heart—
The heart which love of thee alone can bind;
And when thy sons to fetters are consigned—   5
  To fetters, and the damp vault's dayless gloom,
  Their country conquers with their martyrdom,
And freedom's fame finds wings on every wind.
Chillon! thy prison is a holy place,
  And thy sad floor an altar—for 'twas trod,   10
Until his very steps have left a trace
  Worn, as if thy cold pavement were a sod,
By Bonnivard! May none those marks efface!
  For they appeal from tyranny to God.

Chillon: a castle on Lake Geneva.   13 *Bonnivard*: François de Bonnivard, imprisoned at Chillon for aiding the Genevese against Savoy.

Percy Bysshe Shelley   Ozymandias

I met a traveller from an antique land,
Who said: "Two vast and trunkless legs of stone
Stand in the desert. Near them, on the sand,
Half-sunk, a shattered visage lies, whose frown,
And wrinkled lip, and sneer of cold command,   5
Tell that its sculptor well those passions read
Which yet survive, stamped on these lifeless things,
The hand that mocked them and the heart that fed:
And on the pedestal these words appear:
'My name is Ozymandias, king of kings: 10

Look on my works, ye Mighty, and despair!'
Nothing beside remains. Round the decay
Of that colossal wreck, boundless and bare
The lone and level sands stretch far away."

John Keats   On First Looking into Chapman's Homer

Much have I travelled in the realms of gold
And many goodly states and kingdoms seen;
Round many western islands have I been
Which bards in fealty to Apollo hold.
Oft of one wide expanse had I been told   5
That deep-browed Homer ruled as his demesne:
Yet did I never breathe its pure serene
Till I heard Chapman speak out loud and bold:

—Then felt I like some watcher of the skies
When a new planet swims into his ken;   10
Or like stout Cortez—when with eagle eyes
He stared at the Pacific—and all his men
Looked at each other with a wild surmise—
Silent, upon a peak in Darien.

8 *Chapman*: George Chapman (1559?–1634), translator of the
Iliad.   11 *Cortez*: an error for Balboa.   14 *Darien*: the Isthmus
of Panama.

John Keats   On Seeing the Elgin Marbles

My spirit is too weak—mortality
    Weighs heavily on me like unwilling sleep,
    And each imagined pinnacle and steep
Of godlike hardship tells me I must die
Like a sick eagle looking at the sky.   5
    Yet 'tis a gentle luxury to weep
    That I have not the cloudy winds to keep,
Fresh for the opening of the morning's eye.
Such dim-conceived glories of the brain,
    Bring round the heart an indescribable feud;   10
So do these wonders a most dizzy pain,
    That mingles Grecian grandeur with the rude
Wasting of old Time—with a billowy main—
    A sun—a shadow of a magnitude.

Elgin Marbles: ancient Greek sculptures from the Parthenon,
brought to England in 1811 by Thomas Bruce, Lord Elgin.

John Keats "When I Have Fears That I May Cease to Be"

When I have fears that I may cease to be
  Before my pen has gleaned my teeming brain,
Before high-piled books, in charactery,
  Hold like rich garners the full ripened grain;
When I behold, upon the night's starred face,   5
  Huge cloudy symbols of a high romance,
And think that I may never live to trace
  Their shadows, with the magic hand of chance;
And when I feel, fair creature of an hour,
  That I shall never look upon thee more,   10
Never have relish in the faery power
  Of unreflecting love:—then on the shore
Of the wide world I stand alone, and think
Till love and fame to nothingness do sink.

Edgar Allen Poe Sonnet—To Science

Science! true daughter of Old Time thou art!
  Who alterest all things with thy peering eyes.
Why preyest thou thus upon the poet's heart,
  Vulture, whose wings are dull realities?
How should he love thee? or how deem thee wise,   5
  Who wouldst not leave him in his wandering
To seek for treasure in the jewelled skies,
  Albeit he soared with an undaunted wing?
Hast thou not dragged Diana from her car,
  And driven the Hamadryad from the wood   10
To seek a shelter in some happier star?
  Hast thou not torn the Naiad from her flood,
The Elfin from the green grass, and from me
The summer dream beneath the tamarind tree?

9 *Diana*: the goddess of the moon.   *car*: chariot (bearing the moon).   10 *Hamadryad*: a wood nymph.   12 *Naiad*: a water nymph.   14 *tamarind*: a tropical tree.

Jones Very The Dead

I see them—crowd on crowd they walk the earth,
Dry leafless trees no autumn wind laid bare;
And in their nakedness find cause for mirth,
And all unclad would winter's rudeness dare;
No sap doth through their clattering branches flow,   5
Whence springing leaves and blossoms bright appear;
Their hearts the living God have ceased to know

Who gives the spring-time to th'expectant year.
They mimic life, as if from Him to steal
His glow of health to paint the livid cheek;   10
They borrow words for thoughts they cannot feel,
That with a seeming heart their tongue may speak;
And in their show of life more dead they live
Than those that to the earth with many tears they give.

Henry Wadsworth Longfellow   Divina Commedia

Oft have I seen at some cathedral door
    A laborer, pausing in the dust and heat,
    Lay down his burden, and with reverent feet
Enter, and cross himself, and on the floor
Kneel to repeat his paternoster o'er;   5
    Far off the noises of the world retreat;
    The loud vociferations of the street
Become an undistinguishable roar.
So, as I enter here from day to day,
    And leave my burden at this minster gate,   10
Kneeling in prayer, and not ashamed to pray,
    The tumult of the time disconsolate
To inarticulate murmurs dies away,
    While the eternal ages watch and wait.

10 *minster*: church.

Elizabeth Barrett Browning   Two Sonnets from the Portuguese

1

I thought once how Theocritus had sung
Of the sweet years, the dear and wished-for years,
Who each one in a gracious hand appears
To bear a gift for mortals, old or young:
And, as I mused it in its antique tongue,   5
I saw, in gradual vision through my tears,
The sweet, sad years, the melancholy years,
Those of my own life, who by turns had flung
A shadow across me. Straightway I was 'ware,
So weeping, how a mystic shape did move   10
Behind me, and drew me backward by the hair;
And a voice said in mastery, while I strove—
"Guess now who holds thee?" "Death," I said. But, there,
The silver answer rang, "Not Death, but Love."

2

How do I love thee? Let me count the ways.
I love thee to the depth and breadth and height
My soul can reach, when feeling out of sight
For the ends of being and ideal grace.

I love thee to the level of everyday's   5
Most quiet need, by sun and candlelight.
I love thee freely, as men strive for right;
I love thee purely, as they turn from praise.
I love thee with the passion put to use
In my old griefs, and with my childhood's faith.   10
I love thee with a love I seemed to lose
With my lost saints—I love thee with the breath,
Smiles, tears, of all my life! and, if God choose,
I shall but love thee better after death.

Matthew Arnold   To a Friend

Who prop, thou askest, in these bad days, my mind?
He much, the old man, who, clearest-souled of men,
Saw The Wide Prospect, and the Asian Fen,
And Tmolus hill, and Smyrna bay, though blind.

Much he, whose friendship I not long since won,   5
That halting slave, who in Nicopolis
Taught Arrian, when Vespasian's brutal son
Cleared Rome of what most shamed him. But be his

My special thanks, whose even-balanced soul,
From first youth tested up to extreme old age,   10
Business could not make dull, nor passion wild;

Who saw life steadily, and saw it whole;
The mellow glory of the Attic stage,
Singer of sweet Colonus, and its child.

2 old man: Homer.   *3 The Wide Prospect*: Europe.   *Asian
Fen*: Asia Minor.   *4 Tmolus*: in Asia Minor.   *Smyrna*: seaport
of Asia Minor.   *5 he*: Epictetus, a Stoic philosopher.   *7
Arrian*: a Greek historian.   *son*: Emperor Domitian.   *8 what*:
that is, Epictetus and his teachings.   *his*: Sophocles'.   *14* Referring to *Oedipus at Colonus*.

Matthew Arnold   To a Republican Friend, 1848

God knows it, I am with you. If to prize
Those virtues, prized and practised by too few,
But prized, but loved, but eminent in you,
Man's fundamental life; if to despise

The barren optimistic sophistries   5
Of comfortable moles, whom what they do
Teaches the limit of the just and true
(And for such doing they require not eyes);

If sadness at the long heart-wasting show
Wherein earth's great ones are disquieted;   10
If thoughts, not idle, while before me flow

The armies of the homeless and unfed—
If these are yours, if this is what you are,
Then am I yours, and what you feel, I share.

Friend: Arthur Hugh Clough.   *1848*: referring to the revolution
which overthrew the French monarchy.

George Meredith   Lucifer in Starlight

On a starred night Prince Lucifer uprose.
Tired of his dark dominion, swung the fiend
Above the rolling ball, in cloud part screened,
Where sinners hugged their specter of repose.
Poor prey to his hot fit of pride were those.   5
And now upon his western wing he leaned.
Now his huge bulk o'er Afric's sands careened,
Now the black planet shadowed Arctic snows.
Soaring through wider zones that pricked his scars
With memory of the old revolt from Awe,   10
He reached a middle height, and at the stars,
Which are the brain of heaven, he looked, and sank.
Around the ancient track marched, rank on rank,
The army of unalterable law.

Dante Gabriel Rossetti   The Sonnet

A sonnet is a moment's monument—
    Memorial from the soul's eternity
    To one dead deathless hour. Look that it be,
Whether for lustral rite or dire portent,
Of its own arduous fulness reverent: 5
    Carve it in ivory or in ebony,
    As day or night may rule; and let time see
Its flowering crest impearled and orient.

A sonnet is a coin: its face reveals
    The soul—its converse, to what power 'tis due—   10
Whether for tribute to the august appeals
    Of life, or dower in love's high retinue,
It serve; or, 'mid the dark wharf's cavernous breath,
In Charon's palm it pay the toll to Death.

4 lustral: purifying.   *14 Charon*: ferryman of the dead to Hades.

Dante Gabriel Rossetti   Heart's Compass

Sometimes thou seemest not as thyself alone,
But as the meaning of all things that are;
A breathless wonder, shadowing forth afar

Some heavenly solstice hushed and halcyon;
Whose unstirred lips are music's visible tone;   5
Whose eyes the sun-gate of the soul unbar,
Being of its furthest fires oracular—
The evident heart of all life sown and mown.
Even such love is; and is not thy name Love?
Yea, by thy hand the love-god rends apart   10
All gathering clouds of night's ambiguous art;
Flings them far down, and sets thine eyes above;
And simply, as some gage of flower or glove,
Stakes with a smile the world against thy heart.

13 *gage:* pledge (of love or defiance).

Gerard Manley Hopkins   God's Grandeur

The world is charged with the grandeur of God.
    It will flame out, like shining from shook foil;
    It gathers to a greatness, like the ooze of oil
Crushed. Why do men then now not reck his rod?
Generations have trod, have trod, have trod;   5
    And all is seared with trade; bleared, smeared with toil;
    And wears man's smudge and shares man's smell: the soil
Is bare now, nor can foot feel, being shod.

And for all this, nature is never spent;
    There lives the dearest freshness deep down things;   10
And though the last lights off the black West went
    Oh, morning, at the brown brink eastward, springs—
Because the Holy Ghost over the bent
    World broods with warm breast and with ah! bright wings.

4 *reck:* heed.   14 *broods:* with the added meaning, "brings forth young."

Gerard Manley Hopkins   The Windhover: To Christ Our Lord

I caught this morning morning's minion, king-
    dom of daylight's dauphin, dapple-dawn-drawn Falcon, in
        his riding
    Of the rolling level underneath him steady air, and striding
High there, how he rung upon the rein of a wimpling wing
In his ecstasy! then off, off forth on swing,   5
    As a skate's heel sweeps smooth on a bow-bend: the hurl
        and gliding
    Rebuffed the big wind. My heart in hiding
Stirred for a bird—the achieve of, the mastery of the thing!

Brute beauty and valor and act, oh, air, pride, plume, here
    Buckle! AND the fire that breaks from thee then, a billion   10

Times told lovelier, more dangerous, O my chevalier!
   No wonder of it: sheer plod makes plough down sillion
Shine, and blue-bleak embers, ah my dear,
   Fall, gall themselves, and gash gold-vermillion.

Windhover: a small hawk.   *4 rung*: rose spirally, though attached
to a rein.   *wimpling*: rippling.   *12 sillion*: furrow.

Christina Rossetti   Remember

Remember me when I am gone away,
Gone far away into the silent land;
When you can no more hold me by the hand,
Nor I half turn to go yet turning stay.
Remember me when no more day by day   5
You tell me of our future that you planned:
Only remember me; you understand
It will be late to counsel then or pray.
Yet if you should forget me for a while
And afterwards remember, do not grieve: 10
For if the darkness and corruption leave
A vestige of the thoughts that once I had,
Better by far you should forget and smile
Than that you should remember and be sad.

George Santayana   On the Death of a Metaphysician

Unhappy dreamer, who outwinged in flight
The pleasant region of the things I love,
And soared beyond the sunshine, and above
The golden cornfields and the dear and bright
Warmth of the hearth—blasphemer of delight,   5
Was your proud bosom not at peace with Jove,
That you sought, thankless for his guarded grove,
The empty horror of abysmal night?
Ah, the thin air is cold above the moon!
I stood and saw your fall, befooled in death,   10
As, in your numbed spirit's fatal swoon,
You cried you were a god, or were to be;
I heard with feeble moan your boastful breath
Bubble from depths of the Icarian sea.

14 Icarian Sea: sea of Greece, named for Icarus, son of Daedalus,
who fell to his death when he flew too near the sun with wings
attached by wax.

Rupert Brooke   The Soldier

If I should die, think only this of me:
   That there's some corner of a foreign field

That is for ever England. There shall be
   In that rich earth a richer dust concealed;
A dust whom England bore, shaped, made aware,   5
   Gave, once, her flowers to love, her ways to roam,
A body of England's breathing English air,
   Washed by the rivers, blest by suns of home.

And think, this heart, all evil shed away,
   A pulse in the eternal mind, no less   10
      Gives somewhere back the thoughts by England given;
Her sights and sounds; dreams happy as her day;
   And laughter, learnt of friends; and gentleness,
      In hearts at peace, under an English heaven.

Edwin Arlington Robinson   Cliff Klingenhagen

Cliff Klingenhagen had me in to dine
With him one day; and after soup and meat,
And all the other things there were to eat,
Cliff took two glasses and filled one with wine
And one with wormwood. Then, without a sign   5
For me to choose at all, he took the draught
Of bitterness himself, and lightly quaffed
It off, and said the other one was mine.

And when I asked him what the deuce he meant
By doing that, he only looked at me   10
And grinned, and said it was a way of his.
And though I know the fellow, I have spent
Long time a-wondering when I shall be
As happy as Cliff Klingenhagen is.

Edwin Arlington Robinson   How Annandale Went Out

"They called it Annandale—and I was there
To flourish, to find words, and to attend:
Liar, physician, hypocrite, and friend,
I watched him; and the sight was not so fair
As one or two that I have seen elsewhere: 5
An apparatus not for me to mend—
A wreck, with hell between him and the end,
Remained of Annandale; and I was there.

"I knew the ruin as I knew the man;
So put the two together, if you can,   10
Remembering the worst you know of me.
Now view yourself as I was, on the spot,
With a slight kind of engine. Do you see?
Like this . . . You wouldn't hang me? I thought not."

Elinor Wylie   Puritan Sonnet

Down to the Puritan marrow of my bones
There's something in this richness that I hate.
I love the look, austere, immaculate,
Of landscape drawn in pearly monotones.
There's something in my very blood that owns   5
Bare hills, cold silver on a sky of slate,
A thread of water, churned to milky spate
Streaming through slanted pastures fenced with stones.

I love those skies, thin blue or snowy gray,
Those fields sparse-planted, rendering meager sheaves;   10
That spring, briefer than apple-blossom's breath,
Summer, so much too beautiful to stay,
Swift autumn, like a bonfire of leaves,
And sleepy winter, like the sleep of death.

William Butler Yeats   Leda and the Swan

A sudden blow: the great wings beating still
Above the staggering girl, her thighs caressed
By the dark webs, her nape caught in his bill,
He holds her helpless breast upon his breast.

How can those terrified vague fingers push   5
The feathered glory from her loosening thighs?
And how can body, laid in that white rush,
But feel the strange heart beating where it lies?

A shudder in the loins engenders there
The broken wall, the burning roof and tower   10
And Agamemnon dead.
                              Being so caught up,
So mastered by the brute blood of the air,
Did she put on his knowledge with his power
Before the indifferent beak could let her drop?

Leda and the Swan: Jove descended to the mortal Leda in the guise
of a swan; she bore Helen and Clytemnestra, who became the
wives of the brothers Menelaus and Agamemnon. Helen's abduc-
tion by Paris brought on the Trojan War.

Robert Frost   The Silken Tent

She is as in a field a silken tent
At midday when a sunny summer breeze
Has dried the dew and all its ropes relent,
So that in guys it gently sways at ease,
And its supporting central cedar pole,   5

That is its pinnacle to heavenward
And signifies the sureness of the soul,
Seems to owe naught to any single cord,
But strictly held by none, is loosely bound
By countless silken ties of love and thought   10
To everything on earth the compass round,
And only by one's going slightly taut
In the capriciousness of summer air
Is of the slightest bondage made aware.

Archibald MacLeish   The End of the World

Quite unexpectedly as Vasserot
The armless ambidextrian was lighting
A match between his great and second toe
And Ralph the lion was engaged in biting
The neck of Madame Sossman while the drum   5
Pointed, and Teeny was about to cough
In waltz-time swinging Jocko by the thumb—
Quite unexpectedly the top blew off.

And there, there overhead, there, there, hung over
Those thousands of white faces, those dazed eyes,   10
There in the starless dark, the poise, the hover,
There with vast wings across the cancelled skies,
There in the sudden blackness, the black pall
Of nothing, nothing, nothing—nothing at all.

e. e. cummings   sonnet

a wind has blown the rain away and blown
the sky away and all the leaves away,
and the trees stand.   I think i too have known
autumn too long

                    (and what have you to say,
wind wind wind—did you love somebody   5
and have you the petal of somewhere in your heart
pinched from dumb summer?

                    O crazy daddy
of death dance cruelly for us and start

the last leaf whirling in the final brain
of air!)Let us as we have seen see   10
doom's integration . . . . a wind has blown the rain

away and the leaves and the sky and the
trees stand:
            the trees stand. The trees,
suddenly wait against the moon's face.

Allen Tate   Sonnets at Christmas

1

This is the day His hour of life draws near,
Let me get ready from head to foot for it
Most handily with eyes to pick the year
For small feed to reward a feathered wit.
Some men would see it an epiphany   5
At ease, at food and drink, others at chase
Yet I, stung lassitude, with ecstasy
Unspent argue the season's difficult case
So: Man, dull critter of enormous head,
What would he look at in the coiling sky?   10
But I must kneel again unto the Dead
While Christmas bells of paper white and red,
Figured with boys and girls spilt from a sled,
Ring out the silence I am nourished by.

2

Ah, Christ, I love you rings to the wild sky
And I must think a little of the past:
When I was ten I told a stinking lie
That got a black boy whipped; but now at last
The going years, caught in an accurate glow,   5
Reverse like balls englished upon green baize—
Let them return, let the round trumpets blow
The ancient crackle of the Christ's deep gaze.
Deafened and blind, with senses yet unfound,
Am I, untutored to the after-wit   10
Of knowledge, knowing a nightmare has no sound;
Therefore with idle hands and head I sit
In late December before the fire's daze
Punished by crimes of which I would be quit.

Robinson Jeffers   Compensation

Solitude that unmakes me one of men
In snow-white hands brings singular recompense,
Evening me with kindlier natures when
On the needled pinewood the cold dews condense
About the hour of Rigel fallen from heaven   5
In wintertime, or when the long night tides
Sigh blindly from the sand-dune backward driven,
Or when on stormings of the northwind rides
The foamscud with the cormorants, or when passes
A horse or dog with brown affectionate eyes,   10
Or autumn frosts are pricked by earliest grasses,
Or whirring from her covert a quail flies.

Why, even in humanity, beauty and good
Show from the mountainside of solitude.

5 *Rigel*: a star in the constellation Orion.

Irwin Stark   Poets of My Epoch

It matters not. Be lean as Bengal beef,
pound image plastic tight, cast metaphor
coral perfection like a lonely reef,
and speech wave-metrical against the shore,
be blunt as tank treads in an alien land,   5
hazy as cloud and wanton as a flake,
wind-loose, archaic as a sarabande
or calm as summer on a little lake,
it matters not. History has room for all.
Unmask the weaver, set the pattern free   10
in time: eccentric and conventional,
craftsman and cheat, life proves the tapestry.
Forgive the syllable, the hell with tone,
suck out the marrow dry, hew to the bone!

1: Cows are sacred in India, but food is meager.

Dylan Thomas   "When All My Five and Country
    Senses See"

When all my five and country senses see,
The fingers will forget green thumbs and mark
How, through the halfmoon's vegetable eye,
Husk of young stars and handfull zodiac,
Love in the frost is pared and wintered by,   5
The whispering ears will watch love drummed away
Down breeze and shell to a discordant beach,
And, lashed to syllables, the lynx tongue cry
That her fond wounds are mended bitterly.
My nostrils see her breath burn like a bush.   10

My one and noble heart has witnesses
In all love's countries, that will grope awake;
And when blind sleep drops on the spying senses,
The heart is sensual, though five eyes break.

George Barker   Sonnet to My Mother

Most near, most dear, most loved and most far,
Under the window where I often found her
Sitting as huge as Asia, seismic with laughter,
Gin and chicken helpless in her Irish hand,

Irresistible as Rabelais but most tender for   5
The lame dogs and hurt birds that surround her—
She is a procession no one can follow after
But be like a little dog following a brass band.

She will not glance up at the bomber or condescend
To drop her gin and scuttle to a cellar,   10
But lean on the mahogany table like a mountain
Whom only faith can move, and so I send
O all my faith and all my love to tell her
That she will move from mourning into morning.

9–10: During World War II and the Battle of Britain.

George Starbuck   Esthetique du Machiavel

There is nothing at all pretty about death.
One does what one can to make a pretty poem.
One writes, in fact, of death—the grace of the poem
does one the greater credit. Why waste breath
in neoaeolian yodelings for love   5
of the lark, when what goes best is the dead bird?
Of course, there are other subjects. Take my word,
there is nothing all that pretty about love.

(Not that you less than levitate me, love,
or that your sweet surprise has lost its savor: 10
you are the killings I could carol of
if I were someone more than merely clever
who dared own up to his good luck and leave
the Love-and-Death boys to their heavy labor.)

5 neoaeolian: referring to a new version of classical lyric poetry.

Other Types

Barnabe Googe   To Doctor Bale

Good aged Bale, that with thy hoary hairs
Dost yet persist to turn the painful book,
O happy man, that hast obtained such years,
And leav'st not yet on papers pale to look,
Give over now to beat thy wearied brain,   5
And rest thy pen that long hath labored sore;
For aged men unfit sure is such pain,
And thee beseems to labor now no more.
But thou, I think, Don Plato's part will play,
With book in hand to have thy dying day.   10

Doctor Bale: John Bale (1495–1563), Bishop of Ossory, a playwright and author of Illustrium Majoris Britanniae Scriptorum
Summarium, the earliest history of English literature (1548).
9 Don Plato's part: that is, teacher and philosopher.

John Milton   On the Forcers of Conscience

Because you have thrown off your prelate lord
   And with stiff vows renounced his liturgy
   To seize the widowed whore plurality
From them whose sin ye envied, not abhorred,
Dare ye for this adjure the civil sword   5
   To force our consciences that Christ set free,
   And ride us with a classic hierarchy
   Taught ye by mere A. S. and Rutherford?
Men whose life, learning, faith and pure intent
   Would have been held in high esteem with Paul   10
   Must now be named and printed heretics
By shallow Edwards and Scotch what d'ye call;
   But we do hope to find out all your tricks,
   Your plots and packings worse than those of Trent,
                That so the Parliament   15
May with their wholesome and preventive shears
Clip your phylacteries though bauk your ears
                  And succor our just fears
When they shall read this clearly in your charge
New Presbyter is but old Priest writ large.   20

1: Referring to the abolition of episcopacy in July 1643.   **3**
plurality: the holding of multiple clerical posts.   **7** *classic:* referring to the division of the country into classes urged by the Presbyterians. Each classis would be under the jurisdiction of the elders of the district.   **8** *A. S.:* Adam Stewart, a Scotch pamphleteering Presbyterian. *Rutherford:* Samuel Rutherford, author of *Plea for Presbytery* (1642).   **12** *Edwards:* Thomas Edwards, author of *Gangraena* (1646), which alludes to Milton derogatorily.   **13** *Scotch what d'ye call:* Robert Baillie, a Scotch Presbyterian.   **14** *Trent:* The Council of Trent attempted to reform the Church in three synods, but dogmatic decisions and a packing of the Council in the Pope's favor militated against reconciliation.   **17** *phylacteries:* square leather boxes containing scriptural passages, worn by Jews at prayer. The Pharisees only wore them, and thus they became symbols of hypocrisy.   *bauk:* spare. The reference is to the cutting off of William Prynne's ears in 1637 for his opposition to the prelates; symbolically, he could not now hear and preach the word of God.   **20:** "Presbyter" and "Priest" derive from the same Greek word.

George Meredith   Nine Sonnets
FROM *Modern Love*

I

By this he knew she wept with waking eyes:
That, at his hand's light quiver by her head,
The strange low sobs that shook their common bed
Were called into her with a sharp surprise,

And strangled mute, like little gaping snakes,   5
Dreadfully venomous to him. She lay
Stone-still, and the long darkness flowed away
With muffled pulses. Then, as midnight makes
Her giant heart of Memory and Tears
Drink the pale drug of silence, and so beat   10
Sleep's heavy measure, they from head to feet
Were moveless, looking through their dead black years,
By vain regret scrawled over the blank wall.
Like sculptured effigies they might be seen
Upon their marriage-tomb, the sword between;   15
Each wishing for the sword that severs all.

2
It ended, and the morrow brought the task.
Her eyes were guilty gates, that let him in
By shutting all too zealous for their sin:
Each sucked a secret, and each wore a mask.
But, oh, the bitter taste her beauty had!   5
He sickened as at breath of poison-flowers:
A languid humor stole among the hours,
And if their smiles encountered, he went mad,
And raged deep inward, till the light was brown
Before his vision, and the world, forgot,   10
Looked wicked as some old dull murder-spot.
A star with lurid beams, she seemed to crown
The pit of infamy: and then again
He fainted on his vengefulness, and strove
To ape the magnanimity of love,   15
And smote himself, a shuddering heap of pain.

3
This was the woman; what now of the man?
But pass him. If he comes beneath a heel,
He shall be crushed until he cannot feel,
Or, being callous, haply till he can.
But he is nothing:—nothing? Only mark   5
The rich light striking out from her on him!
Ha! what a sense it is when her eyes swim
Across the man she singles, leaving dark
All else! Lord God, who madest the thing so fair,
See that I am drawn to her even now!   10
It cannot be such harm on her cool brow
To put a kiss? Yet if I meet him there!
But she is mine! Ah, no! I know too well
I claim a star whose light is overcast:
I claim a phantom-woman in the Past.   15
The hour has struck, though I heard not the bell!

1 *man:* the wife's lover.

4
All other joys of life he strove to warm,
And magnify, and catch them to his lip:

But they had suffered shipwreck with the ship,
And gazed upon him sallow from the storm.
Or if Delusion came, 'twas but to show   5
The coming minute mock the one that went.
Cold as a mountain in its star-pitched tent,
Stood high Philosophy, less friend than foe:
Whom self-caged Passion, from its prison-bars,
Is always watching with a wondering hate.   10
Not till the fire is dying in the grate,
Look we for any kinship with the stars.
Oh, wisdom never comes when it is gold,
And the great price we pay for it full worth:
We have it only when we are half earth.   15
Little avails that coinage to the old!

14

What soul would bargain for a cure that brings
Contempt the nobler agony to kill?
Rather let me bear on the bitter ill,
And strike this rusty bosom with new stings!
It seems there is another veering fit,   5
Since on a gold-haired lady's eyeballs pure
I looked with little prospect of a cure,
The while her mouth's red bow loosed shafts of wit.
Just heaven! can it be true that jealousy
Has decked the woman thus? and does her head   10
Swim somewhat for possessions forfeited?
Madam, you teach me many things that be.
I open an old book and there I find
That "Women still may love whom they deceive."
Such love I prize not, madam: by your leave,   15
The game you play at is not to my mind.

6 *lady*: the husband's loved one, the fourth character of the sequence.

23

'Tis Christmas weather, and a country house
Receives us: rooms are full: we can but get
An attic-crib. Such lovers will not fret
At that, it is half-said. The great carouse
Knocks hard upon the midnight's hollow door,   5
But when I knock at hers, I see the pit.
Why did I come here in that dullard fit?
I enter, and lie couched upon the floor.
Passing, I caught the coverlet's quick beat:
Come, Shame, burn to my soul! and Pride, and Pain—   10
Foul demons that have tortured me, enchain!
Out in the freezing darkness that lambs bleat.
The small bird stiffens in the low starlight.
I know not how, but shuddering as I slept,
I dreamed a banished angel to me crept: 15
My feet were nourished on her breasts all night.

6 *the pit*: hell.

26

Love ere he bleeds, an eagle in high skies,
Has earth beneath his wings: from reddened eve
He views the rosy dawn. In vain they weave
The fatal web below while for he flies.
But when the arrow strikes him, there's a change.   5
He moves but in the track of his spent pain,
Whose red drops are the links of a harsh chain,
Binding him to the ground, with narrow range.
A subtle serpent then has Love become.
I had the eagle in my bosom erst: 10
Henceforward with the serpent I am cursed.
I can interpret where the mouth is dumb.
Speak, and I see the side-lie of a truth.
Perchance my heart may pardon you this deed:
But be no coward—you that made Love bleed,   15
You must bear all the venom of his tooth!

10 *erst:* formerly.   13 *side-lie:* false impression (which the truth can nonetheless give).

41

He found her by the ocean's moaning verge,
Nor any wicked change in her discerned;
And she believed his old love had returned,
Which was her exultation, and her scourge.
She took his hand, and walked with him, and seemed   5
The wife he sought, though shadow-like and dry.
She had one terror, lest her heart should sigh,
And tell her loudly she no longer dreamed.
She dared not say, "This is my breast: look in."
But there's a strength to help the desperate weak.   10
That night he learned how silence best can speak
The awful things when Pity pleads for Sin.
About the middle of the night her call
Was heard, and he came wondering to the bed.
"Now kiss me, dear! it may be, now!" she said.   15
Lethe had passed those lips, and he knew all.

1: The wife has decided to commit suicide.   16 *Lethe:* the river of forgetfulness.

50

Thus piteously Love closed what he begat:
The union of this ever-diverse pair!
These two were rapid falcons in a snare,
Condemned to do the flitting of the bat.
Lovers beneath the singing sky of May,   5
They wandered once; clear as the dew on flowers:
But they fed not on the advancing hours:
Their hearts held cravings for the buried day.
Then each applied to each that fatal knife,
Deep questioning, which probes to endless dole.   10
Ah, what a dusty answer gets the soul

When hot for certainties in this our life!
In tragic hints here see what evermore
Moves dark as yonder midnight ocean's force,
Thundering like ramping hosts of warrior horse,   15
To throw that faint thin line upon the shore!

George Barker   To Any Member of My Generation

What was it you remember—the summer mornings
Down by the river at Richmond with a girl,
And as you kissed, clumsy in bathing costumes,
History guffawed in a rosebush. O what a warning—
If only we had known, if only we had known!   5
And when you looked in mirrors was this meaning
Plain as the pain in the center of a pearl?
Horrible tomorrow in Teutonic postures
Making absurd the past we cannot disown?

Whenever we kissed we cocked the future's rifles   10
And from our wild-oat words, like dragon's teeth,
Death underfoot now arises; when we were gay
Dancing together in what we hoped was life,
Who was it in our arms but the whores of death
Whom we have found in our beds today, today?   15

2 *Richmond*: a city on the Thames, west of London.   11 *dragon's teeth*: Cadmus strew behind him dragon's teeth that sprang up armed men. The seven who survived the ensuing battle founded Thebes.

SPECIFIC VERSE FORMS: THE ODE

Another lyric form is the ode. Although generally stanzaic and patterned, the ode is also distinguished by subject matter and tone. The Greek odes of Pindar were songs honoring gods or heroes, victorious accomplishment on the field of battle or in athletic contests. The tone was exalted and uplifting; it was inspired and inspiring; and there was always a strong choric quality in its lines. While maintaining some of this attitude, Horace's odes reinterpreted the subject matter to celebrate patriotism in various ways and then love not only of country and public affairs but of woman. The tone became less exalted and less inspiring; thwarted love might indeed create a quite opposed tone. The ode in English therefore follows all these previous examples but also continues the breakdown in rigidity of content and tone. Like most labels the term ode has at times been applied by poets rather indiscriminately. For example, see Michael Drayton's "The Crier," which he printed as an ode. We find it as title of almost any manner of short lyric today, although stanzaic and patterned form still generally differentiates the ode from other lyrics such as we have already examined.

The Pindaric ode consists of several stanzas, each stanza containing a strophe, an antistrophe, and an epode (each of which might in itself be considered a stanza). Lines are of uneven length as are the stanzas and each of their parts. Patterns are not developed for repetition either between stanzas or between any one of their parts. The ode does not require specific prosodic or rhyme patterns. A strophe was originally a stanza sung by the Greek chorus as it moved across the stage from an earlier position. An antistrophe was a stanza sung by the chorus as it returned across the stage to its former position. One was not simply the reversal of the other in length or time, but some contrast in rhythm was observable. The epode was a stanza sung by the chorus when it was standing still in position. An excellent example of the strict Pindaric ode is Ben Jonson's "To the Immortal Memory . . . of . . . Sir Lucius Cary and Sir H. Morrison." Jonson translates the terms as "Turn," "Counterturn," and "Stand."

In English poetry the threefold nature of the Pindaric ode early disappeared from some odes, and in its stead we find a series of irregular stanzas. The number of stanzas was not fixed; the stanzas specifically varied their patterns amongst themselves; and the line lengths and rhyme schemes were purposely irregular. Better called the "irregular ode," it was derived from the Pindaric through such experiments as Abraham Cowley's "The Praise of Pindar." Cowley's aim was to capture the feeling and general sense of Pindar rather than produce an exact translation. In Allen Tate's "Ode to the Confederate Dead" we see how even the irregular ode is further unpatterned in its stanzaic form, while it maintains the subject matter and tone appropriate to the classic lyric.

The Horatian ode consisted of several repeated four-line stanzas. Andrew Marvell's "An Horatian Ode Upon Cromwell's Return from Ireland," with the apparent celebration of patriotism and heroic action, fits the pattern even though it is printed without breaks between the four-line stanzas. The use of a rhyme pattern is predictable in this form of ode. Yet a sharp variation also developed when this odic form came into English poetry. The regular patterning of repeated short stanzas (not only those of four lines) came to constitute a kind of Horatian ode. Here the several stanzas were of the same length and line and rhyme patterns. We may note such diverse stanzaic forms as Shelley's "Ode to the West Wind" or Auden's "Ode: To My Pupils."

The final breakdown of the classic odic form was the development of a single stanza (seldom two) of irregular line lengths and pattern. This so-called English ode is represented by Milton's "On Time" or Joseph Warton's "Ode to Fancy," in 148 lines of tetrameter couplets.

The "Pindaric" Ode

Ben Jonson To the Immortal Memory and Friendship
of That Noble Pair, Sir Lucius Cary and Sir H. Morison

THE TURN

Brave infant of Saguntum, clear
Thy coming forth in that great year,
When the prodigious Hannibal did crown
His rage with razing your immortal town.
Thou, looking then about,   5
Ere thou wert half got out,
Wise child, didst hastily return,
And madest thy mother's womb thine urn.
How summed a circle didst thou leave mankind
Of deepest lore, could we the center find!   10

THE COUNTERTURN

Did wiser nature draw thee back,
From out the horror of that sack,
Where shame, faith, honor, and regard of right
Lay trampled on; the deeds of death and night,
Urged, hurried forth, and hurled   15
Upon the affrighted world:
Sword, fire, and famine, with fell fury met;
And all on utmost ruin set;
As, could they but life's misery foresee,
No doubt all infants would return like thee?   20

THE STAND

For, what is life, if measured by the space,
Not by the act?
Or masked man, if valued by his face,
Above his fact?
Here's one outlived his peers,   25
And told forth fourscore years;
He vexed time and busied the whole state;
Troubled both foes and friends;
But ever to no ends:
What did this stirrer, but die late?   30
How well at twenty had he fallen or stood!
For three of his fourscore, he did no good.

THE TURN

He entered well, by virtuous parts,
Got up and thrived with honest arts:
He purchased friends, and fame, and honors then,   35

And had his noble name advanced with men:
But weary of that flight,
He stooped in all men's sight
To sordid flatteries, acts of strife,
And sunk in that dead sea of life   40
So deep, as he did then death's waters sup;
But that the cork of title buoyed him up.

THE COUNTERTURN

Alas, but Morison fell young:
He never fell, thou fallest, my tongue.
He stood, a soldier to the last right end,   45
A perfect patriot and a noble friend,
But most a virtuous son.
All offices were done
By him, so ample, full, and round,
In weight, in measure, number, sound,   50
As though his age imperfect might appear,
His life was of humanity the sphere.

THE STAND

Go now, and tell out days summed up with fears,
And make them years;
Produce thy mass of miseries on the stage,   55
To swell thine age;
Repeat of things a throng,
To show thou hast been long,
Not lived; for life doth her great actions spell,
By what was done and wrought   60
In season, and so brought
To light: her measures are, how well
Each syllable answered, and was formed, how fair;
These make the lines of life and that's her air.

THE TURN

It is not growing like a tree   65
In bulk doth make man better be;
Or standing long an oak, three hundred year,
To fall a log, at last, dry, bald, and sear:
A lily of a day
Is fairer far in May,   70
Although it fall and die that night;
It was the plant and flower of light.
In small proportions we just beauties see:
And in short measures, life may perfect be.

THE COUNTERTURN

Call, noble Lucius, then for wine,   75
And let thy looks with gladness shine:
Accept this garland, plant it on thy head,

And think, nay know, thy Morison's not dead.
  He leaped the present age,
  Possessed with holy rage,   80
To see that bright eternal day:
Of which we priests and poets say
Such truths as we expect for happy men,
And there he lives with memory; and Ben

THE STAND

Jonson, who sung this of him ere he went   85
  Himself to rest,
Or taste a part of the full joy he meant
  To have expressed,
  In this bright asterism:
  Where it were friendship's schism   90
(Were not his Lucius long with us to tarry),
  To separate these twi-
  Lights, the Dioscuri;
And keep the one half from his Harry.
But fate doth so alternate the design,   95
Whilst that in heaven, this light on earth must shine.

THE TURN

And shine as you exalted are;
Two names of friendship, but one star:
Of hearts the union. And those not by chance
Made, or indentured, or leased out to advance   100
  The profits for a time.
  No pleasures vain did chime,
Of rimes, or riots, at your feasts,
Orgies of drink, or feigned protests:
But simple love of greatness, and of good;   105
That knits brave minds and manners more than blood.

THE COUNTERTURN

This made you first to know the Why
You liked, then after, to apply
That liking; and approach so one the tother,
Till either grew a portion of the other: 110
  Each stiled by his end,
  The copy of his friend.
You lived to be the great surnames,
And titles, by which all made claims
Unto the virtue. Nothing perfect done,   115
But as a Cary or a Morison.

THE STAND

And such a force the fair example had,
  As they that saw
The good, and durst not practise it, were glad
  That such a law   120

Was left yet to mankind;
Where they might read and find
Friendship, in deed, was written, not in words:
And with the heart, not pen,
Of two so early men,   *125*
Whose lines her rolls were and records.
Who, ere the first down bloomed on the chin,
Had sowed these fruits, and got the harvest in.

Sir Lucius Cary: Viscount Falkland (1610?–1643).   *Sir H. Morrison:* Henry (1608?-1629), Cary's brother-in-law.   1 *Saguntum:* town captured by Hannibal in 219 B.C., beginning the second Punic War.   9 *summed:* complete.   25 *one:* perhaps the lawyer Sir Edward Coke.   53 *tell:* count.   89 *asterism:* constellation.   93 *Dioscuri:* the Gemini, Castor and Pollux. 109 *tother:* other.

Abraham Cowley   The Praise of Pindar

IN IMITATION OF HORACE HIS SECOND ODE, BOOK 4

1
Pindar is imitable by none;
   The phoenix Pindar is a vast species alone.
Whoe'er but Daedalus with waxen wings could fly
And neither sink too low nor soar too high?
   What could he who followed claim   5
But of vain boldness the unhappy fame,
   And by his fall a sea to name?
   Pindar's unnavigable song,
Like a swollen flood from some steep mountain, pours along;
   The ocean meets with such a voice   10
From his enlarged mouth as drowns the ocean's noise.

2
So Pindar does new words and figures roll
Down his impetuous dithyrambic tide,
   Which in no channel deigns to abide,
   Which neither banks nor dikes control.   15
   Whether the immortal gods he sings
   In a no less immortal strain,
Or the great acts of god-descended kings,
Who in his numbers still survive and reign,
   Each rich embroidered line,   20
   Which their triumphant brows around
   By his sacred hand is bound,
Does all their starry diadems outshine.

3
Whether at Pisa's race he please
To carve in polished verse the conquerors' images,   25
Whether the swift, the skilful, or the strong

Be crowned in his nimble, artful, vigorous song,
Whether some brave young man's untimely fate
In words worth dying for he celebrate,
   Such mournful and such pleasing words   30
As joy to his mother's and his mistress' grief affords,
    He bids him live and grow in fame;
    Among the stars he sticks his name;
The grave can but the dross of his devour,
So small is death's, so great the poet's power.   35

      4
Lo, how the obsequious wind and swelling air
   The Theban swan does upwards bear
Into the walks of clouds, where he does play,
And with extended wings opens his liquid way,
    Whilst, alas, my timorous Muse   40
    Unambitious tracks pursues;
    Does, with weak, unballast wings,
    About the mossy brooks and springs,
    About the trees' new-blossomed heads,
    About the gardens' painted beds,   45
    About the fields and flowery meads,
    And all inferior beauteous things,
      Like the laborious bee,
   For little drops of honey flee,
And there with humble sweets contents her industry.   50

2 *phoenix:* a fabulous, unique bird, reborn only from its own ashes.
3 *Daedalus:* the inventor who devised wings attached to the body
by wax, in order to escape from Crete; his son Icarus, using them,
flew too near the sun and fell to his death in the sea. Icaria is an
island and section of the Aegean Sea.   13 *dithyrambic:* referring
to wildly lyrical poetry (in honor of Dionysius).   19 *numbers:*
verses.   24 *Pisa's race:* the Olympic games. Pisa was near
Olympia.   36 *obsequious:* compliant, following in attendance.
37 *Theban swan:* Pindar.

William Collins   Ode to Fear

Thou, to whom the world unknown
With all its shadowy shapes is shown;
Who seest appalled the unreal scene,
While Fancy lifts the veil between:
   Ah Fear! Ah frantic Fear!   5
   I see, I see thee near.
I know thy hurried step, thy haggard eye!
Like thee I start, like thee disordered fly,
   For lo what monsters in thy train appear!
   Danger, whose limbs of giant mold   10
   What mortal eye can fixed behold?
   Who stalks his round, an hideous form,

Howling amidst the midnight storm,
Or throws him on the ridgy steep
Of some loose hanging rock to sleep: 15
And with him thousand phantoms joined,
Who prompt to deeds accursed the mind:
And those, the fiends, who near allied,
O'er Nature's wounds, and wrecks preside;
Whilst Vengeance, in the lurid air,   20
Lifts her red arm, exposed and bare:
On whom that ravening brood of fate,
    Who lap the blood of sorrow, wait;
Who, Fear, this ghastly train can see,
And look not madly wild, like thee?   25

ANTISTROPHE

Thou who such weary lengths hast past,
Where wilt thou rest, mad nymph, at last?
Say, wilt thou shroud in haunted cell,
Where gloomy Rape and Murder dwell?
Or, in some hollowed seat,   30
'Gainst which the big waves beat,
Hear drowning seamen's cries in tempests brought!
Dark power, with shuddering meek submitted thought
Be mine, to read the visions old,
Which thy awakening bards have told: 35
And lest thou meet my blasted view,
Hold each strange tale devoutly true;
Ne'er be I found, by thee o'erawed,
In that thrice-hallowed eve abroad,
When ghosts, as cottage-maids believe,   40
Their pebbled beds permitted leave,
And goblins haunt from fire, or fen,
Or mine, or flood, the walks of men!
    O thou whose spirit most possessed
The sacred seat of Shakespeare's breast!   45
By all that from thy prophet broke,
In thy divine emotions spoke:
Hither again thy fury deal,
Teach me but once like him to feel:
His cypress wreath my need decree,   50
And I, O Fear, will dwell with thee!

EPODE

In earliest Greece to thee with partial choice,
    The grief-full Muse addressed her infant tongue;
The maids and matrons, on her awful voice,
    Silent and pale in wild amazement hung.   55

Yet he, the bard who first invoked thy name,
    Disdained in Marathon its power to feel:
For not alone he nursed the poet's flame,
    But reached from Virtue's hand the patriot's steel.

But who is he whom later garlands grace,   60
  Who left awhile o'er Hybla's dews to rove,
With trembling eyes thy dreary steps to trace,
  Where thou and Furies shared the baleful grove?

Wrapt in thy cloudy veil the incestuous queen
  Sighed the sad call her son and husband heard,   65
When once alone it broke the silent scene,
  And he the wretch of Thebes no more appeared.

O Fear, I know thee by my throbbing heart,
  Thy withering power inspired each mournful line,
Though gentle Pity claim her mingled part,   70
  Yet all the thunders of the scene are thine!

21 *red arm:* see *Paradise Lost,* II 173–74: "Should intermitted
vengeance arm again/His [God's] red right hand to plague us?"
Red was the color of the horse of war in Rev. vi.4.   39 *thrice-
hallowed eve:* Hallowe'en, which ushers in All Saints' Day.   50
cypress: an evergreen, but one signifying death.   56 *bard:*
Aeschylus, who wrote of the *Seven Against Thebes.*   57 *Mara-
thon:* a town in Greece, site of an important battle in 490 B.C.
61 *Hybla:* a town of Sicily, famous for honey.   64 *incestuous
queen:* Jocasta, mother and wife of Oedipus, king of Thebes. See
Sophocles' play.

William Wordsworth   Ode: Intimations of Immortality
  from Recollections of Early Childhood

        The Child is father of the Man;
        And I could wish my days to be
        Bound each to each by natural piety.

      1
There was a time when meadow, grove, and stream,
The earth, and every common sight,
      To me did seem
    Apparelled in celestial light,
The glory and the freshness of a dream.   5
It is not now as it hath been of yore—
    Turn wheresoe'er I may,
      By night or day,
The things which I have seen I now can see no more.

      2
    The rainbow comes and goes,   10
    And lovely is the rose,
    The moon doth with delight
Look round her when the heavens are bare,
    Waters on a starry night
    Are beautiful and fair;   15
  The sunshine is a glorious birth;

But yet I know, where'er I go,
That there hath passed away a glory from the earth.

3
Now, while the birds thus sing a joyous song,
    And while the young lambs bound   20
        As to the tabor's sound,
To me alone there came a thought of grief:
A timely utterance gave that thought relief,
        And I again am strong:
The cataracts blow their trumpets from the steep;   25
No more shall grief of mine the season wrong;
I hear the echoes through the mountains throng,
The winds come to me from the fields of sleep,
        And all the earth is gay;
            Land and sea   30
        Give themselves up to jollity,
            And with the heart of May
        Doth every beast keep holiday—
            Thou child of joy,
Shout round me; let me hear thy shouts, thou happy
    shepherd-boy!   35

4
Ye blessed creatures, I have heard the call
    Ye to each other make; I see
The heavens laugh with you in your jubilee;
    My heart is at your festival,
    My head hath its coronal,   40
The fullness of your bliss, I feel—I feel it all.
    Oh, evil day! if I were sullen
    While earth herself is adorning,
        This sweet May morning,
    And the children are culling   45
        On every side,
    In a thousand valleys far and wide,
    Fresh flowers; while the sun shines warm,
And the babe leaps up on his mother's arm—
    I hear, I hear, with joy I hear!   50
    —But there's a tree, of many, one,
A single field which I have looked upon,
Both of them speak of something that is gone:
    The pansy at my feet
    Doth the same tale repeat: 55
Whither is fled the visionary gleam?
Where is it now, the glory and the dream?

5
Our birth is but a sleep and a forgetting:
The soul that rises with us, our life's star,
    Hath had elsewhere its setting,   60
        And cometh from afar:
    Not in entire forgetfulness,

And not in utter nakedness,
But trailing clouds of glory do we come
   From God, who is our home: 65
Heaven lies about us in our infancy!
Shades of the prison-house begin to close
   Upon the growing boy
But he beholds the light, and whence it flows,
   He sees it in his joy;   70
The youth, who daily farther from the east
   Must travel, still is nature's priest,
   And by the vision splendid
   Is on his way attended;
At length the man perceives it die away,   75
And fade into the light of common day.

6

Earth fills her lap with pleasures of her own;
Yearnings she hath in her own natural kind,
And, even with something of a mother's mind,
   And no unworthy aim,   80
   The homely nurse doth all she can
To make her foster-child, her inmate man,
   Forget the glories he hath known,
And that imperial palace from whence he came.

7

Behold the child among his newborn blisses,   85
A six-years' darling of a pygmy size!
See, where 'mid work of his own hand he lies,
Fretted by sallies of his mother's kisses,
With light upon him from his father's eyes!
See, at his feet, some little plan or chart,   90
Some fragment from his dream of human life,
Shaped by himself with newly-learned art;
   A wedding or a festival,
   A mourning or a funeral;
    And this hath now his heart,   95
   And unto this he frames his song;
    Then will he fit his tongue
To dialogues of business, love, or strife;
   But it will not be long
   Ere this be thrown aside,   100
   And with new joy and pride
The little actor cons another part;
Filling from time to time his "humorous stage"
With all the persons, down to palsied age,
That life brings with her in her equipage;   105
   As if his whole vocation
   Were endless imitation.

8

Thou, whose exterior semblance doth belie
   Thy soul's immensity;

Thou best philosopher, who yet dost keep   110
Thy heritage, thou eye among the blind,
That, deaf and silent, readest the eternal deep,
Haunted forever by the eternal mind—
    Mighty prophet! seer blest!
    On whom those truths do rest,   115
Which we are toiling all our lives to find,
In darkness lost, the darkness of the grave;
Thou, over whom thy immortality
Broods like the day, a master o'er a slave,
A presence which is not to be put by;   120
Thou little child, yet glorious in the might
Of heaven-born freedom on thy being's height,
Why with such earnest pains does thou provoke
The years to bring the inevitable yoke,
Thus blindly with thy blessedness at strife?   125
Full soon thy soul shall have her earthly freight,
And custom lie upon thee with a weight,
Heavy as frost, and deep almost as life!

    9
    O joy! that in our embers
    Is something that doth live,   130
    That nature yet remembers
    What was so fugitive!
The thought of our past years in me doth breed
Perpetual benedictions: not indeed
For that which is most worthy to be blest;   135
Delight and liberty, the simple creed
Of childhood, whether busy or at rest,
With new-fledged hope still fluttering in his breast—
    Not for these I raise
    The song of thanks and praise;   140
    But for those obstinate questionings
    Of sense and outward things,
    Fallings from us, vanishings;
    Blank misgivings of a creature
Moving about in worlds not realized,   145
High instincts before which our mortal nature
Did tremble like a guilty thing surprised;
    But for those first affections,
    Those shadowy recollections,
    Which, be they what they may,   150
Are yet the fountain light of all our day,
Are yet a master light of all our seeing;
    Uphold us, cherish, and have power to make
Our noisy years seem moments in the being
Of our eternal silence: truths that wake,   155
    To perish never;
Which neither listlessness, nor mad endeavor,
    Nor man nor boy,
Nor all that is at enmity with joy,
Can utterly abolish or destroy!   160

Hence in a season of calm weather
  Though inland far we be,
Our souls have sight of that immortal sea
  Which brought us hither,
  Can in a moment travel thither,   *165*
And see the children sport upon the shore,
And hear the mighty waters rolling evermore.

  10
Then sing, ye birds, sing, sing a joyous song!
  And let the young lambs bound
  As to the tabor's sound!   *170*
We in thought will join your throng,
  Ye that pipe and ye that play,
  Ye that through your hearts today
  Feel the gladness of the May!
What though the radiance which was once so bright *175*
Be now forever taken from my sight,
  Though nothing can bring back the hour
Of splendor in the grass, of glory in the flower;
  We will grieve not, rather find
  Strength in what remains behind;   *180*
  In the primal sympathy
  Which having been must ever be;
  In the soothing thoughts that spring
  Out of human suffering;
  In the faith that looks through death,   *185*
In years that bring the philosophic mind.

  11
And O, ye fountains, meadows, hills, and groves,
Forebode not any severing of our loves!
Yet in my heart of hearts I feel your might;
I only have relinquished one delight   *190*
To live beneath your more habitual sway.
I love the brooks which down their channels fret,
Even more than when I tripped lightly as they;
The innocent brightness of a newborn day
  Is lovely yet;   *195*
The clouds that gather round the setting sun
Do take a sober coloring from an eye
That hath kept watch o'er man's mortality;
Another race hath been, and other palms are won.
Thanks to the human heart by which we live, 200
Thanks to its tenderness, its joys, and fears,
To me the meanest flower that blows can give
Thoughts that do often lie too deep for tears.

Epigraph: ll. 7–10 of Wordsworth's "My Heart Leaps Up."
102 cons: commits to memory. *103 humorous stage:* see Jaques'
speech in *As You Like It,* II, vii, 139 ff., which describes life as a
play with various scenes according to varying moods.

Percy Bysshe Shelley   Ode to Naples

EPODE I

I stood within the city disinterred;
  And heard the autumnal leaves like light footfalls
Of spirits passing through the streets; and heard
  The Mountain's slumberous voice at intervals
    Thrill through those roofless halls;   5
The oracular thunder penetrating shook
  The listening soul in my suspended blood;
I felt that Earth out of her deep heart spoke—
  I felt, but heard not—through white columns glowed
    The isle-sustaining Ocean-flood,   10
A plane of light between two heavens of azure:
  Round me gleamed many a bright sepulchre
Of whose pure beauty, Time, as if his pleasure
Were to spare Death, had never made erasure;
  But every living lineament was clear   15
  As in the sculptor's thought; and there
The wreaths of stony myrtle, ivy and pine,
  Like winter leaves o'ergrown by moulded snow,
  Seemed only not to move and grow
Because the crystal silence of the air   20
  Weighed on their life; even as the Power divine,
  Which then lulled all things, brooded upon mine.

EPODE II

    Then gentle winds arose,
    With many a mingled close
Of wild Aeolian sound and mountain odors keen;   25
    And where the Baian ocean
    Welters with air-like motion,
Within, above, around its bowers of starry green,
  Moving the sea-flowers in those purple caves
    Even as the ever stormless atmosphere   30
    Floats o'er the Elysian realm,
  It bore me, like an Angel o'er the waves
    Of sunlight, whose swift pinnace of dewy air
    No storm can overwhelm;
    I sailed, where ever flows   35
    Under the calm Serene
    A spirit of deep emotion
    From the unknown graves
    Of the dead kings of Melody.
  Shadowy Aornos darkened o'er the helm   40
  The horizontal ether; Heaven stripped bare
Its depth over Elysium, where the prow
Made the invisible water white as snow;
From that Typhaean mount, Inarimé,
  There streamed a sun-bright vapor, like the standard   45

Of some ethereal host;
  Whilst from all the coast,
  Louder and louder, gathering round, there wandered
Over the oracular woods and divine sea
Prophesyings which grew articulate—   50
They seize me—I must speak them—be they fate!

STROPHE I

Naples! thou Heart of men, which ever pantest
  Naked, beneath the lidless eye of Heaven!
Elysian City, which to calm enchantest
  The mutinous air and sea! they round thee, even   55
  As sleep round Love, are driven!
Metropolis of a ruined Paradise
  Long lost, late won, and yet but half regained!
Bright Altar of the bloodless sacrifice,
  Which armed Victory offers up unstained   60
  To Love the flower-enchained!
Thou which wert once, and then didst cease to be,
Now art, and henceforth ever shalt be, free,
  If Hope, and Truth, and Justice can avail.
    Hail, hail, all hail!   65

STROPHE II

  Thou youngest giant birth,
  Which from the groaning earth
Leapest, clothed in armor of impenetrable scale!
  Last of the Intercessors
  Who 'gainst the Crowned Transgressors   70
Pleadest before God's love! Arrayed in Wisdom's mail,
  Wave thy lightning-lance in mirth!
  Nor let thy high heart fail,
Though from their hundred gates the leagued Oppressors
  With hurried legions move!   75
  Hail, hail, all hail!

ANTISTROPHE I

What though Cimmerian Anarchs dare blaspheme
  Freedom and thee? thy shield is as a mirror
To make their blind slaves see, and with fierce gleam
  To turn his hungry sword upon the wearer;   80
    A new Actaeon's error
Shall theirs have been—devoured by their own hounds!
  Be thou like the imperial Basilisk,
Killing thy foe with unapparent wounds!
  Gaze on oppression, till, at that dread risk   85
  Aghast she pass from the Earth's disk;
Fear not, but gaze—for freemen mightier grow,
And slaves more feeble, gazing on their foe;
  If Hope, and Truth, and Justice may avail,
    Thou shalt be great. All hail!   90

ANTISTROPHE II

From Freedom's form divine,
From Nature's inmost shrine,
Strip every impious gawd, rend Error veil by veil:
O'er Ruin desolate,
O'er Falsehood's fallen state,   95
Sit thou sublime, unawed; be the Destroyer pale!
And equal laws be thine,
And winged words let sail,
Freighted with truth even from the throne of God:
That wealth, surviving fate,   100
Be thine. All hail!

ANTISTROPHE I

Didst thou not start to hear Spain's thrilling paean
From land to land re-echoed solemnly,
Till silence became music? From the Aeaean
To the cold Alps, eternal Italy   105
Starts to hear thine! the Sea,
Which paves the desert streets of Venice, laughs
In light and music; widowed Genoa wan
By moonlight spells ancestral epitaphs,
Murmuring, Where is Doria? fair Milan,   110
Within whose veins long ran
The viper's palsying venom, lifts her heel
To bruise his head. The signal and the seal
If Hope, and Truth, and Justice can avail
Art Thou of all these hopes. O hail!   115

ANTISTROPHE II

Florence! beneath the sun,
Of cities fairest one,
Blushes within her bower for Freedom's expectation:
From eyes of quenchless hope
Rome tears the priestly cope,   120
As ruling once by power, so now by admiration—
An athlete stripped to run
From a remoter station
For the high prize lost on Philippi's shore—
As then Hope, Truth, and Justice did avail,   125
So now many Fraud and Wrong! O hail!

EPODE I

Hear ye the march as of the Earth-born Forms
Arrayed against the ever-living Gods?
The crash and darkness of a thousand storms
Bursting their inaccessible abodes   130
Of crags and thunder clouds?
See ye the banners blazoned to the day,
Inwrought with emblems of barbaric pride?

Dissonant threats kill Silence far away,
   The Serene Heaven which wraps our Eden wide   *135*
      With iron light is dyed,
The Anarchs of the North lead forth their legions
   Like Chaos o'er creation, uncreating;
An hundred tribes nourished on strange religions
And lawless slaveries—down the aerial regions   *140*
   Of the white Alps, desolating,
     Famished wolves that bide no waiting,
Blotting the glowing footsteps of old glory,
Trampling our columned cities into dust,
     Their dull and savage lust   *145*
   On Beauty's corse to sickness satiating—
They come! The fields they tread look blue and hoary
With fire—from their red feet the streams run gory!

   EPODE II

   Great Spirit, deepest Love!
     Which rulest and dost move   *150*
All things which live and are, within the Italian shore
     Who spreadest Heaven around it,
     Whose words, rocks, waves, surround it;
Who sittest in thy star, o'er Ocean's western floor;
Spirit of beauty! at whose soft command   *155*
   The sunbeams and the showers distil its foison
     From the Earth's bosom chill;
Oh, bid those beams be each a blinding brand
   Of lightning! bid those showers be dews of poison!
     Bid the Earth's plenty kill!   *160*
     Bid thy bright Heaven above
     Whilst light and darkness bound it,
     Be their tomb who planned
     To make it ours and thine!

   Or, with thine harmonizing ardors fill   *165*
And raise thy sons, as o'er the prone horizon
Thy lamp feeds every twilight wave with fire—
Be man's high hope and unextinct desire
The instrument to work thy will divine!
   Then clouds from sunbeams, antelopes from leopards,   *170*
     And frowns and fears from Thee,
     Would not more swiftly flee,
   Than Celtic wolves from the Ausonian shepherds.
Whatever, Spirit, from thy starry shrine
   Thou yieldest or withholdest, oh let be   *175*
     This City of thy worship, ever free!

1 the city: Pompeii, an ancient city at the foot of Mt. Vesuvius.
25 Aeolian: borne as by the wind.   *26 Baian:* referring to Baia,
a resort village near Naples.   *39 dead kings of Melody:* Homer
and Vergil.   *40 Aornos:* Lake Avernus, beneath which was
Hades.   *44 Typhaean:* referring to a monster with a hundred
heads.   *Inarimé:* Ischia, a volcanic island in the Bay of Naples
where Typhoeus was supposed to be buried.   *58:* Alluding to

Orpheus' loss of his wife Eurydice through death, his winning her back from Pluto through his song, and his loss of her again when he unwisely looked back as they were ascending from Hades.   77 *Cimmerian*: those living in total darkness.   *Anarchs*: those who believe in anarchy; the Austrians who were gathering for an invasion of the Kingdom of Naples in 1821.   81 Actaeon: a hunter who was changed into a stag by Diana for having spied her bathing. 83 *Basilisk*: a fabulous serpent whose look killed.   104 *Aeaean*: referring to Circe's island.   110 *Doria*: Andrea Doria (1468–1560), who led Genoa to independence; it and Milan were given to Austria by the Congress of Vienna (1814–1815).   112 *viper*: the armorial device of the Visconti, tyrants of Milan. 112–113: Alluding to the Judgment on the serpent in Gen. iii.15: "I will put enmity between thee and the woman, and between thy seed and her seed; it shall bruise thy head, and thou shalt bruise his heel." Eve's seed brought forth Jesus.   124 *Philippi*: a town in Greece where adherents of the republic of Rome were defeated by Caesar in 42 B.C.   127 *Earth-born Forms*: the Giants, sons of Gaia, goddess of Earth, who tried to assault Olympus.   156 *foison*: abundance.   173 *Ausonian*: Italian.

Ralph Waldo Emerson   Ode: Inscribed to
   W. H. Channing

Though loath to grieve
The evil time's sole patriot,
I cannot leave
My honied thought
For the priest's cant,   5
Or statesman's rant.

If I refuse
My study for their politique,
Which at the best is trick,
The angry Muse   10
Puts confusion in my brain.

But who is he that prates
Of the culture of mankind,
Of better arts and life?
Go, blindworm, go,   15
Behold the famous States
Harrying Mexico
With rifle and with knife!

Or who, with accent bolder,
Dare praise the freedom-loving mountaineer?   20
I found by thee, O rushing Contoocook!
And in thy valleys, Agiochook!
The jackals of the negro-holder.

The God who made New Hampshire
Taunted the lofty land   25

With little men;
Small bat and wren
House in the oak:
If earth-fire cleave
The upheaved land, and bury the folk,   30
The southern crocodile would grieve.
Virtue palters; Right is hence;
Freedom praised, but hid;
Funeral eloquence
Rattles the coffin-lid.   35

What boots thy zeal,
O glowing friend,
That would indignant rend
The northland from the south?
Wherefore? to what good end?   40
Boston Bay and Bunker Hill
Would serve things still;
Things are of the snake.

The horseman serves the horse,
The neatherd serves the neat,
The merchant serves the purse,   45
The eater serves his meat;
'Tis the day of the chattel,
Web to weave, and corn to grind;
Things are in the saddle,   50
And ride mankind.

There are two laws discrete,
Not reconciled—
Law for man, and law for thing;
The last builds town and fleet,   55
But it runs wild,
And doth the man unking.

'Tis fit the forest fall,
The steep be graded,
The mountain tunnelled,   60
The sand shaded,
The orchard planted,
The glebe tilled,
The prairie granted,
The steamer built.   65

Let man serve law for man;
Live for friendship, live for love,
For truth's and harmony's behoof;
The state may follow how it can,
As Olympus follows Jove.   70

    Yet do not I implore
The wrinkled shopman to my sounding woods,
Nor bid the unwilling senator
Ask votes of thrushes in the solitudes.
Every one to his chosen work;   75
Foolish hands may mix and mar;

Wise and sure the issues are.
Round they roll till dark is light,

Sex to sex, and even to odd;
The over-god   80
Who marries Right to Might,
Who peoples, unpeoples,
He who exterminates
Races by stronger races,
Black by white faces,   85
Knows to bring honey
Out of the lion;
Grafts gentlest scion
On pirate and Turk.

The Cossack eats Poland,   90
Like stolen fruit;
Her last noble is ruined,
Her last poet mute:
Straight, into double band
The victors divide;   95
Half for freedom strike and stand;
The astonished Muse finds thousands at her side.

W. H. Channing: William Henry Channing, Unitarian preacher,
editor, and Christian Socialist; he was partisan toward many causes,
including the abolitionist movement. The ode, written in 1846,
argues against mere activism and for individualism.   31: The
crocodile was supposed to cry false tears while it devoured its
victim.   36 *What boots:* of what use is.   45 *neat:* ox.   63
glebe: soil.   86–87: Referring to Samson's riddle and its answer
(Judges xiv.14, 18).   90: Russia overran Poland in 1796; Emerson also refers to the Polish insurrection of 1830–1831.

Ezra Pound   Trahison des Clercs; Against the Perversion
   of Language
      FROM *The Confucian Odes*
      PART II, BOOK 4, NO. viii

            1
Frost's nimble silk
beneath a summer moon
cuts heart, men's talk the more.
Double-talk on the up,
I am alone,   5
My heart, ai! ai!
gnawed to the bone.

            2
Begat me, you twain, to pain

in the mid cult of mouth-talk,
nor before, nor yet shall be   10
that grief, the more it's real,
draws more insult.

3
In doleful dumps, having no salary,
vacant in thought, this thought comes over me:
other non-criminals may soon be vexed   15
—hack-driving—to find paid jobs,
nor know where crow lights next.

4
Mid-wood now scrub and bare deforested,
Mere fagot-twigs where once the tall trees stood;
the heaven 's in nightmare, yet it once was able   20
to run smooth course, to all men merciable,
none to withstand it. And it hates what man?

5
Call mountain mole-hill, the high crest says: you lie.
Double-talk runs, not even in jeopardy.
Call the diviners, and their vapid blocks   25
emit: We're wise, who knows crow-hens from -cocks?

6
"The heaven's lid high," not dare to stand up straight;
"The earth's crust thick," not dare to not tread light;
and mark these words that have both order and spine,
while you chameleons turn more serpentine: 30

7
Thick wheat mid rocks upon the terraced hill,
The sky-shake knocks, as though it could not fix me,
seeking my style, and yet cannot annex me,
hating at length
yet using not my strength.   35

8
Sorrow at heart, as though by cords constricted;
grind of his reign whereby are all afflicted
to quench that lamp whereby wide earth was lit,
Proud hall of Chou.
                    Pao Sy 'll abolish it.

9
Thought's tread at end beneath the cold of rain,   40
knock off the cart-props till the load fall out,
and then cry: Lord, is there no help about?

10
not slip the cart poles, that be true spokes-men?

Keep eye on driver in perils, and you won't overturn
but reach hard track's end.
                         That's not your concern.   *45*

           11
A shallow basin gives the fish no shade,
dive as they will, there's flash of fin's knife-blade;
Sorrow in heart for any shred or flaw
to see the state, and all, 'neath tiger's claw.

           12
Good wine, good victuals;   *50*
neighbors, come to dine,
praise from feeding kin.
I've but my skin
alone, to keep grief in.

           13
The low have houses and the mean get tips,   *55*
Folk with no salary
the heavens swat,
While ploots can manage
and the "outs" cannot.

Trahison des Clercs: treason of the clerks (scholars and writers).
6 ai: a sound of sorrow; alas.   *21 merciable:* able to give mercy.
58 ploots: plutocrats.

The "Horatian" Ode

Ben Jonson   An Ode: To Himself

          Where dost thou careless lie
             Buried in ease and sloth?
          Knowledge, that sleeps, doth die;
          And this security,
             It is the common moth,   *5*
    That eats on wits and arts and destroys them both.

          Are all the Aonian springs
             Dried up? lies Thespia wast?
          Doth Clarius' harp want strings,
          That not a nymph now sings?   *10*
             Or droop they as disgraced,
    To see their seats and bowers by chattering pies defaced?

          If hence thy silence be,
             As 'tis too just a cause;
          Let this thought quicken thee,   *15*
          Minds that are great and free,
             Should not on fortune pause,
    'Tis crown enough to virtue still, her own applause.

What though the greedy fry
   Be taken with false baits   20
Of worded balladry,
And think it poesy?
   They die with their conceits,
And only piteous scorn upon their folly waits.

Then take in hand thy lyre,   25
   Strike in thy proper strain,
With Japheth's line, aspire
Sol's chariot for new fire,
   To give the world again:
Who aided him will thee, the issue of Jove's brain.   30

And since our dainty age
   Cannot endure reproof,
Make not thyself a page
To that strumpet the stage,
   But sing high and aloof,   35
Safe from the wolf's black jaw and the dull ass's hoof.

7 *Aonian*: sacred to the Muses.   8 *Thespia*: region near Mount
Helicon.   9 *Clarius*: Apollo.   12 *pies*: magpies.   21 *worded*:
wordy.   27 *Japheth's line*: the Ionian Greeks; specifically, Prome-
theus.   28 *Sol*: the sun.   30 *the issue of Jove's brain*: wisdom;
Athena, goddess of wisdom, was born full-grown from Jove's head.

Andrew Marvell   An Horation Ode Upon Cromwell's Return from Ireland

The forward youth that would appear
Must now forsake his muses dear,
   Nor in the shadows sing
   His numbers languishing.
'Tis time to leave the books in dust,   5
And oil the unused armor's rust:
   Removing from the wall
   The corslet of the hall.
So restless Cromwell could not cease
In the inglorious arts of peace,   10
   But through adventurous war
   Urged his active star:
And, like the three-forked lightning, first
Breaking the clouds where it was nursed,
   Did thorough his own side   15
   His fiery way divide.
For 'tis all one to courage high,
The emulous or enemy;
   And with such to inclose
   Is more than to oppose.   20
Then burning through the air he went,
And palaces and temples rent:

And Caesar's head at last
Did through his laurels blast.
'Tis madness to resist or blame   25
The force of angry heaven's flame:
  And, if we would speak true,
  Much to the man is due;
Who, from his private gardens, where
He lived reserved and austere,   30
  As if his highest plot
  To plant the bergamot,
Could by industrious valor climb
To ruin the great work of time,
  And cast the kingdom old   35
  Into another mold;
Though justice against fate complain,
And plead the ancient right in vain:
  But those do hold or break
  As men are strong or weak,   40
Nature that hateth emptiness,
Allows of penetration less:
  And therefore must make room
  Where greater spirits come.
What field of all the Civil Wars,   45
Where his were not the deepest scars?
  And Hampton shows what part
  He had of wiser art;
Where, twining subtile fears with hope,
He wove a net of such a scope,   50
  That Charles himself might chase
  To Carisbrooke's narrow case;
That thence the royal actor borne
The tragic scaffold might adorn:
  While round the armed bands   55
  Did clap their bloody hands.
He nothing common did or mean
Upon that memorable scene:
  But with his keener eye
  The axe's edge did try: 60
Nor called the gods with vulgar spite
To vindicate his helpless right,
  But bowed his comely head,
  Down as upon a bed.
This was that memorable hour   65
Which first assured the forced power.
  So when they did design
  The Capitol's first line,
A bleeding head where they begun,
Did fright the architects to run;   70
  And yet in that the state
  Foresaw its happy fate.
And now the Irish are ashamed
To see themselves in one year tamed:
  So much one man can do,   75

That does both act and know.
They can affirm his praises best,
And have, though overcome, confest
   How good he is, how just,
    And fit for highest trust: 80
Nor yet grown stiffer with command
But still in the Republic's hand:
   How fit he is to sway
    That can so well obey.
He to the Commons' feet presents   85
A kingdom for his first year's rents:
   And, what he may, forbears
    His fame to make it theirs:
And has his sword and spoils ungirt,
To lay them at the public's skirt.   90
   So when the falcon high
    Falls heavy from the sky,
She, having killed, no more does search,
But on the next green bough to perch;
   Where, when he first does lure,   95
    The falconer has her sure.
What may not then our isle presume
While victory his crest does plume!
   What may not others fear
    If thus he crown each year!   100
A Caesar he ere long to Gaul,
To Italy an Hannibal,
   And to all states not free
    Shall climacteric be.
The Pict no shelter now shall find   105
Within his party-colored mind;
   But from this valor sad
    Shrink underneath the plaid:
Happy if in the tufted brake
The English hunter him mistake;   110
   Nor lay his hounds in near
    The Caledonian deer.
But thou the wars' and fortune's son
March indefatigably on;
   And for the last effect   115
    Still keep thy sword erect:
Besides the force it has to fright
The spirits of the shady night,
   The same arts that did gain
    A power must it maintain.   120

Cromwell's Return: Oliver Cromwell, head of the Commonwealth,
returned to England from a campaign in Ireland in May 1650. In
the ode Marvell tries to dissuade him from an invasion of Scotland
(ll. 91 ff.), which however was undertaken on July 22.   1
forward: ambitious.   *appear:* receive public recogntion.   4
numbers: poetry.   15 *thorough:* through.   *side:* political party
(the Army and the Independents).   23 *Caesar's:* Charles I's,

who was beheaded in January 1649 by action of the Commons, after a trial dominated by Cromwell's party.   32 *the bergamot:* a pear.   42 *penetration:* occupation of the same space by two bodies at the same time.   47 *Hampton:* Hampton Court Palace where Charles was held prisoner.   52 *Carisbrooke:* Carisbrooke Castle on the Isle of Wight, to which Charles escaped.   54 *tragic scaffold:* gallows.   66 *the forced power:* the establishment of the Commonwealth by force.   67–70: Referring to the building of the Temple of Jupiter in Rome, during which a head was found in the excavated ground. It was interpreted as a favorable omen. 104 *climacteric:* referring to that critical period when significant change is about to take place.   105 *Pict:* Scot.   106 *party-colored:* changeable (since the Scotch had supported both Charles and the Parliament at different times); there is also a pun on Scottish tartans and clans.   107 *sad:* resolute.   112 *Caledonian:* Scottish.   116: The sword thus takes on the sign of the cross.

Abraham Cowley   Ode: Of Wit

Tell me, O tell, what kind of thing is wit,
   Thou who master art of it.
For the first matter loves variety less;
Less women lov't, either in love or dress.
    A thousand different shapes it bears,   5
    Comely in thousand shapes appears.
Yonder we saw it plain; and here 'tis now,
Like spirits in a place, we know not how.

London that vents of false ware so much store,
   In no ware deceives us more.   10
For men led by the color and the shape
Like Zeuxis' birds fly to the painted grape;
    Some things do through our judgment pass
    As through a multiplying glass.
And sometimes, if the object be too far,   15
We take a falling meteor for a star.

Hence 'tis a wit that greatest word of fame
   Grow such a common name,
And wits by our creation they become,
Just so, as titular bishops made at Rome.   20
    'Tis not a tale, 'tis not a jest
    Admired with laughter at a feast,
Nor florid talk which can that title gain;
The proofs of wit forever must remain.

'Tis not to force some lifeless verses meet   25
   With their five gouty feet.
All everywhere, like man's, must be the soul,
And reason the inferior powers control.
    Such were the numbers which could call

The stones into the Theban wall.   30
Such miracles are ceased; and now we see
No towns or houses raised by poetry.

Yet 'tis not to adorn and gild each part;
    That shows more cost than art.
Jewels at nose and lips but ill appear;   35
Rather than all things wit, let none be there.
        Several lights will not be seen,
        If there be nothing else between.
Men doubt, because they stand so thick i'th'sky,
If those be stars which paint the Galaxy.   40

'Tis not when two like words make up one noise,
    Jests for Dutch men, and English boys,
In which who finds out wit, the same may see
In anagrams and acrostics poetry.
        Much less can that have any place   45
        At which a virgin hides her face,
Such dross and fire must purge away; 'tis just
The author blush, there where the reader must.

'Tis not such lines as almost crack the stage
    When Bajazet begins to rage.   50
Nor a tall metaphor in the bombast way,
Nor the dry chips of short lunged Seneca.
        Nor upon all things to obtrude,
        And force some odd similitude.
What is it then, which like the power divine   55
We only can by negatives define?

In a true piece of wit all things must be,
    Yet all things there agree.
As in the Ark, joined without force or strife,
All creatures dwelt, all creatures that had life.   60
        Or as the primitive forms of all
        (If we compare great things with small)
Which without discord or confusion lie,
In that strange mirror of the deity.

But love that molds one man up out of two   65
    Makes me forget and injure you.
I took you for myself sure when I thought
That you in anything were to be taught.
        Correct my error with thy pen;
        And if any ask me then,   70
What thing right wit and height of genius is,
I'll only show your lines, and say, 'Tis this.

12 *Zeuxis*: a Greek painter of the fifth century, B.C.   14 *multiply-
ing glass*: telescope.   20 *titular bishops*: those in infidel countries
and thus without sees.   29–30: Referring to the music of
Amphion's lyre, which charmed stones to form themselves into the
walls of Thebes.   50 *Bajazet*: the conquered emperor in Mar-
low's *Tamburlaine*.   52 *Seneca*: the Roman author of declama-
tory tragedies, frequently imitated by English dramatists.

Alexander Pope   Ode on Solitude

Happy the man, whose wish and care
 And few paternal acres bound,
Content to breathe his native air,
    In his own ground.

Whose herds with milk, whose fields with bread,   5
 Whose flocks supply him with attire,
Whose trees in summer yield him shade,
    In winter fire.

Blest, who can unconcernedly find
 Hours, days, and years slide soft away,   10
In health of body, peace of mind,
    Quiet by day,

Sound sleep by night; study and ease,
 Together mixed; sweet recreation;
And innocence, which most does please   15
    With meditation.

Thus let me live, unseen, unknown,
 Thus unlamented let me die,
Steal from the world, and not a stone
    Tell where I lie.   20

Thomas Gray   Ode on a Distant Prospect of Eton College

Ye distant spires, ye antique towers,
 That crown the watery glade,
Where grateful Science still adores
 Her Henry's holy shade;
And ye, that from the stately brow   5
Of Windsor's heights the expanse below
Of grove, of lawn, of mead survey,
Whose turf, whose shade, whose flowers among
Wanders the hoary Thames along
 His silver-winding way: 10

Ah happy hills! ah pleasing shade!
 Ah fields beloved in vain!
When once my careless childhood strayed,
 A stranger yet to pain!
I feel the gales that from ye blow   15
A momentary bliss bestow,
As waving fresh their gladsome wing
My weary soul they seem to soothe
And, redolent of joy and youth,
 To breathe a second spring.   20

Say, Father Thames, for thou hast seen
 Full many a sprightly race

Disporting on thy margent green
   The paths of pleasure trace;
Who foremost now delight to cleave   25
With pliant arm, thy glassy wave?
The captive linnet which enthrall?
What idle progeny succeed
To chase the rolling circle's speed
   Or urge the flying ball?   30

While some on earnest business bent
   Their murmuring labors ply
'Gainst graver hours that bring constraint
   To sweeten liberty:
Some bold adventurers disdain   35
The limits of their little reign
And unknown regions dare descry:
Still as they run they look behind,
They hear a voice in every wind,
   And snatch a fearful joy.   40

Gay Hope is theirs by fancy fed,
   Less pleasing when possessed;
The tear forgot as soon as shed,
   The sunshine of the breast:
Theirs buxom Health, of rosy hue,   45
Wild Wit, Invention ever new,
And lively Cheer, of Vigor born;
The thoughtless day, the easy night,
The spirits pure, the slumbers light
   That fly the approach of morn.   50

Alas! regardless of their doom
   The little victims play!
No sense have they of ills to come
   Nor care beyond today:
Yet see how all around 'em wait   55
The ministers of human fate
And black Misfortune's baleful train!
Ah shew them where in ambush stand
To seize their prey, the murderous band!
   Ah, tell them they are men!   60

These shall the fury Passions tear,
   The vultures of the mind,
Disdainful Anger, pallid Fear,
   And shame that sculks behind;
Or pining Love shall waste their youth,   65
Or jealousy with rankling tooth
That inly gnaws the secret heart,
And Envy wan, and faded Care,
Grim-visaged comfortless Despair,
   And Sorrow's piercing dart.   70

Ambition this shall tempt to rise,
   Then whirl the wretch from high

To bitter Scorn a sacrifice
  And grinning Infamy.
The stings of Falsehood those shall try   75
And hard Unkindness' altered eye,
That mocks the tear it forced to flow;
And keen Remorse with blood defiled,
And moody Madness laughing wild
  Amid severest woe.   80

Lo, in the Vale of Years beneath
  A grisly troop are seen,
The painful family of Death,
  More hideous than their Queen:
This racks the joints, this fires the veins,   85
That every laboring sinew strains,
Those in the deeper vitals rage:
Lo! Poverty, to fill the band,
That numbs the soul with icy hand,
  And slow-consuming Age.   90

To each his sufferings: all are men,
  Condemned alike to groan;
The tender for another's pain,
  The unfeeling for his own.
Yet, ah! why should they know their fate,   95
Since sorrow never comes too late,
And happiness too swiftly flies?
Though would destroy their paradise!
No more;—where ignorance is bliss,
  'Tis folly to be wise.   100

4 *Henry:* Henry VI, founder of Eton College in 1440.   6:
Windsor Castle lies on the Thames opposite Eton.

John Keats   Ode to a Nightingale

My heart aches, and a drowsy numbness pains
  My sense, as though of hemlock I had drunk,
Or emptied some dull opiate to the drains
  One minute past, and Lethe-wards had sunk:
'Tis not through envy of thy happy lot,   5
  But being too happy in thine happiness—
    That thou, light-winged Dryad of the trees,
      In some melodious plot
  Of beechen green, and shadows numberless,
    Singest of summer in full-throated ease.   10

O, for a draught of vintage! that hath been
  Cooled a long age in the deep-delved earth,
Tasting of Flora and the country green,
  Dance, and Provençal song, and sunburnt mirth!
O for a beaker full of the warm South,   15
  Full of the true, the blushful Hippocrene,

With beaded bubbles winking at the brim,
   And purple-stained mouth;
That I might drink, and leave the world unseen,
   And with thee fade away into the forest dim: 20

Fade far away, dissolve, and quite forget
  What thou among the leaves hast never known.
The weariness, the fever, and the fret
  Here, where men sit and hear each other groan;
Where palsy shakes a few, sad, last grey hairs,   25
   Where youth grows pale, and specter-thin, and dies;
     Where but to think is to be full of sorrow
        And leaden-eyed despairs,
   Where Beauty cannot keep her lustrous eyes,
     Or new Love pine at them beyond tomorrow.   30

Away! away: for I will fly to thee,
  Not charioted by Bacchus and his pards,
But on the viewless wings of Poesy,
  Though the dull brain perplexes and retards:
Already with thee! tender is the night,   35
   And haply the Queen Moon is on her throne,
     Clustered around by all her starry Fays;
       But here there is no light,
   Save what from heaven is with the breezes blown
     Through verduous glooms and winding mossy ways.   40

I cannot see what flowers are at my feet,
  Nor what soft incense hangs upon the boughs,
But, in embalmed darkness, guess each sweet
  Wherewith the seasonable month endows
The grass, the thicket, and the fruit tree wild;   45
   White hawthorn, and the pastoral eglantine;
     Fast fading violets covered up in leaves:
        And mid-May's eldest child,
   The coming musk-rose, full of dewy wine,
     The murmurous haunt of flies on summer eves.   50

Darkling I listen; and for many a time
  I have been half in love with easeful Death,
Called him soft names in many a mused rhyme,
  To take into the air my quiet breath;
Now more than ever seems it rich to die,   55
   To cease upon the midnight with no pain,
     While thou art pouring forth thy soul abroad
       In such an ecstasy!
Still wouldst thou sing, and I have ears in vain—
   To thy high requiem become a sod.   60

Thou wast not born for death, immortal Bird!
  No hungry generations tread thee down;
The voice I hear this passing night was heard
  In ancient days by emperor and clown:
Perhaps the selfsame song that found a path   65
   Through the sad heart of Ruth, when, sick for home,

She stood in tears amid the alien corn;
    The same that ofttimes hath
Charmed magic casements, opening on the foam
    Of perilous seas, in faery lands forlorn.   70

Forlorn! the very word is like a bell
    To toll me back from thee to my sole self!
Adieu! the fancy cannot cheat so well
    As she is famed to do, deceiving elf.
Adieu! adieu! thy plaintive anthem fades   75
    Past the near meadows, over the still stream,
        Up the hillside; and now 'tis buried deep
            In the next valley-glades:
    Was it a vision, or a waking dream?
        Fled is that music—Do I wake or sleep?   80

2 *hemlock:* a poisonous shrub.   4 *Lethe:* the river of forgetfulness in Hell.   7 *Dryad:* a wood nymph.   13 *Flora:* goddess of
flowers.   16 *Hippocrene:* a fountain on Mt. Helicon, sacred to
the Muses.   32 *pards:* leopards.   49 *coming:* soon to be blooming.   64 *clown:* rustic person.   66 *Ruth:* daughter-in-law of
Naomi; see Ruth ii.2: "Let me now go to the field, and glean ears
of corn after him in whose sight I shall find grace."   67 *corn:*
wheat.

John Keats   Ode on a Grecian Urn

Thou still unravished bride of quietness,
    Thou foster-child of silence and slow time,
Sylvan historian, who canst thus express
    A flowery tale more sweetly than our rhyme:
What leaf-fringed legend haunts about thy shape   5
    Of deities or mortals, or of both,
        In Tempe or the dales of Arcady?
What men or gods are these? What maidens loath?
    What mad pursuit? What struggle to escape?
        What pipes and timbrels? What wild ecstasy?   10

Heard melodies are sweet, but those unheard
    Are sweeter; therefore, ye soft pipes, play on;
Not to the sensual ear, but, more endeared,
    Pipe to the spirit ditties of no tone:
Fair youth, beneath the trees, thou canst not leave   15
    Thy song, nor ever can those trees be bare;
        Bold lover, never, never canst thou kiss,
Though winning near the goal—yet, do not grieve;
    She cannot fade, though thou hast not thy bliss,
        Forever wilt thou love, and she be fair!   20

Ah, happy, happy boughs! that cannot shed
    Your leaves, nor ever bid the spring adieu;
And, happy melodist, unwearied,
    Forever piping songs forever new;

More happy love! more happy, happy love!   25
    Forever warm and still to be enjoyed,
      Forever panting, and forever young;
All breathing human passion far above,
    That leaves a heart high-sorrowful and cloyed,
      A burning forehead, and a parching tongue.   30

Who are these coming to the sacrifices?
    To what green altar, O mysterious priest,
Leadest thou that heifer lowing at the skies,
    And all her silken flanks with garlands dressed?
What little town by river or sea shore,   35
    Or mountain-built with peaceful citadel,
      Is emptied of this folk, this pious morn?
And, little town, thy streets forevermore
    Will silent be; and not a soul to tell
      Why thou art desolate, can e'er return.   40

O Attic shape! Fair attitude! with brede
    Of marble men and maidens overwrought,
With forest branches and the trodden weed;
    Thou, silent form, dost tease us out of thought
As doth eternity: Cold Pastoral!   45
    When old age shall this generation waste,
      Thou shalt remain, in midst of other woe
Than ours, a friend to man, to whom thou sayest
    "Beauty is truth, truth beauty,"—that is all
      Ye know on earth, and all ye need to know.   50

7 *Tempe*: a valley in Greece.   *Arcady*: a mountainous district of
Greece, sacred to the Muses.   10 *timbrels*: tambourines.   41
brede: border.

Allen Tate   Ode to Fear

VARIATION ON A THEME BY COLLINS

Let the day glare: O memory, your tread
Beats to the pulse of suffocating night—
Night peering from his dark but fire-lit head
Burns on the day his tense and secret light.

Now they dare not to gloss your savage dream,   5
O beast of the heart, those saints who cursed your name;
You are the current of the frozen stream,
Shadow invisible, ambushed and vigilant flame.

My eldest companion present in solitude,
Watch-dog of Thebes when the blind hero strove: 10
You, omniscient, at the cross-roads stood
When Laius, the slain dotard, drenched the grove.

Now to the eye of prophecy immune,
Fading and harried, you stalk us in the street

From the recesses of the August noon,   15
Alert world over, crouched on the air's feet.

You are our surety to immortal life,
God's hatred of the universal strain—
The heritage, O Fear, of ancient strife
Compounded with the tissue of the vein.   20

And I when all is said have seen your form
Most agile and most treacherous to the world
When, on a child's long day, a dry storm
Burst on the cedars, lit by the sun and hurled!

10 blind hero: Oedipus.   *12 Laius*: Oedipus' father who was
unknowingly slain by his son when Oedipus attacked and robbed
his caravan.

The "English" Ode

Michael Drayton   The Crier

Good folk, for gold or hire,
But help me to a crier;
For my poor heart is run astray
After two eyes that passed this way.
    Oyes, oyes, oyes,   5
    If there be any man
    In town or country can
    Bring me my heart again,
    I'll please him for his pain;
And by these marks I will you show   10
That only I this heart do owe.
    It is a wounded heart,
Wherein yet sticks the dart;
Every piece sore hurt throughout it,
Faith and truth writ round about it;   15
It was a tame heart, and a dear,
    And never used to roam;
But having got this haunt, I fear
    'Twill hardly stay at home.
For God's sake, walking by the way,   20
    If you my heart do see,
Either impound it for a stray,
    Or send it back to me.

The Crier: the officer of the law court whose "Oyes" (l. 5) called
for silence before a proclamation.   *11 owe*: own.

Ben Jonson   An Ode

                    High spirited friend,
I send nor balms nor corrosives to your wound:

Your fate hath found
A gentler and more agile hand to tend
The cure of that, which is but corporal,   5
And doubtful days (which were named critical)
Have made their fairest flight,
And now are out of sight.
Yet doth some wholesome physic for the mind,
Wrapped in this paper lie,   10
Which in the taking if you misapply,
You are unkind.

Your covetous hand,
Happy in that fair honor it hath gained,
Must now be reined.   15
True valor doth her own renown command
In one full action; nor have you now more
To do than be a husband of that store.
Think but how dear you bought
This same which you have caught,   20
Such thoughts will make you more in love with truth:
'Tis wisdom and that high,
For men to use their fortune reverently,
Even in youth.

John Milton   At a Solemn Music

Blest pair of Sirens, pledges of Heaven's joy,
Sphere-borne, harmonious sisters, Voice and Verse,
Wed your divine sounds and mixed power employ
Dead things with inbreathed sense able to pierce
And to our high-raised phantasy present   5
That undisturbed song of pure concent
Ay sung before the sapphire-colored throne
To him that sits thereon
With saintly shout and solemn jubilee,
Where the bright seraphim in burning row   10
Their loud uplifted angel trumpets blow,
And the cherubic host in thousand quires
Touch their immortal harps of golden wires
With those just spirits that wear victorious palms,
Hymns devout and holy psalms   15
Singing everlastingly;
That we on earth with undiscording voice
May rightly answer that melodious noise
As once we did, till disproportioned sin
Jarred against nature's chime, and with harsh din   20
Broke the fair music that all creatures made
To their great Lord, whose love their motion swayed
In perfect diapason, whilst they stood
In first obedience, and their state of good.
O may we soon again renew that song,   25
And keep in tune with Heaven, till God erelong

To his celestial consort us unite
    To live with him, and sing in endless morn of light.

Solemn Music: that sung before the throne of God by those who
reach salvation.   2 *Sphere-borne:* each of the eight (sometimes
nine) sirens was supposed to inhabit one of the planets and sing
one tone which made up the music of the spheres.   6 *concent:*
harmony.   13: See Rev. xiv.2–3: "and I heard the voice of
harpers harping with their harps: and they sung as it were a new
song before the throne."   14: See Rev. vii.9: "After this I beheld,
and, lo, a great multitude . . . stood before the throne, and before
the Lamb, clothed with white robes, and palms in their hands."
27 *consort:* concert; close associates; consortium with Christ the
Bridegroom.

William Collins   Ode Written in 1746

How sleep the brave, who sink to rest
By all their country's wishes blest!
When spring, with dewy fingers cold,
Returns to deck their hallowed mould,
She there shall dress a sweeter sod   5
Than fancy's feet have ever trod.

By fairy hands their knell is rung,
By forms unseen their dirge is sung:
There honor comes, a pilgrim gray,
To bless the turf that wraps their clay;   10
And freedom shall awhile repair
To dwell, a weeping hermit, there!

1746: The English had fought the French at Fontenoy, Belgium
(May 1745), in the War of the Austrian Succession, and the
army of Charles Stuart, the Young Pretender, at Prestonpans,
Scotland (September 1745) and Falkirk, Scotland (January
1746).

Joseph Warton   Ode to Fancy

O parent of each lovely Muse,
Thy spirit o'er my soul diffuse,
O'er all my artless songs preside,
My footsteps to thy temple guide,
To offer at thy turf built shrine,   5
In golden cups no costly wine.
No murdered fatling of the flock,
But flowers and honey from the rock.
O nymph with loosely-flowing hair,
With buskined leg, and bosom bare,   10
Thy waist with myrtle-girdle bound,
Thy brows with Indian feathers crowned,

Waving in thy snowy hand
An all-commanding magic wand,
Of power to bid fresh gardens blow,   15
'Mid cheerless Lapland's barren snow,
Whose rapid wings thy flight convey
Through air, and over earth and sea,
While the vast various landscape lies
Conspicuous to thy piercing eyes.   20
O lover of the desert, hail!
Say, in what deep and pathless vale,
Or on what hoary mountain's side,
'Mid fall of waters, you reside,
'Mid broken rocks, a rugged scene,   25
With green and grassy dales between.
'Mid forests dark of aged oak,
Ne'er echoing with the woodman's stroke,
Where never human art appeared,
Nor even one straw-roofed cot was reared,   30
Where Nature seems to sit alone,
Majestic on a craggy throne;
Tell me the path, sweet wanderer, tell.
To thy unknown sequestered cell,
Where woodbines cluster round the door,   35
Where shells and moss o'erlay the floor,
And on whose top an hawthorn blows,
Amid whose thickly-woven boughs
Some nightingale still builds her nest,
Each evening warbling thee to rest: 40
Then lay me by the haunted stream,
Rapt in some wild, poetic dream,
In converse while methinks I rove
With Spenser through a fairy grove;
Till, suddenly awaked, I hear   45
Strange whispered music in my ear,
And my glad soul in bliss is drowned
By the sweetly-soothing sound!
Me, goddess, by thy right hand lead
Sometimes through the yellow mead,   50
Where Joy and white-robed Peace resort,
And Venus keeps her festive court,
Where Mirth and Youth each evening meet,
And lightly trip with nimble feet,
Nodding their lily-crowned heads,   55
Where Laughter, rose-lipped Hebe, leads;
Where Echo walks steep hills among,
Listening to the shepherd's song:
Yet not these flowery fields of joy
Can long my pensive mind employ,   60
Haste, Fancy, from the scenes of folly,
To meet the matron Melancholy,
Goddess of the tearful eye,
That loves to fold her arms, and sigh;
Let us with silent footsteps go   65

To charnels and the house of woe,
To Gothic churches, vaults, and tombs,
Where each sad night some virgin comes,
With throbbing breast, and faded cheek,
Her promised bridegroom's urn to seek;   70
Or to some abbey's mouldering towers,
Where, to avoid cold wintry showers,
The naked beggar shivering lies,
While whistling tempests round her rise,
And trembles lest the tottering wall   75
Should on her sleeping infants fall.
Now let us louder strike the lyre,
For my heart glows with martial fire,
I feel, I feel, with sudden heat,
My big tumultuous bosom beat;   80
The trumpet's clangors pierce my ear,
A thousand widows' shrieks I hear,
Give me another horse, I cry,
Lo! the base Gallic squadrons fly;
Whence is this rage?—what spirit, say   85
To battle hurries me away?
'Tis Fancy, in her fiery car,
Transports me to the thickest war,
There whirls me o'er the hills of slain,
Where Tumult and Destruction reign;   90
Where mad with pain, the wounded steed
Tramples the dying and the dead;
Where giant Terror stalks around,
With sullen joy surveys the ground,
And, pointing to the ensanguined field,   95
Shakes his dreadful gorgon shield!
O guide me from this horrid scene,
To high-arched walks and alleys green,
Which lovely Laura seeks to shun
The fervors of the midday sun;   100
The pangs of absence, O remove!
For thou canst place me near my love,
Canst fold in visionary bliss,
And let me think I steal a kiss,
While her ruby lips dispense   105
Luscious nectar's quintessence!
When young-eyed Spring profusely throws
From her green lap the pink and rose,
When the soft turtle of the dale
To Summer tells her tender tale,   110
When Autumn cooling caverns seeks,
And stains with wine his jolly cheeks;
When Winter, like poor pilgrim old,
Shakes his silver beard with cold;
At every season let my ear   115
Thy solemn whispers, Fancy, hear.
O warm, enthusiastic maid,
Without thy powerful, vital aid,

That breathes an energy divine,
That gives a soul to every line,   *120*
Ne'er may I strive with lips profane
To utter an unhallowed strain,
Nor dare to touch the sacred string,
Save when with smiles thou bidd'st me sing.
O hear our prayer, O hither come   *125*
From thy lamented Shakespeare's tomb,
On which thou lovest to sit at eve,
Musing o'er thy darling's grave;
O queen of numbers, once again
Animate some chosen swain,   *130*
Who, filled with unexhausted fire,
May boldly smite the sounding lyre,
Who with some new unequalled song,
May rise above the rhyming throng,
O'er all our listening passions reign,   *135*
O'erwhelm our souls with joy and pain,
With terror shake, and pity move,
Rouse with revenge, or melt with love,
O deign to attend his evening walk,
With him in groves and grottos talk;   *140*
Teach him to scorn with frigid art
Feebly to touch the unraptured heart;
Like lightning, let his mighty verse
The bosom's inmost foldings pierce;
With native beauties win applause   *145*
Beyond cold critics' studied laws;
I let each Muse's fame increase,
O bid Britannia rival Greece.

10 buskined: tragic.

SPECIFIC VERSE FORMS: OTHER FORMS*

The Ballade

Geoffrey Chaucer   The Complaint of Chaucer to His
    Purse

To you, my purse, and to noon other wight
Complain I, for ye be my lady dear!
I am so sorry, now that ye been light;
For certes, but ye make me heavy chere,
Me were as lief be laid upon my bier;   5

* See the *Glossary of Poetical and Critical Terms* for descriptions
of each specific verse form illustrated on the following pages.

For which unto your mercy thus I cry:
Beeth heavy again, or else might I die!

Now voucheth safe this day, or it be night,
That I of you the blissful sound may hear,
Or see your color like the sunne bright,   10
That of yellowness had never peer.
Ye be my life, ye be mine hearte's stere,
Queen of comfort and of good company:
Beeth heavy again, or else might I die!

Now purse, that been to me my life's light   15
And savior, as down in this world here,
Out of this town help me through your might,
Sin that ye will not been my treasurer;
For I am shave as nigh as any frere.
But yet I pray unto your courtesy: 20
Beeth heavy again, or else might I die!

    L'Envoy de Chaucer

O conqueror of Brute's Albion,
Which that by line and free election
Been very king, this song to you I send;
And ye, that mowen all our harms amend,   25
Have mind upon my supplication!

1 noon: no.   *wight: person.*   *3 been:* are.   *4 certes:* surely.
chere: face.   *5 lief:* willingly.   *12 stere:* rudder.   *18 Sin
that:* since.   *been:* be.   *19 shave:* shaven.   *nigh:* close.
frere: friar.   *22 Brute's Albion:* England, named for Albion, son
of its reputed founder Brutus.   *24 very:* true.   *25 mowen:* may.

Dante Gabriel Rossetti   The Ballad of Dead Ladies

Tell me now in what hidden way is
   Lady Flora the lovely Roman?
Where's Hipparchia, and where is Thais,
   Neither of them the fairer woman?
    Where is Echo, beheld of no man,   5
Only heard on river and mere—
   She whose beauty was more than human? . . .
But where are the snows of yester-year?

Where's Héloïse, the learned nun,
   For whose sake Abeillard, I ween,   10
Lost manhood and put priesthood on?
   (From Love he won such dule and teen!)
    And where, I pray you, is the Queen
Who willed that Buridan should steer
   Sewed in a sack's mouth down the Seine? . . .   15
But where are the snows of yester-year?

White Queen Blanche, like a queen of lilies,
   With a voice like any mermaiden—
Bertha Broadfoot, Beatrice, Alice,
    And Ermengarde the Lady of Maine—   20
    And that good Joan whom Englishmen
At Rouen doomed and burned her there—
   Mother of God, where are they then? . . .
But where are the snows of yester-year?

Nay, never ask this week, fair lord,   25
   Where they are gone, nor yet this year,
Save with thus much for an overword—
   But where are the snows of yester-year?

2 *Lady Flora:* a courtezan of Rome.   3 *Hipparchia:* a courtezan
of Greece.   *Thais:* a courtezan of Athens.   6 *mere:* pond.
9 *Héloise:* she eloped with her teacher Pierre Abelard (1079–
1142). Her uncle, an official of the church, had Abelard emascu-
lated. He thereafter became a monk, and Heloise, a nun.   10
ween: suppose.   12 *dule:* dole.   *teen:* pain.   13 *Queen:* Margaret of Burgundy, who disposed of her castoff lovers by the method
cited.   14 *Buridan:* a scholar once beloved by Margaret.   17
Queen Blanche: Blanche of Castille has been suggested. "Blanche"
means "white."   19 *Bertha Broadfoot:* mother of Charlemagne.
Beatrice, Alice: uncertain.   20 *Ermengarde:* countess of Anjou.
Maine: a region of France bordering Normandy and Brittany.
21 *Joan:* Joan of Arc.

Austin Dobson   The Ballade of Prose and Rhyme

When the ways are heavy with mire and rut,
   In November fogs, in December snows,
When the North Wind howls, and the doors are shut—
   There is place and enough for the pains of prose;
   But whenever a scent from the whitehorn blows,   5
And the jasmine-stars at the casement climb,
   And a Rosalind-face at the lattice shows,
Then hey!—for the ripple of laughing rhyme!

When the brain gets dry as an empty nut,
   When the reason stands on its squarest toes,   10
When the mind (like a beard) has a "formal cut"—
   There is place and enough for the pains of prose;
   But whenever the May-blood stirs and glows,
And the young year draws to the "golden prime,"
   And Sir Romeo sticks in his ear a rose,   15
Then hey!—for the ripple of laughing rhyme!

In a theme where the thoughts have a pedant-strut,
   In a changing quarrel of "Ayes" and "Noes,"
In a starched procession of "If" and "But"—
   There is place and enough for the pains of prose;   20

But wherever a soft glance softer grows,
And the light hours dance to the trysting-time,
   And the secret is told "that no one knows,"
Then hey!—for the ripple of laughing rhyme!

   ENVOY

In the work-a-day world, for its needs and woes,   25
There is place and enough for the pains of prose;
But whenever the May-bells clash and chime,
Then hey!—for the ripple of laughing rhyme!

Ezra Pound   Villonaud for This Yule

Towards the Noel that morte saison
(*Christ make the shepherds' homage dear!*)
Then when the grey wolves everychone
Drink of the winds their chill small-beer
And lap o' the snows food's gueredon   5
Then makyth my heart his yule-tide cheer
(Skoal! with the dregs if the clear be gone!)
Wining the ghosts of yester-year.

Ask ye what ghosts I dream upon?
(*What of the magians' scented gear?*)   10
The ghosts of dead loves everyone
That make the stark winds reek with fear
Lest love return with the foison sun
And slay the memories that me cheer
(Such as I drink to mine fashion)   15
Wining the ghosts of yester-year.

Where are the joys my heart had won?
(*Saturn and Mars to Zeus drawn near!*)
Where are the lips mine lay upon,
Aye! where are the glances feat and clear   20
That bade my heart his valor don?
I skoal to the eyes as grey-blown mere
(Who knows whose was that paragon?)
Wining ghosts of yester-year.

Prince: ask me not what I have done   25
Nor what God hath that can me cheer
But ye ask first where the winds are gone
Wining the ghosts of yester-year.

1 morte saison: dead season.   *3 everychone:* every one.   *10 magians' scented gear:* the frankincense and myrrh of the Magi. *13 foison:* vigorous.   *20 feat:* skillful.   *22 mere:* pool.

The Canzone

Edmund Bolton   A Canzone Pastoral in Honor of
Her Majesty

Alas, what pleasure, now the pleasant spring
   Hath given place
To harsh black frosts the sad ground covering,
   Can we, poor we, embrace?
When every bird on every branch can sing   5
   Nought but this note of woe, alas!
Alas, this note of woe why should we sound?
With us, as May, September hath a prime;
Then, birds and branches, your alas is fond,
Which call upon the absent summertime.   10
   For did flowers make our May
   Or the sunbeams your day,
When night and winter did the world embrace,
Well might you wail your ill, and sing, alas!

Lo, matron-like the earth herself attires   15
   In habit grave;
Naked the fields are, bloomless are the briers,
   Yet we a summer have,
Who in our clime kindleth these living fires,
   Which blooms can on the briers save.   20
No ice doth crystallize the running brook,
No blast deflowers the flower-adorned field;
Crystal is clear, but clearer is the look
Which to our climes these living fires doth yield;
   Winter, though everywhere,   25
   Hath no abiding here,
On brooks and briers she doth rule alone—
The sun which lights our world is always one.

The Débat

Anonymous   The Debate of the Body and the Soul
(*excerpt*)

As I lay in a winter's night
   In a droopening before the day,
Forsooth I saw a seely sight,
   A body on a bier lay,
That haved been a moody knight   5
   And little served God to pay;

Loren he haved the life's light,
   The ghost was out and should away.

When the ghost it should go,
   It bewent and withstood,   10
Beheld the body there it came fro
   So serfully with dreadly mood;
It said, 'Weil and walawo!
   Woe worth thy flesh, thy foul blood.
Wretched body why list thou so,   15
   That whilen were so wild and wood?

'Thou that were woned to ride
   High on horse in and out,
So quaint knight ycouth so wide,
   As a lion fierce and proud,   20
Where is all thy mickel pride,
   And thy lede that was so loud?
Why list thou there so bare o' side
   Ypricked in that poor shroud?

'Where been thy worthly weeds,   25
   Thy somers with thy riche beds,
Thy proud palfreys and thy steeds?
   That thou about in dester leads?
Thy falcons that were wont to grede
   And thine hounds that thou feed?   30
Methinketh God is to thee too gnede,
   That all thine friend been fro thee fled.

'Where been thy castles and thy towers,
   Thy chambers and thy riche halls
Ypainted with so riche flowers,   35
   And thy riche robes all?
Thine cowltes and thy covertures,
   Thy cendels and thy rich palls?
Wretch, full dark is now thy bower;
   Tomorrow thou shalt therein fall.   40

'Where been thine cookes snell
   That should gon to greith thy meat
With spices sweet for to smell,
   That thou never were full of frete,
To do that foul flesh to swell   45
   That foul wormes shoulden eat?
And thou havest the pain of hell
   With gluttony me beget . . .'

'For God thee schop after his schaft,
   And gave thee both wit and skill;   50
In thy looking was I laft
   To wisse after thine own will.
Ne tock I never witchecraft,
   Ne wist I what was good nor ill,
But as a wretche dumb and daft,   55
   But as thou taughtst me theretil.

'Set to serven thee to queme
   Both at even and at morn,
Sithin I was thee betaught to geme,
   Fro the time that thou was born.   60
Thou that deeds couthest deem
   Shouldst habbe be ware beforn
Of my folly, as it seem;
   Now with thyself thou art forlorn.'

The ghost it said, 'Body be still!   65
   Who hath lered thee all this wit
That givest me these wordes grill,
   That list there bollen as a bit?
Weenest thou, wretch, though thou fill
   With thy foul flesh a pit,   70
Of all deeds thou didest ill
   That thou so lightly shalt be quit?

'Weenest thou now to get the grith
   There thou list rotten in the clay?
Though thou be rotten pile and pith,   75
   And blowen with the wind away,
That shalt thou come with limb and lith
   Again to me on doomesday,
And come to court and I thee with
   For to keepen our hard pay.   80
     . . . . .
'Ne nis no levedy bright on blee,
   That well were woned of thee too lete,
That woulde lie a night by thee
   For nought that men might her bihete.
Thou art unseemly for to see,   85
   Uncomely for to kissen sweet;
Thou ne havest friend that ne woulde flee,
   Come thou sterlinde in the street.'

The body it said, 'Ic saith,
   Ghost, thou hast wrong iwys   90
All the guilt on me to laith,
   That thou hast lorn thy mickle bliss.
Were was I by wood or waith,
   Sat or stood or did ought miss,
That I ne was ay under thine eyeth?   95
   Well thou wost that sooth it is.

'Whether I ede up or down,
   That I ne bar thee on my back,
As thine ass fro town to town,
   Also thou me lete have rap and rack?   100
That thou ne were and rede roun
   Nevere did I thing ne spack;
Here thee sooth see men mowen
   On me that ligge so blo and black.
     . . . . .

The ghost it said, 'Is no doubt;   *105*
   Abouten, body, thou me bar;
Thou mostist need, I was without
   Hand and foot, I was well war.
But as thou bear me about
   Ne might I do the least char;   *110*
Therefore must I need lout,
   So doth that non other dare.

'Of a woman born and bred,
   Body, were we bothe two;
Together fostered fair and fed   *115*
   Till thou couldest speak and go.
Soft thee for love I led,
   Ne durst I never do thee woe;
To lese thee so sore I dread,
   And well I wist to get no moe.   *120*

For me thou wouldest somewhat do
   While thou were young a little first,
For friends eythe that thee stood too,
   Thee while thou were beaten and birst;
Oh when thou were thriven and thro,   *125*
   And knew hunger, cold and thirst,
And yhwilk was ease, rest and ro,
   All thine own will thou didst.

'I saw thee fair in flesh and blood
   And all my love on thee I cast;   *130*
That thou thrive me thoughte good,
   And let thee haven ro and rest.
That made thee so stern of mood,
   And of works so unwrest;
To fight with thee ne was no boot   *135*
   Me that thou bar in thy breast.

'Glotery and lechery,
   Pride and wicke covetise,
Nithe and onde and envy
   To God of heaven and all hise,   *140*
And in unlust for to lie,
   Was thy wone in alle wise;
That I shall now full dear abie,
   Ah, well! sore may me grise.
     · · · · ·

'To sin thou wistest was my kind,   *145*
   As mankind it is also,
And to the wretched world so mind,
   And to thy fiend that is your foe.
Thou shouldst ere have late me bind
   When I misdid and done me woe;   *150*
Ah ywanne the blind lat the blind,
   In dike he fallen both two.

Then began the ghost to weep,
   And said, 'Body, alas, alas,

That I thee loved ever yet,   *155*
   For all my love on thee I las.
That thou lovedst me thou let,
   And madest me an houve of glass;
I did all that to thee was set,
   And thou my traitor ever was.   *160*

The fiend of hell that haveth envy
   To mankind, and ever hath had,
Was in us as is a spy
   To do some good ywan I thee bade.
The world he took to company,   *165*
   That many a soul haved forrad;
They three wisten thy folly,
   And maden, wretched, thee all mad.

'When I bade thee rest take,
   Forsake sin ay and oo,   *170*
Do penance, fast and wake,
   The fiend said, 'Thou shalt nought so,
Thus soone all thy bliss forsake,
   To liven ay in pine and woe!
Joy and bliss I rede thou make,   *175*
   And thinke to live yeares moe.

     . . . . .

The foul fiends that were fain,
   By top and tail he slungen hit,
And casten it with might and main
   Down into the devil's pit,   *180*
There sun ne shall never be seen;
   Himself he sonken in theremit;
The earth himself it leck again,
   Anon the donge it was fordit.

When it was forth, that foule lod   *185*
   To hellewell or it were day,
On ilk a hair a droppe stood
   For fright and fear there as I lay;
To Jesu Christ with milde mood
   Yerne I called and looked ay,   *190*
When the fiends hot and wood
   Come to fet me away.

I thonk him that tholede death,
   His mickle mercy and his ore,
That shield me from many a qued,   *195*
   A sinful man as I lay thore.
To all sinful I rede him red
   To shriven hem and rewen sore;
Never was sin idon so great
   That Christ's mercy ne is well more.   200

2 *droopening*: dejection.   3 *seely*: strange.   5 *moody*: brave.
6 *pay*: satisfaction.   7 *Loren*: lost.   8 *ghost*: soul.   10 *bewent*: turned away.   *withstood*: stood by.   12 *serfully*: sorrow-

fully.   *mood:* courage.   13 *Weil and walawo:* woe and alas.
16 *whilen:* once.   *wood:* angry.   17 *woned:* accustomed.
19 *quaint:* famous (a).   *ycouth:* known.   21 *mickel:* great.
22 *lede:* speech.   24 *Ypricked:* clothed.   25 *weeds:* clothes.
26 *somers:* sumpter horses.   *beds:* bedding.   28 *dester:* the
right hand.   29 *grede:* cry out.   31 *gnede:* stingy.   37
cowltes: quilts.   *covertures:* bed clothes.   38 *cendels, palls:*
rich cloths.   41 *snell:* quick.   42 *greith:* prepare.   44 *frete:*
food.   45 *do:* cause.   48 *beget:* received.   49 *schop:* created.
schaft: image.   51 *laft:* permitted.   52 *To wisse:* to be guided.
53 *tock:* touched.   54 *wist:* knew.   55 *daft:* stupid.   57 *to
queme:* for pleasure.   59 *Sithin:* since.   *betaught:* assigned.
geme: guard.   61 *couthest deem:* can judge.   62 *habbe be
ware:* have been aware.   64 *with:* through.   67 *grill:* harsh.
68 *bollen:* swollen.   *bit:* bottle.   73 *grith:* peace.   75 *pile
and pith:* outside and inside.   76 *with:* by.   77 *lith:* joint.
80 *keepen:* receive.   81 *nis:* do not think.   *levedy:* lady.   *on
blee:* in color.   82 *were woned:* remained.   *lete:* think.   84
bihete: promise.   88 *sterlinde:* rushing.   90 *iwys:* certainly.
92 *lorn:* lost.   93 *waith:* way.   94 *miss:* amiss.   97 *ede:* went.
100 *rap and rack:* beating and blow.   101 *rede roun:* directed the
conversation.   103 *mowen:* make attacks.   104 *ligge:* lie.
blo: livid.   106 *bar:* bear.   107 *mostist need:* must allow.
108 *war:* aware.   110 *char:* piece of work.   111 *lout:* bow.
119 *lese:* lose.   123 *eythe:* fear.   124 *birst:* bruised.   125
thro: strong.   127 *yhwilk:* which.   *ro:* quilt.   132 *haven:*
have.   133 *mood:* pride.   134 *unwrest:* weak.   135 *boot:*
use.   139 *Nithe:* contention.   *onde:* malice.   141 *unlust:*
pleasure.   142 *wone:* custom.   143 *abie:* pay for.   144 *grise:*
terrify.   145 *wistest:* know.   *kind:* nature.   147 *mind:* mindful.   149 *late me bind:* caused me to be bound.   151 *ywanne:*
when.   *lat:* leads.   152 *dike:* ditch.   156 *las:* shower.   157
let: admit.   158 *houve:* cap ["cap of glass" signifies something
ridiculous].   159 *set:* pleasing.   166 *forrad:* deceived.   167
They three: Satan, Sin, and Death.   *wisten:* knew.   170 *ay
and oo:* forever and ever.   171 *wake:* watch.   175 *rede:* counsel.   178 *hit:* the body.   182 *theremit:* therewith.   183 *leck:*
locked.   184 *donge:* dungeon.   *fordit:* shut up.   185 *lod:*
journey.   186 *hellewell:* abyss of hell.   *or:* before.   187 *ilk a:*
every.   189 *mood:* courage.   190 *Yerne:* earnestly.   191
wood: angry.   192 *fet:* fetch.   193 *tholede:* suffered.   194
ore: favor.   195 *qued:* evil.   196 *thore:* there.   197 *him:*
them.   *red:* advice.   198 *hem:* themselves.   *rewen:* repent.
199 *idon:* done.

Samuel Daniel   Ulysses and the Siren

SIREN

Come, worthy Greek! Ulysses, come;
  Possess these shores with me!

The winds and seas are troublesome
   And here we may be free.
Here may we sit and view their toil   5
   That travail in the deep,
And joy the day in mirth the while
   And spend the night in sleep.

ULYSSES

Fair nymph, if fame or honor were
   To be attained with ease,   10
Then would I come and rest me there,
   And leave such toils as these.
But here it dwells, and here must I
   With danger seek it forth:
To spend the time luxuriously   15
   Becomes not men of worth.

SIREN

Ulysses, Oh! be not deceived
   With that unreal name;
This honor is a thing conceived
   And rests on others' fame.   20
Begotten only to molest
   Our peace, and to beguile
The best thing of our life, our rest,
   And give us up to toil.

ULYSSES

Delicious nymph, suppose there were   25
   Nor honor nor report,
Yet manliness would scorn to wear
   The time in idle sport;
For toil doth give a better touch
   To make us feel our joy,   30
And ease finds tediousness as much
   As labor yields annoy.

SIREN

Then pleasure likewise seems the shore,
   Whereto tends all your toil
Which you forgo to make it more,   35
   And perish oft the while.
Who may disport them diversely
   Find never tedious day,
And ease may have variety,
   As well as action may.   40

ULYSSES

But natures of the noblest frame
   These toils and dangers please;

And they take comfort in the same
    As much as you in ease;
And with the thought of actions past   *45*
    Are recreated still;
When pleasure leaves a touch at last,
    To show that it was ill.

   SIREN

That doth opinion only cause,
    That's out of custom bred,   *50*
Which makes us many other laws,
    Than ever nature did.
No widows wail for our delights,
    Our sports are without blood;
The world we see by warlike wights   *55*
    Receives more hurt than good.

   ULYSSES

But yet the state of things require
    These motions of unrest;
And these great spirits of high desire
    Seem born to turn them best;   *60*
To purge the mischiefs that increase
    And all good order mar,
For oft we see a wicked peace
    To be well changed for war.

   SIREN

Well, well, Ulysses, then I see   *65*
    I shall not have thee here;
And therefore I will come to thee
    And take my fortunes there.
I must be won that cannot win,
    Yet lost were I not won,   *70*
For beauty hath created been
    To undo, or be undone.

6 travail: travel, labor.   *55 wights*: men.

Andrew Marvell   A Dialogue Between the Resolved
   Soul and Created Pleasure

Courage my Soul, now learn to wield
The weight of thine immortal shield.
Close on thy head thy helmet bright.
Balance thy sword against the fight.
See where an army, strong as fair,   *5*
With silken banners spreads the air.
Now, if thou beest that thing divine,
In this day's combat let it shine:

And show that nature wants an art
To conquer one resolved Heart.   10

PLEASURE

Welcome the Creation Guest,
Lord of Earth and Heaven's Heir.
Lay aside that warlike crest,
And of nature's banquet share:
Where the souls of fruits and flowers   15
Stand prepared to heighten yours.

SOUL

I sup above, and cannot stay
To bait so long upon the way.

PLEASURE

On these downy pillows lie,
Whose soft plumes will thither fly: 20
On these roses strewed so plain
Lest one leaf thy side should strain.

SOUL

My gentler rest is on a thought,
Conscious of doing what I ought.

PLEASURE

If thou beest with perfumes pleased,   25
Such as oft the gods appeased,
Thou in fragrant clouds shalt show
Like another god below.

SOUL

A soul that knows not to presume
Is Heaven's and its own perfume.   30

PLEASURE

Every thing does seem to vie
Which should first attract thine eye:
But since none deserves that grace,
In this crystal view *thy* face.

SOUL

When the Creator's skill is prized,   35
The rest is all but earth disguised.

PLEASURE

Hark how music then prepares
For thy stay these charming airs;
Which the posting winds recall,
And suspend the rivers' fall.   40

SOUL

Had I but any time to lose,
On this I would it all dispose.
Cease tempter. None can chain a mind
Whom this sweet chordage cannot bind.

CHORUS

Earth cannot show so brave a sight   45
As when a single Soul does fence
The batteries of alluring sense,
And Heaven views it with delight.
    Then persevere: for still new charges sound:
    And if thou overcomest thou shalt be crowned.   50

PLEASURE

All this fair, and cost, and sweet,
    Which scatteringly doth shine,
Shall within one beauty meet,
    And she be only thine.

SOUL

If things of sight such heavens be,   55
What heavens are those we cannot see?

PLEASURE

Wheresoe're thy foot shall go
    The minted gold shall lie;
Till thou purchase all below,
    And want new worlds to buy.   60

SOUL

Were't not a price who'd value gold?
And that's worth nought that can be sold.

PLEASURE

Wilt thou all the glory have
    That war or peace commend?
Half the world shall be thy slave,   65
    The other half thy friend.

SOUL

What friends, if to myself untrue?
What slaves, unless I captive you?

PLEASURE

Thou shalt know each hidden cause;
    And see the future time: 70

Try what depth the center draws;
   And then Heaven climb.

SOUL

None thither mounts by the degree
Of Knowledge, but Humility.

CHORUS

Triumph, triumph, victorious Soul;   75
The world has not one Pleasure more:
The rest does lie beyond the pole,
And is thine everlasting store.

18 *bait:* rest to take refreshment.   45 *brave:* excellent.
46 *fence:* ward off.

Edward Weismiller   The Soliloquies

The body says:
   The mind: my moonlight.
   It holds nothing real.
   It entertains the dead.
   Cold, what can it know?   5

   Let it wake.
   I turn from it to my possessions.

The mind says:
   Not for long can the hands grasp.
      The nerves   10
   Dance, whirl with, freeze to; but the song
      Vanishes;

   Helpless at length, the eyes their opals
      Relinquish;
   With what thing pleases us we struggle to couple,   15
      And from it fall.

      It is late now:
   And how should the body learn to be wise?
   Desire is for the red bird on the bough.
   It flies.   20

The Epigram

John Heywood   Of Loving a Dog

Love me, love my dog: by love to agree
I love thy dog as well as I love thee.

John Heywood   Of Late and Never

Better late than never: yea, mate,
But as good never as too late.

Sir John Harington   Comparison of the Sonnet
   and the Epigram

Once by mishap two poets fell a-squaring,
The sonnet and our epigram comparing;
And Faustus, having long demurred upon it,
Yet at the last gave sentence for the sonnet.
Now for such censure this his chief defence is,   5
Their sugared taste best likes his lickerous senses.
   Well, though I grant sugar may please the taste,
   Yet let my verse have salt to make it last.

6 *lickerous:* lecherous.   8 *salt:* wit.

John Weever   Translated out of Martial

Sabidi, I love thee not, nor why I wot,
But this I wot, Sabidi: I love thee not.

1 wot: know.

Ben Jonson   To the Ghost of Martial

Martial, thou gavest far nobler Epigrams
   To thy Domitian than I can my James:
But in my royal subject I pass thee;
   Thou flatteredest thine, mine cannot flattered be.

Ben Jonson   On My First Son

Farewell, thou child of my right hand, and joy;
   My sin was too much hope of thee, loved boy,
Seven years thou wert lent to me, and I thee pay,
   Exacted by thy fate on the just day.
O, could I lose all father now. For why   5
   Will man lament the state he should envy?
To have so soon scaped world's and flesh's rage,
   And, if no other misery, yet age?
Rest in soft peace, and, asked, say here doth lie

Ben Jonson his best piece of poetry. 10
For whose sake, henceforth, all his vows be such,
   As what he loves may never like too much.

1 child of my right hand: the meaning of Benjamin, in Hebrew; he
died in 1603. "Right hand" signifies strength and goodness. 4
the just day: Judgment Day. 9 *Rest in soft peace*: translation of
"Requiescat in pace."

Richard Crashaw   Upon the Infant Martyrs

To see both blended in one flood,
The mothers' milk, the children's blood,
Makes me doubt if Heaven will gather
Roses hence, or lilies rather.

Richard Crashaw   On the Saviour's Wounds

Whatever story of their cruelty,
Or nails, or thorn, or spear have writ in Thee,
    Are in another sense
      Still legible;
    Sweet is the difference: 5
      Once I did spell
    Every red letter
      A wound of thine,
    Now (what is better)
      Balsam for mine.   10

10 Balsam: balm.

Sir Edward Sherburne   The Happy Life

    TO JULIUS MARTIALIS

    MARTIAL X, 47

Those things which make life truly blest,
Sweetest Martial, hear expressed:
Wealth left, and not from labor growing;
A grateful soil, a hearth still glowing;
No strife, small business, peace of mind,   5
Quick wit, a body well inclined,
Wise innocence, friends of one heart,
Cheap food, a table without art;
Nights which nor cares nor surfeits know,
No dull, yet a chaste bedfellow;   10
Sleeps which the tedious hours contract;
Be what thou mayst be, nor exact

Aught more; nor with thy last hour of breath
Fear, nor with wishes hasten death.

Alexander Pope   Epigram

> Engraved on the Collar of a Dog which I
> gave to his Royal Highness

I am his Highness' dog at Kew;
Pray tell me, sir, whose dog are you?

His Royal Highness: Frederick, Prince of Wales.   *1 Kew:* Kew
Gardens, on the Thames, and Frederick's royal residence.

Samuel Taylor Coleridge   On Donne's Poetry

With Donne, whose muse on dromedary trots,
Wreathe iron pokers into true-love knots;
Rhyme's sturdy cripple, fancy's maze and clue,
Wit's forge and fire-blast, meaning's press and screw.

3 clue: the means to get out of the maze.   *4 press and screw:* the
press squeezes out the meaning by its weight and density; the screw
derives meaning by turning in upon itself. Both were instruments
of torture used to extract information.

Walter Savage Landor   To My Ninth Decade

To my ninth decade I have tottered on,
And no soft arm bends now my steps to steady;
She, who once led me where she would, is gone,
So when he calls me, Death shall find me ready.

Walter Savage Landor   On Living Too Long

Is it not better at an early hour
    In its calm cell to rest the weary head,
While birds are singing and while blooms the bower,
    Than sit the fire out and go starved to bed?

Ezra Pound   The New Cake of Soap

Lo, how it gleams and glistens in the sun
Like the cheek of a Chesterton.

2 Chesterton: G. K. Chesterton (1874–1936), the English author.

Haiku

Basho   Haiku

New moon in the sky
And on the earth the faintly
White flowers of wheat.

> *Nobuyuki Yuasa, Translator*

Masaoka Shiki   Haiku

All the hot night
The quail
Sleepless in his cage.

> *Kenneth Rexroth, Translator*

The Rondeau

Sir Thomas Wyatt   Rondeau

Help me to seek, for I lost it there,
And if that ye have found it, ye that be here,
And seek to convey it secretly,
Handle it soft and treat it tenderly,
Or else it will plain and then appear: 5

But rather restore it mannerly,
Since that I do ask it thus honestly:
For to lose it, it sitteth me too near.
      Help me to seek.

Alas, and is there no remedy?   10
But have I thus lost it wilfully?
Iwis it was a thing all too dear
To be bestowed and wist not where:
It was my heart, I pray you heartily
      Help me to seek.   15

5 plain: lament.   *12 Iwis:* certainly.

George Ellis   Rondeau

> Humbly inscribed to the Right Hon. Wil-
> liam Eden, Minister Plenipotentiary of
> Commercial Affairs at the court of Ver-
> sailles.

Of Eden lost, in ancient days,
If we believe what Moses says,

A paltry pippin was the price,
    One crab was bribe enough to entice
Frail human kind from virtue's ways.   5
But now, when Pitt, the all-perfect, sways,
No such vain lures the tempter lays,
    Too poor to be the purchase twice
        Of Eden lost.

The Dev'l grown wiser, to the gaze   10
Six thousand pounds a year displays,
    And finds success from the device;
    Finds this fair fruit too well suffice
To pay the peace, and honest praise,
        Of Eden lost.   15

William Eden, later Lord Auckland, had acted for Prime Minister
Pitt in the negotiation of a commercial treaty with France in 1786.
His salary was £6,000.   *4 crab*: crabapple.

Leigh Hunt   Rondeau

Jenny kissed me when we met,
    Jumping from the chair she sat in;
Time, you thief, who love to get
    Sweets into your list, put that in:
Say I'm weary, say I'm sad.   5
    Say that health and wealth have missed me,
Say I'm growing old, but add,
    Jenny kissed me.

The Rondel

Geoffrey Chaucer   Merciless Beauty

A TRIPLE RONDEL

I

Your yen two will slay me suddenly;
I may the beauty of hem not sustene,
So woundeth hit throughout my hearte keen.

And but your word will helen hastily
My hearte's wound, while that hit is green,   5
    Your yen two will slay me suddenly;
    I may the beauty of hem not sustene.

Upon my troth I say you faithfully
That ye been of my life and death the queen;
For with my death the troth shall be seen.   10
    Your yen two will slay me suddenly;
    I may the beauty of hem not sustene,
        So woundeth it throughout my hearte keen.

2

So hath your beauty fro your hearte chased
Pity, that me ne availeth not to plain;   15
For Danger halt your mercy in his chain.

Guiltless my death thus han ye me purchased;
I say you sooth, me needeth not to feign
    So hath your beauty fro your hearte chased
    Pity, that me ne availeth not to plain.   20

Alas! that Nature hath in you compassed
So great beauty, that no man may attain
To mercy, though he sterve for the pain.
    So hath your beauty fro your hearte chased
    Pity, that me ne availeth not to plain;   25
    For Danger halt your mercy in his chain.

3

Sin I fro Love escaped am so fat,
I never think to ben in his prison lean;
Sin I am free, I count him not a bean.

He may answer, and say this and that;   30
I do no fors, I speak right as I mean.
    Sin I fro Love escaped am so fat,
    I never think to ben in his prison lean.

Love hath my name ystrike out of his sclat,
And he is strike out of my bookes clean   35
For evermo; there is non other mean.
    Sin I fro Love escaped am so fat,
    I never think to ben in his prison lean;
    Sin I am free, I count him not a bean.

1 *yen:* eyes.   2 *hem:* them.   *sustene:* sustain, endure.   4
helen: heal.   5 *green:* fresh.   9 *been:* are.   10 *troth:* truth.
14 *fro:* from.   15 *plain:* lament.   16 *Danger:* disdain.   *halt:*
held.   17 *han:* have.   23 *sterve:* die.   27 *Sin:* since.   31
do no fors: care not.   34 *ystrike:* struck.   *sclat:* slate.

Austin Dobson   Rondel: The Wanderer

Love comes back to his vacant dwelling—
    The old, old Love that we knew of yore!
    We see him stand by the open door,
With his great eyes sad, and his bosom swelling.

He makes as though in our arms repelling,   5
    He fain would lie as he lay before—
Love comes back to his vacant dwelling—
    The old, old Love that we knew of yore!

Ah, who shall help us from over-spelling
    That sweet, forgotten, forbidden lore!   10

E'en as we doubt in our heart once more,
With a rush of tears to our eyelids welling,
Love comes back to his vacant dwelling.

Algernon Charles Swinburne Rondel

Kissing her hair I sat against her feet,
Wove and unwove it, wound and found it sweet;
Made fast therewith her hands, drew down her eyes,
Deep as deep flowers and dreamy like dim skies;
With her own tresses bound and found her fair,   5
       Kissing her hair.

Sleep were no sweeter than her face to me,
Sleep of cold sea-bloom under the cold sea;
What pain could get between my face and hers?
What new sweet thing would love not relish worse?   10
Unless, perhaps, white death had kissed me there,
       Kissing her hair?

The Roundelay

Edmund Spenser
"August," FROM *The Shepheardes Calender*

PERIGOT. It fell upon a holy eve,
WILLY.   hey ho holiday,
PERIGOT. When holy fathers wont to shrieve:
WILLY.   now ginneth this roundelay.
PERIGOT. Sitting upon a hill so high   5
WILLY.   hey ho the high hill,
PERIGOT. The while my flock did feed thereby,
WILLY.   the while the shepherd's self did spill:
PERIGOT. I saw the bouncing Bellibone,
WILLY.   hey ho Bonibell,   10
PERIGOT. Tripping over the dale alone,
WILLY.   she can trip it very well:
PERIGOT. Well decked in a frock of gray,
WILLY.   hey ho gray is greet,
PERIGOT. And in a kirtle of green say,   15
WILLY.   the green is for maidens meet:
PERIGOT. A chapelet on her head she wore,
WILLY.   hey ho chapelet,
PERIGOT. Of sweet violets therein was store,
WILLY.   she sweeter than the violet.   20
PERIGOT. My sheep did leave their wonted food,
WILLY.   hey ho seely sheep,
PERIGOT. And gazed on her, as they were wood,
WILLY.   wood as he, that did them keep.

PERIGOT.	As the bonilass passed by,	25
WILLY.	hey ho bonilass,	
PERIGOT.	She rode at me with glancing eye,	
WILLY.	as clear as the crystal glass:	
PERIGOT.	All as the sunny beam so bright,	
WILLY.	hey ho the sun beam,	30
PERIGOT.	Glanceth from Phoebus' face forthright,	
WILLY.	so love into thy heart did stream:	
PERIGOT.	Or as the thunder cleaves the clouds,	
WILLY.	hey ho the thunder,	
PERIGOT.	Wherein the lightsome levin shrouds,	35
WILLY.	so cleaves thy soul asunder:	
PERIGOT.	Or as Dame Cynthia's silver ray	
WILLY.	hey ho the moonlight,	
PERIGOT.	Upon the glittering wave doth play:	
WILLY.	such play is a piteous plight.	40
PERIGOT.	The glance into my heart did glide,	
WILLY.	hey ho the glider,	
PERIGOT.	Therewith my soul was sharply gride,	
WILLY.	such wounds soon waxen wider.	
PARIGOT.	Hasting to raunch the arrow out,	45
WILLY.	hey ho Perigot.	
PERIGOT.	I left the head in my heart root:	
WILLY.	it was a desperate shot.	
PERIGOT.	There it rankleth ay more and more,	
WILLY.	hey ho the arrow,	50
PERIGOT.	Ne can I find salve for my sore:	
WILLY.	love is a cureless sorrow.	
PERIGOT.	And though my bale with death I bought,	
WILLY.	hey ho heavy cheer,	
PERIGOT.	Yet should thilk lass not from my thought:	55
WILLY.	so you may buy gold too dear.	
PERIGOT.	But whether in painful love I pine,	
WILLY.	hey ho pinching pain,	
PERIGOT.	Or thrive in wealth, she shall be mine.	
WILLY.	but if thou can her obtain.	60
PERIGOT.	And if for graceless grief I die,	
WILLY.	hey ho graceless grief,	
PERIGOT.	Witness, she slew me with her eye:	
WILLY.	let thy folly be the prief.	
PERIGOT.	And you, that saw it, simple sheep,	65
WILLY.	hey ho the fair flock,	
PERIGOT.	For prief thereof, my death shall weep,	
WILLY.	and moan with many a mock.	
PERIGOT.	So learned I love on a holy eve,	
WILLY.	hey ho holiday,	70
PERIGOT.	That ever since my heart did grieve.	
WILLY.	Now endeth our roundelay.	

14 *greet*: lamentation.   15 *kirtle*: girdle.   22 *seely*: simple.
25 *bonilass*: pretty girl.   35 *levin*: lightning.   43 *gride*: cut.
44 *waxen*: grow.   45 *raunch*: pluck.   53 *bale*: release.   55
thilk: this.   64 *prief*: proof.

William Cowper   To Mary

The twentieth year is well-nigh past,
Since our first sky was overcast;
Ah, would that this might be the last!
                    My Mary!

Thy spirits have a fainter flow,   5
I see thee daily weaker grow—
'Twas my distress that brought thee low,
                    My Mary!

Thy needles, once a shining store,
For my sake restless heretofore,   10
Now rust disused, and shine no more,
                    My Mary!

For though thou gladly wouldst fulfill
The same kind office for me still,
Thy sight now seconds not thy will,   15
                    My Mary!

But well thou playedest the housewife's part,
And all thy threads with magic art
Have wound themselves about this heart,
                    My Mary!   20

Thy indistinct expressions seem
Like language uttered in a dream;
Yet me they charm, whate'er the theme,
                    My Mary!

Thy silver locks, once auburn bright,   25
Are still more lovely in my sight
Than golden beams of orient light,
                    My Mary!

For, could I view nor them nor thee,
What sight worth seeing could I see?   30
The sun would rise in vain for me,
                    My Mary!

Partakers of thy sad decline,
Thy hands their little force resign;
Yet, gently pressed, press gently mine,   35
                    My Mary!

And then I feel that still I hold
A richer store ten thousandfold
Than misers fancy in their gold,
                    My Mary!   40

Such feebleness of limbs thou provest,
That now at every step thou movest
Upheld by two; yet still thou lovest,
                    My Mary!

And still to love, though pressed with ill,   *45*
In wintry age to feel no chill,
With me is to be lovely still,
           My Mary!

But ah! by constant heed I know,
How oft the sadness that I show   *50*
Transforms thy smiles to looks of woe,
           My Mary!

And should my future lot be cast
With much resemblance of the past,
Thy worn-out heart will break at last,   *55*
           My Mary!

Mary: Mrs. Mary Unwin.   *2:* Referring to a violent attack of
insanity in 1773.

The Sestina

Sir Philip Sidney   Sestina

Farewell, Oh sun, Arcadia's clearest light;
Farewell, Oh pearl, the poor man's plenteous treasure;
Farewell, Oh golden staff, the weak man's might;
Farewell, Oh joy the joyful's only pleasure;
Wisdom, farewell, the skilless man's direction;   *5*
Farewell, with thee farewell, all our affection.

For what place now is left for our affection,
Now that of purest lamp is quenched the light
Which to our darkened minds was best direction?
Now that the mine is lost of all our treasure;   *10*
Now death hath swallowed up our worldly pleasure,
We orphans made, void of all public might!

Orphans, indeed, deprived of father's might,
For he our father was in all affection,
In our well-doing placing all his pleasure,   *15*
Still studying how to us to be a light;
As well he was in peace a safest treasure,
In war his wit and word was our direction.

Whence, whence, alas, shall we seek our direction,
When that we fear our hateful neighbor's might,   20
Who long have gaped to get Arcadians' treasure?
Shall we now find a guide of such affection,
Who for our sakes will think all travail light,
And make his pain to keep us safe his pleasure?

No, no; forever gone is all our pleasure,   25
For ever wandering from all good direction,
For ever blinded of our clearest light,

For ever lamed of our sured might,
For ever banished from well placed affection,
For ever robbed of all our royal treasure.   30

Let tears for him therefore be all our treasure,
And in our wailful naming him our pleasure;
Let hating of our selves be our affection,
And unto death bend still our thought's direction;
Let us against our selves employ our might,   35
And putting out our eyes seek we our light.

Farewell, our light; farewell, our spoiled treasure;
Farewell, our might; farewell, our daunted pleasure;
Farewell, direction; farewell, all affection.

23 *travail*: labor.

Rudyard Kipling   Sestina of the Tramp-Royal

Speakin' in general, I'ave tried 'em all—
The 'appy roads that take you o'er the world.
Speakin' in general, I'ave found them good
For such as cannot use one bed too long,
But must get 'ence, the same as I'ave done,   5
An' go observin' matters till they die.

What do it matter where or 'ow we die,
So long as we've our 'ealth to watch it all—
The different ways that different things are done,
An' men an' women lovin' in this world;   10
Takin' our chances as they come along,
An' when they ain't, pretendin' they are good?

In cash or credit—no, it aren't no good;
You 'ave to 'ave the 'abit or you'd die,
Unless you lived your life but one day long,   15
Nor didn't prophesy nor fret at all,
But drew your tucker some'ow from the world,
An' never bothered what you might ha' done.

But, Gawd, what things are they I'aven't done!
I've turned my 'and to most, an' turned it good,   20
In various situations round the world—
For 'im that doth not work must surely die;
But that's no reason man should labor all
'Is life on one same shift—life's none so long.

Therefore, from job to job I've moved along.   25
Pay couldn't 'old me when my time was done,
For something in my 'ead upset it all,
Till I 'ad dropped whatever 't was for good,
An' out at sea, be'eld the dock-lights die,
An' met my mate—the wind that tramps the world!   30

It's like a book, I think, this bloomin' world,
Which you can read and care for just so long,
But presently you feel that you will die
Unless you get the page you're readin' done,
An' turn another—likely not so good;   35
But what you're after is to turn 'em all.

Gawd bless this world! Whatever she 'ath done—
Excep' when awful long—I've found it good.
So write, before I die, ' 'E liked it all!'

17 *tucker:* energy.

Tanka

Noin Hoshi   Tanka

In the evening
Quiet of the country town
I came to notice
The cherry blossoms falling
To the tolling temple bell.   5

Nobuyuki Yuasa, Translator

Adelaide Crapsey   Three Cinquains

NOVEMBER NIGHT

Listen . . .
With faint dry sound,
Like steps of passing ghosts,
The leaves, frost-crisped, break from the trees
And fall.   5

SUSANNA AND THE ELDERS

"Why do
You thus devise
Evil against her?" "For that
She is beautiful, delicate.
Therefore."   5

Susanna and the Elders: She was spied by old councillors while
bathing. But because she resisted their advances, they told lies
about her. The story is found in the Apocrypha.

TRIAD

These be
Three silent things:

The falling snow . . . the hour
Before the dawn . . . the mouth of one
Just dead.   5

Akiko No Yosano   Two Tanka

1
Once, far over the breakers,
I caught a glimpse
Of a white bird
And fell in love
With this dream which obsesses me.   5

2
Swifter than hail,
Lighter than a feather,
A vague sorrow
Crossed my mind.

Kenneth Rexroth, Translator

The Triolet

Austin Dobson   Urceus Exit

I intended an Ode,
    And it turned to a Sonnet.
It began à la mode,
I intended an Ode;
But Rose crossed the road   5
    In her latest new bonnet;
I intended an Ode;
    And it turned to a Sonnet.

Urceus Exit: the water-pot goes dry.

Thomas Hardy   At a Hasty Wedding

If hours be years the twain are blest,
For now they solace swift desire
By bonds of every bond the best,
If hours be years. The twain are blest
Do eastern stars slope never west,   5
Nor pallid ashes follow fire:
If hours be years the twain are blest,
For now they solace swift desire.

The Villanelle

Ernest Dowson Villanelle of the Poet's Road

Wine and woman and song,
    Three things garnish our way:
Yet is day over long.

Lest we do our youth wrong,
    Gather them while we may: 5
Wine and woman and song.

Three things render us strong,
    Vine leaves, kisses, and bay;
Yet is day over long.

Unto us they belong,   10
    Us the bitter and gay,
Wine and woman and song.

We, as we pass along,
    Are sad that they will not stay;
Yet is day over long.   15

Fruits and flowers among,
    What is better than they:
Wine and woman and song?
    Yet is day over long.

8 *bay*: laurel (reward for poetry).

John Davidson The Unknown
(VILLANELLE)

To brave and to know the unknown
    Is the high world's motive and mark,
Though the way with snares be strewn.

The earth itself alone
    Wheels through the light and the dark   5
Onward to meet the unknown.

Each soul, upright or prone,
    While the owl sings or the lark,
Must pass where the bones are strewn.

Power on the loftiest throne   10
    Can fashion no certain ark
That shall stem and outride the unknown.

Beauty must doff her zone,
    Strength trudge unarmed and stark
Though the way with eyes be strewn.   15

This only can atone,
  The high world's motive and mark,
To brave and to know the unknown
Though the way with fire be strewn.

William Empson   Missing Dates

Slowly the poison the whole blood stream fills.
It is not the effect nor the failure tires.
The waste remains, the waste remains and kills.

It is not your system or clear sight that mills
Down small to the consequence of life requires;   5
Slowly the poison the whole blood stream fills.

They bled an old dog dry yet the exchange rills
Of young dog blood gave but a month's desires;
The waste remains, the waste remains and kills.

It is the Chinese tombs and the slag hills   10
Usurp the soil, and not the soil retires.
Slowly the poison the whole blood stream fills.

Not to have fire is to be a skin that shrills.
The complete fire is death. From partial fires
The waste remains, the waste remains and kills.   15

It is the poems you have lost, the ills
From missing dates, at which the heart expires.
Slowly the poison the blood stream fills.
The waste remains, the waste remains and kills.

Dylan Thomas   "Do Not Go Gentle into That
  Good Night"

Do not go gentle into that good night,
Old age should burn and rave at close of day;
Rage, rage against the dying of the light.

Though wise men at their end know dark is right,
Because their words had forked no lightning they   5
Do not go gentle into that good night.

Good men, the last wave by, crying how bright
Their frail deeds might have danced in a green bay,
Rage, rage against the dying of the light.

Wild men who caught and sang the sun in flight,   10
And learn, too late, they grieved it on its way,
Do not go gentle into that good night.

Grave men, near death, who see with blinding sight
Blind eyes could blaze like meteors and be gay,
Rage, rage against the dying of the light.   15

And you, my father, there on the sad height,
Curse, bless, me now with your fierce tears, I pray.
Do not go gentle into that good night.
Rage, rage against the dying of the light.

James Merrill   The World and the Child

Letting his wisdom be the whole of love,
The father tiptoes out, backwards. A gleam
Falls on the child awake and wearied of,

Then, as the door clicks shut, is snuffed. The glove-
Gray afterglow appalls him. It would seem   5
That letting wisdom be the whole of love

Were pastime even for the bitter grove
Outside, whose owl's white hoot of disesteem
Falls on the child awake and wearied of.

He lies awake in pain, he does not move,   10
He will not scream. Any who heard him scream
Would let their wisdom be the whole of love.

People have filled the room he lies above.
Their talk, mild variation, chilling theme,
Falls on the child. Awake and wearied of   15

Mere pain, mere wisdom also, he would have
All the world waking from its winter dream,
Letting its wisdom be. The whole of love
Falls on the child awake and wearied of.

Denise Levertov   Obsessions

Maybe it is true we have to return
to the black air of ashcan city
because it is there the most life was burned,

as ghosts or criminals return?
But no, the city has no monopoly   5
of intense life. The dust burned

golden or violet in the wide land
to which we ran away, images
of passion sprang out of the land

as whirlwinds or red flowers, your hands   10
opened in anguish or clenched in violence
under that sun, and clasped my hands

in that place to which we will not return
where so much happened that no one else noticed,
where the city's ashes that we brought with us   15
flew into the intense sky still burning.

The Virelay

John Dryden   A Rondelay

Chloe found Amyntas lying,
   All in tears upon the plain;
Sighing to himself, and crying,
   Wretched I, to love in vain!
Kiss me, dear, before my dying;   5
   Kiss me once, and ease my pain!

Sighing to himself, and crying,
   Wretched I, to love in vain!
Ever scorning, and denying
   To reward your faithful swain: 10
Kiss me, dear, before my dying;
   Kiss me once, and ease my pain!

Ever scorning, and denying
   To reward your faithful swain.
Chloe, laughing at his crying,   15
   Told him, that he loved in vain:
Kiss me, dear, before my dying;
   Kiss me once, and ease my pain!

Chloe, laughing at his crying,
   Told him, that he loved in vain: 20
But, repenting, and complying,
   When he kissed, she kissed again:
Kissed him up before his dying;
   Kissed him up, and eased his pain.

Anonymous   Man, Man, Man

Man, man, man is for the woman made,
And the woman made for man;
As the spur is for the jade,
As the scabbard for the blade,
As for digging is the blade,   5
   As for liquor is the can,
So man, man, man, is for the woman made,
   And the woman made for man.

As the sceptre's to be swayed,
As for Night's the serenade,   10
   As for pudding is the pan,
   As to cool us is the fan,
So man, man, man, is for the woman made,
   And the woman made for man.

Be she widow, wife or maid,   *15*
Be she wanton, be she staid,
Be she well or ill-arrayed,
   Shrew, slut, or harridan,
Yet man, man, man, is for the woman made,
   And the woman made for man.   *20*

Dorothy Parker   One Perfect Rose

A single flow'r he sent me, since we met.
   All tenderly his messenger he chose;
Deep-hearted, pure, with scented dew still wet—
   One perfect rose.

I knew the language of the floweret;   *5*
   "My fragile leaves," it said, "his heart enclose."
Love long has taken for his amulet
   One perfect rose.

Why is it no one ever sent me yet
   One perfect limousine, do you suppose?   *10*
Ah no, it's always just my luck to get
   One perfect rose.

NONSTANZAIC FORMS: GENERAL

George Turberville   Verse in Praise of Lord Henry
   Howard, Earl of Surrey

What should I speak in praise of Surrey's skill
Unless I had a thousand tongues at will?
No one is able to depaint at full
The flowing fountain of his sacred skull,
Whose pen approved what wit he had in mew,   *5*
Where such a skill in making sonnets grew.
Each word in place with such a sleight is couched,
Each thing whereof he treats so firmly touched,
As Pallas seemed within his noble breast
To have sojourned and been a daily guest.   *10*
Our mother tongue by him hath got such light
As ruder speech thereby is banished quite.
Reprove him not for fancies that he wrought,
For fame thereby, and nothing else, he sought.
What though his verse with pleasant toys are fright?   *15*
Yet was his honor's life a lamp of light.
A mirror he, the simple mort to train,
That ever beat his brain for Britain's gain.
By him the nobles had their virtues blazed,

When spiteful death their honors' lives had razed;   20
Each that in life had well deserved aught,
By Surrey's means an endless fame hath caught.
To quite his boon and aye well-meaning mind,
Whereby he did his sequel seem to bind,
Though want of skill to silence me procures,   25
I write of him whose fame for aye endures;
A worthy wight, a noble for his race,
A learned lord that had an earl's place.

5 *approved:* demonstrated.   *mew:* keeping.   9 *Pallas:* Minerva.
15 *toys:* trifles.   *fright:* freighted.   23 *quite:* acquit.   *boon:*
gifts.

Anonymous   Madrigal

My love in her attire doth show her wit,
    It doth so well become her;
For every season she hath dressings fit,
    For winter, spring, and summer.
    No beauty she doth miss   5
    When all her robes are on;
    But beauty's self she is
    When all her robes are gone.

John Donne   The Apparition

When by thy scorn, O murderess, I am dead,
    And that thou thinkest thee free
From all solicitation from me,
Then shall my ghost come to thy bed,
And thee, feigned vestal, in worse arms shall see;   5
Then thy sick taper will begin to wink,
And he whose thou art then, being tired before,
Will, if thou stir or pinch to wake him, think
    Thou callest for more,
And in false sleep will from thee shrink,   10
And then, poor aspen wretch, neglected thou
Bathed in a cold quicksilver sweat wilt lie
    A verier ghost than I.
What I will say, I will not tell thee now,
Lest that preserve thee; and since my love is spent,   15
I had rather thou shouldst painfully repent,
Than by my threatenings rest still innocent.

11 *aspen:* quaking.   13 *verier:* truer.

Richard Lovelace   A Black Patch on Lucasta's Face

Dull as I was to think that a court fly
   Presumed so near her eye,
   When 'twas the industrious bee
Mistook her glorious face for paradise,
To sum up all his chemistry of spice;   5
   With a brave pride and honor led,
   Near both her suns he makes his bed,
And though a spark, struggles to rise as red:
     Then emulates the gay
     Daughter of day,   10
   Acts the romantic phoenix' fate:
When now with all his sweets laid out in state,
   Lucasta scatters but one heat,
And all the aromatic pills do sweat,
And gums calcined themselves to powder beat,   15
     Which a fresh gale of air
     Conveys into her hair;
   Then chaffed he's set on fire,
And in these holy flames doth glad expire;
   And that black marble tablet there   20
     So near her either sphere,
   Was placed; nor foil, nor ornament,
But the sweet little bee's large monument.

15 *calcined*: made powdery by heat.

Andrew Marvell   On a Drop of Dew

See how the orient dew,
Shed from the bosom of the morn
   Into the blowing roses,
Yet careless of its mansion new;
For the clear region where 'twas born   5
   Round in itself incloses:
   And in its little globe's extent,
Frames as it can its native element.
   How it the purple flower does slight,
     Scarce touching where it lies,   10
   But gazing back upon the skies,
     Shines with a mournful light
       Like its own tear
Because so long divided from the sphere.
   Restless it rolls and unsecure,   15
     Trembling lest it grow impure:
   Till the warm sun pity its pain,
And to the skies exhale it back again.
     So the soul, that drop, that ray
Of the clear fountain of eternal day,   20

Could it within the human flower be seen,
  Remembering still its former height,
  Shuns the sweet leaves and blossoms green;
  And, recollecting its own light,
Does in its pure and circling thoughts express   25
The greater heaven in an heaven less.
  In how coy a figure wound,
  Every way it turns away:
  So the world excluding round,
  Yet receiving in the day.   30
  Dark beneath, but bright above:
  Here disdaining, there in love.
 How loose and easy hence to go:
 How girt and ready to ascend.
 Moving but on a point below,   35
 It all about does upwards bend.
Such did the manna's sacred dew distill;
White, and entire, though congealed and chill.
Congealed on earth: but does, dissolving, run
Into the glories of the Almighty Sun.   40

Henry Vaughan The Relapse

My God, how gracious art thou! I had slipped
    Almost to hell,
And on the verge of that dark, dreadful pit
    Did hear them yell,
But O thy love! thy rich, almighty love   5
    That saved my soul,
And checked their fury, when I saw them move,
    And heard them howl;
O my sole comfort, take no more these ways,
    This hideous path,   10
And I will mend my own without delays,
    Cease thou thy wrath!
I have deserved a thick, Egyptian damp,
    Dark as my deeds,
Should mist within me, and put out that lamp   15
    Thy spirit feeds;
A darting conscience full of stabs and fears;
    No shade but yew,
Sullen and sad eclipses, cloudy spheres,
    These are my due.   20
But he that with his blood (a price too dear)
    My scores did pay,
Bid me, by virtue from him, challenge here
    The brightest day;
Sweet, downy thoughts, soft lily-shades, calm streams,   25
    Joys full and true,
Fresh, spicy mornings, and eternal beams
    These are his due.

John Dryden   To the Memory of Mr. Oldham

Farewell, too little and too lately known,
Whom I began to think and call my own;
For sure our souls were near allied, and thine
Cast in the same poetic mould with mine.
One common note on either lyre did strike,   *5*
And knaves and fools we both abhorred alike.
To the same goal did both our studies drive,
The last set out the soonest did arrive.
Thus Nisus fell upon the slippery place,
Whilst his young friend performed and won the race.   *10*
Oh, early ripe! to thy abundant store
What could advancing age have added more?
It might (what Nature never gives the young)
Have taught the numbers of thy native tongue.
But satire needs not those, and wit will shine   *15*
Through the harsh cadence of a rugged line.
A noble error, and but seldom made,
When poets are by too much force betrayed.
Thy generous fruits, though gathered ere their prime,
Still showed a quickness; and maturing time   *20*
But mellows what we write to the dull sweets of rhyme.
Once more, hail and farewell! farewell, thou young,
But ah! too short, Marcellus of our tongue!
Thy brow's with ivy and with laurels bound;
But fate and gloomy night encompass thee around.   *25*

Mr. Oldham: John Oldham (1653–1683), a satiric poet.   *9*
Nisus: he slipped in a pool of blood as he was about to win a foot
race (*Aeneid* V.315–339).   23 *Marcellus:* nephew of Augustus,
he died young (see *Aeneid* VI.854–886).

Matthew Prior   To Cloe Weeping

See, whilst thou weep'st, fair Cloe, see
The world in sympathy with thee.
The cheerful birds no longer sing,
Each drops his head, and hangs his wing.
The clouds have bent their bosom lower,   *5*
And shed their sorrows in a shower.
The brooks beyond their limits flow;
And louder murmurs speak their woe.
The nymphs and swains adopt thy cares:
They heave thy sighs, and weep thy tears.   *10*
Fantastic nymph! that grief should move
Thy heart, obdurate against love.
Strange tears! whose power can soften all,
But that dear breast on which they fall.

Anne Finch, Countess of Winchilsea To the Nightingale

Exert thy voice, sweet harbinger of Spring!
    This moment is thy time to sing,
    This moment I attend to praise,
And set my numbers to thy lays.
    Free as thine shall be my song;   5
    As thy music, short, or long.
Poets, wild as thee, were born,
    Pleasing best when unconfined,
    When to please is least designed,
Soothing but their cares to rest;   10
    Cares do still their thoughts molest,
    And still th'unhappy poet's breast,
Like thine, when best he sings, is placed against a thorn.
She begins; let all be still!
    Muse, thy promise now fulfill!   15
Sweet, oh! sweet, still sweeter yet!
Can thy words such accents fit?
Canst thou syllables refine,
Melt a sense that shall retain
Still some spirit of the brain,   20
Till with sounds like these it join?
    'Twill not be! then change thy note;
Let division shake thy throat.
Hark! division now she tries;
Yet as far the muse outflies.   25
Cease then, prithee, cease thy tune;
Trifler, wilt thou sing till June?
Till thy business all lies waste,
And the time of building's past!
    Thus we poets that have speech,   30
Unlike what thy forests teach,
    If a fluent vein be shown
    That's transcendent to our own,
Criticize, reform, or preach,
Or censure what we cannot reach.   35

Jonathan Swift A Description of the Morning

Now hardly here and there a hackney-coach
Appearing showed the ruddy morn's approach.
Now Betty from her master's bed had flown,
And softly stole to discompose her own;
The slipshod 'prentice from his master's door   5
Had pared the dirt and sprinkled around the floor.
Now Moll had whirled her mop with dexterous airs,
Prepared to scrub the entry and the stairs.

The youth with broomy stumps began to trace
The kennel-edge, where wheels had worn the place.   10
The small-coal man was heard with cadence deep,
Till drowned in shriller notes of chimney-sweep:
Duns at his lordship's gate began to meet;
And brickdust Moll had screamed through half the street.
The turnkey now his flock returning sees,   15
Duly let out a-nights to steal for fees:
The watchful bailiffs take their silent stands,
And schoolboys lag with satchels in their hands.

13 Duns: debt collectors.

Samuel Taylor Coleridge   This Lime-Tree Bower My Prison

Well, they are gone, and here I must remain,
This lime-tree bower my prison! I have lost
Beauties and feelings, such as would have been
Most sweet to my remembrance, even when age
Had dimmed mine eyes to blindness! They, meanwhile,   5
Friends, whom I never more may meet again,
On springy heath, along the hill-top edge,
Wander in gladness, and wind down, perchance,
To that still roaring dell, of which I told;
The roaring dell, o'erwooded, narrow, deep,   10
And only speckled by the mid-day sun;
Where its slim trunk the ash from rock to rock
Flings arching like a bridge—that branchless ash,
Unsunned and damp, whose few poor yellow leaves
Ne'er tremble in the gale, yet tremble still,   15
Fanned by the waterfall! and there my friends
Behold the dark green file of long lank weeds,
That all at once (a most fantastic sight!)
Still nod and drip beneath the dripping edge
Of the blue clay-stone.
          Now, my friends emerge   20
Beneath the wide wide Heaven, and view again
The many-steepled track magnificent
Of hilly fields and meadows, and the sea,
With some fair bark, perhaps whose sails light up
The slip of smooth clear blue betwixt two isles   25
Of purple shadow! Yes! they wander on
In gladness all; but thou, methinks, most glad,
My gentle-hearted Charles! for thou hast pined
And hungered after Nature, many a year,
In the great city pent, winning thy way   30
With sad yet patient soul, through evil and pain
And strange calamity! Ah! slowly sink
Behind the western ridge, thou glorious sun!
Shine in the slant beams of the sinking orb,

Live in the yellow light, ye distant groves!   35
Ye purple heath-flowers! richlier burn, ye clouds!
And kindle, thou blue ocean! So my friend
Struck with deep joy may stand, as I have stood,
Silent with swimming sense; yea, gazing round
On the wide landscape, gaze till all doth seem   40
Less gross than bodily; and of such hues
As veil the Almighty Spirit, when He makes
Spirits perceive His presence.
                          A delight
Comes sudden on my heart, and I am glad
As I myself were there! Nor in this bower,   45
This little lime-tree bower, have I not marked
Much that hath soothed me. Pale beneath the blaze
Hung the transparent foliage; and I watched
Some broad and sunny leaf, and loved to see
The shadow of the leaf and stem above   50
Dappling its sunshine! And that walnut-tree
Was richly tinged, and deep radiance lay
Full on the ancient ivy, which usurps
Those fronting elms, and now, with blackest mass
Makes their dark branches gleam a lighter hue   55
Through the late twilight: and though now the bat
Wheels silent by, and not a swallow twitters,
Yet still the solitary humble bee
Sings in the bean-flower! Henceforth I shall know
That Nature ne'er deserts the wise and pure;   60
No plot so narrow, be but Nature there,
No waste so vacant, but may well employ
Each faculty of sense, and keep the heart
Awake to love and beauty! and sometimes
'Tis well to be bereft of promised good,   65
That we may lift the soul, and contemplate
With lively joys we cannot share.
My gentle-hearted Charles! when the last rook
Beat its straight path along the dusky air
Homewards, I blessed it! deeming its black wing   70
(Now a dim speck, now vanishing in light)
Had crossed the mighty orb's dilated glory,
While thou stood'st gazing; or when all was still,
Flew creaking o'er thy head, and had a charm
For thee, my gentle-hearted Charles, to whom   75
No sound is dissonant which tells of life.

1: Written when Coleridge was confined to his home in June 1797
because boiling milk had been spilled on his foot. "They" were
Wordsworth, Dorothy Wordsworth, and Charles Lamb.

Ralph Waldo Emerson   "Give All to Love"

Give all to love;
Obey thy heart;

Friends, kindred, days,
Estate, good-fame,
Plans, credit and the Muse—   5
Nothing refuse.

'Tis a brave master;
Let it have scope:
Follow it utterly,
Hope beyond hope: 10
High and more high
It dives into noon,
With wing unspent,
Untold intent;
But it is a god,   15
Knows its own path
And the outlets of the sky.

It was never for the mean;
It requireth courage stout.
Souls above doubt,   20
Valor unbending,
It will reward—
They shall return
More than they were,
And ever ascending.   25

Leave all for love;
Yet, hear me, yet,
One word more thy heart behoved,
One pulse more of firm endeavor—
Keep thee today,   30
Tomorrow, forever,
Free as an Arab
Of thy beloved.

Cling with life to the maid;
But when the surprise,   35
First vague shadow of surmise,
Flits across her bosom young,
Of a joy apart from thee,
Free be she, fancy-free;
Nor thou detain her vesture's hem,   40
Nor the palest rose she flung
From her summer diadem.

Though thou loved her as thyself,
As a self of purer clay,
Though her parting dims the day,   45
Stealing grave from all alive;
Heartily know,
When half-gods go,
The gods arrive.

Ralph Waldo Emerson   Days

Daughters of Time, the hypocritic Days,
Muffled and dumb like barefoot dervishes,
And marching single in an endless file,
Bring diadems and fagots in their hands.
To each they offer gifts after his will,   5
Bread, kingdoms, stars, and sky that holds them all.
I, in my pleached garden, watched the pomp,
Forgot my morning wishes, hastily
Took a few herbs and apples, and the Day
Turned and departed silent. I, too late,   10
Under her solemn fillet saw the scorn.

7 *pleached*: interlaced.

Walt Whitman   "A Noiseless, Patient Spider"

A noiseless, patient spider,
I marked, where, on a little promontory, it stood isolated;
Marked how, to explore the vacant, vast surrounding,
It launched forth filament, filament, filament, out of itself;
Ever unreeling them—ever tirelessly speeding them.   5

And you, O my Soul, where you stand,
Surrounded, surrounded, in measureless oceans of space,
Ceaselessly musing, venturing, throwing—seeking the spheres, to
    connect them;
Till the bridge you will need, be formed—till the ductile anchor
    hold;
Till the gossamer thread you fling, catch somewhere, O my
    Soul.   10

Walt Whitman   "As Toilsome I Wandered
    Virginia's Woods"

As toilsome I wandered Virginia's woods,
To the music of rustling leaves kicked by my feet (for 'twas
    autumn)
I marked at the foot of a tree the grave of a soldier;
Mortally wounded he and buried on the retreat (easily all could I
    understand),
The halt of a midday hour, when up! no time to lose—yet this
    sign left,   5
On a tablet scrawled and nailed on the tree by the grave,
Bold, cautious, true, and my loving comrade.

Long, long I muse, then on my way go wandering,
Many a changeful season to follow, and many a scene of life,

Yet at times through changeful season and scene, abrupt, alone, or
   in the crowded street,   10
Comes before me the unknown soldier's grave, comes the inscription rude in Virginia's woods,
Bold, cautious, true, and my loving comrade.

Robert Browning   Prospice

Fear death?—to feel the fog in my throat,
   The mist in my face;
When the snows begin, and the blasts denote
   I am nearing the place—
The power of the night, the press of the storm,   5
   The post of the foe;
Where he stands, the Arch Fear in a visible form:
   Yet the strong man must go.
For the journey is done and the summit attained,
   And the barriers fall;   10
Though a battle's to fight ere the guerdon be gained,
   The reward of it all.
I was ever a fighter, so—one fight more,
   The best and the last!
I would hate that death bandaged my eyes, and forbore,   15
   And bade me creep past.
No! let me taste the whole of it, fare like my peers
   The heroes of old—
Bear the brunt, in a minute pay glad life's arrears
   Of pain, darkness, and cold.   20
For sudden the worst turns the best, to the brave:
   The black minute's at end,
And the elements' rage, the field-voices that rave,
   Shall dwindle, shall blend,
Shall change, shall become first a peace out of pain,   25
   Then a light, then thy breast,
O thou soul of my soul! I shall clasp thee again;
   And with God be the rest!

Prospice: anticipation, look into the future.

Arthur Hugh Clough   Epi-Strauss-ium

Matthew and Mark and Luke and holy John
Evanished all and gone!
Yea, he that erst, his dusky curtains quitting,
Through Eastern pictured panes his level beams transmitting,
With gorgeous portraits blent,   5
On them his glories intercepted spent,
Southwestering now, through windows plainly glassed,
On the inside face his radiance keen hath cast,
And in the lustre lost, invisible and gone,

Are, say you, Matthew, Mark and Luke and holy John?   10
Lost, is it? lost, to be recovered never?
However,
The place of worship the meantime with light
Is, if less richly, more sincerely bright,
And in blue skies the Orb is manifest to sight.   15

Epi-Strauss-ium: a work discussing the ideas of David Strauss, a
German theologian.

Gerard Manley Hopkins   Pied Beauty

Glory be to God for dappled things—
    For skies of couple-color as a brinded cow;
        For rose-moles all in stipple upon trout that swim;
Fresh-firecoal chestnut-falls; finches' wings;
    Landscape plotted and pieced—fold, fallow, and plough;   5
        And all Trades, their gear and tackle and trim
All things counter, original, spare, strange;
    Whatever is fickle, freckled (who knows how?)
        With swift, slow; sweet, sour; adazzle, dim;
He fathers forth whose beauty is past change: 10
                    Praise him.

Gerard Manley Hopkins   Spring and Fall:
   To a Young Child

Márgarét, are you gríeving
Over Goldengrove unleaving?
Léaves, like the things of man, you
With your fresh thoughts care for, can you?
Ah! ás the heart grows older   5
It will come to such sights colder
By and by, nor spare a sigh
Though worlds of wanwood leafmeal lie;
And yet you wíll weep and know why.
Now no matter, child, the name: 10
Sórrow's spríngs áre the same.
Nor mouth had, no nor mind, expressed
What heart heard of, ghost guessed:
It ís the blight man was born for,
It is Margaret you mourn for.   15

Coventry Patmore   The Toys

My little Son, who looked from thoughtful eyes,
And moved and spoke in quiet grown-up wise,
Having my law the seventh time disobeyed,
I struck him, and dismissed

With hard words and unkissed,   5
—His Mother, who was patient, being dead.
Then, fearing lest his grief should hinder sleep,
I visited his bed,
But found him slumbering deep,
With darkened eyelids, and their lashes yet   10
From his late sobbing wet.
And I, with moan,
Kissing away his tears, left others of my own;
For, on a table drawn beside his head,
He had put, within his reach,   15
A box of counters and a red-veined stone,
A piece of glass abraded by the beach,
And six or seven shells,
A bottle with bluebells,
And two French copper coins, ranged there with careful art,   20
To comfort his sad heart.
So when that night I prayed
To God, I wept, and said;
Ah, when at last we lie with tranced breath,
Not vexing Thee in death,   25
And Thou rememberest of what toys
We made our joys,
How weakly understood
Thy great commanded good,
Then fatherly not less   30
Than I whom Thou hast moulded from the clay,
Thou'lt leave Thy wrath, and say,
"I will be sorry for their childishness."

Emily Dickinson   "Title Divine Is Mine"

Title divine is mine
The Wife without
The Sign.
Acute degree
Conferred on me—   5
Empress of Calvary.
Royal all but the
Crown—
Betrothed, without the swoon
God gives us women   10
When two hold Garnet to garnet,
Gold to gold—
Born—Bridalled—
Shrouded—
In a day Tri-Victory—   15
"My Husband"
Women say
Stroking the melody,
Is this the way?

Thomas Hulme   Autumn

A touch of cold in the Autumn night—
I walked abroad,
And saw the ruddy moon lean over a hedge
Like a red-faced farmer.
I did not stop to speak, but nodded,   5
And round about were the wistful stars
With white faces like town children.

H. D.   At Baia

I should have thought
In a dream you would have brought
Some lovely perilous thing,
Orchids piled in a great sheath,
As who would say (in a dream)   5
I send you this,
Who left the blue veins
Of your throat unkissed.
Why was it that your hands
(That never took mine)   10
Your hands that I could see
Drift over the orchid heads
So carefully,
Your hands, so fragile, sure to lift
So gently, the fragile flower stuff—   15
Ah, ah, how was it

You never sent (in a dream)
The very form, the very scent,
Not heavy, not sensuous.
But perilous—perilous—   20
Of orchids, piled in a great sheath,
And folded underneath on a bright scroll
Some word:
Flower sent to flower;
For white hands, the lesser white,   25

Or
Lover to lover, no kiss,
No touch, but forever and ever this.

e. e. cummings   "o sweet spontaneous earth"

o sweet spontaneous
earth how often have
the
doting

           fingers of   5
prurient philosophers pinched
and
poked

thee
, has the naughty thumb   10
of science prodded
thy

      beauty, how
often have religions taken
thee upon their scraggy knees   15
squeezing and

buffeting thee that thou mightest conceive
gods
          (but
true   20

to the incomparable
couch of death thy
rhythmic
lover

      thou answerest   25

them only with

           spring)

Delmore Schwartz   In the Naked Bed, in Plato's Cave

In the naked bed, in Plato's cave,
Reflected headlights slowly slid the wall,
Carpenters hammered under the shaded window,
Wind troubled the window curtains all night long,
A fleet of trucks strained uphill, grinding,   5
Their freights covered, as usual.
The ceiling lightened again, the slanting diagram
Slid slowly forth.
                    Hearing the milkman's chop,
His striving up the stair, the bottle's chink,
I rose from bed, lit a cigarette,   10
And walked to the window. The stony street
Displayed the stillness in which buildings stand,
The street-lamp's vigil and the horse's patience.
The winter sky's pure capital
Turned me back to bed with exhausted eyes.   15

Strangeness grew in the motionless air. The loose
Film grayed. Shaking wagons, hooves' waterfalls,
Sounded far off, increasing, louder and nearer.
A car coughed, starting. Morning, softly

Melting the air, lifted the half-covered chair   20
From underseas, kindled the looking-glass,
Distinguished the dresser and the white wall.
The bird called tentatively, whistled, called,
Bubbled and whistled, so! Perplexed, still wet
With sleep, affectionate, hungry and cold. So, so,   25
O son of man, the ignorant night, the travail
Of early morning, the mystery of beginning
Again and again,
            while History is unforgiven.

Charles Olson   Maximus, to Gloucester, Letter 19

  (A PASTORAL LETTER

relating
to the care of souls,
it says)

        He had smiled at us,
        each time we were in town, inquired   5
        how the baby was, had two cents
        for the weather, wore
        (besides his automobile)
        good clothes.
                And a pink face.   10

        It was yesterday
        it all came out. The gambit
        (as he crossed the street,
        after us): "I don't believe
        I know your name." Given.   15
        How do you do,
        how do you do. And then:
        "Pardon me, but
        what church
        do you belong to,   20
        may I ask?"

And the whole street, the town, the cities, the nation
blinked, in the afternoon sun, as the gun
was held at them. And I wavered
in the thought.   25

        I sd, you may, sir.
        He sd, what, sir.
        I sd, none,
        sir.

And the light was back.   30
For I am no merchant.
Nor so young I need to take a stance
to a loaded
smile.

I have known the face   35
of God.
And turned away,
turned,
as He did,
his backside   40

2
And now it is noon
of a cloudy sunday.
And a bird sings
loudly

And my daughter, naked   45
on the porch, sings
as best she can, and loudly,
back

    She wears her own face
    as we do not,   50
    until we cease to wear
    the clouds
    of all confusion,

    of all confusers
    who wear the false face
    He never wore, Whose   55
    is terrible. Is
    perfection

35–40: Referring to Exodus xxxiii. 20, 23: "Thou canst not see my face: for there shall no man see me, and live. / . . . And I will take away mine hand, and thou shalt see my back parts: but my face shall not be seen."

Lawrence Ferlinghetti   In Goya's Greatest Scenes

In Goya's greatest scenes we seem to see
                        the people of the world
   exactly at the moment when
      they first attained the title of
                'suffering humanity'   5
     They writhe upon the page
               in a veritable rage
                  of adversity
    Heaped up
           groaning with babies and bayonets   10
                  under cement skies
     in an abstract landscape of blasted trees
       bent statues bats' wings and beaks
            slippery gibbets
      cadavers and carnivorous cocks   15

and all the final hollering monsters
    of the
        'imagination of disaster'
they are so bloody real
        it is as if they really still existed   20

And they do
    Only the landscape is changed

They still are ranged along the roads
    plagued by legionnaires
        false windmills and demented roosters 25
They are the same people
        only further from home
on freeways fifty lanes wide
        on a concrete continent
            spaced with bland billboards   30
    illustrating imbecile illusions of happiness

The scene shows fewer tumbrils
        but more maimed citizens
            in painted cars
    and they have strange license plates   35
    and engines
        that devour America.

32 *tumbrils:* carts transporting those to be executed.

Alan Dugan   On Finding the Meaning of "Radiance"

The dreamed Grail found as if in dreams
was not as had been dreamed when found.
The blasted pot, so early in the earth
that it was nearly dirt in dirt, was fired
either in a kiln or a volcano: who can tell   5
a thumb or tool mark from an earthquake's
pressure in time, and what's the difference?
It is all part of the same process. In
the crater of the natural or potter's pot
there still is some of the first fluid.   10
It is, and why not say it, Perceval?,
piss-like, with a float of shit on top,
body and blood having changed in time
to what the beasts give back to the ground
with their personalities. Once drained,   15
the treasure is there in the lees, changed.
The gold filigree, once dreamed to be
a fine vein in the ore with the ore removed,
has run back into its rock, and the gems,
chipped facet by facet from their shells,   20
are back fast in their stones again, asleep;
but the gold lightning and jewels of fire
are freed in the finding of them, freed

by the nauseous draught: the fire balled
in the skull, the lightning veining the veins.   25
So I am freed to say, as a piece of dirt
to the body of earth: "Here is where love is,"
and, "This is the meaning of 'Radiance'."

Jay Wright   "This Morning"

This morning I threw the windows
of my room open, the light burst
in like crystal gauze and I hung
it on my wall to frame.
And here I am watching it take possession   5
of my room, watching the obscure love
match of light and shadow—of cold and warmth.
It is a matter of acceptance, I guess.
It is a matter of finding some room
with shadows to embrace, open. Now   10
the light has settled in. I don't think
I shall ever close my windows again.

Paul Blackburn   The Watchers

It's going to rain
Across the avenue a crane
whose name is
          CIVETTA LINK-BELT
dips, rises and turns in a   5
     graceless geometry

     But grace is slowness   /   as
ecstasy is some kind of speed or madness   /
The crane moves slowly, that
much it is graceful   /   The men   10
     watch and the leaves

Cranes make letters in the sky
     as the wedge flies
          The scholar's function is

               Mercury, thief and poet,   15
               invented the first 7 letters,
               5 of them vowels, watching
               cranes   .   after got

The men watch and the rain does not come
          HC-108B CIVETTA LINK-BELT   20
In the pit below a yellow cat,
          CAT-933
          pushes the debris
and earth to load CIVETTA HC-108B

Cat's name is PASCO and   25
   there is an ORegon phone number,
moves its load toward 3 piles
Let him leave the building to us

   Palamedes, son of Nauplius,
   invented 11 more   30
           (consonant)
   Also invented the lighthouse, and
   measures, the scales, the disc, and
   "the art of posting sentinels"
   Ruled over the Mysians,   35
        Cretan stock, al-
        though his father was Greek
        Took part in the Trojan trouble on the
Greek side . The scholar's function in fact . Let him
   quarry cleanly . All   40
   THOSE INVENTIONS CRETAN
   so that a Greek   /   alpha-beta-tau
   based on a Cretan, not a Phoenician
      model
      Three different piles: 45

earth   /   debris   /   & schist, the stud/stuff of the island
   is moved by this
PASCO
CAT-933
ORegon 6–   50
it does not rain   .   smoke, the
               alpha-beta-tau

raised from   5 vowels, 13 consonants to
         5 vowels, 15 consonants
         (Epicharmus) not   55
the Sicilian writer of comedies, 6 A.D., but
his ancestor   /
the Aesculapius family at Cos, a couple are
mentioned in the Iliad as physicians to
the Greeks before the equipotent walls   60
of Troy

        No, it does not rain, smoke
        rises from the engines, the
        leaves   .   The men watch
        before the walls of Troy   65

Apollo in cithaera ceteras literas adjecit
      7 strings on that zither
      & for each string a letter
      Thence to Simonides,
native of Ceos in the service of Dionysus   70
which god also at home in Delphos
both gods of the solar year as were   /   Aesculapius
                    & Hercules
                    Let's
    get all of this into one pot, 6–700 years B.C.   75

Simonides, well-known poet, introduced into Athens 4 more letters .   the
    unnecessary double-consonants PSI
               (earlier written Pi-Sigma)
   and XI (earlier written Kappa-Sigma)   80
plus (plus) two vowels   :   OMEGA, a distinction from
   t h e   o m i c r o n   H e r m e s   c o n n e d
   f r o m   t h e   3   C r o n e s ,   a n d
EPSILON, as distinct from their eta
& that's the long & the short of it.   85

Cranes fly in V-formation & the
Tyrrhenians, or Etruscans, were
also of Cretan stock, held
the crane in reverence   /   The men watch
        LINK-BELT move up its load, the
        pile to the left near 24th St., the   90
        permanent erection moves
        slow-ly, almost sensually, al-most
          gracefully

The scholar's function   /   fact . Let him quarry   95
cleanly   /   leave the building to us   /   Poems
nicked with a knife onto the bark of a stick (Hesiod)
   or upon tablets of clay
        Perseus cuts off the Gorgon-head
         (Medusa)   100
        and carries it off in a bag   .   But
the head's a ritual mask and a protection, we
frighten children with it
and trespassers
when we perform the rites   .   It is   105
        no murder,
            she has given him power of sight

p o e t r y,
     the gorgons no pursuers
     are escort, and the mask   110
            (his protection)
Hermes / Car / Mercury / Perseus / Palamedes / Thoth / or
   whatever his original name was,
winged sandals and helmet, you bet!
the swiftness of poetic thought   /   And the bag   115
T H E   A L P H A B E T ' S   I N   T H E   B A G!

Almost sensually, almost
gracefully . The men watch
and know not what they watch
The cat pushes . the crane . the bud   120
lifts upward . above the

      Pillars of Hercules, desti-
nation, where he is going, bringing the secret in the bag
     The tree at Gades (Cádiz)
   principal city of Tartessus, the   125

Aegean colony on the Guadalquivir
From there the Milesians will take it to Ireland?
The older city is on the western shore with its
      Temple of Cronus . island,
      the island of the goddess,   *130*
      Red Island   /   & Cronus

god of the middle finger, the fool's finger   /   It is
    his father he kills not his mother, his mother
    gives him
          the secret   *135*
              Scholar's function is
                      The men watch

Hercules' shrine set up by colonists, 1100 B.C.
400 years before the Phoenicians
coming from Tyre in painted ships   *140*
    and their oracle
        HERCULES = PALAMEDES (?)

7 & 2
9 steps to the goddess
& everyone lives to 110 years   *145*
5 years to a lustrum
          (Etruscan)
22   lustra = 110
          (alpha-beta-tau)
& the circumference of the circle when   *150*
    the diameter is   7   is
22
proportion known as π
22 (plus) over 7
a neat recurrent sequence   *155*
which does not work out because it never
ends   /
7 lustra is 35 years   .   Maturity,
or the age at which a man may be elected
President of the United States   /   a convention   *160*
or a Roman might be elected Consul   /   a convention
        $\dfrac{22}{7}$
These numbers no longer a secret   /   But in Crete
               or Spain . . .

Spanish, the mother's family name   *165*
still is set down last, and
still in Crete descent is matrilineal
The Greeks have accomplished nothing
    but death   beauty
        (Troy)   *170*
The men watch the cat push
keeping the piles discrete
earth / debris / & schist
the stuff of the island, the crane, the bud
lifts upward . above the   *175*

> And at Cádiz, Caius Julius Hyginus,
> a Spaniard and Ovid's friend,
> curator of the Palantine Library,
> exiled from the court of Augustus

sitting under a tree in Cádiz   *180*
over the problem, over a millennium later,
traces Greek letters in the spelt of wine at his table
watches the cranes fly over toward Africa
wedge in the sunset   /   set down the score:

> Mercury (or the Fates) 7   *185*
> Palamedes   11
> Epicharmus   2
> Simonides   4

Say that he used Etruscan sources,
    does that explain it?   *190*
Let them quarry cleanly
    Let them leave
Cranes winging over toward Africa
    a wedge.
Hyginus traces π on the wooden table in wine spelt   *195*

> The cat pushes, the crane, the bud
> lifts upward   /   above the
> rain comes finally
The watchers leave the construction site,
the men leave their machines   *200*
    at 323 Third Avenue
    an old drunk (Hyginus)
sits in a doorway and downs a whole
pint of Sacramento Tomato Juice

> The watchers are the gods

> The leaves burgeon

21 cat: caterpillar tractor.   *66:* "Apollo played other poems on
his zither." Apollo was the god of music and poetry.

Roger Mitchell   Riding with Some North Vietnamese Students in a Polish Elevator, 1966

Perhaps they wonder who the tall man is,
wedged elbow deep in silence, briefcase zipped,
holding the limp bouquet of his gaze high
above them, a pale torch stiff-arming the night.
I think of Shapiro riding with his nuns,   5
having his silent Jewish way with them.
I think of all the undressed girls in the street
taking the easy elevator to the top
of a world where lovers watch themselves at work.
I think of all the professional innocents,   10

of the hungry state eating the inside
of its smile, of fattened fathers smiling back;
and I keep, with the rest, the same zipped silence,
getting off, as politely as I can,
here.   *15*

SPECIFIC NONSTANZAIC TYPES

The Distich

Robert Herrick   Slavery

'Tis liberty to serve one lord, but he
Who many serves, serves base servility.

Robert Herrick   Ill Government

Preposterous is that government, and rude,
When kings obey the wilder multitude.

The Tristich

Timothy Kendall   To a Married Couple That Could Not Agree

Sith that you both are like in life—
A naughty man, a wicked wife—
I muse ye live not void of strife.

1 *Sith that*: since.

Langston Hughes   Winter Moon

How thin and sharp is the moon tonight!
How thin and sharp and ghostly white
Is the slim curved crook of the moon tonight!

The Skeltonic

John Skelton   To Mistress Margaret Hussey

Merry Margaret,
    As midsummer flower,

Gentle as falcon
Or hawk of the tower:
With solace and gladness,   5
Much mirth and no madness,
All good and no badness;
    So joyously,
    So maidenly,
    So womanly   10
    Her demeaning
    In every thing,
    Far, far passing
    That I can indite,
    Or suffice to write   15
    Of Merry Margaret
      As midsummer flower
Gentle as falcon
Or hawk of the tower.
      As patient and still   20
And as full of good will
As fair Isaphill,
Coliander,
Sweet pomander,
Good Cassander,   25
Steadfast of thought,
Well made, well wrought,
Far may be sought
Ere that he can find
So courteous, so kind   30
As Merry Margaret,
    This midsummer flower,
Gentle as falcon
Or hawk of the tower.

Rolfe Humphries   A Sad Song, This Time

Now our joy
Dries, or goes
Underground
In the way
Water does: 5
Who can tell
Where it lay
Sweet and fair

Who can say
How far under?   10
Down-a-down
Past the clay,
Past the rock,
Deeper yet,
Deeper still,—   15
In that fire.

Doggerel

John Betjeman   Late-Flowering Lust

My head is bald, my breath is bad,
    Unshaven is my chin,
I have not now the joys I had
    When I was young in sin.

I run my fingers down your dress   5
    With brandy-certain aim
And you respond to my caress
    And maybe feel the same.

But I've a picture of my own
    On this reunion night,   10
Wherein two skeletons are shown
    To hold each other tight;

Dark sockets look on emptiness
    Which once was loving-eyed,
The mouth that opens for a kiss   15
    Has got no tongue inside.

I cling to you inflamed with fear
    As now you cling to me,
I feel how frail you are my dear
    And wonder what will be—   20

A week? or twenty years remain?
    And then—what kind of death?
A losing fight with frightful pain
    Or a gasping fight for breath?

Too long we let our bodies cling,   25
    We cannot hide disgust
At all the thoughts that in us spring
    From this late-flowering lust.

Hudibrastic Verse

Samuel Butler

PART I, CANTO I (excerpt)
FROM *Hudibras*

When civil fury first grew high,
And men fell out, they knew not why;
When hard words, jealousies, and fears
Set folks together by the ears
And made them fight, like mad or drunk,   5
For Dame Religion as for punk,
Whose honesty they all durst swear for,
Though not a man of them knew wherefore;
When gospel-trumpeter, surrounded
With long-eared rout, to battle sounded,   10
And pulpit, drum ecclesiastic,
Was beat with fist instead of a stick—
Then did Sir Knight abandon dwelling,
And out he rode a-colonelling.
   A Wight he was whose very sight would   15
Entitle him Mirror of Knighthood;
That never bent his stubborn knee
To anything but chivalry,
Nor put up blow but that which laid
Right Worshipful on shoulder-blade;   20
Chief of domestic knights and errant,
Either for chartel or for warrant;
Great on the bench, great in the saddle,
That could as well bind o'er as swaddle:
Mighty he was at both of these,   25
And styled of war as well as peace.
(So some rats of amphibious nature
Are either for the land or water.)
But here our authors make a doubt
Whether he were more wise or stout.   30
Some hold the one and some the other;
But howsoe'er they make a pother,
The difference was so small his brain
Outweighed his rage but half a grain;
Which made some take him for a tool   35
That knaves do work with, called a fool.
And offer to lay wagers that
As Montaigne, playing with his cat,
Complains she thought him but an ass,
Much more she would Sir Hudibras   40
(For that's the name our valiant knight

To all his challenges did write);
But they're mistaken very much,
'Tis plain enough he was no such.
We grant, although he had much wit,   45
He was very shy of using it;
As being loth to wear it out,
And therefore bore it not about,
Unless on holidays, or so
As men their best apparel do.   50
Beside, 'tis known he could speak Greek
As naturally as pigs squeak;
That Latin was no more difficile
Than to a blackbird 'tis to whistle.
Being rich in both, he never scanted   55
His bounty unto such as wanted,
But much of either would afford
To many that had not one word.
For Hebrew roots, although they're found
To flourish most in barren ground,   60
He had such plenty as sufficed
To make some think him circumcised;
And truly so perhaps he was,
'Tis many a pious Christian's case.
He was in logic a great critic,   65
Profoundly skilled in analytic:
He could distinguish and divide
A hair 'twixt south and southwest side;
On either which he would dispute,
Confute, change hands, and still confute: 70
He'd undertake to prove, by force
Of argument, a man's no horse;
He'd prove a buzzard is no fowl,
And that a lord may be an owl,
A calf an alderman, a goose a justice,   75
And rooks committee-men and trustees.
He'd run in debt by disputation,
And pay with ratiocination.
All this by syllogism true,
In mood and figure, he would do.   80
    For rhetoric, he could not ope
His mouth but out there flew a trope;
And when he happened to break off
In the middle of his speech, or cough,
He had hard words ready to show why,   85
And tell what rules he did it by.
Else, when with greatest art he spoke,
You'd think he talked like other folk;
For all a rhetorician's rules
Teach nothing but to name his tools.   90
His ordinary rate of speech
In loftiness of sound was rich,
A Babylonish dialect,
Which learned pedants much affect.
It was a parti-colored dress   95

Of patched and piebald languages:
'Twas English cut on Greek and Latin,
Like fustian heretofore on satin.
It has an odd promiscuous tone,
As if he'd talked three parts in one;   100
Which made some think, when he did gabble,
They'd heard three laborers of Babel,
Or Cerberus himself pronounce
A least of languages at once.
This he as volubly would vent   105
As if his stock would ne'er be spent;
And truly, to support that charge,
He had supplies as vast and large.
For he could coin or counterfeit
New words with little or no wit;   110
Words so debased and hard no stone
Was hard enough to touch them on.
And when with hasty noise he spoke 'em,
The ignorant for current took 'em;
That had the orator, who once   115
Did fill his mouth with pebble-stones
When he harangued, but known his phrase,
He would have used no other ways. . . .

6 *punk*: whore.   22 *chartel*: challenge.   76 *trustees*: of prop-
erty, as appointed by Parliament.   93 *Babylonish*: because the
name was derived from the word Babel.   98: Coarse fustian had
holes cut in it to allow the satin beneath to shine through.   103
Cerberus: the three-headed watchdog of Hell.   115 *orator*:
Demosthenes.

The Macaronic

John Donne   In Eundem Macaronicon

Quot, dos *haec*, LINGUISTS perfetti, *Disticha* fairont,
   Tot cuerdos STATES-MEN, *hic* livre fara *tuus*.
Es *sat* a MY l'honneur estre *hic* inteso; Car I LEAVE
   L'honra, de parsonne nestre creduto, *tibi*.

TRANSLATION:

On the same macaronic composition.

As these two double verses, perfect linguists, create
so many prudent statesmen, this book will fashion your book.
It is enough to my credit to be understood herein; for I leave
the reverence of anyone not to be believed to you.

In eundem Macaronicon: Thomas Coryat's fanciful, multilingual
account of his travels, *Coryat's Crudities* (1611).

THE PATTERN POEM

Shaped Verse

George Herbert   Easter Wings

My   tender   age   in   sorrow   did   begin:
   And still with sickness and shame
      Thou didst so punish sin,
         That   I   became
           Most thin.   5
           With thee
        Let   me   combine,
   And feel this day thy victory:
 For, if I imp my wing on thine,
Affliction shall advance the flight in me.   10

Lord, who createdst man in wealth and store,
   Though foolishly he lost the same,
      Decaying more and more,
         Till   he   became
           Most poor: 15
           With thee
        O   let   me   rise
   As   larks,   harmoniously,
   And sing this day thy victories:
Then shall the fall further the flight in me.   20

9 *imp*: repair (by insertion of feathers where needed).

Robert Herrick   This Cross-Tree Here

This   cross-tree   here
Doth   JESUS   bear,
Who   sweatened   first,
The   Death   accursed.

Here all things ready are, make haste, make haste away;   5
For, long this work will be, and very short this day.
Why then, go on to act: Here's wonders to be done,
Before the last least sand of Thy ninth hour be run;
Or ere dark clouds do dull, or dead the midday's sun.

Act when Thou wilt,   10
Blood   will   be   spilt;
Pure   balm,   that   shall
Bring   health   to   all.
Why   then,   begin
To   pour   first   in   15
Some   drops   of   wine,
Instead   of   brine,
To search the wound,
So   long   unsound:
And, when that's done,   20
Let   oil,   next,   run,
To   cure   the   sore
Sin   made   before.
And O! Dear Christ,
E'en   as   Thou   di'st,   25
Look   down   and   see
Us   weep   for   Thee.
And tho (Love knows)
Thy   dreadful   woes
We   cannot   ease;   30
Yet   do   Thou   please,
Who   mercy   art,
To accept each heart,
That   gladly   would
Help,   if   it   could.   35
Meanwhile,   let   me,
Beneath   this   tree,
This   honor   have,
To   make   my   grave.

Rolfe Humphries   Looking Up at Airplanes, Always

High   overhead,
High overhead   the planes go over.
I   lift   my   eyes
To see them, always.

Having been there,   5
Having been there at that great height
I   rise   up   swiftly
Am   there   again.

Like   dragon-flies,
Like dragon-flies how brief their season!   10
A   hundred   hours,
So   I   have   heard.

Patterned Verse

Philip Booth   The Tower

Strangers ask,
always, how tall
it is. Taller,
the natives say,
than any other.   5
Watching it sway,
slightly, in a brisk
wind, you believe
them and feel,
well, smaller   10
than you once
did, or would have,
even had they woken
somebody's father,
who remembers   15
every specification,
they say, having fought
against this location,
in the last elections
before it was built.   20
It is enough
to see it, canted
over you, as
you approach
the strange base: 25
a cement stilt
set in a rough
patch of marsh;

on that, a ball
with numbers   30
etched on it,
perhaps a date,
on which the steel
frame, in one
brave unbroken   35
line, seems to stretch
for heaven itself,
in three diminishing
sections. The balance
is fantastic,   40
or seems so, until
you recall the elastic
web of guy wires
that, slanted
beyond you, support   45
the tower in nine equal directions.
The local women,
hanging their wash
on a wet line,
Monday, report   50
that it's hidden
in clouds, out
of mind, until,
in a sudden
wind and vanishing   55
fog, they look up:
not to worship,
but, more, from habit;
the way, once left
home when their men   60
went to rivet
the thing, they said
morning prayers.
Even on Sunday,
now, of course,   65
they accept how
the shadow swings
down, leaning
in and away
in elliptic rings   70
like a sundial.
Or so a high
state official
told them it did,
when they, craning   75
that broken sky,
sat assembled
there for the long
dedication:
it resembled,   80
he said, nothing

so much; and laughing
then, said if you
knew where you were
(they laughed too),   85
and perhaps how far
from the solstice,
you could almost tell
what time it was,
by when the shadow   90
fell on your house.
Not that the tower
itself would fall,
ever, on such
a quiet meadow   95
of homes, nor would
the isogonic reaction
affect, even touch,
their elm trees;
the theta conductors   100
were shielded, at
his personal direction,
he said, so not
to entail any risk
for them, or their families.   105
A man, then, stood
tall, as if to ask
a first question, but
near him a guard
preserved order.   110
There was, the speaker
admitted, an odor
caused by the breaker
circuits, but this
was the new power,   115
in essence, and, as
designed, wouldn't last,
A solar device,
he called it, strong
as the Nation   120
itself, which, because
of such structures,
would stand until
Kingdom Come.
They were proud there,   125
then; and still are,
when their children,
or children's children,
home from municipal
lectures, recite,   130
without prompting,
the smallest detail:
the interval
of each warning light,

and how, just   *135*
at dawn, the strange
orange glow
on top will go
out, with something
suspended, like   *140*
lazing snow
in the morning air;
not much, a flake
here, a flake there,
which dissolves   *145*
to a kind of dust
and settles, daily,
around the globular
base. And, daily,
the child who puts up   *150*
the flag is assigned,
also, to sweep.
Once every year
they make wreaths
(of jagged cut felt,   *155*
shaped like elm leaves)
and lay them here,
between the new sidewalk
and Main Street.
Otherwise, nothing   *160*
is changed: home
is the same, talk
still revolves
around the same
people. Government   *165*
studies, given
every control,
have proven
this. The report
is unanimous,   *170*
to every intent:
there's been neither
famine nor war.
Their original
fear of the fall   *175*
is gone, the range
of the shadow
seems less, the weather
more clear. The meadows
are full of new flowers;   *180*
stakes are aligned
on most lawns, shaped
like sundials.
Women count hours
still; they repeat   *185*
household trials,
and gossip. But except for

the fool who tried
climbing the tower,
few have died;   190
most have escaped
the usual town
diseases; misbegotten
children are
fewer, the suicide   195
rate is down.
Indeed, nothing
is ominous
here, unless
you take stock   200
of their dreams:
waking, sometimes,
they say, it hangs
over them: not
exactly the tower   205
itself, but what
they've forgotten,
something above
the tower, like
a dance tune   210
they can't quite
remember, or name.
They are used to
the circuit breakers
now; they admit   215
it, even to
Government
census-takers,
who wake them—
women weeping   220
over their sleeping
men, at dawn—
since only then,
before day
begins, will they   225
try to show
without words,
but pointing towards
the tower, that what
they can't name   230
is, like waking
itself, or making
love, not different,
no, but in spite
of the Government,   235
yes, not quite
the same.

97 *isogonic:* having equal angles.

Edwin Honig

W

A

L

WHITMAN

Prophet of the body's
roving magnitude, he still
commands   a   hope   elusive   as
the Jewish savior—not dying, not yet
born, but always imminent: coming in a   *5*
blaze one sunny afternoon, defying winter, to
everyone's distinct advantage, then going on to Eden,
half sham, half hearsay, like California or Miami golden.

All   his   life   was
squandered   in   his   poverty   *10*
when he became the body's prime
reunionist,   bankrupt   exploiter,   from
early   middle   age,   of   the   nation's   largest
unexploited enterprise—baggy, queer, a Johnny
Appleseed freely planting selves the future mashes into   *15*
commonplaces, lops off as flourishes, an unweaned appetite

Yet   who   can   shape   his
mouth's beard brimming bubble,
that violent honey sound? Afterwards
they just blew hard, Tarzans hammering   *20*
through   the   swamp   lots.   His   patent,   never
filed, was being man quixotically alive against the
hoax of sin & dying. Paradise is now. America, whose
greatest war was civil, must be born from Abel's wound

&   Cain   be   welcomed   *25*
home by Adam—Father Abraham
opening   his   blood   to   continents,   all
armies,   lovers,   tramps.   A   time   for   heroes,
but the captains, shot or dowdy, died. (Had old
Abe really smiled & tipped his hat or had he merely   *30*
grimaced? Ulysses, finished, promptly sighed & chompèd
cigars & toured the capitals. The people yea'd & shambled

to   the   greatest   fortunes   made,
while   he   conveyed   the   lippy   cop,   the
whistling   streetcar   man,   the   ferry   pilot   *35*
billowing upon the apron of his praise. Nakedly at
last he flailed his own paralysis with mud & flesh-
brush. A man, all man himself alone, a rugged blue-eyed
testament, his looks in Brady's lens are calm with after-rages.

"The   real   war   *40*
will   never   get
in   the   books."
Below   the   ragged
line   he   signed
his chummy name.   *45*

31 *Ulysses:* General and later President Ulysses S. Grant.   39
Brady: Matthew Brady, an important photographer of the Civil
War.

Emblematic Verse

Francis Quarles   Emblem III from the Fifth Book

Canticles ii.16: My beloved is mine, and
I am his; he feedeth among the lilies.

Ev'n like two little bank-dividing brooks
   That wash the pebbles with their wanton streams,
And having ranged and searched a thousand nooks,
   Meet both at length in silver-breasted Thames,
     Where in a greater current they conjoin,   5
So I my best beloved's am; so He is mine.

Ev'n so we met, and after long pursuit,
   Ev'n so we joined; we both became entire.
No need for either to renew a suit,
   For I was flax, and He was flames of fire.   10
     Our firm-united souls did more than twine;
So I my best beloved's am; so He is mine.

If all those glitt'ring monarchs that command
   The servile quarters of this earthly ball
Should tender, in exchange, their shares of land,   15
   I would not change my fortunes for them all;
     Their wealth is but a counter to my coin;
The world's but theirs; but my beloved's mine.

Nay more, if the fair Thespian ladies all
   Should heap together their diviner treasure,   20
That treasure should be deemed a price too small
   To buy a minute's lease of half my pleasure.
     'Tis not the sacred wealth of all the Nine
Can buy my heart from Him, or from being mine.

Nor time, nor place, nor chance, nor death, can bow   25
   My least desires unto the least remove;
He's firmly mine by oath, I His by vow;
   He's mine by faith, and I am His by love;
     He's mine by water, I am His by wine;
Thus I my best beloved's am; thus He is mine.   30

He is my altar; I, His holy place;
   I am His guest, and He my living food;
I'm His by penitence, He mine by grace;
   I'm His by purchase, He is mine by blood.
     He's my supporting elm, and I His vine;   35
Thus I my best beloved's am; thus He is mine.

He gives me wealth, I give Him all my vows;
   I give Him songs, He gives me length of days;
With wreaths of grace He crowns my conqu'ring brows,
   And I His temples with a crown of praise;   40
     Which He accepts as an everlasting sign
That I my best beloved's am, that He is mine.

EPIGRAM 3

Sing, Hymen, to my soul: what, lost and found?
Welcomed, espoused, enjoyed so soon and crowned!
He did but climb the cross, and then came down
To th' gates of hell; triumphed, and fetched a crown.

43 *Hymen:* the god of marriage.

Edward Taylor   Sacramental Meditations VIII

JOHN VI.51: I AM THE LIVING BREAD.

I kenning through astronomy divine
   The world's bright battlement, wherein I spy
A golden path my pencil cannot line
   From that bright throne unto my threshold lie.
    And while my puzzled thoughts about it pore,   5
    I find the bread of life in't at my door.

When that this bird of Paradise put in
   This wicker cage (my corpse) to tweedle praise
Had peckt the fruit forbid: and so did fling
   Away its food and lost its golden days,   10
    It fell into celestial famine sore,
    And never could attain a morsel more.

Alas! alas! poor bird, what wilt thou do?
   This creature's field no food for souls e'er gave:
And if thou knock at angels' doors, they show   15
   An empty barrel: they no soul bread have.
    Alas! poor bird, the world's white loaf is done,
    And cannot yield thee here the smallest crumb.

In this sad state, God's tender bowels run
   Out streams of grace: and he to end all strife,   20
The purest wheat in Heaven, his dear-dear Son
   Grinds and kneads up into this bread of life:
    Which bread of life from Heaven down came and stands
    Disht in thy table up by angels' Hands.

Did God mould up this bread in Heaven, and bake,   25
   Which from his table came, and to thine goeth?
Doth he bespeak thee thus: This soul bread take;
   Come, eat thy fill of this, thy God's white loaf?
    It's food too fine for angels; yet come, take
    And eat thy fill! It's Heaven's sugar cake.   30

What grace is this knead in this loaf? This thing
   Souls are but petty things it to admire.
Ye angels, help: this fill would to the brim
   Heaven's whelmed-down crystal meal bowl, yea and higher.
    This bread of life dropt in thy mouth doth cry: 35
    Eat, eat me, soul, and thou shalt never die.

The Nonverbal Poem

Kenneth Patchen

HOW TO BE AN ARMY

 MANY SHOES   POTATOES   FLAGS & FLEAS

 RIFLES   TRENCHES   DETERMINATION

》》》》》》》》》》》》》》》》》
KNOWLEDGE OF MARCHING

$$\frac{58207}{27850} = BLOOD$$

+(GENERALS)

AND A FAITH IN THE RIGHT

† †
† †
† †
† †
† †
† † † † † † † † † † † † † † † † † † † †

Richard Kostelanetz   Tribute to Henry Ford

TRIBUTE TO HENRY FORD 1

TRIBUTE TO HENRY FORD 2

TRIBUTE TO HENRY FORD 3

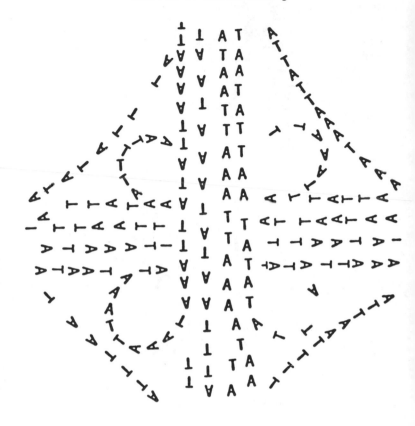

The Concrete Poem

Hansjörg Mayer [Composition]

Pedro Xisto Epithalamium—II

      & = e   S = serpens
     he = êle   h = homo
   she = ela   e = eva

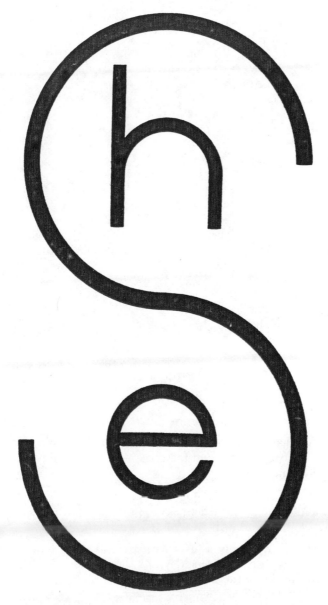

Vito Hannibal Acconci   Re

```
(here) (          ) (        )
(    ) (there) (                          )
(    ) (              ) (here and there—I say here)
(                      ) (I do not say now) (      )
(I do not say it now) (        ) (            )   5
(        ) ( then and there—I say there) (      )
(        ) (            ) (say there)
(        ) (I do not say then) (            )
(I do not say, then, this) (      ) (      )
(                ) (then I say) (        )      10
(      ) (          ) (here and there)
(      ) (first here) (        )
(I said here second) (      ) (        )
(          ) (I do not talk first) (      )
(          ) (          ) (there then)       15
(          ) (here goes) (          )
(I do not say what goes) (      ) (        )
(          ) (I do not go on saying) (      )
(          ) (            ) (there is)
(          ) (That is not to say) (        )      20
(I do not say that) (        ) (        )
(          ) (here below) (          )
(      ) (            ) (I do not talk down)
(          ) (under my words) (          )
(under discussion) (        ) (      )      25
(          ) (all there) (        )
(    ) (      ) (I do not say all)
(          ) (all I say) (      )
```

The Prose Poem

Carl Sandburg   Cool Tombs

When Abraham Lincoln was shoveled into the tombs, he
   forgot the copperheads and the assassin . . . in the dust, in
   the cool tombs.

And Ulysses Grant lost all thought of con men and Wall street,
   cash and collateral turned ashes . . . in the dust, in the cool   5
   tombs.

Pocahontas' body, lovely as a poplar, sweet as a red haw in
   November or a pawpaw in May, did she wonder? does she
   remember? . . . in the dust, in the cool tombs?

Take any streetful of people buying clothes and groceries,   10
   cheering a hero or throwing confetti and blowing tin horns
   . . . tell me if the lovers are losers . . . tell me if any get more
   than the lovers . . . in the dust . . . in the cool tombs.

William Carlos Williams   The Dance

In Breughel's great picture, The Kermess,
the dancers go round, they go round and
around, the squeal and the blare and the
tweedle of bagpipes, a bugle and fiddles
tipping their bellies (round as the thick-   5
sided glasses whose wash they impound)
their hips and their bellies off balance
to turn them. Kicking and rolling about
the Fair Grounds, swinging their butts, those
shanks must be sound to bear up under such   10
rollicking measures, prance as they dance
in Breughel's great picture, The Kermess.

Ted Joans   It Is Time

It is time for the United States to spend money on education so
 that every American would be hipper, *thus no war!*

It is time for the garbage men to treat garbage cans as they treat
 their mothers

It is time for the Union of the Soviet Socialist Republic to raise   5
 the Iron Curtain and let the world dig 'em

It is time for all museums of art to stop charging admission fees

It is time for the electric chair to give birth to an electric couch
 thus enabling the entire family to go together

It is time for Madison Avenue to tell the truth and nothing but   10
 the truth so help them Mr. Clean

It is time for square jivey leaguers to stop saying 'he's sick, she's
 sick, they're sick, sick sick sick'

It is time for the Brooklyn bridge to fall on a boat load of DAR
 fair ladies
                     15

It is time for the races of the world to ball and ball and ball and
 then there will be no reason for war at all

It is time for the Statue of Liberty to be replaced by a Statue of
 Uncle Tom

It is time for the Post Office to employ only the blind to sort   20
 out the mail

It is time for the police headquarters to share their building
 with young nuns

It is time for Steve Allen to be the next president of the United
 States, Dizzy Gillespie Sec of State and Kim Novak   25
 our Minister of Foreign Affairs

It is time for jazz and more jazz and some more jazz and still
    some more jazz

It is time for the American Indians to be made multimillionaires

It is time for the keys to be left in the mail box again   30

It is time for rhinoceroses to roam the streets of Little Rock and
    spread joy

It is time for a moral revolution in America

It is time for the world to love and Love and LOVE

It is time for everybody to swing (Life don't mean a thing if it 35
    don't swing) yes that is right because

It's time it is time to straighten up and fly right tonight

POEMS EMPLOYING DEVICES

The Acrostic

Sir John Davies   Of Astraea

E arly before the day doth spring
L et us awake, my muse, and sing,
I t is no time to slumber;
S o many joys this time doth bring
A s time will fail to number.   5

B ut whereto shall we bend our lays?
E ven up to heaven, again to raise
T he maid which thence descended,
H ath brought again the golden days
A nd all the world amended.   10

R udeness itself she doth refine,
E ven like an alchemist divine,
G ross times of iron turning
I nto the purest form of gold,
N ot to corrupt till heaven wax old,   15
A nd be refined with burning.

Astraea: the goddess of Justice, who fled from Earth at the beginning
of the Bronze Age because of man's evil and greed. Queen Elizabeth
was sometimes called Astraea because of the justice which she
was credited with reinstituting.   *13–14 iron, gold:* referring to
the current corrupt times (the Age of Iron) and to the earliest,
idyllic times (the Age of Gold).

The Echo Poem

Edward Herbert, Lord Cherbury   Echo to a Rock

Thou heaven-threatening rock, gentler than she!
    Since of my pain
  Thou still more sensible wilt be,
Only when thou givest leave but to complain—
                        Echo. Complain.   5
But thou dost answer too, although in vain
  Thou answerest when thou canst no pity show.
                     Echo. Oh.
    What, canst thou speak, and pity too?
    Then yet a further favor do,   10
And tell if of my griefs I any end shall know.
                     Echo. No.
Sure she will pity him that loves her so truly.
                     Echo. You lie.
    Vile rock, thou now growest so unruly,   15
    That hadst thou life as thou hast voice,
      That shouldst die at my foot.
                     Echo. Die at my foot.
    Thou canst not make me do't,
    Unless thou leave it to my choice,   20
    Who thy hard sentence shall fulfill,
When thou shalt say I die to please her only will.
                     Echo. I will.
  When she comes hither, then, I pray thee tell
Thou art my monument, and this my last farewell.   25
                     Echo. Well.

The Pruning Poem

George Herbert   Paradise

I bless thee, Lord, because I GROW
Among thy trees, which in a ROW
To thee both fruit and order OW.

What open force, or hidden CHARM
Can blast my fruit, or bring me HARM
While the inclosure is thine ARM?   5

Inclose me still for fear I START.
Be to me rather sharp and TART,
Than let me want thy hand and ART.

When thou dost greater judgments SPARE,   10
And with thy knife but prune and PARE,
Ev'n fruitful trees more fruitful ARE.

Such sharpness shows the sweetest FREND:
Such cuttings rather heat than REND:
And such beginnings touch their END.   15

PART II

Poetic Conventions: Major Themes

THE PASTORAL

The word "pastoral" is from the Latin word for shepherd, *pastor;* hence, any poem having to do with shepherds may be called a pastoral poem. The pastoral tradition in poetry stems from the writing of the Greek poet Theocritus (third century B.C.), who wrote verse about the life of Sicilian herdsmen, and whose poetry established the three main divisions within the pastoral tradition. The Dialogue, or Eclogue, is a singing-match—a debate—between two shepherds. The Monologue is a poem expressing the complaints of a lovesick shepherd because of the coldness or aloofness of his mistress. The monologue, at times, is used in order to praise some notable person. The third type of pastoral is the Elegy—the praise of a dead shepherd.*

Poets after Theocritus contrast the unspoiled and hence superior nature of rural life to that of the overly civilized life the poet is himself a part of, retaining, very often, the traditional setting in Arcadia, a mountainous area of Greece that was noted for its simple, happy life. But the Christian tradition, adopting elements of the pastoral, sometimes fused the classical tradition

---

* The pastoral elegy is considered in greater detail under The Elegy.

with the Christian, and the shepherd is sometimes seen as the holy man: David and Christ become shepherds.

Pastoral poetry was at its height between 1550 and 1750, despite the fact that a number of pastoral poets employed an artificiality of language, a language that was both courtly and elegant, and which depicted dress more appropriate to the court than to the countryside. By the time of the Romantic Age, however, a new poetic sensibility sought new meanings in nature than those afforded by the pastoral vision, and the pastoral tradition became increasingly less important to English poets, except for the pastoral elements associated with the pastoral elegy.

In our own century, the critic William Empson has suggested that the pastoral mode is a method of literary inversion, a way of "putting the complex into the simple." According to Empson, through a simplification of people and setting, the artist is better able to express complex ideas. Empson expands the traditional notion of the pastoral, and considers, for example, the proletarian novel and even *Alice in Wonderland* to be essentially pastoral.

There are a number of other terms frequently associated with poetry having a rural setting. The word "idyll" (or Idyl), because it served as the title for Theocritus's selection of poetry, has been used to refer to pastoral poetry. This term, however, generally applies to poetry that presents its pastoral elements in a consciously literary manner. The point of view of the idyll is that of the urbane man glancing out his picture window upon the picturesque that lies just beyond. The distinction between the idyll and the pastoral is not clear-cut, and the term is seemingly further confused by its use in Tennyson's *Idylls of the King,* a work which is at times picturesque but seldom pastoral.

The word "bucolic" refers to setting, the rural atmosphere of the pastoral poem; Robert Frost is often referred to as a bucolic poet. The term "georgic" refers to poetry that deals with rural life as a life of labor—that is, it treats more realistically life in the country.

Edmund Spenser

FROM *"The Shepheardes Calender"*

JUNE

ÆGLOGA SEXTA

ARGUMENT

This Æglogue is wholly vowed to the complayning of Colins ill successe in his love. For being (as is aforesaid) enamoured of a country lasse, Rosalind, and having (as seemeth) founde place in her heart, he lamenteth to his deare frend Hobbinoll, that he is nowe forsaken unfaithfully, and in his steede Menalcas, another shepheard, received disloyally. And this is the whole argument of this Æglogue.

HOBBINOL. COLIN CLOUTE.

Hob. Lo, Collin, here the place whose pleasaunt syte
From other shades hath weand my wandring mynde.
Tell me, what wants me here to worke delyte?
The simple ayre, the gentle warbling wynde,
So calme, so coole, as no where else I fynde,   5
The grassye ground with daintye daysies dight,
The bramble bush, where byrds of every kynde
To the waters fall their tunes attemper right.

Col. O happy Hobbinoll! I blesse thy state,
That Paradise hast found, whych Adam lost.   10
Here wander may thy flock, early or late,
Withouten dreade of wolves to bene ytost:
Thy lovely layes here mayst thou freely boste.
But I, unhappy man, whom cruell Fate
And angry gods pursue from coste to coste,   15
Can nowhere fynd to shroude my lucklesse pate.

Hob. Then if by me thou list advised be,
Forsake the soyle that so doth the bewitch;
Leave me those hilles, where harbrough nis to see,
Nor holybush, nor brere, nor winding witche,   20
And to the dales resort, where shepheards ritch,
And fruictfull flocks, bene every where to see.
Here no night ravens lodge, more black then pitche,
Nor elvish ghosts, nor gastly owles doe flee.

But frendly Faeries, met with many Graces,   25
And lightfote Nymphes, can chace the lingring night
With heydeguyes and trimly trodden traces,
Whilst systers nyne, which dwell on Parnasse hight,
Doe make them musick for their more delight;
And Pan himselfe, to kisse their christall faces,   30
Will pype and daunce, when Phœbe shineth bright:
Such pierlesse pleasures have we in these places.

Col. And I, whylst youth and course of carelesse yeeres
Did let me walke withouten lincks of love,
In such delights did joy amongst my peeres: 35
But ryper age such pleasures doth reprove;
My fancye eke from former follies move
To stayed steps: for time in passing weares,
(As garments doen, which wexen old above)
And draweth newe delightes with hoary heares.   40

Tho couth I sing of love, and tune my pype
Unto my plaintive pleas in verses made;
Tho would I seeke for queene apples unrype,
To give my Rosalind, and in sommer shade
Dight gaudy girlonds was my comen trade,   45

To crowne her golden locks; but yeeres more rype,
And losse of her, whose love as lyfe I wayd,
Those weary wanton toyes away dyd wype.

   Hob. Colin, to heare thy rymes and roundelayes,
Which thou were wont on wastefull hylls to singe,   50
I more delight then larke in sommer dayes:
Whose echo made the neyghbour groves to ring,
And taught the byrds, which in the lower spring
Did shroude in shady leaves from sonny rayes,
Frame to thy songe their cherefull cheriping,   55
Or hold theyr peace, for shame of thy swete layes.

I sawe Calliope wyth Muses moe,
Soone as thy oaten pype began to sound,
Theyr yvory luyts and tamburins forgoe,
And from the fountaine, where they sat around,   60
Renne after hastely thy silver sound.
But when they came where thou thy skill didst showe,
They drewe abacke, as halfe with shame confound,
Shepheard to see, them in theyr art outgoe.

   Col. Of Muses, Hobbinol, I conne no skill: 65
For they bene daughters of the hyghest Jove,
And holden scorne of homely shepheards quill.
For sith I heard that Pan with Phœbus strove,
Which him to much rebuke and daunger drove,
I never lyst presume to Parnasse hyll,   70
But, pyping lowe in shade of lowly grove,
I play to please my selfe, all be it ill.

Nought weigh I, who my song doth prayse or blame,
Ne strive to winne renowne, or passe the rest:
With shepheard sittes not followe flying fame,   75
But feede his flocke in fields where falls hem best.
I wote my rymes bene rough, and rudely drest:
The fytter they my carefull case to frame:
Enough is me to paint out my unrest,
And poore my piteous plaints out in the same.   80

The god of shepheards, Tityrus, is dead,
Who taught me, homely as I can, to make.
He, whilst he lived, was the soveraigne head
Of shepheards all that bene with love ytake:

Well couth he wayle his woes, and lightly slake   85
The flames which love within his heart had bredd,
And tell us mery tales, to keepe us wake,
The while our sheepe about us safely fedde.

Nowe dead he is, and lyeth wrapt in lead,
(O why should Death on hym such outrage showe?)   90
And all hys passing skil with him is fledde,
The fame whereof doth dayly greater growe.
But if on me some little drops would flowe
Of that the spring was in his learned hedde,

I soone would learne these woods to wayle my woe,   95
And teache the trees their trickling teares to shedde.

Then should my plaints, causd of discurtesee,
As messengers of all my painfull plight,
Flye to my love, where ever that she bee,
And pierce her heart with poynt of worthy wight,   100
As shee deserves, that wrought so deadly spight.
And thou Menalcas, that by trecheree
Didst underfong my lasse to wexe so light,
Shouldest well be knowne for such thy villanee.

But since I am not as I wish I were,   105
Ye gentle shepheards, which your flocks do feede,
Whether on hylls, or dales, or other where,
Beare witnesse all of thys so wicked deede;
And tell the lasse, whose flowre is woxe a weede,
And faultlesse fayth is turned to faithlesse fere,   100
That she the truest shepheards hart made bleede
That lyves on earth, and loved her most dere.

  Hob. O carefull Colin! I lament thy case:
Thy teares would make the hardest flint to flowe.
Ah, faithlesse Rosalind, and voide of grace,   115
That art the roote of all this ruthfull woe
But now is time, I gesse, homeward to goe:
Then ryse, ye blessed flocks, and home apace,
Least night with stealing steppes doe you forsloe,
And wett your tender lambes that by you trace.   120

COLINS EMBLEME.

Già Speme Spenta.

GLOSSE [Spenser's]

1 syte: situation and place.   *10 Paradise:* A Paradise in Greeke
signifieth a garden of pleasure, or place of delights. So he com-
pareth the soile wherin Hobbinoll made his abode, to that earthly
Paradise, in Scripture called Eden, wherein Adam in his first
creation was placed: which, of the most learned, is thought to be
in Mesopotamia, the most fertile and pleasaunte country in the
world (as may appeare by Diodorus Syculus description of it, in
the hystorie of Alexanders conquest thereof;) lying betweene the
two famous ryvers, (which are sayd in Scriptures to flowe out of
Paradise) Tygris and Euphrates, whereof it is so denominate.
18 Forsake the soyle: This is no poetical fiction, but unfeynedly
spoken of the poete selfe, who for speciall occasion of private
affayres, (as I have bene partly of himselfe informed) and for his
more preferment, removing out of the Northparts, came into the
South, as Hobbinoll indeed advised him privately.   *19 those
hilles:* that is the North countrye, where he dwelt.   *nis:* is
not.   *21 the dales:* the Southpartes, where he nowe abydeth,
which thoughe they be full of hylles and woodes (for Kent is very
hyllye and woodye; and therefore so called: for *Kantsh* in the

Saxons tongue signifieth woodie,) yet in respecte of the North-partes they be called dales. For indede the North is counted the higher countrye.   23 *night ravens,* &c: by such hateful byrdes, hee meaneth all misfortunes (whereof they be tokens) flying every where.   25 *frendly Faeries:* The opinion of faeries and elfes is very old, and yet sticketh very religiously in the myndes of some. But to roote that rancke opinion of elfes oute of mens hearts, the truth is, that there be no such thinges, nor yet the shadowes of the things, but onely by a sort of bald friers and knavish shavelings so feigned; which, as in all other things, so in that, soughte to nousell the comen people in ignoraunce, least, being once ac-quainted with the truth of things, they woulde in tyme smell out the untruth of theyr packed pelfe and massepenie religion. But the sooth is, that when all Italy was distraicte into the factions of the Guelfes and the Gibelins, being two famous houses in Flor-ence, the name began, through their great mischiefes and many outrages, to be so odious, or rather dreadfull, in the peoples eares, that if theyr children at any time were frowarde and wanton, they would say to them that the Guelfe or the Gibeline came. Which words nowe from them (as many thinge els) be come into our usage, and, for Guelfes and Gibelines, we say elfes and goblins. No otherwise then the Frenchmen used to say of that valiaunt captain, the very scourge of Fraunce, the Lord Thalbot, afterward Erle of Shrewsbury; whose noblesse bred such a terrour in the hearts of the French, that oft times even great armies were defaicted and put to flyght at the onely hearing of hys name. In somuch that the French wemen, to affray theyr chyldren, would tell them that the Talbot commeth.   25 *many Graces:* Though there be indeede but three Graces or Charites (as afore is sayd) or at the utmost but foure, yet in respect of many gyftes of bounty, there may be sayde more. And so Musæus sayth, that in Heroes eyther eye there satte a hundred Graces. And by that authoritye, thys same poete, in his Pageaunts, saith 'An hundred Graces on her eye-ledde satte,' &c.   27 *heydeguyes:* a country daunce or rownd. The conceipt is, that the Graces and Nymphes doe daunce unto the Muses and Pan his musicke all night by moonelight. To signifie the pleasauntnesse of the soyle.   35 *peeres:* equalles and felow shepheards.   43 *queene apples unripe:* imitating Vergils verse,
              'Ipse ego cana legam tenera lanugine mala.'
52 *neyghbour groves,* a straunge phrase in English, but word for word expressing the Latine *vicina nemora.*   53 *spring:* not of water, but of young trees springing.   57 *Calliope:* afforesayde. Thys staffe is full of verie poetical invention.   59 *tamburins,* an old kind of instrument, which of some is supposed to be the clarion.   68 *Pan with Phœbus:* The tale is well knowne, howe that Pan and Apollo, striving for excellencye in musicke, chose Midas for their judge. Who, being corrupted wyth partiall affec-tion, gave the victorye to Pan undeserved: for which Phœbus sette a payre of asses eares upon hys head, &c.   81 *Tityrus:* That by Tityrus is meant Chaucer, hath bene already sufficiently sayde, and by thys more playne appeareth, that he sayth, he tolde merye tales. Such as be hys Canterburie Tales. Whom he calleth the god of poetes for hys excellencie, so as Tullie

calleth Lentulus, *Deum vitæ suæ*, sc. the god of hys lyfe.
82 *to make*: to versifie.   90 *O why*: a pretye epanorthosis or cor-
rection.   97 *discurtese*: He meaneth the falsenesse of his lover
Rosalinde, who, forsaking hym, hadde chosen another.   100
poynte of worthy wight: the pricke of deserved blame.   102 *Menalcas*: the name of a shephearde in Virgile; but here is meant a person unknowne and secrete, agaynst whome he often bitterly
invayeth.   103 *underfong*: undermynde and deceive by false
suggestion.   *Colins Embleme*: You remember that in the fyrst
Æglogue, Colins poesie was *Anchora speme*: ["the meaning
whereof is, that notwithstanding his extreme passion and lucklesse
love, yet, leaning on hope, he is somewhat recomforted!"—Spenser]
for that as then there was hope of favour to be found in tyme. But
nowe being cleane forlorne and rejected of her, as whose hope,
that was, is cleane extinguished and turned into despeyre, he re-
nounceth all comfort, and hope of goodnesse to come: which is all
the meaning of thys embleme.

Nicholas Breton   A Pastoral of Phillis and Coridon

On a hill there grows a flower,
  Fair befall the dainty sweet!
By that flower there is a bower
  Where the heavenly Muses meet.

In that bower there is a chair   5
  Fringed all about with gold,
Where doth sit the fairest fair
  That did ever eye behold.

It is Phillis fair and bright,
  She that is the shepherds' joy,   10
She that Venus did despite
  And did blind her little boy.

This is she, the wise, the rich,
  And the world desires to see;
This is *ipsa quae* the which   15
  There is none but only she.

Who would not this face admire?
  Who would not this saint adore?
Who would not this sight desire,
  Though he thought to see no more?   20

O fair eyes, yet let me see!
  One good look, and I am gone,
Look on me, for I am he—
  Thy poor silly Coridon.

Thou that art the shepherd's queen,   25
  Look upon thy silly swain;

By thy comfort have been seen
   Dead men brought to life again.

15 *ipsa quae:* she herself.

Christopher Marlowe   The Passionate Shepherd
   to His Love

Come live with me and be my love,
And we will all the pleasures prove
That hills and valleys, dales and fields
Woods, or steepy mountain yields.

And we will sit upon the rocks,   5
Seeing the shepherds feed their flocks,
By shallow rivers, to whose falls
Melodious birds sing madrigals.

And I will make thee beds of roses
And a thousand fragrant posies;   10
A cap of flowers, and a kirtle
Embroidered all with leaves of myrtle;

A gown made of the finest wool
Which from our pretty lambs we pull;
Fair lined slippers for the cold,   15
With buckles of the purest gold;

A belt of straw and ivy buds,
With coral clasps and amber studs:
And if these pleasures may thee move,
Come live with me, and be my love.   20

The shepherd swains shall dance and sing
For thy delight each May morning:
If these delights thy mind may move,
Then live with me and be my love.

Robert Herrick   The Wake

Come Anthea, let us two
Go to feast as others do;
Tarts and custards, creams and cakes,
Are the junkets still at wakes,
Unto which the tribes resort,   5
Where the business is the sport;
Morris-dancers thou shalt see,
Marian too in pageantry,
And a mimic to devise
Many grinning properties.   10
Players there will be, and those

Base in action as in clothes;
Yet with strutting they will please
The incurious villages.
Near the dying of the day   *15*
There will be a cudgel-play,
Where a coxcomb will be broke
Ere a good word can be spoke;
But the anger ends all here,
Drenched in ale, or drowned in beer.   *20*
Happy rustics, best content
With the cheapest merriment,
And possess no other fear
Than to want the wake next year.

Andrew Marvell   Clorinda and Damon

C. Damon, come drive thy flocks this way.
D. No, 'tis too late, they went astray.
C. I have a grassy scutcheon spied,
 Where Flora blazons all her pride;
 The grass I aim to feast thy sheep,   *5*
 The flowers I for thy temples keep.
D. Grass withers and the flowers too fade.
C. Seize the short joys then, ere they vade.
 See'st thou that unfrequented cave?
D. That den? C. Love's shrine. D. But virtue's grave.   *10*
C. In whose cool bosom we may lie
 Safe from the sun. D. Not heaven's eye.
C. Near this a fountain's liquid bell
 Tinkles within the concave shell.
D. Might a soul bathe there and be clean,   *15*
 Or slake its drought? C. What is't you mean?
D. These once had been enticing things,
 Clorinda, pastures, caves, and springs.
C. And what late change? D. The other day
 Pan met me. C. What did Great Pan say?   *20*
D. Words that transcend poor shepherd's skill,
 But he e'er since my songs does fill,
 And his name swells my slender oat.
C. Sweet must Pan sound in Damon's note.
D. Clorinda's voice might make it sweet.   *25*
C. Who would not in Pan's praises meet?

 CHORUS

Of Pan the flow'ry pastures sing,
Caves echo, and the fountains ring;
Sing then while he doth us inspire,
For all the world is our Pan's choir.   *30*

8 *vade*: fade, wither.   20 *Pan*: Christ.

Alexander Pope   Winter

THE FOURTH PASTORAL, OR DAPHNE
TO THE MEMORY OF MRS. TEMPEST

LYCIDAS

Thyrsis, the music of that murmuring spring,
Is not so mournful as the strains you sing.
Nor rivers winding through the vales below,
So sweetly warble, or so smoothly flow.
Now sleeping flocks on their soft fleeces lie,   5
The moon, serene in glory, mounts the sky,
While silent birds forget their tuneful lays,
Oh sing of Daphne's fate, and Daphne's praise!

THYRSIS

Behold the groves that shine with silver frost,
Their beauty withered, and their verdure lost.   10
Here shall I try the sweet Alexis' strain,
That called the listening Dryads to the plain?
Thames heard the numbers as he flowed along,
And bade his willows learn the moving song.

LYCIDAS

So may kind rains their vital moisture yield,   15
And swell the future harvest of the field.
Begin; this charge the dying Daphne gave,
And said: "Ye shepherds, sing around my grave!
Sing, while beside the shaded tomb I mourn,
And with fresh bays her rural shrine adorn."   20

THYRSIS

Ye gentle Muses, leave your crystal spring,
Let Nymphs and Sylvans cypress garlands bring;
Ye weeping Loves, the stream with myrtles hide,
And break your bows, as when Adonis died;
And with your golden darts, now useless grown,   25
Inscribe a verse on this relenting stone:
"Let nature change, let heaven and earth deplore,
Fair Daphne's dead, and love is now no more!"
'Tis done, and nature's various charms decay,
See gloomy clouds obscure the cheerful day!   30
Now hung with pearls the dropping trees appear,
Their faded honours scattered on her bier.
See, where on earth the flowery glories lie,
With her they flourished, and with her they die.
Ah what avail the beauties nature wore?   35
Fair Daphne's dead, and beauty is no more!
For her the flocks refuse their verdant food,
Nor thirsty heifers seek the gliding flood.

The silver swans her hapless fate bemoan,
In notes more sad than when they sing their own;   40
In hollow caves sweet Echo silent lies,
Silent, or only to her name replies;
Her name with pleasure once she taught the shore,
Now Daphne's dead, and pleasure is no more!
    No grateful dews descend from evening skies,   45
Nor morning odours from the flowers arise;
No rich perfumes refresh the fruitful field,
Nor fragrant herbs their native incense yield.
The balmy Zephyrs, silent since her death,
Lament the ceasing of a sweeter breath;   50
Th' industrious bees neglect their golden store!
Fair Daphne's dead, and sweetness is no more!
    No more the mounting larks, while Daphne sings,
Shall listening in mid air suspend their wings;
No more the birds shall imitate her lays,   55
Or hushed with wonder, hearken from the sprays:
No more the streams their murmur shall forbear,
A sweeter music than their own to hear,
But tell the reeds, and tell the vocal shore,
Fair Daphne's dead, and music is no more!   60
    Her fate is whispered by the gentle breeze,
And told in sighs to all the trembling trees;
The trembling trees, in every plain and wood,
Her fate remurmur to the silver flood;
The silver flood, so lately calm, appears   65
Swelled with new passion, and o'erflows with tears;
The winds and trees and floods her death deplore,
Daphne, our grief! our glory now no more!
    But see! where Daphne wondering mounts on high
Above the clouds, above the starry sky   70
Eternal beauties grace the shining scene,
Fields ever fresh, and groves for ever green!
There while you rest in Amaranthine bowers,
Or from those meads select unfading flowers,
Behold us kindly, who your name implore,   75
Daphne, our Goddess, and our grief no more!

LYCIDAS

    How all things listen, while thy Muse complains!
Such silence waits on Philomela's strains,
In some still evening, when the whispering breeze
Pants on the leaves, and dies upon the trees.   80
To thee, bright goddess, oft a lamb shall bleed,
If teeming ewes increase my fleecy breed.
While plants their shade, or flowers their odours give,
Thy name, thy honour, and thy praise shall live!

THYRSIS

    But see, Orion sheds unwholesome dews,   85
Arise, the pines a noxious shade diffuse;

Sharp Boreas blows, and Nature feels decay,
Time conquers all, and we must Time obey.
Adieu, ye vales, ye mountains, streams and groves,
Adieu, ye shepherd's rural lays and loves;   90
Adieu, my flocks, farewell ye sylvan crew,
Daphne, farewell, and all the world adieu!

title: This Lady was of an ancient family in Yorkshire, and particularly admired by the Author's friend Mr. Walsh, who, having celebrated her in a Pastoral Elegy, desired his friend to do the same, as
appears from one of his letters, dated September 9, 1706: "Your
last Eclogue being on the same subject with mine on Mrs.
Tempest's death, I should take it very kindly in you to give it a
little turn as if it were to the memory of the same lady." Her death
having happened on the night of the great storm in 1703, gave a
propriety to this eclogue, which in its general turn alludes to it.
The scene of the Pastoral lies in a grove, the time at midnight.
[Pope's note.]   89–92 These four last lines allude to the several
subjects of the four Pastorals, and to the several scenes of them,
particularized before in each. [Pope's note.]

Louis Simpson   The Green Shepherd

Here sit a shepherd and a shepherdess,
He playing on his melancholy flute;
The sea wind ruffles up her simple dress
And shows the delicacy of her foot.

And there you see Constantinople's wall   5
With arrows and Greek fire, molten lead;
Down from a turret seven virgins fall,
Hands folded, each one praying on her head.

The shepherd yawns and puts his flute away.
It's time, she murmurs, we were going back.   10
He offers certain reasons she should stay—
But neither sees the dragon on their track.

A dragon like a car in a garage
Is in the wood, his long tail sticking out.
Here rides St. George, swinging his sword and targe,   15
And sticks the grinning dragon in the snout.

Puffing a smoke ring, like the cigarette
Over Times Square, Sir Dragon snorts his last.
St. George takes off his armor in a sweat.
The Middle Ages have been safely passed.   20

What is the sail that crosses the still bay,
Unnoticed by the shepherds? It could be
A caravel that's sailing to Cathay,
Westward from Palos on the unknown sea.

But the green shepherd travels in her eye   25
And whispers nothings in his lady's ear,

And sings a little song, that roses die,
Carpe diem, which she seems pleased to hear.

The vessel they ignored still sails away
So bravely on the water, Westward Ho!   30
And murdering, in a religious way,
Brings Jesus to the Gulf of Mexico.

Now Portugal is fading, and the state
Of Castile rising purple on Peru;
Now England, now America grows great—   35
With which these lovers have nothing to do.

What do they care if time, uncompassed, drift
To China, and the crew is a baboon?
But let him whisper always, and her lift
The oceans in her eyelids to the moon.   40

The dragon rises crackling in the air,
And who is god but Dagon? Wings careen,
Rejoicing, on the Russian hemisphere.
Meanwhile, the shepherd dotes upon her skin.

Old Aristotle, having seen this pass,   45
From where he studied in the giant's cave,
Went in and shut his book and locked the brass
And lay down with a shudder in his grave.

The groaning pole had gone more than a mile;
These shepherds did not feel it where they loved.   50
For time was sympathetic all the while
And on the magic mountain nothing moved.

15 *targe:* an archaic word for shield or buckler.   28 *Carpe diem:*
"Seize the day."

Robert Hillyer   Pastorals

2

So soft in the hemlock wood
The phoenix sang his lullaby,
Shepherds drowsed where they stood,
Slumber felled each passerby,
And lovers at their first caress   5
Slept in virgin loneliness.

Nor for mortal eye to see
Naked life arise from embers;
Only the dark hemlock tree,
Evergreen itself, remembers   10
How the Word came into being,
No man hearing, no man seeing.

From the taut bow of sleep
Shoots the phoenix toward the day,

Shepherds wake and call their sheep,   15
Wanderers go on their way.
Unaware how death went by,
Lovers under the hemlocks lie.

THE ELEGY

In Greek and Latin verse, an elegy was a poem in alternate
lines of dactylic hexameters and dactylic pentameters—the
elegaic meter (see Glossary). The term "elegy" in post-Roman
poetry came to denote either a melancholy formal poem, a
lament, or a poem of grave meditation. Sustained and formal,
the meditation was often occasioned by the death of a particular
person; by contrast, the earlier Greek and Latin elegies concerned themselves with the subjects of death, love, or war.

In the Middle Ages and during the Renaissance, the term
"elegy" referred to long songs, and Elizabethan poets frequently
used the term to denote love poems (there was a precedent in
Ovid and Catullus for this). These love poems, however, are
often of the "complaint" type (see Index). Since the sixteenth
century, the term has generally been used to describe poetry
about death, though Thomas Gray's "Elegy Written in a
Country Churchyard" is not about a particular death so much
as it is a generalized reflection upon the unfulfilled lives of
ordinary people buried in the graveyard. The contemporary
poetry of Rainer Maria Rilke's *Duino Elegies* (originally
in German) serves as a reminder that the elegy need not necessarily deal with the subject of the death of a friend or important person.

Terms also associated with wailing and death in poetry are
the "coronach," the "monody," the "dirge," and the "threnody."
These types, however, are wailing songs, originally meant to be
sung at a funeral or in the commemoration of a death; they are
distinguished, usually, from the elegy in that they are shorter,
more lyrical and poignant, and less meditative than the elegy.
A monody is a mourning poem, sung by one singer, and
Milton refers to "Lycidas" as a monody.

The elegy, even when it does concern itself with death, is
more than an outpouring of personal grief. Generalizing from
a particular death, the writer of the elegy concludes with a
reflection on the meaning of death and life. The tone of an
elegy is serious; the level of diction, the syntax, and the style
are then suited to this mood. The movement of the poem is
from great sadness to a sense of consolation and the acceptance
of death and the loss of the particular person whose death
seemingly initiated the poem. The elegy, like mourning, is a
consolation for the surviving.

The Love Elegy

John Donne   The Anagram

Marry and love thy Flavia, for she
Hath all things whereby others beauteous be;
For though her eyes be small, her mouth is great,
Though they be ivory, yet her teeth be jet,
Though they be dim, yet she is light enough,   5
And though her harsh hair fall, her skin is rough;
What though her cheeks be yellow, her hair's red;
Give her thine, and she hath a maidenhead.
These things are beauty's elements; where these
Meet in one, that one must, as perfect, please.   10
If red and white and each good quality
Be in thy wench, ne'er ask where it doth lie.
In buying things perfumed we ask if there
Be musk and amber in it, but not where.
Though all her parts be not in the usual place,   15
She hath yet an anagram of a good face.
If we might put the letters but one way,
In the lean dearth of words, what could we say?
When by the gamut some musicians make
A perfect song, others will undertake   20
By the same gamut changed, to equal it.
Things simply good can never be unfit.
She's fair as any if all be like her,
And if none be, then she is singular.
All love is wonder; if we justly do   25
Account her wonderful, why not lovely too?
Love built on beauty, soon as beauty, dies;
Choose this face, changed by no deformities.
Women are all like angels: the fair be
Like those which fell to worse; but such as she,   30
Like to good angels, nothing can impair;
'Tis less grief to be foul than to have been fair.
For one night's revels silk and gold we choose,
But in long journeys cloth and leather use.
Beauty is barren oft; best husbands say   35
There is best land where there is foulest way.
O what a sovereign plaster will she be
If thy past sins have taught thee jealousy!
Here needs no spies nor eunuchs; her commit
Safe to thy foes, yea to a marmosit.   40
When Belgia's cities the round countries drown,
That dirty foulness guards and arms the town;
So doth her face guard her; and so for thee,
Which, forced by business, absent oft must be,
She, whose face, like clouds, turns the day to night,   45
Who, mightier than the sea, makes Moors seem white,
Who, though seven years she in the stews had laid,

A nunnery durst receive and think a maid,
And though in childbed's labor she did lie,
Midwives would swear 'twere but a tympany,   50
Whom if she accuse herself I credit less
Than witches which impossibles confess,
Whom dildoes, bedstaves, and her velvet glass
Would be as loath to touch as Joseph was;
One like none, and liked of none, fittest were,   55
For things in fashion every man will wear.

5 *they*: her eyes.   8 *thine*: hair; sexual organ (head).   14
amber: ambergris   16 *anagram*: that is, the parts of her face can
be rearranged into a good face.   19 *gamut*: octave of notes.   22
unfit: also, taken apart.   35 *husbands*: farmers.   40 *marmosit*:
an ugly little fellow.   41 *When*: until.   *round*: not flat (the
Lowlands); surrounding (Spain and France).   41–42 Referring to
the hostilities between the Lowlands and Spain toward the end of
the sixteenth century.   42 *foulness*: referring to the canals of the
Lowlands, filled with sewage.   47 *stews*: brothels.   50 *tympany*: swelling. 53 *dildoes*: phalluses.   *velvet glass*: mirror with a
velvet backing. 54 *Joseph*: he refused to sleep with his master Poti-
phar's wife (Gen. xxxix. 7–20).

Henry King   The Exequy. To His Matchless Never to Be Forgotten Friend

Accept thou Shrine of my dead Saint,
Instead of Dirges this complaint;
And for sweet flowers to crown thy hearse,
Receive a strew of weeping verse
From thy griev'd friend, whom thou might'st see   5
Quite melted into tears for thee.

　　Dear loss! since thy untimely fate
My task hath been to meditate
On thee, on thee: thou art the book,
The library whereon I look   10
Though almost blind. For thee (lov'd clay)
I languish out, not live, the day,
Using no other exercise
But what I practise with mine eyes:
By which wet glasses I find out   15
How lazily time creeps about
To one that mourns: this, only this
My exercise and business is:
So I compute the weary hours
With sighs dissolved into showers.   20

　　Nor wonder if my time go thus
Backward and most preposterous;
Thou hast benighted me, thy set
This Eve of blackness did beget,

Who was't my day, though overcast   25
Before thou had'st thy Noon-tide past;
And I remember must in tears,
Thou scarce had'st seen so many years
As Day tells houres. By the clear Sun
My love and fortune first did run;   30
But thou wilt never more appear
Folded within my hemisphere,
Since both thy light and motion
Like a fled Star is fall'n and gone;
And twixt me and my soul's dear wish   35
The earth now interposed is,
Which such a strange eclipse doth make
As ne'er was read in almanac.

 I could allow thee for a time
To darken me and my sad clime,   40
Were it a month, a year, or ten,
I would thy exile live till then;
And all that space my mirth adjourn,
So thou wouldst promise to return;
And putting off thy ashy shroud   45
At length disperse this sorrow's cloud.

 But woe is me! the longest date
Too narrow is to calculate
These empty hopes: never shall I
Be so much blest as to descry   50
A glimpse of thee, till that day come
Which shall the earth to cinders doom,
And a fierce fever must calcine
The body of this world like tine,
My little world! That fit of fire   55
Once off, our bodies shall aspire
To our souls' bliss: then we shall rise,
And view our selves with clearer eyes
In that calm Region, where no night
Can hide us from each others sight.   60

 Meantime, thou hast her, earth; much good
May my harm do thee. Since it stood
With Heavens will I might not call
Her longer mine, I give thee all
My short-lived right and interest   65
In her whom living I lov'd best;
With a most free and bounteous grief,
I give thee what I could not keep.
Be kind to her, and prithee look
Thou write into thy doomsday book   70
Each parcel of this Rarity
Which in thy Casket shrin'd doth lie:
See that thou make thy reck'ning straight,
And yield her back again by weight;
For thou must audit on thy trust   75

Each grain and atom of this dust,
As thou wilt answer Him that lent,
Not give thee, my dear monument
So close the ground, and 'bout her shade
Black curtains draw, my bride is laid.   80

   Sleep on my Love in thy cold bed
Never to be disquieted!
My last good night! Thou wilt not wake
Till age, or grief, or sickness must
Marry my body to that dust   85
It so much loves; and fill the room
My heart keeps empty in thy Tomb.
Stay for me there, I will not fail
To meet thee in that hollow vale.
And think not much of my delay;   90
I am already on the way,
And follow thee with all the speed
Desire can make, or sorrows breed.
Each minute is a short degree,
And ev'ry hour a step towards thee.   95
At night when I betake to rest,
Next morn I rise nearer my West
Of life, almost by eight hours sail,
Then when sleep breath'd his drowsy gale.

   Thus from the Sun my Bottom steers,   100
And my day's Compass downward bears;
Nor labour I to stem the tide
Through which to thee I swiftly glide.

   'Tis true, with shame and grief I yield,
Thou like the vans first tookst the field,   105
And gotten hath the victory
In thus adventuring to die
Before me, whose more years might crave
A just precedence in the grave.
But hark! my pulse like a soft Drum   110
Beats my approach, tell thee I come;
And slow howe'er my marches be,
I shall at last sit down by thee.

   The thought of this bids me go on,
And wait my dissolution   115
With hope and comfort. Dear, forgive
The crime, I am content to live
Divided, with but half a heart,
Till we shall meet and never part.

title: the "Matchless . . . Friend" of the title is Anne, the author's
first wife, who died about 1624.   105 *van:* an abbreviation of
"vanguard," the foremost position.

The Pastoral Elegy

The pastoral elegy, a subtype of the elegy, was popular in English from about the time of the Renaissance and had its origin with the Greek poets Theocritus, Bion, and Moschus. Written in a dignified, serious language, and expressing grief at the loss of an important person or of a friend, it is an elegy that employs conventional pastoral imagery.

The usual divisions within the pastoral elegy are the invocation of the muse; an expression of the anguish caused by the loss of a friend; a solemn procession of mourners; a digression—usually upon a subject of topical interest, such as the abuses of the church in Milton's "Lycidas"; a consolation which involves the poet's submission to the inevitable fact of death; and an acceptance of that death and its meaning.

In addition, other conventions that are often present in pastoral elegies are the presence of the poet as a shepherd, praise of the dead person as a "shepherd," an expression of deeply felt grief and an inability to comprehend why Nature or the Gods allowed the death to take place, the use of much flower imagery and symbolism and an expression of belief in some form of immortality toward the conclusion of the poem. The use of a refrain and rhetorical questions is not-uncommon. In addition to those pastoral elegies reprinted in this section of the anthology, Shelley's "Adonais," and Matthew Arnold's "Thyrsis" are among the longer and best-known examples of pastoral elegies. The "November" Eclogue of Edmund Spenser's *The Shepheardes Calender* is a shorter example of the type, and it uses many of the conventions already mentioned.

John Milton   Lycidas

*In this monody the author bewails a
learned friend, unfortunately drowned in
his passage from Chester on the Irish Seas,
1637. And by occasion foretells the ruin of
our corrupted clergy then in their height.*

Yet once more, O ye laurels, and once more
Ye myrtles brown, with ivy never-sear,
I come to pluck your berries harsh and crude,
And with forced fingers rude,
Shatter your leaves before the mellowing year.   5
Bitter constraint, and sad occasion dear,
Compels me to disturb your season due:
For *Lycidas* is dead, dead ere his prime
Young *Lycidas,* and hath not left his peer:
Who would not sing for *Lycidas?* he knew   10
Himself to sing, and build the lofty rhyme.

He must not float upon his watery bier
Unwept, and welter to the parching wind,
Without the meed of some melodious tear.
  Begin then, sisters of the sacred well,   15
That from beneath the seat of *Jove* doth spring,
Begin, and somewhat loudly sweep the string.
Hence with denial vain, and coy excuse,
So may some gentle muse
With lucky words favor my destin'd urn,   20
And as he passes turn,
And bid fair peace be to my sable shroud.
For we were nursed upon the self-same hill,
Fed the same flock, by fountain, shade, and rill.
  Together both, ere the high lawns appeared   25
Under the opening eyelids of the morn,
We drove afield, and both together heard
What time the gray-fly winds her sultry horn,
Battening our flocks with the fresh dews of night.
Oft till the star that rose, at evening, bright   30
Toward heaven's descent had sloped his westering wheel.
Meanwhile the rural ditties were not mute,
Tempered to the'oaten flute,
Rough *satyrs* danced, and *fauns* with cloven heel,
From the glad sound would not be absent long,   35
And old *Damœtas* loved to hear our song.
  But O the heavy change, now thou art gone,
Now thou art gone, and never must return!
Thee shepherd, thee the woods, and desert caves,
With wild thyme and the gadding vine o'ergrown,   40
And all their echoes mourn.
The willows, and the hazel copses green,
Shall now no more be seen,
Fanning their joyous leaves to thy soft lays.
As killing as the canker to the rose,   45
Or taint-worm to the weanling herds that graze,
Or frost to flowers, that their gay wardrop wear,
When first the white thorn blows;
Such, *Lycidas,* thy loss to shepherds' ear.
  Where were ye, Nymphs, when the remorseless deep 50
Closed o'er the head of your loved *Lycidas?*
For neither were ye playing on the steep,
Where your old *Bards,* the famous *Druids* lie,
Nor on the shaggy top of *Mona* high,
Nor yet where *Deva* spreads her wizard stream: 55
Ay me, I fondly dream!
Had you been there—for what could that have done?
What could the Muse herself that *Orpheus* bore,
The Muse herself, for her enchanting son
Whom universal nature did lament,   60
When by the rout that made the hideous roar,
His goary visage down the stream was sent,
Down the swift *Hebrus* to the *Lesbian* shore.
  Alas! What boots it with incessant care

To tend the homely slighted shepherd's trade,   65
And strictly meditate the thankless muse,
Were it not better done as others use,
To sport with *Amaryllis* in the shade,
Or with the tangles of *Neæra's* hair?
Fame is the spur that the clear spirit doth raise   70
(That last infirmity of noble mind)
To scorn delights, and live laboriously days;
But the fair guerdon when we hope to find,
And think to burst out into sudden blaze,
Comes the blind *Fury* with th'abhorred shears,   75
And slits the thin-spun life. But not the praise,
Phœbus repli'd, and touched my trembling ears;
Fame is no plant that grows on mortal soil,
Nor in the glistering foil
Set off to th'world, nor in broad rumor lies,   80
But lives and spreads aloft by those pure eyes,
And perfect witness of all–judging *Jove;*
As he pronounces lastly on each deed,
Of so much fame in Heaven expect thy meed.

    O Fountain *Arethuse,* and thou honored flood,   85
Smooth-sliding *Mincius,* crowned with vocal reeds
The strain I heard was of a higher mood:
But now my oat proceeds,
And listens to the herald of the sea
That came in *Neptune's* plea,   90
He asked the waves, and asked the felon winds,
What hard mishap hath doomed this gentle swain?
And questioned every gust of rugged wings
That blows from off each beaked promontory.
They knew not of his story,   95
And sage *Hippotades* their answer brings,
That not a blast was from his dungeon strayed,
The air was calm, and on the level brine,
Sleek *Panope* with all her sisters played.
It was that fatal and perfidious bark   100
Built in the'eclipse, and rigged with curses dark,
That sunk so low that sacred head of thine.

    Next *Camus,* reverend sire, went footing slow,
His mantle hairy, and his bonnet sedge,
Inwrought with figures dim, and on the edge   105
Like to that sanguine flower inscribed with woe.
Ah! Who hath reft (quoth he) my dearest pledge?
Last came, and last did go,
The Pilot of the *Galilean* lake,
Two massy keys he bore of metals twain,   110
(The golden opes, the iron shuts amain)
He shook his mitered locks, and stern bespake,
How well could I have spared for thee young swain,
Anow of such as for their bellies' sake,
Creep and intrude, and climb into the fold?   115
Of other care they little reckoning make,
Then how to scramble at the shearers' feast,

And shove away the worthy bidden guest.
Blind mouths! that scarce themselves know how to hold
A sheephook, or have learned ought else the least   120
That to the faithful herdman's art belongs!
What recks it them? What need they? They are sped;
And when they list, their lean and flashy songs
Grate on their scrannel pipes of wretched straw,
The hungry sheep look up, and are not fed,   125
But swol'n with wind, and the rank mist they draw,
Rot inwardly, and foul contagion spread:
Besides what the grim wolf with privy paw
Daily devours apace, and nothing said,
But that two-handed engine at the door,   130
Stands ready to smite once, and smite no more.
    Return *Alpheus*, the dread voice is past,
That shrunk thy streams; return *Sicilian* muse,
And call the vales, and bid them hither cast
Their bells, and flowerets of a thousand hues.   135
Ye valleys low where the mild whispers use,
Of shades and wanton winds, and gushing brooks,
On whose fresh lap the swart star sparely looks,
Throw hither all your quaint enameled eyes,
That on the green turf suck the honeyed showers,   140
And purple all the ground with vernal flowers.
Bring the rathe primrose that forsaken dies.
The tufted crow-toe, and pale gessamine,
The white pink, and the pansy freaked with jet,
The glowing violet.   145
The musk-rose, and the well attired woodbine,
With cowslips wan that hang the pensive head,
And every flower that sad embroidery wears:
Bid *Amaranthus* all his beauty shed,
And daffadillies fill their cups with tears,   150
To strew the laureate hearse where *Lycid'* lies.
For so to interpose a little ease,
Let our frail thoughts dally with false surmise,
Ay me! whilst thee the shores, and sounding seas
Wash far away, where e'er thy bones are hurled,   155
Whether beyond the stormy *Hebrides*,
Where thou perhaps under the whelming tide
Visit'st the bottom of the monstrous world;
Or whether thou to our moist vows denied,
Sleep'st by the fable of *Bellerus* old,   160
Where the great vision of the guarded mount
Looks toward *Namancos* and *Bayona's* hold;
Look homeward, angel, now, and melt with ruth.
And, O ye dolphins, waft the hapless youth.
    Weep no more, woeful shepherds weep no more,   165
For *Lycidas* your sorrow is not dead,
Sunk though he be beneath the watery floor,
So sinks the day-star in the ocean bed,
And yet anon repairs his drooping head,
And tricks his beams, and with new–spangled ore,   170

Flames in the forehead of the morning sky:
So *Lycidas* sunk low, but mounted high,
Through the dear might of him that walked the waves
Where other groves, and other streams along,
With nectar pure his oozy locks he laves,   *175*
And hears the unexpressive nuptial song,
In the blest kingdoms meek of joy and love.
There entertain him all the saints above,
In solemn troops, and sweet societies
That sing, and singing in their glory move,   *180*
And wipe the tears for ever from his eyes.
Now *Lycidas* the shepherds weep no more;
Henceforth thou art the genius of the shore
In thy large recompense, and shalt be good
To all that wander in that perilous flood.   *185*
　　Thus sang the uncouth swain to th'oaks and rills,
While the still morn went out with sandals gray,
He touched the tender stops of various quills,
With eager thought warbling his *Doric* lay:
And now the sun had stretched out all the hills,   *190*
And now was dropt into the western bay;
At last he rose, and twitched his mantle blue:
Tomorrow to fresh woods, and pastures new.

title: The name Lycidas occurs in the *Idyll* of Theocritus. The
"learned friend" referred to in Milton's note was Edward King of
Christ's College, Cambridge.　　*5:* Milton was forced to break his
resolve not to write until he felt his poetic powers were matured.
15 sisters: Muses of the Pierian spring.　　*29 Battening:* feeding.
30 the star . . . bright: Hesperus, which appears at evening.　　*36
Damoetas:* a conventional pastoral name.　　*53–56:* These names
refer to places near the scene where King's shipwreck occurred.
56 fondly: foolishly.　　*58 Muse:* Calliope, the Muse of eloquence
and epic poetry. Orpheus, the "enchanting son," was torn to pieces
by Thracian women; his head was thrown into the river Hebrus.
75 Fury: Atropos, a Fate.　　*79 foil:* a setting for a gem.　　*88 oat:*
a shepherd's pipe.　　*96 Hippotades:* Aeolus, god of winds.　　*99
Panope:* one of the Nereids or sea nymphs.　　*103 Camus:* the
god of the Cam, the river at Cambridge.　　*106 flower . . . woe:*
the hyacinth.　　*107 reft . . . pledge:* bereaved me of my dearest
child.　　*109 Pilot of the Galilean lake:* St. Peter.　　*111 amain:*
with force.　　*122 recks:* concerns.　　*sped:* provided for.　　*124
scrannel:* thin.　　*132 Alpheus:* river of Arcadia.　　*138 swart
star:* the dog-star, supposed to be injurious to plants.　　*142 rathe:*
early.　　*144 freaked:* sprinkled.　　*160 Bellerus:* Land's End.
161 mount: St. Michael's Mount, near Land's End.　　*162 Namancos:* an ancient town in Spain opposite St. Michael's Mount
and near the Spanish castle of Bayona.　　*163 angel:* St. Michael,
probably, who is urged to turn his gaze from Spain to England.
164 dolphins . . . youth: alludes to the Greek legend of the rescue
of the bard Arion by dolphins.　　*170 tricks:* dresses, adorns.
176 unexpressive: inexpressible.　　*188 quills:* reeds in his pastoral
pipe.　　*189 Doric lay:* pastoral poetry.　　*192 twitched:* pulled
about him.

Alexander Pope   Elegy to the Memory of an
    Unfortunate Lady
    1717

What beckoning ghost, along the moonlight shade
Invites my steps, and points to yonder glade?
'Tis she!—but why that bleeding bosom gored,
Why dimly gleams the visionary sword?
Oh ever beauteous, ever friendly! tell,   5
Is it, in heaven, a crime to love too well?
To bear too tender, or too firm a heart,
To act a Lover's or a Roman's part?
Is there no bright reversion in the sky,
For those who greatly think, or bravely die?   10
    Why bade ye else, ye Powers! her soul aspire
Above the vulgar flight of low desire?
Ambition first sprung from your blest abodes;
The glorious fault of Angels and of Gods:
Thence to their images on earth it flows,
And in the breasts of Kings and Heroes glows.   20
Most souls, 'tis true, but peep out once an age,
Dull sullen prisoners in the body's cage:
Dim lights of life, that burn a length of years
Useless, unseen, as lamps in sepulchres;
Like Eastern Kings a lazy state they keep,   25
And close confined to their own palace, sleep.
    From these perhaps (ere nature bade her die)
Fate snatched her early to the pitying sky.
As into air the purer spirits flow,
And separate from their kindred dregs below;   30
So flew the soul to its congenial place,
Nor left one virtue to redeem her Race.
    But thou, false guardian of a charge too good,
Thou, mean deserter of thy brother's blood!
See on these ruby lips the trembling breath,   35
These cheeks, now fading at the blast of death;
Cold is that breast which warmed the world before,
And those love-darting eyes must roll no more.
Thus, if Eternal justice rules the ball,
Thus shall your wives, and thus your children fall: 40
On all the line a sudden vengeance waits,
And frequent hearses shall besiege your gates.
There passengers shall stand, and pointing say,
(While the long funerals blacken all the way)
Lo these were they, whose souls the Furies steeled,   45
And cursed with hearts unknowing how to yield.
Thus unlamented pass the proud away,
The gaze of fools, and pageant of a day!
So perish all, whose breast ne'er learned to glow
For others' good, or melt at others' woe.   50

What can atone (oh ever-injured shade!)
Thy fate unpitied, and thy rites unpaid?
No friend's complaint, no kind domestic tear
Pleased thy pale ghost, or graced thy mournful bier.
By foreign hands thy dying eyes were closed,   55
By foreign hands decent limbs composed,
By foreign hands thy humble grave adorned,
By strangers honoured, and by strangers mourned!
What though no friends in sable weeds appear,
Grieve for an hour, perhaps, then mourn a year,   60
And bear about the mockery of woe
To midnight dances, and the public show?
What though no weeping Loves thy ashes grace,
Nor polished marble emulate thy face?
What though no sacred earth allow thee room,   65
Nor hallowed dirge be muttered o'er thy tomb?
Yet shall thy grave with rising flowers be drest,
And the green turf lie lightly on thy breast:
There shall the morn her earliest tears bestow,
There the first roses of the year shall blow;   70
While Angels with their silver wings o'ershade
The ground, now sacred by thy reliques made.
   So peaceful rests, without a stone, a name,
What once had beauty, titles, wealth, and fame.
How loved, how honoured once, avails thee not,   75
To whom related, or by whom begot;
A heap of dust alone remains of thee,
'Tis all thou art, and all the proud shall be!
   Poets themselves must fall, like those they sung,
Deaf the praised ear, and mute the tuneful tongue.   80
Even he, whose soul now melts in mournful lays,
Shall shortly want the generous tear he pays;
Then from his closing eyes thy form shall part,
And the last pang shall tear thee from his heart,
Life's idle business at one gasp be o'er,   85
The Muse forgot, and thou beloved no more!

Thomas Gray   Elegy Written in a Country Churchyard

The curfew tolls the knell of parting day;
   The lowing herd winds slowly o'er the lea;
The ploughman homeward plods his weary way,
   And leaves the world to darkness and to me.

Now fades the glimmering landscape on the sight,   5
   And all the air a solemn stillness holds,
Save where the beetle wheels his droning flight,
   And drowsy tinklings lull the distant folds;

Save that from yonder ivy-mantled tower,
   The moping owl does to the moon complain   10

Of such as, wandering near her secret bower,
   Molest her ancient solitary reign.

Beneath those rugged elms, that yew-tree's shade,
   Where heaves the turf in a mouldering heap,
Each in his narrow cell forever laid,   15
   The rude forefathers of the hamlet sleep.

The breezy call of incense-breathing Morn,
   The swallow twittering from the straw-built shed,
The cock's shrill clarion, or the echoing horn,
   No more shall rouse them from their lowly bed.   20

For them no more the blazing hearth shall burn,
   Or busy housewife ply her evening care;
No children run to lisp their sire's return,
   Or climb his knees the envied kiss to share.

Oft did the harvest to their sickle yield.   25
   Their furrow oft the stubborn glebe has broke;
How jocund did they drive their team afield!
   How bowed the woods beneath their sturdy stroke!

Let not Ambition mock their useful toil,
   Their homely joys, and destiny obscure;   30
Nor Grandeur hear with a disdainful smile
   The short and simple annals of the poor.

The boast of heraldry, the pomp of power,
   And all that beauty, all that wealth e'er gave,
Awaits alike th' inevitable hour: 35
   The paths of glory lead but to the grave.

Nor you, ye proud, impute to these the fault,
   If Memory o'er their tomb no trophies raise,
Where through the long-drawn aisle and fretted vault
   The pealing anthem swells the note of praise.   40

Can storied urn, or animated bust,
   Back to its mansion call the fleeting breath?
Can Honor's voice provoke the silent dust,
   Or Flattery soothe the dull cold ear of Death?

Perhaps in this neglected spot is laid   45
   Some heart once pregnant with celestial fire;
Hands that the rod of empire might have swayed,
   Or waked to ecstasy the living lyre.

But Knowledge to their eyes her ample page,
   Rich with the spoils of time, did ne'er unroll;   50
Chill Penury repressed their noble rage,
   And froze the genial current of the soul.

Full many a gem of purest ray serene
   The dark unfathomed caves of ocean bear;
Full many a flower is born to blush unseen,   55
   And waste its sweetness on the desert air.

Some village Hampden that with dauntless breast,
    The little tryant of his fields withstood,
Some mute inglorious Milton here may rest,
    Some Cromwell guiltless of his country's blood.   60

Th' applause of listening senates to command,
    The threats of pain and ruin to despise,
To scatter plenty o'er a smiling land,
    And read their history in a nation's eyes,

Their lot forbade: nor circumscribed alone   65
    Their growing virtues, but their crimes confined
Forbade to wade through slaughter to a throne,
    And shut the gates of mercy on mankind,

The struggling pangs of conscious truth to hide,
    To quench the blushes of ingenuous shame,   70
Or heap the shrine of Luxury and Pride
    With incense kindled at the Muse's flame.

Far from the madding crowd's ignoble strife,
    Their sober wishes never learned to stray;
Along the cool sequestered vale of life   75
    They kept the noiseless tenor of their way.

Yet even these bones from insult to protect,
    Some frail memorial still erected nigh,
With uncouth rhymes and shapeless sculpture decked,
    Implores the passing tribute of a sigh.   80

Their name, their years, spelt by th' unlettered Muse,
    The place of fame and elegy supply;
And many a holy text around she strews,
    That teach the rustic moralist to die.

For who, to dumb Forgetfulness a prey,   85
    This pleasing anxious being e'er resigned,
Left the warm precincts of the cheerful day,
    Nor cast one longing, lingering look behind?

On some fond breast the parting soul relies,
    Some pious drops the closing eye requires;   90
E'en from the tomb the voice of Nature cries,
    E'en in our ashes live their wonted fires.

For thee, who, mindful of th' unhonored dead,
    Dost in these lines their artless tale relate,
If chance, by lonely Contemplation led,   95
    Some kindred spirit shall require thy fate—

Haply some hoary-headed swain may say,
    "Oft have we seen him at the peep of dawn
Brushing with hasty steps the dews away,
    To meet the sun upon the upland lawn.   100

"There, at the foot of yonder nodding beech,
    That wreathes its old fantastic roots so high,

His listless length at noontide would he stretch,
    And pore upon the brook that babbles by.

"Hard by yon wood, now smiling as in scorn,   *105*
    Muttering his wayward fancies, he would rove;
Now drooping, woeful-wan, like one forlorn,
    Or crazed with care, or crossed in hopeless love.

"One morn I missed him on the customed hill,
    Along the heath, and near his favorite tree;   *110*
Another came; nor yet beside the rill,
    Nor up the lawn, nor at the wood was he;

"The next, with dirges due, in sad array
Slow through the church-way path we saw him borne:
Approach and read (for thou can'st read) the lay   *115*
    Graved on the stone beneath yon aged thorn."

THE EPITAPH

Here rests his head upon the lap of Earth
    A youth, to Fortune and to Fame unknown:
Fair Science frowned not on his humble birth,
    And Melancholy marked him for her own.   *120*

Large was his bounty, and his soul sincere;
    Heaven did a recompense as largely send:
He gave to Misery all he had, a tear,
    He gained from Heaven ('twas all he wished) a friend.

No farther seek his merits to disclose,   *125*
    Or draw his frailties from their dread abode
(There they alike in trembling hope repose),
    The bosom of his Father and his God.

16 rude: simple-living.   *26 glebe*: soil.   *57 Hampden*: John Hampden (1594–1643), English patriot and statesman; he refused to pay ship-money to Charles I.   *95 chance*: perchance.   *116 thorn*: hawthorn.

Ralph Waldo Emerson   Threnody

The South-wind brings
Life, sunshine and desire,
And on every mount and meadow
Breathes aromatic fire;
But over the dead he has no power,   *5*
The lost, the lost, he cannot restore;
And, looking over the hills, I mourn
The darling who shall not return.

I see my empty house,
I see my trees repair their boughs;   *10*
And he, the wondrous child,
Whose silver warble wild

Outvalued every pulsing sound
Within the air's cerulean round,—
The hyacinthine boy, for whom   15
Morn well might break and April bloom,
The gracious boy, who did adorn
The world whereinto he was born,
And by his countenance repay
The favor of the loving Day,—   20
Has disappeared from the Day's eye;
Far and wide she cannot find him;
My hopes pursue, they cannot bind him.
Returned this day, the South-wind searches,
And finds young pines and budding birches;   25
But finds not the budding man;
Nature, who lost, cannot remake him;
Fate let him fall, Fate can't retake him;
Nature, Fate, men, him seek in vain.

And whither now, my truant wise and sweet,   30
O, whither tend thy feet?
I had the right, few days ago,
Thy steps to watch, thy place to know:
How have I forfeited the right?
Hast thou forgot me in a new delight?   35
I hearken for thy household cheer,
O eloquent child!
Whose voice, an equal messenger,
Conveyed thy meaning mild.
What though the pains and joys   40
Whereof it spoke were toys
Fitting his age and ken,
Yet fairest dames and bearded men,
Who heard the sweet request,
So gentle, wise and grave,   45
Bended with joy to his behest
And let the world's affairs go by,
A while to share his cordial game,
Or mend his wicker wagon-frame,
Still plotting how their hungry ear   50
That winsome voice again might hear;
For his lips could well pronounce
Words that were persuasions.

Gentlest guardians marked serene
His early hope, his liberal mien;   55
Took counsel from his guiding eyes
To make this wisdom earthly wise.
Ah, vainly do these eyes recall
The school-march, each day's festival,
When every morn my bosom glowed   60
To watch the convoy on the road;
The babe in willow wagon closed,
With rolling eyes and face composed;
With children forward and behind,

Like Cupids studiously inclined;   65
And he the chieftain paced beside,
The center of the troop allied,
With sunny face of sweet repose,
To guard the babe from fancied foes.
The little captain innocent   70
Took the eye with him as he went;
Each village senior paused to scan
And speak the lovely caravan.
From the window I look out
To mark thy beautiful parade,   75
Stately marching in cap and coat
To some tune by fairies played;—
A music heard by thee alone
To works as noble led thee on.

Now Love and Pride, alas! in vain,   80
Up and down their glances strain.
The painted sled stands where it stood;
The kennel by the corded wood;
His gathered sticks to stanch the wall
Of the snow-tower, when snow should fall;   85
The ominous hole he dug in the sand,
And childhood's castles built or planned;
His daily haunts I well discern,—
The poultry-yard, the shed, the barn,—
And every inch of garden ground   90
Paced by the blessed feet around,
From the roadside to the brook
Whereinto he loved to look.
Step the meek fowls where erst they ranged;
The wintry garden lies unchanged;   95
The brook into the stream runs on;
But the deep-eyed boy is gone.

On that shaded day,
Dark with more clouds than tempests are,
When thou didst yield thy innocent breath   100
In birdlike heavings unto death,
Night came, and Nature had not thee;
I said, "We are mates in misery."
The morrow dawned with needless glow;
Each snowbird chirped, each fowl must crow;   105
Each tramper started; but the feet
Of the most beautiful and sweet
Of human youth had left the hill
And garden,—they were bound and still.
There's not a sparrow or a wren,   110
There's not a blade of autumn grain,
Which the four seasons do not tend
And tides of life and increase lend;
And every chick of every bird,
And weed and rock-moss is preferred.   115
O ostrich-like forgetfulness!

O loss of larger in the less!
Was there no star that could be sent,
No watcher in the firmament,
No angel from the countless host   120
That loiters round the crystal coast,
Could stoop to heal that only child,
Nature's sweet marvel undefiled,
And keep the blossom of the earth,
Which all her harvests were not worth?   125
Not mine,—I never called thee mine,
But Nature's heir,—if I repine,
And seeing rashly torn and moved
Not what I made, but what I loved,
Grow early old with grief that thou   130
Must to the wastes of Nature go,—
'Tis because a general hope
Was quenched, and all must doubt and grope.
For flattering planets seemed to say
This child should ills of ages stay,   135
By wondrous tongue, and guided pen,
Bring the flown Muses back to men.
Perchance not he but Nature ailed,
The world and not the infant failed.
It was not ripe yet to sustain   140
A genius of so fine a strain,
Who gazed upon the sun and moon
As if he came unto his own,
And, pregnant with his grander thought,
Brought the old order into doubt.   145
His beauty once their beauty tried;
They could not feed him, and he died,
And wandered backward as in scorn,
To wait an aeon to be born.
Ill day which made this beauty waste,   150
Plight broken, this high face defaced!
Some went and came about the dead;
And some in books of solace read;
Some to their friends the tidings say;
Some went to write, some went to pray;   155
One tarried here, there hurried one;
But their heart abode with none.
Covetous death bereaved us all,
To aggrandize one funeral.
The eager fate which carried thee   160
Took the largest part of me:
For this losing is true dying;
This is lordly man's down-lying,
This his slow but sure reclining
Star by star his world resigning.   165

O child of paradise,
Boy who made dear his father's home,
In whose deep eyes

Men read the welfare of the times to come,
I am too much bereft.   *170*
The world dishonored thou hast left.
O truth's and nature's costly lie!
O trusted broken prophecy!
O richest fortune sourly crossed!
Born for the future, to the future lost!   *175*

The deep Heart answered, "Weepest thou?
Worthier cause for passion wild
If I had not taken the child.
And deemest thou as those who pore,
With aged eyes, short way before—   *180*
Think'st Beauty vanished from the coast
Of matter, and thy darling lost?
Taught he not thee—the man of eld,
Whose eyes within his eyes beheld
Heaven's numerous hierarchy span   *185*
The mystic gulf from God to man?
To be alone wilt thou begin
When worlds of lovers hem thee in?
Tomorrow, when the masks shall fall
That dizen Nature's carnival,   *190*
The pure shall see by their own will,
Which overflowing Love shall fill,
'Tis not within the force of fate
The fate-conjoined to separate.
But thou, my votary, weepest thou?   *195*
I gave thee sight—where is it now?
I taught thy heart beyond the reach
Of ritual, bible, or of speech;
Wrote in thy mind's transparent table,
As far as the incommunicable;   *200*
Taught thee each private sign to raise
Lit by the supersolar blaze.
Past utterance, and past belief,
And past the blasphemy of grief,
The mysteries of Nature's heart;   *205*
And though no Muse can these impart,
Throb thine with Nature's throbbing breast,
And all is clear from east to west.

"I came to thee as to a friend;
Dearest, to thee I did not send   *210*
Tutors, but a joyful eye,
Innocence that matched the sky,
Lovely locks, a form of wonder,
Laughter rich as woodland thunder,
That thou might'st entertain apart   *215*
The richest flowering of all art:
And, as the great all-loving Day
Through smallest chambers takes its way,
That thou might'st break thy daily bread
With prophet, savior and head;   *220*
That thou might'st cherish for thine own

The riches of sweet Mary's Son,
Boy-Rabbi, Israel's paragon.
And thoughtest thou such guest
Would in thy hall take up his rest?   225
Would rushing life forget her laws,
Fate's glowing revolution pause?
High omens ask diviner guess;
Not to be conned to tediousness
And know my higher gifts unbind   230
The zone that girds the incarnate mind.
When the scanty shores are full
With Thought's perilous, whirling pool;
When frail Nature can no more,
Then the Spirit strikes the hour: 235
My servant Death, with solving rite,
Pours finite into infinite.
Wilt thou freeze love's tidal flow,
Whose streams through Nature circling go?
Nail the wild star to its track   240
On the half-climbed zodiac?
Light is light which radiates,
Blood is blood which circulates,
Life is life which generates,
And many-seeming life is one,—   245
Wilt thou transfix and make it none?
Its onward force too starkly pent
In figure, bone and lineament?
Wilt thou, uncalled, interrogate,
Talker! the unreplying Fate?   250
Nor see the genius of the whole
Ascendant in the private soul,
Beckon it when to go and come,
Self-announced its hour of doom?
Fair the soul's recess and shrine,   255
Magic-built to last a season;
Masterpiece of love benign;
Fairer that expansive reason
Whose omen 'tis, and sign.
Wilt thou not ope thy heart to know   260
What rainbows teach, and sunsets show?
Verdict which accumulates
From lengthening scroll of human fates,
Voice of earth to earth returned,
Prayers of saints that inly burned,—   265
Saying, *What is excellent,*
As God lives, is permanent;
Hearts are dust, hearts' loves remain;
Heart's love will meet thee again.
Revere the Maker; fetch thine eye   270
Up to his style, and manners of the sky.
Not of adamant and gold
Built he heaven stark and cold;
No, but a nest of bending reeds,

Flowering grass and scented weeds;   275
Or like a traveler's fleeing tent,
Or bow above the tempest bent;
Built of tears and sacred flames,
And virtue reaching to its aims;
Built of furtherance and pursuing,   280
Not of spent deeds, but of doing.
Silent rushes the swift Lord
Through ruined systems still restored,
Broadsowing, bleak and void to bless,
Plants with worlds the wilderness;   285
Waters with tears of ancient sorrow
Apples of Eden ripe tomorrow.
House and tenant go to ground,
Lost in God, in Godhead found."

Walt Whitman   When Lilacs Last in the Dooryard
   Bloomed

         1
When lilacs last in the dooryard bloomed,
And the great star early drooped in the western sky in the night,
I mourned, and yet shall mourn with ever-returning spring.

Ever-returning spring, trinity sure to me you bring,
Lilac blooming perennial and drooping star in the west,   5
And thought of him I love.

         2
O powerful western fallen star!
O shades of night—O moody, tearful night!
O great star disappeared—O the black murk that hides the star!
O cruel hands that hold me powerless—O helpless soul of me!   10
O harsh surrounding cloud that will not free my soul.

         3
In the dooryard fronting an old farm-house near the white-
    washed palings,
Stands the lilac-bush tall-growing with heart-shaped leaves of
    rich green,
With many a pointed blossom rising delicate, with the perfume
    strong I love,
With every leaf a miracle—and from this bush in the door-
    yard,   15
With delicate-colored blossoms and heart-shaped leaves of rich
    green,
A sprig with its flower I break.

         4
In the swamp in secluded recesses,
A shy and hidden bird is warbling a song.

Solitary the thrush,   20
The hermit withdrawn to himself, avoiding the settlements,
Sings by himself a song.

Song of the bleeding throat,
Death's outlet song of life (for well, dear brother, I know,
If thou wast not granted to sing thou would'st surely die).   25

5
Over the breast of the spring, the land, amid cities,
Amid lanes and through old woods, where lately the violets
  peeped from the ground, spotting the gray debris,
Amid the grass in the fields each side of the lanes, passing
  the endless grass,
Passing the yellow-speared wheat, every grain from its shroud
  in the dark-brown fields uprisen,
Passing the apple-tree blows of white and pink in the
  orchards,   30
Carrying a corpse to where it shall rest in the grave,
Night and day journeys a coffin.

6
Coffin that passes through lanes and streets,
Through day and night with the great cloud darkening the
  land,
With the pomp of the inlooped flags with the cities draped in
  black,   35
With the show of the States themselves as of crepe-veiled
  women standing,
With processions long and winding and the flambeaus of the
  night,
With the countless torches lit, with the silent sea of faces and
  the unbared heads,
With the waiting depot, the arriving coffin, and the somber
  faces,
With dirges through the night, with the thousand voices
  rising strong and solemn,   40
With all the mournful voices of the dirges poured around the
  coffin,
The dim-lit churches and the shuddering organs—where amid
  these you journey,
With the tolling tolling bells' perpetual clang,
Here; coffin that slowly passes,
I give you my sprig of lilac.   45

7
(Nor for you, for one alone,
Blossoms and branches green to coffins all I bring,
For fresh as the morning, thus would I chant a song for you
  O sane and sacred death.

All over bouquets of roses,
O death, I cover you over with roses and early lilies,   50

But mostly and now the lilac that blooms the first,
Copious I break, I break the sprigs from the bushes,
With loaded arms I come, pouring for you,
For you and the coffins all of you O death.)

8

O western orb sailing the heaven,   55
Now I know what you must have meant as a month since I
    walked,
As I walked in silence the transparent shadowy night,
As I saw you had something to tell as you bent to me night
    after night,
As you drooped from the sky low down as if to my side (while
    the other stars all looked on),
As we wandered together the solemn night (for something I
    know not what kept me from sleep),   60
As the night advanced, and I saw on the rim of the west how
    full you were of woe,
As I stood on the rising ground in the breeze in cool trans-
    parent night,
As I watched where you passed and was lost in the nether-
    ward black of the night,
As my soul in its trouble dissatisfied sank, as where you, sad
    orb,
Concluded, dropped in the night, and was gone.   65

9

Sing on there in the swamp,
O singer bashful and tender, I hear your notes, I hear your call,
I hear, I come presently, I understand you,
But a moment I linger, for the lustrous star has detained me,
The star, my departing comrade, holds and detains me.   70

10

O how shall I warble myself for the dead one there I loved?
And how shall I deck my song for the large sweet soul that
    has gone?
And what shall my perfume be for the grave of him I love?

Sea-winds blown from east and west,
Blown from the eastern sea and blown from the western sea,
    till there on the prairies meeting,   75
These and with these and the breath of my chant,
I'll perfume the grave of him I love.

11

O what shall I hang on the chamber walls?
And what shall the pictures be that I hang on the walls,
To adorn the burial-house of him I love?   80

Pictures of growing spring and farms and homes,
With the fourth-month eve at sundown, and the gray smoke
    lucid and bright,

With floods of the yellow gold of the gorgeous, indolent, sink-
    ing sun, burning, expanding the air,
With the fresh sweet herbage under foot, and the pale green
    leaves of the trees prolific,
In the distance the flowing glaze, the breast of the river, with
    a wind-dapple here and there,   85
With ranging hills on the banks, with many a line against the
    sky, and shadows,
And the city at hand with dwellings so dense, and stacks of
    chimneys,
And all the scenes of life and the workshops, and the work-
    men homeward returning.

                12
Lo, body and soul—this land,
My own Manhattan with spires, and the sparkling and hur-
    rying tides, and the ships,   90
The varied and ample land, the South and the North in the
    light, Ohio's shores and flashing Missouri,
And ever the far-spreading prairies covered with grass and
    corn.
Lo, the most excellent sun so calm and haughty,
The violet and purple morn with just-felt breezes,
The gentle soft-born measureless light,   95
The miracle spreading, bathing all, the fulfilled noon,
The coming eve delicious, the welcome night and the stars,
Over my cities shining all, enveloping man and land.

                13
Sing on, sing on you gray-brown bird,
Sing from the swamps, the recesses, pour your chant from the
    bushes,   100
Limitless out of the dusk, out of the cedars and pines.

Sing on dearest brother, warble your reedy song,
Loud human song, with voice of uttermost woe.

O liquid and free and tender!
O wild and loose to my soul—O wondrous singer!   105
You only I hear—yet the star holds me (but will soon depart),
Yet the lilac with mastering odor holds me.

                14
Now while I sat in the day and looked forth,
In the close of the day with its light and the fields of spring,
    and the farmers preparing their crops,
In the large unconscious scenery of my land with its lakes and
    forests,   110
In the heavenly aerial beauty (after the perturbed winds and
    the storms),
Under the arching heavens of the afternoon swift passing, and
    the voices of children and women,

The many-moving sea-tides, and I saw the ships how they
    sailed,
And the summer approaching with richness, and the fields all
    busy with labor,
And the infinite separate houses, how they all went on, each
    with its meals and minutia of daily usages,   *115*
And the streets how their throbbings throbbed, and the cities
    pent—lo, then and there,
Falling upon them all and among them all, enveloping me
    with the rest,
Appeared the cloud, appeared the long black trail,
And I knew death, its thought, and the sacred knowledge of
    death.

Then with the knowledge of death as walking one side of
    me,   *120*
And the thought of death close-walking the other side of me,
And I in the middle as with companions, and as holding the
    hands of companions,
I fled forth to the hiding receiving night that talks not,
Down to the shores of the water, the path by the swamp in the
    dimness,
To the solemn shadowy cedars and ghostly pines so still.   *125*

And the singer so shy to the rest received me,
The gray-brown bird I know received us comrades three,
And he sang the carol of death, and a verse for him I love.

From deep secluded recesses,
From the fragrant cedars and the ghostly pines so still,   *130*
Came the carol of the bird.

And the charm of the carol rapt me,
As I held as if by their hands my comrades in the night,
And the voice of my spirit tallied the song of the bird.

Come lovely and soothing death,   *135*
Undulate round the world, serenely arriving, arriving,
In the day, in the night, to all, to each,
Sooner or later delicate death.

Praised be the fathomless universe,
For life and joy, and for objects and knowledge curious,   *140*
And for love, sweet love—but praise! praise! praise!
For the sure-enwinding arms of cool-enfolding death.

Dark mother always gliding near with soft feet,
Have none chanted for thee a chant of fullest welcome?
Then I chant it for thee, I glorify thee above all,   *145*
I bring thee a song that when thou most indeed come, come
    unfalteringly.

Approach strong deliveress,
When it is so, when thou hast taken them, I joyously sing the
    dead,
Lost in the loving floating ocean of thee,
Laved in the flood of thy bliss, O death.   *150*

From me to thee glad serenades,
Dances for thee I propose saluting thee, adornments and
  feastings for thee,
And the sights of the open landscape and the high-spread sky
  are fitting,
And life and the fields, and the huge and thoughtful night.

The night in silence under many a star,   155
The ocean shore and the husky whispering wave whose voice I
  know,
And the soul turning to thee, O vast and well-veiled death,
And the body gratefully nestling close to thee.

Over the tree-tops I float thee a song,
Over the rising and sinking waves, over the myriad fields and
  the prairies wide,   160
Over the dense-packed cities all and the teeming wharves and
  ways
I float this carol with joy, with joy to thee, O death.

15

To the tally of my soul,
Loud and strong kept up the gray-brown bird,
With pure deliberate notes spreading, filling the night,   165

Loud in the pines and cedars dim,
Clear in the freshness moist and the swamp-perfume,
And I with my comrades there in the night.

While my sight that was bound in my eyes unclosed,
As to long panoramas of visions.   170

And I saw askant the armies,
I saw as in noiseless dreams hundreds of battle-flags,
Borne through the smoke of the battles and pierced with
    missiles I saw them,
And carried hither and yon through the smoke, and torn and
    bloody,
And at last but a few shreds left on the staffs (and all in
    silence),   175
And the staffs all splintered and broken.

I saw battle-corpses, myriads of them,
And the white skeletons of young men, I saw them,
I saw the debris and debris of all the slain soldiers of the war,
But I saw they were not as was thought,   180
They themselves were fully at rest, they suffered not,
The living remained and suffered, the mother suffered,
And the wife and the child and the musing comrade suffered,
And the armies that remained suffered.

16

Passing the visions, passing the night,   185
Passing, unloosing the hold of my comrades' hands,
Passing the song of the hermit bird and the tallying song of
    my soul,

Victorious song, death's outlet song, yet varying, ever-altering
    song,
As low and wailing, yet clear the notes, rising and falling,
    flooding the night,
Sadly sinking and fainting, as warning and warning, and yet
    again bursting with joy,   190
Covering the earth and filling the spread of the heaven,
As that powerful psalm in the night I heard from recesses,
Passing, I leave thee lilac with heart-shaped leaves,
I leave thee there in the dooryard, blooming, returning with
    spring.

I cease from my song for thee,   195
From my gaze on thee in the west, fronting the west, com-
    muning with thee,
O comrade lustrous with silver face in the night.

Yet each to keep and all, retrievements out of the night,
The song, the wondrous chant of the gray-brown bird,
And the tallying chant, the echo aroused in my soul,   200
With the lustrous and drooping star with the countenance
    full of woe,
With the holders holding my hand nearing the call of the
    bird,
Comrades mine and I in the midst, and their memory ever to
    keep, for the dead I loved so well,
For the sweetest, wisest soul of all my days and lands—and
    this for his dear sake,
Lilac and star and bird twined with the chant of my soul,   205
There in the fragrant pines and the cedars dusk and dim.

6 *him:* President Lincoln, assassinated April, 1865.   37 *flambeaus:* torches.   63 *netherward:* downward.   72 *deck:* adorn.
106 *yet:* still.   116 *pent:* confined.   136 *Undulate:* move with
the motion of the wave.   160 *myriad:* countless.   163 *tally:*
record.   171 *askant:* with misgivings.

Ezra Pound   Elegy VII

FROM *Homage to Sextus Propertius*

THE CYNTHIA EPISTLES

Me happy, night, night full of brightness;
Oh couch made happy by my long delectations;
How many words talked out with abundant candles;
Struggles when the lights were taken away;
Now with bared breasts she wrestled against me,   5
        Tunic spread in delay;
And then opening my eyelids fallen in sleep,
Her lips upon them; and it was her mouth saying:
    Sluggard!

In how many varied embraces, our changing arms,   10
Her kisses, how many, lingering on my lips.
"Turn not Venus into a blinded motion,
  Eyes are the guides of love,
Paris took Helen naked coming from the bed of Menelaus,
Endymion's naked body, bright bait for Diana,"   15
  —such at least is the story.

While our fates twine together, sate we our eyes with love:
For long night comes upon you
  and a day when no day returns.
Let the gods lay chains upon us   20
  so that no day shall unbind them.

Fool who would set a term to love's madness,
For the sun shall drive with black horses,
  earth shall bring wheat from barley,
The flood shall move toward the fountain   25
  Ere love know moderations,
  The fish shall swim in dry streams.

No, now while it may be, let not the fruit of life cease.

  Dry wreaths drop their petals,
   their stalks are woven in baskets,   30
  To-day we take the great breath of lovers,
    to-morrow fate shuts us in.

Though you give all your kisses
    you give but few.

Nor can I shift my pains to other,   35
  Hers will I be dead,
If she confers such nights upon me,
  long is my life, long in years,
If she give me many,
  God am I for the time.   40

title: Sextus Propertius, the Roman elegaic poet, was born in
Umbria about 51 B.C. Pound translated twelve elegaic lyrics.
15 *Endymion's . . . Diana:* Endymion was sleeping on Mount
Latmos in the moonlight, when Diana, goddess of the moon, came
down and lay beside him.

George Barker Secular Elegies—III

Satan is on your tongue, sweet singer, with
Your eye on the income and the encomium:
Angels rhapsodise for and from their faith.
And in the studies of chromium
Lucifer seduces Orpheus with a myth.   5

But the principle of evil is not autonomous.
Like the Liberty Horse with a plume at a circus
Under the whipmaster it steps proud in its circles.

When I let slip one instant the whip of the will
All hell's scot free with fire at the nostril.   10

Thus if the crux and judgment never is
Left to our own to do with as we will,
But the decision, like a master key, lies
Wholly in the higher hands that hold all—
How can we be as innocent as this?   15

Everything that is proud loves the mask,
Said the Dionysian who never wore one.
Thus our damnation and our condemnation,
Wiser than Nietzsche, never taking a risk,
Wears the mask of a necessary satisfaction.   20

Not, Love, when we kiss do the archangels weep
For we are naked then wherever we are,
Like tigers in the night; but in our sleep
The masks go down, and the beast is bare:
It is not Love but double damnation there.   25

Marooned on the islands of pride, lonely
And mad on the pyramids of achievement,
Disillusioned in the cathedrals of doxology,
The sad man senses his continual bereavement:
God has just died, and now there is only   30

Us. The gold bull with its horns of finances
Over the sensual mountains goes gallivanting
In glory: all night and all day it dances,
Absurd and happy because nothing is wanting.
The sad man hides his grief in his five senses.   35

W. H. Auden   In Memory of W. B. Yeats
        (*died* Jan. 1939)

                    I
He disappeared in the dead of winter:
The brooks were frozen, the air-ports almost deserted,
And snow disfigured the public statues;
The mercury sank in the mouth of the dying day.
O all the instruments agree   5
The day of his death was a dark cold day.

Far from his illness
The wolves ran on through the evergreen forests,
The peasant river was untempted by the fashionable quays;
By mourning tongues   10
The death of the poet was kept from his poems.

But for him it was his last afternoon as himself,
An afternoon of nurses and rumours;
The provinces of his body revolted,
The squares of his mind were empty,   15

Silence invaded the suburbs,
The current of his feeling failed: he became his admirers.

Now he is scattered among a hundred cities
And wholly given over to unfamiliar affections;
To find his happiness in another kind of wood   20
And be punished under a foreign code of conscience.
The words of a dead man
Are modified in the guts of the living.

But in the importance and noise of to-morrow
When the brokers are roaring like beasts on the floor of the   25
    Bourse,
And the poor have the sufferings to which they are fairly ac-
    customed,
And each in the cell of himself is almost convinced of his
    freedom;

A few thousand will think of this day
As one thinks of a day when one did something slightly un-
    usual.

O all the instruments agree   30
The day of his death was a dark cold day.

        2
You were silly like us: your gift survived it all;
The parish of rich women, physical decay,
Yourself; mad Ireland hurt you into poetry.
Now Ireland has her madness and her weather still,   35
For poetry makes nothing happen: it survives
In the valley of its saying where executives
Would never want to tamper; it flows south
From ranches of isolation and the busy griefs,
Raw towns that we believe and die in; it survives,   40
A way of happening, a mouth.

        3
Earth, receive an honoured guest;
William Yeats is laid to rest:
Let the Irish vessel lie
Emptied of its poetry.   45

Time that is intolerant
Of the brave and innocent,
And indifferent in a week
To a beautiful physique,

Worships language and forgives   50
Everyone by whom it lives;
Pardons cowardice, conceit,
Lays its honours at their feet.

Time that with this strange excuse
Pardoned Kipling and his views,   55

And will pardon Paul Claudel,
Pardons him for writing well.

In the nightmare of the dark
All the gods of Europe bark,
And the living nations wait,   60
Each sequestered in its hate;

Intellectual disgrace
Stares from every human face,
And the seas of pity lie
Locked and frozen in each eye.   65

Follow, poet, follow right
To the bottom of the night,
With your unconstraining voice
Still persuade us to rejoice;

With the farming of a verse   70
Make a vineyard of the curse,
Sing of human unsuccess
In a rapture of distress;

In the deserts of the heart
Let the healing fountain start,   75
In the prison of his days
Teach the free man how to praise.

1 He . . . winter: Yeats died on January 28, 1939.   *25 Bourse:*
the stock exchange.   *55 Pardoned . . . views:* Rudyard Kipling
had said some nasty things about the Conservatives of his time; his
political views probably prevented his being named poet laureate.
56 Paul Claudel: French poet, playwright, and diplomat (1868–
1955).

John Crowe Ransom   Bells for John Whiteside's Daughter

There was such speed in her little body,
And such lightness in her footfall,
It is no wonder that her brown study
Astonished us all.

Her wars were bruited in our high window.   5
We looked among orchard trees and beyond,
Where she took arms against her shadow,
Or harried unto the pond

The lazy geese, like a snow cloud
Dripping their snow on the green grass,   10
Tricking and stopping, sleepy and proud,
Who cried in goose, Alas,

For the tireless heart within the little
Lady with rod that made them rise

From their noon apple-dreams, and scuttle   *15*
Goose-fashion under the skies!

But now go the bells, and we are ready;
In one house we are sternly stopped
To say we are vexed at her brown study,
Lying so primly propped.   *20*

3 *brown study*: daydream or reverie.

Robert Lowell   In Memory of Arthur Winslow

I. DEATH FROM CANCER

This Easter, Arthur Winslow, less than dead,
Your people set you up in Phillips' House
To settle off your wrestling with the crab—
The claws drop flesh upon your yachting blouse
Until longshoreman Charon come and stab   *5*
Through your adjusted bed
And crush the crab. On Boston Basin, shells
Hit water by the Union Boat Club wharf:
You ponder why the coxes squeakings dwarf
The *resurrexit dominus* of all the bells.   *10*

Grandfather Winslow, look, the swanboats coast
That island in the Public Gardens, where
The bread-stuffed ducks are brooding, where with tub
And strainer the mid-Sunday Irish scare
The sun-struck shallows for the dusky chub   *15*
This Easter, and the ghost
Of risen Jesus walks the waves to run
Arthur upon a trumpeting black swan
Beyond Charles River to the Acheron
Where the wide waters and their voyager are one.   *20*

II. DUNBARTON

The stones are yellow and the grass is gray
Past Concord by the rotten lake and hill
Where crutch and trumpet meet the limousine
And half-forgotten Starks and Winslows fill
The granite plot and the dwarf pines are green   *25*
From watching for the day
When the great year of the little yeomen come
Bringing its landed Promise and the faith
That made the Pilgrim Makers take a lathe
And point their wooden steeples lest the Word be dumb.   *30*

O fearful witnesses, your day is done:
The minister from Boston waves your shades,
Like children, out of sight and out of mind.
The first selectman of Dunbarton spreads

Wreaths of New Hampshire pine cones on the lined   35
Casket where the cold sun
Is melting. But, at last, the end is reached;
We start our cars. The preacher's mouthing still
Deafen my poor relations on the hill:
Their sunken landmarks echo what our fathers preached.   40

III. *FIVE YEARS LATER*

This Easter, Arthur Winslow, five years gone
I came to mourn you, not to raise the craft
That netted you a million dollars, late
Hosing out gold in Colorado's waste,
Then lost it all in Boston real estate.   45
Now from the train, at dawn
Leaving Columbus in Ohio, shell
On shell of our stark culture strikes the sun
To fill my head with all our fathers won
When Cotton Mather wrestled with the fiends from hell.   50

You must have hankered for our family's craft:
The block-house Edward made, the Governor,
At Marshfield, and the slight coin-silver spoons
The Sheriff beat to shame the gaunt Revere,
And General Stark's coarse bas-relief in bronze   55
Set on your granite shaft
In rough Dunbarton; for what else could bring
You, Arthur, to the veined and alien West
But devil's notions that your gold at least
Could give back life to men who whipped or backed the
  King?   60

IV. *A PRAYER FOR MY GRANDFATHER TO OUR LADY*

Mother, for these three hundred years or more
Neither our clippers nor our slavers reached
The haven of your peace in this Bay State:
Neither my father nor his father. Beached
On these dry flats of fishy real estate,   65
O Mother, I implore
Your scorched, blue thunderbreasts of love to pour
Buckets of blessings on my burning head
Until I rise like Lazarus from the dead:
Lavabis nos et super nivem dealbabor.   70

"On Copley Square, I saw you hold the door
To Trinity, the costly Church, and saw
The painted Paradise of harps and lutes
Sink like Atlantis in the Devil's jaw
And knock the Devil's teeth out by the roots;   75
But when I strike for shore
I find no painted idols to adore:
Hell is burned out, heaven's harp-strings are slack.

Mother, run to the chalice, and bring back
Blood on your finger-tips for Lazarus who was poor."   80

title: Arthur Winslow, the poet's grandfather on his mother's side.
He was a financial adventurer, a Boston Brahmin, and an autocrat
who was proud of descent from the Stark family of Dunbarton,
N.H., as well as the Winslows of Massachusetts, a colonial family.
3 crab: the Latin word is "Cancer," referred to in the section
title.   *5 Charon*: Charon, in Greek mythology, ferried the
souls of the dead across the River Styx, the river of death.
9 coxes: coxswains, the steersmen of ships' boats or racing
shells.   *10 resurrexit dominus*: Easter liturgical message, "The
Lord is risen."   *15 chub*: a form of carp that on Easter recalls
the fact that the fish became a Christian symbol.   *17 Jesus
. . . run*: Matthew xiv. 25; the miracle of Jesus walking on
the sea.   *19 Charles . . . Acheron*: The Charles is a river in
Boston. Acheron, a river in Hades in Greek mythology.   *27
yeomen*: freeholders of land, commoners but of the highest
level.   *28 Promise*: i.e., the Promised Land of the redeemed
on the final day of judgment.   *40 landmarks . . . preached*:
Bible texts that were carved on tombstones.   *44 Hosing . . .
waste*: a reference to placer mining, a form of mining gold in
which, under high-pressure hoses, worthless deposits are separated
from the gold.   *47–50* Contemporary buildings, representative
of our material wealth, are in these lines compared with the message
of salvation preached by Cotton Mather. Mather (1663–1728)
has come to represent the archetypal Puritan.   *52 Governor*:
Edward Winslow, a Mayflower Pilgrim, was three times elected
governor.   *54 Revere*: Paul Revere, famed for his midnight
ride, was a silversmith and engraver of great ability.   *55 General
Stark*: General John Stark (1728–1822), another ancestor and
famous soldier of the American Revolution.   *69 Lazarus*: Lowell
refers to two Lazarus figures in this section. The reference here
is to the Lazarus raised by Jesus from the dead (John xi. 11–43).
70 Lavabis . . . dealbabor: "You shall wash us and I shall be made
whiter than snow."   *71 Copley Square*: an old Boston square
associated at one time with great elegance and social refinement.
74 Atlantis: an island civilization that is supposed to have sunk
beneath the ocean.   *80 Lazarus . . . poor*: The second Lazarus
referred to in this section. This one is the beggar in Jesus' parable
(Luke xvi: 19–31) of the rich man who is selfish.

Theodore Roethke   Elegy for Jane

(MY STUDENT, THROWN BY A HORSE)

I remember the neckcurls, limp and damp as tendrils;
And her quick look, a sidelong pickerel smile;
And how, once startled into talk, the light syllables leaped for
     her,
And she balanced in the delight of her thought,
A wren, happy, tail into the wind,   5

Her song trembling the twigs and small branches.
The shade sang with her;
The leaves, their whispers turned to kissing,
And the mould sang in the bleached valleys under the rose.

Oh, when she was sad, she cast herself down into such a pure
        depth,   10
Even a father could not find her:
Scraping her cheek against straw,
Stirring the clearest water.

My sparrow, you are not here,
Waiting like a fern, making a spiney shadow.   15
The sides of wet stones cannot console me,
Nor the moss, wound with the last light.

If only I could nudge you from this sleep,
My maimed darling, my skittery pigeon.
Over this damp grave I speak the words of my love: 20
I, with no rights in this matter,
Neither father nor lover.

VERSE SATIRE

Verse satire is a literary manner, a critical attitude toward human institutions and humanity. Through laughter, the satirist
attempts to inspire a remodeling or restructuring of man's
values. Still appropriate as a definition is Dr. Johnson's remark
that a satire is "a poem in which wickedness or folly is
censured." Ezra Pound Literary Essays notes that "Satire
reminds one that certain things are not worth while. It draws
one to consider time wasted." Whether the satirist succeeds in
his effort is doubtful, for "Satire is a sort of glass wherein be-
holders do generally discover everybody's face but their own"
(Jonathan Swift).

The word "satire" is derived from satura, a "medley," and
the writing of satire has its roots in the works of Horace, Persius,
and Juvenal. Formal verse satire is a quasi-dramatic poem that
contains an encounter between the Satirist, or his persona,
and an Adversarius who elicits speech from the Satirist.
Through this dramatic convention, vice and folly are exposed
to analysis. But since there are few conventions for the satirist to
follow, the author is free to present his materials in an almost
unlimited number of ways. A satiric intention may be couched
in the presentation of beast fables, homilies, Theophrastian
"characters," narrative and dramatic incidents, or proverbs.
Tone is established through invective, irony, mockery, exaggeration, understatement, or one of the many shadings of the
word "wit."

In formal verse satire, there is a general movement from the
arraignment of vice and folly to an appeal to virtue or rational
behavior. Alexander Pope is generally regarded as perhaps the

only English poet to write formal verse satire with distinction, and his satires include the classical use of a discursive, colloquial tone and language, and a justification within the work of the satirical art.

In formal verse satire there is no real story present, and the only speaker is the author. By contrast, satire that is not "formal" is often referred to as "indirect" satire. In indirect satire, the author presents a story with invented characters. Another method by which satire is sometimes distinguished, however, is to refer to the Roman poets whose works serve as examples of the type. Classified thus, Horatian satire (Horace, 65–8 B.C.) usually attacks foibles and follies. Juvenalian satire (Juvenal, 55–130 A.D.) attacks vices and crimes. Whereas Horatian satire is easy-going, urbane, and gentle—its method to correct by sympathetic laughter—Juvenalian satire is biting, caustic, and angry. With a sense of outrage and anger, it contemptuously points an accusing finger at corruption and evil. A third form of satire has recently been given attention by the critic Northrop Frye, who suggests that Menippean satire (Menippus, fl. 290 B.C., but whose work has been lost) and the satire of his followers deals "less with people . . . than with mental attitudes." Frye, in his *Anatomy of Criticism,* thus places Swift's *Gulliver, Gulliver's Travels* and the works of Lewis Carroll in this category. According to Frye, this form of satire often makes fun of the wise or learned man, e.g., the pedant, the philosopher, and it presents characters as spokesmen for learned ideas. Frye suggests that this sort of satire might more aptly be named "the anatomy," since the characters usually congregate in order to anatomize ideas. Menippean satire should be regarded as indirect satire, since the story is told not by the author (or his persona) but by invented characters.

Great satire—in prose as well as in verse—is the product of periods of time when there are reasonably well-established ethical and rational norms. These norms gain widespread support, though there is not a strict or absolute adherence to these norms. The satirist, consequently, is both a part of his society and apart from his society. He measures attitudes and institutions against societal norms. Today, however, the poet is alienated from his society. His concern for his society's norms is but slight, since too often he feels his society and its values have rejected him and his values. Nevertheless, a verse satirist such as T. S. Eliot in "The Wasteland" can be cited as an example of a poet who is able to measure his contemporary society by the standards of a religious vision and a concern for the classical and literary heritage of Western civilization.

John Donne   Satire III

Kind pity chokes my spleen; brave scorn forbids
Those tears to issue which swell my eyelids;

I must not laugh, nor weep sins and be wise;
Can railing then cure these worn maladies?
Is not our mistress, fair religion,   5
As worthy of all our souls' devotion
As virtue was in the first blinded age?
Are not heaven's joys as valiant to assuage
Lusts as earth's honor was to them? Alas,
As we do them in means, shall they surpass   10
Us in the end? and shall thy father's spirit
Meet blind philosophers in heaven, whose merit
Of strict life may be imputed faith, and hear
Thee, whom he taught so easy ways and near
To follow, damned? Oh, if thou dar'st, fear this;   15
This fear great courage and high valor is.
Dar'st thou aid mutinous Dutch, and dar'st thou lay
Thee in ships, wooden sepulchers, a prey
To leaders' rage, to storms, to shot, to dearth?
Dar'st thou dive seas, and dungeons of the earth?   20
Hast thou courageous fire to thaw the ice
Of frozen North discoveries? and thrice
Colder than salamanders, like divine
Children in th' oven, fires of Spain and the Line,
Whose countries limbecs to our bodies be,   25
Canst thou for gain bear? and must every he
Which cries not, Goddess, to thy mistress, draw
Or eat thy poisonous words? Courage of straw!
O desperate coward, wilt thou seem bold and
To thy foes and His, who made thee to stand   30
Sentinel in his world's garrison, thus yield,
And for forbidden wars leave th' appointed field?
Know thy foes: the foul devil, whom thou
Strivest to please, for hate, not love, would allow
Thee fain his whole realm to be quit; and as   35
The world's all parts wither away and pass,
So the world's self, thy other loved foe, is
In her decrepit wane, and thou, loving this,
Dost love a withered and worn strumpet; last,
Flesh, itself death, and joys which flesh can taste   40
Thou lovest, and thy fair goodly soul, which doth
Give this flesh power to taste joy, thou dost loathe.
Seek true religion. Oh, where? Mirreus,
Thinking her unhoused here and fled from us,
Seeks her at Rome; there, because he doth know   45
That she was there a thousand years ago;
He loves her rags so, as we here obey
The statecloth where the prince sat yesterday.
Crantz to such brave loves will not be enthralled,
But loves her only, who at Geneva is called   50
Religion, plain, simple, sullen, young,
Contemptuous, yet unhandsome; as among
Lecherous humors, there is one that judges
No wenches wholesome, but coarse country drudges.
Graius stays still at home here, and because   55

Some preachers, vile ambitious bawds, and laws
Still new like fashions, bid him think that she
Which dwells with us is only perfect; he
Embraceth her, whom his godfathers will
Tender to him, being tender, as wards still   60
Take such wives as their guardians offer, or
Pay values. Careless Phrygius doth abhor
All, because all cannot be good, as one,
Knowing some women whores, dares marry none.
Graccus loves all as one, and thinks that so   65
As women do in divers countries go
In divers habits, yet are still one kind,
So doth, so is religion; and this blind-
ness too much light breeds; but unmoved, thou
Of force must one, and forced but one allow,   70
And the right; ask thy father which is she,
Let him ask his; though truth and falsehood be
Near twins, yet truth a little elder is;
Be busy to seek her; believe me this,
He's not of none, nor worst, that seeks the best.   75
To adore, or scorn an image, or protest,
May all be bad. Doubt wisely; in strange way
To stand inquiring right is not to stray;
To sleep, or run wrong, is. On a huge hill,
Cragged and steep, Truth stands, and he that will   80
Reach her, about must and about must go,
And what the hill's suddenness resists win so.
Yet strive so that before age, death's twilight,
Thy soul rest, for none can work in that night.
To will implies delay, therefore now do   85
Hard deeds, the body's pains; hard knowledge too
The mind's endeavors reach, and mysteries
Are like the sun, dazzling, yet plain to all eyes.
Keep the truth which thou hast found; men do not stand
In so ill case, that God hath with his hand   90
Signed kings blank charters to kill whom they hate;
Nor are they vicars, but hangmen, to fate.
Fool and wretch, wilt thou let thy soul be tied
To man's laws, by which she shall not be tried
At the last day? Will it then boot thee   95
To say a Philip or a Gregory,
A Harry or a Martin taught thee this?
Is not this excuse for mere contraries
Equally strong? Cannot both sides say so?
That thou mayest rightly obey power, her bounds know;   100
Those past, her nature and name is changed; to be
Then humble to her is idolatry.
As streams are, power is; those blest flowers that dwell
At the rough stream's calm head, thrive and do well,
But having left their roots, and themselves given   105
To the stream's tyrannous rage, also, are driven
Through mills and rocks and woods, and at last, almost
Consumed in going, in the sea are lost.

So perish souls, which more choose men's unjust
Power from God claimed than God himself to trust.   110

1 *spleen*: anger.   7 *first, blinded age*: before the light of God's
religious revelation shone.   9 *them*: worthies of the blinded age.
23 *salamanders*: supposed to be able to withstand fire.   24 *Children*: Shadrach, Meshach, and Abednego.   *fires of Spain*: autos-
da-fé of the Inquisition.   *the Line*: the equator.   25 *limbecs*:
alembics.   43 *Mirreus*: representing the Roman Catholic.   44
here: England.   49 *Crantz*: representing the Calvinist.   55
Graius: representing the Anglican.   62 *Pay values*: pay a sum
that was equal to the dowry when a ward refused marriage to a
girl selected by his guardian.   *Phrygius*: representing the atheist.
65 *Graccus*: representing the eclectic, who accepts all religions
as one.   96 *Philip*: Philip II of Spain, a Roman Catholic.
Gregory: Pope Gregory XIII.   97 *Harry*: Henry VIII of England,
a Protestant.   *Martin*: Martin Luther.

John Wilmot, Earl of Rochester   Satire

  Were I (who to my cost already am
One of those strange prodigious creatures Man),
A spirit free, to choose for my own share
What case of flesh and blood I please to wear,
I'd be a dog, a monkey, or a bear.   5
Or anything but that vain animal
Who is so proud of being rational.
The senses are too gross, and he'll contrive
A sixth, to contradict the other five;
And before certain instinct, will prefer   10
Reason, which fifty times for one does err.
Reason, an *ignis fatuus* in the mind,
Which leaving light of Nature, sense behind,
Pathless and dangerous wandering ways it takes,
Through errors, fenny bogs, and thorny breaks;   15
Whilst the misguided follower climbs with pain
Mountains of whimseys heaped in his own brain:
Stumbling from thought to thought, falls headlong down
Into doubt's boundless sea where, like to drown,
Books bear him up awhile and make him try   20
To swim with bladders of philosophy.
In hopes still t' o'ertake th' escaping light,
The vapor dances in his dazzling sight,
Till spent, it leaves him to eternal night.
Then old age and experience, hand in hand   25
Lead him to death, and make him understand
After a search so painful, and so long,
That all his life he has been in the wrong;
Huddled in dirt the reasoning engine lies,
Who was so proud, so witty, and so wise.   30
Pride drew him in, as cheats their bubbles catch,
And makes him venture to be made a wretch.

His wisdom did his happiness destroy,
Aiming to know what world he should enjoy;
And wit was his vain frivolous pretense   35
Of pleasing others at his own expense.
For wits are treated just like common whores,
First they're enjoyed, and then kicked out of doors:
The pleasure past, a threatening doubt remains,
That frights th' enjoyer with succeeding pains: 40
Women and men of wit are dangerous tools
And ever fatal to admiring fools.
Pleasure allures, and when the fops escape,
'Tis not that they're beloved, but fortunate,
And therefore what they fear at last they hate.   45
　　But now methinks some formal band and beard
Takes me to task; come on, Sir, I'm prepared.
　　Then by your favor, anything that's writ
Against this gibing jingling knack called wit,
Likes me abundantly, but you take care   50
Upon this point not to be too severe.
Perhaps my Muse were fitter for this part,
For I profess, I can be very smart
On wit, which I abhor with all my heart:
I long to lash it in some sharp essay,   55
But your grand indiscretion bids me stay,
And turns my tide of ink another way.
What rage ferments in your degenerate mind,
To make you rail at reason and mankind?
Blessed glorious Man! to whom alone kind Heaven   60
An everlasting soul has freely given;
Whom his great Maker took such care to make,
That from himself he did the image take;
And this fair frame, in shining reason dressed
To dignify his nature above beast.   65
Reason, by whose aspiring influence
We take a flight beyond material sense,
Dive into mysteries, then soaring pierce
The flaming limits of the universe,
Search Heaven and Hell, find out what's acted there,   70
And give the world true grounds of hope and fear.
　　Hold mighty Man, I cry, all this we know,
From the pathetic pen of Ingelo;
From P——— *Pilgrim*, S——— replies,
And 'tis this very reason I despise.   75
This supernatural gift, that makes a mite
Think he is the image of the Infinite:
Comparing his short life, void of all rest,
To the Eternal and the ever-blessed.
This busy, puzzling, stirrer-up of doubt,   80
That frames deep mysteries, then finds 'em out;
Filling with frantic crowds of thinking fools
Those reverend bedlams: colleges and schools;
Borne on whose wings, each heavy sot can pierce
The limits of the boundless universe.   85

So charming ointments make an old witch fly,
And bear a crippled carcass through the sky.
'Tis exalted power whose business lies
In nonsense and impossibilities.
This made a whimsical philosopher, 90
Before the spacious world, his tub prefer,
And we have modern cloistered coxcombs, who
Retire to think 'cause they have naught to do.
But thoughts are given for action's government,
Where action ceases, thought's impertinent: 95
Our sphere of action is life's happiness,
And he who thinks beyond thinks like an ass.
Thus, whilst 'gainst false reasoning I inveigh,
I own right reason, which I would obey:
That reason that distinguishes by sense 100
And gives us rules of good and ill from thence:
That bounds desires with a reforming will,
To keep 'em more in vigor, not to kill.
Your reason hinders, mine helps t'enjoy,
Renewing appetites yours would destroy 105
My reason is my friend, yours is a cheat,
Hunger calls out, my reason bids me eat;
Perversely yours, your appetite does mock,
This asks for food, that answers what's a clock?
This plain distinction, Sir, your doubt secures, 110
'Tis not true reason I despise but yours.
Thus I think reason righted but for Man.
I'll ne'er recant; defend him if you can.
For all his pride and his philosophy,
'Tis evident beasts are in their degree 115
As wise, at least, and better far than he.
Those creatures are the wisest who attain
By surest means the ends at which they aim.
If therefore Jowler finds and kills his hares,
Better than M——— supplies committee chairs, 120
Though one's a statesman, th' other but a hound,
Jowler, in justice, would be wiser found.
You see how far Man's wisdom here extends,
Look next, if human nature makes amends;
Whose principles most generous are, and just, 125
And to whose morals you would sooner trust,
Be judge yourself, I'll bring it to the test.
Which is the basest creature, man or beast?
Birds feed on birds, beasts on each other prey,
But savage Man alone does Man betray: 130
Pressed by necessity, they kill for food;
Man undoes Man, to do himself no good.
With teeth and claws by Nature armed they hunt,
Nature's allowance to supply their want.
But Man, with smiles, embraces, friendships, praise, 135
Unhumanly his fellow's life betrays;
With voluntary pains works his distress,
Not through necessity, but wantonness.

For hunger, or for love, they fight, or tear,
Whilst wretched Man is still in arms for fear.   140
For fear he arms, and is of arms afraid,
By fear to fear successively betrayed.
Base fear, the source whence his best passion came,
His boasted honor, and his dear bought fame,
That lust of power to which he's such a slave,   145
And for the which alone he dares be brave:
To which his various projects are designed,
Which makes him generous, affable, and kind.
For which he takes such pains to be thought wise
And screws his actions in a forced disguise: 150
Leading a tedious life in misery,
Under laborious, mean hypocrisy.
Look to the bottom of his vast design,
Wherein Man's wisdom, power, and glory join;
The good he acts, the ill he does endure,   155
'Tis all for fear, to make himself secure.
Merely for safety, after fame we thirst,
For all men would be cowards if they durst,
And honesty's against all common sense,
Men must be knaves, 'tis in their own defense.   160
Mankind's dishonest; if you think it fair
Amongst known cheats to play upon the square,
You'll be undone . . .
Nor can weak truth your reputation save,
The knaves will all agree to call you knave.   165
Wronged shall he live, insulted o'er, oppressed,
Who dares be less a villain than the rest.
Thus, Sir, you see what human nature craves,
Most men are cowards, all men should be knaves:
The difference lies (as far as I can see)   170
Not in the thing itself, but the degree;
And all the subject matter of debate
Is only, who's a knave of the first rate?
   All this with indignation have I hurled
At the pretending part of the proud world,   175
Who swollen with selfish vanity, devise
False freedoms, holy cheats, and formal lies
Over their fellow slaves to tyrannize.
   But if in court, so just a man there be
(In court, a just man, yet unknown to me)   180
Who does his needful flattery direct,
Not to oppress and ruin, but protect;
Since flattery, which way soever laid,
Is still a tax on that unhappy trade.
If so upright a statesman you can find,   185
Whose passions bend to his unbiased mind;
Who does his arts and policies apply,
To raise his country, not his family;
Nor while his pride, owned avarice withstands,
Receives aureal bribes, from friends' corrupted hands.   190
   Is there a churchman who on God relies?

Whose life his faith and doctrine justifies?
Not one blown up with vain prelatic pride,
Who for reproof of sins does Man deride;
Whose envious heart with his obstreperous saucy eloquence   *195*
Dares chide at kings and rail at men of sense;
Who from his pulpit vents more peevish lies,
More bitter railings, scandals, calumnies,
Than at a gossiping are thrown about
When the good wives get drunk and then fall out;   *200*
None of that sensual tribe, whose talents lie
In avarice, pride, sloth, and gluttony.
Who hunt good livings, but abhor good lives,
Whose lust exalted, to that height arrives,
They act adultery with their own wives   *205*
And ere a score of years completed be,
Can from a lofty pulpit proudly see
Half a large parish their own progeny.
   Nor doting B——— who would be adored
For domineering at the council board;   *210*
A greater fop in business at fourscore,
Fonder of serious toys, affected more
Than the gay glittering fool at twenty proves,
With all his noise, his tawdry clothes, and loves.
   But a meek humble man, of modest sense,   *215*
Who preaching peace, does practice continence;
Whose pious life's a proof he does believe
Mysterious truths which no man can conceive.
If upon Earth there dwell such God-like men,
I'll here recant my paradox to them.   *220*
Adore those shrines of virtue, homage pay,
And with the rabble world, their laws obey.
If such there are, yet grant me this at least,
Man differs more from man than man from beast.

title: commonly cited as "The Satire Against Mankind."   12
ignis fatuus: will-o'-the-wisp.   23 *dazzling:* dimming.   29
reasoning engine expresses the current view of man as a machine.
31 *bubbles:* dupes, or gulls.   73 *Ingelo:* Rev. Nathaniel Ingelo
(1621?–1683), whose religious romance, *Bentivolio and Urania*
(1660–1664), went through four editions by 1682.   74 *P———
Pilgrim:* Patrick's *Pilgrim,* a reference to *The Parable of the
Pilgrim:* a religious allegory by Simon Patrick, Bishop of Ely.
S——— replies: Richard Sibbes (1577–1635), author of religious
works, including a collection of sermons entitled *Bowels Opened.*
90–91: Diogenes (fourth century B.C.), principal representative of
the Cynic School of Philosophy.   108: That is, despite the fact that
it belongs to you, your appetite mocks you.   119 *Jowler:* common
name for a hound.   120 *M———:* Sir Thomas Meres (1635–
1715), M. P. in the Restoration period and Commissioner for the
Admiralty, 1679–84.   190 *aureal bribes:* bribes of gold.   209
B———: possibly Thomas Barlow, Bishop of Lincoln, who early
declared his loyalty to James II but as quickly turned Whig when
William III succeeded James.

Jonathan Swift   A Satirical Elegy on the Death
of a Late Famous General

His Grace! impossible! what, dead!
Of old age too, and in his bed!
And could that Mighty Warrior fall?
And so inglorious, after all!
Well, since he's gone, no matter how,   5
The last loud trump must wake him now;
And, trust me, as the noise grows stronger,
He'd wish to sleep a little longer.
And could he be indeed so old
As by the newspapers we're told?   10
Threescore, I think, is pretty high;
'Twas time in conscience he should die.
This world he cumbered long enough;
He burnt his candle to the snuff;
And that's the reason, some folks think,   15
He left behind so great a stink.
Behold his funeral appears,
Nor widow's sighs, nor orphans' tears,
Wont at such times each heart to pierce,
Attend the progress of his hearse.   20
But what of that, his friends may say,
He had those honors in his day.
True to his profit and his pride,
He made them weep before he died.

Come hither, all ye empty things,   25
Ye bubbles raised by breath of Kings;
Who float upon the tide of state,
Come hither, and behold your fate.
Let pride be taught by this rebuke,
How very mean a thing's a Duke;   30
From all his ill-got honors flung,
Turned to that dirt from whence he sprung.

1 *His Grace:* Duke of Marlborough (1650–1722), hero of Blen-
heim and various other battles in the War of Spanish Succession,
1701–1714.

Alexander Pope   An Epistle from Mr. Pope,
to Dr. Arbuthnot

SHUT, shut the door, good John! fatigued I said,
Tie up the knocker, say I'm sick, I'm dead.
The Dog-star rages! nay 'tis past a doubt,
All Bedlam, or Parnassus, is let out:
Fire in each eye, and papers in each hand,   5

They rave, recite, and madden round the land.
　　What walls can guard me, or what shades can hide?
They pierce my thickets, thro' my grot they glide,
By land, by water, they renew the charge,
They stop the chariot, and they board the barge.   10
No place is sacred, not the Church is free,
Ev'n Sunday shines no Sabbath-day to me:
Then from the Mint walks forth the Man of rhyme,
Happy! to catch me, just at dinner-time.
　　Is there a parson, much bemused in beer,   15
A maudlin poetress, a rhyming peer,
A clerk, foredoomed his father's soul to cross,
Who pens a stanza when he should *engross*?
Is there, who locked from ink and paper, scrawls
With desp'rate charcoal round his darkened walls?   20
All fly to Twit'nam, and in humble strain
Apply to me, to keep them mad or vain.
Arthur, whose giddy son neglects the laws.
Imputes to me and my damned works the cause:
Poor Cornus sees his frantic wife elope,   25
And curses wit, and poetry, and Pope.
　　Friend to my life! (which did not you prolong,
The world had wanted many an idle song)
What *drop* or *nostrum* can this plague remove?
Or which must end me, a fool's wrath or love?   30
A dire dilemma, either way I'm sped,
If foes, they write, if friends, they read me dead.
Seized and tied down to judge, how wretched I!
Why can't be silent, and who will not lie;
To laugh were want of goodness and of grace,   35
And to be grave exceeds all power of face.
I sit with sad civility, I read
With honest anguish, and an aching head;
And drop at last, but in unwilling ears,
This saving counsel, "Keep your piece nine years."   40
　　Nine years! cries he, who high in Drury Lane
Lulled by soft zephyrs thro' the broken pane,
Rhymes ere he wakes, and prints before *Term* ends,
Obliged by hunger, and request of friends:
"The piece you think is incorrect? why take it,   45
"I'm all submission, what you'd have it, make it."
Three things another's modest wishes bound,
My friendship, and a prologue, and ten pound.
　　Pitholeon sends to me: "You know his Grace,
"I want a patron; ask him for a place."   50
Pitholeon libelled me—"but here's a letter
"Informs you, sir, 'twas when he knew no better.
"Dare you refuse him? Curll invites to dine,
"He'll write a *Journal*, or he'll turn divine."
Bless me! a packet.—" 'Tis a stranger sues,   55
"A virgin tragedy, an orphan muse."
If I dislike it, "Furies, death, and rage!"
If I approve, "Commend it to the stage."

There (thank my stars) my whole commission ends,
The players and I are, luckily, no friends.   60
Fired that the house reject him, "S'death I'll print it,
"And shame the fools—your int'rest, sir, with Lintot."
Lintot, dull rogue! will think your price too much:
"Not sir, If you revise it, and retouch."
All my demurs but double his attacks,   65
At last he whispers, "Do, and we go snacks."
Glad of a quarrel, strait I clap the door,
Sir, let me see your works and you no more.
   'Tis sung, when Midas' ears began to spring,
(Midas, a sacred person and a king)   70
His very minister who spied them first,
(Some say his queen) was forced to speak, or burst.
And is not mine, my friend, a sorer case,
When every coxcomb perks them in my face?
"Good friend forbear! you deal in dang'rous things,   75
"I'd never name queens, ministers, or kings;
"Keep close to ears, and those let asses prick,
" 'Tis nothing."—Nothing? if they bite and kick?
Out with it, *Dunciad!* let the secret pass,
That secret to each fool, that he's an ass: 80
The truth once told, (and wherefore should we lie?)
The queen of Midas slept, and so may I.
   You think this cruel? take it for a rule,
No creature smarts so little as a fool.
Let peals of laughter, Codrus! round thee break,   85
Thou unconcerned canst hear the mighty crack:
Pit, box, and gallery in convulsions hurled,
Thou stand'st unshook amidst a bursting world.
Who shames a scribler? break one cobweb thro',
He spins the slight, self-pleasing thread anew: 90
Destroy his fib or sophistry, in vain,
The creature's at his dirty work again,
Throned in the center of his thin designs,
Proud of a vast extent of flimsy lines!
Whom have I hurt? has poet yet, or peer,   95
Lost the arched eyebrow, or Parnassian sneer?
And has not Coley still his lord, and whore?
His butchers Henley, his free-masons Moore?
Does not one table Bavius still admit?
Still to one Bishop Philips seems a wit?   100
Still Sappho—"Hold! for God sake—you'll offend,
"No names—be calm—learn prudence of a friend:
"I too could write, and I am twice as tall;
"But foes like these!—One flatt'rer's worse than all;
Of all mad creatures, if the learned are right,   105
It is the slaver kills, and not the bite.
A fool quite angry is quite innocent,
Alas! 'tis ten times worse when they *repent*.
   One dedicates in high heroic prose,
And ridicules beyond a hundred foes;   110
One from all Grubstreet will my fame defend,

And more abusive, calls himself my friend.
This prints my *Letters,* that expects a bribe,
And others roar aloud, "Subscribe, subscribe."
 There are, who to my person pay their court,   *115*
I cough like *Horace,* and tho' lean, am short,
Ammon's great son one shoulder had too high,
Such *Ovid's* nose, and "Sir! you have an eye—"
Go on, obliging creatures, make me see
All that disgraced my betters, met in me.   *120*
Say for my comfort, languishing in bed,
"Just so immortal *Maro* held his head":
And when I die, be sure you let me know
Great *Homer* died three thousand years ago.
 Why did I write? what sin to me unknown   *125*
Dipt me in ink, my parents, or my own?
As yet a child, nor yet a fool to fame,
I lisped in numbers, for the numbers came.
I left no calling for this idle trade,
No duty broke, no father disobeyed.   *130*
The muse but served to ease some friend, not wife,
To help me thro' this long disease, my Life,
To second, Arbuthnot! thy Art and Care,
And teach, the being you preserved, to bear.
 But why then publish? *Granville* the polite,   *135*
And knowing *Walsh,* would tell me I could write;
Well-natured *Garth* inflam'd with early praise,
And *Congreve* loved, and *Swift* endured my lays;
The courtly *Talbot, Somers, Sheffield* read,
Ev'n mitred *Rochester* would nod the head.   *140*
And St. *John's* self (great *Dryden's* friend before)
With open arms received one poet more.
Happy my studies, when by these approved!
Happier their author, when by these beloved!
From these the world will judge of men and books, *145*
Not from the *Burnets, Oldmixons,* and *Cooks.*
 Soft were my numbers; who could take offence
While pure description held the place of sense?
Like gentle *Fanny's* was my flowery theme,
A painted mistress, or a purling stream.   *150*
Yet then did *Gildon* draw his venal quill;
I wished the man a dinner, and sat still.
Yet then did *Dennis* rave in furious fret;
I never answered, I was not in debt.
If want provoked, or madness made them print, *155*
I waged no war with *Bedlam* or the *Mint.*
 Did some more sober Critic come abroad?
If wrong, I smiled; if right, I kissed the rod.
Pains, reading, study, are their just pretence,
And all they want is spirit, taste, and sense.   *160*
Commas and points they set exactly right,
And 'twere a sin to rob them of their mite.
Yet ne'er one sring of laurel graced these ribalds,
From slashing *Bentley* down to pidling *Tibalds:*

Each wight, who reads not, and but scans and spells,   *165*
Each word-catcher, that lives on syllables,
Ev'n such small critics some regard may claim,
Preserved in *Milton's* or in *Shakespeare's* name.
Pretty! in amber to observe the forms
Of hairs, or straws, or dirt, or grubs, or worms!   *170*
The things, we know, are neither rich nor rare,
But wonder how the devil they got there?
    Were others angry? I excused them too;
Well might they rage, I gave them but their due.
A man's true merit 'tis not hard to find,   *175*
But each man's secret standard in his mind,
That casting-weight pride adds to emptiness,
This, who can gratify? for who can *guess*?
The bard whom pilfered pastorals renown,
Who turns a Persian tale for half a crown,   *180*
Just writes to make his barrenness appear,
And strains from hard-bound brains, eight lines a year;
He, who still wanting, tho' he lives on theft,
Steals much, spends little, yet has nothing left:
And he, who now to sense, now nonsense leaning,   *185*
Means not, but blunders round about a meaning:
And he, whose fustian's so sublimely bad,
It is not poetry, but prose run mad:
All these, my modest satire bad *translate*,
And owned, that nine such poets made a *Tate*.   *190*
How did they fume, and stamp, and roar, and chafe?
And swear, not *Addison* himself was safe.
    Peace to all such! but were there one whose fires
True genius kindles, and fair fame inspires;
Blest with each talent and each art to please,   *195*
And born to write, converse, and live with ease:
Should such a man, too fond to rule alone,
Bear, like the Turk, no brother near the throne,
View him with scornful, yet with jealous eyes,
And hate for arts that caused himself to rise;   *200*
Damn with faint praise, assent with civil leer,
And without sneering, teach the rest to sneer;
Willing to wound, and yet afraid to strike,
Just hint a fault, and hesitate dislike;
Alike reserved to blame, or to commend,   *205*
A timorous foe, and a suspicious friend:
Dreading ev'n fools, by flatterers besieged,
And so obliging, that he ne'er obliged;
Like *Cato*, gave his little Senate laws,
And sit attentive to his own applause;   *210*
While wits and templers every sentence raise,
And wonder with a foolish face of praise—
Who but must laugh, if such a man there be?
Who would not weep, if *Atticus* were he!
    What tho' my name stood rubric on the walls,   *215*
Or plaistered posts, with claps in capitals?
Or smoking forth, a hundred hawkers load,

On wings of winds came flying all abroad?
I sought no homage from the race that write;
I kept, like *Asian* Monarch, from their sight: 220
Poems I heeded (now be-rhymed so long)
No more than thou, great GEORGE! a birthday song.
I ne'er with wits or witlings past my days,
To spread about the itch of verse and praise;
Nor like a puppy, daggled thro' the town,   225
To fetch and carry sing-song up and down;
Nor at rehearsals sweat, and mouthed, and cried,
With handkerchief and orange at my side;
But sick of fops, and poetry, and prate,
To *Bufo* left the whole *Castalian* state.   230
    Proud, as *Apollo* on his forked hill,
Sat full-blown *Bufo,* puffed by every quill;
Fed with soft dedication all day long,
Horace and he went hand in hand in song.
His library, (where busts of poets dead   235
And a true *Pindar* stood without a head)
Received of wits an undistinguished race,
Who first his judgment asked, and then a place:
Much they extoll'd his pictures, much his seat,
And flattered every day, and some days eat: 240
Till grown more frugal in his riper days,
He paid some bards with port, and some with praise,
To some a dry rehearsal was assigned.
And others (harder still) he paid in kind.
Dryden alone (what wonder?) came not nigh,   245
Dryden alone escaped this judging eye:
But still the great have kindness in reserve,
He helped to bury whom he helped to starve.
    May some choice patron bless each grey goose quill!
May every *Bavius* have his *Bufo* still!   250
So when a Statesman wants a day's defence,
Or envy holds a whole week's war with sense,
Or simple pride for flattery makes demands,
May dunce by dunce be whistled off my hands!
Blest be the *Great!* for those they take away,   255
And those they left me; For they left me GAY;
Left me to see neglected Genius bloom,
Neglected die, and tell it on his tomb:
Of all thy blameless life the sole return
My Verse, and QUEENSB'RY weeping o'er thy urn!   260
    Oh let me live my own, and die so too!
("To live and die is all I have to do")
Maintain a poet's dignity and ease,
And see what friends, and read what books I please:
Above a patron, tho' I condescend   265
Sometimes to call a minister my friend.
I was not born for courts or great affairs:
I pay my debts, believe, and say my prayers;
Can sleep without a poem in my head,
Nor know, if *Dennis* be alive or dead.   270

    Why am I asked what next shall see the light;
Heavens! was I born for nothing but to write?
Has life no joys for me? or (to be grave)
Have I no friend to serve, no soul to save?
"I found him close with *Swift*—Indeed? no doubt   275
"(Cries prating *Balbus*) something will come out.
'Tis all in vain, deny it as I will.
"No, such a genius never can lie still;
And then for mine obligingly mistakes
The first lampoon *Sir Will* or *Bubo* makes.   280
Poor guiltless I! and can I choose but smile,
When every coxcomb knows me by my *style*?
    Curst be the verse, how well soe'er it flow,
That tends to make one worthy man my foe,
Give virtue scandal, innocence a fear,   285
Or from the soft-eyed virgin steal a tear!
But he who hurts a harmless neighbor's peace,
Insults fallen worth, or beauty in distress,
Who loves a lie, lame slander helps about,
Who writes a libel, or who copies out: 290
The fop, whose pride affects a patron's name,
Yet absent, wounds an author's honest fame:
Who can *your* merit *selfishly* approve,
And show the *sense* of it without the *love*;
Who has the vanity to call you friend,   295
Yet wants the honor injured to defend;
Who tells whate'er you think, whate'er you say,
And, if he lie not, must at least betray;
Who to the *Dean*, and *silver bell* can swear,
And sees at *Cannon*'s what was never there;   300
Who reads, but with a lust to misapply,
Make satire a lampoon, and fiction lie.
A lash like mine no honest man shall dread,
But all such babbling blockheads in his stead.
    Let *Sporus* tremble—"What? that thing of silk,   305
"*Sporus*, that mere white curd of ass's milk?
"Satire or sense alas! can *Sporus* feel?
"Who breaks a butterfly upon a wheel?"
Yet let me flap this bug with gilded wings,
This painted child of dirt, that stinks and stings;   310
Whose buzz the witty and the fair annoys,
Yet wit ne'er tastes, and beauty ne'er enjoys:
So well-bred spaniels civilly delight
In mumbling of the game they dare not bite.
Eternal smiles his emptiness betray,   315
As shallow streams run dimpling all the way,
Whether in florid impotence he speaks,
And, as the prompter breathes, the puppet squeaks,
Or at the ear of *Eve*, familiar toad,
Half froth, half venom, spits himself abroad,   320
In puns, or politics, or tales, or lies,
Or spite, or smut, or rhymes, or blasphemies,

His wit all see-saw, between *that* and *this*,
Now high, now low, now master up, now miss,
And he himself one vile antithesis.   325
Amphibious thing! that acting either part,
The trifling head, or the corrupted heart,
Fop at the toilet, flatterer at the board,
Now trips a lady, and now struts a lord.
Eve's tempter thus the Rabbins have exprest,   330
A Cherub's face, a reptile all the rest,
Beauty that shocks you, parts that none will trust,
Wit that can creep, and pride that licks the dust.
   Not fortune's worshipper, nor fashion's fool,
Not lucre's madman, nor ambition's tool,   335
Not proud, nor servile; be one poet's praise,
That, if he pleased, he pleased by manly ways;
That flattery, ev'n to kings, he held a shame,
And thought a lie in verse or prose the same.
That not in fancy's maze he wandered long,   340
But stooped to truth, and moralized his song:
That not for fame, but virtue's better end,
He stood the furious foe, the timid friend,
The damning critic, half-approving wit,
The coxcomb hit, or fearing to be hit;   345
Laughed at the loss of friends he never had,
The dull, the proud, the wicked, and the mad;
The distant threats of vengeance on his head,
The blow unfelt, the tear he never shed;
The tale revived, the lie so oft o'erthrown,   350
Th' imputed trash, and dulness not his own;
The morals blackened when the writings scape,
The libeled person, and the pictured shape;
Abuse, on all he loved, or loved him, spread,
A friend in exile, or a father, dead;   355
The whisper, that to greatness still too near,
Perhaps, yet vibrates on his SOVEREIGN's ear—
Welcome for thee, fair Virtue! all the past:
For thee, fair Virtue! welcome ev'n the *last!*
   "But why insult the poor, affront the great?"   360
A knave's a knave, to me, in every state:
Alike my scorn, if he succeed or fail,
Sporus at court, or *Japhet* in a jail,
A hireling scribbler, or a hireling peer,
Knight of the post corrupt, or of the shire;   365
If on a pillory, or near a throne,
He gain his prince's ear, or lose his own.
   Yet soft by nature, more a dupe than wit,
Sappho can tell you how this this man was bit:
This dreaded satirist *Dennis* will confess   370
Foe to his pride, but friend to his distress:
So humble, he has knocked at *Tibbald's* door,
Has drunk with *Cibber,* nay has rhymed for *Moor.*
Full ten years slandered, did he once reply?
Three thousand suns went down on *Welsted's* lie.   375

To please a Mistress one aspersed his life;
He lashed him not, but let her be his wife:
Let *Budgell* charge low Grubstreet on his quill,
And write whate'er he pleased, except his will;
Let the two *Curlls* of town and court, abuse   380
His father, mother, body, soul and muse.
Yet why? that father held it for a rule,
It was a sin to call our neighbor fool:
That harmless mother thought no wife a whore:
Hear this, and spare his family, *James Moore!*   385
Unspotted names, and memorable long!
If there be force in virtue, or in song.
   Of gentle blood (part shed in honor's cause,
While yet in *Britain* honor had applause)
Each parent sprung—"What fortune, pray?—Their own,   390
And better got, than *Bestia's* from the throne.
Born to no pride, inheriting no strife,
Nor marrying discord in a noble wife,
Stranger to civil and religious rage,
The good man walked innoxious thro' his age.   395
No courts he saw, no suits would ever try,
Nor dared an oath, nor hazarded a lie.
Unlearned, he knew no schoolman's subtile art,
No language, but the language of the heart.
By nature honest, by experience wise,   400
Healthy by temperance, and by exercise;
His life, tho' long, to sickness past unknown,
His death was instant, and without a groan.
O grant me, thus to live, and thus to die!
Who sprung from kings shall know less joy than I.   405
   O friend! may each domestic bliss be thine!
Be no unpleasing melancholy mine:
Me, let the tender office long engage,
To rock the cradle of reposing age,
With lenient arts extend a mother's breath,   410
Make languor smile, and smooth the bed of death,
Explore the thought, explain the asking eye,
And keep a while one parent from the sky!
On cares like these if length of days attend,
May heaven, to bless those days, preserve my friend,   415
Preserve his social, cheerful, and serene,
And just as rich as when he served a QUEEN.
Whether that blessing be denied or given,
Thus far was right, the rest belongs to Heaven.

title: Dr. John Arbuthnot (1667–1735), physician to Queen Anne,
a leading figure of the Scriblerus Club, which included Swift,
Gay, and Pope. Arbuthnot, mortally ill, asked Pope to continue to
write satire "more to reform than chastise," and the following
poem is Pope's response to Arbuthnot's request.   *1 John:* John
Searle, his old servant.   *13 Mint:* the district of the Mint, from
which debtors were exempt from arrest. Debtors in all London
were exempt from arrest on Sunday.   *23 Arthur:* Arthur Moore,

a politician.   25 *Cornus:* Latin for "horn" (*i.e.,* cuckold). Sir
Robert Walpole's wife left him in 1734.   43 *Term:* a session of
the law courts.   49 *Pitholeon:* a poetaster of Rhodes.   53 *Curll:*
Edmund Curll, a piratical publisher.   62 *Lintot:* Bernard Lintot,
the publisher of many of Pope's works.   85 *Codrus:* a poet
satirized by Juvenal.   96 *Colley:* Colley Cibber, actor, dramatist
and poet laureate.   98 *Henley:* "Orator" John Henley preached to
the "butchers" and various other tradesmen.   *Moor:* James
Moore, the son of Arthur Moore (line 23).   99 *Bavius:* a poetaster of the first century A.D.   100 *Philips:* Ambrose Philips,
famous for his *Pastorals,* patronized by Bishop Hugh Boulter.   101
Sappho: Lady Mary Wortley Montague. Pope believed Lady Mary,
a former friend, in part responsible for the attack upon him.
117 *Ammon's great son:* Alexander the Great was supposed to be
descended from Jupiter Ammon.   135 *Granville:* George Granville, a politician to whom Pope dedicated his topographical poem
Windsor Forest.   139: Charles Talbot, Duke of Shrewsbury;
John, Baron Sommers, Lord Chancellor; and John Sheffield Duke
of Buckingham.   140 *Rochester:* Francis Atterbury, Bishop of
Rochester.   146 Authors of secret and scandalous history. [Pope]
149: Fanny and Sporus were names used by Pope for Lord Hervey,
a friend of Lady Mary Wortley Montagu.   151 *Gildon:* Charles
Gildon. Pope believed Gildon to be in part responsible for the *True
Character of Mr. Pope.*   164 *Bentley . . . Tibbalds:* Richard
Bentley, who made what Pope took to be slighting remarks upon
Pope's translation of the *Iliad.* Lewis Theobald was the hero of
Pope's first *Dunciad.*   180 *Persian tale:* Ambrose Philips had
printed a volume of *Persian Tales.*   190 *Tate:* Nahum Tate was
laureate from 1692 to 1715.   193 *one who fires:* a reference to
Pope's celebrated portrait of Atticus, or Addison.   216 *claps:*
posters.   222 *George:* King George II.   230 *Bufo:* Charles
Montagu, Lord Halifax, the patron of Thomas Tickell, who
had translated the *Iliad* and was hence a rival.   260 *Queensb'ry:*
The Duke of Queensbury. He and his wife were John Gay's
patrons.   276 *Balbus:* possibly George Hay, Earl of Kinnoul.
280 *Sir Will or Bubo:* Sir William Yonge, a Whig politician;
Bubb Dodington, a politician of little merit and a patron of the
arts with slight taste.   299: Meaning the man who would have
persuaded the Duke of Chandos that Mr. P. meant him in those
circumstances ridiculed in the Epistle on Taste. [Pope]   305
Sporus: a reference to the famous attack on Lord Hervey.   353
pictur'd shape: a reference to the caricatures that depicted Pope as
hunchbacked.   363 *Japhet:* Japhet Crook, a forger who was
punished by having his nose and ears cut off.   365 *Knight of the
post:* one who hung about near sheriffs' posts in order to sell his
testimony to whoever would buy it.   375 *Welsted's lye:* Leonard
Welsted had attacked Pope a number of times.   377 *wife:* the
reference is obscure but possibly refers to Teresa Blount.   379
his will: a reference to Eustace Budgell (l. 378), who had attacked
Pope and who was suspected of having forged a will.   380
Curlls: Edmund Curll and Lord Hervey were both associated with
the publication of scandal.   385 *James Moore:* James Moore,
another man who had attacked Pope, was thought to be illegitimate.

391 *Bestia's:* L. Capurnius Bestia was a Roman pro-consul who took bribes. Critics suggest that the reference may be to the Duke of Marlborough.   393 *discord . . . wife:* Addison had married the Countess of Warwick. Pope implies that their marriage was not a happy one.   413 *one parent . . . sky:* this poem was published in January, 1735; Pope's mother died in 1733.

George Gordon, Lord Byron

FROM *Beppo*

[ITALY AND ENGLAND]

41

With all its sinful doings, I must say,
    That Italy's a pleasant place to me,
Who love to see the sun shine every day,
    And vines (not nailed to walls) from tree to tree
Festooned, much like the back scene of a play,   5
    Or melodrame, which people flock to see,
When the first act is ended by a dance
In vineyards copied from the south of France.

42

I like on autumn evenings to ride out,
    Without being forced to bid my groom be sure   10
My cloak is round his middle strapped about,
    Because the skies are not the most secure;
I know too that, if stopped upon my route,
    Where the green alleys windingly allure,
Reeling with *grapes* red wagons choke the way,—   15
In England 'twould be dung, dust, or a dray.

43

I also like to dine on becaficas,
    To see the sun set, sure he'll rise tomorrow,
Not through a misty morning twinkling weak as
    A drunken man's dead eye in maudlin sorrow,   20
But with all Heaven t'himself: the day will break as
    Beauteous as cloudless, nor be forced to borrow
That sort of farthing candlelight which glimmers
Where reeking London's smoky cauldron simmers.

44

I love the language, that soft bastard Latin,   25
    Which melts like kisses from a female mouth,
And sounds as if it should be writ on satin,
    With syllables which breathe of the sweet South,
And gentle liquids gliding all so pat in,
    That not a single accent seems uncouth,   30
Like our harsh northern whistling, grunting guttural,
Which we're obliged to hiss, and spit, and sputter all.

45

I like the women too (forgive my folly!)
  From the rich peasant cheek of ruddy bronze,
And large black eyes that flash on you a volley   35
  Of rays that say a thousand things at once,
To the high Dama's brow, more melancholy,
  But clear, and with a wild and liquid glance,
Heart on her lips, and soul within her eyes,
Soft as her clime, and sunny as her skies.   40

46

Eve of the land which still is Paradise!
  Italian Beauty! Did'st thou not inspire
Raphael, who died in thy embrace, and vies
  With all we know of Heaven, or can desire,
In what he hath bequeathed us?—in what guise,   45
  Though flashing from the fervor of the lyre,
Would *words* describe thy past and present glow,
While yet Canova can create below?

47

"ENGLAND! with all thy faults I love thee still,"
  I said at Calais, and have not forgot it;   50
I like to speak and lucubrate my fill;
  I like the government (but that is not it);
I like the freedom of the press and quill;
  I like the Habeas Corpus (when we've got it);
I like a parliamentary debate,   55
Particularly when 'tis not too late;

48

I like the taxes, when they're not too many;
  I like a sea-coal fire, when not too dear;
I like a beef-steak, too, as well as any;
  Have no objection to a pot of beer;   60
I like the weather, when it is not rainy,
  That is, I like two months of every year,
And so God save the Regent, Church, and King!
Which means that I like all and everything.

49

Our standing army, and disbanded seamen,   65
  Poor's rate, Reform, my own, the nation's debt,
Our little riots just to show we're free men,
  Our trifling bankruptcies in the Gazette,
Our cloudy climate, and our chilly women,
  All these I can forgive, and those forget,   70
And greatly venerate our recent glories,
And wish they were not owing to the Tories.

title: Beppo is a Venetian tale in ninety-nine stanzas.   *17 beca-*
ficas: small songbirds, eaten as a delicacy in Italy.

James Russell Lowell
  FROM *A Fable for Critics*
  [EMERSON]

"There comes Emerson first, whose rich words, every one,
Are like gold nails in temples to hang trophies on,
Whose prose is grand verse, while his verse, the Lord knows,
Is some of it pr—No, 'tis not even prose;
I'm speaking of metres; some poems have welled   5
From those rare depths of soul that have ne'er been excelled;
They're not epics, but that doesn't matter a pin,
In creating, the only hard thing's to begin;
A glass-blade's no easier to make than an oak;
If you've once found the way, you've achieved the grand   10
    stroke;
In the worst of his poems are mines of rich matter,
But thrown in a heap with a crash and a clatter;
Now it is not one thing nor another alone
Makes a poem, but rather the general tone,
The something pervading, uniting the whole,   15
The before unconceived, unconceivable soul,
So that just in removing this trifle or that, you
Take away, as it were, a chief limb of the statue;
Roots, wood, bark, and leaves singly perfect may be,
But, clapt hodge-podge together, they don't make a tree.   20

"But, to come back to Emerson (whom, by the way,
I believe we left waiting),—his is, we may say,
A Greek head on right Yankee shoulders, whose range
Has Olympus for one pole, for t'other the Exchange;
He seems, to my thinking (although I'm afraid   25
The comparison must, long ere this, have been made),
A Plotinus-Montaigne, where the Egyptian's gold mist
And the Gascon's shrewd wit cheek-by-jowl coexist;
All admire, and yet scarcely six converts he's got
To I don't (nor they either) exactly know what;   30
For though he builds glorious temples, 'tis odd
He leaves never a doorway to get in a god.
'Tis refreshing to old-fashioned people like me
To meet such a primitive Pagan as he,
In whose mind all creation is duly respected   35
As parts of himself—just a little projected;
And who's willing to worship the stars and the sun,
A convert to—nothing but Emerson.
So perfect a balance there is in his head,
That he talks of things sometimes as if they were dead;   40
Life, nature, love, God, and affairs of that sort,
He looks at as merely ideas; in short,
As if they were fossils stuck round in a cabinet,
Of such vast extent that our earth's a mere dab in it;

Composed just as he is inclined to conjecture her,   45
Namely, one part pure earth, ninety-nine parts pure lecturer;
You are filled with delight at his clear demonstration,
Each figure, word, gesture, just fits the occasion,
With the quiet precision of science he'll sort 'em,
But you can't help suspecting the whole a *post mortem*.   50

"There are persons, mole-blind to the soul's make and style,
Who insist on a likeness 'twixt him and Carlyle;
To compare him with Plato would be vastly fairer,
Carlyle's the more burly, but E. is the rarer;
He sees fewer objects, but clearlier, trulier,   55
If C.'s as original, E.'s more peculiar;
That he's more of a man you might say of the one,
Of the other he's more of an Emerson;
C.'s the Titan, as shaggy of mind as of limb,—
E. the clear-eyed Olympian, rapid and slim;   60
The one's two thirds Norseman, the other half Greek,
Where the one's most abounding, the other's to see;
C.'s generals require to be seen in the mass,—
E.'s specialties gain if enlarged by the glass;
C. gives nature and God his own fits of the blues,   65
And rimes common-sense things with mystical hues,—
E. sits in a mystery calm and intense,
And looks coolly around him with sharp common-sense;
C. shows you how every-day matters unite
With the dim transdiurnal recesses of night,—   70
While E., in a plain, preternatural way,
Makes mysteries matters of mere every day;
C. draws all his characters quite *à la* Fuseli,—
Not sketching their bundles of muscles and thews illy,
He paints with a brush so untamed and profuse   75
They seem nothing but bundles of muscles and thews;
E. is rather like Flaxman, lines strait and severe,
And a colorless outline, but full, round, and clear;—
To the men he thinks worthy he frankly accords
The design of a white marble statue in words.   80
C. labors to get at the centre, and then
Take a reckoning from there of his actions and men;
E. calmly assumes the said centre as granted,
And, given himself, has whatever is wanted.

"He has imitators in scores, who omit   85
No part of the man but his wisdom and wit,—
Who go carefully o'er the sky-blue of his brain,
And when he has skimmed it once, skim it again;
If at all they resemble him, you may be sure it is
Because their shoals mirror his mists and obscurities,   90
As a mud-puddle seems deep as heaven for a minute,
While a cloud that floats o'er is reflected within it."

title: Lowell's *Fable* appeared in 1848 and is a witty criticism of
contemporary American writers. Loosely modeled upon Alexander
Pope's critical essay in verse, *The Dunciad, A Fable* pokes fun

at such figures as Bryant, Whittier, Cooper, Poe, Hawthorne, Irving, and the author himself. The excerpt that follows compares Ralph Waldo Emerson (1803–1882), American essayist, transcendentalist and poet with Thomas Carlyle (1795–1881), English essayist, transcendentalist, and historian.   24 *Exchange:* Stock Exchange. The ideal and practical aspects of Emerson are here contrasted.   27 *Plotinus-Montaigne:* Plotinus (205–270), a Roman Neo-platonic philosopher. Michel Eyquem de Montaigne (1533–1592), French essayist, noted for his skeptical wit and urbane style.   73 *Fuseli:* Johann Heinrich Füssli (1742–1825), German-Swiss painter and engraver whose depiction of anatomical details in his *Paradise Lost* illustrations are extravagant in the extreme.   77 *Flaxman:* John Flaxman (1755–1826), English sculptor and draftsman; his work is in the classical tradition.

Emily Dickinson   "He Preached upon 'Breadth' "

He preached upon "Breadth" till it argued him narrow—
The Broad are too broad to define
And of "Truth" until it proclaimed him a Liar—
The Truth never flaunted a Sign—

Simplicity fled from his counterfeit presence   5
As Gold the Pyrites would shun—
What confusion would cover the innocent Jesus
To meet so enabled a Man!

6 *Pyrites:* mock gold; here contrasted with gold, a symbol of integrity.

Stephen Crane   War Is Kind

Do not weep, maiden, for war is kind.
Because your lover threw wild hands toward the sky
And the affrighted steed ran on alone,
Do not weep.
War is kind.   5

    Hoarse, booming drums of the regiment,
    Little souls who thirst for fight,
    These men were born to drill and die.
    The unexplained glory flies above them,
    Great is the Battle-God, great, and his Kingdom—   10
    A field where a thousand corpses lie.

Do not weep, babe, for war is kind.
Because your father tumbled in the yellow trenches,
Raged at his breast, gulped and died,
Do not weep.   15
War is kind.

Swift blazing flag of the regiment,
Eagle with crest of red and gold,
These men were born to drill and die.
Point for them the virtue of slaughter,   20
Make plain to them the excellence of killing
And a field where a thousand corpses lie.

Mother whose heart hung humble as a button
On the bright splendid shroud of your son,
Do not weep.   25
War is kind.

T. S. *Eliot*   Sweeney Among the Nightingales

Apeneck Sweeney spreads his knees
Letting his arms hang down to laugh,
The zebra stripes along his jaw
Swelling to maculate giraffe.

The circles of the stormy moon   5
Slide westward to the River Plate,
Death and the Raven drift above
And Sweeney guards the hornèd gate.

Gloomy Orion and the Dog
Are veiled, and hushed the shrunken seas;   10
The person in the Spanish cape
Tried to sit on Sweeney's knees,

Slips and pulls the table cloth,
Overturns a coffee cup;
Reorganized upon the floor   15
She yawns and draws a stocking up;

The silent man in mocha brown
Sprawls at the window-sill and gapes;
The waiter brings in oranges,
Bananas, figs and hot-house grapes;   20

The silent vertebrate exhales,
Contracts and concentrates, withdraws;
Rachel *née* Rabinovitch
Tears at the grapes with murderous paws;

She and the lady in the cape   25
Are suspect, thought to be in league;
Therefore the man with heavy eyes
Declines the gambit, shows fatigue,

Leaves the room and reappears
Outside the window, leaning in,   30
Branches of wistaria
Circumscribe a golden grin;

The host with someone indistinct
Converses at the door apart,
The nightingales are singing near   35
The Convent of the Sacred Heart,

And sang within the bloody wood
When Agamemnon cried aloud,
And let their liquid siftings fall
To stain the stiff dishonoured shroud.   40

4 *maculate*: spotted.   6 *River Plate*: lying between Uruguay and
Argentina   8 *hornèd*: symbolizing cuckoldry. The two gates of
dreams were ivory (false dreams) and horn (true dreams); the
dreams entered into one's mind from Hell.

Wallace Stevens   A High-Toned Old Christian Woman

Poetry is the supreme fiction, madame.
Take the moral law and make a nave of it
And from the nave build haunted heaven. Thus,
The conscience is converted into palms,
Like windy citherns hankering for hymns.   5
We agree in principle. That's clear. But take
The opposing law and make a peristyle,
And from the peristyle project a masque
Beyond the planets. Thus, our bawdiness,
Unpurged by epitaph, indulged at last,   10
Is equally converted into palms,
Squiggling like saxophones. And palm for palm,
Madame, we are where we began. Allow,
Therefore, that in the planetary scene
Your disaffected flagellants, well-stuffed,   15
Smacking their muzzy bellies in parade,
Proud of such novelties of the sublime,
Such tink and tank and tunk-a-tunk-tunk,
May, merely may, madame, whip from themselves
A jovial hullabaloo among the spheres.   20
This will make widows wince. But fictive things
Wink as they will. Wink most when widows wince.

2 *nave*: the main part of a church interior.   5 *citherns*: citterns,
a guitar with a pear-shaped flat-backed body; popular in Renaissance
England.   7 *peristyle*: an open space enclosed by a colonnade,
i.e., a space bounded by a series of columns set at regular intervals.

e. e. cummings   "i sing of Olaf glad and big"

i sing of Olaf glad and big
whose warmest heart recoiled at war:
a conscientious object-or

his wellbelovéd colonel(trig
westpointer most succinctly bred)   5
took erring Olaf soon in hand;
but—though an host of overjoyed
noncoms(first knocking on the head
him)do through icy waters roll
that helplessness which others stroke   10
with brushes recently employed
anent this muddy toiletbowl,
while kindred intellects evoke
allegiance per blunt instruments—
Olaf(being to all intents   15
a corpse and wanting any rag
upon what God unto him gave)
responds, without getting annoyed
"I will not kiss your f.ing flag"

straightway the silver bird looked grave   20
(departing hurriedly to shave)

but—though all kinds of officers
(a yearning nation's blueeyed pride)
their passive prey did kick and curse
until for wear their clarion   25
voices and boots were much the worse,
and egged the firstclassprivates on
his rectum wickedly to tease
by means of skillfully applied
bayonets roasted hot with heat—   30
Olaf(upon what were once knees)
does almost ceaselessly repeat
"there is some s. I will not eat"

our president, being of which
assertions duly notified   35
threw the yellowsonofabitch
into a dungeon,where he died

Christ(of His mercy infinite)   ?
i pray to see; and Olaf, too

preponderatingly because   40
unless statistics lie he was
more brave than me:more blond than you.

e. e. cummings   Poem, or Beauty Hurts Mr. Vinal

take it from me kiddo
believe me
my country, 'tis of

you, land of the Cluett
Shirt Boston Garter and Spearmint   5

Girl With the Wrigley Eyes(of you
land of the Arrow Ide
and Earl & Wilson
Collars)of you i
sing:land of Abraham Lincoln and Lydia E. Pinkham,   10
land above all of Just Add Hot Water And Serve—
from every B. V. D.

let freedom ring

amen.   i do however protest, anent the un
-spontaneous and otherwise scented merde which   15
greets one(Everywhere Why) as divine poesy per
that and this radically defunct periodical.   i would
suggest that certain ideas gestures
rhymes, like Gillette Razor Blades
having been used and reused   20
to the mystical moment of dullness emphatically are
Not To Be Resharpened.   (Case in point

if we are to believe these gently O sweetly
melancholy trillers amid the thrillers
these crepuscular violinists among my and your   25
skyscrapers—Helen & Cleopatra were Just Too Lovely,
The Snail's On the Thorn enter Morn and God's
In His andsoforth

do you get me?)according
to such supposedly indigenous   70
throstles Art if O World O Life
a formula:example, Turn Your Shirttails Into
Drawers and If It Isn't An Eastman It Isn't A
Kodak therefore my friends let
us now sing each and all fortissimo A-   35
mer
i
ca, I
love,
You. And there're a   40
hun-dred-mil-lion-oth-ers, like
all of you successfully if
delicately gelded(or spaded)
gentlemen(and ladies)—pretty

littleliverpill-   45
hearted-Nujolneeding-There's-A-Reason
americans(who tensetendoned and with
upward vacant eyes, painfully
perpetually crouched, quivering, upon the
sternly allotted sandpile   50
—how silently
emit a tiny violetflavoured nuisance:Odor?
ono.
comes out like a ribbon lies flat on the brush

W. H. Auden   The Unknown Citizen

(To JS/07/M/378
This Marble Monument
Is Erected by the State)

He was found by the Bureau of Statistics to be
One against whom there was no official complaint,
And all the reports on his conduct agree
That, in the modern sense of an old-fashioned word, he was a
    saint,
For in everything he did he served the Greater Community.   5
Except for the War till the day he retired
He worked in a factory and never got fired,
But satisfied his employers, Fudge Motors Inc.
Yet he wasn't a scab or odd in his views,
For his Union reports that he paid his dues,   10
(Our report on his Union shows it was sound)
And our Social Psychology workers found
That he was popular with his mates and liked a drink.
The Press are convinced that he bought a paper every day
And that his reactions to advertisements were normal in every 15
    way.
Policies taken out in his name prove that he was fully insured,
And his Health-card shows he was once in hospital but left it
    cured.
Both Producers Research and High-Grade Living declare
He was fully sensible to the advantages of the Instalment
    Plan
And had everything necessary to the Modern Man,   20
A phonograph, a radio, a car and a frigidaire.
Our researchers into Public Opinion are content
That he held the proper opinions for the time of year;
When there was peace, he was for peace; when there was war,
    he went.
He was married and added five children to the population,   25
Which our Eugenist says was the right number for a parent of
    his generation,
And our teachers report that he never interfered with their
    education.
Was he free? Was he happy? The question is absurd:
Had anything been wrong, we should certainly have heard.

THE VERSE EPISTLE

The verse epistle is a poem addressed to a particular patron or
friend, usually written in the familiar style. The two traditional
types of the verse epistle derive from Roman models. From
Horace's *Epistles* there developed the tradition of the moral
and philosophical content of the verse letter. Widely influential
in the Renaissance, the Horatian tradition was brought before

English readers by Ben Jonson in "Forest" (1616), and was employed by later writers such as Vaughan, Dryden, and Congreve. This tradition reached its highest level of distinction in Alexander Pope's "Moral Essay" and in his "Epistle to Dr. Arbuthnot." Pope's "Epistle" is an excellent example of how the verse may be used as a vehicle for a satiric intention.

The second traditional category of the verse epistle is the romantic and sentimental, which derives from Ovid's "Heroides." Again, Pope may serve as a model of excellence, and his "Eloisa to Abelard" remains among the finest poems written in this tradition.

By the time of the Romantic Age, the writing of verse epistles decreased, though the poets Shelley, Keats, and Landor did attempt the form. Among the more notable examples of the verse epistle today, in addition to those included in this anthology, are W. H. Auden's "New Year's Letter" and Louis MacNeice's "Letters from Iceland."

John Donne   To Sir Henry Wotton

Here's no more news than virtue: I may as well
Tell you Cales' or Saint Michael's tale for news, as tell
That vice doth here habitually dwell.

Yet, as to'get stomachs we walk up and down,
And toil to sweeten rest, so, may God frown   5
If, but to loathe both, I haunt court or town.

For here no one is from extremity
Of vice by any other reason free,
But that the next to'him still is worse than he.

In this world's warfare, they whom rugged Fate,   10
God's commissary, doth so throughly hate
As in'the court's squadron to marshal their state;

If they stand armed with seely honesty,
With wishing prayers, and neat integrity,
Like Indians 'gainst Spanish host they be.   15

Suspicious boldness to this place belongs,
And to'have as many ears as all have tongues;
Tender to know, tough to acknowledge wrongs.

Believe me, Sir, in my youth's giddiest days,
When to be like the court was a play's praise,   20
Plays were not so like courts as courts'are like plays.

Then let us at these mimic antics jest,
Whose deepest projects and egregious gests
Are but dull morals of a game at chests.

But now 'tis incongruity to smile,   25
Therefore I end, and bid farewell awhile;
At court; though From court were the better style.

2 *Cales'*: Cadiz.   *St. Michael's*: the Azores. Donne is referring to
the Cadiz expedition of 1596 and the Island Voyage of 1597.
13 *seely*: blind.   24 *chests*: chess.

John Donne   To the Countess of Bedford

Madam,
Reason is our soul's left hand, faith her right;
By these we reach divinity, that's you.
Their loves, who have the blessings of your light,
Grew from their reason; mine from fair faith grew.

But as, although a squint lefthandedness   5
Be ungracious, yet we cannot want that hand,
So would I, not to increase, but to express
My faith, as I believe, so understand.

Therefore I study you first in your saints,
Those friends whom your election glorifies,   10
Then in your deeds, accesses, and restraints,
And what you read, and what yourself devise.

But soon the reasons why you are loved by all
Grow infinite, and so pass reason's reach;
Then back again to implicit faith I fall,   15
And rest on what the catholic voice doth teach:

That you are good. And not one heretic
Denies it: if he did, yet you are so,
For rocks which, high topped and deep rooted stick,
Waves wash, not undermine nor overthrow.   20

In everything there naturally grows
A balsamum to keep it fresh and new,
If 'twere not injured by extrinsic blows;
Your birth and beauty are this balm in you.

But you of learning and religion   25
And virtue and such ingredients have made
A mithridate whose operation
Keeps off or cures what can be done or said.

Yet this is not your physic, but your food,
A diet fit for you, for you are here   30
The first good angel, since the world's frame stood,
That ever did in woman's shape appear.

Since you are then God's masterpiece, and so
His factor for our loves, do as you do;
Make your return home gracious, and bestow   35
This life on that; so make one life of two.

   For so God help me, I would not miss you there
   For all the good which you can do me here.

title: Lucy Harington Russell, a patroness of Donne from 1608
until around 1614.   1 *left hand*: the weaker, more forced.

right: the stronger, more active.   6 *want:* lack.   10 *election:*
reference to the Calvinist doctrine of the elect.   11 *accesses:*
fits of passion.   16 *catholic:* universal, but also Roman Catholic
in teaching salvation through goodness.   22 *balsamum:* balm.
27 *mithridate:* antidote.   34 *factor:* creative agent.   35 *home:*
Twickenham; the countess was married to Edward, third Earl of
Bedford, and they lived at Twickenham Park.

Sir John Suckling   An Epistle

Sir,
Whether these lines do find you out,
Putting or clearing of a doubt;
Whether predestination,
Or reconciling three in one,
Or the unriddling how men die,   5
And live at once eternally,
Now take you up, know 'tis decreed
You straight bestride the college steed,
Leave Socinus and the schoolmen
(Which Jack Bond swears do but fool men),   10
And come to town: 'tis fit you show
Yourself abroad, that men may know
(Whate'er some learned men have guessed)
That oracles are not yet ceased:
There you shall find the wit and wine   15
Flowing alike, and both divine;
Dishes, with names not known in books,
And less amongst the college-cooks,
With sauce so pregnant that you need
Not stay till hunger bids you feed.   20
The sweat of learned Jonson's brain,
And gentle Shakespeare's easier strain,
A hackney-coach conveys you to,
In spite of all that rain can do;
And for your eighteenpence you sit   25
The lord and judge of all fresh wit.
News in one day as much we have here,
As serves all Windsor for a year,
And which the carrier brings to you,
After't has here been found not true,   30
Then think what company's designed
To meet you here, men so refined,
Their very common talk at board
Makes wise or mad a young court-lord,
And makes him capable to be   35
Umpire in's father's company;
Where no disputes, nor forced defence
Of a man's person for his sense
Take up the time: all strive to be
Masters of truth, as victory;   40

And where you come, I'd boldly swear
A synod might as easily err.

3 *predestination:* Calvinist doctrine of the elect.   4 *three in one:*
the Trinity.   9 *Socinus:* Italian theologian who argued against
the divinity of Christ (1539–1604).   *schoolmen:* the Scho-
lastics, known for their hair-splitting arguments over theological
questions.   10 *Jack Bond:* Unidentified.   28 *Windsor:* the
royal residence.

Abraham Cowley   An Answer to an Invitation
    to Cambridge

   Nichols, my better self, forbear,
For if thou tellest what Cambridge pleasures are,
   The schoolboy's sin will light on me,
I shall in mind at least a truant be.
   Tell me not how you feed your mind   5
   With dainties of philosophy,
   In Ovid's nut I shall not find
   The taste once pleased me.
O tell me not of logic's diverse cheer,
I shall begin to loathe our crambe here.   10

   Tell me not how the waves appear
Of Cam, or how it cuts the learned shire.
   I shall contemn the troubled Thames
On her chief holiday, even when her streams
   Are with rich folly gilded, when   15
   The quondam dungboat is made gay,
   Just like the bravery of the men,
   And graces with fresh paint that day.
When the City shines with flags and pageants there,
And satin doublets, seen not twice a year.   20

   Why do I stay then? I would meet
Thee there, but plummets hang upon my feet:
   'Tis my chief wish to live [with] thee,
But not till I deserve thy company:
   Till then we'll scorn to let that toy,   25
   Some forty miles, divide our hearts:
   Write to me, and I shall enjoy
   Friendship and wit, thy better parts.
Though envious fortune larger hindrance brings,
We'll easily see each other: Love hath wings.   30

1 *Nichols:* a Cambridge friend.   10 *crambe:* i.e., *crambe repetita,*
cabbage served up again; a distasteful repetition. The poet suggests
what we today would call ennui or boredom.   12 *Cam: the*
river from which Cambridge gets its name.   16 *quondam dungboat:* the barge used to transport sewage across the Thames.

John Milton   "Cyriack, Whose Grandsire on the
  Royal Bench"

SONNET XXI

Cyriack, whose Grandsire on the Royal Bench
  Of British *Themis,* with no mean applause
  Pronounc't and in his volumes taught our Lawes,
  Which others at their Bar so often wrench;
Today deep thoughts resolve with me to drench   5
  In mirth, that after no repenting draws;
  Let *Euclid* rest and *Archimedes* pause,
  And what the *Swede* intend, and what the *French.*
To measure life, learn thou betimes, and know
  Toward solid good what leads the nearest way;   10
  For other things mild Heav'n a time ordains,
And disapproves that care, though wise in show,
  That with superfluous burden loads the day,
  And when God sends a cheerful hour, refrains.

1 Cyriack: Cyriack Skinner, grandson of Sir Edward Coke, Chief
Justice of the King's Bench: he consistently championed Parliament
against the usurpations of James I. Cyriack Skinner was Milton's
pupil.

Matthew Prior   A Letter to the Honourable Lady

  Miss Margaret Cavendish Holles-Harley

My noble, lovely, little PEGGY,
Let this, my FIRST-EPISTLE, beg ye,
At dawn of morn, and close of even,
To lift your heart and hands to heaven:
In double beauty say your pray'r,   5
Our father first, then *notre pere;*
And dearest CHILD, along the day,
In ev'ry thing you do and say,
Obey and please my LORD and LADY,
So GOD shall love, and ANGELS aid, Ye.   10

    If to these PRECEPTS YOU attend,
No SECOND-LETTER need I send,
And so I rest Your constant Friend,
                    M.P.

Alexander Pope   An Essay on Man

EPISTLE I

 Awake, my St. John! leave all meaner things
To low ambition, and the pride of kings.

Let us (since life can little more supply
Than just to look about us and to die)
Expatiate free o'er all this scene of Man;   5
A mighty maze! but not without a plan;
A wild, where weeds and flowers promiscuous shoot;
Or garden, tempting with forbidden fruit.
Together let us beat this ample field,
Try what the open, what the covert yield;   10
The latent tracts, the giddy heights, explore
Of all who blindly creep, or sightless soar;
Eye nature's walks, shoot folly as it flies,
And catch the manners living as they rise;
Laugh where we must, be candid where we can,   15
But vindicate the ways of God to man.
   I. Say first, of God above, or man below,
What can we reason but from what we know?
Of man, what see we but his station here,
From which to reason, or to which refer?   20
Through worlds unnumbered though the God be known,
'Tis ours to trace him only in our own.
He who through vast immensity can pierce,
See worlds on worlds compose one universe,
Observe how system into system runs,   25
What other planets circle other suns,
What varied being peoples every star,
May tell why Heaven has made us as we are.
But of this frame the bearings and the ties,
The strong connections, nice dependencies,   30
Gradations just, has thy pervading soul
Looked through? or can a part contain the whole?
   Is the great chain that draws all to agree,
And drawn supports, upheld by God, or thee?
   II. Presumptuous man! the reason wouldst thou find,   35
Why formed so weak, so little, and so blind?
First, if thou canst, the harder reason guess,
Why formed no weaker, blinder, and no less!
Ask of thy mother earth, why oaks are made
Taller or stronger than the weeds they shade!   40
Or ask of yonder argent fields above,
Why Jove's satellites are less than Jove.
   Of systems possible, if 'tis confessed
That wisdom infinite must form the best,
Where all must full or not coherent be,   45
And all that rises, rise in due degree;
Then, in the scale of reasoning life, 'tis plain,
There must be, somewhere, such a rank as man:
And all the question (wrangle e'er so long)
Is only this, if God has placed him wrong.   50
   Respecting man, whatever wrong we call,
May, must be right, as relative to all.
In human works, though labored on with pain,
A thousand movements scarce one purpose gain;
In God's, one single can its end produce;   55

Yet serves to second too some other use.
So man, who here seems principal alone,
Perhaps acts second to some sphere unknown,
Touches some wheel, or verges to some goal;
'Tis but a part we see, and not a whole.   60
     When the proud steed shall know why man restrains
His fiery course, or drives him o'er the plains:
When the dull ox, why now he breaks the clod,
Is now a victim, and now Egypt's god:
Then shall man's pride and dullness comprehend   65
His actions', passions; being's, use and end;
Why doing, suffering, checked, impelled; and why
This hour a slave, the next a deity.
     Then say not man's imperfect, Heaven in fault;
Say rather, man's as perfect as he ought: 70
His knowledge measured to his state and place;
His time a moment, and a point his space.
If to be perfect in a certain sphere,
What matter, soon or late, or here or there?
The blest today is as completely so,   75
As who began a thousand years ago.
     III. Heaven from all creatures hides the book of fate,
All but the page prescribed, their present state:
From brutes what men, from men what spirits know:
Or who could suffer being here below?   80
The lamb thy riot dooms to bleed today,
Had he thy reason, would he skip and play?
Pleased to the last, he crops the flowery food,
And licks the hand just raised to shed his blood.
Oh blindness to the future! kindly given,   85
That each may fill the circle marked by Heaven:
Who sees with equal eye, as God of all,
A hero perish, or a sparrow fall,
Atoms or systems into ruin hurled,
And now a bubble burst, and now a world.   90
     Hope humbly then; with trembling pinions soar;
Wait the great teacher death; and God adore.
What future bliss, He gives not thee to know,
But gives that hope to be thy blessing now.
Hope springs eternal in the human breast: 95
Man never is, but always to be blest:
The soul, uneasy and confined from home,
Rests and expatiates in a life to come.
     Lo, the poor Indian! whose untutored mind
Sees God in clouds, or hears Him in the wind;   100
His soul, proud science never taught to stray
Far as the solar-walk, or milky way;
Yet simple Nature to his hope has given,
Behind the cloud-topped hill, an humbler heaven;
Some safer world in depth of woods embraced,   105
Some happier island in the watery waste,
Where slaves once more their native land behold,
No fiends torment, no Christians thirst for gold.

To be, contents his natural desire,
He asks no angel's wings, no seraph's fire;   110
But thinks, admitted to that equal sky,
His faithful dog shall bear him company.
    IV. Go, wiser thou! and in thy scale of sense,
Weigh thy opinion against Providence;
Call imperfection what thou fanciest such,   115
Say, here He gives too little, there too much:
Destroy all creatures for thy sport or gust,
Yet cry, If man's unhappy, God's unjust;
If man alone engross not Heaven's high care,
Alone made perfect here, immortal there: 120
Snatch from his hand the balance and the rod,
Rejudge his justice, be the God of God.
In pride, in reasoning pride, our error lies;
All quit their sphere, and rush into the skies.
Pride still is aiming at the blessed abodes,   125
Men would be angels, angels would be gods.
Aspiring to be gods, if angels fell,
Aspiring to be angels, men rebel:
And who but wishes to invert the laws
Of order, sins against th' Eternal Cause.   130
    V. Ask for what end the heavenly bodies shine,
Earth for whose use? Pride answers, " 'Tis for mine:
For me kind Nature wakes her genial power,
Suckles each herb, and spreads out every flower;
Annual for me, the grape, the rose renew,   135
The juice nectareous, and the balmy dew;
For me, the mine a thousand treasures brings;
For me, health gushes from a thousand springs;
Seas roll to waft me, suns to light me rise;
My footstool earth, my canopy the skies."   140
    But errs not Nature from this gracious end,
From burning suns when livid deaths descend,
When earthquakes swallow, or when tempests sweep
Towns to one grave, whole nations to the deep?
"No" ('tis replied) "the first Almighty Cause   145
Acts not by partial, but by general laws;
Th' exceptions few; some change since all begin:
And what created perfect?"—Why then man?
If the great end by human happiness,
Then Nature deviates; and can man do less?   150
As much that end a constant course requires
Of showers and sunshine, as of man's desires;
As much eternal springs and cloudless skies,
As men forever temperate, calm, and wise.
If plagues or earthquakes break not Heaven's design,   155
Why then a Borgia, or a Catiline?
Who knows but He, whose hand the lightning forms,
Who heaves old ocean, and who wings the storms;
Pours fierce ambition in a Caesar's mind,
Or turns young Ammon loose to scourge mankind?   160
From pride, from pride, our very reasoning springs;

Account for moral as for natural things;
Why charge we Heaven in those, in these acquit?
In both, to reason right is to submit.
Better for us, perhaps, it might appear,   165
Were there all harmony, all virtue here;
That never air or ocean felt the wind;
That never passion discomposed the mind.
But all subsists by elemental strife;
And passions are the elements of life.   170
The general order, since the whole began,
Is kept by Nature, and is kept in man.
　　VI. What would this man? Now upward will he soar,
And little less than angel, would be more;
Now looking downwards, just as grieved appears,   175
To want the strength of bulls, the fur of bears.
Made for his use all creatures if he call,
Say what their use, had he the powers of all?
Nature to these, without profusion, kind,
The proper organs, proper powers assigned;   180
Each seeming want compensated of course,
Here with degrees of swiftness, there of force;
All in exact proportion to the state;
Nothing to add, and nothing to abate.
Each beast, each insect, happy in its own: 185
Is Heaven unkind to man, and man alone?
Shall he alone, whom rational we call,
Be pleased with nothing, if not blessed with all?
　　The bliss of man (could pride that blessing find)
Is not to act or think beyond mankind;   190
No powers of body or of soul to share,
But what his nature and his state can bear.
Why has not man a microscopic eye?
For this plain reason, man is not a fly.
Say what the use, were finer optics given,   195
To inspect a mite, not comprehend the heaven?
Or touch, if tremblingly alive all o'er,
To smart and agonize at every pore?
Or quick effluvia darting through the brain,
Die of a rose in aromatic pain?   200
If Nature thundered in his opening ears,
And stunned him with the music of the spheres,
How would he wish that Heaven had left him still
The whispering zephyr, and the purling rill?
Who finds not Providence all good and wise,   205
Alike in what it gives, and what it denies?
　　VII.　Far as creation's ample range extends,
The scale of sensual, mental powers ascends:
Mark how it mounts, to man's imperial race,
From the green myriads in the peopled grass: 210
What modes of sight betwixt each wide extreme,
The mole's dim curtain, and the lynx's beam:
Of smell, the headlong lioness between,
And hound sagacious on the tainted green:

Of hearing, from the life that fills the flood,   215
To that which warbles through the vernal wood:
The spider's touch, how exquisitely fine!
Feels at each thread, and lives along the line:
In the nice bee, what sense so subtly true
From poisonous herbs extract the healing dew?   220
How instinct varies in the groveling swine,
Compared, half-reasoning elephant, with thine!
Twixt that, and reason, what a nice barrier;
For ever separate, yet for ever near!
Remembrance and reflection how allied;   225
What thin partitions sense from thought divide:
And middle natures, how they long to join,
Yet never pass th' insuperable line!
Without this just gradation, could they be
Subjected, these to those, or all to thee?   230
The powers of all subdued by thee alone,
Is not thy reason all these powers in one?
    VIII. See, through this air, this ocean, and this earth,
All matter quick, and bursting into birth.
Above, how high, progressive life may go!   235
Around, how wide! how deep extend below!
Vast chain of being! which from God began,
Natures ethereal, human, angel, man,
Beast, bird, fish, insect, what no eye can see,
No glass can reach; from Infinite to thee,   240
From thee to nothing—On superior powers
Were we to press, inferior might on ours:
Or in the full creation leave a void,
Where, one step broken, the great scale's destroyed:
From Nature's chain whatever link you strike,   245
Tenth, or ten thousandth, breaks the chain alike.
    And, if each system in gradation roll
Alike essential to th' amazing whole,
The least confusion but in one, not all
That system only, but the whole must fall.   250
Let earth unbalanced from her orbit fly,
Planets and suns run lawless through the sky;
Let ruling angels from their spheres be hurled,
Being on being wrecked, and world on world;
Heaven's whole foundations to their center nod,   255
And Nature tremble to the throne of God.
All this dread order break—for whom? for thee?
Vile worm!—oh madness! pride! impiety!
    IX. What if the foot, ordained the dust to tread,
Or hand, to toil, aspired to be the head?   260
What if the head, the eye, or ear repined
To serve mere engines to the ruling mind?
Just as absurd for any part to claim
To be another, in this general frame:
Just as absurd, to mourn the tasks or pains,   265
The great directing Mind of all ordains.
    All are but parts of one stupendous whole,

Whose body Nature is, and God the soul;
That, changed through all, and yet in all the same;
Great in the earth, as in th' ethereal frame;   270
Warms in the sun, refreshes in the breeze,
Glows in the stars, and blossoms in the trees,
Lives through all life, extends through all extent,
Spreads undivided, operates unspent;
Breathes in our soul, informs our mortal part,   275
As full, as perfect, in a hair as heart;
As full, as perfect, in vile man that mourns,
As the rapt seraph that adores and burns:
To Him no high, no low, no great, no small;
He fills, He bounds, connects, and equals all.   280
    X. Cease then, nor older imperfection name:
Our proper bliss depends on what we blame.
Know thy own point: this kind, this due degree
Of blindness, weakness, Heaven bestows on thee.
Submit.—In this, or any other sphere,   285
Secure to be as blessed as thou canst bear:
Safe in the hand of one disposing Power,
Or in the natal, or the mortal hour.
All Nature is but art, unknown to thee;
All chance, direction, which thou canst not see;   290
All discord, harmony not understood;
All partial evil, universal good:
And, spite of pride, in erring reason's spite,
One truth is clear, Whatever is, is right.

1 St. John: Henry St. John, Viscount Bolingbroke.   *41 argent:*
silver.   *117 gust:* appetite.   *142 burning suns:* once believed
the cause of plague.   *156 Borgia:* the evil Cesare Borgia (1476–
1507).   *Catiline:* a conspirator against the government, de-
nounced by Cicero.   *160 young Ammon:* Alexander the Great.
194 fly: which was supposed to have microscopic vision.   *199
effluvia:* invisible streams by which odor was indicated to the brain.
212: The mole is blind; the lynx was supposed to have the keenest
sight.   *213 lioness:* which had the dullest sense of smell.   *214
tainted:* by animal smells.   *220 healing dew:* honey, used med-
icinally.

Emily Dickinson   "This Is My Letter to the World"

This is my letter to the world,
    That never wrote to me,—
The simple news that Nature told,
    With tender majesty.

Her message is committed   5
    To hand I cannot see,
For love of her, sweet countrymen,
    Judge tenderly of me!

D. H. Lawrence   Letter from Town: The Almond Tree

You promised to send me some violets. Did you forget?
   White ones and blue ones from under the orchard hedge?
   Sweet dark purple, and white ones mixed for a pledge
Of our early love that hardly has opened yet.

Here there's an almond tree—you have never seen   5
   Such a one in the north—it flowers on the street, and I stand
   Every day by the fence to look up at the flowers that expand
At rest in the blue, and wonder at what they mean.

Under the almond tree, the happy lands
   Provence, Japan, and Italy repose;   10
   And passing feet are charter and clapping of those
Who play around us country girls clapping their hands.

You, my love, the foremost, in a flowered gown,
   All your unbearable tenderness, you with the laughter
   Startled upon your eyes now so wide with hereafter,   15
You with loose hands of abandonment hanging down.

Ezra Pound   The River-Merchant's Wife: A Letter

While my hair was still cut straight across my forehead
I played about the front gate, pulling flowers.
You came by on bamboo stilts, playing horse,
You walked about my seat, playing with blue plums.
And we went on living in the village of Chokan: 5
Two small people, without dislike or suspicion.

At fourteen I married My Lord you.
I never laughed, being bashful.
Lowering my head, I looked at the wall.
Called to, a thousand times, I never looked back.   10

At fifteen I stopped scowling,
I desired my dust to be mingled with yours
For ever and for ever and for ever.
Why should I climb the look out?

At sixteen you departed,   15
You went into far Ku-to-yen, by the river of swirling eddies,
And you have been gone five months.
The monkeys make sorrowful noise overhead.

You dragged your feet when you went out.
By the gate now, the moss is grown, the different mosses,   20
Too deep to clear them away!
The leaves fall early this autumn, in wind.
The paired butterflies are already yellow with August
Over the grass in the West garden;

They hurt me. I grow older.   25
If you are coming down through the narrows of the river
    Kiang,
Please let me know beforehand,
And I will come out to meet you
            As far as Cho-fu-Sa.

Archibald MacLeish   Epistle to Be Left in the Earth

. . . It is colder now
                    there are many stars
                            we are drifting
North by the Great Bear
                    the leaves are falling   5
The water is stone in the scooped rocks
                            to southward
Red sun grey air
                    the crows are
Slow on their crooked wings   10
                    the jays have left us
Long since we passed the flares of Orion
Each man believes in his heart he will die
Many have written last thoughts and last letters
None know if our deaths are now or forever   15
None know if this wandering earth will be found

We lie down and the snow covers our garments
I pray for you
            you (if any open this writing)
Make in your mouths the words that were our names   20
I will tell you all we have learned
                            I will tell you everything
The earth is round
                    there are springs under the orchards
The loam cuts with a blunt knife   25
                            beware of
Elms in thunder
                    the lights in the sky are stars
We think they do not see
                            we think also   30
The trees do not know nor the leaves of the grasses
                                    hear us
The birds too are ignorant
                    Do not listen
Do not stand at dark in the open windows   35
We before you have heard this
                    they are voices
They are not words at all but the wind rising
Also none among us has seen God
(. . . We have thought often   40
The flaws of sun in the late and driving weather

Pointed to one tree but it was not so.)
As for the nights I warn you the nights are dangerous
The wind changes at night and the dreams come

It is very cold   *45*
       there are strange stars near Arcturus

Voices are crying an unknown name in the sky

Frank Horne

   FROM *"Letters Found Near a Suicide"*

   TO JAMES

Do you remember
How you won
That last race . . . ?
How you flung your body
At the start . . .   5
How your spikes
Ripped the cinders
In the stretch . . .
How you catapulted
Through the tape . . .   *10*
Do you remember . . . ?
Don't you think
I lurched with you
Out of those starting holes . . . ?
Don't you think   *15*
My sinews tightened
At those first
Few strides . . .
And when you flew into the stretch
Was not all my thrill   20
Of a thousand races
In your blood . . . ?
At your final drive
Through the finish line
Did not my shout   25
Tell of the
Triumphant ecstasy
Of victory . . . ?
Live
As I have taught you   30
To run, Boy—
It's a short dash
Dig your starting holes
Deep and firm
Lurch out of them   35
Into the straightaway
With all the power

That is in you
Look straight ahead
To the finish line   40
Think only of the goal
Run straight
Run high
Run hard
Save nothing   45
And finish
With an ecstatic burst
That carries you
Hurtling
Through the tape   50
To victory .

Robert Hillyer   A Letter to a Teacher of English

YOUR learning, James, in classics and romance,
Sits lightlier than most men's ignorance.
It is yourself, an undivided part
Of you as man, not only mind but heart.
How often do I see in our profession   5
Learning a mere extraneous possession,
A self-sufficient mass of dates and sources
Roll'd round in academe's diurnal courses,
Where scholars prepare scholars, not for life
But gaudy footnotes and a threadbare wife,—   10
Keen eyes for errors in a worthless text,
But none at all for this world or the next.
I fall between two stools—I can't say Chairs—
A bard too learn'd, a scholar in arrears.
The critical reviewers, week by week,   15
Damn poets who command their own technique.
A careful rhyme, a spondee nobly planned
Is academic, and the work unmanned.
Would that these critics lived in houses fashioned
By carpenters congenially impassioned.   20
I'd love to see the rooftree fall on . . . no,
The name is legion; let us leave it so.
But as a teacher I have equal luck,—
In ponds a chicken and on shore a duck.
My wretched memory, for all my pains,   25
Drops tons for every ounce that it retains;
Far wiser now, I have less factual knowledge
At forty-one than when I was in college.
With eyes astonished, I peruse the rant
My younger self delivered against Kant.   30
The *Critique of Pure Reason* was to me
Mere holiday from Greek philosophy.
The Greeks I can remember in due season,
But where now is the *Critique of Pure Reason?*

Alas, that educated men should find   35
Their memory not equal to their mind!
But since I have to choose, the lifeless fact
Must yield before the will to write and act.
Though I salute my past for what he knew
Let him return the bow for what I do;—   40
Thus to reverse, and much more truly say:
Si vieillesse savait, si jeunesse pouvait.

Yet there is recompense for knowing well
One language, if it be incomparable.
Disdainful, the Athenian would speak   45
No other language than his native Greek.
Now his provincial literature is prized
In every barbarous tongue that he despised.
The learned Roman, who knew Greek by heart,
Had twice the scholarship, and half the art.   50
The great Elizabethans' education
Thrived less on lore than on superb translation.
Our scholars, to whom every root is known,
Command all languages, except their own;
For confirmation, but consult the theses   55
That year by year bankrupt the college presses.

When poets go, grammarians arrive.
Is Virgil dead? Let commentators thrive.
The gift of tongues without the Holy Ghost
Is but a Babel, not a Pentecost.   60
Research in science may produce the answer
To love or wealth, to authorship or cancer;
Research in language? What is there to cure?
Some languages are dead and some endure,
Some fossil bones, some living literature.   65
Science in language is a game, designed
As rare Ben Jonson said, to break a mind;
One lives in words or knows them not at all
And weeps at the grammarian's funeral.
Romantic doctrine if you will, but who   70
Knowing his Gothic, knows his English too?
Mere English, mightiest tongue, whose cadences
Roar with the tides and murmur with the trees,
Since I hear living beauty, what care I
What tongues dared frame thy fearful symmetry?   75
I will not see thee petrified, my native
Language frozen to a fossil dative.
In short, dear James, by now you plainly see
I find no virtue in philology;
At best a sterile hobby, often worse,   80
The plumes, when language dies, upon its hearse.

Besides Illisus under the cool trees
Youth answered questions put by Socrates.
It does not matter what the questions were,

Suffice the youth and the philosopher.   85
Both, doubtless, would have thought it very odd
To trace the genitives in Hesiod;
Their works were intermingled with their days,
It was enough to know, not paraphrase.
Their voices reach me this calm afternoon   90
Through the bright air honeyed with ample June
More clearly than the meaningless confusion
That dominates the modern world's illusion.
Clearest of all, one question rouses me:
"Why have you lost the old simplicity   95
In life and learning, politics and art,
While wisdom, peace, and innocence depart?"

Though we who teach cry out against the mesh
Spread by the world, the Devil, and the flesh
To entrap the moneyed in material things   100
While we at lofty altitude spread wings,
Yet are we not materialists ourselves?
They build their mansions, we extend our shelves;
They flaunt possessions, we a weary text,
One-tenth original, nine-tenths indexed,   105
Both of us sharing in a common loss
Of life's essentials smothered by a gloss.

Now, James, I stop complaining, I will plan
An education to produce a man.
Make no mistake, I do not want this done,—   110
My limitations are the cornerstone.
Plato's *Republic* may have served some use
In manuscript, but not in Syracuse,
So let my dream Academy remain
A dream;—I'm sure I do not ask in vain.   115

First would I have my scholar learn the tongue
He never learned to speak when he was young;
Then would I have him read therein, but merely
In the great books, to understand them clearly.
At present, for no earthly good, we ask   120
A deadly and unnecessary task:
A knowledge of small names that time has taken
And put to bed—and whom we vainly waken.
O that our living literature could be
Our sustenance, not archaeology!   125
Time is the wisest judge, who folds away
The surplus of a too-abundant day.
My scholar shall be brilliantly forbidden
To dig old garbage from a kitchen midden;
Old it may be, and curious as old,   130
But I would have him dig for purest gold:
The text itself, no footnotes but his own,
And critics who let well enough alone.
Far better Alexandria in flames

Than buried beneath unimportant names;   135
And even Sappho, glory that was Greece's,
Lives best, I blasphemously think, in pieces.
Surely our sprite, who over Amherst hovered,
Would gain if no more poems were discovered.
That Chinese emperor who burned the books   140
Succumbed to madness shrewder than it looks;
The minor poets and the minor sages
Went up in smoke; the great shine down the ages.
The Harvard Library's ungainly porch
Has often made me hunger for a torch,   145
But this not more to simplify a lecture
Than to appease the Muse of architecture.

When music and sweet poetry agree,
Who would be thinking of a Ph.D.?
O who would ablauts bear, when Brahms's First   150
Is soon to be performed or but rehearsed?
My scholar must have music in his heart,
Bach and Beethoven, Schumann and Mozart,
Handel, Vivaldi, Purcell, Couperin,
Dowland, Corelli, Mendelssohn, Chopin.   155
Ah, James, I missed my calling; I would turn
To that one art toward which the others yearn,—
But I observe my neighbor's cow, who leaves
Her fertile pasture for my barren sheaves.
The field next-door, the next-door art, will thus   160
Always attract the mildly covetous.
Yet some day I will play you the main theme
Of the immortal counterpoint I dream:
Clear melody in fugue and canon rises
On strings, with many structural surprises.   165
No letter, but a prelude, for your sake
I would compose beside this tranquil lake.
Its line should rise toward heaven until it broke
Half-way between the sky and the great oak;
Then waver, like a flock of homing birds,   170
In slow descending flights of minor thirds.
Music alone can set the spirit free
From the dark past and darker things to be.
I'd live for ever in an atmosphere
Of high harmonics where all tones are clear.   175
Could Man be judged by music, then the Lord
Would quench the angel of the flaming sword.
Alas, the final tones so soon disperse
Their echoes through the empty universe,
And hearers, weak from following Beethoven,   180
Relax with Gershwin, Herbert, and de Koven.

But to return to Polyhymnia,
And incidentally to my student. Ah,
Where is the creature? Nay, but is that he?
A saxophone is nuzzling on his knee!   185
His eyes pop out, his bellied cheeks expand,

His foot taps "Alexander's Ragtime Band."
Ungraceful and unpardonable wretch!
Was it for you my eager pen would sketch
A new, a sensible curriculum?   *190*
Burst with your panpipes! and we'll both be dumb.

I was about to urge philosophy,
Especially the Greek. I was to be
Your godfather in recommending Faith
To you, fit godson for a Sigmund Spaeth!   *195*
Of history and time I was to tell,
Things visible and things invisible,
But what to you are echoes from Nicaea,
Who never prayed nor cherished an idea?
And what have you to gain from education,   *200*
Blown bellows for unceasing syncopation?
Learning and life are too far wrenched apart,
I can not reconcile, for all my art,
Studies that go one way and life another,
Tastes that demoralize, and tests that smother.   *205*

James, what is this I find? an angry scowl
Sits on my brow like a Palladian owl!
Let me erase it, lest it should transform
The soft horizon with a thunder storm.
I would you were beside me now, to share   *210*
The sound of falling water, the sweet air.
Under the yew a vacant easy chair
Awaits your coming; and long-planted seeds
Begin to bloom amid the encircling weeds.
I bade my student an abrupt adieu   *215*
But find it harder to take leave of you.

May we not some day have a mild carouse
In Pontefract instead of Warren House?
The distance nothing,—in two hours' time
Another land where that word's but a rhyme.   *220*
Would I were Marvell, then you could not harden
Your heart against a visit to my garden.
I'd write those happy lines about the green
Annihilation, and you'd soon be seen
Hatless and coatless, bootless,—well, my soul!   *225*
He's in the lake with nothing on at all!
Farewell, and yours sincerely, and yours ever,
The time has come for the initial shiver.
When into lakes, as into life, we dive,
We're fortunate if we come up alive.   *230*

title: "Delivered as the Phi Beta Kappa poem at the Tercentenary
of Harvard College in 1936. The 'Teacher of English' is my friend,
Professor James Buell Munn, of Harvard." [R.H.]   *42 Si vieil-*
lesse savait, si jeunesse pouvait: "If old age had the wisdom, if youth
had the power." The poet has reversed the terms of an old French
proverb, "If youth had the wisdom, if old age had the power."

Robert Lowell   After the Surprising Conversions

September twenty-second, Sir: today
I answer. In the latter part of May,
Hard on our Lord's Ascension, it began
To be more sensible. A gentleman
Of more than common understanding, strict   5
In morals, pious in behavior, kicked
Against our goad. A man of some renown,
An useful, honored person in the town,
He came of melancholy parents; prone
To secret spells, for years they kept alone—   10
His uncle, I believe, was killed of it:
Good people, but of too much or little wit.
I preached one Sabbath on a text from Kings;
He showed concernment for his soul. Some things
In his experience were hopeful. He   15
Would sit and watch the wind knocking a tree
And praise this countryside our Lord has made.
Once when a poor man's heifer died, he laid
A shilling on the doorsill; though a thirst
For loving shook him like a snake, he durst   20
Not entertain much hope of his estate
In heaven. Once we saw him sitting late
Behind his attic window by a light
That guttered on his Bible; through that night
He meditated terror, and he seemed   25
Beyond advice or reason, for he dreamed
That he was called to trumpet Judgment Day
To Concord. In the latter part of May
He cut his throat. And though the coroner
Judged him delirious, soon a noisome stir   30
Palsied our village. At Jehovah's nod
Satan seemed more let loose amongst us: God
Abandoned us to Satan, and he pressed
Us hard, until we thought we could not rest
Till we had done with life. Content was gone.   35
All the good work was quashed. We were undone.
The breath of God had carried out a planned
And sensible withdrawal from this land;
The multitude, once unconcerned with doubt,
Once neither callous, curious nor devout,   40
Jumped at broad noon, as though some peddler groaned
At it in its familiar twang: "My friend,
Cut your own throat. Cut your own throat. Now! Now!"
September twenty-second, Sir, the bough
Cracks with the unpicked apples, and at dawn   45
The small-mouth bass breaks water, gorged with spawn.

title: Jonathan Edwards (1703–1758), the last great defender of
Calvinism in America, wrote "Narrative of Surprising Conversions"
as a letter to the Reverend Benjamin Colman on May 30, 1735.

In this work, he described the religious awakening which was taking place in Northampton. On June 3, 1735, in addition to his letter, he described the suicide of his uncle:

"Since I wrote the foregoing Letter, there has Happen'd a thing of a very awfull nature in the Town; My Uncle Hawley, the Last Sabbath day morning, Laid violent Hands on himself, & Put an End to his Life, by Cutting his own throat. He had been for a Considerable Time Greatly Concern'd about the Condition of his soul. . . . We have appointed a day of Fasting in the Town this week, by Reason of this & other appearances of satans Rage amongst us against Poor souls. . . ."

Alan Dugan   Letter to Eve

The lion and lioness are intractable,
the leaves are covered with dust,
and even the peacocks will not
preen. You should come back,
burnish us with your former look,   5
and let the search for truth
go. After a loud sleep last night
I got up late and saw a new
expression on the faces of the deer;
the shrews and wolves are gaunt   10
and out of sorts: they nosed
their usual fruits and do not know
what they intend to do. The dogs
got tangled up in an unusual way:
one put its urinary tube   15
into the other's urinary tract
and could not get it out.
Standing tail to tail for hours,
they looked at me with wise,
supplicatory eyes. I named   20
two new sounds: snarl and shriek,
and hitherto unnoticed bells,
which used to perform the air,
exploded!, making a difference.
Come back before the garden does   25
what I'll call "die," not that it
matters. Rib, Rib, I have a new
opinion of your Eve, called "lust"
or Love, I don't know which,
and want to know how I will choose.   30

PART III

Poetic Conventions: The Poem as Narrative

A narrative is an account of events. Unlike exposition, which tells the reader about that which has already taken place in order to make sense of that action, narrative unfolds an advancing action. Narrative poetry, then, is verse that tells a story, which is presented without the use of dramatic conventions, such as speakers' names. Plot, an aspect of the story, is the organization of the incidents within the narrative. Though narrative verse may have dramatic values, and dramatic verse may have story-telling interest, the distinction, finally, between these modes of literature is one of emphasis, and the methods by which the content is presented to the reader. In narrative verse, the "what-happens-next" quality is the primary appeal of the work.

Narrative verse has had a long and honorable history, and the epics of the Greeks, Chaucer's *Canterbury Tales,* and Milton's *Paradise Lost* are still regarded as among the highest achievements of Western civilization. In our own century, however, the novel has become the favored medium for telling stories.

But if in general narrative poetry has fallen somewhat into disfavor, the popular, or traditional (folk) ballad still retains a universality of appeal.

THE BALLAD

Popular ballads are narrative songs that originated among the people rather than at the courts of kings or in the halls of the educated and aristocratic class. Ballads existed orally for many years before they were committed to paper; when they were later written down, they were reproduced in a language that today seems fairly modern. Ballads, however, have been traced back to the latter half of the fourteenth century.

There are a number of theories as to the original composition of the popular ballads. Some critics maintain that ballads were composed by individual authors. Other critics insist that they were "communal," i.e., composed by the community as a whole. Still other writers contend that they were composed on an improvisational basis before an assembled crowd.

Popular ballads are usually about the lives of ordinary people. Domestic complications, murder, love, the use of the supernatural—all these subjects and themes are found in the ballads. Absent to a significant degree, however, is characterization and description. Transitions are usually abrupt, and action in the ballads generally develops through dialogue. The emphasis in the popular ballad is upon action rather than reflection. Commonly incremental repetition is used in the ballad, a stanza repeating the preceding one with a variation that adds to the developing of the story.

The ballad often focuses attention on a moment of climax or on some deeply felt human involvement that follows the climax of an action. However, because of an avoidance of polysyllabic words, and through the use of direct and vigorous language, the ballad appears to depict the quality of simplicity. Further, the use of conventional epithets and the impersonality and objectivity of nearly all popular ballads, combined with a general avoidance of sentimentality, tend to create the impression of the absence of the author: the ballad seems to be almost "authorless." By contrast, "minstrel" ballads, written for an aristocratic class by bards familiar with the tastes of the people, are often recognizable because of their subjectivity, their greater concern with description and character.

The ballad consists of any number of four-line stanzas. Usually, the first and third lines are tetrameter (four accented syllables); the second and fourth are trimeter (three accented syllables). The meter is iambic, and the rhyme scheme is abcb, defe, etc. The use of a refrain is not uncommon, and rhymes are often only approximate.

In the sixteenth century, there appeared a special form of ballad—the broadside ballad. Poems were printed on a single folded sheet of paper, and the subject matter usually dealt with public affairs, often treated in a humorous or satiric way. Offered for sale, these ballads were usually intended to be sung to music already known by the public. By the eighteenth century, the term "ballad" became generalized to the extent that the word often meant simply a "song."

In addition to being a folk form, the ballad has found a place as a literary type. Poets such as Keats, Tennyson, Pound, and Yeats have been attracted to the vigor and directness of the ballad, and a substantial body of literary, or "art," ballads now exists. The ballad, however, whether folk or literary, is difficult of easy classification, despite its simplicity and directness, since it usually combines elements of the lyric, the narrative, and the dialogue of dramatic verse. Traditionally, it has been grouped with narrative poetry because, finally, in the ballad it is the story that is emphasized.

Anonymous   Lord Randal

"O where hae ye been, Lord Randal, my son?
O where hae ye been, my handsome young man?"
"I hae been to the wild wood; mother, make my bed soon,
For I'm weary wi hunting, and fain wald lie down."

"Where gat ye your dinner, Lord Randal, my son?   5
Where gat ye your dinner, my handsome young man?"
"I din'd wi my true-love; mother, make my bed soon,
For I'm weary wi hunting, and fain wald lie down."

"What gat ye to your dinner, Lord Randal, my son?
What gat ye to your dinner, my handsome young man?"   10
"I gat eels boild in broo; mother, make my bed soon,
For I'm weary wi hunting and fain wald lie down."

"What became of your bloodhounds, Lord Randal, my son?
What became of your bloodhounds, my handsome young
     man?"
"O they swelld and they died; mother, make my bed soon,   15
For I'm weary wi hunting and fain wald lie down."

"O I fear ye are poisond, Lord Randal, my son!
O I fear ye are poisond, my handsome young man!"
"O yes! I am poisond; mother, make my bed soon,
For I'm sick at the heart, and I fain wald lie down."   20

Anonymous   Sir Patrick Spence

The king sits in Dumferling toune,
    Drinking the blude-reid wine:
"O whar will I get guid sailor,
    To sail this schip of mine?"

Up and spak an eldern knicht,   5
    Sat at the kings richt kne:
"Sir Patrick Spence is the best sailor
    That sails upon the se."

The king has written a braid letter,
    And signed it wi his hand,   10
And sent it to Sir Patrick Spence,
    Was walking on the sand.

The first line that Sir Patrick red,
    A loud lauch lauched he;
The next line that Sir Patrick red,   15
    The teir blinded his ee.

"O what is this has don this deid,
    This ill deid don to me,
To send me out this time o' the yeir,
    To sail upon the se!   20

"Mak hast, mak hast, my mirry men all,
    Our guid schip sails the morne:"
"O say na sae, my master deir,
    For I feir a deadlie storme.

"Late late yestreen I saw the new moone,   25
    Wi the auld moone in hir arme,
And I feir, I feir, my deir master,
    That we will cum to harme."

O our Scots nobles wer richt laith
    To weet their cork-heild schoone;   30
Bot lang owre a' the play wer playd,
    Thair hats they swam aboone.

O lang, lang may their ladies sit,
    Wi thair fans into their hand,
Or eir they se Sir Patrick Spence   35
    Cum sailing to the land.

O lang, lang may the ladies stand,
    Wi thair gold kems in their hair,
Wating for thair ain deir lords,
    For they'll se thame na mair.   40

Haf owre, haf owre to Aberdour,
    It's fiftie fadom deip,

And thair lies guid Sir Patrick Spence,
   Wi the Scots lords at his feit.

9 *braid letter*: a letter written on a long or broad sheet.   16 *ee*:
eye.   25–26 *Late . . . arme*: a bad omen because the new moon
was seen late in the evening. The "auld moone in hir arme" refers
to the semiluminous surface of the moon, visible between the
horns of the new moon.   29 *laith*: loath.   30 *cork-heild
schoone*: shoes with heels of cork.   31 *owre*: before.   32
aboone: above; their hats floating above their bodies.   38 *Kems*:
combs.   41 *haf . . . Aberdour*: halfway home.

Anonymous   Get up and Bar the Door

There livd a man in yonder glen,
   And John Blunt was his name; O
He maks gude maut and he brews gude ale,
   And he bears a wondrous fame. O

The wind blew in the hallan ae night,   5
   Fu snell out oer the moor;
"Rise up, rise up, auld Luckie," he says,
   "Rise up, and bar the door."

They made a paction tween them twa,
   They made it firm and sure,   10
Whaeer sud speak the foremost word
   Should rise and bar the door.

Three travelers that had tint their gate,
   As thro the hills they foor,
They airted by the line o light   15
   Fu straught to Johnie Blunt's door.

They haurld auld Luckie out o her bed
   And laid her on the floor,
But never a word auld Luckie wad say,
   For barrin o the door.   20

"Ye've eaten my bread, ye hae druken my ale,
   And ye'll make my auld wife a whore!"
"A ha, Johnie Blunt! ye hae spoke the first word,
   Get up and bar the door."

3 *maut*: malt beer.   5 *ae*: all.   6 *Fu snell*: full bitter cold.
13 *tint*: lost.   *gate*: way.   14 *foor*: fared.   15 *airted*: were
directed.

Anonymous   The Twa Corbies

As I was walking all alane,
I heard twa corbies making a mane;

The tane unto the t'other say,
"Where sall we gang and dine to-day?"

"In behint yon auld fail dyke,   5
I wot there lies a new slain knight;
And naebody kens that he lies there,
But his hawk, his hound, and lady fair.

"His hound is to the hunting gane,
His hawk to fetch the wild-fowl hame,   10
His lady's ta'en another mate,
So we may mak our dinner sweet.

"Ye'll sit on his white hause bane,
And I'll pike out his bonny blue een;
Wi ae lock o his gowden hair   15
We'll theek our nest when it grows bare.

"Mony a one for him makes mane,
But nane sall ken where he is gane;
Oer his white banes, when they are bare,
The wind sal blaw for evermair."   20

title: The Two Ravens.   2 *mane:* moan.   5 *fail:* turf.   7
kens: knows.   13 *hause-bane:* neck bone.   16 *theek:* thatch.

Anonymous   Babylon; or, The Bonnie Banks o' Fordie

There were three ladies lived in a bower,
   Eh vow bonnie
And they went out to pull a flower.
   On the bonnie banks o Fordie.

They hadna pu'ed a flower but ane,   5
When up started to them a banisht man.

He's taen the first sister by her hand,
And he's turned her round and made her stand.

"It's whether will ye be a rank robber's wife,
Or will ye die by my wee pen-knife?"   10

"It's I'll not be a rank robber's wife,
But I'll rather die by your wee pen-knife."

He's killed this may, and he's lay her by,
For to bear the red rose company.

He's taken the second ane by the hand,   15
And he's turned her round and made her stand.

"It's whether will ye be a rank robber's wife,
Or will ye die by my wee pen-knife?"

"I'll not be a rank robber's wife,
But I'll rather die by your wee pen-knife."   20

He's killed this may, and he's laid her by,
For to bear the red rose company.

He's taken the youngest ane by the hand,
And he's turned her round and made her stand.

Says, "Will ye be a rank robber's wife,   25
Or will ye die by my wee pen-knife?"

"I'll not be a rank robber's wife,
Nor will I die by your wee pen-knife.

"For I hae a brother in this wood,
And gin ye kill me, it's he'll kill thee."   30

"What's thy brother's name? come tell to me."
"My brother's name is Baby Lon."

"O sister, sister, what have I done!
O have I done this ill to thee!

"O since I've done this evil deed,   35
Good sall never be seen o me."

He's taken out his wee pen-knife,
And he's twyned himsel of his ain sweet life.

13 *may*: maid.   38 *twyned*: separated.

Anonymous   Bonny Barbara Allan

It was in and about the Martinmas time,
    When the green leaves were a falling,
That Sir John Graeme, in the West Country,
    Fell in love with Barbara Allan.

He sent his man down through the town,   5
    To the place where she was dwelling:
"O haste and come to my master dear,
    Gin ye be Barbara Allan."

O hooly, hooly rose she up,
    To the place where he was lying,   10
And when she drew the curtain by,
    "Young man, I think you're dying."

"O it's I'm sick, and very, very sick,
    And 'tis a' for Barbara Allan;"
"O the better for me ye's never be,   15
    Tho your heart's blood were a spilling.

"O dinna ye mind, young man," said she,
    "When ye was in the tavern a drinking,
That ye made the healths gae round and round,
    And slighted Barbara Allan?"   20

He turned his face unto the wall,
    And death was with him dealing:

"Adieu, adieu, my dear friends all,
   And be kind to Barbara Allan."

And slowly, slowly raised she up,   25
   And slowly, slowly left him,
And sighing said, she could not stay,
   Since death of life had reft him.

She had not gane a mile but twa,
   When she heard the dead-bell ringing,   30
And every jow that the dead-bell geid,
   It cry'd "Woe to Barbara Allan!"

"O mother, mother, make my bed!
   O make it soft and narrow!
My love has died for me today,   35
   I'll die for him tomorrow."

8 *Gin*: if.   9 *hooly*: slowly and softly.   *17 mind*: remember.
31 jow: stroke (of a bell).   *geid*: gave.

Anonymous   Mary Hamilton

Word's gane to the kitchen,
   And word's gane to the ha,
That Marie Hamilton gangs wi' bairn
   To the hichest Stewart of a'.

He's courted her in the kitchen;   5
   He's courted her in the ha';
He's courted her in the laigh cellar,
   And that was warst of a'.

She's tyed it in her apron,
   And she's thrown it in the sea;   10
Says, "Sink ye, swim ye, bonny wee babe,
   You'll neer get mair of me!"

Down then came the auld queen,
   Goud tassels tying her hair:
"O Marie, where's the bonny wee babe   15
   That I heard greet sae sair?"

"There was never a babe intill my room,
   As little designs to be;
It was but a touch o my sair side,
   Come oer my fair bodie."   20

"O Marie, put on your robes o black,
   Or else your robes o brown,
For ye maun gang wi me the night,
   To see fair Edinbro town."

"I winna put on my robes o black,   25
   Nor yet my robes o brown;
But I'll put on my robes o white,
   To shine through Edinbro town."

When she gaed up the Cannogate,
    She laughed loud laughters three;   30
But when she cam down the Cannogate,
    The tear blinded her ee.

When she gaed up the Parliament stair,
    The heel came aff her shee;
And lang or she cam down again,   35
    She was condemnd to dee.

When she cam down the Cannogate,
    The Cannogate sae free,
Many a ladie look oer her window,
    Weeping for this ladie.   40

"Ye need nae weep for me," she says,
    "Ye need nae weep for me;
For had I not slain mine own sweet babe,
    This death I wadna dee.

"Bring me a bottle of wine," she says,   45
    "The best that eer ye hae,
That I may drink to my weil-wishers,
    And they may drink to me.

"Here's a health to the jolly sailors,
    That sail upon the main;   50
Let them never let on to my father and mother
    But what I'm coming hame.

"Here's a health to the jolly sailors,
    That sail upon the sea;
Let them never let on to my father and mother   55
    That I cam here to dee.

"Oh little did my mother think,
    The day she cradled me,
What lands I was to travel through,
    What death I was to dee.   60

"Oh little did my father think,
    The day he held up me,
What lands I was to travel through,
    What death I was to dee.

"Last night I washd the queen's feet,   65
    And gently laid her down;
And a' the thanks I've gotten the nicht
    To be hangd in Edinbro town!

"Last nicht there was four Maries;
    The nicht there'll be but three: 70
There was Marie Seton and Marie Beton
    And Marie Carmichael and me."

title: Mary Stuart, Queen of Scots, had four well-born ladies as
her attendants, though none met the fate ascribed to Mary Hamilton in this ballad. The poem probably reflects a scandalous incident

at the court.   3 *bairn*: child (goes with child).   4 *hichest*:
highest, that is, the king, Henry Stuart, Lord Darnley, Queen
Mary's husband.   7 *laigh*: low.   16 *greet*: cry.   23 *night*:
tonight.   29 *Cannogate*: an avenue leading from Holyrood
Palace to the city of Edinburgh.   38 *free*: noble, fine.

Anonymous   Giles Corey and Goodwyfe Corey—
   A Ballad of 1692

Come all New England men,
   And hearken unto me,
And I will tell what did befalle
   Upon ye Gallows Tree.

In Salem Village was the Place   5
   As I did heare them saye,
And Goodwyfe Corey was her Name,
   Upon that paynfull Daye:

This Goody Corey was a Witch
   The people did believe,   10
Afflicting of the Godly Ones
   Did make them sadly Greave.

There were two pyous Matron Dames
   And goodly Maidens Three,
That cryed upon this heynous Witch   15
   As you shall quicklie see.

Goodwyfe Bibber, she was one,
   And Goodwyfe Goodall two,
These were the sore afflicted ones
   With Fyts and Pynchings too: 20

And those three Damsels faire,
   She worried them full sore,
As all could see upon their Arms
   The divers Marks they bore.

And when before the Magistrates   25
   For Tryall she did stand,
This Wicked Witch did lye to them
   While holding up her Hand.

'I pray you all Good Gentlemen
   Come listen unto me,   30
I never harmed those two Goodwyfes
   Nor yet these Children Three.

'I call upon my Savior Lord,'
   (Blasphemously she sayed)
'As Witness of my Innocence,   35
   In this my Hour of Need.'

The goodly Ministers were shockt
   This Witch-prayer for to hear,
And some did see ye Black Man there
   A-whispering in her Eare.   40

The Magistrates did say to her
   'Most surely thou dost lye!
Convess thou here thy hellish Deeds
   Or ill Death thou must dye.'

This Goodwyfe had a Goodman too,   45
   Giles Corey was his Name,
In Salem Gaol they shut him in
   With his blasphemous Dame.

Giles Corey was a Wizzard strong,
   A stubborn Wretch was he,   50
And fitt was he to hang on high
   Upon ye Locust Tree.

So when before ye Magistrates
   For Tryall he did come,
He would no true Confession make   55
   But was compleatlie dumbe.

'Giles Corey,' said ye Magistrate,
   'What hast thou heare to pleade,
To those who now accuse thy Soule
   Of Crymes and horrid Deed?'   60

Giles Corey—he sayde not a Word,
   No single Word spake he;
'Giles Corey,' sayeth ye Magistrate,
   'We'll press it out of thee.'

They got them then a heavy Beam,   65
   They layde it on his Breast,
They loaded it with heavy Stones,
   And hard upon him presst.

'More weight!' now sayde this wretched Man,
   'More weight!' again he cryde,   70
And he did no Confession make
   But wickedly he dyed.

Dame Corey lived but six Days more,
   But six Days more lived she,
For she was hung at Gallows Hill   75
   Upon ye Locust Tree.

Rejoyce all true New England men,
   Let Grace still more abounde,
Go search ye Land with myght and maine
   Till all these Imps be founde.   80

And that will be a glorious Daye,
   A goodlie sight to see,

When you shall hang these Brands of Fyre
  Upon ye Gallows Tree.

title: This ballad collected by Olive W. Burt, ed., *American Murder Ballads,* Oxford Univ. Press, 1958.   64 *'We'll press it out of thee'*: an old judicial torture, *peine forte et dure,* based on the assumption that a sufficiently heavy weight could actually press the truth from an accused man.

John Keats   La Belle Dame Sans Merci

O what can ail thee, Knight at arms,
  Alone and palely loitering?
The sedge has withered from the Lake
  And no birds sing!

O what can ail thee, Knight at arms,   5
  So haggard, and so woebegone?
The squirrel's granary is full
  And the harvest's done.

I see a lily on thy brow
  With anguish moist and fever dew,   10
And on thy cheeks a fading rose
  Fast withereth too.

I met a Lady in the Meads,
  Full beautiful, a faery's child,
Her hair was long, her foot was light   15
  And her eyes were wild.

I made a Garland for her head,
  And bracelets too, and fragrant Zone;
She looked at me as she did love
  And made sweet moan.   20

I set her on my pacing steed
  And nothing else saw all day long,
For sidelong would she bend and sing
  A faery's song.

She found me roots of relish sweet,   25
  And honey wild, and manna dew,
And sure in language strange she said,
  "I love thee true."

She took me to her elfin grot
  And there she wept and sighed full sore,   30
And there I shut her wild wild eyes
  With kisses four.

And there she lulléd me asleep,
  And there I dreamed, Ah Woe betide!
The latest dream I ever dreamt   35
  On the cold hillside.

I saw pale Kings, and Princes too,
    Pale warriors, death-pale were they all;
They cried, "La belle dame sans merci
    Thee hath in thrall!"   *40*

I saw their starved lips in the gloam
    With horrid warning gapéd wide,
And I awoke, and found me here
    On the cold hill's side.

And this is why I sojourn here,   *45*
    Alone and palely loitering;
Though the sedge is withered from the Lake
    And no birds sing.

18 *Zone:* girdle.   35 *latest:* last.

John Davidson   A Ballad of a Nun

From Eastertide to Eastertide
    For ten long years her patient knees
Engraved the stones—the fittest bride
    Of Christ in all the diocese.

She conquered every earthly lust;   *5*
    The abbess loved her more and more;
And, as a mark of perfect trust,
    Made her the keeper of the door.

High on a hill the convent hung,
    Across a duchy looking down,   *10*
Where everlasting mountains flung
    Their shadows over tower and town.

The jewels of their lofty snows
    In constellations flashed at night;
Above their crests the moon arose;   *15*
    The deep earth shuddered with delight.

Long ere she left her cloudy bed,
    Still dreaming in the orient land,
On many a mountain's happy head
    Dawn lightly laid her rosy hand.   *20*

The adventurous sun took heaven by storm;
    Clouds scattered largesses of rain;
The sounding cities, rich and warm,
    Smouldered and glittered in the plain.

Sometimes it was a wandering wind,   *25*
    Sometimes the fragrance of the pine,
Sometimes the thought how others sinned,
    That turned her sweet blood into wine.

Sometimes she heard a serenade
    Complaining sweetly far away.   *30*

She said, "A young man woos a maid";
   And dreamt of love till break of day.

Then would she ply her knotted scourge
   Until she swooned; but evermore
She had the same red sin to purge,   35
   Poor, passionate keeper of the door!

For still night's starry scroll unfurled,
   And still the day came like a flood:
It was the greatness of the world
   That made her long to use her blood.   40

In winter-time when Lent drew nigh,
   And hill and plain were wrapped in snow,
She watched beneath the frosty sky
   The nearest city nightly glow.

Like peals of airy bells outworn   45
   Faint laughter died above her head
In gusts of broken music borne:
   "They keep the Carnival," she said.

Her hungry heart devoured the town:
   "Heaven save me by a miracle!   50
Unless God sends an angel down,
   Thither I go though it were Hell."

She dug her nails deep in her breast,
   Sobbed, shrieked, and straight withdrew the bar:
A fledgling flying from the nest,   55
   A pale moth rushing to a star.

Fillet and veil in strips she tore;
   Her golden tresses floated wide;
The ring and bracelet that she wore
   As Christ's betrothed, she cast aside.   60

"Life's dearest meaning I shall probe;
   Lo! I shall taste of love at last!
Away!" She doffed her outer robe,
   And sent it sailing down the blast.

Her body seemed to warm the wind;   65
   With bleeding feet o'er ice she ran:
"I leave the righteous God behind;
   I go to worship sinful man."

She reached the sounding city's gate;
   No question did the warder ask: 70
He passed her in: "Welcome, wild mate!"
   He thought her some fantastic mask.

Half-naked through the town she went;
   Each footstep left a bloody mark;
Crowds followed her with looks intent;   75
   Her bright eyes made the torches dark.

Alone and watching in the street
   There stood a grave youth nobly dressed;
To him she knelt and kissed his feet;
   Her face her great desire confessed.   80

He healed her bosom with a kiss;
   She gave him all her passion's hoard;
And sobbed and murmured ever, "This
   Is life's great meaning, dear, my lord.

"I care not for my broken vow;   85
   Though God should come in thunder soon,
I am sister to the mountains now,
   And sister to the sun and moon."

Through all the towns of Belmarie
   She made a progress like a queen.
"She is," they said, "whate'er she be,   90
   The strangest woman ever seen.

"From fairyland she must have come,
   Or else she is a mermaiden."
Some said she was a ghoul, and some   95
   A heathen goddess born again.

But soon her fire to ashes burned;
   Her beauty changed to haggardness;
Her golden hair to silver turned;
   The hour came of her last caress.   100

At midnight from her lonely bed
   She rose, and said, "I have had my will."
The old ragged robe she donned, and fled
   Back to the convent on the hill.

Half-naked as she went before,   105
   She hurried to the city wall,
Unnoticed in the rush and roar
   And splendour of the Carnival.

No question did the warder ask:
   Her ragged robe, her shrunken limb,
Her dreadful eyes! "It is no mask;   110
   It is a she-wolf, gaunt and grim!"

She ran across the icy plain;
   Her worn blood curdled in the blast;
Each footstep left a crimson stain;   115
   The white-faced moon looked on aghast.

She said between her chattering jaws,
   "Deep peace is mine; I cease to strive.
Oh, comfortable convent laws
   That bury foolish nuns alive!   120

"A trowel for my passing-bell,
   A little bed within the wall

A coverlet of stones—how well
 I there shall keep the Carnival!"

Like tired bells chiming in their sleep,   *125*
 The wind faint peals of laughter bore;
She stopped her ears and climbed the steep,
 And thundered at the convent door.

It opened straight; she entered in,
 And at the wardress' feet fell prone: *130*
"I come to purge away my sin.
 Bury me; close me up in stone."

The wardress raised her tenderly;
 She touched her wet and fast-shut eyes.
"Look, sister; sister, look at me.   *135*
 Look, can you see through my disguise?"

She looked and saw her own sad face,
 And trembled, wondering, "Who art thou?"
"God sent me down to fill your place:
 I am the Virgin Mary now."   *140*

And with the word, God's mother shone.
 The wanderer whispered, "Mary, hail!"
The vision helped her to put on
 Bracelet and fillet, ring and veil.

"You are sister to the mountains now,   *145*
 And sister to the day and night:
Sister to God." And on the brow
 She kissed her thrice, and left her sight.

While dreaming in her cloudy bed,
 Far in the crimson orient land,   *150*
On many a mountain's happy head
 Dawn lightly laid her rosy hand.

William Butler Yeats The Ballad of Father Gilligan

The old priest Peter Gilligan
Was weary night and day;
For half his flock were in their beds,
Or under green sods lay.

Once, while he nodded on a chair,   5
At the moth-hour of eve,
Another poor man sent for him,
And he began to grieve.

"I have no rest, nor joy, nor peace,
For people die and die";   10
And after cried he, "God forgive!
My body spake, not I!"

He knelt, and leaning on the chair
He prayed and fell asleep;
And the moth-hour went from the fields,   *15*
And stars began to peep.

They slowly into millions grew,
And leaves shook in the wind;
And God covered the world with shade,
And whispered to mankind.   20

Upon the time of sparrow-chirp
When moths came once more,
The old priest Peter Gilligan
Stood upright on the floor.

"Mavrone, mavrone! the man has died   25
While I slept on the chair";
He roused his horse out of its sleep,
And rode with little care.

He rode now as he never rode,
By rocky lane and fen;   30
The sick man's wife opened the door:
"Father! you come again!"

"And is the poor man dead?" he cried.
"He died an hour ago."
The old priest Peter Gilligan   35
In grief swayed to and fro.

"When you were gone, he turned and died
As merry as a bird."
The old priest Peter Gilligan
He knelt him at that word.   40

"He Who hath made the night of stars
For souls who tire and bleed,
Sent one of His great angels down
To help me in my need.

"He Who is wrapped in purple robes,   45
With planets in His care,
Had pity on the least of things
Asleep upon a chair."

25 *mavrone*: ochone; an exclamation of grief or regret.

Ezra Pound   Ballad of the Goodly Fere

SIMON ZELOTES SPEAKETH IT SOMEWHILE

AFTER THE CRUCIFIXION

Ha' we lost the goodliest fere o' all
For the priests and the gallows tree?

Aye, lover he was of brawny men,
O' ships and the open sea.

When they came wi' a host to take Our Man   5
His smile was good to see,
"First let these go!" quo' our Goodly Fere,
"Or I'll see ye damned," says he.

Aye, he sent us out through the crossed high spears,
And the scorn of his laugh rang free,   10
"Why took ye not me when I walked about
Alone in the town?" says he.

Oh we drank his "Hale" in the good red wine
When we last made company,
No capon priest was the Goodly Fere   15
But a man o' men was he.

I ha' seen him drive a hundred men
Wi' a bundle o' cords swung free,
When they took the high and holy house
For their pawn and treasury.   20

They'll no get him a' in a book I think
Though they write it cunningly;
No mouse of the scrolls was the Goodly Fere
But aye loved the open sea.

If they think they ha' snared our Goodly Fere   25
They are fools to the last degree.
"I'll go to the feast," quo' our Goodly Fere,
"Though I go to the gallows tree."

"Ye ha' seen me heal the lame and the blind,
And wake the dead," says he,   30
"Ye shall see one thing to master all:
'Tis how a brave man dies on the tree."

A son of God was the Goodly Fere
That bade us his brothers be.
I ha' seen him cow a thousand men.   35
I ha' seen him upon the tree.

He cried no cry when they drave the nails
And the blood gushed hot and free,
The hounds of the crimson sky gave tongue
But never a cry cried he.   40

I ha' seen him cow a thousand men
On the hills o' Galilee,
They whined as he walked out calm between,
Wi' his eyes like the gray o' the sea.

Like the sea that brooks no voyaging   45
With the winds unleashed and free,
Like the sea that he cowed at Gennesaret
Wi' twey words spoke' suddenly.

A master of men was the Goodly Fere,
A mate of the wind and sea,   50
If they think they ha' slain our Goodly Fere
They are fools eternally.

I ha' seen him eat o' the honey-comb
Sin' they nailed him to the tree.

1 fere: mate, companion.

Yvor Winters   Sir Gawaine and the Green Knight

Reptilian green the wrinkled throat,
Green as a bough of yew the beard;
He bent his head, and so I smote;
Then for a thought my vision cleared.

The head dropped clean; he rose and walked;   5
He fixed his fingers in the hair;
The head was unabashed and talked;
I understood what I must dare.

His flesh, cut down, arose and grew.
He bade me wait the season's round,   10
And then, when he had strength anew,
To meet him on his native ground.

The year declined; and in his keep
I passed in joy a thriving yule;
And whether waking or in sleep,   15
I lived in riot like a fool.

He beat the woods to bring me meat.
His lady, like a forest vine,
Grew in my arms; the growth was sweet;
And yet what thoughtless force was mine!   20

By practice and conviction formed,
With ancient stubbornness ingrained,
Although her body clung and swarmed,
My own identity remained.

Her beauty, lithe, unholy, pure   25
Took shapes that I had never known;
And had I once been insecure,
Had grafted laurel in my bone.

And then, since I had kept the trust,
Had loved the lady, yet was true,   30
The knight withheld his giant thrust
And let me go with what I knew.

I left the green bark and the shade,
Where growth was rapid, thick, and still;
I found a road that men had made   35
And rested on a drying hill.

Anonymous   Sinking of the Titanic

It was 1912 when the awful news got around
That the great Titanic was sinking down.
Shine came running up on deck, told the Captain, "Please,
The water in the boiler room is up to my knees."

Captain said, "Take your black self on back down there!   5
I got a hundred-fifty pumps to keep the boiler room clear."
Shine went back in the hole, started shovelling coal,
Singing, "Lord, have mercy, Lord, on my soul!"
Just then half the ocean jumped across the boiler room deck.
Shine yelled to the Captain, "The water's 'round my neck!"   10
Captain said, "Go back! Neither fear nor doubt!
I got a hundred more pumps to keep the water out."

"Your words sound happy and your words sound true,
But this is one time, Cap, your words won't do.
I don't like chicken and I don't like ham—   15
And I don't believe your pumps is worth a damn!"

The old Titanic was beginning to sink.
Shine pulled off his clothes and jumped in the brink.
He said, "Little fish, big fish, and shark fishes, too,
Get out of my way because I'm coming through."   20

Captain on bridge hollered, "Shine, Shine, save poor me,
And I'll make you as rich as any man can be."
Shine said, "There's more gold on land than there is on sea."
And he swimmed on.

Jay Gould's millionary daughter came running up on deck   25
With her suitcase in her hand and her dress 'round her neck.
She cried, "Shine, Shine, save poor me!
I'll give you everything your eyes can see."
Shine said, "There's more on land than there is on sea."
And he swimmed on.   30

Big fat banker begging, "Shine, Shine, save poor me!
I'll give you a thousand shares of T and T."
Shine said, "More stocks on land than there is on sea."
And he swimmed on.

When all them white folks went to heaven,   35
Shine was in Sugar Ray's Bar drinking Seagrams Seven.

title: "According to Negro belief, persons of color, even servants,
were barred from the Titanic on its ill-fated maiden voyage. But
folk versifiers insist that there was one Negro aboard. This is a
Harlem variant of his story as heard by Langston Hughes on
Eighth Avenue in 1956." [collected in *The Book of Negro Folklore,* ed. Langston Hughes and Arna Bontemps, Dodd, Mead and
Co., 1959]

X. J. Kennedy   In a Prominent Bar in Secaucus
   One Day

(TO THE *tune of 'Tho Old Orange Flute' or the
      tune of 'Sweet Betsy from Pike'*)

In a prominent bar in Secaucus one day
Rose a lady in skunk with a topheavy sway,
Raised a knobby red finger—all turned from their beer—
While with eyes bright as snowcrust she sang high and clear:

'Now who of you'd think from an eyeload of me   5
That I once was a lady as proud as could be?
Oh I'd never sit down by a tumbledown drunk
If it wasn't, my dears, for the high cost of junk.

'All the gents used to swear that the white of my calf
Beat the down of the swan by a length and a half.   10
In the kerchief of linen I caught to my nose
Ah, there never fell snot, but a little gold rose.

'I had seven gold teeth and a toothpick of gold,
My Virginia cheroot was a leaf of it rolled
And I'd light it each time with a thousand in cash—   15
Why the bums used to fight if I flicked them an ash.

'Once the toast of the Biltmore, the belle of the Taft,
I would drink bottle beer at the Drake, never draught,
And dine at the Astor on Salisbury steak
With a clean tablecloth for each bite I did take.   20

'In a car like the Roxy I'd roll to the track,
A steel-guitar trio, a bar in the back,
And the wheels made no noise, they turned over so fast
Still it took you ten minutes to see me go past.

'When horses bowed down to me that I might choose,   25
I bet on them all, for I hated to lose.
Now I'm saddled each night for my butter and eggs
And the broken threads race down the backs of my legs.

'Let you hold in mind, girls, that your beauty must pass
Like a lovely white clover that rusts with its grass.   30
Keep your bottoms off barstools and marry you young
Or be left—an old barrel with many a bung.

'For when time takes you out for a spin in his car
You'll be hard-pressed to stop him from going too far
And be left by the roadside, for all your good deeds.   35
Two toadstools for tits and a face full of weeds.'

All the house raised a cheer, but the man at the bar
Made a phonecall and up pulled a red patrol car
And she blew us a kiss as they copped her away
From that prominent bar in Secaucus, N.J.   40

THE NARRATIVE

Geoffrey Chaucer
    THE FRIAR'S TALE
    FROM *The Canterbury Tales*

Heere bigynneth the Freres Tale.

Whilom ther was dwellynge in my contree
An erchedekene, a man of heigh degree,
That boldely dide execucioun
In punysshynge of fornicacioun,
Of wicchecraft, and eek of bawderye,   5
Of diffamacioun, and avowtrye,
Of chirche reves, and of testamentz,
Of contractes, and of lakke of sacramentz,
Of usure, and of symonye also.
But, certes, lecchours dide he grettest wo;   10
They sholde syngen, if that they were hent;
And smale tytheres weren foule yshent,
If any persone wolde upon hem pleyne.
Ther myghte asterte hym no pecunyal peyne.
For smale tithes and for smal offrynge   15
He made the peple pitously to synge.
For er the bisshope caughte hem with his hook,
They weren in the erchedeknes book;
And thanne hadde he thurgh his jurisdiccioun,
Power to doon on hem correccioun.   20
    He hadde a somonour redy to his hond.
A slyer boye nas noon in Engelond;
For subtilly he hadde his espiaille,
That taughte hym wel wher mighte availle.
He koude spare of lecchours oon or two,   25
To techen hym to foure and twenty mo.
For thogh this Somonour wood were as an hare,
To telle his harlotrye I wol nat spare;
For we been out of his correccioun.
They han of us no juridiccioun,   30
Ne nevere shullen, terme of alle hir lyves.
    "Peter! so been wommen of the styves,"
Quod the Somonour, "yput out of oure cure."
    "Pees, with myschance, and with mysaventure!"
Thus seyde oure Hoost; "and lat hym telle his tale.   35
Now telleth forth, thogh that the Somonour gale;
Ne spareth nat, myn owene maister deere!"
    This false theef, this somonour—quod the Frere—
Hadde alwey bawdes redy to his hond
As any hauk to lure in Engelond,   40
That tolde hym al the secree that they knewe.

For hire acqueytance was nat come of newe;
They weren his approwours prively.
He took hymself a greet profit therby;
His maister knew nat alwey what he wan.   45
Withouten mandement a lewed man
He koude somne, on peyne of Cristes curs.
And they were glade for to fille his purs
And make hym grete feestes atte nale.
And right as Judas hadde purses smale   50
And was a theef, right swich a theef was he;
His maister hadde but half his duëtee.
He was, if I shal yeven hym his laude,
A theef, and eek a somnour, and a baude.
He hadde eek wenches at his retenue,   55
That wheither that Sir Robert, or Sir Huwe,
Or Jakke, or Rauf, or whoso that it were
That lay by hem, they tolde it in his ere.
Thus was the wenche and he of oon assent;
And he wolde fecche a feyned mandement,   60
And somne hem to the chapitre bothe two,
And pile the man and lete the wenche go.
Thanne wolde he seye, "Freend, I shal for thy sake
Do striken hire out of oure lettres blake.
Thee thar namoore as in this cas travaille.   65
I am thy freend ther I thee may availle."
Certeyn, he knew of briberyes mo
Than possible is to telle in yeres two;
For in this world nys dogge for the bowe
That kan an hurt deer from an hool yknowe   70
Bet than this somnour knew a sly lecchour,
Or an avowtier, or a paramour.
And for that was the fruyt of al his rente,
Therefore on it he sette al his entente.
    And so bifel that ones on a day   75
This somnour, evere waityng on his pray,
Rood for to somne an old wydwe, a ribibe,
Feynynge a cause, for he wolde brybe.
And happed that he saugh bifore hym ryde
A gay yeman, under a forest syde.   80
A bowe he bar and arwes brighte and kene;
He hadde upon a courtepy of grene,
An hat upon his heed with frenges blake.
"Sire," quod this somnour, "hayle, and wel atake!"
    "Welcome," quod he, "and every good felawe!   85
Wher rydestow, under this grene-wode shawe?"
Seyde this yeman; "wiltow fer today?"
    This somnour hym answerde, and seyde, "Nay.
Heere faste by," quod he, "is myn entente
To ryden, for to reysen up a rente   90
That longeth to my lordes duëtee."
    "Artow thanne a bailly?" "Ye," quod he.
He dorste nat, for verray filthe and shame,
Seye that he was a somonour, for the name.

"*Depardieux*," quod this yeman, "deere broother,   95
Thou art a bailly, and I am another.
I am unknowen as in this contree;
Of thyn aqueyntance I wolde praye thee,
And eek of bretherhede, if that yow leste.
I have gold and silver in my cheste;   100
If that thee happe to comen in oure shire,
Al shal be thyn, right as thou wolt desire."
    "Grantmercy," quod this somonour, "by my feith!"
Everych in ootheres hand his trouthe leith,
For to be sworne bretheren till they deye.   105
In daliance they ryden forth and pleye.
This somonour, which that was as ful of jangles,
As ful of venym been thise waryangles,
And evere enqueryng upon every thyng,
"Brother," quod he, "where is now youre dwellyng,   110
Another day if that I sholde yow seche?"
    This yeman hym answerde in softe speche,
"Brother," quod he, "fer in the north contree,
Where-as I hope somtyme I shal thee see.
Er we departe, I shal thee so wel wisse   115
That of myn hous ne shaltow nevere mysse."
    "Now, brother," quod this somonour, "I yow preye,
Teche me, whil that we ryden by the weye,
Syn that ye been a baillif as am I,
Som subtiltee, and tel me feithfully   120
In myn office how that I may moost wynne;
And spareth nat for conscience ne synne,
But as my brother tel me how do ye."
    "Now by my trouthe, brother deere," seyd he,
"As I shal tellen thee a feithful tale.   125
My wages been ful streite and ful smale,
My lord is hard to me, and daungerous,
And myn office is ful laborious,
And therfore by extorcions I lyve.
For sothe, I take all that men wol me yive.   130
Algate, by sleyghtë or by violence,
Fro yeer to yeer I wynne al my dispence.
I kan no bettre telle, feithfully."
    "Now certes," quod this somonour, "so fare I,
I spare nat to taken, God it woot,   135
But-if it be to hevy or to hoot.
What I may gete in conseil prively,
No manner conscience of that have I.
Nere myn extorcioun, I myghte nat lyven,
Nor of swiche japes wol I nat be shryven;   140
Stomak ne conscience ne knowe I noon;
I shrewe thise shrifte-fadres everychoon.
Wel be we met, by God and by Seint Jame!
But, leeve brother, tel me thanne thy name,"
Quod this somonour. In this meene while,   145
This yeman gan a litel for to smyle.
    "Brother," quod he, "wiltow that I thee telle?

I am a feend; my dwellyng is in helle.
And heere I ryde aboute my purchasyng,
To wite wher men wol yeve me anythyng.   150
My purchas is th'effect of al my rente.
Looke how thou rydest for the same entente,
To wynne good, thou rekkest nevere how;
Right so fare I, for ryde wolde I now
Unto the worldes ende for a preye."   155
  "A!" quod this somonour, "benedicite! what say ye?
I wende ye were a yeman trewely;
Ye han a mannes shape as wel as I.
Han ye a figure thanne determinat
In helle, ther ye been in youre estat?"   160
  "Nay, certeinly," quod he; "ther have we noon;
But whan us liketh we kan take us oon,
Or elles make you seme we been shape
Somtyme lyk a man or lyk an ape,
Or lyk an angel kan I ryde or go.   165
It is no wonder thyng thogh it be so;
A lowsy jogelour kan deceyve thee,
And pardee, yet kan I moore craft than he."
  "Why," quod this somonour, "ryde ye thanne or goon
In sondry shape, and nat alwey in oon?"   170
  "For we," quod he, "wol us swiche formes make
As moost able is oure preyes for to take."
  "What maketh yow to han al this labour?"
  "Ful many a cause, leeve sire somonour,"
Seyde this feend. "But alle thyng hath tyme;   175
The day is short, and it is passed pryme,
And yet ne wan I nothyng in this day.
I wol entende to wynnyng, if I may,
And nat entende oure wittes to declare.
For, brother myn, thy wit is al to bare   180
To understonde, althogh I tolde hem thee.
But, for thou axest why labouren we—
For somtyme we been Goddes instrumentz,
And meenes to doon his comandementz,
Whan that hym list, upon his creatures,   185
In divers art and in diverse figures.
Withouten hym we have no myght, certayn,
If that hym list to stonden ther-agayn.
And somtyme, at oure prayere, han we leve
Oonly the body and nat the soule greve;   190
Witnesse on Job, whom that we diden wo.
And somtyme han we myght of bothe two,
This is to seyn, of soule and body eke.
And somtyme be we suffred for to seke
Upon a man and doon his soule unreste   195
And nat his body. And al is for the beste.
Whan he withstandeth oure temptacioun,
It is a cause of his savacioun;
Al be it that it was nat oure entente
He sholde be sauf, but that we wolde hym hente.   200

And somtyme be we servant unto man;
As to the ercebisshope, Seint Dunstan;
And to the apostles servant eek was I."
   "Yet tel me," quod the somonour, "feithfully,
Make ye yow newe bodies thus alway   205
Of elementz?" The feend answerde, "Nay.
Somtyme we feyne; and somtyme we aryse
With dede bodyes, in ful sondry wyse,
And speke as renably and faire and wel
As to the Phitonissa dide Samuel.   210
(And yet wol som men seye it was nat he;
I do no fors of youre dyvynytee.)
But o thyng warne I thee, I wol nat jape:
Thou wolt algates wite how we been shape;
Thou shalt herafterward, my brother deere,   215
Come there thee nedeth nat of me to leere;
For thou shalt, by thyn owene experience,
Konne in a chayre rede of this sentence
Bet than Virgile while he was on lyve,
Or Dant also. Now lat us ryde blyve,   220
For I wole holde compaignye with thee
Til it be so that thou forsake me."
   "Nay," quod this somonour, "that shal nat bityde.
I am a yeman, knowen is ful wyde;
My trouthe wol I holde, as in this cas.   225
For though thou were the devel Sathanas,
My trouthe wol I holde to my brother,
As I am sworn, and ech of us til oother,
For to be trewe brother in this cas.
And bothe we goon abouten oure purchas.   230
Taak thou thy part, what that men wol thee yive,
And I shal myn; thus may we bothe lyve.
And if that any of us have moore than oother,
Lat hym be trewe and parte it with his brother."
   "I graunte," quod the devel, "by my fey!"   235
And with that word, they ryden forth hir wey.
And right at the entryng of the townes ende,
To which this somonour shoope hym for to wende,
They saugh a cart that charged was with hey,
Which that a cartere droof forth in his wey.   240
Deep was the wey, for which the carte stood.
   The cartere smoot, and cryde as he were wood,
"Hayt, Brok! Hayte, Scot! what spare ye for the stones?
The feend," quod he, "yow fecche, body and bones,
As ferforthly as evere were ye foled,   245
So muche wo as I have with yow tholed!
The devel have al, bothe hors and cart and hey!"
   This somonour seyde, "Heere shal we have a pley."
And neer the feend he drough, as noght ne were,
Ful prively, and rowned in his ere: 250
"Herkne, my brother! herkne, by thy feith!
Herestow nat how that the cartere seith?
Hent it anon, for he hath yeve it thee—

Bothe hey and cart, and eek his caples thre."
"Nay," quod the devel, "God woot, never a deel.   255
It is nat his entente, trust me weel.
Axe hym thyself, if thou nat trowest me;
Or elles stynt a while, and thou shalt see."
   This cartere thakketh his hors upon the croupe,
And they bigonne to drawen and to stoupe.   260
"Heyt now!" quod he, "ther Jesu Crist yow blesse,
And al his handwerk, bothe moore and lesse!
That was wel twight, myn owene lyard boy.
I pray God save thee, and Seinte Loy!
Now is my cart out of the slow, pardee."   265
   "Lo, brother," quod the feend, "what tolde I thee?
Heere may ye se, myn owene deere brother,
The carl spak oo thing, but he thoghte another.
Lat us go forth abouten oure viage;
Heere wynne I nothyng upon carriage."   270
   Whan that they coomen somwhat out of towne,
This somonour to his brother gan to rowne:
"Brother," quod he, "heere woneth an old rebekke,
That hadde almost as lief to lese hire nekke
As for to yeve a peny of hir good.   275
I wole han twelf pens, though that she be wood,
Or I wol sompne hire unto oure office;
And yet, God woot, of hire knowe I no vice.
But, for thou kanst nat as in this contree
Wynne thy cost, taak heer ensample of me."   280
   This somonour clappeth at the wydwes gate.
"Com out," quod he, "thou olde virytrate!
I trowe thou hast som frere or preest with thee."
   "Who clappeth there?" seyde this wyf, "benedicite!
God save you, sire. What is youre sweete wille?"   285
   "I have," quod he, "of somonce here a bille.
Up peyne of cursyng, looke that thou be
To-morn bifore the erchedeknes knee,
T'answere to the court of certeyn thynges."
   "Now, Lord," quod she, "Crist Jhesu, kyng of kynges,   290
So wisly helpe me, as I ne may.
I have been syk, and that ful many a day.
I may nat go so fer," quod she, "ne ryde,
But I be deed, so priketh it in my syde.
May I nat axe a libel, sire somonour,   295
And answere there by my procuratour
To swich thyng as men wole opposen me?"
   "Yis," quod this somonour, "pay anon, lat se,
Twelf pens to me, and I wol thee acquite.
I shal no profit han thereby but lite;   300
My maister hath the profit and nat I.
Com of, and lat me ryden hastily;
Yif me twelf pens; I may no lenger tarye."
   "Twelf pens!" quod she, "now, lady Seinte Marie
So wisly help me out of care and synne,   305
This wyde world thogh that I sholde wynne,

Ne have I nat twelf pens withinne myn hoold.
Ye knowen wel that I am povre and oold;
Kithe youre almesse on me povre wrecche."
   "Nay thanne," quod he, "the foule feend me fecche   310
If I th'excuse, though thou shul be spilt!"
   "Allas!" quod she; "God woot, I have no gilt."
   "Pay me," quod he, "or by the sweete Seinte Anne,
As I wol bere awey thy newe panne
For dette which thou owest me of old.   315
Whan that thou madest thyn housbonde cokewold,
I payde at hoom for thy correccioun."
   "Thou lixt!" quod she; "by my savacioun,
Ne was I nevere er now, wydwe ne wyf,
Somoned unto youre court in al my lyf;   320
Ne nevere I nas but of my body trewe.
Unto the devel, blak and rough of hewe,
Yeve I thy body and my panne also!"
   And whan the devel herde hire cursen so
Upon hir knees, he seyde in this manere: 325
"Now, Mabely, myn owene moder deere,
Is this youre wyl in ernest that ye seye?"
   "The devel," quod she, "so fecche hym er he deye,
And panne and al, but he wol hym repente!"
   "Nay, olde stot, that is nat myn entente,"   330
Quod this somonour, "for to repente me
For any thyng that I have had of thee.
I wolde I hadde thy smok and every clooth."
   "Now, brother," quod the devel, "be nat wrooth.
Thy body and this panne been myne by right;   335
Thou shalt with me to helle yet to-nyght,
Where thou shalt knowen of oure privetee
Moore than a maister of dyvyntee."
   And with that word this foule feend hym hente;
Body and soule he with the devel wente   340
Where-as that somonours han hir heritage.
And God, that maked after his ymage
Mankynde, save and gyde us, alle and some,
And leve thise somonours goode men bicome!
   "Lordynges, I koude han toold yow," quod this Frere,   345
"Hadde I had leyser, for this Somnour heere,
After the text of Crist, Poul, and John,
And of oure othere doctours many oon,
Swiche peynes that youre hertes myghte agryse;
Al be it so no tonge may it devyse,   350
Thogh that I myghte a thousand wynter telle
The peynes of thilke cursed hous of helle.
But, for to kepe us fro that cursed place,
Waketh, and preyeth Jhesu for his grace
So kepe us fro the temptour, Sathanas.   355
Herketh this world! beth war, as in this cas:
The leoun sit in his awayt alway
To sle the innocent, if that he may.
Disposeth ay youre hertes to withstonde

The feend, that yow wolde make thral and bonde.   360
He may nat tempte yow over youre myght,
For Crist wol be youre champion and knyght.
And prayeth that thise somonours hem repente
Or hir mysdedes, er that the feend hem hente!"

Heere endeth the Freres Tale.

1 *Whilom:* formerly.   6 *avowtrye:* adultery.   7 *chirche reves:*
church robberies.   *testamentz:* wills.   9 *symonye:* the buying
and selling of ecclesiastical appointments.   11 *hent:* caught.
12 *yshent:* injured, ruined.   13 *persone:* parson.   *pleyne:* complain.   14 *pecunyal peyne:* monetary penalty, i.e., he always
imposed a fine.   17 *hook:* bishop's staff.   23 *espiaille:* corps of
spies.   27 *wood . . . hare:* "mad as a March hare."   28 *harlotrye:*
rascality.   32 *styves:* brothels (stews).   33 *cure:* care.   34
Pees . . . mysaventure: i.e., mischance and trouble be yours if you
are not silent.   36 *gale:* exclaim.   42 *hire:* their.   43 *approwours:* informers.   46 *mandement:* writ of summons.   *lewed:*
ignorant or ordinary.   47 *curs:* excommunication.   49 *nale:*
an alehouse.   52 *duëtee:* fees.   61 *chapitre:* chapter, an assem-
bly of diocese officials.   62 *pile:* pillage.   65 *Thee . . . travaille:*
i.e., trouble yourself no longer.   67 *briberyes:* ways to steal.
69 *nys:* is not.   *bowe:* refers to the dog that accompanies a
hunter.   72 *avowtier:* adulterer.   73 *And . . . rente:* because
that was the substance of his income.   77 *ribibe:* an old woman.
82 *courtepy:* a jacket.   86 *shawe:* wood.   92 *bailly:* bailiff, a
man in charge of a lord's estate.   95 *Depardieux:* By God!
103 *Grantmercy:* many thanks.   104 *trouthe:* promise.   107
jangles: jabber or nonsense.   108 *waryangles:* shrikes.   115
departe: separate.   *wisse:* inform.   126 *streite:* scanty.   127
daungerous: difficult to please.   131 *Algate:* in every way.   139
Nere: were it not for.   141 *Stomak:* compassion.   142 *I
shrewe . . . ever ychoon:* I curse each of these father confessors.
149 *purchasyng:* procuring.   150 *wite:* learn, discover.   151
rente: income, i.e., what I pick up is my entire income.   156
benedicite: bless thee.   157 *wende:* supposed, thought.   159
determinat: fixed.   167 *jogelour:* juggler.   176 *pryme:* 9 a.m.
188 *ther-agayn:* thereagainst.   200 *hente:* seize.   209 *renably:*
readily.   210 *Phitonissa:* Pythoness, the Witch of Endor (see I
Sam. 28:7–20).   212 *dyvynytee:* divinity, i.e., I don't believe
in your (I take no stock in your) theology.   213 *jape:* jest.
218 *Konne . . . sentence:* You can in a professorial chair read about
this subject.   220 *blyve:* quickly.   235 *fey:* faith.   238
shoope . . . wende: planned to go.   239 *charged:* loaded.   241
stood: the wagon stuck because of the deep mud on the road.   243
Hayt: Get up!   *Brok:* badger, a common name for a gray horse.
246 *tholed:* endured.   249 *as . . . were:* as though nothing were
up.   250 *rowned:* whispered.   254 *caples:* horses used to pull
carts.   255 *never a deel:* never a bit.   257 *trowest:* believe.
263 *twight:* pulled.   *lyard:* gray.   265 *slow:* mudhole.   268
carl: churl, fellow.   270 *Heere . . . carriage:* as payment (by the
carter) on consideration of my giving up my claim on the cart and
horses.   273 *woneth:* dwells.   *rebekke:* old woman.   274

lese: lose.   281 *clappeth:* knocks.   282 *virytrate:* seemingly a
contemptuous term for an old woman.   291 *wisly:* surely.   294
But I be deed: without its causing my death.   295 *libel:* a bill
of indictment.   296 *procuratour:* attorney.   302 *Com of:* come
off it, i.e., stop holding back.   309 *Kithe youre almesse:* Show
your alms.   311 *spilt:* destroyed.   318 *lixt:* liest.   330 *stot:*
horse, the term here used as abuse.   341 *Where-as . . . heritage:*
where summonors have their heritage.   344 *leve:* let.   349
agryse: shudder.   356 *beth war:* be wary.   357 *awayt:* ambush.
361 *He . . . myght:* He can not tempt you above your power to
resist.

John Keats   The Eve of St. Agnes

1

St. Agnes' Eve—Ah, bitter chill it was!
The owl, for all his feathers, was a-cold;
The hare limped trembling through the frozen grass,
And silent was the flock in woolly fold:
Numb were the Beadsman's fingers, while he told   5
His rosary, and while his frosted breath,
Like pious incense from a censer old,
Seemed taking flight for heaven, without a death,
Past the sweet Virgin's picture, while his prayer he saith.

2

His prayer he saith, this patient, holy man;   10
Then takes his lamp, and riseth from his knees,
And back returneth, meager, barefoot, wan,
Along the chapel aisle by slow degrees:
The sculptured dead, on each side, seem to freeze,
Imprisoned in black, purgatorial rails: 15
Knights, ladies, praying in dumb orat'ries,
He passeth by; and his weak spirit fails
To think how they may ache in icy hoods and mails.

3

Northward he turneth through a little door,
And scarce three steps, ere Music's golden tongue   20
Flattered to tears this aged man and poor;
But no—already had his deathbell rung:
The joys of all his life were said and sung:
His was harsh penance on St. Agnes' Eve:
Another way he went, and soon among   25
Rough ashes sat he for his soul's reprieve,
And all night kept awake, for sinner's sake to grieve.

4

That ancient Beadsman heard the prelude soft;
And so it chanced, for many a door was wide,

From hurry to and fro. Soon, up aloft,   30
The silver, snarling trumpets 'gan to chide:
The level chambers, ready with their pride,
Were glowing to receive a thousand guests:
The carvéd angels, ever eager-eyed,
Stared, where upon their heads the cornice rests,   35
With hair blown back, and wings put cross-wise on their breasts.

5

At length burst in the argent revelry,
With plume, tiara, and all rich array,
Numerous as shadows haunting fairily
The brain, new stuffed, in youth, with triumphs gay   40
Of old romance. These let us wish away,
And turn, sole-thoughted, to one Lady there,
Whose heart had brooded, all that wintry day,
On love, and winged St. Agnes' saintly care,
As she had heard old dames full many times declare.   45

6

They told her how, upon St. Agnes' Eve,
Young virgins might have visions of delight,
And soft adorings from their loves receive
Upon the honeyed middle of the night,
If ceremonies due they did aright;   50
As, supperless to bed they must retire,
And couch supine their beauties, lily white;
Nor look behind, nor sideways, but require
Of Heaven with upward eyes for all that they desire.

7

Full of this whim was thoughtful Madeline: 55
The music, yearning like a God in pain,
She scarcely heard: her maiden eyes divine,
Fixed on the floor, saw many a sweeping train
Pass by—she heeded not at all: in vain
Came many a tiptoe, amorous cavalier,   60
And back retired; not cooled by high disdain;
But she saw not: her heart was otherwhere:
She sighed for Agnes' dreams, the sweetest of the year.

8

She danced along with vague, regardless eyes,
Anxious her lips, her breathing quick and short: 65
The hallowed hour was near at hand: she sighs
Amid the timbrels, and the thronged resort
Of whisperers in anger, or in sport;
'Mid looks of love, defiance, hate, and scorn,
Hoodwinked with faery fancy; all amort,   70
Save to St. Agnes and her lambs unshorn,
And all the bliss to be before tomorrow morn.

9

So, purposing each moment to retire,
She lingered still. Meantime, across the moors,
Had come young Porphyro, with heart on fire   75
For Madeline. Beside the portal doors,
Buttressed from moonlight, stands he, and implores
All saints to give him sight of Madeline,
But for one moment in the tedious hours,
That he might gaze and worship all unseen;   80
Perchance speak, kneel, touch, kiss—in sooth such things have
been.

10

He ventures in: let no buzzed whisper tell:
All eyes be muffled, or a hundred swords
Will storm his heart, Love's fev'rous citadel:
For him, those chambers held barbarian hordes,   85
Hyena foemen, and hot-blooded lords,
Whose very dogs would execrations howl
Against his lineage: not one breast affords
Him any mercy, in that mansion foul,
Save one old beldame, weak in body and in soul.   90

11

Ah, happy chance! the aged creature came,
Shuffling along with ivory-headed wand,
To where he stood, hid from the torch's flame,
Behind a broad hall-pillar, far beyond
The sound of merriment and chorus bland: 95
He startled her; but soon she knew his face,
And grasped his fingers in her palsied hand,
Saying, "Mercy, Porphyro! hie thee from this place;
They are all here tonight, the whole bloodthirsty race!

12

"Get hence! get hence! there's dwarfish Hildebrand;   100
He had a fever late, and in the fit
He curséd thee and thine, both house and land:
Then there's that old Lord Maurice, not a whit
More tame for his gray hairs—Alas me! flit!
Flit like a ghost away."—"Ah, Gossip dear,   105
We're safe enough; here in this armchair sit,
And tell me how"—"Good Saints! not here, not here;
Follow me, child, or else these stones will be thy bier."

13

He followed through a lowly archéd way,
Brushing the cobwebs with his lofty plume,
And as she muttered "Well-a—well-a-day!"   110
He found him in a little moonlight room,

Pale, latticed, chill, and silent as a tomb.
"Now tell me where is Madeline," said he,
"O tell me, Angela, by the holy loom   *115*
Which none but secret sisterhood may see,
When they St. Agnes' wool are weaving piously."

14

"St. Agnes! Ah! it is St. Agnes' Eve—
Yet men will murder upon holy days:
Thou must hold water in a witch's sieve,   *120*
And be liege lord of all the Elves and Fays,
To venture so: it fills me with amaze
To see thee, Porphyro!—St. Agnes' Eve!
God's help! my lady fair the conjuror plays
This very night: good angels her deceive!   *125*
But let me laugh awhile, I've mickle time to grieve."

15

Feebly she laugheth in the languid moon,
While Porphyro upon her face doth look,
Like puzzled urchin on an aged crone
Who keepeth closed a wondrous riddle-book,   *130*
As spectacled she sits in chimney nook.
But soon his eyes grew brilliant, when she told
His lady's purpose; and he scarce could brook
Tears, at the thought of those enchantments cold,
And Madeline asleep in lap of legends old.   *135*

16

Sudden a thought came like a full-blown rose,
Flushing his brow, and in his painéd heart
Made purple riot: then doth he propose
A strategem, that makes the beldame start:
"A cruel man and impious thou art: *140*
Sweet lady, let her pray, and sleep, and dream
Alone with her good angels, far apart
From wicked men like thee. Go, go!—I deem
Thou canst not surely be the same that thou didst seem."

17

"I will not harm her, by all saints I swear,"   *145*
Quoth Porphyro: "O may I ne'er find grace
When my weak voice shall whisper its last prayer,
If one of her soft ringlets I displace,
Or look with ruffian passion in her face.
Good Angela, believe me by these tears;   *150*
Or I will, even in a moment's space,
Awake, with horrid shout, my foemen's ears,
And beard them, though they be more fanged then wolves and
      bears."

18

"Ah! why wilt thou affright a feeble soul?
A poor, weak, palsy-stricken, churchyard thing,   *155*
Whose passing bell may ere the midnight toll;
Whose prayers for thee, each morn and evening,
Were never missed."—Thus plaining, doth she bring
A gentler speech from burning Porphyro;
So woeful and of such deep sorrowing,   *160*
That Angela gives promise she will do
Whatever he shall wish, betide her weal or woe.

19

Which was, to lead him, in close secrecy,
Even to Madeline's chamber, and there hide
Him in a closet, of such privacy   *165*
That he might see her beauty unespied,
And win perhaps that night a peerless bride,
While legioned faeries paced the coverlet,
And pale enchantment held her sleepy-eyed.
Never on such a night have lovers met,   *170*
Since Merlin paid his Demon all the monstrous debt.

20

"It shall be as thou wishest," said the Dame:
"All cates and dainties shall be storéd there
Quickly on this feast night: by the tambour frame
Her own lute thou wilt see: no time to spare,   *175*
For I am slow and feeble, and scarce dare
On such a catering trust my dizzy head.
Wait here, my child, with patience; kneel in prayer
The while: Ah! thou must needs the lady wed,
Or may I never leave my grave among the dead."   *180*

21

So saying, she hobbled off with busy fear.
The lover's endless minutes slowly passed:
The dame returned, and whispered in his ear
To follow her; with aged eyes aghast
From fright of dim espial. Safe at last,   *185*
Through many a dusky gallery, they gain
The maiden's chamber, silken, hushed, and chaste;
Where Porphyro took covert, pleased amain.
His poor guide hurried back with agues in her brain.

22

Her falt'ring hand upon the balustrade,   *190*
Old Angela was feeling for the stair,
When Madeline, St. Agnes' charméd maid,
Rose, like a missioned spirit, unaware:
With silver taper's light, and pious care,
She turned, and down the aged gossip led   *195*

To a safe level matting. Now prepare,
  Young Porphyro, for gazing on that bed;
She comes, she comes again, like ringdove frayed and fled.

23

Out went the taper as she hurried in;
  Its little smoke, in pallid moonshine, died: 200
She closed the door, she panted, all akin
  To spirits of the air, and visions wide:
  No uttered syllable, or, woe betide!
  But to her heart, her heart was voluble,
  Paining with eloquence her balmy side;   205
  As though a tongueless nightingale should swell
Her throat in vain, and die, heart-stifled, in her dell.

24

A casement high and triple-arched there was,
  All garlanded with carven imag'ries
Of fruits, and flowers, and bunches of knot-grass,   210
  And diamonded with panes of quaint device,
  Innumerable of stains and splendid dyes,
  As are the tiger moth's deep-damasked wings;
  And in the midst, 'mong thousand heraldries,
  And twilight saints, and dim emblazonings,   215
A shielded scutcheon blushed with blood of queens and kings.

25

Full on this casement shone the wintry moon,
  And threw warm gules on Madeline's fair breast,
As down she knelt for heaven's grace and boon;
  Rose-bloom fell on her hands, together pressed,   220
  And on her silver cross soft amethyst,
  And on her hair a glory, like a saint:
  She seemed a splendid angel, newly dressed,
  Save wings, for heaven—Porphyro grew faint:
She knelt, so pure a thing, so free from mortal taint.   225

26

Anon his heart revives: her vespers done,
  Of all its wreathéd pearls her hair she frees;
Unclasps her warméd jewels one by one;
  Loosens her fragrant bodice; by degrees
  Her rich attire creeps rustling to her knees: 230
  Half-hidden, like a mermaid in sea-weed,
  Pensive awhile she dreams awake, and sees,
  In fancy, fair St. Agnes in her bed,
But dares not look behind, or all the charm is fled.

27

Soon, trembling in her soft and chilly nest,   235
  In sort of wakeful swoon, perplexed she lay,

Until the poppied warmth of sleep oppressed
Her soothéd limbs, and soul fatigued away;
Flown, like a thought, until the morrow-day;
Blissfully havened both from joy and pain;   240
Clasped like a missal where swart Paynims pray;
Blinded alike from sunshine and from rain,
As though a rose should shut, and be a bud again.

28

Stol'n to this paradise, and so entranced,
Porphyro gazed upon her empty dress,   245
And listened to her breathing, if it chanced
To wake into a slumberous tenderness;
Which when he heard, that minute did he bless,
And breathed himself: then from the closet crept,
Noiseless as fear in a wide wilderness,   250
And over the hushed carpet, silent, stepped,
And 'tween the curtains peeped, where, lo!—how fast she slept.

29

Then by the bedside, where the faded moon
Made a dim, silver twilight, soft he set
A table, and, half anguished, threw thereon   255
A cloth of woven crimson, gold, and jet—
O for some drowsy Morphean amulet!
The boisterous, midnight, festive clarion,
The kettledrum, and far-heard clarinet,
Affray his ears, though but in dying tone—   260
The hall door shuts again, and all the noise is gone.

30

And still she slept an azure-lidded sleep,
In blanchéd linen, smooth, and lavendered,
While he from forth the closet brought a heap
Of candied apple, quince, and plum, and gourd;   265
With jellies soother than the creamy curd,
And lucent syrups, tinct with cinnamon;
Manna and dates, in argosy transferred
From Fez; and spicéd dainties, every one,
From silken Samarcand to cedared Lebanon.   270

31

These delicates he heaped with glowing hand
On golden dishes and in baskets bright
Of wreathéd silver: sumptuous they stand
In the retired quiet of the night,
Filling the chilly room with perfume light.—   275
"And now, my love, my seraph fair, awake!
Thou art my heaven, and I thine eremite:
Open thine eyes, for meek St. Agnes' sake,
Or I shall drowse beside thee, so my soul doth ache."

32

Thus whispering, his warm, unnervéd arm   280
Sank in her pillow. Shaded was her dream
By the dusk curtains: 'twas a midnight charm
Impossible to melt as icéd stream:
The lustrous salvers in the moonlight gleam;
Broad golden fringe upon the carpet lies: 285
It seemed he never, never could redeem
From such a steadfast spell his lady's eyes;
So mused awhile, entoiled in wooféd fantasies.

33

Awakening up, he took her hollow lute—
Tumultuous—and, in chords that tenderest be,   290
He played an ancient ditty, long since mute,
In Provence called *"La belle dame sans merci"*:
Close to her ear touching the melody;
Wherewith disturbed, she uttered a soft moan:
He ceased—she panted quick—and suddenly   295
Her blue affrayéd eyes wide open shone:
Upon his knees he sank, pale as smooth-sculptured stone.

34

Her eyes were open, but she still beheld,
Now wide awake, the vision of her sleep:
There was a painful change, that nigh expelled   300
The blisses of her dream so pure and deep,
At which fair Madeline began to weep,
And moan forth witless words with many a sigh;
While still her gaze on Porphyro would keep,
Who knelt, with joinéd hands and piteous eye,   305
Fearing to move or speak, she looked so dreamingly.

35

"Ah, Porphyro!" said she, "but even now
Thy voice was at sweet tremble in mine ear,
Made tunable with every sweetest vow;
And those sad eyes were spiritual and clear: 310
How changed thou art! how pallid, chill, and drear!
Give me that voice again, my Porphyro,
Those looks immortal, those complainings dear!
Oh leave me not in this eternal woe,
For if thou diest, my Love, I know not where to go."   315

36

Beyond a mortal man impassioned far
At these voluptuous accents, he arose,
Ethereal, flushed, and like a throbbing star
Seen mid the sapphire heaven's deep repose;
Into her dream he melted, as the rose   320
Blendeth its odor with the violet—

Solution sweet: meantime the frost-wind blows
Like Love's alarum pattering the sharp sleet
Against the windowpanes; St. Agnes' moon hath set.

37

"'Tis dark: quick pattereth the flaw-blown sleet: 325
"This is no dream, my bride, my Madeline!"
'Tis dark: the icéd gusts still rave and beat:
"No dream, alas! alas! and woe is mine!
Porphyro will leave me here to fade and pine.—
Cruel! what traitor could thee hither bring?   330
I curse not, for my heart is lost in thine,
Though thou forsakest a deceivéd thing—
A dove forlorn and lost with sick unprunéd wing."

38

"My Madeline! sweet dreamer! lovely bride!
Say, may I be for aye thy vassal blest?   335
Thy beauty's shield, heart-shaped and vermeil dyed?
Ah, silver shrine, here will I take my rest
After so many hours of toil and quest,
A famished pilgrim—saved by miracle.
Though I have found, I will not rob thy nest   340
Saving of thy sweet self; if thou think'st well
To trust, fair Madeline, to no rude infidel.

39

"Hark! 'tis an elfin-storm from faery land,
Of haggard seeming, but a boom indeed:
Arise—arise! the morning is at hand—   345
The bloated wassaillers will never heed—
Let us away, my love, with happy speed;
There are no ears to hear, or eyes to see—
Drowned all in Rhenish and the sleepy mead:
Awake! arise! my love, and fearless be,   350
For o'er the southern moors I have a home for thee."

40

She hurried at his words, beset with fears,
For there were sleeping dragons all around,
At glaring watch, perhaps, with ready spears—
Down the wide stairs a darkling way they found.—   355
In all the house was heard no human sound.
A chain-drooped lamp was flickering by each door;
The arras, rich with horseman, hawk, and hound,
Fluttered in the besieging wind's uproar;
And the long carpets rose along the gusty floor.   360

41

They glide, like phantoms, into the wide hall;
Like phantoms, to the iron porch, they glide;

Where lay the Porter, in uneasy sprawl,
With a huge empty flagon by his side:
The wakeful bloodhound rose, and shook his hide,   365
But his sagacious eye an inmate owns:
By one, and one, the bolts full easy slide:
The chains lie silent on the footworn stones;
The key turns, and the door upon its hinges groans.

42

And they are gone: aye, ages long ago   370
These lovers fled away into the storm.
That night the Baron dreamt of many a woe,
And all his warrior-guests, with shade and form
Of witch, and demon, and large coffin-worm,
Were long be-nightmared. Angela the old   375
Died palsy-twitched, with meager face deform;
The Beadsman, after thousand aves told,
For aye unsought for slept among his ashes cold.

---

1 St. Agnes' Eve: St. Agnes, martyred ca. 303 at the age of 13, is the patron saint of virgins. According to legend, a virtuous young girl, if she performs the proper ritual, will dream of her future husband on the evening before St. Agnes' Day, which falls on January 21.   *5 Beadsman . . . told:* a beadsman is paid to pray for his benefactor; he "tells" (counts) the beads of his rosary in order to keep track of his prayers.   *16 orat'ries:* small chapels for private devotion.   *37 argent revelry:* silver-clad revelers.   *67 timbrels:* small drums.   *70 all amort:* as though she were dead.   *71 lambs unshorn:* It was the custom on St. Agnes' Day to offer lambs' wool at the altar, to be made into cloth by nuns.   *77 Buttressed from moonlight:* sheltered from the moonlight by the buttresses, supports that projected from the wall.   *90 beldame:* an old and usually homely woman.   *105 Gossip:* old friend or godmother. *126 mickle:* much.   *158 plaining:* complaining.   *171 Merlin . . . debt:* possibly refers to Merlin, the magician who paid for his magic with his life when Vivien turned one of his spells against him.   *173 cates:* delicacies, sweets.   *174 tambour frame:* an embroidery frame in the shape of a drum.   *188 amain:* mightily. *198 frayed:* frightened.   *218 gules:* the color red in heraldry. *241 swart Paynims:* dark-skinned pagans.   *257 Morphean amulet:* a charm to produce sleep.   *265 gourd:* melon. The legend says that the fantasy lover will bring the virgin a feast of great delicacies.   *266 soother:* softer.   *277 eremite:* a religious hermit.   *288 entoiled in woofèd fantasies:* entangled in a weave of fantasies.   *325 flaw-blown:* gust-blown.   *336 vermeil:* vermilion.   *344 haggard:* unbroken, untamed; wild.   *349 mead:* fermented drink made with honey.   *355 darkling:* in the dark. *366 inmate owns:* i.e., recognizes and accepts a member of the household.   *377 aves:* prayers beginning with "Hail Mary."

Alfred, Lord Tennyson   Morte D'Arthur
FROM *Idylls of the King*

So all day long the noise of battle roll'd
Among the mountains by the winter sea;
Until King Arthur's table, man by man,
Had fall'n in Lyonnesse about their Lord,
King Arthur: then, because his wound was deep,   5
The bold Sir Bedivere uplifted him,
Sir Bedivere, the last of all his knights,
And bore him to a chapel nigh the field,
A broken chancel with a broken cross,
That stood on a dark strait of barren land.   10
On one side lay the Ocean, and on one
Lay a great water, and the moon was full.
    Then spake King Arthur to Sir Bedivere:
'The sequel of to-day unsolders all
The goodliest fellowship of famous knights   15
Whereof this world holds record. Such a sleep
They sleep—the men I loved. I think that we
Shall never more, at any future time,
Delight our souls with talk of knightly deeds,
Walking about the gardens and the halls   20
Of Camelot, as in the days that were.
I perish by this people which I made,—
Tho' Merlin sware that I should come again
To rule once more—but let what will be, be,
I am so deeply smitten thro' the helm   25
That without help I cannot last till morn.
Thou therefore take my brand Excalibur,
Which was my pride: for thou rememberest how
In those old days, one summer noon, an arm
Rose up from out the bosom of the lake,   30
Clothed in white samite, mystic, wonderful,
Holding the sword—and how I row'd across
And took it, and have worn it, like a king:
And, wheresoever I am sung or told
In aftertime, this also shall be known: 35
But now delay not: take Excalibur,
And fling him far into the middle mere:
Watch what thou seëst, and lightly bring me word.'
    To him replied the bold Sir Bedivere:
'It is not meet, Sir King, to leave thee thus,   40
Aidless, alone, and smitten thro' the helm.
A little thing may harm a wounded man.
Yet I thy hest will all perform at full,
Watch what I see, and lightly bring thee word.'
    So saying, from the ruin'd shrine he stept   45
And in the moon athwart the place of tombs,
Where lay the mighty bones of ancient men,
Old knights, and over them the sea-wind sang

Shrill, chill, with flakes of foam. He stepping down
By zig-zag paths, and juts of pointed rock,   50
Came on the shining levels of the lake.
    There drew he forth the brand Excalibur,
And o'er him, drawing it, the winter moon,
Brightening the skirts of a long cloud, ran forth
And sparkled keen with frost against the hilt: 55
For all the haft twinkled with diamond sparks,
Myriads of topaz-lights, and jacinth-work
Of subtlest jewellery. He gazed so long
That both his eyes were dazzled, as he stood,
This way and that dividing the swift mind,   60
In act to throw: but at the last it seem'd
Better to leave Excalibur conceal'd
There in the many-knotted waterflags,
That whistled stiff and dry about the marge.
So strode he back slow to the wounded King.   65
    Then spake King Arthur to Sir Bedivere:
'Hast thou perform'd my mission which I gave?
What is it thou hast seen? or what hast heard?'
    And answer made the bold Sir Bedivere:
'I heard the ripple washing in the reeds,   70
And the wild water lapping on the crag.'
    To whom replied King Arthur, faint and pale:
'Thou hast betray'd thy nature and thy name,
Not rendering true answer, as beseem'd
Thy fëalty, nor like a noble knight: 75
For surer sign had follow'd, either hand,
Or voice, or else a motion of the mere.
This is a shameful thing for men to lie.
Yet now, I charge thee, quickly go again
As thou art lief and dear, and do the thing   80
I bade thee, watch, and lightly bring me word.'
    Then went Sir Bedivere the second time
Across the ridge, and paced beside the mere,
Counting the dewy pebbles, fix'd in thought;
But when he saw the wonder of the hilt,   85
How curiously and strangely chased, he smote
His palms together, and he cried aloud.
    'And if indeed I cast the brand away,
Surely a precious thing, one worthy note,
Should thus be lost for ever from the earth,   90
Which might have pleased the eyes of many men.
What good should follow this, if this were done?
What harm, undone? deep harm to disobey,
Seeing obedience is the bond of rule.
Were it well to obey then, if a king demand   95
An act unprofitable, against himself?
The King is sick, and knows not what he does.
What record, or what relic of my lord
Should be to aftertime, but empty breath
And rumors of a doubt? but were this kept,   100
Stored in some treasure-house of mighty kings,

Some one might show it at a joust of arms,
Saying, "King Arthur's sword, Excalibur,
Wrought by the lonely maiden of the Lake.
Nine years she wrought it, sitting in the deeps   *105*
Upon the hidden bases of the hills."
So might some old man speak in the aftertime
To all the people, winning reverence.
But now much honor and much fame were lost,'
    So spake he, clouded with his own conceit,   *110*
And hid Excalibur the second time,
And so strode back slow to the wounded King.
    Then spoke King Arthur, breathing heavily:
'What is it thou hast seen? or what hast heard?'
    And answer made the bold Sir Bedivere: *115*
'I heard the water lapping on the crag,
And the long-ripple washing in the reeds.'
    To whom replied King Arthur, much in wrath:
'Ah, miserable and unkind, untrue,
Unknightly, traitor-hearted! Woe is me!   *120*
Authority forgets a dying king,
Laid widow'd of the power in his eye
That bow'd the will. I see thee what thou art,
For thou, the latest-left of all my knights,
In whom should meet the offices of all,   *125*
Thou wouldst betray me for the precious hilt;
Either from lust of gold, or like a girl
Valuing the giddy pleasure of the eyes.
Yet, for a man may fail in duty twice,
And the third time may prosper, get thee hence: *130*
But, if thou spare to fling Excalibur,
I will arise and slay thee with my hands.'
    Then quickly rose Sir Bedivere and ran,
And, leaping down the ridges lightly, plunged
Among the bulrush-beds, and clutch'd the sword,   *135*
And strongly wheel'd and threw it. The great brand
Made lightnings in the splendor of the moon,
And flashing round and round, and whirl'd in an arch,
Shot like a streamer of the northern morn,
Seen where the moving isles of winter shock   *140*
By night, with noises of the northern sea.
So flash'd and fell the brand Excalibur:
But ere he dipt the surface, rose an arm
Clothed in white samite, mystic, wonderful,
And caught him by the hilt, and brandish'd him   *145*
Three times, and drew him under in the mere.
And lightly went the other to the King.
    Then spoke King Arthur, drawing thicker breath:
'Now see I by thine eyes that this is done.
Speak out: what is it thou hast heard, or seen?'   *150*
    And answer made the bold Sir Bedivere:
'Sir King, I closed mine eyelids, lest the gems
Should blind my purpose, for I never saw,
Nor shall see, here or elsewhere, till I die,

Not tho' I live three lives of mortal men,   155
So great a miracle as yonder hilt.
Then with both hands I flung him, wheeling him;
But when I look'd again, behold an arm,
Clothed in white samite, mystic, wonderful,
That caught him by the hilt, and brandish'd him   160
Three times, and drew him under in the mere.'
      And answer made King Arthur, breathing hard:
'My end draws nigh; 'tis time that I were gone.
Make broad thy shoulders to receive my weight,
And bear me to the margin; yet I fear   165
My wound hath taken cold, and I shall die.'
      So saying, from the pavement he half rose,
Slowly, with pain, reclining on his arm,
And looking wistfully with wide blue eyes
As in a picture. Him Sir Bedivere   170
Remorsefully regarded thro' his tears,
And would have spoken, but he found not words,
Then took with care, and kneeling on one knee,
O'er both his shoulders drew the languid hands,
And rising bore him thro' the place of tombs.   175
      But, as he walk'd, King Arthur panted hard,
Like one that feels a nightmare on his bed
When all the house is mute. So sigh'd the King,
Muttering and murmuring at his ear, 'Quick, Quick!
I fear it is too late, and I shall die.'   180
But the other swiftly strode from ridge to ridge,
Clothed with his breath, and looking, as he walk'd,
Larger than human on the frozen hills.
He heard the deep behind him, and a cry
Before. His own thought drove him like a goad.   185
Dry clash'd his harness in the icy caves
And barren chasms, and all to left and right
The bare black cliff clang'd round him, as he based
His feet on juts of slippery crag that rang
Sharp-smitten with the dint of armed heels—   190
And on a sudden, lo! the level lake,
And the long glories of the winter moon.
      Then saw they how there hove a dusky barge,
Dark as a funeral scarf from stem to stern,
Beneath them; and descending they were ware   195
That all the decks were dense with stately forms
Black-stoled, black-hooded, like a dream—by these
Three Queens with crowns of gold—and from them rose
A cry that shiver'd to the tingling stars,
And, as it were one voice, an agony   200
Of lamentation, like a wind, that shrills
All night in a waste land, where no one comes,
Or hath come, since the making of the world.
      Then murmur'd Arthur, 'Place me in the barge,'
And to the barge they came. There those three Queens   205
Put forth their hands, and took the King, and wept.
But she, that rose the tallest of them all

And fairest, laid his head upon her lap,
And loosed the shatter'd casque, and chafed his hands,
And call'd him by his name, complaining loud,   210
And dropping bitter tears against his brow
Striped with dark blood: for all his face was white
And colorless, and like the wither'd moon
Smote by the fresh beam of the springing east;
And all his greaves and cuisses dash'd with drops   215
Of onset; and the light and lustrous curls—
That made his forehead like a rising sun
High from the dais-throne—were parch'd with dust;
Or, clotted into points and hanging loose,
Mix'd with the knightly growth that fringed his lips.   220
So like a shatter'd column lay the King;
Not like that Arthur who, with lance in rest,
From spur to plume a star of tournament,
Shot thro' the lists at Camelot, and charged
Before the eyes of ladies and of kings.   225
    Then loudly cried the bold Sir Bedivere,
'Ah! my Lord Arthur, whither shall I go?
Where shall I hide my forehead and my eyes?
For now I see the true old times are dead,
When every morning brought a noble chance,   230
And every chance brought out a noble knight.
Such times have been not since the light that led
The holy Elders with the gift of myrrh.
But now the whole ROUND TABLE is dissolved
Which was an image of the mighty world;   235
And I, the last, go forth companionless,
And the days darken round me, and the years,
Among new men, strange faces, other minds.'
    And slowly answered Arthur from the barge:
'The old order changeth, yielding place to new,   240
And God fulfills Himself in many ways,
Lest one good custom should corrupt the world.
Comfort thyself: what comfort is in me?
I have lived my life, and that which I have done
May He within Himself make pure! but thou,   245
If thou shouldst never see my face again,
Pray for my soul! More things are wrought by prayer
Than this world dreams of. Wherefore, let thy voice
Rise like a fountain for me night and day.
For what are men better than sheep or goats   250
That nourish a blind lie within the brain,
If, knowing God, they lift not hands of prayer
Both for themselves and those who call them friend?
For so the whole round earth is every way
Bound by gold chains about the feet of God.   255
But now farewell. I am going a long way
With these thou seëst—if indeed I go—
(For all my mind is clouded with a doubt)
To the island-valley of Avilion;
Where falls not hail, or rain, or any snow,   260

Nor ever wind blows loudly; but it lies
Deep meadow'd, happy, fair with orchard-lawns
And bowery hollows crown'd with summer sea,
Where I will heal me of my grievous wound.'
   So said he, and the barge with oar and sail   265
Moved from the brink, like some full-breasted swan
That, fluting a wild carol ere her death,
Ruffles her pure cold plume, and takes the flood
With swarthy webs. Long stood Sir Bedivere
Revolving many memories, till the hull   270
Look'd one black dot against the verge of dawn,
And on the mere the wailing died away.

title: The Passing of Arthur. 169 lines of transitional material that
begin this section of the *Idylls*, has been deleted.

Robert Browning   How They Brought the Good News
   from Ghent to Aix

I sprang to the stirrup, and Jorris, and he;
I galloped, Dirck galloped, we galloped all three;
"Good speed!" cried the watch, as the gate bolts undrew,
"Speed!" echoed the wall to us galloping through;
Behind shut the postern, the lights sank to rest,   5
And into the midnight we galloped abreast.

Not a word to each other; we kept the great pace
Neck by neck, stride by stride, never changing our place;
I turned in my saddle and made its girths tight,
Then shortened each stirrup, and set the pique right,   10
Rebuckled the cheek-strap, chained slacker the bit,
Nor galloped less steadily Roland a whit.

'Twas moonset at starting; but while we drew near
Lokeren, the cocks and twilight dawned clear;
At Boom, a great yellow star came out to see;   15
At Düffeld, 'twas morning as plain as could be;
And from Mecheln church-steeple we heard the half-chime,
So Joris broke silence with, "Yet there is time!"

At Aerschot, up leaped of a sudden the sun
And against him the cattle stood black every one,   20
To stare thro' the mist at us galloping past,
And I saw my stout galloper Roland at last,
With resolute shoulders, each butting away
The haze, as some bluff river headland its spray:

And his low head and crest, just one sharp ear bent back   25
For my voice, and the other pricked out on his track;
And one eye's black intelligence—ever that glance
O'er its white edge at me, his own master, askance!
And the thick heavy spume-flakes which aye and anon
His fierce lips shook upwards in galloping on.   30

By Hasselt, Dirck groaned; and cried Joris, "Stay spur!
Your Roos galloped bravely, the fault's not in her,
We'll remember at Aix"—for one heard the quick wheeze
Of her chest, saw the stretched neck and staggering knees,
And sunk tail, and horrible heave of the flank,   35
As down on her haunches she shuddered and sank.

So we were left galloping, Joris and I,
Past Looz and past Tongres, no cloud in the sky;
The broad sun above laughed a pitiless laugh,
'Near our feet broke the brittle bright stubble like chaff;   40
Till over by Dalhem a dome-spire sprang white,
And "Gallop," gasped Joris, "for Aix is in sight!"

"How they'll greet us!"—and all in a moment his roan
Rolled neck and croup over, lay dead as a stone;
And there was my Roland to bear the whole weight   45
Of the news which alone could save Aix from her fate,
With his nostrils like pits full of blood to the brim,
And with circles of red for his eye-sockets' rim.

Then I cast loose my buffcoat, each holster let fall,
Shook off both my jack-boots, let go belt and all,   50
Stood up in the stirrup, leaned, patted his ear,
Called my Roland his pet-name, my horse without peer;
Clapped my hands, laughed and sang, any noise, bad or good,
Till at length into Aix Roland galloped and stood.

And all I remember is—friends flocking round   55
As I sat with his head 'twixt my knees on the ground;
And no voice but was praising this Roland of mine,
As I poured down his throat our last measure of wine,
Which (the burgesses voted by common consent)
Was no more than his due who brought good news from
   Ghent.

William Morris   The Haystack in the Floods

Had she come all the way for this,
To part at last without a kiss?
Yea, had she borne the dirt and rain
That her own eyes might see him slain
Beside the haystack in the floods?   5

Along the dripping leafless woods,
The stirrup touching either shoe,
She rode astride as troopers do;
With kirtle kilted to her knee,
To which the mud splashed wretchedly;   10
And the wet dripped from every tree
Upon her head and heavy hair,
And on her eyelids broad and fair;
The tears and rain ran down her face.

By fits and starts they rode apace,   *15*
And very often was his place
Far off from her; he had to ride
Ahead, to see what might betide
When the roads crossed; and sometimes, when
There rose a murmuring from his men,   20
Had to turn back with promises.
Ah me! she had but little ease;
And often for pure doubt and dread
She sobbed, made giddy in the head
By the swift riding; while, for cold,   25
Her slender fingers scarce could hold
The wet reins; yea, and scarcely, too,
She felt the foot within her shoe
Against the stirrup: all for this,
To part at last without a kiss   30
Beside the haystack in the floods.

For when they neared the old soaked hay,
They saw across the only way
That Judas, Godmar, and the three
Red running lions dismally   35
Grinned from his pennon, under which
In one straight line along the ditch,
They counted thirty heads.
                                  So then
While Robert turned round to his men,
She saw at once the wretched end,   40
And, stooping down, tried hard to rend
Her coif the wrong way from her head,
And hid her eyes; while Robert said:
"Nay, love, 'tis scarcely two to one;
At Poictiers where we made them run   45
So fast—why, sweet my love, good cheer,
The Gascon frontier is so near,
Nought after us."
                          But: "O!" she said
"My God! my God! I have to tread   50
The long way back without you; then
The court at Paris; those six men;
The gratings of the Chatelet;
The swift Seine on some rainy day
Like this, and people standing by,   55
And laughing, while my weak hands try
To recollect how strong men swim.
All this, or else a life with him,
For which I should be damned at last,
Would God that this next hour were past!"   60

He answered not, but cried his cry,
"St. George for Marny!" cheerily;
And laid his hand upon her rein.
Alas! no man of all his train
Gave back that cheery cry again;   65

And, while for rage his thumb beat fast
Upon his sword-hilt, some one cast
About his neck a kerchief long,
And bound him.
     Then they went along   70
To Godmar, who said: "Now, Jehane,
Your lover's life is on the wane
So fast, that, if this very hour
You yield not as my paramour,
He will not see the rain leave off: 75
Nay, keep your tongue from gibe and scoff,
Sir Robert, or I slay you now."

She laid her hand upon her brow,
Then gazed upon the palm, as though
She thought her forehead bled, and: "No!" 80
She said, and turned her head away,
As there was nothing else to say,
And everything was settled: red
Grew Godmar's face from chin to head:
"Jehane, on yonder hill there stands   85
My castle, guarding well my lands;
What hinders me from taking you,
And doing that I list to do
To your fair wilful body, while
Your knight lies dead?"   90
     A wicked smile
Wrinkled her face, her lips grew thin,
A long way out she thrust her chin:
"You know that I should strangle you
While you were sleeping; or bite through 95
Your throat, by God's help: ah!" she said,
"Lord Jesus, pity your poor maid!
For in such wise they hem me in,
I cannot choose but sin and sin,
Whatever happens: yet I think   100
They could not make me eat or drink,
And so should I just reach my rest."

"Nay, if you do not my behest,
O Jehane! though I love you well,"
Said Godmar, "would I fail to tell   105
All that I know?" "Foul lies," she said.
"Eh? lies, my Jehane? By God's head,
At Paris folk would deem them true!
Do you know, Jehane, they cry for you:
'Jehane the brown! Jehane the brown! 110
Give us Jehane to burn or drown!'
Eh! gag me, Robert!—sweet my friend,
This were indeed a piteous end
For those long fingers, and long feet,
And long neck, and smooth shoulders sweet; 115
An end that few men would forget

That saw it. So, an hour yet:
Consider, Jehane, which to take
Of life or death!"
                So, scarce awake,   120
Dismounting, did she leave that place,
And totter some yards: with her face
Turned upward to the sky she lay,
Her head on a wet heap of hay,
And fell asleep: and while she slept,   125
And did not dream, the minutes crept
Around to twelve again; but she,
Being waked at last, sighed quietly,
And strangely childlike came, and said:
"I will not." Straightway Godmar's head,   130
As though it hung on strong wires, turned
Most sharply round, and his face burned.

For Robert, both his eyes were dry,
He could not weep, but gloomily
He seemed to watch the rain; yea, too,   135
His lips were firm; he tried once more
To touch her lips; she reached out, sore
And vain desire so tortured them,
The poor gray lips, and now the hem
Of his sleeve brushed them.   140
                  With a start
Up Godmar rose, thrust them apart;
From Robert's throat he loosed the bands
Of silk and mail. With empty hands
Held out, she stood and gazed, and saw,   145
The long bright blade without a flaw
Glide out from Godmar's sheath, his hand
In Robert's hair; she saw him bend
Back Robert's head; she saw him send
The thin steel down; the blow told well,   150
Right backward the knight Robert fell,
And moaned as dogs do, being half dead,
Unwitting, as I deem: so then
Godmar turned grinning to his men,
Who ran, some five or six, and beat   155
His head to pieces at their feet.

Then Godmar turned again and said:
"So, Jehane, the first fitte is read!
Take note, my lady, that your way
Lies backward to the Chatelet!"   160
She shook her head and gazed awhile
At her cold hands with a rueful smile,
As though this thing had made her mad.

This was the parting that they had
Beside the haystack in the floods.   165

title: Sir Robert de Marny, an English knight, and Jehane, his
mistress, are trying to get to Gascony, which is being held by the

British. The date of this incident is 1356, a short time after the
English victory over the French at Poictiers.   36 *pennon:* Godmar's banner, which bears his family crest.   52 *six men:* the
judges.   53 *gratings of the Chatelet:* the bars of the prison by
this name, located in Paris.   57 *swim:* trial by water. If she sank
and drowned, she would be innocent of being a witch; if she swam,
she would be declared guilty and would be burned.   158 *fitte:*
a part of a song or tale.

Stephen Vincent Benét   Metropolitan Nightmare

It rained quite a lot that spring. You woke in the morning
And saw the sky still clouded, the streets still wet,
But nobody noticed so much, except the taxis
And the people who parade. You don't, in a city.
The parks got very green. All the trees were green   5
Far into July and August, heavy with leaf,
Heavy with leaf and the long roots boring and spreading,
But nobody noticed that but the city gardeners
And they don't talk.
                    Oh, on Sundays, perhaps you'd notice: 10
Walking through certain blocks, by the shut, proud houses
With the windows boarded, the people gone away,
You'd suddenly see the queerest small shoots of green
Poking through cracks and crevices in the stone
And a bird-sown flower, red on a balcony,   15
But then you made jokes about grass growing in the streets
And politics and grass-roots—and there were songs
And gags and a musical show called "Hot and Wet."
It all made a good box for the papers. When the flamingo
Flew into a meeting of the Board of Estimate,   20
The new mayor acted at once and called the photographers.
When the first green creeper crawled upon Brooklyn Bridge,
They thought it was ornamental. They let it stay.

That was the year the termites came to New York
And they don't do well in cold climates—but listen, Joe,   25
They're only ants, and ants are nothing but insects.
It was funny and yet rather wistful, in a way
(As Heywood Broun pointed out in the *World-Telegram*)
To think of them looking for wood in a steel city.
It made you feel about life. It was too divine.   30
There were funny pictures by all the smart, funny artists
And Macy's ran a terribly clever ad:
"The Widow's Termite" or something.
                                 There was no
Disturbance. Even the Communists didn't protest   35
And say they were Morgan hirelings. It was too hot,
Too hot to protest, too hot to get excited,
And even African heat, lush, fertile and steamy,
That soaked into bone and mind and never once broke.

The warm rain fell in fierce showers and ceased and fell.   40
Pretty soon you got used to its always being that way.

You got used to the changed rhythm, the altered beat,
To people walking slower, to the whole bright
Fierce pulse of the city slowing, to men in shorts,
To the new sun-helmets from Best's and the cops' white   45
    uniforms,
And the long noon-rest in the offices, everywhere.
It wasn't a plan or anything. It just happened.
The fingers tapped slower, the office-boys
Dozed on their benches, the bookkeeper yawned at his desk.
The A.T.&T. was the first to change the shifts   50
And establish an official siesta-room;
But they were always efficient. Mostly it just
Happened like sleep itself, like a tropic sleep,
Till even the Thirties were deserted at noon
Except for a few tourists and one damp cop.   55
They ran boats to see the big lilies on the North River
But it was only the tourists who really noticed
The flocks of rose-and-green parrots and parrakeets
Nesting in the stone crannies of the Cathedral.
The rest of us had forgotten when they first came.   60

There wasn't any real change, it was just a heat spell,
A rain spell, a funny summer, a weather-man's joke,
In spite of the geraniums three feet high
In the tin-can gardens of Hester and Desbrosses.
New York was New York. It couldn't turn inside out.   65
When they got the news from Woods Hole about the Gulf
    Stream,
The *Times* ran an adequate story.
But nobody reads those stories but science-cranks.

Until, one day, a somnolent city-editor
Gave a new cub the termite yarn to break his teeth on.   70
The cub was just down from Vermont, so he took his time.
He was serious about it. He went around.
He read all about termites in the Public Library
And it made him sore when they fired him.
                                    So, one evening,   75
Talking with an old watchman, beside the first
Raw girders of the new Planetopolis Building
(Ten thousand brine-cooled offices, each with shower)
He saw a dark line creeping across the rubble
And turned a flashlight on it.   80
                        "Say, buddy," he said,
"You better look out for those ants. They eat wood, you know,
They'll have your shack down in no time."
                            The watchman spat.
"Oh, they've quit eating wood," he said, in a casual voice,   85
"I thought everybody knew that."
                        —And, reaching down,
He pried from the insect's jaws the bright crumb of steel.

Robert Frost   The Star-Splitter

"You know Orion always comes up sideways.
Throwing a leg up over our fence of mountains,
And rising on his hands, he looks in on me
Busy outdoors by lantern-light with something
I should have done by daylight, and indeed,   5
After the ground is frozen, I should have done
Before it froze, and a gust flings a handful
Of waste leaves at my smoky lantern chimney
To make fun of my way of doing things,
Or else fun of Orion's having caught me.   10
Has a man, I should like to ask, no rights
These forces are obliged to pay respect to?"
So Brad McLaughlin mingled reckless talk
Of heavenly stars with hugger-mugger farming,
Till having failed at hugger-mugger farming,   15
He burned his house down for the fire insurance
And spent the proceeds on a telescope
To satisfy a life-long curiosity
About our place among the infinities.

"What do you want with one of those blame things?"   20
I asked him well beforehand. "Don't you get one!"
"Don't call it blamed; there isn't anything
More blameless in the sense of being less
A weapon in our human fight," he said.
"I'll have one if I sell my farm to buy it."   25
There where he moved the rocks to plow the ground
And plowed between the rocks he couldn't move,
Few farms changed hands; so rather than spend years
Trying to sell his farm and then not selling,
He burned his house down for the fire insurance   30
And bought the telescope with what it came to.
He had been heard to say by several:
"The best thing that we're put here for's to see
The strongest thing that's given us to see with's
A telescope. Someone in every town   35
Seems to me owes it to the town to keep one.
In Littleton it may as well be me."
After such loose talk it was no surprise
When he did what he did and burned his house down.

Mean laughter went about the town that day   40
To let him know we weren't the least imposed on,
And he could wait—we'd see to him tomorrow.
But the first thing next morning we reflected
If one by one we counted people out
For the least sin, it wouldn't take us long   45
To get so we had no one left to live with.
For to be social is to be forgiving.
Our thief, the one who does the stealing from us,

We don't cut off from coming to church supper
But what we miss we go to him and ask for.   50
He promptly gives it back, that is if still
Uneaten, unworn out, or undisposed of.
It wouldn't do to be too hard on Brad
About his telescope. Beyond the age
Of being given one's gift for Christmas,   55
He had to take the best way he knew how
To find himself in one. Well, all we said was
He took a strange thing to be roguish over.
Some sympathy was wasted on the house,
A good old-timer dating back along;   60
But a house isn't sentient; the house
Didn't feel anything. And if it did,
Why not regard it as a sacrifice,
And an old-fashioned sacrifice by fire?
Instead of a new-fashioned one at auction?   65

Out of a house and so out of a farm
At one stroke (of a match), Brad had to turn
To earn a living on the Concord railroad,
As under-ticket-agent at a station
Where his job, when he wasn't selling tickets,   70
Was setting out up track and down, not plants
As on a farm, but planets, evening stars
That varied in their hue from red to green.

He got a good glass for six hundred dollars.
His new job gave him leisure for star-gazing.   75
Often he bid me come and have a look
Up the brass barrel, velvet black inside,
At a star quaking in the other end.
I recollect a night of broken clouds
And underfoot snow melted down to ice,   80
And melting further in the wind to mud.
Bradford and I had out the telescope.
We spread our two legs as we spread its three,
Pointed our thoughts the way we pointed it,
And standing at our leisure till the day broke,   85
Said some of the best things we ever said.
That telescope was christened the Star-splitter,
Because it didn't do a thing but split
A star in two or three the way you split
A globule of quicksilver in your hand   90
With one stroke of your finger in the middle.
It's a star-splitter if there ever was one
And ought to do some good if splitting stars
'S a thing to be compared with splitting wood.

We've looked and looked, but after all where are we?   95
Do we know any better where we are,
And how it stands between the night to-night
And a man with a smoky lantern chimney?
How different from the way it ever stood?

Robert Hayden   Middle Passage

I

Jesús, Estrella, Esperanza, Mercy:

> Sails flashing to the wind like weapons,
> sharks following the moans the fever and the dying;
> horror the corposant and compass rose.

Middle Passage   5
        voyage through death
            to life upon these shores.

> "10 April 1800—
> Blacks rebellious. Crew uneasy. Our linguist says
> their moaning is a prayer for death,   10
> ours and their own. Some try to starve themselves.
> Lost three this morning leaped with crazy laughter
> to the waiting sharks, sang as they went under."

Desire, Adventure,Tartar, Ann:

> Standing to America, bringing home   15
> black gold, black ivory, black seed.
> *Deep in the festering hold thy father lies,*
> *of his bones New England pews are made,*
> *those are altar lights that were his eyes.*

Jesus Saviour Pilot Me
Over Life's Tempestuous Sea   20

We pray that Thou wilt grant, O Lord,
safe passage to our vessels bringing
heathen souls unto Thy chastening.

Jesus Saviour

> "8 bells. I cannot sleep, for I am sick   25
> with fear, but writing eases fear a little
> since still my eyes can see these words take shape
> upon the page & so I write, as one
> would turn to exorcism. 4 days scudding,
> but now the sea is calm again. Misfortune   30
> follows in our wake like sharks (our grinning
> tutelary gods). Which one of us
> has killed an albatross? A plague among
> our blacks—Ophthalmia: blindness—& we
> have jettisoned the blind to no avail.   35
> It spreads, the terrifying sickness spreads.
> Its claws have scratched sight from the Capt.'s eyes
> & there is blindness in the fo'c'sle
> & we must sail 3 weeks before we come
> to port."   40
> *What port awaits us, Davy Jones'*

> or home? I've heard of slavers drifting, drifting,
> playthings of wind and storm and chance, their
>   crews
> gone blind, the jungle hatred
> crawling up on deck. 45

Thou Who Walked On Galilee

"Deponent further sayeth *The Bella J*
left the Guinea Coast
with cargo of five hundred blacks and odd
for the barracoons of Florida: 50

"That there was hardly room 'tween-decks for half
the sweltering cattle stowed spoon-fashion there;
that some went mad of thirst and tore their flesh
and sucked the blood:

"That Crew and Captain lusted with the comeliest 55
of the savage girls kept naked in the cabins;
that there was one they called the Guinea Rose
and they cast lots and fought to lie with her:

"That when the Bo's'n piped all hands, the flames
spreading from starboard already were beyond 60
control, the negroes howling and their chains
entangled with the flames:

"That the burning blacks could not be reached,
that the Crew abandoned ship,
leaving their shrieking negresses behind, 65
that the Captain perished drunken with the wenches:

"Further Deponent sayeth not."

Pilot Oh Pilot Me

2

Aye, lad, and I have seen those factories,
Gambia, Rio Pongo, Calabar;
have watched the artful mongos baiting traps 70
of war wherein the victor and the vanquished

Were caught as prizes for our barracoons.
Have seen the nigger kings whose vanity
and greed turned wild black hides of Fellatah, 75
Mandingo, Ibo, Kru to gold for us.

And there was one— King Anthracite we named him—
fetish face beneath French parasols
of brass and orange velvet, impudent mouth
whose cups were carven skulls of enemies: 80

He'd honor us with drum and feast and conjo
and palm-oil glistening wenches deft in love,
and for tin crowns that shone with paste,
red calico and German silver trinkets

Would have the drums talk war and send   85
his warriors to burn the sleeping villages
and kill the sick and old and lead the young
in coffles to our factories.

Twenty years a trader, twenty years,
for there was wealth aplenty to be harvested   90
from those black fields, and I'd be trading still
but for the fevers melting down my bones.

   3
Shuttles in the rocking loom of history,
the dark ships move, the dark ships move,
their bright ironical names   95
like jests of kindness on a murderer's mouth;
plough through thrashing glister toward
fata morgana's lucent melting shore,
weave toward New World littorals that are
mirage and myth and actual shore.   100

Voyage through death,
            voyage whose chartings are
                unlove.
A charnel stench, effluvium of living death
spreads outward from the hold,   105
where the living and the dead, the horribly dying,
lie interlocked, lie foul with blood and excrement.

   Deep in the festering hold thy father lies,
   the corpse of mercy rots with him,
   rats eat love's rotten gelid eyes.   110
   But, oh, the living look at you
   with human eyes whose suffering accuses you,
   whose hatred reaches through the swill of dark
   to strike you like a leper's claw.

   You cannot stare that hatred down   115
   or chain the fear that stalks the watches
   and breathes on you its fetid scorching breath;
   cannot kill the deep immortal human wish,
   the timeless will.

   "But for the storm that flung up barriers   120
   of wind and wave, *The Amistad,* señores,
   would have reached the port of Príncipe in two,
   three days at most; but for the storm we should
   have been prepared for what befell.
   Swift as the puma's leap it came. There was   125
   that interval of moonless calm filled only
   with the water's and the rigging's usual sounds,
   then sudden movement, blows and snarling cries
   and they had fallen on us with machete
   and marlinspike. It was as though the very   130
   air, the night itself were striking us.

Exhausted by the rigors of the storm,
we were no match for them. Our men went down
before the murderous Africans. Our loyal
Celestino ran from below with gun   135
and lantern and I saw, before the cane-
knife's wounding flash, Cinquez,
that surly brute who calls himself a prince,
directing, urging on the ghastly work.
He hacked the poor mulatto down, and then   140
he turned on me. The decks were slippery
when daylight finally came. It sickens me
to think of what I saw, of how these apes
threw overboard the butchered bodies of
our men, true Christians all, like so much jetsam.   145
Enough, enough. The rest is quickly told:
Cinquez was forced to spare the two of us
you see to steer the ship to Africa,
and we like phantoms doomed to rove the sea
voyaged east by day and west by night,   150
deceiving them, hoping for rescue,
prisoners on our own vessel, till
at length we drifted to the shores of this
your land, America, where we were freed
from our unspeakable misery. Now we   155
demand, good sirs, the extradition of
Cinquez and his accomplices to La
Havana. And it distresses us to know
there are so many here who seem inclined
to justify the mutiny of these blacks.   160
We find it paradoxical indeed
that you whose wealth, whose tree of liberty
are rooted in the labor of your slaves
should suffer the august John Quincy Adams
to speak with so much passion of the right   165
of chattel slaves to kill their lawful masters
and with his Roman rhetoric weave a hero's
garland for Cinquez. I tell you that
we are determined to return to Cuba
with our slaves and there see justice done.   170
    Cinquez—
or let us say 'the Prince'—Cinquez shall die."

The deep immortal human wish,
the timeless will:

Cinquez its deathless primaveral image,   175
life that transfigures many lives.

Voyage through death
                    to life upon these shores.

50 *barracoons*: barracks for slaves.   71 *mongos*: Negroes.   81
conjo: booze.   88 *coffles*: lines of slaves shackled together.

James Dickey   Between Two Prisoners

I would not wish to sit
In my shape bound together with wire,
Wedged into a child's sprained desk
In the schoolhouses under the palm tree.
Only those who did could have done it.   5

One bled from a cut on his temple,
And sat with his yellow head bowed,
His wound for him painfully thinking.
A belief in words grew upon them
That the unbound, who walk, cannot know.   10

The guard at the window leaned close
In a movement he took from the palm tree,
To hear, in a foreign tongue,
All things which cannot be said.
In the splintering clapboard room   15

They rested the sides of their faces
On the tops of the desks as they talked.
Because of the presence of children
In the deep signs carved in the desk tops
Signs on the empty blackboard   20

Began, like a rain, to appear.
In the luminous chalks of all colors,
Green face, yellow breast, white sails
Whose wing feathers made the wall burn
Like a waterfall seen in a fever,   25

An angel came boldly to light
From his hands casting green, ragged bolts
Each having the shape of a palm leaf.
Also traced upon darkness in chalk
Was the guard at the rear window leaning   30

Through the red, vital strokes of his tears.
Behind him, men lying with swords
As with women, heard themselves sing.
And woke, then, terribly knowing
That they were a death squad, singing   35

In its sleep, in the middle of a war.
A wind sprang out of the tree.
The guard awoke by the window,
And found he had talked to himself
All night, in two voices, of Heaven.   40

He stood in the sunlit playground
Where the quiet boys knelt together
In their bloodletting trusses of wire,
And saw their mussed, severed heads
Make the ground jump up like a dog.   45

I watched the small guard be hanged
A year later, to the day,
In a closed horse stall in Manila.
No one knows what language he spoke
As his face changed into all colors, 50

And gave off his red, promised tears,
Or if he learned blindly to read
A child's deep, hacked hieroglyphics
Which can call up an angel from nothing,
Or what was said for an instant, there, 55

In the tied, scribbled dark, between him
And a figure drawn hugely in chalk,
Speaking words that can never be spoken
Except in a foreign tongue,
In the end, at the end of a war. 60

THE EPIC

Like the ballad, the epic exists in both the folk and the literary tradition. While no strict definition of an epic may be acceptable to all scholars, in general, an epic is a long verse narrative in which events and incidents are unified by their relation to a central hero. This hero experiences a number of challenges and changes which, in the process of meeting, reflects the history of a race or a nation. Thus, an epic has a range not usually found in other forms of literature. In an epic, the needs, fears, wishes, and aspirations of a people are expressed, and the relationship of man to himself and to his god(s) is defined.

The folk epic presumably developed by accretion in an oral tradition, and is a work of unknown or uncertain authorship. Among the important folk epics are *The Iliad, The Odyssey* (Homer); the Old English *Beowulf:* the Spanish *Cid:* the French *Song of Roland:* and the German *Nibelungenlied.*

Among the best known art epics, or epics for which the authorship is known, is Vergil's *Aeneid,* Dante's *Divine Comedy,* Tasso's *Jerusalem Delivered,* and Milton's *Paradise Lost.* In America, Longfellow attempted to write an Indian epic in his *Hiawatha:* Whitman's *Leaves of Grass* is sometimes regarded as an epic because the central voice is seemingly a representative American; Stephen Vincent Benet's *John Brown's Body* and Hart Crane's *The Bridge* are more recent epic-like works. Hart Crane referred to his poem as an attempt at "a synthesis of America and its structural identity." He has written of his search for materials that might be "organic and active factors in the experience and perceptions of our common race, time, and belief."

In the Middle Ages there were many poems that seemed epic-like in form and purpose but which did not always adhere to the conventional epic formula. Sometimes referred to as epic, sometimes as "Romance," Spenser's *The Faerie Queene* is the best example of this type. Thomas Hardy's *Dynasts,* according to some scholars, has the range and sweep usually associated with the epic.

Conservative scholars maintain that only *The Iliad, The Odyssey,* and *The Aeneid* are true epics; other writers see little need for a work to follow exactly the precedent established by Homer, so long as the basic criteria of the epic are observed. These more permissive scholars allow for the impact of cultural variation upon epic composition.

Epics, both folk and literary, have common characteristics. The central figure of an epic has heroic stature; often he is a national hero, of great historical or legendary significance. The setting is vast, either national, international or, as in *Paradise Lost,* cosmic. The action of the epic includes deeds of great courage. Supernatural forces often are present or intervene on the behalf of the character or characters involved. The style is dignified and elevated, and the poet often employs a simplicity of diction and an objectivity in presentation.

Among the conventions frequently employed is the opening statement of the poet's theme—the epic invocation, appealing to a Muse for inspiration and instruction, and a general statement about the intention of the epic. The narrative opens *in medias res* (in the middle of things). Exposition is given in later portions of the work. The epic includes catalogues of warriors, ships, armies, equipment—these lists help to swell the scope and magnitude of the work. There is often a trip to the Underworld; boasts and challenges; extended formal speeches, stock epithets (e.g., Homer's recurrent "rosy-fingered dawn"); repeated formulas (especially in the oral epic) occurring at a particular position in the line.

In addition, epic poets have often employed, in imitation of Homer, the epic simile, an elaborate comparison in which the secondary object is developed independent of the main object to which it presumably is being compared. The following is an example of the epic simile, from George Chapman's translation of *The Iliad:*

> And as a hilly spring
> Presents a serpent to a man, full underneath his feet,
> Her blue neck, swollen with poison, raised, and her sting out, to greet
> His heedless entry, suddenly his walk he altereth,
> Starts back amazed, is shook with fear, and looks as pale as death;
> So Menelaus Paris scared. . . .

If today we find few "epic" poems, we should remember that epic poets usually assumed a common denominator, a basic mythology that was understood or accepted by their audiences. Since Milton's time, however, the fragmentation of beliefs—both political and religious—has forced poets to create a mythology as a framework for their large poems. One need but turn to the examples of Yeats' *A Vision,* Pound's *Cantos,* and

T. S. Eliot's *Wasteland* to see how the contemporary writer
has created, or attempted to create, mythology or source from
which he might draw in order to express the needs, aspirations,
and values of his age.

Edmund Spenser "Induction"
FROM *The Faerie Queene, Book I*

The Induction to the First Booke, Contayning the Legend of
Sir Guyon or of Temperaunce

1

Right well I wote, most mighty Soveraine,
That all this famous antique history
Of some th' aboundance of an ydle braine
Will judged be, and painted forgery,
Rather then matter of just memory;   5
Sith none that breatheth living aire does know,
Where is that happy land of Faery,
Which I so much doe vaunt, yet no where show,
But vouch antiquities, which no body can know.

2

But let that man with better sense advize,   10
That of the world least part to us is red:
And daily how through hardy enterprize
Many great regions are discovered,
Which to late age were never mentioned.
Who ever heard of th' Indian Peru?   15
Or who in venturous vessell measured
The Amazons huge river, now found trew?
Or fruitfullest Virginia who did ever vew?

3

Yet all these were when no man did them know,
Yet have from wisest ages hidden beene;   20
And later times things more unknowne shall show.
Why then should witlesse man so much misweene,
That nothing is, but that which he hath secne?
What if within the moones fayre shining spheare,
What if in every other starre unseene,   25
Of other worldes he happily should heare?
He wonder would much more; yet such to some appeare.

4

Of Faery Lond yet if he more inquyre,
By certeine signes, here sett in sondrie place,
He may it fynd; ne let him then admyre,   30

But yield his sence to bee too blunt and bace,
That no'te without an hound fine footing trace.
And thou, O fayrest Princesse under sky,
In this fayre mirrhour maist behold thy face,
And thine owne realmes in lond of Faery,   35
And in this antique ymage thy great auncestry.

     5

The which O pardon me thus to enfold
In covert vele, and wrap in shadows light,
That feeble eyes your glory may behold,
Which ells could not endure those beames bright,   40
But would bee dazled with exceeding light.
O pardon! and vouchsafe with patient eare
The brave adventures of this Faery knight,
The good Sir Guyon, gratiously to heare;
In whom great rule of Temp'raunce goodly doth appeare.   45

1 wote: know.   *5 just:* valid.

John Milton

FROM *Paradise Lost, Book I*

THE ARGUMENT

   *The first book proposes first in brief the whole subject, man's dis-
obedience, and the loss thereupon of Paradise wherein he was placed:
then touches the prime cause of his fall, the serpent, or rather Satan in
the serpent; who revolting from God, and drawing to his side many
legions of angels, was by the command of God driven out of Heaven
with all his crew into the great deep. Which action past over, the poem
hastes into the midst of things, presenting Satan with his angels now
fallen into Hell . . .*

  Of man's first disobedience, and the fruit
Of that forbidden tree, whose mortal taste
Brought death into the world, and all our woe,
With loss of *Eden,* till one greater man
Restore us, and regain the blissful seat,   5
Sing Heavenly Muse, that on the secret top
Of *Oreb,* or of *Sinai,* didst inspire
That shepherd, who first taught the chosen seed,
In the beginning how the heavens and earth
Rose out of *Chaos:* or if *Sion* hill   10
Delight thee more, and *Siloa's* brook that flowed
Fast by the oracle of God; I thence
Invoke thy aid to my adventurous song,
That with no middle flight intends to soar
Above th' *Aonian* mount, while it pursues   15
Things unattempted yet in prose or rhyme.
And chiefly Thou O Spirit, that dost prefer
Before all temples th' upright heart and pure,

Instruct me, for Thou know'st; Thou from the first
Wast present, and with mighty wings outspread   20
Dove-like satst brooding on the vast abyss
And mad'st it pregnant: What in me is dark
Illumine, what is low raise and support;
That to the heighth of this great argument
I may assert eternal providence,   25
And justify the ways of God to men.
    Say first, for Heaven hides nothing from thy view
Nor the deep tract of Hell, say first what cause
Moved our grand parents in that happy state,
Favored of Heaven so highly, to fall off   30
From their creator, and transgress His will
For one restraint, lords of the world besides?
Who first seduced them to that foul revolt?
Th' infernal serpent; he it was, whose guile
Stirred up with envy and revenge, deceived   35
The mother of mankind, what time his pride
Had cast him out from Heaven, with all his host
Of rebel angels, by whose aid aspiring
To set himself in glory above his peers,
He trusted to have equalled the most High,   40
If he opposed; and with ambitious aim
Against the throne and monarchy of God
Raised impious war in Heaven and battle proud
With vain attempt. Him the Almighty Power
Hurled headlong flaming from th' ethereal sky   45
With hideous ruin and combustion down
To bottomless perdition, there to dwell
In adamantine chains and penal fire,
Who durst defile th' Omnipotent to arms.
Nine times the space that measures day and night   50
To mortal men, he with his horrid crew
Lay vanquished, rolling in the fiery gulf
Confounded though immortal: But his doom
Reserv'd him to more wrath; for now the thought
Both of lost happiness and lasting pain   55
Torments him; round he throws his baleful eyes
That witnessed huge affliction and dismay
Mixed with obdurate pride and steadfast hate:
At once as far as angel's ken he views
The dismal situation waste and wild,   60
A dungeon horrible, on all sides round
As one great furnace flamed, yet from those flames
No light, but rather darkness visible
Served only to discover sights of woe,
Regions of sorrow, doleful shades, where peace   65
And rest can never dwell, hope never comes
That comes to all; but torture without end
Still urges, and a fiery deluge, fed
With ever-burning sulpher unconsumed:
Such place eternal justice had prepared   70
For those rebellious, here their prison ordained

In utter darkness, and their portion set
As far removed from God and light of Heaven
As from the center thrice to th' utmost pole.
Oh how unlike the place from whence they fell!   75
There the companions of his fall, o'erwhelmed
With floods and whirlwinds of tempestuous fire,
He soon discerns, and welt'ring by his side
One next himself in power, and next in crime,
Long after known in *Palestine,* and named   80
Bëëlzebub. To whom th' arch-enemy,
And thence in Heaven called Satan, with bold words
Breaking the horrid silence thus began.

The Argument: the subject or theme. The poem, Milton states,
"hastes into the midst of things," a reference to the convention (*in
medias res*) that an epic should begin in the midst of an action and
later narrate the antecedent action. *Paradise Lost* consists of 12
books; books five and six (as in the *Odyssey* and *Aeneid*) recount
the earliest part of the action.   6 *Heavenly Muse:* the holy spirit
that inspired Moses, David, and the prophets is here contrasted
with the Greek muses.   8 *That shepherd:* Moses.   15 *Aonian
mount:* Helicon in Boeotia, sacred to the Muses.   25–26: statement by the author of his purpose in writing the epic.

Hart Crane   Proem: To Brooklyn Bridge
FROM *The Bridge*

How many dawns, chill from his rippling rest
The seagull's wings shall dip and pivot him,
Shedding white rings of tumult, building high
Over the chained bay waters Liberty—

Then, with inviolate curve, forsake our eyes   5
As apparitional as sails that cross
Some page of figures to be filed away;
—Till elevators drop us from our day. . .

I think of cinemas, panoramic sleights
With multitudes bent toward some flashing scene   10
Never disclosed, but hastened to again,
Foretold to other eyes on the same screen;

And Thee, across the harbor, silver-paced
As though the sun took step of thee, yet left
Some motion ever unspent in thy stride,—   15
Implicitly thy freedom staying thee!

Out of some subway scuttle, cell or loft
A bedlamite speeds to thy parapets,
Tilting there momently, shrill shirt ballooning,
A jest falls from the speechless caravan.   20

Down Wall, from girder into street noon leaks,
A rip-tooth of the sky's acetylene;

All afternoon the cloud-flown derricks turn . . .
Thy cables breathe the North Atlantic still.

And obscure as that heaven of the Jews,   25
Thy guerdon . . . Accolade thou dost bestow
Of anonymity time cannot raise:
Vibrant reprieve and pardon thou dost show.

O harp and altar, of the fury fused,
(How could mere toil align thy choiring strings!)   30
Terrific threshold of the prophet's pledge,
Prayer of pariah, and the lover's cry,—

Again the traffic lights that skim thy swift
Unfractioned idiom, immaculate sigh of stars,
Beading thy path—condense eternity: 35
And we have seen night lifted in thine arms.

Under thy shadow by the piers I waited;
Only in darkness is thy shadow clear.
The City's fiery parcels all undone,
Already snow submerges an iron year . . .   40

O Sleepless as the river under thee,
Vaulting the sea, the prairies' dreaming sod,
Unto us lowliest sometime sweep, descend
And of the curveship lend a myth to God.

title: The Bridge consists of fifteen parts loosely held together.
8: The dots here and elsewhere in the poem are Crane's; they do
not indicate omissions.   *29 harp and altar:* the Brooklyn Bridge,
which throughout the poem comes to symbolize many things.

Ezra Pound   Canto I

And then went down to the ship,
Set keel to breakers, forth on the godly sea, and
We set up mast and sail on that swart ship,
Bore sheep aboard her, and our bodies also
Heavy with weeping, and winds from sternward   5
Bore us out onward with bellying canvas,
Circe's this craft, the trim-coifed goddess.
Then sat we amidships, wind jamming the tiller,
Thus with stretched sail, we went over sea till day's end.
Sun to his slumber, shadows o'er all the ocean,   10
Came we then to the bounds of deepest water,
To the Kimmerian lands, and peopled cities
Covered with close-webbed mist, unpierced ever
With glitter of sun-ray
Nor with stars stretched, nor looking back from heaven   15
Swartest night stretched over men there.
The ocean flowing backward, came we then to the place
Aforesaid by Circe.

Here did they rites, Perimedes and Eurylochus,
And drawing sword from my hip   20
I dug the ell-square pitkin;
Poured we libations unto each the dead,
First mead and then sweet wine, water mixed with white flour.
Then prayed I many a prayer to the sickly death's-heads;
As set in Ithaca, sterile bulls of the best   25
For sacrifice, heaping the pyre with goods,
A sheep to Tiresias only, black and a bell-sheep.
Dark blood flowed in the fosse,
Souls out of Erebus, cadaverous dead, of brides
Of youths and of the old who had borne much;   30
Souls stained with recent tears, girls tender,
Men many, mauled with bronze lance heads,
Battle spoil, bearing yet dreory arms,
These many crowded about me; with shouting
Pallor upon me, cried to my men for more beasts;   35
Slaughtered the herds, sheep slain of bronze;
Poured ointment, cried to the gods,
To Pluto the strong, and praised Proserpine;
Unsheathed the narrow sword,
I sat to keep off the impetuous impotent dead,   40
Till I should hear Tiresias.
But first Elpenor came, our friend Elpenor,
Unburied, cast on the wide earth,
Limbs that we left in the house of Circe,
Unwept, unwrapped in sepulcher, since toils urged other.   45
Pitiful spirit. And I cried in hurried speech:
"Elpenor, how art thou come to this dark coast?
"Cam'st thou afoot, outstripping seamen?"
                 And he in heavy speech:
"Ill fate and abundant wine. I slept in Circe's ingle.   50
"Going down the long ladder unguarded,
"I fell against the buttress,
"Shattered the nape-nerve, the soul sought Avernus.
"But thou, O King, I bid remember me, unwept, unburied,
"Heap up mine arms, be tomb by sea-bord, and inscribed: 55
" *'A man of no fortune and with a name to come.'*
"And set my oar up, that I swung mid fellows."

And Anticlea came, whom I beat off, and then Tiresias
    Theban,
Holding his golden wand, knew me, and spoke first:
"A second time? why? man of ill star,   60
"Facing the sunless dead and this joyless region?
"Stand from the fosse, leave me my bloody bever
"For soothsay."
              And I stepped back,
And he strong with the blood, said then: "Odysseus   65
"Shalt return through spiteful Neptune, over dark seas,
"Lose all companions." And then Anticlea came.
Lie quiet Divus. I mean, that is Andreas Divus,
In officina Wecheli, 1538, out of Homer.

And he sailed, by Sirens and thence outward and away 70
And unto Circe.
                    Venerandam,
In the Cretan's phase, with the golden crown, Aphrodite,
Cypri munimenta sortita est, mirthful, oricalchi, with golden
Girdles and breast bands, thou with dark eyelids 75
Bearing the golden bough of Argicida. So that:

title: This canto tells the story of Odysseus' visit to the underworld
(Book XI of the Odyssey). Pound's translation is from the Latin
translation by Andreas Divas (published 1538). The speaker is
Odysseus.   12 *Kimmerian lands:* The Cimmerians were a mythi-
cal people. Their land was perpetually in mist and darkness.   27
Tiresias: the blind prophet of Thebes who appears in Sophocles'
Oedipus Rex.   33 *dreory:* Anglo-Saxon word for "bloody."   58
Anticlea: the mother of Odysseus. Odysseus had been told to keep
her spirit away from the blood until Tiresias had drunk and thereby
gained strength to prophesy.   68 *Lie . . . Divus:* The poet himself
begins speaking in the first person; he addresses the Latin translator.
Pound refers at this point to Odysseus as "he."   69 *In officina . . .
1538:* the imprint of the translation Pound has used. "In the work-
shop of Wechel, 1538."   72 *Venerandam:* The phrase, relating
to Aphrodite, means "Compelling adoration."   74 *Cypri . . .
est:* "The citadels of Cyprus were her realm." This phrase is from
the second Homeric hymn to Aphrodite, translated into Latin by
Georgius Dartona Cretensis, the Cretan referred to in the preceding
line.   *oricalchi:* "of copper" (Latin).   76 *golden bough of
Argicida:* Hermes, the messenger god, is here named as the "slayer
of Argus." Aeneas carried a golden bough to the underworld as a
talisman, and Pound apparently identifies Hermes' caduceus with
this talisman. One of Hermes' responsibilities was to conduct the
souls of the dead to Hades.   *So that:* Pound seemingly provides
a transition to the following canto by the use of this phrase.

PART IV

Poetic Conventions: The Poem as Drama

The term dramatic poetry, logically, should be confined in its use to include poetry that makes use of dramatic form or dramatic techniques as a means of presenting poetic materials. The term, however, is often used in a more generalized sense to include any poem that tells an eventful, exciting story. Similarly, we refer to a particular drama as having "dramatic values" in addition to its method of presentation of materials.

In a sense, all poetry is dramatic, since a single speaker is saying something to someone. However. in lyric poetry the speaker is usually assumed to be the poet; in dramatic poetry the poet creates a character or characters. It is from the point of view of these characters that we come to know and evaluate the experience that is the poem.

THE SOLILOQUY

Soliloquy is usually associated with the drama (theater), usually with the plays of the Elizabethan period. The soliloquy, in general, assumes the convention that a character, alone on stage, will give voice to his inner thoughts and feelings. Because the playwright cannot directly comment upon his character's thoughts, the character himself must avail the audience of this information. The soliloquy, then, assumes that the thoughts and feelings a character has are not to be developed in conversation with others but must be shared only with the audience. Hamlet's "To be or not to be" speech is perhaps the best-known example in English drama of the uses and advantages of the soliloquy.

Christopher Marlowe

FROM *The Tragical History of Doctor Faustus*

Faustus.
Ah, Faustus,
Now hast thou but one bare hour to live,
And then thou must be damned perpetually!
Stand still, you ever-moving spheres of heaven,
That time may cease, and midnight never come;   5
Fair Nature's eye, rise, rise again, and make
Perpetual day; or let this hour be but
A year, a month, a week, a natural day,
That Faustus may repent and save his soul!
O *lente, lente currite, noctis equi!*   10
The stars move still, time runs, the clock will strike,
The devil will come, and Faustus must be damned.
Oh, I'll leap up to my God!—Who pulls me down?—
See, see, where Christ's blood streams in the firmament!
One drop would save my soul, half a drop: ah, my Christ!—   15
Ah, rend not my heart for naming of my Christ!
Yet will I call on Him: O spare me, Lucifer!—
Where is it now? 'tis gone: and see, where God
Stretcheth out His arm and bends His ireful brows!
Mountains and hills, come, come, and fall on me,   20
And hide me from the heavy wrath of God!
No, no!
Then will I headlong run into the earth:
Earth, gape! O no, it will not harbor me!
You stars that reigned at my nativity,   25
Whose influence hath allotted death and hell,
Now draw up Faustus, like a foggy mist,
Into the entrails of yon laboring clouds,
That, when you vomit forth into the air,
My limbs may issue from your smoky mouths,   30
So that my soul may but ascend to heaven!
                 [*The clock strikes the half-hour.*
Ah, half the hour is past! 'twill all be past anon.
O God,
If Thou wilt not have mercy on my soul,
Yet for Christ's sake, whose blood hath ransomed me,   35
Impose some end to my incessant pain;
Let Faustus live in hell a thousand years.
A hundred thousand, and at last be saved;

Oh, no end is limited to damnéd souls!
Why wert thou not a creature wanting soul?   40
Or why is this immortal that thou hast?
Ah, Pythagoras' metempsychosis, were that true,
This soul should fly from me, and I be changed
Unto some brutish beast! All beasts are happy,
For, when they die,   45
Their souls are soon dissolved in elements;
But mine must live still to be plagued in hell.
Curst be the parents that engendered me!
No, Faustus, curse thyself; curse Lucifer
That hath deprived thee of the joys of heaven.   50
        [*The clock strikes twelve.*
Oh, it strikes, it strikes! Now, body, turn to air,
Or Lucifer will bear thee quick to hell!
        [*Thunder and lightning.*
O soul, be changed into little water-drops,
And fall into the ocean—ne'er be found!
My God, my God, look not so fierce on me!   55

        Enter Devils.

Adders and serpents, let me breathe a while!
Ugly hell, gape not! come not, Lucifer!
I'll burn my books!—Ah, Mephistophilis!
        [*Exeunt* Devils *with* Faustus.

title: Dr. Faustus, through magic, has raised a devil, Mephistophilis,
servant of Lucifer. Faustus makes a pact with the devil and agrees
to surrender up his soul to the devil on condition that he be spared
for twenty-four years and permitted to live a life of voluptuousness.
The soliloquy here presented is Faustus's final one.   *10: O lente*
... *equi!:* Run slowly, slowly, horses of night (Ovid, *Amores,* i,13).

Robert Browning   Soliloquy of the Spanish Cloister

        1

Gr-r-r—there go, my heart's abhorrence!
    Water your damned flowerpots, do!
If hate killed men, Brother Lawrence,
    God's blood, would not mine kill you!
What? your myrtle bush wants trimming?   5
    Oh, that rose has prior claims—
Needs its leaden vase filled brimming?
    Hell dry you up with its flames!

        2

At the meal we sit together:
    Salve tibi! I must hear   10
Wise talk of the kind of weather,
    Sort of season, time of year:
Not a plenteous cork crop: scarcely

Dare we hope oak-galls, I doubt:
What's the Latin name for "parsley"?   15
 What's the Greek name for Swine's Snout?

  3
Whew! We'll have our platter burnished,
 Laid with care on your own shelf!
With a fire-new spoon we're furnished,
 And a goblet for ourself,   20
Rinsed like something sacrificial
 Ere 'tis fit to touch our chaps—
Marked with L. for our initial!
 (He-he! There his lily snaps!)

  4
Saint, forsooth! While brown Dolores   25
 Squats outside the Convent bank
With Sanchicha, telling stories,
 Steeping tresses in the tank,
Blue-black, lustrous, thick like horsehairs,
 —Can't I see his dead eye glow,   30
Bright as 'twere a Barbary corsair's?
 (That is, if he'd let it show!)

  5
When he finishes refection,
 Knife and fork he never lays
Cross-wise, to my recollection,   35
 As do I, in Jesu's praise.
I the Trinity illustrate,
 Drinking watered orange pulp—
In three sips the Arian frustrate;
 While he drains his at one gulp.   40

  6
Oh, those melons? If he's able
 We're to have a feast! so nice!
One goes to the Abbot's table,
 All of us get each a slice.
How go on your flowers? None double?   45
 Not one fruit-sort can you spy?
Strange!—And I, too, at such trouble,
 Keep them close-nipped on the sly!

  7
There's a great text in Galatians,
 Once you trip on it, entails   50
Twenty-nine distinct damnations,
 One sure, if another fails:
If I trip him just a-dying,
 Sure of heaven as sure can be,

Spin him round and send him flying   55
  Off to hell, a Manichee?

          8

Or, my scrofulous French novel
  On gray paper with blunt type!
Simply glance at it, you grovel
  Hand and foot in Belial's gripe;   60
If I double down its pages
  At the woeful sixteenth print,
When he gathers his greengages,
  Ope a sieve and slip it in't?

          9

Or, there's Satan!—one might venture   65
  Pledge one's soul to him, yet leave
Such a flaw in the indenture
  As he'd miss till, past retrieve,
Blasted lay that rose-acacia
  We're so proud of! *Hy, Zy, Hine* . . .   70
'St, there's Vespers! *Plena, Gratia*
  Ave, Virgo! Gr-r——you swine!

title: The setting of the poem is a Spanish monastery. No particular historical period is specified.   10 *Salve tibi!*: "Hail to
thee!" This and the other speeches in italics are supposed to be
Brother Lawrence's words.   14 *oak-galls*: growths on oak trees.
22 *chaps*: jaws.   31 *Barbary corsair*: pirate of the Barbary Coast
(northern Africa); they were renowned for their fierceness.   33
refection: dinner.   39 *Arian*: heretical followers of Arius (256–
336), who denied the doctrine of the Trinity.   49 *Galatians*:
The speaker hopes to damn Lawrence by getting him to commit
heresy. In Galatians, St. Paul lists a number of fleshly acts
that will lead to damnation; these fleshly works total twenty-nine.
56 *Manichee*: heretical follower of the Persian prophet (3rd century) Mani.   66 *Pledge . . . leave*: The speaker would pledge
his soul to Satan in return for blasting Lawrence; the pledge, however, would be worded in such a way that the speaker would be
exempt from payment of his own debt to Satan.   70 *Hy . . . The*
speaker begins a mysterious curse against Lawrence.   71–72
Plena . . . Virgo! "Full of grace, Hail, Virgin!" The prayer to Mary
is "Ave, Maria, gratia plena" ("Hail, Mary, full of grace").

THE DRAMATIC MONOLOGUE

The dramatic monologue, by contrast with the soliloquy,
usually reveals feelings, thoughts, and character traits that the
speaker himself is unaware of. In dramatic monologue a fictional character (the speaker) is usually placed in a dramatic
situation, a critical moment. The silent listener is sufficiently
present in the poem so that he is identifiable, but he remains

silent, and as the speaker refers to the situation in which he is involved, we learn a great deal about the character of the speaker; at times we learn to understand the character of the speaker in more depth than he understands himself.

Great dramatic monologues seem to have in common the fact that the presence of the second person—the silent character—is felt from the onset of the poem and remains present throughout the poem. Both situation and character retain great interest for the reader of the poem. Robert Browning's dramatic monologues are the most notable examples of the use of this form, and though earlier writers employed the dramatic monologue, Browning's achievement was so great that he is often credited with having created the dramatic monologue.

There are no formal rules for the writing of dramatic monologues, and poets less interested in the revelation of character than in the development of philosophical ideas may use the device of a silent auditor in order to enhance the dramatic values of their poetic materials. In T. S. Eliot's "The Love Song of J. Alfred Prufrock" the speaker's timid self seems to be addressing his aggressive, erotic self, another variant on the form.

Whereas the stage soliloquy establishes time and place prior to the soliloquy proper, the dramatic monologue reveals this information in the context of the poem itself. So, too, the dramatic poem. The dramatic monologue has become a type of poem, a separate category, because of the achievement of Browning's work. The dramatic poem, by contrast, is a rather amorphous classification that would include a wide variety of poems and techniques.

Alfred Lord Tennyson   Ulysses

It little profits that an idle king,
By this still hearth, among these barren crags,
Matched with an aged wife, I mete and dole
Unequal laws unto a savage race,
That hoard, and sleep, and feed, and know not me.   5
I cannot rest from travel; I will drink
Life to the lees. All times I have enjoyed
Greatly, have suffered greatly, both with those
That love me, and alone; on shore, and when
Through scudding drifts the rainy Hyades   10
Vexed the dim sea. I am become a name;
For always roaming with a hungry heart
Much have I seen and known—cities of men
And manners, climates, councils, governments,
Myself not least, but honored of them all—   15
And drunk delight of battle with my peers,
Far on the ringing plains of windy Troy.
I am a part of all that I have met;
Yet all experience is an arch wherethrough

Gleams that untraveled world whose margin fades   20
Forever and forever when I move.
How dull it is to pause, to make an end,
To rust unburnished, not to shine in use!
As though to breathe were life! Life piled on life
Were all too little, and of one to me   25
Little remains; but every hour is saved
From that eternal silence, something more,
A bringer of new things; and vile it were
For some three suns to store and hoard myself,
And this grey spirit yearning in desire   30
To follow knowledge like a sinking star,
Beyond the utmost bound of human thought.
    This is my son, mine own Telemachus,
To whom I leave the scepter and the isle—
Well-loved of me, discerning to fulfill   35
This labor, by slow prudence to make mild
A rugged people, and through soft degrees
Subdue them to the useful and the good.
Most blameless is he, centered in the sphere
Of common duties, decent not to fail   40
In offices of tenderness, and pay
Meet adoration to my household gods,
When I am gone. He works his work, I mine.
    There lies the port; the vessel puffs her sail;
There gloom the dark, broad seas. My mariners,   45
Souls that have toiled, and wrought, and thought with me—
That ever with a frolic welcome took
The thunder and the sunshine, and opposed
Free hearts, free foreheads—you and I are old;
Old age hath yet his honor and his toil.   50
Death closes all; but something ere the end,
Some work of noble note, may yet be done,
Not unbecoming men that strove with gods.
The lights begin to twinkle from the rocks;
The long day wanes; the slow moon climbs; the deep   55
Moans round with many voices. Come, my friends,
'Tis not too late to seek a newer world.
Push off, and sitting well in order smite
The sounding furrows; for my purpose holds
To sail beyond the sunset, and the baths   60
Of all the western stars, until I die.
It may be that the gulfs will wash us down;
It may be we shall touch the Happy Isles,
And see the great Achilles, whom we knew.
Though much is taken, much abides; and though   65
We are not now that strength which in old days
Moved earth and heaven, that which we are, we are—
One equal temper of heroic hearts,
Made weak by time and fate, but strong in will
To strive, to seek, to find, and not to yield.   70

63 Happy Isles: Elysium.

Alfred Lord Tennyson   Rizpah

1

Wailing, wailing, wailing, the wind over land and sea—
And Willy's voice in the wind, "O mother, come out to me!"
Why should he call me to-night, when he knows that I cannot
  go?
For the downs are as bright as day, and the full moon stares at
  the snow.

2

We should be seen, my dear; they would spy us out of the
  town.   5
The loud black nights for us, and the storm rushing over the
  down,
When I cannot see my own hand, but am led by the creak of
  the chain,
And grovel and grope for my son till I find myself drenched
  with the rain.

3

Anything fallen again? nay—what was there left to fall?
I have taken them home, I have number'd the bones, I have
  hidden them all.   10
What am I saying? and what are *you*? do you come as a spy?
Falls? what falls? who knows? As the tree falls so must it lie.

4

Who let her in? how long has she been? you—what have you
  heard?
Why did you sit so quiet? you never have spoken a word.
O—to pray with me—yes—a lady—none of their spies—   15
But the night has crept into my heart, and begun to darken
  my eyes.

5

Ah—you, that have lived so soft, what should *you* know of the
  night,
The blast and the burning shame and the bitter frost and the
  fright?
I have done it, while you were asleep—you were only made for
  the day.
I have gather'd my baby together—and now you may go your
  way.   20

6

Nay—for it's kind of you, madam, to sit by an old dying wife.
But say nothing hard of my boy, I have only an hour of life.

I kiss'd my boy in the prison, before he went out to die.
"They dared me to do it," he said, and he never has told me a
    lie.
I whipt him for robbing an orchard once when he was but a
    child—   25
"The farmer-dared me to do it," he said; he was always so wild—
And idle—and couldn't be idle—my Willy—he never could
    rest.
The King should have made him a soldier, he would have been
    one of his best.

7

But he lived with a lot of wild mates, and they never would let
    him be good;
They swore that he dare not rob the mail, and he swore that he
    would;   30
And he took no life, but he took one purse, and when all was
    done
He flung it among his fellows—"I 'll none of it," said my son.

8

I came into court to the judge and the lawyers. I told them my
    tale,
God's own truth—but they kill'd him, they kill'd him for
    robbing the mail.
They hang'd him in chains for a show—we had always borne
    a good name—   35
To be hang'd for a thief—and then put away—isn't that
    enough shame?
Dust to dust—low down—let us hide! but they set him so high
That all the ships of the world could stare at him, passing by.
God 'ill pardon the hell-black raven and horrible fowls of the
    air,
But not the black heart of the lawyer who kill'd him and hang'd
    him there.   40

9

And the jailer forced me away. I had bid him my last good-bye;
They had fasten'd the door of his cell. "O mother!" I heard him
    cry.
I couldn't get back tho' I tried, he had something further to say,
And now I never shall know it. The jailer forced me away.

10

Then since I couldn't but hear that cry of my boy that was
    dead,   45
They seized me and shut me up: they fasten'd me down on my
    bed.
"Mother, O mother!"—he call'd in the dark to me year after
    year—

They beat me for that, they beat me—you know that I couldn't
　　but hear;
And then at the last they found I had grown so stupid and still
They let me abroad again—but the creatures had worked their
　　will.　　　　　　　　　　　　　　　　　　　　　　　　　　50

11

Flesh of my flesh was gone, but bone of my bone was left—
I stole them all from the lawyers—and you, will you call it a
　　theft?—
My baby, the bones that had suck'd me, the bones that had
　　laughed and had cried—
Theirs? O, no! they are mine—not theirs— they had moved in
　　my side.

12

Do you think I was scared by the bones? I kiss'd 'em, I buried
　　'em all—　　　　　　　　　　　　　　　　　　　　　　　55
I can't dig, I am old—in the night by the churchyard wall.
My Willy 'ill rise up whole when the trumpet of judgement
　　'ill sound,
But I charge you never to say that I laid him in holy ground.

13

They would scratch him up—they would hang him again on
　　the cursed tree.
Sin? O, yes, we are sinners, I know—let all that be,　　　　60
And read me a Bible verse of the Lord's goodwill toward
　　men—
"Full of compassion and mercy, the Lord"—let me hear it
　　again;
"Full of compassion and mercy—long-suffering." Yes, O, yes!
For the lawyer is born but to murder—the Savior lives but to
　　bless.
*He'*ll never put on the black cap except for the worst of the
　　worst,　　　　　　　　　　　　　　　　　　　　　　　　65
And the first may be last—I have heard it in church—and the
　　last may be first.
Suffering—O, long-suffering—yes, as the Lord must know,
Year after year in the mist and the wind and the shower and
　　the snow.

14

Heard, have you? what? they have told you he never repented
　　his sin.
How do they know it? are *they* his mother? are *you* of his
　　kin?　　　　　　　　　　　　　　　　　　　　　　　　　70
Heard! have you ever heard, when the storm on the downs
　　began,
The wind that 'ill wail like a child and the sea that 'ill moan
　　like a man?

15

Election, Election, and Reprobation—it's all very well.
But I go to-night to my boy, and I shall not find him in hell.

Robert Browning   My Last Duchess

That's my last Duchess painted on the wall,
Looking as if she were alive. I call
That piece a wonder, now: Frà Pandolf's hands
Worked busily a day, and there she stands.
Will't please you sit and look at her? I said   5
"Frà Pandolf" by design, for never read
Strangers like you that pictured countenance,
The depth and passion of its earnest glance,
But to myself they turned (since none puts by
The curtain I have drawn for you, but I)   10
And seemed as they would ask me, if they durst,
How such a glance came there; so, not the first
Are you to turn and ask thus. Sir, 'twas not
Her husband's presence only, called that spot
Of joy into the Duchess' cheek: perhaps   15
Frà Pandolf chanced to say "Her mantle laps
Over my lady's wrist too much," or "Paint
Must never hope to reproduce the faint
Half-flush that dies along her throat": such stuff
Was courtesy, she thought, and cause enough   20
For calling up that spot of joy. She had
A heart—how shall I say?—too soon made glad,
Too easily impressed; she liked whate'er
She looked on, and her looks went everywhere.
Sir, 'twas all one! My favor at her breast,   25
The dropping of the daylight in the West,
The bough of cherries some officious fool
Broke in the orchard for her, the white mule
She rode with round the terrace—all and each
Would draw from her alike the approving speech,   30
Or blush, at least. She thanked men—good! but thanked
Somehow—I know not how—as if she ranked
My gift of a nine-hundred-years-old name
With anybody's gift. Who'd stoop to blame
This sort of trifling? Even had you skill   35
In speech—(which I have not)—to make your will
Quite clear to such an one, and say, "Just this
Or that in you disgusts me; here you miss,
Or there exceed the mark"—and if she let
Herself be lessoned so, nor plainly set   40
Her wits to yours, forsooth, and made excuse
—E'en then would be some stooping; and I choose
Never to stoop. Oh sir, she smiled, no doubt,
Whene'er I passed her; but who passed without
Much the same smile? This grew; I gave commands;   45

Then all smiles stopped together. There she stands
As if alive. Will't please you rise? We'll meet
The company below, then. I repeat,
The Count your master's known munificence
Is ample warrant that no just pretense   50
Of mine for dowry will be disallowed;
Though his fair daughter's self, as I avowed
At starting, is my object. Nay, we'll go
Together down, sir. Notice Neptune, though,
Taming a sea horse, thought a rarity,   55
Which Claus of Innsbruck cast in bronze for me!

3 *Frà Pandolf*: Brother Pandolf is an imaginary painter.   56
Claus of Innsbruck: unidentified and probably an imaginary sculptor. Innsbruck is a city in the Tyrol, Austria.

Robert Browning   A Toccata of Galuppi's

1

Oh, Galuppi, Baldassaro, this is very sad to find!
I can hardly misconceive you; it would prove me deaf and
    blind;
But although I take your meaning, 'tis with such a heavy
    mind!

2

Here you come with your old music, and here's all the good it
    brings.
What, they lived once thus at Venice where the merchants
    were the kings,   5
Where Saint Mark's is, where the Doges used to wed the sea
    with rings?

3

Aye, because the sea's the street there; and 'tis arched by . . .
    what you call
. . . Shylock's bridge with houses on it, where they kept the
    carnival:
I was never out of England—it's as if I saw it all.

4

Did young people take their pleasure when the sea was warm
    in May?   10
Balls and masks begun at midnight, burning ever to midday,
When they made up fresh adventures for the morrow, do you
    say?

5

Was a lady such a lady, cheeks so round and lips so red—
On her neck the small face buoyant, like a bellflower on its
    bed,

O'er the breast's superb abundance where a man might base
   his head?   *15*

6

Well, and it was graceful of them—they'd break talk off and
   afford
—She, to bite her mask's black velvet—he, to finger on his
   sword,
While you sat and played toccatas, stately at the clavichord?

7

What? Those lesser thirds so plaintive, sixths diminished, sigh
   on sigh,
Told them something? Those suspensions, those solutions—
   "Must we die?"   *20*
Those commiserating sevenths—"Life's might last! we can but
   try!"

8

"Were you happy?"—"Yes."—"And are you still as happy?"—
   "Yes. And you?"
—"Then, more kisses!"—Did *I* stop them, when a million
   seemed so few?"
Hark, the dominant's persistence till it must be answered to!

9

So, an octave struck the answer. Oh, they praised you, I dare
   say!   *25*
"Brave Galuppi! that was music; good alike at grave and gay!
I can always leave off talking when I hear a master play!"

10

Then they left you for their pleasure: till in due time, one by
   one,
Some with lives that came to nothing, some with deeds as
   well undone,
Death stepped tacitly and took them where they never see the
   sun.   *30*

11

But when I sit down to reason, think to take my stand nor
   swerve,
While I triumph o'er a secret wrung from nature's close
   reserve,
In you come with your cold music till I creep through every
   nerve.

12

Yes, you, like a ghostly cricket, creaking where a house was
   burned:

"Dust and ashes, dead and done with, Venice spent what
Venice earned.   35
The soul, doubtless, is immortal—where a soul can be
discerned.

13

"Yours for instance: you know physics, something of geology,
Mathematics are your pastime; souls shall rise in their degree;
Butterflies may dread extinction—you'll not die, it cannot be!

14

"As for Venice and her people, merely born to bloom and drop, 40
Here on earth they bore their fruitage, mirth and folly were
the crop:
What of soul was left, I wonder, when the kissing had to stop?

15

"Dust and ashes!" So you creak it, and I want the heart to
scold.
Dear dead women, with such hair, too—what's become of all
the gold
Used to hang and brush their bosoms? I feel chilly and grown
old.   45

title: There are three "speakers" in this poem. The first is a 19th-
century scientist in England; he is listening to a musical composition
by Baldassaro Galuppi (1706–85), a Venetian. The music heard
by the scientist evokes the voice of the dead composer who com-
ments upon the meaningless frivolity of his 18th-century contempo-
raries. Galuppi's audience form a second group of voices as they
respond to Galuppi's music, played during a party that is imagined
as having taken place in Venice. A "toccata" is a composition in free
style, designed originally to display the technique of the per-
former.   *6 Doges . . . rings:* The doge, chief magistrate of Venice,
annually threw a ring into the water to symbolize the bond that
existed between Venice, its maritime empire, and the sea.   *8
Shylock's bridge:* the Rialto, a bridge over the Grand Canal.   *21
sevenths:* The musical terms here and elsewhere in the poem refer
to technical devices that Galuppi employs to achieve alternating
moods in his music; conflict in each instance is resolved into harmony.

William Morris   The Defence of Guenevere

But, knowing now that they would have her speak,
She threw her wet hair backward from her brow,
Her hand close to her mouth touching her cheek,

As though she had had there a shameful blow,
And feeling it shameful to feel aught but shame   5
All through her heart, yet felt her cheek burned so,

She must a little touch it; like one lame
She walked away from Gauwaine, with her head
Still lifted up; and on her cheek of flame

The tears dried quick; she stopped at last and said: 10
"O knights and lords, it seems but little skill
To talk of well-known things past now and dead.

"God wot I ought to say, I have done ill,
And pray you all forgiveness heartily!
Because you must be right, such great lords; still   15

"Listen—suppose your time were come to die,
And you were quite alone and very weak;
Yea, laid a-dying, while very mightily

"The wind was ruffling up the narrow streak
Of river through your broad lands running well;   20
Suppose a hush should come, then someone speak:

" 'One of these cloths is heaven, and one is hell;
Now choose one cloth forever—which they be,
I will not tell you; you must somehow tell

" 'Of your own strength and mightiness; here, see!'   25
Yea, yea, my lord, and you to ope your eyes,
At foot of your familiar bed to see

"A great God's angel standing, with such dyes,
Not known on earth, on his great wings, and hands,
Held out two ways, light from the inner skies   30

"Showing him well, and making his commands
Seem to be God's commands, moreover, too,
Holding within his hands the cloth on wands;

"And one of these strange choosing cloths was blue,
Wavy and long, and one cut short and red;   35
No man could tell the better of the two.

"After a shivering half-hour you said:
'God help! heaven's color, the blue'; and he said, 'hell.'
Perhaps you would then roll upon your bed,

"And cry to all good men that loved you well,   40
'Ah, Christ! if only I had known, known, known';
Launcelot went away, then I could tell,

"Like wisest man how all things would be, moan,
And roll and hurt myself, and long to die,
And yet fear much to die for what was sown.   45

"Nevertheless, you, O Sir Gauwaine, lie;
Whatever may have happened through these years,
God knows I speak truth, saying that you lie."

Her voice was low at first, being full of tears,
But as it cleared, it grew loud and shrill,   50
Growing a windy shriek in all men's ears,

A ringing in their startled brains, until
She said that Gauwaine lied, then her voice sunk,
And her great eyes began again to fill,

Though still she stood right up, and never shrunk,   55
But spoke on bravely, glorious lady fair!
Whatever tears her full lips may have drunk,

She stood, and seemed to think, and wrung her hair,
Spoke out at last with no more trace of shame,
With passionate twisting of her body there: 60

"It chanced upon a day that Launcelot came
To dwell at Arthur's court —at Christmastime
This happened; when the heralds sung his name.

"Son of King Ban of Benwick, seemed to chime
Along with all the bells that rang that day,   65
O'er the white roofs, with little change of rime.

"Christmas and whitened winter passed away,
And over me the April sunshine came,
Made very awful with black hail-clouds; yea,

"And in the summer I grew white with flame,   70
And bowed my head down; autumn, and the sick
Sure knowledge things would never be the same,

"However often spring might be most thick
Of blossoms and buds, smote on me, and I grew
Careless of most things, let the clock tick, tick,   75

"To my unhappy pulse, that beat right through
My eager body; while I laughed out loud,
And let my lips curl up at false or true,

"Seemed cold and shallow without any cloud.
Behold, my judges, then the cloths were brought;   80
While I was dizzied thus, old thoughts would crowd,

"Belonging to the time ere I was bought
By Arthur's great name and his little love;
Must I give up forever then, I thought,

"That which I deemed would ever round me move   85
Glorifying all things; for a little word,
Scarce ever meant at all, must I now prove

"Stone-cold forever? Pray you, does the Lord
Will that all folks should be quite happy and good?
I love God now a little, if this cord   90

"Were broken, once for all what striving could
Make me love anything in earth or heaven?
So day by day it grew, as if one should

"Slip slowly down some path worn smooth and even,
Down to a cool sea on a summer day;   95
Yet still in slipping there was some small leaven

"Of stretched hands catching small stones by the way,
Until one surely reached the sea at last,
And felt strange new joy as the worn head lay

"Back, with the hair like sea-weed; yea, all past   100
Sweat of the forehead, dryness of the lips,
Washed utterly out by the dear waves o'ercast,

"In the lone sea, far off from any ships!
Do I not know now of a day in spring?
No minute of that wild day ever slips   105

"From out my memory; I hear thrushes sing,
And wheresoever I may be, straightway
Thoughts of it all come up with most fresh sting.

"I was half mad with beauty on that day,
And went, without my ladies, all alone,   110
In a quiet garden walled round every way;

"I was right joyful of that wall of stone,
That shut the flowers and trees up with the sky,
And trebled all the beauty; to the bone—

"Yea, right through to my heart, grown very shy   115
With wary thoughts—it pierced, and made me glad,
Exceedingly glad, and I knew verily,

"A little thing just then had made me mad;
I dared not think, as I was wont to do,
Sometimes, upon my beauty; if I had   120

"Held out my long hand up against the blue,
And, looked on the tenderly darkened fingers,
Thought that by rights one ought to see quite through,

"There, see you, where the soft still light yet lingers,
Round by the edges; what should I have done,   125
If this had joined with yellow spotted singers,

"And startling green drawn upward by the sun?
But shouting, loosed out, see now! all my hair,
And trancedly stood watching the west wind run

"With faintest half-heard breathing sound—why there   130
I lose my head e'en now in doing this.
But shortly listen: In that garden fair

"Came Launcelot walking; this is true, the kiss
Wherewith we kissed in meeting that spring day,
I scarce dare talk of the remembered bliss,   135

"When both our mouths went wandering in one way,
And aching sorely, met among the leaves;
Our hands, being left behind, strained far away.

"Never within a yard of my bright sleeves
Had Launcelot come before—and now so nigh!   140
After that day why is it Guenevere grieves?"

"Nevertheless, you, O Sir Gauwaine, lie,
Whatever happened on through all those years—
God knows I speak truth, saying that you lie.

"Being such a lady, could I weep these tears   145
If this were true? A great queen such as I,
Having sinned this way, straight her conscience sears;

"And afterwards she liveth hatefully,
Slaying and poisoning—certes never weeps;
Gauwaine, be friends now, speak me lovingly.   150

"Do I not see how God's dear pity creeps
All through your frame, and trembles in your mouth?
Remember in what grave your mother sleeps,

"Buried in some place far down in the south,
Men are forgetting as I speak to you;   155
By her head, severed in that awful drouth

"Of pity that drew Agravaine's fell blow,
I pray your pity! let me not scream out
Forever after, when the shrill winds blow

"Through half your castle-locks! let me not shout   160
Forever after in the winter night
When you ride out alone! in battle-rout

"Let not my rusting tears make your sword light!
Ah! God of mercy, how he turns away!
So, ever must I dress me to the fight,   165

"So—let God's justice work! Gauwaine, I say,
See me hew down your proofs; yea, all men know,
Even as you said, how Mellyagraunce one day,

"One bitter day in *la Fausse Garde*, for so
All good knights held it after, saw—   170
Yea, sirs, by cursed unknightly outrage, though

"You, Gauwaine, held his word without a flaw,
This Mellyagraunce saw blood upon my bed—
Whose blood then pray you? is there any law

"To make a queen say why some spots of red   175
Lie on her coverlet? or will you say,
'Your hands are white, lady, as when you wed,

" 'Where did you bleed?' and must I stammer out—'Nay,
I blush indeed, fair lord, only to rend
My sleeve up to my shoulder, where there lay   180

" 'A knife-point last night': so must I defend
The honor of the Lady Guenevere?
Not so, fair lords, even if the world should end

"This very day, and you were judges here
Instead of God. Did you see Mellyagraunce   185
When Launcelot stood by him?—what white fear

"Curdled his blood, and how his teeth did dance,
His side sink in? as my knight cried and said:
'Slayer of unarmed men, here is a chance!

" 'Setter of traps, I pray you guard your head;   190
By God, I am so glad to fight with you,
Stripper of ladies, that my hand feels lead

" 'For driving weight; hurrah now! draw and do,
For all my wounds are moving in my breast,
And I am getting mad with waiting so.'   195

"He struck his hands together o'er the beast,
Who fell down flat, and groveled at his feet,
And groaned at being slain so young. 'At least,'

"My knight said, 'Rise you, sir, who are so fleet
At catching ladies; half-armed will I fight,   200
My left side all uncovered!' Then, I weet,

"Up sprang Sir Mellyagraunce with great delight
Upon his knave's face; not until just then
Did I quite hate him, as I saw my knight

"Along the lists look to my stake and pen   205
With such a joyous smile, it made me sigh
From agony beneath my waist-chain, when

"The fight began, and to me they draw nigh;
Ever Sir Launcelot kept him on the right,
And traversed warily, and ever high   210

"And fast leapt caitiff's sword, until my knight
Sudden threw up his sword to his left hand,
Caught it, and swung it; that was all the fight,

"Except a spout of blood on the hot land;
For it was hottest summer; and I know   215
I wondered how the fire, while I should stand,

"And burn, against the heat, would quiver so,
Yards above my head; thus these matters went;
Which things were only warnings of the woe

"That fell on me. Yet Mellyagraunce was shent,   220
For Mellyagraunce had fought against the Lord;
Therefore, my lords, take heed lest you be blent

"With all his wickedness—say no rash word
Against me, being so beautiful; my eyes,
Wept all away to gray, may bring some sword   225

"To drown you in your blood; see my breast rise,
"Like waves of purple sea, as here I stand;
And how my arms are moved in wonderful wise;

"Yea, also at my full heart's strong command,
See through my long throat how the words go up   230
In ripples to my mouth; how in my hand

"The shadow lies like wine within a cup
Of marvelously colored gold; yea, now
This little wind is rising, look you up,

"And wonder how the light is falling so   235
Within my moving tresses. Will you dare
When you have looked a little on my brow,

"To say this thing is vile? or will you care
For any plausible lies of cunning woof,
When you can see my face with no lie there   240

"Forever? Am I not a gracious proof?—
'But in your chamber Launcelot was found'—
Is there a good knight then would stand aloof,

"When a queen says with gentle queenly sound,
'O true as steel, come now and talk with me;   245
I love to see your step upon the ground

" 'Unwavering; also well I love to see
That gracious smile light up your face, and hear
Your wonderful words, that all mean verily

" 'The thing they seem to mean. Good friend, so dear   250
To me in everything, come here tonight,
Or else the hours will pass most dull and drear.

" 'If you come not, I fear this time I might
Get thinking overmuch of times gone by,
When I was young, and green hope was in sight;   255

" 'For no man cares now to know why I sigh;
And no man comes to sing me pleasant songs,
Nor any brings me the sweet flowers that lie

" 'So thick in the gardens; therefore one so longs
To see you, Launcelot, that we may be   260
Like children once again, free from all wrongs

" 'Just for one night.' Did he not come to me?
What thing could keep true Launcelot away
If I said, 'Come'? There was one less than three

"In my quiet room that night, and we were gay;   265
Till sudden I rose up, weak, pale, and sick,
Because a bawling broke our dream up; yea,

"I looked at Launcelot's face and could not speak,
For he looked helpless, too, for a little while;
Then I remember how I tried to shriek,   270

"And could not, but fell down; from tile to tile
The stones they threw up rattled o'er my head
And made me dizzier; till within a while

"My maids were all about me, and my head
On Launcelot's breast was being soothed away   275
From its white chattering, until Launcelot said . . .

"By God! I will not tell you more today—
Judge any way you will; what matters it?
You know quite well the story of that fray,

"How Launcclot stilled their bawling, the mad fit   280
That caught up Gauwaine, all, all, verily,
But just that which would save me; these things flit.

"Nevertheless, you, O Sir Gauwaine, lie;
Whatever may have happened these long years,
God knows I speak truth, saying that you lie!   285

"All I have said is truth, by Christ's dear tears."
She would not speak another word, but stood
Turned sideways, listening, like a man who hears

His brother's trumpet sounding through the wood
Of his foes' lances. She leaned eagerly,   290
And gave a slight spring sometimes, as she could

At last hear something really; joyfully
Her cheek grew crimson, as the headlong speed
Of the roan charger drew all men to see,
The knight who came was Launcelot at good need.   295

title: Morris represents King Arthur's queen as defending herself
against the charge of adultery with Sir Launcelot. The charge was
made by Sir Gauwaine. In this, her second trial on the same charge,
she accuses Sir Gauwaine of plotting and perjury. At her first trial
she was rescued by Launcelot, who killed her accuser, Sir Mellyagraunce in a trial by combat, referred to in lines 166–219.   11
skill: reason, wisdom.   13 *wot*: knows.   46 *you . . . lie*:
Gauwaine is presented here as an accuser.   80 the cloths: See ll.
22 ff.   126 *yellow . . . singers*: thrushes.   153 *your mother*:
According to Malory's *Morte Darthur*, from which Morris drew
a great deal of his material, she was Morgawse, Arthur's sister. Her
son, Sir Gaheris (not Agravaine) slew her when he found her un-
faithful to her husband, King Lot.   168 *Mellyagraunce*: See note
to *title*.   169 *la Fausse Garde*: false prison (in which Mellyagraunce had kept her prisoner).   171 *unknightly outrage*: refers
to Mellyagraunce's entrance into Guenevere's chamber while she
was asleep.   190 *Setter of traps*: Mellyagraunce, who had trapped
Launcelot.   201 *weet*: knew, observed.   216–217 *while . . .
burn*: Because of Mellyagraunce's testimony, she was sentenced to
be burned. Launcelot saved her.   220 *shent*: destroyed.   222
blent: blinded.   280 *mad fit*: Gauwaine was not present.   282
that . . . me: her innocence.   291 *as*: as if.

Matthew Arnold   Dover Beach

The sea is calm tonight.
The tide is full, the moon lies fair
Upon the straits—on the French coast the light

Gleams and is gone; the cliffs of England stand,
Glimmering and vast, out in the tranquil bay.   5
Come to the window, sweet is the night air!
Only, from the long line of spray
Where the sea meets the moon-blanched land,
Listen! you hear the grating roar
Of pebbles which the waves draw back, and fling,   10
At their return, up the high strand,
Begin, and cease, and then again begin,
With tremulous cadence slow, and bring
The eternal note of sadness in.

Sophocles long ago   15
Heard it on the Aegean, and it brought
Into his mind the turbid ebb and flow
Of human misery; we
Find also in the sound a thought,
Hearing it by this distant northern sea.   20

The Sea of Faith
Was once, too, at the full, and round earth's shore
Lay like the folds of a bright girdle furled.
But now I only hear
Its melancholy, long, withdrawing roar,   25
Retreating, to the breath
Of the night wind, down the vast edges drear
And naked shingles of the world.

Ah, love, let us be true
To one another! for the world, which seems   30
To lie before us like a land of dreams,
So various, so beautiful, so new,
Hath really neither joy, nor love, nor light,
Nor certitude, nor peace, nor help for pain;
And we are here as on a darkling plain   35
Swept with confused alarms of struggle and flight,
Where ignorant armies clash by night.

23 *Lay . . . furled:* At high tide the sea envelops the land closely, its
forces gathered like the folds of bright clothing ("girdle") which
are compressed ("furled"). At ebb tide, it is unfurled and spread
out. Though still surrounding the shore, it is no longer an "en-
clasping flow."   28 *shingles:* beaches covered with pebbles.

Edwin Arlington Robinson   Mr. Flood's Party

Old Eben Flood, climbing alone one night
Over the hill between the town below
And the forsaken upland hermitage
That held as much as he should ever know
On earth again of home, paused warily.   5
The road was his with not a native near;

And Eben, having leisure, said aloud,
For no man else in Tilbury Town to hear:

'Well, Mr. Flood, we have the harvest moon
Again, and we may not have many more;   10
The bird is on the wing, the poet says,
And you and I have said it here before.
Drink to the bird.' He raised up to the light
The jug that he had gone so far to fill,
And answered huskily: 'Well, Mr. Flood,   15
Since you propose it, I believe I will.'

Alone, as if enduring to the end
A valiant armor of scarred hopes outworn,
He stood there in the middle of the road
Like Roland's ghost winding a silent horn.   20
Below him, in the town among the trees,
Where friends of other days had honored him,
A phantom salutation of the dead
Rang thinly till old Eben's eyes were dim.

Then, as a mother lays her sleeping child   25
Down tenderly, fearing it may awake,
He set the jug down slowly at his feet
With trembling care, knowing that most things break;
And only when assured that on firm earth
It stood, as the uncertain lives of men   30
Assuredly did not, he paced away,
And with his hand extended paused again:

'Well, Mr. Flood, we have not met like this
In a long time; and many a change has come
To both of us, I fear, since last it was   35
We had a drop together. Welcome home!'
Convivially returning with himself,
Again he raised the jug up to the light;
And with an acquiescent quaver said:
'Well, Mr. Flood, if you insist, I might.   40

'Only a very little, Mr. Flood—
For auld lang syne. No more, sir; that will do.'
So, for the time, apparently it did,
And Eben evidently thought so too;
For soon amid the silver loneliness   45
Of night he lifted up his voice and sang,
Secure, with only two moons listening,
Until the whole harmonious landscape rang—

'For auld lang syne.' The weary throat gave out,
The last word wavered, and the song was done.   50
He raised again the jug regretfully
And shook his head, and was again alone.
There was not much that was ahead of him,
And there was nothing in the town below—
Where strangers would have shut the many doors   55
That many friends had opened long ago.

T. S. *Eliot*   The Love Song of J. Alfred Prufrock

S'io credesse che mia risposta fosse
A persona che mai tornasse al mondo,
Questa fiamma staria senza piu scosse.
Ma perciocche giammai di questo fondo
Non torno vivo alcum, s'i'odo il vero,
Senza tema d'infamia ti rispondo.

Let us go then, you and I,
When the evening is spread out against the sky
Like a patient etherised upon a table;
Let us go, through certain half-deserted streets,
The muttering retreats   5
Of restless nights in one-night cheap hotels
And sawdust restaurants with oyster-shells:
Streets that follow like a tedious argument
Of insidious intent
To lead you to an overwhelming question . . .   10
Oh, do not ask, "What is it?"
Let us go and make our visit.

In the room the women come and go
Talking of Michelangelo.

The yellow fog that rubs its back upon the window-panes,   15
The yellow smoke that rubs its muzzle on the window-panes
Licked its tongue into the corners of the evening,
Lingered upon the pools that stand in drains,
Let fall upon its back the soot that falls from chimneys,
Slipped by the terrace, made a sudden leap,   20
And seeing that it was a soft October night,
Curled once about the house, and fell asleep.

And indeed there will be time
For the yellow smoke that slides along the street,
Rubbing its back upon the window-panes;   25
There will be time, there will be time
To prepare a face to meet the faces that you meet;
There will be time to murder and create,
And time for all the works and days of hands
That lift and drop a question on your plate;   30
Time for you and time for me,
And time yet for a hundred indecisions,
And for a hundred visions and revisions,
Before the taking of a toast and tea.

In the room the women come and go   35
Talking of Michelangelo.

And indeed there will be time
To wonder, "Do I dare?" and, "Do I dare?"
Time to turn back and descend the stair,
With a bald spot in the middle of my hair—   40

(They will say: "How his hair is growing thin!")
My morning coat, my collar mounting firmly to the chin,
My necktie rich and modest, but asserted by a simple pin—
(They will say: "But how his arms and legs are thin!")
Do I dare   45
Disturb the universe?
In a minute there is time
For decisions and revisions which a minute will reverse.

For I have known them all already, known them all:—
Have known the evenings, mornings, afternoons,   50
I have measured out my life with coffee spoons;
I know the voices dying with a dying fall
Beneath the music from a farther room.
    So how should I presume?

And I have known the eyes already, known them all—   55
The eyes that fix you in a formulated phrase,
And when I am formulated, sprawling on a pin,
When I am pinned and wriggling on the wall,
Then how should I begin
To spit out all the butt-ends of my days and ways?   60
    And how should I presume?

And I have known the arms already, known them all—
Arms that are braceleted and white and bare
(But in the lamplight, downed with light brown hair!)
Is it perfume from a dress   65
That makes me so digress?
Arms that lie along a table, or wrap about a shawl.
    And should I then presume?
    And how should I begin?

.   .   .   .

Shall I say, I have gone at dusk through narrow streets   70
And watched the smoke that rises from the pipes
Of lonely men in shirt-sleeves, leaning out of windows? . . .

I should have been a pair of ragged claws
Scuttling across the floors of silent seas.

.   .   .   .

And the afternoon, the evening, sleeps so peacefully!   75
Smoothed by long fingers,
Asleep . . tired . . . or it malingers,
Stretched on the floor, here beside you and me.
Should I, after tea and cakes and ices,
Have the strength to force the moment to its crisis?   80
But though I have wept and fasted, wept and prayed,
Though I have seen my head (grown slightly bald) brought in
    upon a platter,
I am no prophet—and here's no great matter;
I have seen the moment of my greatness flicker,
And I have seen the eternal Footman hold my coat, and
    snicker,   85

And in short, I was afraid.
And would it have been worth it, after all,
After the cups, the marmalade, the tea,
Among the porcelain, among some talk of you and me,
Would it have been worth while,   90
To have bitten off the matter with a smile,
To have squeezed the universe into a ball
To roll it toward some overwhelming question,
To say: "I am Lazarus, come from the dead,
Come back to tell you all, I shall tell you all"—   95
If one, settling a pillow by her head,
    Should say: "That is not what I meant at all.
    That is not it, at all."

And would it have been worth it, after all,
Would it have been worth while,   100
After the sunsets and the dooryards and the sprinkled streets,
After the novels, after the teacups, after the skirts that trail
    along the floor—
And this, and so much more?—
It is impossible to say just what I mean!
But as if a magic lantern threw the nerves in patterns on a
    screen: 105
Would it have been worth while
If one, settling a pillow or throwing off a shawl,
And turning toward the window, should say:
    "That is not it at all,
    That is not what I meant, at all."   110

No! I am not Prince Hamlet, nor was meant to be;
Am an attendant lord, one that will do
To swell a progress, start a scene or two,
Advise the prince; no doubt, an easy tool,
Deferential, glad to be of use,   115
Politic, cautious, and meticulous;
Full of high sentence, but a bit obtuse;
At times, indeed, almost ridiculous—
Almost, at times, the Fool.

I grow old . . . I grow old . . .   120
I shall wear the bottoms of my trousers rolled.

Shall I part my hair behind? Do I dare to eat a peach?
I shall wear white flannel trousers, and walk upon the beach.
I have heard the mermaids singing, each to each.

I do not think that they will sing to me.   125

I have seen them riding seaward on the waves
Combing the white hair of the waves blown back
When the wind blows the water white and black.

We have lingered in the chambers of the sea
By sea-girls wreathed with seaweed red and brown   130
Till human voices wake us, and we drown.

title: Eliot establishes an ironic contrast between the romantic sug-
gestions of the "love song" and the prosaic name, "J. Alfred Prufrock."   *epigraph:* In *Inferno,* Canto XXVII, lines 61–66, Dante
asks one of the souls condemned to damnation for its name; it answers: "If I thought my answer were to one who could return to
the world, I would not reply, but as none ever did return alive from
this depth, without fear of infamy I answer thee."   *23 there . . .
time:* Cf. Marvell's "To His Coy Mistress": "Had we but world
enough and time. . . ." Marvell argues in his poem that there is not
sufficient time for "indecisions."   *29 works . . . days:* the title
of a poem by the Greek poet Hesiod (8th century B.C.). The Greek
poet, addressing his brother, urges him to work hard at farming.
Eliot, by contrast, suggests the futility of meaningless social gestures.   *46 Disturb . . . universe:* Cf. Marvell, who suggests that
love can make a new universe.   *52 a . . . fall:* Ironically recalls the
opening speech of Duke Orsino in Shakespeare's "Twelfth Night,"
(I.i.4): "That strain again! It had a dying fall."   *82 Though . . .
platter:* a reference to John the Baptist, beheaded by Herod to
please his step-daughter Salome.   *85 Footman:* Death. Even in
death the speaker believes he will be without dignity or respect.
92 squeezed . . . ball: Cf. Marvell: "Let us roll all our strength
and all/Our sweetness up into a ball,/And tear our pleasures with
rough strife/Thorough the iron gates of life."   *94 Lazarus:* the
brother of Mary and Martha, raised from the dead by Jesus. Cf.
John xi.1–14.   *113 progress:* used in the Elizabethan sense of a
state journey made by a noble or royal person.   *117 sentence:*
used in the older meaning of "sententiousness."

DRAMATIC POETRY

A useful approach to a discussion of dramatic poetry is provided by the distinction that Henry James made in his critical
discussions of the novel. Showing, rather than telling, James
concluded, was the essence of drama and dramatic immediacy.
Our word "drama," it is useful to recall, is from the Greek
word *dram,* "to do." Hence, in dramatic poetry, the fictional
characters make us aware of situation, character, place, time,
and conflict. The poet's voice, his presence in the poem, has
been, to a large extent, removed from the poem. There is of
course a wide latitude left to the poet's discretion, and whereas
one poet may simply employ the formality of giving speakers'
names in his margin—as in the text of a play—another poet
may try to achieve a greater dramatic illusion by allowing
names and other pertinent information to emerge from the
poem itself. Again, many poets combine methods of composition and in part tell (describe, narrate) and in part "show"
(present) through dialogue.

Inherent in that aspect of literature which we label dramatic,
and an element that has more to do with dramatic values than
with formal dramatic techniques, is the element of conflict.
Within the situation of the poem or play there is usually to be

found a struggle, the result of an interplay between opposing forces. This struggle (or conflict) provides the work with a great deal of its interest and suspense. The struggle itself may be with another person, with oneself, against some force in nature, against society, against a devil, or whatever the poet chooses. In addition, there is usually the implication that conflict assumes motivation, goals, and values.

Robert Herrick   The Kiss: A Dialogue

1.   Among thy fancies, tell me this,
        What is the thing we call a kiss?
2.   I shall resolve ye, what it is.

        It is a creature born and bred
        Between the lips, (all cherry-red),   5
        By love and warm desires fed,
Chorus. And makes more soft the bridal bed.

2.   It is an active flame that flies,
        First, to the babies of the eyes;
        And charms them there with lullabies;   10
Chor.   And still the bride too, when she cries.

2.   Then to the chin, the cheek, the ear,
        It frisks, and flies, now here, now there,
        'Tis now far off, and then 'tis near;
Chor.   And here, and there, and everywhere.   15

1.   Has it a speaking virtue? 2. Yes;
1.   How speaks it, say? 2. Do you but this,
        Part your joined lips, then speaks your kiss;
Chor.   And this love's sweetest language is.

1.   Has it a body? 2. Aye, and wings   20
        With thousand rare encolorings:
        And as it flies, it gently sings,
Chor.   Love, honey yields; but never stings.

Andrew Marvell   A Dialogue Between the Soul and Body

SOUL

O who shall, from this dungeon, raise
A soul enslaved so many ways?
With bolts of bones, that fettered stands
In feet; and manacled in hands.
Here blinded with an eye; and there   5
Deaf with the drumming of an ear.
A soul hung up, as 'twere, in chains
Of nerves and arteries, and veins.
Tortur'd, besides each other part,
In a vain head, and double heart.   10

BODY

  O who shall me deliver whole,
From bonds of this tyrannic soul?
Which, stretched up right, impales me so,
That mine own precipice I go;
And warms and moves this needless frame: 15
(A fever could but do the same.)
And, wanting where its spite to try,
Has made me live to let me die.
A body that could never rest,
Since this ill spirit is possessed.   20

SOUL

  What magic could me thus confine
Within another's grief to pine?
Where whatsoever it complain,
I feel, that cannot feel, the pain.
And all my care its self employs,   25
That to preserve, which me destroys:
Constrained not only to endure
Diseases, but, what's worse, the cure:
And ready oft the port to gain,
Am shipwrackt into health aagin.   30

BODY

  But physic yet could never reach
The maladies thou me dost teach;
Whom first the cramp of hope does tear;
And then the palsy shakes of fear.
The pestilence of love does heat: 35
Or hatred's hidden ulcer eat.
Joy's cheerful madness does perplex:
Or sorrow's other madness vex.
Which knowledge forces me to know;
And memory will not forgo.   40
What but a soul could have the wit
To build me up for sin so fit?
So architects do square and hew,
Green trees that in the forest grew.

5 i.e., to spiritual sight.   8 *nerves*: sinews.   15 *needless*: having no need.   17 *where*: somewhere.   24 *I feel, that cannot feel*: the soul has intellectual intuition though not endowed with senses. 43 *square*: square off; cut to squares.

John Dryden   The Secular Masque

JANUS.   Chronos, Chronos, mend thy pace,
                  An hundred times the rolling sun

Around the radiant belt has run
In his revolving race.
Behold, behold, the goal in sight   5
Spread thy fans, and wing thy flight.

CHRONOS.   Weary, weary of my weight,
                      Let me, let me, drop my freight,
                      And leave the world behind.
                  I could not bear,   10
                  Another year,
                  The load of human-kind.

MOMUS.   Ha! ha! ha! ha! ha! ha! well hast thou done
                      To lay down thy pack,
                      And lighten thy back,   15
                  The world was a fool, e'er since it begun,
                  And since neither Janus, nor Chronos, nor I,
                      Can hinder the crimes,
                      Or mend the bad times,
                  'Tis better to laugh than to cry.   20

CHORUS OF
ALL THREE.   'Tis better to laugh than to cry.

JANUS.   Since Momus comes to laugh below,
                      Old Time, begin the show,
                  That he may see, in every scene,
                  What changes in this age have been.   25

CHRONOS.   The goddess of the silver bow begin.

DIANA.   With horns and with hounds, I waken the day:
                      And hie to the woodland-walks away:
                      I tuck up my robe, and am buskined soon,
                      And tie to my forehead a waxing moon. 30
                      I course the fleet stag, unkennel the fox,
                      And chase the wild goats o'er summits of rocks,
                      With shouting and hooting we pierce
                          through the sky,
                      And Echo turns hunter, and doubles the cry.

CHORUS OF
ALL.   With shouting and hooting we pierce
                      through the sky,   35
                  And Echo turns hunter, and doubles the cry.

JANUS.   Then our age was in its prime:

CHRONOS.   Free from rage:

DIANA.   —And free from crime:

MOMUS.   A very merry, dancing, drinking,
                  Laughing, quaffing, and unthinking time. 40

CHORUS OF
ALL.   Then our age was in its prime,
                  Free from rage, and free from crime,

          A very merry, dancing, drinking,
          Laughing, quaffing, and unthinking time.

MARS.   Inspire the vocal brass, inspire;   45
          The world is past its infant age:
             Arms and honor,
             Arms and honor,
          Set the martial mind on fire,
          And kindle manly rage;   50
          Mars has looked the sky to red;
          And Peace, the lazy good, is fled.
          Plenty, peace, and pleasure fly;
             The sprightly green,
          In woodland-walks, no more is seen;   55
          The sprightly green has drunk the
             Tyrian dye.

CHORUS OF
ALL.   Plenty, peace, &c.

MARS.   Sound the trumpet, beat the drum;
          Through all the world around,
          Sound a reveillé, sound, sound,   60
          The warrior god is come.

CHORUS OF
ALL.   Sound the trumpet, &c.

MOMUS.   Thy sword within the scabbard keep,
             And let mankind agree;
          Better the world were fast asleep   65
          Than kept awake by thee,
          The fools are only thinner,
             With all our cost and care;
          But neither side a winner,
             For things are as they were.   70

CHORUS OF
ALL.   The fools are only, &c.

VENUS.   Calms appear, when storms are past;
          Love will have his hour at last:
          Nature is my kindly care;
          Mars destroys, and I repair;   75
          Take me, take me, while you may,
          Venus comes not every day.

CHORUS OF
ALL.   Take her, take her, &c.

CHRONOS.   The world was then so light,
          I scarcely felt the weight;   80
          Joy ruled the day, and Love the night.
          But since the queen of pleasure left the ground,
             I faint, I lag,
             And feebly drag
          The pondrous orb around.   85

MOMUS.	All, all of a piece throughout:
TO DIANA.	Thy chase had a beast in view.
TO MARS.	Thy wars brought nothing about;
TO VENUS.	Thy lovers were all untrue.

| JANUS. | 'Tis well an old age is out. | 90 |

| CHRONOS. | And time to begin a new. |

CHORUS OF
ALL.   All, all of a piece throughout;
                Thy chase had a beast in view::
                Thy wars brought nothing about;
                Thy lovers were all untrue.   95
                'Tis well an old age is out,
                And time to begin a new.

Title: In this poem, Dryden celebrates the turn of the century.
He employs allegorical figures (Janus, the god of beginnings;
Chronos, time; Momus, laughter, etc.) to describe the passing
seventeenth century and his attitude toward it. He treats the
century under three main headings: the early century under
James I, the wars of Charles I, and the gay and licentious courts
of Charles II and James II.

William Morris   Scenes from the Fall of Troy

HELEN ARMING PARIS

PARIS.
So, my sweet thing, a little tighter yet.
Look you, it must not rattle or some blow
Given at hazard on my knee-cap here
Would drive the thin edge in my foot. (*sighing*)
My sweet thing, shall I talk or hold my tongue?   5

HELEN.
Shall I say, Paris, that my heart is faint,
And my head sick? I grow afraid of death:
The Gods are all against us, and some day
The long black ships rowed equal on each side
Shall throng the Trojan bay, and I shall walk   10
From off the green earth to the straining ship;
Cold Agamemnon with his sickly smile
Shall go before me, and behind shall go
My old chain Menelaus: we shall sit
Under the deck amid the oars, and hear   15
From day to day their wretched measured beat
Against the washing surges; they shall sit
There in that twilight, with their faces turned
Away from mine, and we shall say no word;
And I shall be too sick at heart to sing,   20
Though the rough dirt-grimed mariners may sing

Through all their weariness their rowing-song
Of Argo and the Golden Fleece, and Her
That made and marred them all in a short while,
As any potter might do with his clay,   25
Medea the Colchian. We shall come at last
To land in Greece, and all shall cry at me,
"See her who slew the sons of Priamus,
Who threw to earth that right fair town of Troy,
Who slew full many a mother's son of Greece!   30
See how she walks still like a Queen! By the Gods!
Is there no faggot for her false white limbs?
No sack, wherein, close sewn and crying out,
She may roll down the steep gulfs of the sea?
Is there no butcher's knife?"

PARIS.
                              Nay hold, my love!   35
And let Greek butchers butcher their own lambs,
For you are ours: and let the sea-folk roll
Their own sea-calves in sacks of woven sea-weed,
For you are ours: and let the beechen-wood
Bake bread for Greeks: seeing that you are ours.   40
Look Helen, hence upon our walls of stone,
Our great wet ditches where the carp and tench
In spite of arblasts and petrariae
Suck at the floating lilies all day long;
Look at the mighty barriers of fir-wood,   45
And look at Ilium rising over all,
Then at the few white tents and green log-huts
Of the Greek leaguer: listen too, my love
And you shall hear the muster of our men
Down in the streets, and marching toward the gates   50
Of many a captain. Ah! my sweet Helen,
Full many a day shall we kiss thus and thus
Before that last day when you kiss me dead,
An old man lying where the incense burns.

HELEN.
Lips upon lips is surely a sweet game;   55
But I have ruined you, oh poor Paris,
My poor kind knight, who never for himself
Would look a yard before his sweet grey eyes;
Who taught me how to live, when long ago
I had forgotten that the world was fair   60
And I was fair: who made my lying down
Right peaceful to my tired heart and limbs,
Who made my walking sweet to rested eyes,
Who gave me joyful hours day by day.
In turn I give you this: no peace at all,   65
At best your weary anxiousness put off
So that it crushes not, pain and trouble, dear,
To you and all your kin; and at the worst—
O Paris, Paris, what care I for the Greeks?
They will not slay me, as I know full well,   70

And time will stay their babble and hard words.
Yea, I shall live a Queen while you lie slain—
But think of Troy with wolves about the streets,
Some yellow lion couched upon the place
Where first you called out, "Troy, love! this is Troy!"   75
And men all shouted, "Helen! the fair Dame!"
But on their skulls that lion shall look then
And bones of women that looked out at me
Calling out "Helen!"—bones of young children
Born in the siege, who never knew of peace: 80
Fair, tall Andromache gone who knows where,
And Hector fallen dead among the spears,
One man to hundreds, when the rest are slain
And Troy is burning: yea good Helenus
Slain at his altar, and Cassandra mocked   85
Used like a jester, while the Grecian wine
Stains Priam's golden cups: and Priam slain,
And Troilus slain before his withered hope
Can spring afresh: Deiphobus dead, slain,
Thrust in some ditch the salt sea sometimes fills   90
When wind and tide are high: Polyxena,
Younger than me and fairer she is now,
Sadder therefore and longer shall she live
As some man's slave—In what way, love Paris
Will they slay you, I wonder? will they call,   95
"Come Helen, come to this our sacrifice,
For Paris shall be slain at the sea's foot"?
Or will they wake me from my weeping sleep
Dangling your head above me by the hair,
Then all day long send women to dress me,   100
And scent my limbs, and comb my hair and bathe
My dull red eyelids till they grow stone-white,
Then set me at the feast among the wine
In Agamemnon's tent, to hear them tell
Long tales about the war, and hear them sing   105
Right in mine ears forgotten songs of Greece?

PARIS.
Sweet, will you count our love an idle tale,
A thing the years take from us day by day,
A thing that was once but forgotten now?
Love, though indeed the bitter death may come,   110
And unclasp both my arms from round your neck,
Yet have I lived once. Helen, when I think
The fairest thing the Gods have made will sit
Hours together with her cheek laid on mine
And praises my poor doings, and looks pale   115
When from the mellay something scratched I come—
Say, lets me love her—why today, Helen,
I feel so light of heart with my great joy
That I can scarce be sober—shall I say,
Half jesting, half in earnest, as I take   120
Your fair long hand and kiss it, that our folk,

All Trojans, would be glad to die for this?
By God, Helen, but half I deem it true.

HELEN.
Do not believe it, Paris: bitterly
Death comes to all, and they have their own wives, 125
Own loves or children: Paris, you know not
What death can do: pray God you curse me not
When you leave off being happy—do you think
We can be happy in the end, Paris?
I shudder when I think of those fell men 130
Who every day stand round about Troy Town
And every night wipe the rust off their spears.
They have no thoughts of pleasure or of love;
Each day they rise to see the walls of Troy
Still stand unbreached, and in the dead of night 135
Awake or dreaming, still they think of it;
Unspoken vows lie coiled about their hearts,
Unspoken wrath is in their heavy hands,
They are become mine enemies, yet still
I am grieved for their unspoken woes, 140
And longings for the merry fields of Greece:
They know themselves to be but ruined men
Whatever happens—Doubt not they will win
Their dreadful slow revenge at last, Paris.

PARIS.
Look you my love, it is not well to boast 145
Of anything one has, for fear the Gods
Should take it from us: yet I pray you think
Of that great belt of Priam's sons, buckled
By shining Hector the great clasp of all:
The unfailing steadfast hearts of my brothers, 150
Shall they not match the fierce-eyed gloomy Greeks?

HELEN.
O me! my brother Hector, kind and true,
How sweet thou art for ever unto me!
Yet sometime shall Achilles have his day:
Better a live dog than a dead lion, dear. 155

PARIS.
Behold him coming, glancing with a smile
Down on the Grecian tents.

HELEN.
                              Is it farewell
To both of you? Would I could weep for love!
But little ever have I used wet eyes
When hurt I have been. Where go you, sweet lords? 160

HECTOR.
The word is, each in arms we meet straightway
In Priam's Hall, then out at gates go we;
And goodly tilting shall the Trojan dames

See from the walls: right thick the Greeks are set,
And even now the stones begin to fall   *165*
By the Scaean gates from their petrariae.
Why Paris! you look brave in arms today.
See you do well! Helen shall see your works.
                Helen *falls.*
Helen! fair Helen!

PARIS.
          O my God! Hector,
What may all this forbode? She said true now,   *170*
She never wept: I never saw her weep;
But now she lies full length upon the stones
And terrible her weeping is to hear,
And terribly the sobs take half her breath:
              Kneeling by Helen.
For God's sake, Helen! will you kill me, love?   *175*

HELEN.
Go out and fight! I cannot speak with you,
No, no, I cannot kiss you: go, Paris.

PARIS.
I will not leave you, Helen, till you do.
Tell me what ails you?

HELEN.
         O, Paris, Paris!
Let me lie still and leave me!

HECTOR.
          Come, brother!   *180*
For time presses. 'Tis better too for her;
She will weep out her full, and go to sleep,
And wake up in your arms tonight smiling.
              Exeunt.

43 *arblasts:* crossbows.   *petrariae:* ordnance used for throwing
stones, etc.   116 *mellay:* fight.   166 *Scaean:* western.

Gerard Manley Hopkins   The Leaden Echo and the
   Golden Echo
     (*"Maidens' Song"* FROM *"St. Winefred's Well"*)

THE LEADEN ECHO

How to keep—is there any any, is there none such, nowhere
     known some, bow or brooch or braid or brace, lace, latch
     or catch or key to keep
Back beauty, keep it, beauty, beauty, beauty, . . . from vanish-
     ing away?
O is there no frowning of these wrinkles, rankèd wrinkles
     deep,

Down? no waving off of these most mournful messengers, still
   messengers, sad and stealing messengers of grey?—
No there's none, there's none, O no there's none,   5
Nor can you long be, what you now are, called fair,
Do what you may do, what, do what you may,
And wisdom is early to despair:
Be beginning; since, no, nothing can be done
To keep at bay   10
Age and age's evils, hoar hair,
Ruck and wrinkle, drooping, dying, death's worst, winding
   sheets, tombs and worms and tumbling to decay;
So be beginning, be beginning to despair.
O there's none; no no no there's none:
Be beginning to despair, to despair,   15
Despair, despair, despair, despair.

THE GOLDEN ECHO

                        Spare!
There is one, yes I have one (Hush there!),
Only not within seeing of the sun.
Not within the singeing of the strong sun,   20
Tall sun's tingeing, or treacherous the tainting of the earth's
   air,
Somewhere elsewhere there is ah well where! one,
One. Yes I can tell such a key, I do know such a place,
Where whatever's prizèd and passes of us, everything that's
   fresh and fast flying of us, seems to us sweet of us and
   swiftly away with, done away with, undone,
Undone, done with, soon done with, and yet dearly and
   dangerously sweet   25
Of us, the wimpled-water-dimpled, not-by-morning-matchèd
   face,
The flower of beauty, fleece of beauty, too too apt to, ah! to
   fleet,
Never fleets more, fastened with the tenderest truth
To its own best being and its loveliness of youth: it is an
   everlastingness of, O it is an all youth!
Come then, your ways and airs and looks, locks, maidengear,
   gallantry and gaiety and grace,   30
Winning ways, airs innocent, maiden manners, sweet looks,
   loose locks, long locks, lovelocks, gaygear, going gallant,
   girlgrace—
Resign them, sign them, seal them, send them, motion them
   with breath,
And with sighs soaring, soaring sighs deliver
Them; beauty-in-the-ghost, deliver it, early now, long before
   death
Give beauty back, beauty, beauty, beauty, back to God,
   beauty's self and beauty's giver.   35
See; not a hair is, not an eyelash, not the least lash lost; every
   hair
Is, hair of the head, numbered.

Nay, what we had lighthanded left in surly the mere mould
Will have waked and have waxed and have walked with the
   wind what while we slept,
This side, that side hurling a heavyheaded hundredfold   *40*
What while we, while we slumbered.
O then, weary then why should we tread? O why are we so
   haggard at the heart, so care-coiled, care-killed, so fagged,
   so fashed, so cogged, so cumbered,
When the thing we freely forfeit is kept with fonder a care,
Fonder a care kept than we could have kept it, kept
Far with fonder a care (and we, we should have lost it) finer,
   fonder   *45*
A care kept.—Where kept? Do but tell us where kept,
   where.—
Yonder.—What high as that! We follow, now we follow.—
   Yonder, yes yonder, yonder,
Yonder.

12 *Ruck:* crease.   17 *Spare:* an echo of despair, but also meaning
spare yourself this mourning and there is a rare (spare) truth to
be told.   34 *beauty-in-the-ghost:* beauty of spirit.   42 *cogged:*
confused, deceived.   47 *Yonder:* in heaven.

William Butler Yeats   A Dialogue of Self and Soul

    I

    MY SOUL.

I summon to the winding ancient stairs;
Set all your mind upon the steep ascent,
Upon the broken, crumbling battlement,
Upon the breathless starlit air,
Upon the star that marks the hidden pole;   *5*
Fix every wandering thought upon
That quarter where all thought is done:
Who can distinguish darkness from the soul?

    MY SELF.

The consecrated blade upon my knees
Is Sato's ancient blade, still as it was,   *10*
Still razor-keen, still like a looking-glass
Unspotted by the centuries;
That flowering, silken, old embroidery, torn
From some court-lady's dress and round
The wooden scabbard bound and wound,   *15*
Can, tattered, still protect, faded adorn.

    MY SOUL.

Why should the imagination of a man
Long past his prime remember things that are

Emblematical of love and war?
Thing of ancestral night that can,   20
If but imagination scorn the earth
And intellect its wandering
To this and that and t' other thing,
Deliver from the crime of death and birth.

MY SELF.

Montashigi, third of his family, fashioned it   25
Five hundred years ago, about it lie
Flowers from I know not what embroidery—
Heart's purple—and all these I set
For emblems of the day against the tower
Emblematical of the night,   30
And claims as by a soldier's right
A charter to commit the crime once more.

MY SOUL.

Such fullness in that quarter overflows
And falls into the basin of the mind
That man is stricken deaf and dumb and blind,   35
For intellect no longer knows
Is from the *Ought,* or *Knower* from the *Known*—
That is to say, ascends to Heaven;
Only the dead can be forgiven;
But when I think of that my tongue's a stone.   40

2

MY SELF.

A living man is blind and drinks his drop.
What matter if the ditches are impure?
What matter if I live it all once more?
Endure that toil of growing up;
The ignominy of boyhood; the distress   45
Of boyhood changing into man;
The unfinished man and his pain
Brought face to face with his own clumsiness;
The finished man among his enemies?—
How in the name of Heaven can he escape   50
That defiling and disfigured shape
The mirror of malicious eyes
Casts upon his eyes until at last
He thinks that shape must be his shape?
And what's the good of an escape   55
If honor find him in the wintry blast?

I am content to live it all again
And yet again, if it be life to pitch
Into the frog-spawn of a blind man's ditch,
A blind man battering blind men;   60

Or into that most fecund ditch of all,
The folly that man does
Or must suffer, if he woos
A proud woman not kindred of his soul.

I am content to follow to its source   65
Every event in action or in thought;
Measure the lot; forgive myself the lot!
When such as I cast out remorse
So great a sweetness flows into the breast
We must laugh and we must sing,   70
We are blest by everything,
Everything we look upon is blest.

10 *Sato:* Junzo Sato gave a sword to Yeats in 1920; it was covered
with a piece of a Japanese lady's court dress. He was a fellow-
member of a secret society.

Robert Frost   The Witch of Coös

I stayed the night for shelter at a farm
Behind the mountain, with a mother and son,
Two old-believers. They did all the talking.

MOTHER. Folks think a witch who has familiar spirits
She could call up to pass a winter evening,   5
But won't, should be burned at the stake or something.
Summoning spirits isn't 'Button, button,
Who's got the button,' I would have them know.

SON. Mother can make a common table rear
And kick with two legs like an army mule.   10

MOTHER. And when I've done it, what good have I done?
Rather than tip a table for you, let me
Tell you what Ralle the Sioux Control once told me.
He said the dead had souls, but when I asked him
How could that be—I thought the dead were souls,   15
He broke my trance. Don't that make you suspicious
That there's something the dead are keeping back?
Yes, there's something the dead are keeping back.

SON. You wouldn't want to tell him what we have
Up attic, mother?   20

MOTHER. Bones—a skeleton.

SON. But the headboard of mother's bed is pushed
Against the attic door: the door is nailed.
It's harmless. Mother hears it in the night
Halting perplexed behind the barrier   25
Of door and headboard. Where it wants to get
Is back into the cellar where it came from.

MOTHER. We'll never let them, will we, son! We'll never!

SON. It left the cellar forty years ago
And carried itself like a pile of dishes   30
Up one flight from the cellar to the kitchen,
Another from the kitchen to the bedroom,
Another from the bedroom to the attic,
Right past both father and mother, and neither stopped it
Father had gone upstairs; mother was downstairs.   35
I was a baby: I don't know where I was.

MOTHER. The only fault my husband found with me—
I went to sleep before I went to bed,
Especially in winter when the bed
Might just as well be ice and the clothes snow.   40
The night the bones came up the cellar-stairs
Toffile had gone to bed alone and left me,
But left an open door to cool the room off
So as to sort of turn me out of it...
I was just coming to myself enough   45
To wonder where the cold was coming from,
When I heard Toffile upstairs in the bedroom
And thought I heard him downstairs in the cellar.
The board we had laid down to walk dry-shod on
When there was water in the cellar in spring   50
Struck the hard cellar bottom. And then someone
Began the stairs, two footsteps for each step,
The way a man with one leg and a crutch,
Or a little child, comes up. It wasn't Toffile:
It wasn't anyone who could be there.   55
The bulkhead double-doors were double-locked
And swollen tight and buried under snow.
The cellar windows were banked up with sawdust
And swollen tight and buried under snow.
It was the bones. I knew them—and good reason.   60
My first impulse was to get to the knob
And hold the door. But the bones didn't try
The door; they halted helpless on the landing,
Waiting for things to happen in their favor.
The faintest restless rustling ran all through them.   65
I never could have done the thing I did
If the wish hadn't been too strong in me
To see how they were mounted for this walk.
I had a vision of them put together
Not like a man, but like a chandelier.   70
So suddenly I flung the door wide on him.
A moment he stood balancing with emotion,
And all but lost himself. (A tongue of fire
Flashed out and licked along his upper teeth.
Smoke rolled inside the sockets of his eyes.)   75
Then he came at me with one hand outstretched,
The way he did in life once; but this time
I struck the hand off brittle on the floor,
And fell back from him on the floor myself.
The finger-pieces slid in all directions.   80

(Where did I see one of those pieces lately?
Hand me my button-box—it must be there.)
I sat up on the floor and shouted, 'Toffile,
It's coming up to you.' It had its choice
Of the door to the cellar or the hall.   85
It took the hall door for the novelty,
And set off briskly for so slow a thing,
Still going every which way in the joints, though,
So that it looked like lightning or a scribble,
From the slap I had just now given its hand.   90
I listened till it almost climbed the stairs
From the hall to the only finished bedroom,
Before I got up to do anything;
Then ran and shouted, 'Shut the bedroom door,
Toffile, for my sake!' 'Company?' he said,   95
'Don't make me get up; I'm too warm in bed.'
So lying forward weakly on the handrail
I pushed myself upstairs, and in the light
(The kitchen had been dark) I had to own
I could see nothing. 'Toffile, I don't see it.   100
It's with us in the room though. It's the bones.'
'What bones?' 'The cellar bones—out of the grave.'
That made him throw his bare legs out of bed
And sit up by me and take hold of me.
I wanted to put out the light and see   105
If I could see it, or else mow the room,
With our arms at the level of our knees,
And bring the chalk-pile down. 'I'll tell you what—
It's looking for another door to try.
The uncommonly deep snow has made him think   110
Of his old song, The Wild Colonial Boy,
He always used to sing along the tote-road.
He's after an open door to get out-doors.
Let's trap him with an open door up attic.'
Toffile agreed to that, and sure enough,   115
Almost the moment he was given an opening,
The steps began to climb the attic stairs.
I heard them. Toffile didn't seem to hear them.
'Quick!' I slammed to the door and held the knob,
'Toffile, get nails.' I made him nail the door shut,   120
And push the headboard of the bed against it.
Then we asked was there anything
Up attic that we'd ever want again.
The attic was less to us than the cellar.
If the bones liked the attic, let them have it.   125
Let them stay in the attic. When they sometimes
Come down the stairs at night and stand perplexed
Behind the door and headboard of the bed,
Brushing their chalky skull with chalky fingers,   130
With sounds like the dry rattling of a shutter,
That's what I sit up in the dark to say—
To no one any more since Toffile died.
Let them stay in the attic since they went there.

I promised Toffile to be cruel to them   135
For helping them be cruel once to him.

SON. We think they had a grave down in the cellar.

MOTHER. We know they had a grave down in the cellar.

SON. We never could find out whose bones they were.

MOTHER. Yes, we could too, son. Tell the truth for once   140
They were a man's his father killed for me.
I mean a man he killed instead of me.
The least I could do was to help dig their grave.
We were about it one night in the cellar.
Son knows the story: but 'twas not for him   145
To tell the truth, suppose the time had come.
Son looks surprised to see me end a lie
We'd kept all these years between ourselves
So as to have it ready for outsiders.
But tonight I don't care enough to lie—   150
I don't remember why I ever cared.
Toffile, if he were here, I don't believe
Could tell you why he ever cared himself . . .

She hadn't found the finger-bone she wanted
Among the buttons poured out in her lap.   155
I verified the name next morning: Toffile.
The rural letter-box said Toffile Lajway.

Robert Frost   West-running Brook

'Fred, where is north?'

                          'North? North is there, my love.
The brook runs west.'

                          'West-running Brook then call it.'
(West-running Brook men call it to this day.)
'What does it think it's doing running west
When all the other country brooks flow east   5
To reach the ocean? It must be the brook
Can trust itself to go by contraries
The way I can with you—and you with me—
Because we're—we're—I don't know what we are.
What are we?'

               'Young or new?'

                                    'We must be something.   10
We've said we two. Let's change that to we three.
As you and I are married to each other,
We'll both be married to the brook. We'll build
Our bridge across it, and the bridge shall be

Our arm thrown over it asleep beside it.   15
Look, look, it's waving to us with a wave
To let us know it hears me.'

                            'Why, my dear,
That wave's been standing off this jut of shore—'
(The black stream, catching on a sunken rock,
Flung backward on itself in one white wave,   20
And the white water rode the black forever,
Not gaining but not losing, like a bird
White feathers from the struggle of whose breast
Flecked the dark stream and flecked the darker pool
Below the point, and were at last driven wrinkled   25
In a white scarf against the far shore alders.)
'That wave's been standing off this jut of shore
Ever since rivers, I was going to say,
Were made in heaven. It wasn't waved to us.'

'It wasn't, yet it was. If not to you   30
It was to me—in an annunciation.'

'Oh, if you take it off to lady-land,
As't were the country of the Amazons
We men must see you to the confines of
And leave you there, ourselves forbid to enter,—   35
It is your brook! I have no more to say.'

'Yes, you have, too. Go on. You thought of something.'

'Speaking of contraries, see how the brook
In that white wave runs counter to itself.
It is from that in water we were from   40
Long, long before we were from any creature.
Here we, in our impatience of the steps,
Get back to the beginning of beginnings,
The stream of everything that runs away.
Some say existence like a Pirouot   45
And Pirouette, forever in one place,
Stands still and dances, but it runs away,
It seriously, sadly, runs away
To fill the abyss' void with emptiness.
It flows beside us in this water brook,   50
But it flows over us. It flows between us
To separate us for a panic moment.
It flows between us, over us, and *with* us.
And it is time, strength, tone, light, life and love—
The universal cataract of death   55
That spends to nothingness—and unresisted,
Save by some strange resistance in itself,
Not just a swerving, but a throwing back,
As if regret were in it and were sacred.
It has this throwing backward on itself   60
So that the fall of most of it is always
Raising a little, sending up a little.
Our life runs down in sending up the clock.

The brook runs down in sending up our life.
The sun runs down in sending up the brook 65
And there is something sending up the sun.
It is this backward motion toward the source,
Against the stream, that most we see ourselves in,
The tribute of the current to the source.
It is from this in nature we are from. 70
It is most us.'

        'Today will be the day
You said so.'

        'No, today will be the day
You said the brook was called West-running Brook.'

'Today will be the day of what we both said.'

VERSE DRAMA

If poets have often used the formal and informal qualities of drama, dramatists, in turn, have from the earliest days of playwriting used the techniques of poetry. Poetic drama (or verse drama) is the title we give to those plays that employ poetry as the principal medium of language. We have already noted that dramatic poetry may, at times, use speakers' names. In verse drama, the playwright usually provides his written script with stage directions, information as to setting, time, and place. The essence of verse drama, as of any drama (closet drama excepted), is that there is a presentation by actors for spectators; that deeds are rendered by gestures and by words.

Classic drama had its beginning in religious ritual; with the disappearance in western Europe of even a reading of the drama, manuscripts were preserved in libraries and monastic schools. But the instinct for drama remained—that desire to observe a representation by words and gesture of an "action" (Aristotle called drama an "imitated human action").

English drama began to develop in about the ninth century, stemming from the rituals of the Christian church. First there developed the mystery plays, dramas that dealt with stories from the bible; additional materials were found in the lives of the saints, and this type of play was called the miracle play. More allegorical than these forms, however, was the morality play, a play that depicted the spiritual conflicts between good and evil through the presentation of abstract virtues and vices.

By the beginning of the sixteenth century the acting of plays became very popular, and new subjects—primarily secular materials—and kinds of plays were introduced. Noblemen and finally the crown itself became the patrons of the various professional acting companies that began to form.

With the construction of public theaters, an influx into London of professional writers for the stage, and the seemingly limitless public appetite for plays, the period of Elizabethan drama began. The greatest dramatist of the period is of course William Shakespeare, but one should remember that at least thirty years before Shakespeare's plays were produced, the play "Gorboduc" (1562) introduced into English drama the use of blank verse as a substitute for the rhymed doggerel that was customary in the earlier native drama. Blank verse (iambic pentameter lines without rhyme) has generally been regarded as the most natural, flexible, and suitable meter for English poetic drama.

Playwrights during the Elizabethan period favored dramas that mixed verse and prose, a mixture that allowed for greater variety. Hence, in passages depicting philosophical ideas, speeches by men of high rank, and dialogue calling for an elevation or heightening of language, blank verse was used. Comic and light parts, dialect, speeches depicting madness, on the other hand, were usually rendered in prose. Couplets were sometimes used, often to mark the close of a scene, or sometimes to emphasize a highly stylized speech, a speech that the poet wanted to call attention to for its unnaturalness.

In 1642 the Puritans closed the English theaters; when they opened again in 1660 the influence of the Elizabethan Ben Jonson led Restoration and eighteenth-century dramatists to emphasize those qualities we associate with neoclassicism. There was a revival of interest in the classical "rules," and the dominant form in the heroic drama—a play usually about a conflict between love and honor—was the heroic couplet, a pair of rhymed iambic pentameter lines. (Chaucer was the first English poet to use the heroic couplet.) Comedies, erotic and sophisticated comedies of manners, were at times written in couplets, at times in blank verse.

The verse dramas of the Romantic period were closet dramas —plays written to be read rather than acted. In our own century, we need but think of our great dramatists to realize that ours is a prose drama. George Bernard Shaw, John Galsworthy, Lillian Hellman, Tennessee Williams, Arthur Miller, Eugene O'Neill are among our grestest dramatists; each has used prose as his medium. Nevertheless, great poets of the twentieth century have attempted to revive the tradition of the verse drama; and this tradition has been enriched by the plays of W. B. Yeats, T. S. Eliot, Christopher Fry, Archibald MacLeish, and Robert Lowell.

William Butler Yeats   Purgatory

PERSONS IN THE PLAY

A Boy   An Old Man

Scene.—A ruined house and a bare tree in the background.

BOY. Half-door, hall door,
    Hither and thither day and night,
    Hill or hollow, shouldering this pack,

Hearing you talk.
OLD MAN   Study that house.   5
  I think about its jokes and stories;
  I try to remember what the butler
  Said to a drunken gamekeeper
  In mid-October, but I cannot.
  If I cannot, none living can.   10
  Where are the jokes and stories of a house,
  Its threshold gone to patch a pig-sty?
BOY. So you have come this path before?
OLD MAN. The moonlight falls upon the path,
  The shadow of a cloud upon the house,   15
  And that's symbolical; study that tree,
  What is it like?
BOY.   A silly old man.
OLD MAN. It's like—no matter what it's like.
  I saw it a year ago stripped bare as now,   20
  So I chose a better trade.
  I saw it fifty years ago
  Before the thunderbolt had riven it,
  Green leaves, ripe leaves, leaves thick as butter,
  Fat, greasy life. Stand there and look,   25
  Because there is somebody in that house.
       [The Boy puts down pack and stands in the doorway.
BOY. There's nobody here.
OLD MAN.   There's somebody there.
BOY. The floor is gone, the windows gone,
  And where there should be roof there's sky,   30
  And here's a bit of an egg-shell thrown
  Out of a jackdaw's nest.
OLD MAN   But there are some
  That do not care what's gone, what's left:
  The souls in Purgatory that come back   35
  To habitations and familiar spots.
BOY. Your wits are out again.
OLD MAN.   Re-live
  Their transgressions, and that not once
  But many times; they know at last   40
  The consequence of those transgressions
  Whether upon others or upon themselves;
  Upon others, others may bring help,
  For when the consequence is at an end
  The dream must end; if upon themselves,   45
  There is no help but in themselves
  And in the mercy of God.
BOY.   I have had enough!
  Talk to the jackdaws, if talk you must.
OLD MAN. Stop! Sit there upon that stone.   50
  That is the house where I was born.
BOY. The big old house that was burnt down?
OLD MAN. My mother that was your grand-dam owned it,
  This scenery and this countryside,
  Kennel and stable, horse and hound—   55

She had a horse at the Curragh, and there met
My father, a groom in a training stable,
Looked at him and married him.
Her mother never spoke to her again,
And she did right.   60
BOY.   What's right and wrong?
My grand-dad got the girl and the money.
OLD MAN. Looked at him and married him,
And he squandered everything she had.
She never knew the worst, because   65
She died in giving birth to me,
But now she knows it all, being dead.
Great people lived and died in this house;
Magistrates, colonels, members of Parliament,
Captains and Governors, and long ago   70
Men that had fought at Aughrim and the Boyne.
Some that had gone on Government work
To London or to India came home to die,
Or came from London every spring
To look at the may-blossom in the park.   75
They had loved the trees that he cut down
To pay what he had lost at cards
Or spent on horses, drink and women;
Had loved the house, had loved all
The intricate passages of the house,   80
But he killed the house; to kill a house
Where great men grew up, married, died,
I here declare a capital offence.
BOY. My God, but you had luck! Grand clothes,
And maybe a grand horse to ride.   85
OLD MAN. That he might keep me upon his level
He never sent me to school, but some
Half-loved me for my half of her:
A gamekeeper's wife taught me to read,
A Catholic curate taught me Latin.   90
There were old books and books made fine
By eighteenth-century French binding, books
Modern and ancient, books by the ton.
BOY. What education have you given me?
OLD MAN. I gave the education that befits   95
A bastard that a pedlar got
Upon a tinker's daughter in a ditch.
When I had come to sixteen years old
My father burned down the house when drunk.
BOY. But that is my age, sixteen years old,   100
At the Puck Fair.
OLD MAN.   And everything was burnt;
Books, library, all were burnt.
BOY. Is what I have heard upon the road the truth,
That you killed him in the burning house?   105
OLD MAN. There's nobody here but our two selves?
BOY. Nobody, Father.
OLD MAN.   I stuck him with a knife,

That knife that cuts my dinner now,
And after that I left him in the fire.   110
They dragged him out, somebody saw
The knife-wound but could not be certain
Because the body was all black and charred.
Then some that were his drunken friends
Swore they would put me upon trial,   115
Spoke of quarrels, a threat I had made.
The gamekeeper gave me some old clothes,
I ran away, worked here and there
Till I became a pedlar on the roads,
No good trade, but good enough   120
Because I am my father's son,
Because of what I did or may do.
Listen to the hoof-beats! Listen, listen!
BOY. I cannot hear a sound.
OLD MAN.   Beat! Beat!   125
This night is the anniversary
Of my mother's wedding night,
Or of the night wherein I was begotten.
My father is riding from the public-house,
A whisky-bottle under his arm.   130
                    [*A window is lit showing a young girl.*
Look at the window; she stands there
Listening, the servants are all in bed,
She is alone, he has stayed late
Bragging and drinking in the public-house.
BOY. There's nothing but an empty gap in the wall.   135
You have made it up. No, you are mad!
You are getting madder every day.
OLD MAN. It's louder now because he rides
Upon a gravelled avenue
All grass to-day. The hoof-beat stops,   140
He has gone to the other side of the house,
Gone to the stable, put the horse up.
She has gone down to open the door.
This night she is no better than her man
And does not mind that he is half drunk,   145
She is mad about him. They mount the stairs,
She brings him into her own chamber.
And that is the marriage-chamber now.
The window is dimly lit again.

Do not let him touch you! It is not true   150
That drunken men cannot beget,
And if he touch he must beget
And you must bear his murderer.
Deaf! Both deaf! If I should throw
A stick or a stone they would not hear;   155
And that's a proof my wits are out.
But there's a problem: she must live
Through everything in exact detail,
Driven to it by remorse, and yet

Can she renew the sexual act   160
And find no pleasure in it, and if not,
If pleasure and remorse must both be there,
Which is the greater?
                          I lack schooling.
Go fetch Tertullian; he and I   165
Will ravel all that problem out
Whilst those two lie upon the mattress
Begetting me.
                    Come back! Come back!
And so you thought to slip away,   170
My bag of money between your fingers,
And that I could not talk and see!
You have been rummaging in the pack.
                    [*The light in the window has faded out.*
BOY. You never gave me my right share.
OLD MAN. And had I given it, young as you are,   175
    You would have spent it upon drink.
BOY. What if I did? I had a right
    To get it and spend it as I chose.
OLD MAN. Give me that bag and no more words.
BOY. I will not.   180
OLD MAN.   I will break your fingers.
        [*They struggle for the bag. In the struggle it drops,
        scattering the money. The Old Man staggers but
        does not fall. They stand looking at each other. The
        window is lit up. A man is seen pouring whiskey
        into a glass.*
BOY. What if I killed you? You killed my grand-dad,
    Because you were young and he was old.
    Now I am young and you are old.
OLD MAN [*staring at window*]. Better-looking, those sixteen
    years—   185
BOY. What are you muttering?
OLD MAN.   Younger—and yet
    She should have known he was not her kind.
BOY. What are you saying? Out with it! [*Old Man points to
    window.*
    My God! The window is lit up   190
    And somebody stands there, although
    The floorboards are all burnt away.
OLD MAN. The window is lit up because my father
    Has come to find a glass for his whiskey.
    He leans there like some tired beast.   195
BOY. A dead, living, murdered man!
OLD MAN. 'Then the bride-sleep fell upon Adam':
    Where did I read those words?
                          And yet
    There's nothing leaning in the window   200
    But the impression upon my mother's mind;
    Being dead she is alone in her remorse.
BOY. A body that was a bundle of old bones
    Before I was born. Horrible! Horrible!   [*He covers his eyes.*

OLD MAN. That beast there would know nothing, being noth-
    ing,   205
    If I should kill a man under the window
    He would not even turn his head.   [*He stabs the Boy.*
    My father and my son on the same jack-knife!
    That finishes—there—there—there—
        [*He stabs again and again. The window grows dark.*
    'Hush-a-bye, thy father's a knight,
    'Hush-a-bye baby, thy father's a knight,   210
    Thy mother a lady, lovely and bright.'
    No, that is something that I read in a book,
    And if I sing it must be to my mother,
    And I lack rhyme.
      [*The stage has grown dark except where the tree stands
        in white light.*
                        Study that tree.   215
    It stands there like a purified soul,
    All cold, sweet, glistening light.
    Dear mother, the window is dark again,
    But you are in the light because
    I finished all that consequence.   220
    I killed that lad because had he grown up
    He would have struck a woman's fancy
    Begot, and passed pollution on.
    I am a wretched foul old man
    And therefore harmless. When I have stuck   225
    This old jack-knife into a sod
    And pulled it out all bright again,
    And picked up all the money that he dropped,
    I'll to a distant place, and there
    Tell my old jokes among new men.   230
        [*He cleans the knife and begins to pick up money.*
    Hoof-beats! Dear God,
    How quickly it returns—beat—beat—!
    Her mind cannot hold up that dream.
    Twice a murderer and all for nothing,
    And she must animate that dead night   235
    Not once but many times!
                O God,
    Release my mother's soul from its dream!
    Mankind can do no more. Appease
    The misery of the living and the remorse of the dead.   240

    THE END

PART V

Recurrent Strains and Other Occasions

THE ALBA AND THE AUBADE

The alba ("dawn") is a Provençal lament over the coming of the dawn which forces lovers to part. Popular during the medieval period, and inspired in part by Ovid, the tradition of the alba was carried forward by the troubadours. The word "alba" originally ended each refrain of a poem, a convention that may have developed from the night watchman's announcing the approach of dawn. One anonymous alba protests the coming daylight in its refrain in the following manner: "Ah God! Ah God! that dawn should come so soon!" A few early albas were addressed to the Virgin and were religious.

The aubade, related to French forms, is also a morning song, but by contrast it is joyous, a morning serenade, a welcoming of a new day. Today, poets and critics often use the word "aubade" to refer to any poem that concerns itself with the forthcoming of the new day. The distinction between the two moods, however, makes the terms "alba" and "aubade" useful when one reads early poetry, and hence, the distinction is worth preserving.

Geoffrey Chaucer
> FROM *Troilus and Criseyde*
> (BOOK III, LINES 1450–1470)

"O cruel day, accusour of the joie
That nyght and love han stole and faste iwryen,
Acorsed be thi comyng into Troye,
For every bore hath oon of thi bryghte yën!
Envyous day, what list the so to spien?   5
What hastow lost, why sekestow this place,
Ther God thi light so quenche, for his grace?

"Allas! what have thise loveris the agylt,
Dispitous day? Thyn be the peyne of helle!
For many a lovere hastow slayn, and wilt;   10
Thy pourynge in wol nowher lat hem dwelle.
What profrestow thi light here for to selle?
Go selle it hem that smale selys grave;
We wol the nought, us nedeth no day have."

And ek the sonne, Titan, gan he chide,   15
And seyde, "O fool, wel may men the dispise,
That hast the dawyng al nyght by thi syde,
And suffrest hire so soone up fro the rise,
For to disese loveris in this wyse.
What! holde youre bed ther, thow, and ek thi Morwe!   20
I bidde God, so yeve yow bothe sorwe!"

title: Troilus has finally consummated his burning desire for
Criseyde. It is now morning and he must depart. He is the
speaker in these lines.   *2 iwryen:* concealed.   *4 bore:* hole.
oon: one.   *yën:* eyes   *5 the:* thee.   *8 agylt:* offended.   *9
Dispitous:* unmerciful.   *11 pourynge:* peeping.   *12 What profrestow:* why do you proffer.   *13 selys:* seals.   *grave:* engrave.
14 wol: want.   *15 ek:* also.   *19 disease:* discomfort.   *21 yeve:*
give.

William Shakespeare
> FROM *Romeo and Juliet*

JULIET.   Wilt thou be gone? it is not yet near day:
           It was the nightingale and not the lark,
           That pierc'd the fearful hollow of thine ear;
           Nightly she sings on yon pomegranate tree:
           Believe me, love, it was the nightingale.

ROMEO.   It was the lark, the herald of the morn,
             No nightingale: look, love, what envious streaks
             Do lace the severing clouds in yonder east:

Night's candles are burnt out, and jocund day
Stands tiptoe on the misty mountain tops.   *10*

William Shakespeare Song
    FROM *Cymbeline*

Hark, hark! the lark at heaven's gate sings,
    And Phoebus 'gins arise,
His steeds to water at those springs
    On chaliced flowers that lies;
And winking Mary-buds begin   *5*
    To ope their golden eyes,
With every thing that pretty is,
    My lady sweet, arise!
        Arise, arise!

Louis MacNeice   Aubade

Having bitten on life like a sharp apple
Or, playing it like a fish, been happy,

Having felt with fingers that the sky is blue,
What have we after that to look forward to?

Not the twilight of the gods but a precise dawn   *5*
Of sallow and grey bricks, and newsboys crying war.

William Empson   Aubade

Hours before dawn we were woken by the quake.
My house was on a cliff. The thing could take
Bookloads off the shelves, break bottles in a row.
Then the long pause and then the bigger shake.
It seemed the best thing to be up and go.   *5*

And for too large for my feet to step by.
I hoped that various buildings were brought low.
The heart of standing is you cannot fly.

It seemed quite safe till she got up and dressed.
The guarded tourist makes the guide the test.   *10*
Then I said The Garden? Laughing she said No.
Taxi for her and for me healthy rest.
It seemed the best thing to be up and go.

The language problem but you have to try.
Some solid ground for lying could she show?   *15*
The heart of standing is you cannot fly.

None of these deaths were her point at all.
The thing was that being woken he would bawl
And finding her not in earshot he would know.
I tried saying Half an Hour to pay this call.   20
It seemed the best thing to be up and go.

I slept, and blank as that I would yet lie.
Till you have seen what a threat holds below
The heart of standing is you cannot fly.

Tell me again about Europe and her pains,   25
Who's tortured by the drought, who by the rains.
Glut me with floods where only the swine can row
Who cuts his throat and let him count his gains.
It seemed the best thing to be up and go.

A bedshift flight to a Far Eastern sky.   30
Only the same war on a stronger toe.
The heart of standing is you cannot fly.

Tell me more quickly what I lost by this,
Or tell me with less drama what they miss
Who call no die a god for a good throw,   35
Who say after two aliens had one kiss
It seemed the best thing to be up and go.

But as to risings, I can tell you why.
It is on contradiction that they grow.
It seemed the best thing to be up and go.   40
Up was the heartening and the strong reply.
The heart of standing is we cannot fly.

Richard Wilbur   A Late Aubade

You could be sitting now in a carrel
Turning some liver-spotted page,
Or rising in an elevator-cage
Toward Ladies' Apparel.

You could be planting a raucous bed   5
Of Salvia, in rubber gloves,
Or lunching through a screed of someone's loves
With pitying head,

Or making some unhappy setter
Heel, or listening to a bleak   10
Lecture on Schoenberg's serial technique,
Isn't this better?

Think of all the time you are not
Wasting, and would not care to waste,
Such things, thank God, not being to your taste.   15
Think what a lot

Of time, by woman's reckoning,
You've saved, and so may spend on this,

You who had rather lie in bed and kiss
Than anything.   20

It's almost noon, you say? If so,
Time flies, and I need not rehearse
The rosebuds-theme of centuries of verse.
If you *must* go,

Wait for a while, then slip downstairs   25
And bring us up some chilled white wine,
And some blue cheese, and crackers, and some fine
Ruddy-skinned pears.

7 *screed:* a long, tiresome noisy speech or harangue.

CARPE DIEM

The phrase *carpe diem* means "seize the day," and is from
Horace. The term is applied to lyric poems in order to express
an attitude that one should enjoy the present moment. Especially common as a theme in sixteenth- and seventeenth-
century English love poetry, *carpe diem* poems usually implore
the young mistress to take advantage of her youth and beauty
while she still has it.

Thomas Campion   My Sweetest Lesbia

My sweetest Lesbia, let us live and love,
And though the sager sort our deeds reprove,
Let us not weigh them. Heaven's great lamps do dive
Into their west, and straight again revive,
But soon as once set is our little light,   5
Then must we sleep one ever-during night.

If all would lead their lives in love like me,
Then bloody swords and armor should not be,
No drum not trumpet peaceful sleeps should move,
Unless alarm came from the camp of love.   10
But fools do live and waste their little light,
And seek with pain their ever during night.

When timely death my life and fortune ends,
Let not my hearse be vexed with mourning friends,
But let all lovers, rich in triumph, come   15
And with sweet pastimes grace my happy tomb;
And Lesbia, close up thou my little light,
And crown with love my ever-during night.

3 *lamps:* the stars.

Anonymous   Drink Today

FROM JOHN FLETCHER's *The Bloody Brother*

Drink today, and drown all sorrow;
You shall perhaps not do it tomorrow.
Best, while you have it, use your breath;
There is no drinking after death.

Wine works the heart up, wakes the wit,   5
There is no cure 'gainst age but it;
It helps the headache, cough, and tisic,
And is for all diseases physic.

Then let us swill, boys, for our health;
Who drinks well, loves the commonwealth.   10
And he that will to bed go sober
Falls with the leaf still in October.

title: John Fletcher collaborated with a number of other writers in
preparing *The Bloody Brother;* hence, the authorship of this poem
is not certain.   *7 tisic:* phthisic, consumption.

Robert Herrick   To the Virgins, to Make Much of Time

Gather ye rosebuds while ye may,
    Old time is still a-flying,
And this same flower that smiles to-day,
    To-morrow will be dying.

The glorious lamp of heaven, the sun,   5
    The higher he's a-getting,
The sooner will his race be run,
    And nearer he's to setting.

That age is best which is the first,
    When youth and blood are warmer;   10
But being spent, the worse, and worst
    Times still succeed the former.

Then be not coy, but use your time,
    And while we may, go marry;
For having lost but once your prime,   15
    You may for ever tarry.

Thomas Carew   Persuasions to Enjoy

If the quick spirits in your eye
Now languish and anon must die,
If every sweet and every grace
Must fly from that forsaken face,

    Then, Celia, let us reap our joys   5
    Ere Time such goodly fruit destroys.

Or, if that golden fleece must grow
For ever free from agèd snow,
If those bright suns must know no shade,
Nor your fresh beauties ever fade,   10
    Then fear not, Celia, to bestow
    What still being gathered, still must grow.

Thus either Time his sickle brings
In vain, or else in vain his wings.

Andrew Marvell   To His Coy Mistress

Had we but world enough, and time,
This coyness, lady, were no crime.
We would sit down, and think which way
To walk, and pass our long love's day.
Thou by the Indian Ganges' side   5
Shouldst rubies find; I by the tide
Of Humber would complain. I would
Love you ten years before the Flood,
And you should, if you please, refuse
Till the conversion of the Jews.   10
My vegetable love should grow
Vaster than empires, and more slow;
And hundred years should go to praise
Thine eyes and on thy forehead gaze,
Two hundred to adore each breast,   15
But thirty thousand to the rest:
An age at least to every part,
And the last age should show your heart.
For, lady, you deserve this state,
Nor would I love at lower rate.   20
    But at my back I always hear
Time's wingèd chariot hurrying near;
And yonder all before us lie
Deserts of vast eternity.
Thy beauty shall no more be found,   25
Nor in thy marble vault shall sound
My echoing song; then worms shall try
That long preserved virginity,
And your quaint honor turn to dust,
And into ashes all my lust.   30
The grave's a fine and private place,
But none, I think, do there embrace.
    Now, therefore, while the youthful hue
Sits on thy skin like morning dew,
And while thy willing soul transpires   35
At every pore with instant fires,
Now let us sport us while we may,

And now, like am'rous birds of prey,
Rather at once our time devour
Than languish in his slow-chapped power.   40
Let us roll all our strength and all
Our sweetness up into one ball,
And tear our pleasures with rough strife
Thorough the iron gates of life.
Thus, though we cannot make our sun   45
Stand still, yet we will make him run.

19 state: stately procedure.   *29 quaint:* overfastidious.   *40 slow-chapped:* slow-jawed, i.e., slowly devouring.   *46 run:* i.e., run to catch up with us.

Robert Frost   Carpe Diem

Age saw two quiet children
Go loving by at twilight
He knew not whether homeward,
Or outward from the village,
Or (chimes were ringing) churchward.   5
He waited (they were strangers)
Till they were out of hearing
To bid them both be happy.
'Be happy, happy, happy,
And seize the day of pleasure.'   10
The age-long theme is Age's.
'Twas Age imposed on poems
Their gather-roses burden
To warn against the danger
That overtaken lovers   15
From being overflooded
With happiness should have it
And yet not know they have it.
But bid life seize the present?
It lives less in the present   20
Than in the future always,
And less in both together
Than in the past. The present
Is too much for the senses,
Too crowding, too confusing—   25
Too present to imagine.

THE COMPLAINT AND THE LAMENT

The complaint is a lyric poem that was popular in the Middle Ages and during the Renaissance. In the complaint, the poet through monologue complains upon the lack of responsiveness of his mistress; or he complains about his lot; or he bewails the state of the world. Having expressed his mood, the causes, and the possible remedies, the speaker usually concludes with an appeal—often it is to the unresponsive woman—for help.

The variety in subject matter and length of complaints may be seen in such works as Thomas Hoccleve's (c. 1369–c. 1450) "Complaint"; Thomas Sackville's "Complaint of Henry Duke of Buckingham," which appeared in the 1536 edition of the *Mirror for Magistrates;* and Richard Barnfield's "The Complaint of Poetry for the Death of Liberality" (1598). Complaints that are still read and enjoyed by many students of English literature are the nine written by Edmund Spenser, which he gathered in his book *Complaints* (1591), and Chaucer's "The Complaint of Chaucer to His Purse."

By contrast, the lament, is usually very personal, intense, and sad. The lament is more tragic and painful than the complaint. Among the best known examples of the lament are "The Lamentations of Jeremiah" and the Anglo-Saxon "Deor"; a more recent example is Shelley's "Lament."

Anonymous (ca. 900)
    Deor

Weland from wounds underwent hardship,
the cunning kemp bore cares full great,
he had for solace sorrow and longing,
winter-cold want; woe oft enough
he found, after Nithad laid fetters on him,   5
bonds of lithe sinew on the better man.
That now is gone; this too will go.

Beadohild was less for her brother's sake
than sake of herself so sore at heart:
full well was she aware of that,   10
that she was with child; choose she dared not
to think it through in her thoughts to the end.
That now is gone; this too will go.

We know that Mæthild's moans grew boundless,
grievous waxed the plaints of Geat's lady: 15
that ruthless love bereft her of all sleep.
That now is gone; this too will go.

Theodric held for thirty winters
Mæingaburg; to many that was known.
That now is gone; this too will go.   20

We asked and learned Ermanaric's
wolfishness of thought; wide shires he held
of the Gothic realm; he was grim, that lord,
in ween or woe; they wished much to see   25

that king in his realm overcome and fallen.
That now is gone; this too will go.

The man that is wretched sits bereft of gladness,
his soul darkens, it seems to him
the number of his hardships is never-ending;   30
he can bethink him, then, that through this world
God in his wisdom gives and withholds:
to many a man he metes out honor,
fame and fortune; their fill, to some, of woes.
That I will say, of myself to speak,   35
that the Heodenings had me a while for scop,
the king held me dear; Deor they called me.
For many winters my master was kind,
my hap was high, till Heorrenda now,
a good man in song, was given the land   40
that my lord before had lent to me.
That now is gone; this too will go.

Kemp Malone, Translator

1 Weland: mythical smith of Germanic legends; cf. Vulcan.   2
cunning kemp: skilled champion.   *7 this:* the poet's misfortunes
described at close of the poem.   *16 ruthless love:* alludes to a
story told in the Scandinavian ballad of Gaute and Magnhild. The
"ruthless love" is a water-demon's.   *25 ween:* expectation.   *36
scop:* bard or minstrel.   *39 Heorrenda:* most famous of the minstrels in Germanic legend.

Henry Howard, Earl of Surrey   A Complaint by Night
of the Lover Not Beloved

Alas, so all things now do hold their peace,
Heaven and earth disturbëd in nothing;
The beasts, the air, the birds their song do cease,
The nightë's chair the stars about doth bring;
Calm is the sea, the waves work less and less.   5
So am not I, whom love, alas, doth wring,
Bringing before my face the great increase
Of my desires, whereat I weep and sing
In joy and woe, as in a doubtful ease.
For my sweet thoughts sometime do pleasure bring,   10
But by and by the cause of my disease
Gives me pang that inwardly doth sting,
When that I think what grief it is again
To live and lack the thing should rid my pain.

EPITHALAMION

An epithalamion is a poem usually, though not always, of a
solemn nature, written to celebrate a marriage. The biblical

Song of Solomon and Edmund Spenser's "Epithalamion" (1595) are two of the better known examples of the type. Spenser's "Prothalamion"—he coined the word—is also a marriage song, commissioned by the Earl of Worcester for the marriage of his two daughters. But Spenser's "Epithalamion," written to celebrate his own marriage, is the greater of his two marriage poems. In twenty-three strophes, Spenser's great poem registers some twenty hours of an Irish day. Its greatness, as one critic observed, may be seen in the fact that no matter what codes of conduct come and go, the "Epithalamion" always remains in excellent taste.

Edmund Spenser   Epithalamion

Ye learned sisters which have oftentimes
Beene to me ayding, others to adorne
Whom ye thought worthy of your gracefull rymes,
That even the greatest did not greatly scorne
To heare theyr names sung in your simple layes,   5
But joyed in theyr prayse
(And when ye list your owne mishaps to mourne,
Which death or love or fortune's wreck did rayse,
Your string could soon to sadder tenor turne,
And teach the woods and waters to lament   10
Your dolefull dreriment),
Now lay those sorrowfull complaints aside,
And, having all your heads with girland crownd,
Helpe me mine owne love's prayses to resound,
Ne let the same of any be envide!   15
So Orpheus did for his owne bride;
So I unto my selfe alone will sing:
The woods shall to me answer and my Eccho ring.

Early, before the world's light-giving lampe
His golden beame upon the hils doth spred,   20
Having disperst the night's unchearefull dampe,
Doe ye awake, and with fresh lusty-hed
Go to the bowre of my beloved love,
My truest turtledove!
Bid her awake; for Hymen is awake   25
And long since ready forth his maske to move,
With his bright Tead that flames with many a flake,
And many a bachelor to waite on him,
In theyr fresh garments trim!
Bid her awake therefore and soone her dight,   30
For lo! the wished day is come at last,
That shall for al the paynes and sorrowes past
Pay to her usury of long delight!
And whylest she doth her dight,
Doe ye to her of joy and solace sing,   35
That all the woods may answer and your eccho ring!

Bring with you all the Nymphes that you can heare,
Both of the rivers and the forrests greene
And of the sea that neighbours to her neare,
Al with gay girlands goodly wel beseene.   40
And let them also with them bring in hand
Another gay girlánd
For my fayre love of lillyes and of roses,
Bound truelove-wize with a blew silke ribánd.
And let them make great store of bridale poses,   45
And let them eeke bring store of other flowers
To deck the bridale bowers.
And let the ground whereas her foot shall tread,
For feare the stones her tender foot should wrong,
Be strewed with fragrant flowers all along,   50
And diapred lyke the discolored mead.
Which done, doe at her chamber dore awayt,
For she will waken strayt,
The whiles doe ye this song unto her sing:
The woods shall to you answer and your Echo ring.   55

Ye Nymphes of Mulla, which with carefull heed
The silver scaly trouts doe tend full well
And greedy pikes which use therein to feed
(Those trouts and pikes all others doo excell),
And ye likewise which keepe the rushy lake   60
Where none doo fishes take,
Bynd up the locks the which hang scatterd light,
And in his waters which your mirror make
Behold your faces as the christall bright,
That when you come whereas my love doth lie,   65
No blemish she may spie.
And eke ye lightfoot mayds which keepe the dere
That on the hoary mountayne use to towre,
And the wylde wolves which seeke them to devoure
With your steele darts doo chace from comming neer,   70
Be also present heere
To helpe to decke her and to help to sing,
That all the woods may answer and your eccho ring.

Wake now, my love, awake, for it is time;
The Rosy Morne long since left Tithone's bed,   75
All ready to her silver coche to clyme,
And Phoebus gins to shew his glorious hed.
Hark how the cheerefull birds to chaunt theyr laies
And carroll of love's praise.
The merry Larke hir mattins sings aloft,   80
The thrush replyes, the Mavis descant playes,
The Ouzell shrills, the Ruddock warbles soft,
So goodly all agree with sweet consent
To this daye's merriment.
Ah! my deere love, why doe ye sleepe thus long,   85
When meeter were that ye should now awake,
T'awayt the comming of your joyous make,
And hearken to the birds' love-learned song,

The deawy leaves among?
For they of joy and pleasance to you sing,   90
That all the woods them answer and theyr eccho ring.

My love is now awake out of her dreame,
And her fayre eyes, like stars that dimmed were
With darksome cloud, now shew theyr goodly beams
More bright than Hesperus his head doth rere.   95
Come now, ye damzels, daughters of delight,
Helpe quickly her to dight!
But first come ye, fayre Houres, which were begot
In Jove's sweet paradice, of Day and Night,
Which doe the seasons of the yeare allot,   100
And al that ever in this world is fayre
Do make and still repayre.
And ye three handmayds of the Cyprian Queene,
The which doe still adorne her beautie's pride,
Helpe to addorne my beautifullest bride!   105
And as ye her array, still throw betweene
Some graces to be seene;
And, as ye use to Venus, to her sing,
The whiles the woods shal answer and your eccho ring.

Now is my love all ready forth to come.   110
Let all virgins therefore well awayt;
And ye fresh boyes, that tend upon her groome,
Prepare your selves, for he is comming strayt.
Set all your things in seemely good aray,
Fit for so joyfull day,   115
The joyfulst day that ever sunne did see!
Faire Sun, shew forth thy favourable ray,
And let thy lifull heat not fervent be,
For feare of burning her sunshyny face,
Her beauty to disgrace.   120
O fayrest Phoebus, father of the Muse,
If ever I did honour thee aright,
Or sing the thing that mote thy mind delight,
Doe not thy servant's simple boone refuse,
But let this day, let this one day be myne—   125
Let all the rest be thine!
Then I thy soverayne prayses loud wil sing,
That all the woods shal answer and theyr eccho ring.

Harke how the Minstrels gin to shrill aloud
Their merry Musick that resouds from far,   130
The pipe, the tabor, and the trembling Croud,
That well agree withouten breach or jar.
But most of all the Damzels doe delite,
When they their tymbrels smyte,
And thereunto doe daunce and carrol sweet,   135
That all the sences they doe ravish quite,
The whyles the boyes run up and downe the street,
Crying aloud with strong confused noyce,
As if it were one voyce.

"Hymen, Iö Hymen, Hymen!" they do shout,   140
That even to the heavens theyr shouting shrill
Doth reach, and all the firmament doth fill;
To which the people, standing all about,
As in approvance doe thereto applaud,
And loud advaunce her laud,   145
And evermore they "Hymen, Hymen" sing,
That al the woods them answer and theyr eccho ring.

Loe, where she comes along with portly pace,
Lyke Phoebe, from her chamber of the East,
Arysing forth to run her mighty race,   150
Clad all in white, that seemes a virgin best.
So well it her beseemes that ye would weene
Some angell she had beene.
Her long loose yellow locks lyke golden wyre,
Sprinckled with perle, and perling flowres atweene,   155
Doe lyke a golden mantle her attyre,
And being crowned with a girland greene,
Seeme lyke some mayden Queene.
Her modest eyes, abashed to behold
So many gazers as on her do stare,   160
Upon the lowly ground affixed are;
Ne dare lift up her countenance too bold,
But blush to heare her prayses sung so loud,
So farre from being proud.
Nathlesse doe ye still loud her prayses sing,   165
That all the woods may answer and your eccho ring.
Tell me, ye merchants' daughters, did ye see
So fayre a creature in your towne before,
So sweet, so lovely, and so mild as she,
Adornd with beautye's grace and vertue's store?   170
Her goodly eyes lyke Saphyres shining bright,
Her forehead yvory white,
Her cheekes lyke apples which the sun hath rudded,
Her lips lyke cherryes charming men to byte,
Her brest like a bowle of creame uncrudded,   175
Her paps lyke lyllies budded,
Her snowie necke lyke to a marble towre,
And all her body like a pallace fayre,
Ascending uppe with many a stately stayre,
To honor's seat and chastitie's sweet bowre.   180
Why stand ye still, ye virgins, in amaze
Upon her so to gaze,
Whiles ye forget your former lay to sing,
To which the woods did answer and your eccho ring?

But if ye saw that which no eyes can see,   185
The inward beauty of her lively spright,
Garnisht with heavenly guifts of high degree,
Much more then would ye wonder at that sight
And stand astonisht lyke to those which red
Medusae's mazeful hed.   190
There dwels sweet love and constant chastity,

Unspotted fayth and comely womanhood,
Regard of honour and mild modesty;
There vertue raynes as Queene in royal throne,
And giveth lawes alone,   195
The which the base affections doe obay
And yeeld theyr services unto her will;
Ne thought of thing uncomely ever may
Thereto approch to tempt her mind to ill.
Had ye once seene these her celestial threasures   200
And unrevealed pleasures,
Then would ye wonder and her prayses sing,
That al the woods should answer and your eccho ring.

Open the temple gates unto my love,
Open them wide that she may enter in,   205
And all the postes adorne as doth behove,
And all the pillours deck with girlands trim,
For to receyve this Saynt with honour dew,
That commeth in to you!
With trembling steps and humble reverence   210
She commeth in, before th'almightie's vew.
Of her, ye virgins, learne obedience:
When so ye come into those holy places,
To humble your proud faces!
Bring her up to th'high altar, that she may   215
The sacred ceremonies these partake,
The which do endlesse matrimony make;
And let the roring Organs loudly play
The praises of the Lord in lively notes,
The whiles with hollow throates   220
The Choristers the joyous Antheme sing,
That al the woods may answere and their eccho ring!

Behold, whiles she before the altar stands
Hearing the holy priest that to her speakes
And blesseth her with his two happy hands,   225
How the red roses flush up in her cheekes,
And the pure snow with goodly vermill stayne,
Like crimsin dyde in grayne,
That even th'Angels which continually
About the sacred Altare doe remaine   230
Forget their service and about her fly,
Ofte peeping in her face that seemes more fayre,
The more they on it stare.
But her sad eyes still fastened on the ground
Are governed with goodly modesty,   235
That suffers not one looke to glaunce awry
Which may let in a little thought unsownd.
Why blush ye, love, to give to me your hand,
The pledge of all our band?
Sing, ye sweet Angels, Alleluya sing,   240
That all the woods may answere and your ecco ring!

Now al is done; bring home the bride againe,
Bring home the triumph of our victory,

Bring home with you the glory of her gaine,
With joyance bring her and with jollity!   245
Never had man more joyfull day then this,
Whom heaven would heape with blis.
Make feast therefore now all this livelong day—
This day for ever to me holy is—
Poure out the wine without restraint or stay,   250
Poure not by cups, but by the bellyfull,
Poure out to all that wull,
And sprinkle all the postes and wals with wine,
That they may sweat and drunken be withall!
Crowne ye God Bacchus with a coronall,   255
And Hymen also crowne with wreathes of vine,
And let the Graces daunce unto the rest,
For they can doo it best!
The whiles the caydens doe theyr carroll sing,
To which the woods shal answer and theyr eccho ring.   260

Ring ye the bels, ye yong men of the towne,
And leave your wonted labours for this day!
This day is holy: doe ye write it downe,
That ye for ever it remember may!
This day the sunne is in his chiefest hight,   265
With Barnaby the bright,
From whence declining daily by degrees
He somewhat loseth of his heat and light,
When once the Crab behind his back he sees.
But for this time it ill ordained was   270
To chose the longest day in all the yeare
And shortest night, when longest fitter weare;
Yet never day so long, but late would passe.
Ring ye the bels, to make it weare away,
And bonefiers make all day   275
And daunce about them and about them sing,
That all the woods may answer and your eccho ring.

Ah, when will this long, weary day have end
And lende me leave to come unto my love?
How slowly do the houres theyr numbers spend!   280
How slowly does sad Time his feathers move!
Hast thee, O fayrest Planet, to thy home
Within the Westerne fome!
Thy tyred steedes long since have need of rest.
Long though it be, at last I see it gloome,   285
And the bright evening star with golden creast
Appeare out of the East.
Fayre childe of beauty, glorious lampe of love,
That all the host of heaven in rankes doost lead,
And guydest lovers through the nightès dread,   290
How chearefully thou lookest from above
And seemst to laugh atweene thy twinkling light,
As joying in the sight
Of these glad many which for joy doe sing,
That all the woods them answer and theyr eccho ring.   295

Now ceases, ye damsels, your delights forepast;
Enough is it that all the day was youres;
Now day is doen, and night is nighing fast:
Now bring the Bryde into the brydall boures!
The night is come, now soone her disaray,   300
And in her bed her lay;
Lay her in lillies and in violets,
And silken courteins over her display,
And odourd sheetes, and Arras coverlets.
Behold, how goodly my faire love does ly   305
In proud humility,
Like unto Maia, when-as Jove her tooke,
In Tempe, lying on the flowry gras,
Twixt sleepe and wake, after she weary was,
With bathing in the Acidalian brooke!   310
Now it is night; ye damsels may be gon,
And leave my love alone,
And leave likewise your former lay to sing;
The woods no more shal answere nor your eccho ring.

Now welcome, night, thou so long expected,   315
That long daie's labour doest at last defray,
And all my cares, which cruell love collected,
Hast sumd in one and cancelled for aye!
Spread thy broad wing over my love and me,
That no man may us see,   320
And in thy sable mantle us enwrap,
From feare of perrill and foule horror free.
Let no false treason seeke us to entrap,
Nor any dread disquiet once annoy
The safety of our joy;   325
But let the night be calme and quietsome,
Without tempestuous storms or sad afray,
Lyke as when Jove with fayre Alcmena lay,
When he begot the great Tirynthian groome;
Or lyke as when he with thy selfe did lie,   330
And begot Majesty!
And let the mayds and yongmen cease to sing,
Ne let the woods them answer nor theyr eccho ring!

Let no lamenting cryes nor dolefull teares
Be heard all night within nor yet without;   335
Ne let false whispers, breeding hidden feares,
Breake gentle sleepe with misconceived dout!
Let no deluding dreames nor dreadful sights
Make sudden sad affrights;
Ne let housefyres nor lightning's helplesse harmes,   340
Ne let the Pouke nor other evill sprights,
Ne let mischivous witches with theyr charmes,
Ne let hob Goblins, names whose sence we see not,
Fray us with things that be not.
Let not the shriech Oule nor the Storke be heard;   345
Nor the night Raven that still deadly yels,
Nor damned ghosts cald up with mighty spels,

Nor griesly vultures make us once affeard;
Ne let th'unpleasant Quyre of Frogs still croking
Make us to wish theyr choking;   350
Let none of these theyr drery accents sing,
Ne let the woods them answer, nor theyr eccho ring!

But let stil Silence trew night watches keepe,
That sacred peace may in assurance rayne,
And tymely sleep, when it is tyme to sleepe,   355
May poure his limbs forth on your pleasant playne,
The whiles an hundred little winged loves,
Live divers fethered doves,
Shall fly and flutter round about our bed.
And in the secret darke, that none reproves,   360
Their prety stealthes shal worke and snares shal spread
To filch away sweet snatches of delight,
Conceald through covert night.
Ye sonnes of Venus, play your sports at will,
For greedy pleasure, carelesse of your toyes,   365
Thinks more upon her paradise of joyes,
Then what ye do, albe it good or ill.
All night therefore attend your merry play,
For it will soone be day!
Now none doth hinder you, that say or sing,   370
Ne will the woods now answer nor your Eccho ring.

Who is the same which at my window peepes?
Or whose is that faire face that shines so bright?
Is it not Cinthia, she that never sleepes,
But walkes about high heaven al the night?   375
O fayrest goddesse, do thou not envý
My love with me to spy!
For thou likewise didst love, though now unthought,
And for a fleece of woll, which privily
The Latmian shephard once unto thee brought,   380
His pleasures with thee wrought.
Therefore to us be favorable now;
And sith of wemen's labours thou hast charge
And generation goodly dost enlarge,
Encline thy will t' effect our wishfull vow,   385
And the chast wombe informe with timely seed,
That may our comfort breed!
Till which we cease our hopefull hap to sing,
Ne let the woods us answere nor our Eccho ring.

And thou, great Juno, which with awful might   390
The lawes of wedlock still dost patronize,
And the religion of the faith first plight
With sacred rites hast taught to solemnize,
And eeke for comfort often called art
Of women in their smart,   395
Eternally bind thou this lovely band,
And all thy blessings unto us impart!
And thou, glad Genius, in whose gentle hand

The bridale bowre and geniall bed remaine,
Without blemish or staine,   400
And the sweet pleasures of theyr love's delight
With secret ayde dost succour and supply
Till they bring forth the fruitfull progeny,
Send us the timely fruit of this same night!
And thou, fayre Hebe, and thou Hymen free,   405
Grant that it may so be!
Til which we cease your further prayse to sing,
Ne any woods shal answer nor your Eccho ring.

And ye high heavens, the temple of the gods,
In which a thousand torches flaming bright   410
Doe burne, that to us wretched earthly clods
In dreadful darknesse lend desired light,
And all ye powers which in the same remayne,
More then we men can fayne,
Poure out your blessing on us plentiously   415
And happy influence upon us raine,
That we may raise a large posterity,
Which from the earth, which they may long possesse
With lasting happinesse,
Up to your haughty pallaces may mount,   420
And for the guerdon of theyr glorious merit
May heavenly tabernacles there inherit,
Of blessed Saints for to increase the count!
So let us rest, sweet love, in hope of this,
And cease till then our tymely joyes to sing,   425
The woods no more us answer nor our eccho ring.

Song made in lieu of many ornaments
With which my love should duly have bene dect,
Which cutting off through hasty accidents
Ye would not stay your dew time to expect   430
But promist both to recompens,
Be unto her a goodly ornament
And for short time an endlesse moniment!

title: The word *epithalamion* is Greek and means "nuptial song."
2: That is, the nine Muses, who have previously helped the poet to
write verses to others.   7: Spenser alludes to his *The Tears of the
Muses.*   15: Because I show her attention, let not my beloved be
hatred by anyone.   22 *lusty-hed:* lustihood, vigor.   23 *boure:*
bedchamber.   25 *Hymen:* god of marriage.   26 *maske:* celebration, rite.   27 *Tead:* torch, Hymen's symbol.   *flake:* spark.
30 *soone her dight:* quickly dress herself.   39: Spenser married
Elizabeth Boyle, who lived at Kilcoran, County Cork, on the Bay
of Youghal.   40 *beseene:* adorned.   46 *eeke:* also.   51
diapred: patterned.   *discolored mead:* variegated meadow.   56
Mulla: Spenser's name for the River Awbeg, close to his home at
Kilcolman.   67 *mayds:* nymphs. In classical mythology they are
minor nature divinities.   68 *towre:* climb to high altitudes.   75
Tithone's: Tithonus was the mortal who fell in love with Aurora,
goddess of the dawn, and was granted immortality but not youth.

81 Mavis: song thrush.   *descant playes:* sings a "part," which harmonizes.   *82 Ouzell:* blackbird.   *Ruddock:* robin.   *83 consent:* harmony.   *87 Make:* mate.   *95 than Hesperus:* than Hesperus (Venus), the evening star.   *96 damzels:* the brides-maids.   *98 Houres:* goddesses of the seasons and orderliness; daughters of Jove.   *103 handmayds:* the graces, or sister god-desses.   *Cyprian Queene:* Aphrodite (or Venus), who is sup-posed to have been born at Cyprus.   *118 lifull:* lifeful, life-giving. *121 Phoebus:* Apollo, god of poetry and music; not the Muses' father.   *123 Mote:* might.   *131 tabor:* a small drum. *Croud:* crowd, a fiddle-like instrument.   *134 tymbrels:* tambourines. *140:* This is the Romans' joyful cry in honor of Hymen.   *148 pace:* stately step.   *149 Phoebe:* Diana, goddess of the moon. *175 uncrudded:* uncurdled.   *180 bowre:* the head, seat of the mind.   *186 spright:* spirit, soul.   *189 red:* looked at.   *190 Medusae's mazeful hed:* confounding. The Gorgon Medusa, accord-ing to myth, had a head of hair filled with snakes, and whoever gazed upon her was instantly turned to stone.   *196 affections:* passions.   *204 temple gates:* the doors to the church.   *228 grayne:* fast.   *234 sad:* serious.   *239 band:* bond; that is, the marriage bond.   *244 glory of her gaine:* the glory of having won her.   *252 Wull:* will, wish.   *253:* This line refers to a Roman custom.   *266 Barnaby:* St. Barnabas, whose day, June 11, co-incided with the summer solstice (old calendar), the longest day of the year.   *269 Crab:* Cancer, a zodiac sign. The sun leaves it in June.   *282 Planet:* actually the sun.   *304:* Arras was famous for its tapestries.   *307 Maia:* mother of Hermes (Mercury). *308 Tempe:* a vale in Thessaly.   *310 Acidalian brooke:* refers to the fountain Acidalius, in Boeotia.   *329 Tirynthian groome:* Hercules.   *331:* Commentators note that this episode is invented by Spenser.   *340 helpelesse:* irreparable.   *341 Pouke:* a malicious goblin in Celtic folklore.   *344 Fray:* frighten.   *374 Cinthia:* the moon, Diana.   *380 Latmian shephard:* Endymion, a shepherd boy of Mt. Latmos. The moon saw him sleeping and fell in love with him.   *388 hap:* good fortune.   *398 Genius:* guardian spirit.   *399 geniall:* nuptial.   *405 Hebe:* goddess of youth.   *414 fayne:* imagine.   *421 guerdon:* reward.   *430 expect:* await. Lines 429–430 suggest that the date of the mar-riage was advanced, and that not sufficient time remained in order for the poet to present the ornaments to his bride that he had in-tended.

John Donne   Epithalamion Made at Lincoln's Inn

The sunbeams in the East are spread;
Leave, leave, fair bride, your solitary bed;
   No more shall you return to it alone;
It nurseth sadness, and your body's print;
Like to a grave, the yielding down doth dint;   5
      You and your other you meet there anon;
      Put forth, put forth that warm balm-breathing thigh,

Which when next time you in these sheets will smother,
     There it must meet another,
          Which never was, but must be, oft, more nigh;   *10*
Come glad from thence, go gladder than you came,
Today put on perfection, and a woman's name.

Daughters of London, you which be
Our golden mines, and furnished treasury,
     You which are angels, yet still bring with you   *15*
Thousands of angels on your marriage days,
Help with your presence and devise to praise
          These rites, which also unto you grow due;
          Conceitedly dress her, and be assigned,
By you, fit place for every flower and jewel;   20
          Make her for love fit fuel,
          As gay as Flora, and as rich as Inde:
So may she fair, rich, glad, and in nothing lame,
Today put on perfection, and a woman's name.

And you frolic patricians,   25
Sons of these senators, wealth's deep oceans,
     Ye painted courtiers, barrels of others' wits,
Ye country men, who but your beasts love none,
Ye of those fellowships whereof he's one,
          Of study and play made strange hermaphrodites,   30
          Here shine; this bridegroom to the temple bring.
Lo, in yon path, which store of strawed flowers graceth,
          The sober virgin paceth;
               Except my sight fail, 'tis no other thing;
Weep not nor blush, here is no grief nor shame,   35
Today put on perfection, and a woman's name.

Thy two-leaved gates fair temple unfold,
And these two in thy sacred bosom hold,
     Till, mystically joined, but one they be;
Then may thy lean and hunger-starvèd womb   40
Long time expect their bodies and their tomb,
          Long after their own parents fatten thee.
          All elder claims, and all cold barrenness,
All yielding to new loves be far forever,
          Which might these two dissever,   45
               All ways all th'other may each one possess;
For, the best bride, best worthy of praise and fame,
Today puts on perfection, and a woman's name.

Oh winter days bring much delight,
Not for themselves, but for they soon bring night;   50
     Other sweets wait thee than these diverse meats,
Other disports than dancing jollities,
Other love tricks than glancing with the eyes,
          But that the sun still in our half sphere sweats;
          He flies in winter, but he now stands still.   55
Yet shadows turn; noon point he hath attained,
          His steeds will be restrained,
               But gallop lively down the western hill;

Thou shalt, when he hath run the world's half frame,
Tonight put on perfection, and a woman's name.   60

The amorous evening star is rose,
Why then should not our amorous star enclose
   Herself in her wished bed? Release your strings
Musicians, and dancers take some truce
With these your pleasing labors, for great use   65
     As much weariness as perfection brings;
     You, and not only you, but all toiled beasts
Rest duly; at night all their toils are dispensed;
But in their beds commenced
     Arc other labors, and more dainty feasts;   70
She goes a maid, who, lest she turn the same,
Tonight puts on perfection, and a woman's name.

Thy virgin's girdle now untie,
And in thy nuptial bed (love's altar) lie
   A pleasing sacrifice; now dispossess   75
Thee of these chains and robes which were put on
T'adorn the day, not thee; for thou, alone,
     Like virtue and truth, art best in nakedness;
     This bed is only to virginity
A grave, but, to a better state, a cradle;   80
Till now thou wast but able
     To be what now thou art; then that by thee
No more be said "I may be," but "I am,"
Tonight put on perfection, and a woman's name.

Even like a faithful man content   85
That this life for a better should be spent,
   So she a mother's rich style doth prefer,
And at the bridegroom's wished approach doth lie,
Like an appointed lamb, when tenderly
     The priest comes on his knees t'embowed her;   90
     Now sleep or watch with more joy; and O light
Of heaven, tomorrow rise thou hot and early;
This sun will love so dearly
     Her rest, that long, long we shall want her sight;
Wonders are wrought, for she which had no maim,   95
Tonight puts on perfection, and a woman's name.

title: Lincoln's Inn is one of the colleges for lawyers in London.
5 dint: dent.   *16 angels:* coins, dowry.   *19 Conceitedly:* fastidiously.   *22 Flora:* goddess of flowers and fertility.   *Inde:* India.   *52 disports:* merriment.   *58 But:* or else they will.
61 star: Venus.   *71 turn:* return.

John Milton

FROM *Paradise Lost*, BOOK IV (LINES 749–770)

Hail wedded love, mysterious law, true source
Of human offspring, sole propriety,

In Paradise of all things common else.
By thee adulterous lust was driv'n from men
Among the bestial herds to range, by thee   5
Founded in reason, loyal, just, and pure,
Relations dear, and all the charities
Of father, son, and brother first were known.
Far be it that I should write thee sin or blame,
Or think thee unbefitting holiest place,   10
Perpetual fountain of domestic sweets,
Whose bed is undefiled and chaste pronounced,
Present, or past, as saints, and patriarchs used.
Here Love his golden shafts imploys, here lights
His constant lamp, and waves his purple wings,   15
Reigns here and revels; not in the bought smile
Of harlots, loveless, joyless, unendeared,
Casual fruition, nor in court amours
Mixed dance, or wanton mask, or midnight ball,
Or serenade, which the starved lover sings   20
To his proud fair, best quitted with disdain.

William Bell   To a Lady on Her Marriage

My dear, when I was very young
and you not half as much again,
I found you single and unsung.
Oh then I only lived to pen
lamenting elegies, resigned   5
to die of love like better men
for both your body and your mind.

But even when I told you true
(though you would pay no heed to me),
'The days are drawing near when you   10
will ask no more for poetry
or flaming youth, content to find
a steady man, content if he
will love your body, not your mind.

'Joy is the rush of blood, the falling   15
or fallen pride of summer's lark
calling the leaves to hide him, calling
even the snows, even the dark.
Love is a mask, with death behind:
your beauty he will not remark,   20
nor love your body nor your mind.'

And though a torment as intense,
as tyrannous as then I had
awaits, I have learnt too much sense
to let her know when I am sad.   25
I'll say, 'Though love has made me blind
he has forgot to make me mad
to love your body and your mind.'

Vassar Miller   Song for a Marriage

Housed in each other's arms,
Thatched with each other's grace,
Your bodies, flint on steel
Striking out fire to fend
The cold away awhile;   5
With sweat for mortar, brace
Your walls against the sleet
And the rib-riddling wind.

A house, you house yourselves,
Housed, you will house another,   10
Scaled to a subtler blueprint
Than architects can draw—
A triple function yours
In this world's winter weather,
Oh, breathing brick and stone,   15
I look on you with awe.

A fig for praise that calls
Flesh a bundle of sticks,
Kindling for flame that feels
Like swallowing the sun!   20
Yet luxury turned labor's
No old maid's rancid mix,
But how bone-masonry
Outweighs the skeleton.

John Peale Bishop   Epithalamium

When first my beloved came to my bed
It was as though the midnight had seen pass
Morning on the march or that great bird of the
Dayspring, newly mewed, plumed in loud brass.

My breath abandoned me and my breath failed   5
And silence came all sighing to my mouth.
My knees went down before her naked feet.
Love was the cry recovered me from death.

THE HYMN

The Greek poets meant by the term *hymnos* a song praising
heroes or the gods. In England the hymn was a lyric poem
expressing religious emotion, theological doctrine, or religious
aspiration, and was usually sung by a chorus. During the
medieval period the hymn was an important form of poetry.
Latin hymns were important throughout the twelfth and

thirteenth centuries, but with the growing importance of the vernacular, and with the English renaissance, and, finally, the Protestant movement in England, hymns were written in English and sometimes became concerned with more secular matters. The term became generalized and extended, and the word "hymn" came to suggest any song of praise, such as Ben Jonson's humorous "Hymn to Comus," or Shelley's "Hymn to Intellectual Beauty." Famous hymn writers include Wesley, Cowper, Newman, Whittier and Holmes.

Religious hymns often employ *common meter* (see Glossary), which may be distinguisthed from the *ballad stanza* (see Glossary) by the metrical regularity which C.M. (the usual designation for common meter) employs.

John Donne   A Hymn to God the Father

Wilt thou forgive that sin where I begun,
   Which is my sin though it were done before?
Wilt thou forgive those sins through which I run,
   And do them still, though still I do deplore?
     When thou hast done, thou hast not done,   5
      For I have more.

Wilt thou forgive that sin by which I won
   Others to sin? and made my sin their door?
Wilt thou forgive that sin which I did shun
   A year or two, but wallowed in a score?   10
     When thou hast done, thou hast not done,
      For I have more.

I have a sin of fear, that when I've spun
   My last thread, I shall perish on the shore;
Swear by thyself that at my death thy sun   15
   Shall shine as it shines now, and heretofore;
     And having done that thou hast done.
      I have no more.

Ben Jonson   Queen and Huntress

HYMN FROM *"Cynthia's Revels"*

Queen and huntress, chaste, and fair,
Now the sun is laid to sleep,
Seated in thy silver chair,
State in wonted manner keep:
   Hesperus entreats thy light,   5
   Goddess, excellently bright.

Earth, let not thy envious shade
Dare itself to interpose;
Cynthia's shining orb was made
Heaven to clear when day did close: 10

Bless us then with wished sight,
Goddess, excellently bright.

Lay thy bow of pearl apart,
And thy crystal-shining quiver;
Give unto the flying hart   *15*
Space to breathe, how short soever:
   Thou, that makest a day of night,
   Goddess, excellently bright.

1 Queen: Diana, goddess of the moon, hunting, and chastity; known also as Cynthia.

William Cowper   Hymn XXXIX

FROM THE *"Olney Hymns"*

SEEKING THE BELOVED

To those who know the Lord I speak;
   Is my Beloved near?
The Bridegroom of my soul I seek,
   Oh, when will he appear?

Though once a man of grief and shame,   5
   Yet now he fills a throne,
And bears the greatest, sweetest name
   That earth or heaven has known.

Grace flies before, and love attends
   His steps where'er he goes;   *10*
Though none can see him but his friends,
   And they were once his foes.

He speaks;—obedient to his call
   Our warm affections move:
Did he but shine alike on all,   *15*
   Then all alike would love.

Then love in every heart would reign,
   And war would cease to roar;
And cruel and bloodthirsty men
   Would thirst for blood no more.   20

Such Jesus is, and such his grace;
   Oh, may he shine on you!
And tell him, when you see his face,
   I long to see him too.

Owen Dodson   Hymn Written After Jeremiah Preached to Me in a Dream

Nowhere are we safe.
Surely not in love,

Morning ripe at three
Or in the Holy Trinity.

(My God, look after me.)   5

Where does Grace abide,
Whole, whole in surety?
Or does sin abide
Where virtue tries, in shame, to hide?

(My God, have I no pride?)   10

Shall I try the whole,
Crippled in my will,
Spatter where it falls
My carnal fire waterfalls?

(My angel, in compassion, calls.)   15

Secret, knotted shame
Rips me like a curse.
Unction in my dust
Gives me final thrust.

(My God, consider dust!)   20

John Betjeman   Harvest Hymn

We spray the fields and scatter
    The poison on the ground
So that no wicked wild flowers
    Upon our farm be found.
We like whatever helps us   5
    To line our purse with pence;
The twenty-four-hour broiler-house
    And neat electric fence.

All concrete sheds around us
    And Jaguars in the yard,   10
The telly lounge and deep-freeze
    Are ours from working hard.

We fire the fields for harvest,
    The hedges swell the flame,
The oak trees and the cottages   15
    From which our fathers came.
We give no compensation,
    The earth is ours today,
And if we lose on arable,
    Then bungalows will pay.   20

    All concrete sheds . . . etc.

OCCASIONAL VERSE

Occasional verse is poetry written to commemorate important events. To celebrate man's first landing upon the surface of the moon, for example, Archibald MacLeish wrote "Voyage to the Moon." Occasional verse often succumbs to the passing of the years, but such poems as Marvell's "Horatian Ode upon Cromwell's Return from Ireland" and John Milton's "On the Late Massacre in Piedmont" have stood the test of time. Poets laureate are usually expected to write appropriate poems for important public events in the fulfilling of their office.

William Butler Yeats   Easter 1916

I have met them at close of day
Coming with vivid faces
From counter or desk among grey
Eighteenth-century houses.
I have passed with a nod of the head   5
Or polite meaningless words,
Or have lingered awhile and said
Polite meaningless words,
And thought before I had done
Of a mocking tale or a gibe   10
To please a companion
Around the fire at the club,
Being certain that they and I
But lived where motley is worn:
All changed, changed utterly: 15
A terrible beauty is born.

That woman's days were spent
In ignorant good-will,
Her nights in argument
Until her voice grew shrill.   20
What voice more sweet than hers
When, young and beautiful,
She rode to harriers?
This man had kept a school
And rode our wingèd horse;   25
This other his helper and friend
Was coming into his force;
He might have won fame in the end,
So sensitive his nature seemed,
So daring and sweet his thought.   30
This other man I had dreamed
A drunken, vainglorious lout.
He had done most bitter wrong
To some who are near my heart,

Yet I number him in the song;   35
He, too, has resigned his part
In the casual comedy;
He, too, has been changed in his turn,
Transformed utterly:
A terrible beauty is born.   40

Hearts with one purpose alone
Through summer and winter seem
Enchanted to a stone
To trouble the living stream.
The horse that comes from the road,   45
The rider, the birds that range
From cloud to tumbling cloud,
Minute by minute they change;
A shadow of cloud on the stream
Changes minute by minute;   50
A horse-hoof slides on the brim,
And a horse plashes within it;
The long-legged moor-hens dive,
And hens to moor-cocks call;
Minute by minute they live: 55
The stone's in the midst of all.

Too long a sacrifice
Can make a stone of the heart.
O when may it suffice?
That is Heaven's part, our part   60
To murmur name upon name,
As a mother names her child
When sleep at last has come
On limbs that had run wild.
What is it but nightfall?   65
No, no, not night but death;
Was it needless death after all?
For England may keep faith
For all that is done and said.
We know their dream; enough   70
To know they dreamed and are dead;
And what if excess of love
Bewildered them till they died?
I write it out in a verse—
MacDonagh and MacBride   75
And Connolly and Pearse
Now and in time to be,
Wherever green is worn,
Are changed, changed utterly:
A terrible beauty is born.   80

title: The occasion of this poem was the insurrection of the Irish
nationalists that took place on Easter Monday, 1916. The English
repressed the Easter Rising, and fifteen of the leaders, including
four men named in the poem, were executed.   *17 That woman:*
Countess Markiewicz, who was active in the Easter Rebellion and

was given a sentence of life imprisonment.   24 *This man*: Patrick Pearse was in command of the rebel forces.   26 *This other*:
Thomas MacDonagh, a writer admired by Yeats.   31 *This . . .
man*: Major John MacBride, husband of Maud Gonne.   76 *Connolly*: Pearse's partner in leading the insurrection.

ON POETS AND POETRY

It has become a fairly common practice among editors of
poetry anthologies to include groupings of poems based upon
general categories such as Love, War, Nature, and Beauty.
These categories, useful for comparison and contrast, may be
presented in smaller groupings and labeled poems about
Painting, Music, Character, the City, Landscape, Time,
Space, the Wind, the Moon, Faith, and so forth.

For the student of poetry, however, we believe that no
general grouping is more useful or interesting than those
poems that are concerned with the nature of poetry, or those
poems in which the poet speaks about another poet's art. The
poems that follow in this section have been selected on the
basis of chronology and diversity.

William Shakespeare   "The Lunatic, the Lover, and
   the Poet"
   FROM   *A Midsummer Night's Dream*

The lunatic, the lover, and the poet
Are of imagination all compact.
One sees more devils than vast hell can hold:
That is the madman. The lover, all as frantic,
Sees Helen's beauty in a brow of Egypt.   5
The poet's eye, in a fine frenzy rolling,
Doth glance from heaven to earth, from earth to heaven;
And as imagination bodies forth
The forms of things unknown, the poet's pen
Turns them to shapes, and gives to airy nothing   10
A local habitation and a name.
Such tricks hath strong imagination
That, if it would but apprehend some joy,
It comprehends some bringer of that joy;
Or in the night, imagining some fear,   15
How easy is a bush suppos'd a bear!

Robert Herrick   Discontents in Devon

More discontents I never had
   Since I was born, than here,

Where I have been, and still am sad,
    In this dull Devonshire;
Yet justly too I must confess,   5
    I ne'er invented such
Ennobled numbers for the press,
    Than where I loathed so much.

John Keats   On the Sonnet

If by dull rhymes our English must be chained,
And, like Andromeda, the Sonnet sweet
Fettered, in spite of pained loveliness,
Let us find out, if we must be constrained,
Sandals more interwoven and complete   5
To fit the naked foot of Poesy:
Let us inspect the Lyre, and weigh the stress
Of every chord, and see what may be gained
By ear industrious, and attention meet;
Misers of sound and syllable, no less   10
Than Midas of his coinage, let us be
Jealous of dead leaves in the bay wreath crown;
So, if we may not let the Muse be free,
She will be bound with garlands of her own.

2 *Andromeda*: in Greek legend, the daughter of Cepheus and Cassiopeia. To satisfy Poseidon, who had been offended, Andromeda was chained to a rock and exposed to a sea monster. Perseus found her, killed the monster, and married her.

Ralph Waldo Emerson   Terminus

It is time to be old,
To take in sail:—
The god of bounds,
Who sets to seas a shore,
Came to me in his fatal rounds,   5
And said: "No more!
No farther shoot
Thy broad ambitious branches, and thy root.
Fancy departs: no more invent;
Contract thy firmament   10
To compass of a tent.
There's not enough for this and that,
Make thy option which of two;
Economize the failing river,
Not the less revere the Giver,   15
Leave the many and hold the few.
Timely wise accept the terms,
Soften the fall with wary foot;
A little while

Still plan and smile,   20
And,—fault of novel germs,—
Mature the unfallen fruit.
Curse, thou wilt, thy sires,
Bad husbands of their fires,
Who, when they gave thee breath,   25
Failed to bequeath
The needful sinew stark as once,
The Baresark marrow to thy bones,
But left a legacy of ebbing veins,
Inconstant heat and nerveless reins,—   30
Amid the Muses, left thee deaf and dumb,
Amid the gladiators, halt and numb."

    As the bird trims her to the gale,
I trim myself to the storm of time,
I man the rudder, reef the sail,   35
Obey the voice at eve obeyed at prime:
"Lowly faithful, banish fear,
Right onward drive unharmed;
The port, well worth the cruise, is near,
And every wave is charmed."   40

title: Terminus is the Roman god of boundaries.

Henry Wadsworth Longfellow   Chaucer

An old man in a lodge within a park;
The chamber walls depicted all around
With portraitures of huntsman, hawk, and hound,
And the hurt deer. He listeneth to the lark,
Whose song comes with the sunshine through the dark   5
Of painted glass in leaden lattice bound;
He listeneth and he laugheth at the sound,
Then writeth in a book like any clerk.
He is the poet of the dawn, who wrote
The Canterbury Tales, and his old age   10
Made beautiful with song; and as I read
I hear the crowing cock, I hear the note
Of lark and linnet, and from every page
Rise odors of ploughed field or flowery mead.

14 mead: meadow.

James Weldon Johnson   O Black and Unknown Bards

O black and unknown bards of long ago,
How came your lips to touch the sacred fire?
How, in your darkness, did you come to know
The power and beauty of the minstrel's lyre?
Who first from midst his bonds lifted his eyes?   5

Who first from out the still watch, lone and long,
Feeling the ancient faith of prophets rise
Within his dark-kept soul, burst into song?

Heart of what slave poured out such melody
As "Steal away to Jesus"? On its strains   10
His spirit must have nightly floated free,
Though still about his hands he felt his chains.
Who heard great "Jordan roll"? Whose starward eye
Saw chariot "swing low"? And who was he
That breathed that comforting, melodic sigh,   15
"Nobody knows de trouble I see"?

What merely living clod, what captive thing,
Could up toward God through all its darkness grope,
And find within its deadened heart to sing
These songs of sorrow, love and faith, and hope?   20
How did it catch that subtle undertone,
That note in music heard not with the ears?
How sound the elusive reed so seldom blown,
Which stirs the soul or melts the heart to tears.

Not that great German master in his dream   25
Of harmonies that thundered amongst the stars
At the creation, ever heard a theme
Nobler than "Go down, Moses." Mark its bars
How like a mighty trumpet-call they stir
The blood. Such are the notes that men have sung   30
Going to valorous deeds; such tones there were
That helped make history when Time was young.

There is a wide, wide wonder in it all,
That from degraded rest and servile toil
The fiery spirit of the seer should call   35
These simple children of the sun and soil.
O black slave singers, gone, forgot, unfamed,
You—you alone, of all the long, long line
Of those who've sung untaught, unknown, unnamed,
Have stretched out upward, seeking the divine.   40

You sang not deeds of heroes or of kings;
No chant of bloody war, no exulting paean
Of arms-won triumphs; but your humble strings
You touched in chord with music empyrean.
You sang far better than you knew; the songs   45
That for your listeners' hungry hearts sufficed
Still live,—but more than this to you belongs:
You sang a race from wood and stone to Christ.

Ezra Pound   A Pact

I make a pact with you, Walt Whitman—
I have detested you long enough.

I come to you as a grown child
Who has had a pig-headed father;
I am old enough now to make friends.   5
It was you that broke the new wood,
Now is a time for carving.
We have one sap and one root—
Let there be commerce between us.

Archibald MacLeish   Ars Poetica

A poem should be palpable and mute
As a globed fruit

Dumb
As old medallions to the thumb

Silent as the sleeve-worn stone   5
Of casement ledges where the moss has grown—

A poem should be wordless
As the flight of birds

A poem should be motionless in time
As the moon climbs   10

Leaving, as the moon releases
Twig by twig the night-entangled trees,

Leaving, as the moon behind the winter leaves,
Memory by memory the mind—

A poem should be motionless in time   15
As the moon climbs

A poem should be equal to:
Not true

For all the history of grief
An empty doorway and a maple leaf   20

For love
The meaning grasses and two lights above the sea—

A poem should not mean
But be

Archibald MacLeish   L'An Trentiesme de Mon Age

And I have come upon this place
By lost ways, by a nod, by words,
By faces, by an old man's face
At Morlaix lifted to the birds,

By hands upon the tablecloth   5
At Aldebori's, by the thin

Child's hands that opened to the moth
And let the flutter of the moonlight in,

By hands, by voices, by the voice
Of Mrs. Whitman on the stair,   10
By Margaret's "If we had the choice
To choose or not—" through her thick hair,

By voices, by the creak and fall
Of footsteps on the upper floor,
By silence waiting in the hall   15
Between the doorbell and the door,

By words, by voices, a lost way—
And here above the chimney stack
The unknown constellations sway—
And by what way shall I go back?   20

title: "The thirtieth year of my age." This title is taken from François Villon's "The Testament."

Wallace Stevens   Of Modern Poetry

The poem of the mind in the act of finding
What will suffice. It has not always had
To find: the scene was set; it repeated what
Was in the script.
                    Then the theater was changed   5
To something else. Its past was a souvenir.
It has to be living, to learn the speech of the place.
It has to face the men of the time and to meet
The women of the time. It has to think about war
To construct a new stage. It has to be on that stage   10
And, like an insatiable actor, slowly and
With meditation, speak words that in the ear,
In the delicatest ear of the mind, repeat,
Exactly, that which it wants to hear, at the sound
Of which, an invisible audience listens,   15
Not to the play, but to itself, expressed
In an emotion as of two people, as of two
Emotions becoming one. The actor is
A metaphysician in the dark, twanging
An instrument, twanging a wiry string that gives   20
Sounds passing through sudden rightnesses, wholly
Containing the mind, below which it cannot descend,
Beyond which it has no will to rise.
                            It must
Be the finding of a satisfaction, and may   25
Be of a man skating, a woman dancing, a woman
Combing. The poem of the act of the mind.

Marianne Moore   Poetry

I, too, dislike it; there are things that are important beyond all
        this fiddle.
    Reading it, however, with a perfect contempt for it, one dis-
        covers in it after all, a place for the genuine.
        Hands that can grasp, eyes
        that can dilate, hair that can rise   5
            if it must, these things are important not because a

high-sounding interpretation can be put upon them but be-
        cause they are
    useful. When they become so derivative as to become unintel-
        ligible,
    The same thing may be said for all of us, that we
        do not admire what   10
        we cannot understand: the bat
            holding on upside down or in quest of something to

eat, elephants pushing, a wild horse taking a roll, a tireless wolf
        under
    a tree, the immovable critic, twitching his skin like a horse that
        feels a flea, the base-   15
        ball fan, the statistician—
            nor is it valid
                to discriminate against 'business documents and

school-books'; all these phenomena are important. One must
        make a distinction
    however; when dragged into prominence by half poets, the re-
        sult is not poetry,
nor till the poets among us can be
        'literalists of
        the imagination'—above
            insolence and triviality and can present

for inspection, 'imaginary garden with real toads in them',   25
        shall we have
    it. In the meantime, if you demand on the one hand, the raw
        material of poetry in
        all its rawness and
        that which is on the other hand
            genuine, then you are interested in poetry.   30

Elder Olson   A Valentine for Marianne Moore

The hardest thing to imagine is
The fact perfectly seen. Tannhauser's miracle
repeated, certainly; the blossoming
Pilgrim's-staff, thought dead wood. Anyone sees
The wintry stick; a few can fancy flowers   5
And are called poets; the truly rare

Eye sees what is really there:
The dry stick shaken with implicit spring,

Imagination
More precise than sensation   *10*
Because it is governed by an intellect
More precise than either. Pleasure, said Aristotle,
Is perfect when the perfect organ finds
Its worthiest object; pleasure then
Perfects the perfected activity   *15*
As youth is perfected by the bloom of youth.
This is your perfection, Madam; there is
Nothing more beautiful than perfect truth

Except the mind that sees it. Poetry, to be
Poetry truly, must be more than poetry; in perfection   *20*
It is never fiction,
It never falsifies. Detestable the eloquence
That must turn every pebble to a jewel
To make it a fit subject; yes, and hateful
The raging of a false poetic fire,   *25*
The bellows working audibly; but Plato
Would have loved your poems; would have wondered, too, to
    see
Poems ordered like his Perfect State.

True beauty is most truly praised
By the glass which is most true.   *30*
Madam, this glass is mine,
The loveliness within is you.
Accept this for your valentine.
It has my heart's shape, and no more;
I scorn to dress it with the common lace;   *35*
Let it have no grace but your grace.

2 *Tannhauser*: a legendary German knight. Having repented for
the loose life he has led, Tannhauser seeks forgiveness from the
Pope. A staff flowers miraculously, convincing the Pope to grant
forgiveness, but Tannhauser disappears before being granted his
forgiveness. He is never seen again.

Dylan Thomas   "In My Craft or Sullen Art"

In my craft or sullen art
Exercised in the still night
When only the moon rages
And the lovers lie abed
With all their griefs in their arms,   *5*
I labor by singing light
Not for ambition or bread
Or the strut and trade of charms
On the ivory stages
But for the common wages   *10*

Of their most secret heart.
Not for the proud man apart
From the raging moon I write
On these spindrift pages
Not for the towering dead   15
With their nightingales and psalms
But for the lovers, their arms
Round the griefs of the ages,
Who pay no praise or wages
Nor heed my craft or art.   20

John Wain   Reason for Not Writing Orthodox
     Nature Poetry

The January sky is deep and calm.
The mountain sprawls in comfort, and the sea
Sleeps in the crook of that enormous arm.

And nature from a simple recipe—
Rocks, water, mist, a sunlit winter's day—   5
Has brewed a cup whose strength has dizzied me.

So little beauty is enough to pay;
The heart so soon yields up its store of love,
And where you love you cannot break away.

So sages never found it hard to prove   10
Nor prophets to declare in metaphor
That God and Nature must be hand in glove.

And this became the basis of their lore.
Then later poets found it easy going
To give the public what they bargained for,   15

And like a spectacled curator showing
The wares of his museum to the crowd,
They yearly waxed more eloquent and knowing

More slick, more photographic, and more proud:
From Tennyson with notebook in his hand   20
(His truth to Nature fits him like a shroud)

To moderns who devoutly hymn the land.
So be it: each is welcome to his voice;
They are gentle, if a useless, band.

But leave me free to make a sterner choice;   25
Content, without embellishment, to note
How little beauty bids the heart rejoice,

How little beauty catches at the throat,
Simply, I love this mountain and this bay
With love that I can never speak by rote,   30

And where you love you cannot break away.

Lawrence Ferlinghetti   Constantly Risking Absurdity

Constantly risking absurdity
                        and death
        whenever he performs
                        above the heads
                                of his audience   5
        the poet like an acrobat
                    climbs on rime
                        to a high wire of his own making
        and balancing on eyebeams
                        above a sea of faces   10
            paces his way
                        to the other side of day
        performing entrechats
                        and slight-of-foot tricks
        and other high theatrics
                        and all without mistaking
                    any thing
                        for what it may not be
        For he's the super realist
                        who must perforce perceive   20
            taut truth
                        before the taking of each stance or step
        in his supposed advance
                        toward that still higher perch
where Beauty stands and waits   25
                    with gravity
                        to start her death-defying leap
        And he
            a little charleychaplin man
                        who may or may not catch   30
            her fair eternal form
                        spreadeagled in the empty air
            of existence

TOPOGRAPHICAL POETRY

Significantly introduced into English poetry by Ben Jonson's
"To Penshurst," which appeared in the author's collected
works in 1616, topographical poetry had a vogue throughout
the seventeenth and eighteenth centuries. It ceased to be
popular when the romantic poets of the nineteenth century
used descriptive details of nature for newer, different purposes.
Samuel Johnson, the great writer and critic of the eighteenth
century, defined topographical poetry as "local poetry, of
which the fundamental subject is some particular landscape
. . . with the addition of . . . historical retrospection or inci-

dental meditation." Topographical poetry is essentially descriptive poetry with a great amount of moral reflection.

Among some of the most noteworthy topographical poems are Sir John Denham's "Cooper's Hill" (1642), Waller's "Poem on St. James' Park," and his two poems "At Penshurst," Marvell's "Upon Appleton House," Tickell's "Kensington Garden," Alexander Pope's "Windsor Forest," Garth's "Claremont," Dyer's "Grongar Hill," and James Thomson's "The Seasons," completed in 1730.

In Thomson's "The Seasons," the reader is apt to detect a changing attitude toward nature from that of the earlier topographical poems. Whereas nature was formerly a picturesque prospect, to be captured in details supplied by the poet, in Thomson's poem nature is for contemplation, a book to be studied with reverence.

Topographical poets did not necessarily limit themselves to describing nature in topographical poems, and it is possible though not profitable to recognize some nine sub-categories of the genre, including poems about rivers, caves, hills, towns, and buildings. In our own century, the poetry of John Betjeman at times resembles topographical poetry.

Ben Jonson   To Penshurst

Thou are not, Penshurst, built to envious show
   Of touch, or marble; nor canst boast a row
Of polished pillars, or a roof of gold:
   Thou hast no lanthorn, whereof tales are told;
Or stair, or courts; but standest an ancient pile,   5
   And these grudged at, art reverenced the while.
Thou joyest in better marks, of soil, of air,
   Of wood, of water: therein thou art fair.
Thou hast thy walks for health, as well as sport:
   Thy Mount, to which the Dryads do resort,   10
Where Pan and Bacchus their high feasts have made
   Beneath the broad beech and the chestnut shade;
The taller tree, which of a nut was set,
   At his great birth, where all the Muses met.
There, in the writhed bark, are cut the names   15
   Of many a Sylvan, taken with his flames.
And thence, the ruddy Satyrs oft provoke
   The lighter Fauns, to reach thy Lady's oak.
Thy copse, too, named of Gamage, thou hast there,
   That never fails to serve thee seasoned deer   20
When thou wouldst feast, or exercise thy friends.
   The lower land that to the river bends,
Thy sheep, thy bullocks, kine, and calves do feed:
   The middle grounds thy mares and horses breed.
Each bank doth yield thee coneys; and the tops   25
   Fertile of wood, Ashore and Sidney's copse,
To crown thy open table doth provide
   The purpled pheasant with the speckled side:

The painted partridge lies in every field,
   And, for thy mess, is willing to be killed.   30
And if the high swollen Medway fail thy dish,
   Thou hast thy ponds that pay thee tribute fish,
Fat, aged carps, that run into thy net.
   And pikes, now weary their own kind to eat,
As loath, the second draught or cast to stay,   35
   Officiously, at first, themselves betray.
Bright eels that emulate them and leap on land,
   Before the fisher or into his hand.
Then hath thy orchard fruit, thy garden flowers,
   Fresh as the air and new as are the hours.   40
The early cherry, with the later plum,
   Fig, grape and quince, each in his time doth come:
The blushing apricot and woolly peach
   Hang on thy walls that every child may reach.
And though thy walls be of the country stone,   45
   They are reared with no man's ruin, no man's groan.
There's none that dwell about them wish them down;
   But all came in, the farmer, and the clown:
And no one empty-handed to salute
   Thy lord and lady, though they have no suit.   50
Some bring a capon, some a rural cake,
   Some nuts, some apples; some that think they make
The better cheeses bring them; or else send
   By their ripe daughters whom they would commend
This way to husbands; and whose baskets bear   55
   An emblem of themselves, in plum or pear.
But what can this (more than express their love)
   Add to thy free provisions, far above
The need of such? whose liberal board doth flow
   With all that hospitality doth know!   60
Where comes no guest, but is allowed to eat
   Without his fear, and of thy Lord's own meat:
Where the same beer and bread and self-same wine
   That is his Lordship's shall be also mine.
And I not fain to sit (as some, this day,   65
   At great men's tables) and yet dine away.
Here no man tells my cups; nor, standing by,
   A waiter doth my gluttony envy:
But gives me what I call and lets me eat,
   He knows, below, he shall find plenty of meat,   70
Thy tables hoard not up for the next day,
   Nor when I take my lodging need I pray
For fire, or lights, or livery: all is there;
   As if thou, then, wert mine, or I resigned here:
There's nothing I can wish, for which I stay.   75
   That found King James, when hunting late this way,
With his brave son, the Prince, they saw thy fires
   Shine bright on every hearth as the desires
Of thy Penates had been set on flame
   To entertain them; or the country came,   80
With all their zeal, to warm their welcome here.
   What (great, I will not say, but) sudden cheer

Didst thou, then, make them! and what praise was heaped
  On thy good lady, then! who, therein, reaped
The just reward of her high huswifery;   85
  To have her linen, plate, and all things nigh,
When she was far: and not a room, but dressed,
  As if it had expected such a guest!
These, Penshurst, are thy praise, and yet not all.
  Thy lady's noble, fruitful, chaste withall.   90
His children thy great lord may call his own:
  A fortune in this age but rarely known.
They are and have been taught religion: thence
  Their gentler spirits have sucked innocence.
Each morn and even they are taught to pray   95
  With the whole household, and may, every day,
Read, in their virtuous parent's noble parts,
  The mysteries of manners, arms, and arts.
Now Penshurst, they that will proportion thee
  With other edifices, when they see   100
Those proud, ambitious heaps, and nothing else,
  May say, their lords have built, but thy lord dwells.

title: Penshurst was the country estate of the Sidney family in
Kent. The poem praises a bucolic home or the owners, and plays
upon the *beata ille* theme, or the happy life to be gained by re-
tirement from the tensions of the city. The simplicity and freedom
of the surroundings are stressed.   2 *touch*: touchstone, black
siliceous stone.   4 *lanthorn*: a structure on a roof, letting in light
and air.   6: "And while these attributes are envied, you (without them) are admired."   7 *marks*: marches, boundaries.   10
Mount: apparently a hill on the grounds.   14 *his*: Sir Philip
Sidney's, born November 30, 1554.   16 *Sylvan*: rustic swain.
18 *Lady's oak*: the tree under which, according to tradition, Lady
Leicester, wife of Robert Sidney, began giving birth to their son
Robert, 1595.   19 *Gamage*: named for Sir Robert Sidney's wife
Barbara Gamage.   25 *coneys*: rabbits.   26 *Ashore and
Sidney's copse*: two wooded areas.   31 *Medway*: a river bordering Penshurst.   35 *draught*: drawing of a net. *stay*: await.
36 *Officiously*: obligingly.   44 *Hang on thy walls*: that is, they
are espaliered.   48 *clown*: rustic.   50 *no suit*: nothing to ask
for.   56 *emblem*: symbol.   62 *his fear*: fear of being poisoned.
66 *yet dine away*: yet must dine elsewhere to be well fed.   67
tells my cups: counts how much I drink.   70 *below*: stored in
the cellar.   73 *livery*: food.   77 *Prince*: Henry, who died in
November 1612.   78 *as*: as if.   79 *Penates*: gods of the
household.   99 *proportion*: compare.

Sir John Denham
    Cooper's Hill (excerpt)

My eye descending from the hill, surveys
Where Thames amongst the wanton valleys strays.

Thames, the most loved of all the ocean's sons
By his old sire, to his embraces runs
Hasting to pay his tribute to the sea,   5
Like mortal life to meet eternity.
Though with those streams he no resemblance hold,
Whose foam is amber, and their gravel gold,
His genuine and less guilty wealth t'explore,
Search not his bottom, but survey his shore,   10
O'er which he kindly spreads his spacious wing,
And hatches plenty for th' ensuing spring;
Nor then destroys it with too fond a stay,
Like mothers which their infants overlay;
Now with a sudden and impetuous wave,   15
Like profuse kings, resumes the wealth he gave.
No unexpected inundations spoil
The mower's hopes, nor mock the plowman's toil;
But godlike his unwearied bounty flows,
First loves to do, then loves the good he does.   20
Nor are his blessings to the banks confined,
But free and common as the sea or wind:
When he, to boast or to disperse his stores,
Full of the tributes of his grateful shores,
Visits the world, and in his flying towers   25
Brings home to us, and makes both Indies ours;
Finds wealth where 'tis, bestows it where it wants,
Cities in deserts, woods in cities plants;
So that to us no thing, no place is strange,
While his fair bosom is the world's exchange.   30
Oh, could I flow like thee, and make thy stream
My great example, as it is my theme!
Though deep, yet clear; though gentle, yet not dull.
Strong without rage, without o'erflowing full.
Here nature, whether more intent to please   35
Us or herself with strange varieties,
(For things of wonder give no less delight
To the wise maker's than beholder's sight,
Though these delights from several causes move,
For so our children, thus our friends, we love)   40
Wisely she knew the harmony of things,
As well as that of sounds, from discord springs.
Such was the discord which did first disperse.
Form, order, beauty, through the universe;
While dryness moisture, coldness heat, resists,   45
All that we have, and that we are, subsists,
While the steep horrid roughness of the wood
Strives with the gentle calmness of the flood;
Such huge extremes when nature doth unite,
Wonder from thence results, from thence delight.   50
The stream is so transparent, pure, and clear,
That had the self-enamoured youth gazed here,
So fatally deceived he had not been,
While he the bottom, not his face, had seen.
But his proud head the airy mountain hides   55

Among the clouds; his shoulders and his sides
A shady mantle clothes; his curlëd brows
Frown on the gentle stream, which calmly flows,
While winds and storms his lofty forehead beat,
The common fate of all that's high or great.   60
Low at his foot a spacious plain is placed,
Between the mountain and the stream embraced,
Which shade and shelter from the hill derives,
While the kind river wealth and beauty gives,
And in the mixture of all these appears   65
Variety, which all the rest endears.
This scene had some bold Greek or British bard
Beheld of old, what stories had we heard
Of fairies, satyrs, and the nymphs, their dames,
Their feasts, their revels, and their amorous flames?   70
'Tis still the same, although their airy shape
All but a quick poetic sight escape.
There Faunus and Sylvanus keep their courts,
And thither all the horned host resorts
To gaze the ranker mead: that noble herd   75
On whose sublime and shady fronts is reared
Nature's great masterpiece, to show how soon
Great things are made, but sooner are undone.

title: "Cooper's Hill" is a poem of 342 lines; we have printed
lines 159–236 of the poem.

John Dyer   Grongar Hill

Silent Nymph, with curious eye!
Who, the purple ev'ning, lie
On the mountain's lonely van,
Beyond the noise of busy man,
Painting fair the form of things,   5
While the yellow linnet sings;
Or the tuneful nightingale
Charms the forest with her tale;
Come with all thy various hues,
Come, and aid thy sister Muse;   10
Now while Phœbus riding high
Gives luster to the land and sky!
Grongar Hill invites my song,
Draw the landskip bright and strong;
Grongar, in whose mossy cells   15
Sweetly-musing Quiet dwells;
Grongar, in whose silent shade,
For the modest Muses made,
So oft I have, the evening still,
At the fountain of a rill,   20
Sat upon a flow'ry bed,
With my hand beneath my head;

While stray'd my eyes o'er Towy's flood,
Over mead, and over wood,
From house to house, from hill to hill,   25
'Till Contemplation had her fill.
  About his chequer'd sides I wind,
And leave his brooks and meads behind,
And groves, and grottoes where I lay,
And vistoes shooting beams of day: 30
Wide and wider spreads the vale;
As circles on a smooth canal:
The mountains round, unhappy fate!
Sooner or later, of all height,
Withdraw their summits from the skies,   35
And lessen as the others rise:
Still the prospect wider spreads.
Adds a thousand woods and meads,
Still it widens, widens still,
And sinks the newly-risen hill.   40
  Now, I gain the mountain's brow,
What a landskip lies below!
No clouds, no vapors intervene,
But the gay, the open scene
Does the face of nature show,   45
In all the hues of heaven's bow!
And, swelling to embrace the light,
Spreads around beneath the sight.
  Old castles on the cliffs arise,
Proudly tow'ring in the skies!   50
Rushing from the woods, the spires
Seem from hence ascending fires!
Half his beams Apollo sheds
On the yellow mountain-heads!
Gilds the fleeces of the flocks: 55
And glitters on the broken rocks!
  Below me trees unnumber'd rise,
Beautiful in various dyes:
The gloomy pine, the poplar blue,
The yellow beech, the sable yew,   60
The slender fir, that taper grows,
The sturdy oak with broad-spread boughs.
And beyond the purple grove,
Haunt of Phyllis, queen of love!
Gaudy as the op'ning dawn,   65
Lies a long and level lawn
On which a dark hill, steep and high,
Holds and charms the wand'ring eye!
Deep are his feet in Towy's flood,
His sides are cloath'd with waving wood,   70
And ancient towers crown his brow,
That cast an awful look below;
Whose ragged walls the ivy creeps,
And with her arms from falling keeps;
So both a safety from the wind   75

On mutual dependence find.
   'Tis now the raven's bleak abode;
'Tis now th' apartment of the toad;
And there the fox securely feeds;
And there the pois'nous adder breeds   80
Conceal'd in ruins, moss and weeds;
While, ever and anon, there falls
Huge heaps of hoary moulder'd walls.
Yet time has seen, that lifts the low,
And level lays the lofty brow,   85
Has seen this broken pile complete,
Big with the vanity of state;
But transient is the smile of fate!
A little rule, a little sway,
A sun beam in a winter's day,   90
Is all the proud and mighty have
Between the cradle and the grave.
   And see the rivers how they run,
Thro' woods and meads, in shade and sun,
Sometimes swift, sometimes slow,   95
Wave succeeding wave, they go
A various journey to the deep,
Like human life to endless sleep!
Thus nature's vesture wrought,
To instruct our wand'ring thought;   100
Thus she dresses green and gay,
To disperse our cares away.
   Ever charming, ever new,
When will the landskip tire the view!
The fountain's fall, the river's flow,   105
The woody valleys, warm and low;
The windy summit, wild and high,
Roughly rushing on the sky!
The pleasant seat, the ruin'd tow'r,
The naked rock, the shady bow'r;   110
The town and village, dome and farm,
Each give each a double charm,
As pearls upon an Æthiop's arm.
   See on the mountain's southern side,
Where the prospect opens wide,   115
Where the evening gilds the tide;
How close and small the hedges lie!
What streaks of meadows cross the eye!
A step methinks may pass the stream,
So little distant dangers seem;   120
So we mistake the future's face,
Ey'd thro' hope's deluding glass;
As yon summits soft and fair
Clad in colors of the air,
Which to those who journey near,   125
Batten, brown, and rough appear;
Still we tread the same coarse way,
The present's still a cloudy day.

        O may I with myself agree,
And never covet what I see: *130*
Content me with an humble shade,
My passions tam'd, my wishes laid;
For while our wishes wildly roll,
We banish quiet from the soul:
'Tis thus the busy beat the air;   *135*
And misers gather wealth and care.
        Now, ev'n now, my joys run high,
As on the mountain-turf I lie;
While the wanton Zephyr sings,
And in the vale perfumes his wings;   *140*
While the waters murmur deep;
While the shepherd charms his sheep;
While the birds unbounded fly,
And with music fill the sky,
Now, ev'n now, my joys run high.   *145*
        Be full, ye courts, be great who will;
Search for Peace with all your skill:
Open wide the lofty door,
Seek her on the marble floor,
In vain you search, she is not there;   *150*
In vain ye search the domes of care!
Grass and flowers Quiet treads,
On the meads, and mountain-heads,
Along with Pleasure, close ally'd,
Ever by each other's side: *155*
And often, by the murm'ring rill,
Hears the thrush, while all is still,
Within the groves of Grongar Hill.

30 vistoes: vistas.

John Betjeman   Cornish Cliffs

Those moments, tasted once and never done,
Of long surf breaking in the mid-day sun,
A far-off blow-hole booming like a gun—

The seagulls plane and circle out of sight
Below this thirsty, thrift-encrusted height,   *5*
The veined sea-campion buds burst into white

And gorse turns tawny orange, seen beside
Pale drifts of primroses cascading wide
To where the slate falls sheer into the tide.

More than in gardened Surrey, nature spills   *10*
A wealth of heather, kidney-vetch and squills
Over these long-defended Cornish hills.

A gun-emplacement of the latest war
Looks older than the hill fort built before
Saxon or Norman headed for the shore.   *15*

And in the shadowless, unclouded glare
Deep blue above us fades to whiteness where
A misty sea-line meets the wash of air.

Nut-smell of gorse and honey-smell of ling
Waft out to sea the freshness of the spring   20
On sunny shallows, green and whispering.

The wideness which the lark-song gives the sky
Shrinks at the clang of sea-birds sailing by
Whose notes are tuned to days when the seas are high.

From today's calm, the lane's enclosing green   25
Leads inland to a usual Cornish scene—
Slate cottages with sycamore between,

Small fields and tellymasts and wires and poles
With, as the everlasting ocean rolls,
Two chapels built for half a hundred souls.   30

UBI SUNT FORMULA

Both theme and formula, this type of poem, especially
popular in French forms, asks "where are" (*ubi sunt*) such
and such things today. The general effect of the *ubi sunt*
formula is to suggest the transitory quality of life. The most
famous example in English is Dante Gabriel Rossetti's translation of a François Villon ballade (see Glossary), "The
Ballade of Dead Ladies," which asks:
> "But where are the snows of yester-year?"
Some further examples often cited for the use of this theme
are Justin McCarthy's poem, "I Wonder in What Isle of
Bliss," in which the formula is slightly altered in each stanza,
as follows:
> "Where are the Gods (the Dreams; the Girls; the Snows)
> of Yesterday?"
and Edmund Gosse's "The Ballad of Dead Cities," written in
three stanzas.

Anonymous ca. 1350   Ubi Sunt Qui Ante Nos Fuerunt?

Were beth they that biforen us weren,
Houndes ladden and havekes beren,
  And hadden feld and wode?
    The riche levedies in here bour,
      That wereden gold in here tressour,   5
  With here brighte rode;

Eten and drounken, and maden hem glad;
Here lif was al with gamen y-lad,
  Men kneleden hem biforen;

They beren hem wel swithe heye;   10
And in a twincling of an eye
Here soules weren forloren.

Were is that lawhing and that song,
That trayling and that proude gong,
   Tho havekes and tho houndes?   15
      Al that joye is went away,
      That wele is comen to weylaway
   To manye harde stoundes.

Here paradis they nomen here,
And nou they lyen in helle y-fere;   20
   The fyr hit brennes evere:
      Long is ay, and long is o,
      Long is wy, and long is wo;
   Thennes ne cometh they nevere.

title: "Where are they who were before us?"   *1 Were beth:* where
are.   *2 ladden:* led. *havekes beren:* hawks borne.   *4 levedies:*
ladies. *here:* their. *bour:* chamber.   *5 tressour:* tresses.   *6*
brighte rode: fair complexions.   *8 gamen y-lad:* pleasures led.
9 hem: them.   *10:* They carried themselves very high.   *12*
forloren: lost.   *13 lawhing:* laughing.   *14:* that trailing (of
garments) and that proud walk.   *17 wele . . . weylaway:* weal has
come to woe.   *18 stoundes:* times.   *19:* Their paradise they
took here.   *20 y-fere:* together.   *21 brennes:* burns.

VERS DE SOCIÉTÉ

The distinction between light verse and *vers de société* is
worth preserving, though at times readers may disagree upon
individual poems. Light verse, an inclusive term, is designed
primarily to entertain, and includes parodies and limericks.
Vers de société may be complimentary, often makes reference
to the manners and morals of the day, and is usually marked
by its grace, elegance, wit, and sophistication.

George Wither   "Shall I Wasting in Despair"

Shall I wasting in despair,
Die because a woman's fair?
Or make pale my cheeks with care,
'Cause another's rose are?
Be she fairer than the day,   5
Or the flowery meads in May;
   If she be not so to me,
   What care I how fair she be.

Should my heart be grieved or pined,
'Cause I see a woman kind?   10

Or a well disposed nature,
Joined with a lovely feature?
Be she meeker, kinder than
Turtle-dove or pelican:
   If she be not so me,   15
   What care I how kind she be.

Shall a woman's virtues move
Me to perish for her love?
Or, her well-deserving known,
Make me quite forget mine own?   20
Be she with that goodness blest,
Which may gain her name of best:
   If she be not such to me,
   What care I how good she be.

'Cause her fortune seems too high,   25
Shall I play the fool and die?
Those that bear a noble mind,
Where they want of riches find,
Thine, what with them, they would do,
That without them, dare to woo.   30
   And, unless that mind I see,
   What care I for whom she be.

Great, or good, or kind, or fair,
I will ne'er the more despair,
If she love me, this believe;   35
I will die ere she shall grieve.
If she slight me when I woo;
I can scorn, and let her go.
   For, if she be not for me,
   What care I for whom she be.

Ogden Nash   The Anatomy of Happiness

Lots of truisms don't have to be repeated but there is one that
   has got to be,
Which is that it is much nicer to be happy than it is not to be,
And I shall even add to it by stating unequivocally and
   without restraint
That you are much happier when you are happy than when
   you ain't.
Some people are just naturally Pollyanna,   5
While others call for sugar and cream and strawberries on
   their manna.
Now, I think we all ought to say a fig for the happiness
   that comes of thinking helpful thoughts and searching your
   soul,
The most exciting happiness is the happiness generated by
   forces beyond your control,
Because if you just depend on your helpful thoughts for your

happiness and would just as soon drink buttermilk as
champagne, and if mink is no better than lapin to you,
Why you don't even deserve to have anything nice and
exciting happen to you.   10
If you are really Master of your Fate,
It shouldn't make any difference to you whether Cleopatra or
the Bearded Lady is your mate,
So I hold no brief for the kind of happiness or the kind of
unhappiness that some people constantly carry around in
their breast,
Because that kind of happiness simply consists of being
resigned to the worst just as that kind of unhappiness
consists of being resentful of the best.
No, there is only one kind of happiness that I take the stump
for,   15
Which is the kind that comes when something so wonderful
falls in your lap that joy is what you jump for,
Something not of your own doing,
When the blue sky opens and out pops a refund from the
Government or an invitation to a terrapin dinner or an
unhoped-for Yes from the lovely creature you have been
disconsolately wooing.
And obviously such miracles don't happen every day,
But here's hoping they may,   20
Because then everybody would be happy except the people
who pride themselves on creating their own happiness who
as soon as they saw everybody who didn't create their own
happiness happy they would probably grieve over sharing
their own heretofore private sublimity,
A condition which I could face with equanimity.

PART VI

Poetic Fusions of Form and Theme

As previous examples have illustrated, form and theme, narrative and drama fuse within a poem, for a theme must be expressed in some form. The choice of theme frequently limits the form, although at times a specific form is chosen to enhance the theme, its treatment, or its meaning. Among the specific fusions of form and theme which occur often enough for separate categorization in this text are comic imitations of specific poems, authors' style, narrative conventions, and serious themes; lyrics which relate or imply stories or character studies; lyrics which have dramatic presence or are actually set up in dialogue form; and single poems which are constituted by a number of smaller, seemingly independent poems or by a series of interrelated units.

Comic imitations depend upon the author's intent of satirizing a form, a theme, an author, a specific poem, or an idea. Unconscious satire—such as may occur in derivative work of an inferior writer—does not qualify as burlesque, mock-epic, parody, or travesty. Intent, difficult though it may be to determine in other cases, is fairly obvious in comic imitation. Narrative or dramatic lyrics, depend primarily on the author's removal of himself from the poem; that is, they depend on perspective toward the subject, despite the presence, often of the first person singular. Much poetry read cursorily as personal statement proves not to be personal, and should be classified

here; for example, poem 11 from Whitman's *Song of Myself*
is obviously a lyric as narrative (the whole being a sequence),
for the "I" is a woman, or look at Donne's *The Good-Morrow*,
which should be read as a dramatic lyric rather than an auto-
biographical poem.

Poems as sequence most fully allow all forms—either in
single, repeated forms for the entire sequence, or in various
forms in the same sequence—and all themes and conventions.
At times the sequence is structurally united, as in Gascoigne's
Memories IV, or thematically united, as in Sandburg's *Four
Preludes;* but at times units may be excerpted as unified poems,
for example, the first of Aiken's *Preludes to Attitude* (not
included here), although the title of the sequence demands all
ten units be considered before that "attitude" can be fully
determined.

COMIC IMITATIONS

Burlesque

John Philips   The Splendid Shilling

AN IMITATION OF MILTON

Happy the man who, void of cares and strife,
In silken or in leathern purse retains
A Splendid Shilling: he nor hears with pain
New oysters cried, nor sighs for cheerful ale;
But with his friends, when nightly mists arise,   5
To Juniper's, Magpye, or Town-Hall repairs:
Where, mindful of the nymph whose wanton eye
Transfixed his soul and kindled amorous flames,
Chloe, or Phyllis, he each circling glass
Wisheth her health, and joy, and equal love.   10
Meanwhile he smokes, and laughs at merry tale,
Or pun ambiguous, or conundrum quaint.
But I, whom griping penury surrounds,
And hunger, sure attendant upon want,
With scanty offals, and small acid tiff   15
(Wretched repast!) my meager corpse sustain:
Then solitary walk, or doze at home
In garret vile, and with a warming puff
Regale chilled fingers; or from tube as black
As winter chimney or well polished jet   20
Exhale Mundungus, ill-perfuming scent:
Not blacker tube nor of a shorter size
Smokes Cambro-Britain (versed in pedigree,
Sprung from Cadwalader and Arthur, kings
Full famous in romantic tale) when he   25
O'er many a craggy hill and barren cliff

Upon a cargo of famed Cestrian cheese
High over-shadowing rides, with a design
To vend his wares, or at the Arvonian mart,
Or Maridunum, or the ancient town   30
Yclept Brechinia, or where Vaga's stream
Encircles Ariconium, fruitful soil,
Whence flow nectareous wines, that well may vie
With Massic, Setin, or renowned Falern.
   Thus while my joyless minutes tedious flow   35
With looks demure and silent pace, a dun,
Horrible monster! hated by gods and men,
To my aerial citadel ascends;
With vocal heel thrice thundering at my gates,
With hideous accent thrice he calls; I know   40
The voice ill-boding and the solemn sound.
What should I do? or whither turn? Amazed,
Confounded, to the dark recess I fly
Of woodhole; straight my bristling hairs erect
Through sudden fear; a chilly sweat bedews   45
My shuddering limbs, and, wonderful to tell,
My tongue forgets her faculty of speech,
So horrible he seems; his faded brow
Entrenched with many a frown and conic beard
And spreading band, admired by modern saints,   50
Disastrous acts forebode; in his right hand
Long scrolls of paper solemnly he waves,
With characters and figures dire inscribed
Grievous to mortal eyes; (ye gods avert
Such plagues from righteous men!) behind him stalks   55
Another monster, not unlike himself,
Sullen of aspect, by the vulgar called
A catchpole, whose polluted hands the gods
With force incredible and magic charms
Erst have indued; if he his ample palm   60
Should haply on ill-fated shoulder lay
Of debtor, straight his body to the touch
Obsequious, as whilom knights were wont,
To some enchanted castle is conveyed,
Where gates impregnable and coercive chains   65
In durance strict detain him, till in form
Of money Pallas sets the captive free.
   Beware, ye debtors, when ye walk beware,
Be circumspect; oft with insidious ken
This caitiff eyes your steps aloof, and oft   70
Lies perdue in a nook or gloomy cave,
Prompt to enchant some inadvertent wretch
With his unhallowed touch, So, poets sing,
Grimalkin, to domestic vermin sworn
An everlasting foe, with watchful eye   75
Lies nightly brooding o'er a chinky gap,
Protending her fell claws, to thoughtless mice
Sure ruin. So her disemboweled web
Arachne in a hall or kitchen spreads,

Obvious to vagrant flies: she secret stands   80
Within her woven cell; the humming prey,
Regardless of their fate, rush on the toils
Inextricable, nor will aught avail
Their arts, nor arms, nor shapes of lovely hue:
The wasp insidious, and the bussing drone,   85
And butterfly proud of expanded wings
Distinct with gold, entangled in her snares,
Useless resistance make. With eager strides
She towering flies to her expected spoils;
Then with envenomed jaws the vital blood   90
Drinks of reluctant foes, and to her cave
Their bulky carcasses triumphant drags.
    So pass my days. But when nocturnal shades
This world envelop, and the inclement air
Persuades men to repel benumbing frosts   95
With pleasant wines and crackling blaze of wood,
Me lonely sitting, nor the glimmering light
Of make-weight candle, nor the joyous talk
Of loving friend delights; distressed, forlorn,
Amidst the horrors of the tedious night   100
Darkling I sigh, and feed with dismal thoughts
My anxious mind; or sometimes mournful verse
Indite, and sing of groves and myrtle shades,
Or desperate lady near a purling stream,
Or lover pendent on a willow tree.   105
Meanwhile I labor with eternal drought,
And restless wish and rave; my parched throat
Finds no relief, nor heavy eyes repose:
But if a slumber haply does invade
My weary limbs, my fancy's still awake,   110
Thoughtful of drink, and eager in a dream
Tipples imaginary pots of ale;
In vain; awake, I find the settled thirst
Still gnawing, and the pleasant phantom curse.
    Thus do I live from pleasure quite debarred,   115
Nor taste the fruits that the sun's genial rays
Mature, John-apple, nor the downy peach,
Nor walnut in rough-furrowed coat secure,
Nor medlar, fruit delicious in decay.
Afflictions great! yet greater still remain: 120
My galligaskins that have long withstood
The winter's fury and encroaching frosts,
By time subdued (what will not time subdue!),
An horrid chasm disclose, with orifice
Wide, discontinuous; at which the winds   125
Eurus and Auster, and the dreadful force
Of Boreas, that congeals the Cronian waves,
Tumultuous enter with dire chilling blasts
Protending agues. Thus a well-fraught ship
Long sailed secure, or through the Aegean deep,   130
Or the Ionian, till cruising near

The Lilybean shore, with hideous crush
On Scylla or Charybdis, dangerous rocks,
She strikes rebounding, whence the shattered oak,
So fierce a shock unable to withstand,   135
Admits the sea; in at the gaping side
The crowding waves gush with impetuous rage,
Resistless, overwhelming; horrors seize
The mariners, death in their eyes appears,
They stare, they lave, they pump, they swear, they pray: 140
Vain efforts! still the battering waves rush in
Implacable, till deluged by the foam,
The ship sinks foundering in the vast abyss.

An Imitation of Milton: that is, of the verse and language of *Paradise Lost.*   15 *tiff:* weak liquor.   21 *Mundungus:* offensive-
smelling tobacco.   23 *Cambro-Britain:* the Welsh part of Britain.   27 *Cestrian:* from Cheshire.   29 *Arvonian:* of Caernar-
von, Wales.   30 *Maridunum:* section of southern Wales.   31
Yclept: called. *Brechinia:* an area of Scotland. *Vaga:* a Russian
river.   32 *Ariconium:* a city in Hereford.   34 *Massic:* of the
Massican Hills in Italy. *Setin:* a section of ancient Latium. *Falern:*
a wine-producing area of Italy.   36 *dun:* bill-collector.   58
catchpole: a sheriff's officer.   60 *Erst:* formerly.   63 *whilom
knights:* knights of earlier days.   67 *Pallas:* Minerva.   71
perdue: lost.   74 *Grimalkin:* a cat.   77 *Protending:* extend-
ing.   79 *Arachne:* a spider.   105 *pendent:* suspended.   121
galligaskins: breeches.   126 *Eurus:* the southeast wind. *Auster:*
the south wind.   127 *Boreas:* the north wind. *Cronian:* of the
Arctic Sea.   129 *Protending:* portending.   132 *Lilybean:*
Libyan.

George Gordon, Lord Byron   Epilogue

There's something in a stupid ass:
And something in a heavy dunce;
But never since I went to school
I saw or heard so damned a fool
As William Wordsworth is for once.   5

And now I've seen so great a fool
As William Wordsworth is for once,
I really wish that Peter Bell
And he who wrote it were in hell,
For writing nonsense for the nonce.   10

I saw the "light in ninety-eight,"
Sweet Babe of one and twenty years!
And then he gave it to the nation,
And deems himself of Shakespeare's peers.
He gives the perfect works to light!   15
William Wordsworth—if I might advise,
Content you with the praise you get

From Sir George Beaumont, Baronet,
And with your place in the excise.

8 *Peter Bell*: a poetical tale by Wordsworth (1819).   18 *Beaumont*: English landscape painter and patron of art.

Bayard Taylor   Camerados

Everywhere, everywhere, following me;
Taking me by the buttonhole, pulling off my boots, hustling
     me with the elbows;
Sitting down with me to clams and the chowder-kettle;
Plunging naked at my side into the sleek, irascible surges;
Soothing me with the strain that I neither permit nor
     prohibit;   5
Flocking this way and that, reverent, eager, orotund,
     irrepressible;
Denser than sycamore leaves when the north-winds are
     scouring Paumanok;
What can I do to restrain them? Nothing, verily nothing.
Everywhere, everywhere, crying aloud for me;
Crying, I hear; and I satisfy them out of my nature;   10
And he that comes at the end of the feast shall find
     something over.
Whatever they want I give; though it be something else,
     they shall have it.
Drunkard, leper, Tammanyite, small-pox and cholera patient,
     shoddy and codfish millionaire,
And the beautiful young men, and the beautiful young
     women, all the same,
Crowding, hundreds of thousands, cosmical multitudes,   15
Buss me and hang on my hips and lean up to my shoulders,
Everywhere listening to my yawp and glad whenever they
     hear it;
Everywhere saying, say it, Walt, we believe it:
Everywhere, everywhere.

Ezra Pound   Mr. Housman's Message

O woe, woe,
People are born and die,
We also shall be dead pretty soon
Therefore let us act as if we were
               dead already.   5

The birds sits on the hawthorn tree
But he dies also, presently.
Some lads get hung, and some get shot.
Woeful is this human lot.
          Woe! woe, etcetera . . .   10

Louis Untermeyer   Edna St. Vincent Millay Exhorts Little Boy Blue

From that last acre on oblivion's heap
Come, lad tricked out in bold and trumpery blue;
Come, blow your idle horn, and send the few
Notes with no name against the night. Here sheep
Trample the fetid meadow; here cows creep,   5
Raising their eyes wherever one or two
Crushing the corn, pause to admire the view;
Come, doubtful dreamer, spurn ignoble sleep.

I tell you this, Boy Blue, lift up your horn
Against the world's deliberate apathy,   10
Or what we held so dear will be the scorn
Of casual rats and roaches; life will be
A town not worth the taking, a spent call.
Grimly I tell you this. And this is all.

Mock-Heroic

Ben Jonson   On the Famous Voyage

No more let Greece her bolder fables tell
    Of Hercules, or Theseus going to hell,
Orpheus, Ulysses: or the Latin Muse,
    With tales of Troy's just knight, our faiths abuse:
We have a Shelton and a Heyden got,   5
    Had powers to act, what they to feign had not.
All that they boast of Styx, of Acheron,
    Cocytus, Phlegethon, our have proved in one;
The filth, stench, noise: save only what was there
    Subtly distinguished was confused here.   10
Their wherry had no sail, too; ours had none:
    And in it, two more horrid knaves than Charon.
Arses were heard to croak instead of frogs;
    And for one Cerberus, the whole coast was dogs.
Furies there wanted not: each scold was ten.   15
    And, for the cries of ghosts, women, and men,
Laden with plague-sores, and their sins, were heard,
    Lashed by their consciences, to die, afeared.
Then let the former age, with this content her,
    She brought the poets forth, but ours the adventer.   20

The Voyage Itself

I sing the brave adventure of two wights,
And pity 'tis, I cannot call 'em knights:
One was; and he, for brawn and brain, right able

To have been styled of King Arthur's table.
The other was a squire of fair degree;   25
But in the action greater man than he:
Who gave, to take at his return from Hell,
His three for one. Now, lordings, listen well.
    It was the day, what time the powerful moon
Makes the poor bankside creature wet its shoon   30
In its own hall; when these (in worthy scorn
Of those, that put out moneys, on return
From Venice, Paris, or some inland passage
Of six times to, and fro, without embassage,
Or him that backward went to Berwick, or which   35
Did dance the famous Morris, unto Norwich)
At Bread Street's Mermaid, having dined, and merry,
Proposed to go to Holborn in a wherry:
A harder task than either his to Bristo',
Or his to Antwerp. Therefore, once more, list ho'.   40
    A dock there is, that called is Avernus,
Of some Bridewell, and may, in time, concern us
All, that are readers: but, methinks 'tis odd,
That all this while I have forgot some god
Or goddess to invoke, to stuff my verse;   45
And with both bombard-style, and phrase rehearse
The many perils of this port, and how
Sans help of Sybil, or a golden bough,
Or magic sacrifice, they passed along!
Alcides, be thou succoring to my song.   50
Thou hast seen hell (some say) and knowest all nooks there,
Canst tell me best, how every Fury looks there,
And art a god, if Fame thee not abuses,
Always at hand, to aid the mercy Muses.
Great club-fist, though thy back and bones be sore,   55
Still, with thy former labors; yet, once more,
Act a brave work, call it thy last adventry:
But hold my torch, while I describe the entry
To this dire passage. Say, thou, stop thy noise:
'Tis but light pains: indeed this dock's no rose.   60
    In the first jaws appeared that ugly monster,
Ycleped Mud, which, when their oars did once stir,
Belched forth an air, as hot, as at the muster
Of all your night-tubs, when the carts do cluster,
Who shall discharge first his merde-urinous load: 65
Through her womb they make their famous road,
Between two walls; where, on one side, to scare men,
Were seen your ugly Centaurs, ye call carmen,
Gorgonian scolds, and Harpies; on the other
Hung stench, diseases, and old filth, their mother,   70
With famine, wants, and sorrows many a dozen,
The least of which was to the plague a cousin.
But they unfrighted pass, though many a privy
Spake to 'em louder than the ox in Livy.
And many a sink poured out her rage anenst 'em;   75
But still their valor and their virtue fenced 'em,

And on they went, like Castor brave and Pollux:
Plowing the main. When, see (the worst of all lucks)
They met the second prodigy, would fear a
Man that had never heard of a chimaera. 80
One said, it was bold Briareus, or the beadle
(Who hath the hundred hands when he doth meddle);
The other thought it Hydra, or the rock
Made of the trull that cut her father's lock;
But, coming near, they found it but a lighter, 85
So huge, it seemed, they could by no means quiet her.
Back, cried their brace of Charons: they cried no,
No going back; on still you rogues, and row.
How hight the place? A voice was heard, Cocytus.
Row close then slaves. Alas, they will beshite us. 90
No matter, stinkards, row. What croaking sound
Is this we hear? of frogs? No, guts windbound,
Over your heads: Well, row. At this a loud
Crack did report itself, as if a cloud
Had burst with storm, and down fell, *ab excelsis,* 95
Poor Mercury, crying out on Paracelsus,
And all his followers, that had so abused him:
And, in so shitten sort, so long had used him:
For (where he was the god of eloquence,
And subtlety of metals) they dispense 100
His spirits, now, in pills, and eke in potions,
Suppositories, cataplasms, and lotions.
But many moons there shall not wane, quoth he;
In the meantime, let 'em imprison me,
But I will speak (and know I shall be heard) 105
Touching this cause, where they will be afeared
To answer me. And sure, it was the intent
Of the grave fart, late let in parliament,
Had it been seconded, and not in fume
Vanished away: as you must all presume 110
Their Mercury did now. By this, the stem
Of the hulk touched, and, as by Polypheme
The sly Ulysses stole in a sheepskin,
The well-greased wherry now had got between,
And bade her farewell sough, unto the lurden: 115
Never did bottom more betray her burden;
The meat-boat of Bears' college, Paris Garden,
Stunk not so ill; nor, when she kissed, Kate Arden.
Yet, one day in the year, for swect 'tis voiced
And that is when it is the Lord Mayor's foist. 120
   By this time had they reached the Stygian pool,
By which the Masters swear, when, on the stool
Of worship, they their nodding chins do hit
Against their breasts. Here, several ghosts did flit
About the shore, of farts, but late departed, 125
White, black, blue, green, and in more forms outstarted
Than all those atomi ridiculous,
Whereof old Democrite, and Hill Nicholas,
One said, the other swore, the world consists.

These be the cause of those thick frequent mists   130
Arising in that place, through which, who goes,
Must try the unused valor of a nose:
And that ours did. For, yet, no nare was tainted,
Nor thumb, nor finger to the stop acquainted,
But open, and unarmed encountered all;   135
Whether it languishing stuck upon the wall,
Or were precipitated down the jakes,
And, after, swum abroad in ample flakes,
Or, that it lay, heaped like an usurer's mass,
All was to them the same, they were to pass,   140
And so they did, from Styx to Acheron,
The ever-boiling flood, whose banks upon
Your Fleet Lane Furies; and hot cooks do dwell,
That, with still-scalding steams, makes the place hell.
The sinks ran grease, and hair of measled hogs,   145
The heads, houghs, entrails, and the hides of dogs:
For to say truth, what scullion is so nasty,
To put the skins and offal in a pasty?
Cats there lay divers had been flead, and roasted,
And, after moldy grown, again were toasted,   150
Then, selling not, a dish was ta'en to mince 'em,
But still it seemed the rankness did convince 'em.
For here they were thrown in with the melted pewter,
Yet drowned they not. They had five lives in future.
    But 'mongst these tiberts, who do you think there was?   155
Old Banks, the juggler, our Pythagoras,
Grave tutor to the learned horse. Both which,
Being beyond sea, burned for one witch,
Their spirits transmigrated to a cat:
And now above the pool, a face right fat   160
With great gray eyes, are filled up and mewed;
Thrice did it spit: thrice dived. At last it viewed
Our brave heroes with a milder glare
And in a piteous tune began. How dare
Your dainty nostrils (in so hot a season,   165
When every clerk eats artichokes and peason,
Laxative lettuce, and such windy meat)
Tempt such passage? when each privy's seat
Is filled with buttocks? And the walls do sweat
Urine and plasters? when the noise doth beat   170
Upon your ears of discords so unsweet?
And outcries of the damned in the Fleet?
Cannot the plague-bill keep you back? nor bells
Of loud Sepulchre's with their hourly knells,
But you will visit grisly Pluto's hall?   175
Behold where Cerberus, reared on the wall
Of Holborn (three sergeants' heads) looks o'er,
And stays but till you come unto the door!
Tempt not his fury, Pluto is away:
And Madame Caesar, great Proserpina,   180
Is now from home. You lose your labors quite,
Were you Jove's sons, or had Alcides' might.

They cried out, Puss. He told them he was Banks,
That had so often showed 'em merry pranks.
They laughed at his laugh-worthy fate, and passed   *185*
The triple head without a sop. At last,
Calling for Rhadamanthus, that dwelt by,
A soap-boiler; and Aeacus him nigh,
Who kept an alehouse; with my little Minos,
An ancient purblind fletcher, with a high nose;   *190*
They took 'em all to witness of their action:
And so went bravely back, without protraction.
   In memory of which most liquid deed,
The city since hath raised a pyramid.
And I could wish for their eternized sakes,   *195*
My Muse had plowed with his that sung A-jax.

4 *knights:* Aeneas.   5 *Shelton:* Sir Ralph Shelton.   *Heyden:*
unknown.   7–8: The four rivers of Hell.   8 *one:* Fleet Ditch,
carrying London's sewage to the Thames.   11 *Their:* those cited
in ll. 2–4. *wherry:* rowboat.   12 *Charon:* ferryman of the Styx.
14 *Cerberus:* the three-headed watchdog of Hell.   20 *adventer:*
adventure.   28 *His three for one:* i. e., with high return.   30
bankside: southern side of the Thames, a disreputable district.
shoon: shoes.   35 *backward went:* a well-known contemporary
stunt.   *which:* Will Kempe, a comic actor.   37 *Mermaid:* a
tavern.   38 *Holborn:* an area to the northwest.   39–40: Referring to attempts to row the Channel.   41 *dock:* 1) a basin to
receive vessels; its name should be read "Bride's Well." 2) a prisoner's platform in court; Brideswell was also a prison on the way
to Holborn.   *Avernus:* a cavernous entry into Hell.   48 *Sans:*
without. *Sybil, golden bough:* they aided Aeneas' descent to Hell.
50 *Alcides:* Hercules.   62 *Ycleped:* called. *Mud:* punning on
mother.   65 *merde:* excremental.   68 *carmen:* drivers of dung
carts.   74 *ox:* which thereby foretold the future.   75 *sink:* sewage conduit. *anenst:* against.   76 *fenced:* protected.   77 *Castor, Pollux:* twins, one in Hell, one in Heaven.   80 *chimaera:*
a creature with a lion's head, a goat's body, and a serpent's tail.
81 *Briareus:* a hundred-handed monster.   83 *Hydra:* a nine-
headed serpent. *the rock:* Scylla, but it was the daughter of Nisus
of Megara, who cut off her father's life-giving hair to win Minos.
86 *quiet:* avoid.   89 *How hight:* What is [the place] called?
95 *ab excelsis:* from the heavens.   96: Mercury was conductor of
the dead to the afterworld. Followers of Paracelsus used mercury
as a purgative.   102 *cataplasms:* poultices.   108: Referring to
an event in 1607.   115 *sough:* sigh. *lurden:* heaviness.   117:
Referring to the boat that carried offal across the Thames to be
used as food for the bears kept for bear-baiting shows.   118 *Kate
Arden:* a well-known whore.   120 *foist:* barge; stink.   127
atomi: atoms.   128 *Democrite:* Democritus. *Hill Nicholas:* Nicholas Hill (1570?–1610).   137 *jakes:* toilet.   145 *measled:* lep-
rous.   146 *houghs:* hocks.   149 *flead:* flayed.   150 *toasted:*
with a pun on "passed excrement."   155 *tiberts:* cats.   156
Banks: a showman of the 1590's using a horse, an ape, and an
elephant in his act.   *Pythagoras:* because he believed in trans-

migration.   *161 mewed*: imprisoned   *166 peason*: peas.   *172
Fleet*: a debtor's prison.   *174 Sepulchre's*: a church's.   *180
Caesar*: ruler.   *187 Rhadamanthus*: one of the three judges of
Hell, the others being Aeacus and Minos (ll. 187–189). They
were Jove's sons (l. 182).   *190 fletcher*: arrow-maker.   *196
his*: Sir John Harington, the author of the *Metamorphosis of Ajax*
(1596), i.e., of the Greek hero. *A-jax*: i.e., a jakes.

Parody

George Gordon, Lord Byron   "Strahan, Tonson, Lintot of the Times"

Strahan, Tonson, Lintot of the times,
Patron and publisher of rhymes,
For thee the bard up Pindus climbs,
   My Murray.

To thee, with hope and terror dumb,   5
The unfledged MS. authors come;
Thou printest all—and sellest some—
   My Murray.

Upon thy table's baize so green
The last new *Quarterly* is seen;   10
But where is thy new Magazine,
   My Murray.

Along thy sprucest bookshelves shine
The works thou deemest most divine—
The *Art of Cookery*, and mine,   15
   My Murray.

Tours, Travels, Essays, too, I wist,
And Sermons, to thy mill bring grist;
And then thou hast the *Navy List*,
   My Murray.   20

And Heaven forbid I should conclude
Without "the Board of Longitude,"
Although this narrow paper would,
   My Murray.

Strahan, Tonson, Lintot: William Strahan (1715–1785), Jacob
Tonson (1565?–1736), Barnaby Lintot (1675–1736), important
publishers in *their* times. Compare William Cowper's "To Mary."
3 *Pindus*: a Greek mountain range.   4 *Murray*: John Murray
(1778–1843), Byron's publisher and founder of the *Edinburgh
Review*.   10 *Quarterly*: organ of the Whig party, started in opposition to the *Edinburgh Review*.   11 *new Magazine: Black-
wood's Edinburgh Monthly Magazine*, in which Murray bought an
interest in August 1818.   15 *Art of Cookery*: a cookbook by Mrs.
Maria Eliza Rundell, entitled *Family Receipt-Book* and later *Domestic Cookery*.   17 *wist*: knew.   19 *Navy List*: for the Ad-

miralty.   22 *the Board of Longitude:* in the sixth ed. of *Childe Harold's Pilgrimage* (1813), the title page lists Murray as "Bookseller to the Admiralty, and Board of Longitude."

Algernon Charles Swinburne   The Higher Pantheism in a Nutshell

One, who is not, we see; but one, whom we see not, is;
Surely this is not that; but that is assuredly this.

What, and wherefore, and whence? for under is over and under;
If thunder could be without lightning, lightning could be without thunder.

Doubt is faith in the main; but faith, on the whole, is doubt;   5
We cannot believe by proof; but could we believe without?

Why, and whither, and how? for barley and rye are not clover;
Neither are straight lines curves; yet over is under and over.

Two and two may be four; but four and four are not eight;
Fate and God may be twain; but God is the same thing as fate.   10

Ask a man what he thinks, and get from a man what he feels;
God, once caught in the fact, shows you a fair pair of heels.

Body and spirit are twins; God only knows which is which;
The soul squats down in the flesh, like a tinker drunk in a ditch.

More is the whole than a part; but half is more than the whole;   15
Clearly, the soul is the body; but is not the body the soul?

One and two are not one; but one and nothing is two;
Truth can hardly be false, if falsehood cannot be true.

Once the mastodon was; pterodactyls were common as cocks;
Then the mammoth was God; now is He a prize ox.   20

Parallels all things are; yet many of these are askew;
You are certainly I; but certainly I am not you.

Springs the rock from the plain, shoots the stream from the rock;
Cocks exist for the hen; but hens exist for the cock.

God, whom we see not, is; and God, who is not, we see;   25
Fiddle, we know, is diddle; and diddle, we take it, is dee.

Morris Bishop   Ozymandias Revisited

I met a traveller from an antique land
Who said: Two vast and trunkless legs of stone

Stand in the desert. Near them on the sand,
Half sunk, a shattered visage lies, whose frown
And wrinkled lip and sneer of cold command   5
Tell that its sculptor well those passions read
Which yet survive, stamped on these lifeless things,
The hand that mocked them and the heart that fed;
And on the pedestal these words appear:
'My name is Ozymandias, king of kings!   10
Look on my works, ye Mighty, and despair!'
Also the names of Emory P. Gray,
Mr. and Mrs. Dukes, and Oscar Baer,
Of 17 West 4th Street, Oyster Bay.

Anthony Hecht   The Dover Bitch

So there stood Matthew Arnold and this girl
With the cliffs of England crumbling away behind them,
And he said to her, "Try to be true to me,
And I'll do the same for you, for things are bad
All over, etc., etc."   5
Well now, I knew this girl. It's true she had read
Sophocles in a fairly good translation
And caught that bitter allusion to the sea,
But all the time he was talking she had in mind
The notion of what his whiskers would feel like   10
On the back of her neck. She told me later on
That after a while she got to looking out
At the lights across the channel, and really felt sad,
Thinking of all the wine and enormous beds
And blandishments in French and the perfumes.   15
And then she got really angry. To have been brought
All the way down from London, and then be addressed
As a sort of mournful cosmic last resort
Is really tough on a girl, and she was pretty.
Anyway, she watched him pace the room   20
And finger his watch-chain and seem to sweat a bit,
And then she said one or two unprintable things.
But you mustn't judge her by that. What I mean to say is,
She's really all right. I still see her once in a while
And she always treats me right. We have a drink   25
And I give her a good time, and perhaps it's a year
Before I see her again, but there she is,
Running to fat, but dependable as they come.
And sometimes I bring her a bottle of *Nuit d' Amour*.

W.D. Snodgrass   Vampire's Aubade

Why so drawn, so worn,
  My dearest;

Should this sun-drenched morn
Find you so burned out and so pale?
Until now I've had no fear lest   5
    You'd be quick to fail.

Just last night, your glowing
    Cheek and breast
Entranced me, overflowing
With their young love, warm and strong.   10
Not to freely give your best,
    Dear—you'd think that wrong.

Then rise; shine; yet your laughter
    Fill the air.
When I do need looking after   15
And there's so much to be done,
Dear, it surely isn't fair
    So to hang on everyone.

    Or don't you care?

Travesty

G. K. Chesterton   A Ballade of Suicide

The gallows in my garden, people say,
Is new and neat and adequately tall.
I tie the noose on in a knowing way
As one that knots his necktie for a ball;
But just as all the neighbors—on the wall—   5
Are drawing a long breath to shout "Hurray!"
The strangest whim has seized me . . . After all
I think I will not hang myself today.

Tomorrow is the time I get my pay—
My uncle's sword is hanging in the hall—   10
I see a little cloud all pink and grey—
Perhaps the Rector's mother will *not* call—
I fancy that I heard from Mr. Gall
That mushrooms could be cooked another way—
I never read the works of Juvenal—   15
I think I will not hang myself today.

The world will have another washing day;
The decadents decay; the pedants pall;
And H. G. Wells has found that children play,
And Bernard Shaw discovered that they squall;   20
Rationalists are growing rational—
And through thick woods one finds a stream astray,
So secret that the very sky seems small—
I think I will not hang myself today.

ENVOI

Prince, I can hear the trumpet of Germinal,   25
The tumbrils toiling up the terrible way;
Even today your head may fall—
I think I will not hang myself today.

25 *Germinal*: a month of the French Revolutionary Calendar (corresponding to March 21 and meaning "seed").   26 *tumbrils*: carts transporting the condemned to the guillotine.

Leonard Bacon   Richard Tolman's Universe

Eddington's universe goes phut.
Richard Tolman's can open and shut.
Eddington's bursts without grace or tact,
But Tolman's swells and perhaps may contract.
All that Eddington can see   5
Is entropy, entropy, entropy.
But Tolman throws a punch to the jaw
Of the second thermodynamic law.
His heart, indeed, is comforted
When he sees a displacement toward the red,   10
And he at once sets up an equation
Which wholly alters the situation.
Give more rope! Give more rope!
Give more rope to the spectroscope.
Then catch Andromeda and hang her.   15
Tolman's a first-chop Doppleganger.
Tell me what Newton never knew,
Things about Messier 42.
In words of one syllable display
How Cepheid variables get that way.   20
Bring the criminal to the bar,
That stripped the atoms of Van Maanen's star.
Let me hear alpha particles clank.
Serve my electrons on a Planck.
And, no matter what sort of Hell has popped,   25
Let not the constant h be dropped
For things grow nebulous to me,
Especially the nebulae.
Astrophysics is perfectly grand.
There's nothing in it I understand   30
Except that I'm stuck for better or worse
In Tolman's elastic universe.

Richard Tolman: a physicist, whose relativistic thermodynamic theory reversed the second law of thermodynamics in a contracting universe, thus allowing for re-formation of matter from radiation.   1 *Eddington*: Sir Arthur Stanley Eddington, who investigated the stars and who championed the theory of relativity.

6 *entropy:* a measure of the unavailable energy in thermodynamics.   8 *law:* heat cannot pass of itself from a colder to a hotter
body.   10: That is, in the spectrum of light.   15 *Andromeda:*
a northern constellation.   16 *chop:* class. *Doppleganger:* an unreal double of oneself.   18 *Messier 42:* Orion; referring to
Charles Messier's catalogue of celestial objects.   20 *Cepheid:*
a meteor emanating from the constellation Cepheus. Cepheus was
Andromeda's father.   22 *Van Maanen:* Adrian Van Maanen,
Dutch astronomer, who proved that nuclear matter flows along
arms of spiral nebulae.   24 *Planck:* punning on physicist Max
Planck, who developed the quantum theory (i.e., that radiation is
an interrupted process, with equal amounts of energy being radi-
ated; their value depends on the universal constant h [l. 26] and
the frequency of vibration).

Richard L. Greene   Ubi Iam Sunt?

Where in what strange Elysium is now the *Literary Digest?*
  Where now the *Century* and the old *Review of Reviews?*
Where is the *Boston Transcript?* Where, oh where is *Leslie's?*
  Where are *Ballyhoo, Puck,* and *Judge* with their raffish
    crews?

They all are gone to that far land of the Marmon;   5
  The Locomobile, Pierce-Arrow, and Packard are in that
    place,
The leafy hunting-ground where snarls the fierce Stutz Bear-
    cat,
  Showing his fangs to the Mercer, the Kissel, the Cord, and
    the Case.
There sound the hollow whistles of *Aquitania, Celtic,*
  Paris, Olympic, Vaterland, Mauretania, Rex,   10
Conte Rosso, Britannic, Ile de France, and *Duilio,*
  Their spectral multiple funnels high above ghostly decks.

They are all gone forever, gone with the spat and the bustle,
  Gone with the open trolley and the fifty-cent gallery rush,
Gone with the celluloid collar, gone with the virtuous hatpin,   15
  Vanished and gone with the whalebone, the curtsey, the
    fan, and the blush.

Ubi Iam Sunt? where are they now?

THE LYRIC AS NARRATIVE

Andrew Marvell   The Nymph Complaining for the
Death of Her Fawn

The wanton troopers riding by
Have shot my fawn, and it will die.

Ungentle men! they cannot thrive
To kill thee. Thou ne'er didst alive
Them any harm; alas, nor could   5
Thy death yet do them any good.
I'm sure I never wished them ill;
Nor do I for all this, nor will:
But if my simple prayers may yet
Prevail with Heaven to forget   10
Thy murder, I will join my tears,
Rather than fail. But, O my fears!
It cannot die so. Heaven's king
Keeps register of everything,
And nothing may we use in vain;   15
Even beasts must be with justice slain,
Else men are made their deodands.
Though they should wash their guilty hands
In this warm life-blood which doth part
From thine, and wounds me to the heart,   20
Yet could they not be clean; their stain
Is dyed in such a purple grain.
There is not such another in
The world, to offer for their sin.
    Unconstant Sylvio, when yet   25
I had not found him counterfeit,
One morning (I remember well),
Tied in this silver chain and bell,
Gave it to me: nay, and I know
What he said then, I'm sure I do: 30
Said he, "Look how your huntsman here
Hath taught a fawn to hunt his deer."
But Sylvio soon had me beguiled;
This waxed tame, while he grew wild,
And quite regardless of my smart,   35
Left me his fawn, but took his heart.
    Thenceforth set myself to play
My solitary time away
With this; and, very well content,
Could so mine idle life have spent;   40
For it was full of sport, and light
Of foot and heart, and did invite
Me to its game: it seemed to bless
Itself in me; how could I less
Than love it? O, I cannot be   45
Unkind t' a beast that loveth me.
    Had it lived long I do not know
Whether it too might have done so
As Sylvio did; his gifts might be
Perhaps as false, or more, than he;   50
But I am sure, for ought that I
Could in so short a time espy,
Thy love was far more better than
The love of false and cruel men.
    With sweetest milk and sugar, first,   55

I it at my own fingers nursed;
And as it grew, so every day
It waxed more white and sweet than they.
It had so sweet a breath! and oft
I blushed to see its foot more soft   60
And white, shall I say than my hand?
Nay, and lady's of the land.
   It is a wondrous thing how fleet
'Twas on those little silver feet;
With what a pretty skipping grace   65
It oft would challenge me the race;
And, when't had left me far away,
'Twould stay, and run again, and stay;
For it was nimbler much than hinds,
And trod as on the four winds.   70
   I have a garden of my own,
But so with roses overgrown,
And lilies, that you would it guess
To be a little wilderness;
And all the springtime of the year   75
It only loved to be there.
Among the beds of lilies I
Have sought it oft, where it should lie,
Yet could not, till itself would rise,
Find it, although before mine eyes;   80
For, in the flaxen lilies' shade,
It like a bank of lilies laid.
Upon the roses it would feed,
Until its lips even seemed to bleed;
And then to me 'twould boldly trip,   85
And print those roses on my lip.
But all its chief delight was still
On roses thus itself to fill,
And its pure virgin limbs to fold
In whitest sheets of lilies cold: 90
Had it lived long, it would have been
Lilies without, roses within.
   O help! O help! I see it faint
And die as calmly as a saint!
See how it weeps! the tears do come   95
Sad, slowly, dropping like a gum.
So weeps the wounded balsam; so
The holy frankincense doth flow;
The brotherless Heliades
Melt in such amber tears as these.   100
   I in a golden vial will
Keep these two crystal tears, and fill
It till it do o'erflow with mine;
Then place it in Diana's shrine.
   Now my sweet fawn is vanished to   105
Whither the swans and turtles go;
In fair Elysium to endure,
With milk-white lambs and ermines pure.

O do not run too fast: for I
Will but bespeak thy grave, and die.   110
  First, my unhappy statue shall
Be cut in marble; and withal,
Let it be weeping too; but there
The engraver sure his art may spare;
For I so truly thee bemoan,   115
That I shall weep, though I be stone,
Until my tears, still dropping, wear
My breast, themselves engraving there;
There at my feet shalt thou be laid,
Of purest alabaster made;   120
For I would have thine image be
White as I can, though not as thee.

3 *Ungentle:* ungentlemanly, ignoble.   17 *deodands:* forlfeits for
being the cause of an innocent person's death.   36 *heart:* with
a pun on "hart."   99 *Heliades:* sisters of Phaeton; when they
mourned his death, they were turned into poplars that dripped
amber tears.   104 *Diana:* goddess of chastity and the hunt.
106 *turtles:* turtledoves, male symbols of faithfulness.

Robert Browning   Meeting at Night

The gray sea and the long black land;
And the yellow half-moon large and low;
And the startled little waves that leap
In fiery ringlets from their sleep,
As I gain the cove with pushing prow,   5
And quench its speed i' the slushy sand.

Then a mile of warm sea-scented beach;
Three fields to cross till a farm appears;
A tap at the pane, the quick sharp scratch
And blue spurt of a lighted match,   10
And a voice less loud, through its joys and fears,
Than the two hearts beating each to each!

Robert Browning   Parting at Morning

Round the cape of a sudden came the sea,
And the sun looked over the mountain's rim:
And straight was a path of gold for him,
And the need of a world of men for me.

Ralph Hodgson   Eve

Eve, with her basket, was
Deep in the bells and grass,

Wading in bells and grass
Up to her knees.
Picking a dish of sweet   5
Berries and plums to eat,
Down in the bells and grass
Under the trees.

Mute as a mouse in a
Corner the cobra lay,   10
Curled round a bough of the
Cinnamon tall. . . .
Now to get even and
Humble proud heaven and
Now was the moment or   15
Never at all.

"Eva!" Each syllable
Light as a flower fell,
"Eva!" he whispered the
Wondering maid,   20
Soft as a bubble sung
Out of a linnet's lung,
Soft and most silverly
"Eva!" he said.

Picture that orchard sprite;   25
Eve, with her body white,
Supple and smooth to her
Slim finger tips;
Wondering, listening,
Listening, wondering,   30
Eve with a berry
Half-way to her lips.

Oh, had our simple Eve
Seen through the make-believe!
Had she but known the   35
Pretender he was!
Out of the boughs he came,
Whispering still her name,
Tumbling in twenty rings
Into the grass.   40

Here was the strangest pair
In the world anywhere,
Eve in the bells and grass
Kneeling, and he
Telling his story low . . .
Singing birds saw them go   45
Down the dark path to
The Blasphemous Tree.

Oh, what a clatter when
Titmouse and Jenny wren
Saw him successful and   50
Taking his leave!

How the birds rated him,
How they all hated him!
How they all pitied   55
Poor motherless Eve!

Picture her crying
Outside in the lane,
Eve, with no dish of sweet
Berries and plums to eat,   60
Haunting the gate of the
Orchard in vain . . .
Picture the lewd delight
Under the hill tonight—
"Eva!" the toast goes round,   65
"Eva!" again.

Edwin Arlington Robinson   Richard Cory

Whenever Richard Cory went down town,
    We people on the pavement looked at him:
He was a gentleman from sole to crown,
    Clean favored, and imperially slim.

And he was always quietly arrayed,   5
    And he was always human when he talked;
But still he fluttered pulses when he said,
    "Good-morning," and he glittered when he walked.

And he was rich—yes, richer than a king—
    And admirably schooled in every grace: 10
In fine, we thought that he was everything
    To make us wish that we were in his place.

So on we worked, and waited for the light,
    And went without the meat, and cursed the bread;
And Richard Cory, one calm summer night,   15
    Went home and put a bullet through his head.

Kenneth Fearing   American Rhapsody (4)

First you bite your fingernails. And then you comb your hair
    again. And then you wait. And wait.
(They say, you know, that first you lie. And then you steal,
    they say. And then, they say, you kill.)

Then the doorbell rings. Then Peg drops in. And Bill. And
    Jane. And Doc.
And first you talk, and smoke, and hear the news and have
    a drink. Then you walk down the stairs.
And you dine, then, and go to a show after that, perhaps, and
    after that a night spot, and after that come home again, and
    climb the stairs again, and again go to bed.   5

But first Peg argues, and Doc replies. First you dance the
   same dance and you drink the same drink you always drank
   before.
And the piano builds a roof of notes above the world.
And the trumpet weaves a dome of music through space. And
   the drum makes a ceiling over space and time and night.
And then the table-wit. And then the check. Then home
   again to bed.
But first, the stairs.   10

And do you now, baby, as you climb the stairs, do you still
   feel as you felt back there?
Do you feel again as you felt this morning? And the night
   before? And the night before that?

(They say, you know, that first you hear voices. And then
   you have visions, they say. Then, they say, you kick and
   scream and rave.)

Or do you feel: What is one more night in a lifetime of
   nights?
What is one more death, or friendship, or divorce out of two,
   or three? Or four? Or five?   15
One more face among so many, many faces, one more life
   among so many million lives?

But first, baby, as you climb and count the stairs (and they
   total the same) did you, sometime or somewhere, have a
   different idea?
Is this, baby, what you were born to feel, and do, and be?

THE LYRIC AS DRAMA

John Donne   Break of Day

'Tis true, 'tis day, what though it be?
O wilt thou therefore rise from me?
Why should we rise because 'tis light?
Did we lie down because 'twas night?
Love which in spite of darkness brought us hither,   5
Should in despite of light keep us together.

Light hath no tongue, but is all eye;
If it could speak as well as spy,
This were the worst that it could say,
That being well, I fain would stay,   10
And that I loved my heart and honor so,
That I would not from him that had them go.

Must business thee from hence remove?
Oh, that's the worst disease of love,
The poor, the foul, the false, love can   15

Admit, but not the busied man.
He which hath business and makes love doth do
Such wrong as when a married man doth woo.

Break of Day: spoken by a woman.

John Donne   The Flea

Mark but this flea, and mark in this
How little that which thou deniest me is;
It sucked me first, and now sucks thee,
And in this flea our two bloods mingled be.
Thou knowest that this cannot be said   5
A sin, nor shame, nor loss of maidenhead;
    Yet this enjoys before it woo,
    And pampered, swells with one blood made of two,
    And this, alas, is more than we would do.

O stay, three lives in one flea spare,   10
Where we almost, yea more than married are.
This flea is you and I, and this
Our marriage bed and marriage temple is;
Though parents grudge, and you, we're met
And cloistered in these living walls of jet.   15
    Though use make you apt to kill me,
    Let not to that, self-murder added be,
    And sacrilege, three sins in killing three.

Cruel and sudden, hast thou since
Purpled thy nail in blood of innocence?   20
Wherein could this flea guilty be,
Except in that drop which it sucked from thee?
Yet thou triumphest, and sayest that thou
Findest not thyself nor me the weaker now.
    'Tis true. Then learn how false fears be: 25
    Just so much honor, when thou yieldest to me,
    Will waste, as this flea's death took life from thee.

A. E. Housman   "Is My Team Ploughing?"

"Is my team ploughing,
    That I was used to drive
And hear the harness jingle
    When I was man alive?"

Ay, the horses trample,   5
    The harness jingles now;
No change though you lie under
    The land you used to plough.

"Is football playing
    Along the river shore,   10

With lads to chase the leather,
  Now I stand up no more?"

Ay, the ball is flying,
  The lads play heart and soul;
The goal stands up, the keeper   15
  Stands up to keep the goal.

"Is my girl happy,
  That I thought hard to leave,
And has she tired of weeping
  As she lies down at eve?"   20

Ay, she lies down lightly,
  She lies not down to weep:
Your girl is well contented.
  Be still, my lad, and sleep.

"Is my friend hearty,   25
  Now I am thin and pine,
And has he found to sleep in
  A better bed than mine?"

Ay, lad, I lie easy,
  I lie as lads would choose;   30
I cheer a dead man's sweatheart.
  Never ask me whose.

John Crowe Ransom   Piazza Piece

—I am a gentleman in a dustcoat trying
To make you hear. Your ears are soft and small
And listen to an old man not at all;
They want the young men's whispering and sighing.
But see the roses on your trellis dying   5
And hear the spectral singing of the moon—
For I must have my lovely lady soon.
I am a gentleman in a dustcoat trying.

—I am a lady young in beauty waiting
Until my truelove comes, and then we kiss.   10
But what gray man among the vines is this
Whose words are dry and faint as in a dream?
Back from my trellis, sir, before I scream!
I am a lady young in beauty waiting.

Langston Hughes   Mulatto
   I am your son, white man!

Georgia dusk
And the turpentine woods.

One of the pillars of the temple fell.

>   *You are my son!*   5
>   *Like hell!*

The moon over the turpentine woods.
The Southern night
Full of stars,
Great big yellow stars.   10
  What's a body but a toy?
    Juicy bodies
    Of nigger wenches
    Blue black
    Against black fences.   15
    O, you little bastard boy,
    What's a body but a toy?
The scent of pine wood stings the soft night air.
    What's the body of your mother?
Silver moonlight everywhere.   20
    What's the body of your mother?
Sharp pine scent in the evening air.
      A nigger night,
      A nigger joy,
      A little yellow   25
      Bastard boy.
    Naw, you ain't my brother.
    Niggers ain't my brother.
    Not ever.
    Niggers ain't my brother.   30
The Southern night is full of stars,
Great big yellow stars.
        O, sweet as earth,
        Dusk dark bodies
        Give sweet birth   35
To little yellow bastard boys.
      Git on back there in the night,
      You ain't white.
The bright stars scatter everywhere.
Pine wood scent in the evening air.   40
      A nigger night,
      A nigger joy.
    I am your son, white man!
      A little yellow
      Bastard boy.   45

Kenneth Patchen   Do the Dead Know What Time It Is?

The old guy put down his beer.
Son, he said
  (and a girl came over to the table where we were:
  asked us by Jack Christ to buy her a drink.)

Son, I am going to tell you something   5
The like of which nobody ever was told.
   (and the girl said, I've got nothing on tonight:
   how about you and me going to your place?)
I am going to tell you the story of my mother's
Meeting with God.   10
   (and I whispered to the girl: I don't have a room,
   but maybe . . .)
She walked up to where the top of the world is
And He came right up to her and said
So at last you've come home.   15
   (but maybe what?
   I thought I'd like to stay here and talk to you.)
My mother started to cry and God
Put His arms around her.
   (about what?   20
   Oh, just talk . . . we'll find something.)
She said it was like a fog coming over her face
And light was everywhere and a soft voice saying
You can stop crying now.
   (what can we talk about that will take all night?   25
   and I said that I didn't know.)
You can stop crying now.

Malcolm Lowry   Sestina in a Cantina

Scene: A waterfront tavern in Vera Cruz at daybreak.

LEGION

Watching this dawn's mnemonic of old dawning:
Jonquil-coloured, delicate, some in prison,
Green dawns of drinking tenderer than sunset,
But clean and delicate like dawns of ocean
Flooding the heart with pale light in which horrors   5
Stampede like plump wolves in distorting mirrors.

Oh, we have seen ourselves in many mirrors;
Confusing all our sunsets with the dawning,
Investing every tongue and leaf with horrors,
And every stranger overtones for prison,   10
And seeing mainly in the nauseous ocean
The last shot of our life before the sunset.

ST. LUKE (*a ship's doctor*)

How long since you have really seen a sunset?
The mind has many slanting lying mirrors,
The mind is like that sparkling greenhouse ocean   15
Glass-deceptive in the Bengal dawning;
The mind has ways of keeping us in prison,
The better there to supervise its horrors.

SIR PHILLIP SIDNEY

Why do you not, sir, organize your horrors
And shoot them one day, preferably at sunset   20
That we may wake up next day not in prison,
No more deceived by lies and many mirrors,
And go down to the old beach at dawning
To lave away the past in colder ocean?

ST. LUKE

No longer is there freedom on the ocean.   25
And even if there were, he likes his horrors,
And if he shot them would do so at dawning
That he might have acquired some more by sunset,
Breaking them in by that time before mirrors
To thoughts of spending many nights in prison.   30

LEGION

The fungus-colored sky of dawns in prison,
The fate that broods on every pictured ocean,
The fatal conversations before mirrors,
The friends and all the spindly breeds of horrors,
Have shattered by their beauty every sunset   35
And rendered quite intolerable old dawning.

The oxen standing motionless at dawning—
Outside our tavern now, outside our prison—
Red through the wagon wheels, jalousies like sunset,
Swinging now in a sky as calm as ocean,   40
Where Venus hangs her obscene horn of horrors
For us now swaying in a hall of mirrors—

Such horrid beauty maddened all my mirrors,
Has burst in heart's eye sanity of dawning,
No chamber in my house brimful of horrors   45
But does not whisper of some dreadful prison,
Worse than all ships dithering through the ocean
Tottering like drunkards, arms upraised at sunset.

RICHARD III (a barman)

Vain derelict all avid for the sunset!
Shine out fair sun till you have bought new mirrors   50
That you may see your shadow pass the ocean,
And sunken no more pass our way at dawning,
But lie on the cold stone sea floor of some prison,
A chunk of sodden driftwood gnawed by horrors.

LEGION

At first I never looked on them as horrors;   55
But one day I was drinking hard near sunset,
And suddenly saw the world as a giant prison,

Ruled by tossing moose-heads, with hand mirrors,
And heard the voice of the idiot speak at dawning,
And since that time have dwelt beside the ocean.   60

EL UNIVERSAL (EARLY EDITION)

Did no one speak of love beside the ocean,
Have you not felt, even among your horrors,
Granting them, there was such a thing as dawning,
A dawning for man whose star seems now at sunset,
Like million-sheeted scarlet dusty mirrors,   65
But one day must be led out of his prison?

LEGION

I see myself as all mankind in prison,
With hands outstretched to lanterns by the ocean;
I see myself as all mankind in mirrors,
Babbling of love while at his back rise horrors   70
Ready to suck the blood out of the sunset
And amputate the godhead of the dawning.

THE SWINE

And now the dawning drives us from our prison
Into the dawn like sunset, into the ocean,
Bereaving him of horrors, but leaving him his mirrors. . . .   75

1 mnemonic: memory.

POEMS AS SEQUENCE

George Gascoigne   Memories: IV

1

In haste, post haste, when first my wandering mind
Beheld the glistering court with gazing eye,
Such deep delights I seemed therein to find
As might beguile a graver guest than I.
The stately pomp of Princes and their peers   5
Did seem to swim in floods of beaten gold;
The wanton world of young delightful years
Was not unlike a heaven for to behold,
Wherein did swarm, for every saint, a Dame—
So fair of hue, so fresh of their attire,   10
As might excel Dame Cynthia for fame,
Or conquer Cupid with his own desire.
These and such like were baits that blazed still
Before mine eye to feed my greedy will.

2

Before mine eye to feed my greedy will,   15

Gan muster eke mine old acquainted mates,
Who helped the dish of vain delight to fill
My empty mouth with dainty delicates;
And foolish boldness took the whip in hand
To lash my life into this trustless trace,   20
Till all in haste I leaped aloof from land,
And hoist up soil to catch a courtly grace.
Each lingering day did seem a world of woe,
Till in that hapless haven my head was brought;
Waves of wanhope so tossed me to and fro   25
In deep despair to drown my dreadful thought:
Each hour a day, each day a year did seem,
And every year a world my will did deem.

3
And every year a world my will did deem,
Till lo, at last to court now am I come,   30
A seemly swain that might the place beseem,
A gladsome guest embraced of all and some.
Not there content with common dignity,
My wandering eye in haste—yea, post, post, haste—
Beheld the blazing badge of bravery,   35
For want whereof I thought my self disgraced.
Then peevish pride puffed up my swelling heart
To further forth so hot an enterprise,
And comely cost began to play his part
In praising patterns of mine own devise.   40
Thus all was good that might be got in haste,
To prink me up, and make me higher placed.

4
To prink me up and make me higher placed,
All came too late that tarried any time;
Pills of provision pleased not my taste;   45
They made my heels too heavy for to climb.
Me thought it best that boughs of boisterous oak
Should first be shred to make my feathers gay,
Till at the last a deadly dinting stroke
Brought down the bulk with edgetools of decay.   50
Of every farm I then let fly a lease
To feed the purse that paid for peevishness,
Till rent and all were fallen in such disease
As scarce could serve to maintain cleanliness.
The bough, the body, fine, farm, lease, and land—   55
All were too little for the merchant's hand.

5
All were too little for the merchant's hand,
And yet my bravery bigger than his book:
But when this hot account was coldly scanned,
I thought high time about me for to look.   60
With heavy cheer I cast my head aback
To see the fountain of my furious race;

Compared my loss, my living, and my lack,
In equal balance with my jolly grace,
And saw expenses grating on the ground   65
Like lumps of lead to press my purse full oft,
When light reward and recompence were found
Fleeting like feathers in the wind aloft.
These thus compared, I left the court at large;
For why? The gains doth seldom quit the charge.   70

        6
For why? The gains doth seldom quit the charge;
And so say I, by proof too dearly bought.
My haste made waste, my brave and brainsick barge
Did float too fast to catch a thing of nought;
With leisure, measure, mean, and many mo,   75
I might have kept a chair of quiet state,
But hasty heads can not be settled so
Till crooked Fortune give a crabbed mate.
As busy brains must beat on tickle toys,
As rash invention breeds a raw device,   80
So sudden falls do hinder hasty joys;
And as swift baits do fleetest fish entice,
So haste makes waste; and therefore now I say,
No haste but good, where wisdom makes the way.

        7
No haste but good, where wisdom makes the way—   85
For proof whereof, behold the simple snail,
Who sees the soldier's carcass cast away,
With hot assault the castle to assail;
By line and leisure climbs the lofty wall
And wins the turret's top more cunningly   90
Than doughty Dick, who lost his life and all
With hoisting up his head too hastily.
The swiftest bitch brings forth the blindest whelps;
The hottest fevers coldest cramps ensue;
The naked'st need hath ever lastest helps: 95
With Neville, then, I find this proverb true:
That haste makes waste, and therefore still I say
No haste but good, where wisdom makes the way.

16 Gan: began.   eke: also.   25 wanhope: hopelessness.   42
prink: bedeck, preen.   96 Neville: Alexander Neville (1544–
1614), a poet and translator; he had given Gascoigne this proverb
in Latin, whereupon Gascoigne is reputed to have written this
poem.

Carl Sandburg   Four Preludes on Playthings of the Wind

        I
The woman named Tomorrow
sits with a hairpin in her teeth

and takes her time
and does her hair the way she wants it
and fastens at last the last braid and coil   5
and puts the hairpin where it belongs
and turns and drawls; Well, what of it?
My grandmother, Yesterday, is gone.
What of it? Let the dead be dead.

    2
The doors were cedar   10
and the panel strips of gold
and the girls were golden girls
and the panels read and the girls chanted:
    We are the greatest city,
    and the greatest nation: 15
    nothing like us ever was.
The doors are twisted on broken hinges,
Sheets of rain swish through on the wind
    Where the golden girls ran and the panels read:
    We are the greatest city,   20
    the greatest nation,
    nothing like us ever was.

    3
It has happened before.
Strong men put up a city and got
    a nation together,   25
And paid singers to sing and women
    to warble: We are the greatest city,
    the greatest nation,
    nothing like us ever was.

And while the singers sang   30
and the strong men listened
and paid the singers well,
    there were rats and lizards who listened
    . . . and the only listeners left now
    . . . are . . . the rats . . . and the lizards.   35
    And there are black crows
    crying, "Caw, caw,"
    bringing mud and sticks
    building a nest
    over the words carved   40
    on the doors where the panels were cedar
    and the strips on the panels were gold
    and the golden girls came singing:
    We are the greatest city,
    the greatest nation: 45
    nothing like us ever was.

The only singers now are crows crying, "Caw, caw,"
And the sheets of rain whine in the wind and doorways.
And the only listeners now are . . . the rats . . . and the
    lizards.

4
The feet of the rats 50
scribble on the doorsills;
the hieroglyphs of the rat footprints
chatter the pedigrees of the rats
and babble of the blood
and gabble of the breed 55
of the grandfathers and the great-grandfathers
of the rats.

And the wind shifts
and the dust on the doorsills shifts
and even the writing of the rat footprints 60
tells us nothing, nothing at all
   about the greatest city, the greatest nation
   where the strong men listened
   and the women warbled: Nothing like us ever was.

Wallace Stevens   Peter Quince at the Clavier

1
Just as my fingers on these keys
Make music, so the selfsame sounds
On my spirit make a music, too.

Music is feeling, then, not sound;
And thus it is that what I feel, 5
Here in this room, desiring you,

Thinking of your blue-shadowed silk,
Is music. It is like the strain
Waked in the elders by Susanna.

Of a green evening, clear and warm, 10
She bathed in her still garden, while
The red-eyed elders watching, felt

The basses of their beings throb
In witching chords, and their thin blood
Pulse pizzicatti of Hosanna. 15

2
In the green water, clear and warm,
Susanna lay.

She searched
The touch of springs,
And found 20
Concealed imaginings.
She sighed,
For so much melody.

Upon the bank, she stood
In the cool

Of spent emotions.
She felt, among the leaves,
The dew
Of old devotions.

She walked upon the grass,   30
Still quavering.
The winds were like her maids,
On timid feet,
Fetching her woven scarves,
Yet wavering.   35

A breath upon her hand
Muted the night.
She turned—
A cymbal crashed,
And roaring horns.   40

        3
Soon, with a noise like tambourines,
Came her attendant Byzantines.

They wondered why Susanna cried
Against the elders by her side;

And as they whispered, the refrain   45
Was like a willow swept by rain.

Anon, their lamps' uplifted flame
Revealed Susanna and her shame.

And then, the simpering Byzantines
Fled, with a noise like tambourines.   50

        4
Beauty is momentary in the mind—
The fitful tracing of a portal;
But in the flesh it is immortal.

The body dies; the body's beauty lives.
So evenings die, in their green going,   55
A wave, interminably flowing.
So gardens die, their meek breath scenting
The cowl of winter, done repenting.
So maidens die, to the auroral
Celebration of a maiden's choral.   60

Susanna's music touched the bawdy strings
Of those elders; but, escaping,
Left only Death's ironic scraping.
Now, in its immortality, it plays
On the clear viol of her memory,   65
And makes a constant sacrament of praise.

Peter Quince: one of the boorish characters in *A Midsummer Night's Dream.*

John L'Heureux   St. Ignatius Loyola, Founder of the
Jesuits: His Autobiography
[with directions for reading]

1. "The Early Years"
Manresa and the mango trees and the sterile landscape
stretching out like an unimaginative hell.
It was a good place to begin. (Beginnings
always look that way, viewed from the end) The cave bit
came much later after whores and horses and a ball   5
in the knees (for a switch) and some literary quarter-lies.
   [he is resigned]
Well, you work with what you've got.

2. This is a reflection
and you can't expect Palestrina   10
for Christ's sake
when it's only a priest humming while he scans the land-
      scape
casually on a Saturday afternoon
without even a telescope.

3. Yes   well   I suppose   15
it's been a good thirty years—
no acceptance   no warmth   no tenderness   no
(can even a psychiatrist say it seriously,
be serious when he says it?)   no love—
   [he sighs]   20
a good thirty years for writing and thinking
   [he smiles]
and stuff like that.
(It's a tough thing when you're a saint to write
your autobiography)   25

4. "The Augustine Syndrome"
   [to be read only while drinking]

You have to smile a little, don't you?
Because it's funny. It is.
   [am I drinking too much?]
I mean we get off the subject if it hurts. No one
cares about the great excess; it's the little secret dirt   30
they want. The slip.
   [he drinks, frowning]
We're all alike and, what the hell, it all . . .
   [he forgets]
it all comes down to the same thing.   35
You know what I mean? I mean
it's important to be yourself. Your
   [he is drunk]
real

genu-wine (I'm just saying it that way to be funny)   40
self.
   [he knows what they are thinking]
I mean
   [he goes on anyway]
I mean that's the most important thing.   45
I mean,
Christ,
if you're not yourself
   [he screws up his face]
what are you?   50
I mean, really.
But anyway mirrors are very important
in the ultimate scheme of things.
   [he is talking to the mirror]
Ultimately, the most important things   55
are love. I mean that's what they resolve
down to—the important things—love.
And I think that's a very important thing
ultimately.
   [he is lost]   60
I do. I mean—honest to God, no shit—
what are you, what is anybody
except himself? You know?
Excuse me. I have to go to the bathroom.
Even saints have kidneys.   65

5. "Alarums and Fanfares for the King's Supper"

Professional help, Cripes, yes!
You've got a clear mind
and a good body
and being a saint wears the hell out of you.
Out of me   70
is what I mean.
There was this girl,
see,
with long black hair and everything.
(This is complicated, I think)   75
Well, anyhow, her hair was long and black
and always moving
like a black light or a dark water
or a mind looking and looking
but the thing is it was moving   changing   forming   80
(on the wind) a new word
to tell me
ask me
what   what
what do you want   85
what is it
what   what
say it   only say it
then—

you know how it is—   90
the darkness was too much or something
and I said,
hell,
what about having a peanut butter sandwich
for lunch tomorrow   95
while she stood there
handing me pieces of her heart that she had chunked out
with her thumbnail and—
understandably—
she turned away, sick.   100
Well hell, yes.
Bring it on. I could use
some professional help.
    [he lapses]
(Move a little and I'll slip it in)   105

6. "Conversion"

Up on those goddam battlements with the wind
freezing your ass off, you really wonder about things.
You know you've had it anyway
and you say what the hell, dying's not so bad,
it's living screws you up.   110
    [he is factual]
Here you are standing around
waiting to make roast beef out of guys
you don't even know well enough to hate. So they play
the Star Spangled Banner   115
and baby
you fight to the death.
(They say that in the Army. I know. I was in the Army)
So meanwhile I'm back on the battlements
freezing my etceteras   120
when this pistol ball comes whizzing around a corner
and takes my kneecap with it.
They find me among the living,
more or less,
and I am here to tell you all today: 125
    [he proclaims]
support your local draft board in its hour of need.
I did.
My Cardinal, right or wrong.

7. "Interlude"

Purists get upset now   130
that I've dropped control: easy fun, they say, but cheap.
Dear Purists, it wasn't easy;
have you ever tried to drop control?
(Drop, I said. I've never lost anything)
it wasn't fun; hop into the showers   135
at Buchenwald and smile, baby, smile.
(Smiles don't come easy to me. Honest!)
it wasn't cheap; twenty-five bucks an hour

and somebody you'd like to love
treating you like a complicated hernia   *140*
(That's the worst part; it's called living)
Dear Purists, get your non-fucking hands off me.
I've earned my dropped control.

8. "A Philosophical Excursus on 'Gift, Giving, To Give'
   According to St. Thomas' *Commentary on the Sentences*"

A real gift is never something that you need
like teeth   *145*
or a turkey on Thanksgiving
or a pail of money.
A real gift is when you crawl in through my eyes
   [he speaks in a monotone because this is philosophy]
and sit around for longer than you want   *150*
until you forget you're there
and I forget you're there
except sometimes.
A real gift is when that doggy who had everything
sighed and said: *155*
"It's true. I do have everything.
But there must be more to life than just having everything."
You can always tell a real gift
because you know that to keep it you've got to give it away.
(That's how philosophy is; it's difficult)   *160*
And so in this, the income tax season, I discover
I have given you seven non-gifts, three partial-gifts,
and now, I think, one gift.
Non-gifts:
      1. my sex life   *165*
      2. my intellectual life
      3. my emotional life
      4. my mother
      5. my father
      6. my brother   *170*
      7. my hatred, anger, and associated virtues.
Partial-gifts:
      1. the three times we laughed
      2. the love you had already
      3. the weaknesses you had not known about.   *175*
One gift:
      1. Some words, these, which no one ever said
         before—not in this order anyway.
Is this a poem? Hell, no. It's reality, a gift.
You can't keep a gift.   *180*

9. "Spiritual Consolations and the Gift of Tears"

Madam, this requires a little explanation.
   [he is patient throughout, almost]
This water I have drawn, painfully,
out of my eyes,
out of my brain,   *185*
(a doctor got some out of my spine

with needles and a headache)
out of my heart
(which holds very little blood). I have prepared
this water carefully and, as I said, with pain.   190
To be honest,
Madam,
I hoped for holy water.
I had planned a pool, perhaps,
or a fountain   195
(if we can find equipment)
or simply some nice thing. Just a nice good thing.
   [he is almost patient]
and now look.
You've got your beautiful broad-bottomed fat little baby   200
smack on its ass
in the middle of my water.
   [for a moment he forgets the lady's age and rank]
Lady, take your goddam baby quick.
I want my bath water.   205
   [he ponders her mystery]
Besides, how'd you ever get a baby without loving?

10. "Pilgrimage"

   Yes   well   I suppose
it's good to be back. Once you've seen Christ's feet
printed deep   210
in the Rock of the Ascension
you're pretty willing to settle for a Paris grammar school.
   [he—does he sneer?]
(What the hell, it will look romantic in the history books)
And I like kids. They're closer to where   215
it's at.
If it's at anywhere.
   [he pauses, making everybody get serious]
Christ is.
I'd like that in Italics. Because—   220
there's always a because and it never makes sense—
because it's been hard, damned hard.
Thirty years of pressing my goddam Basque nose
against Parisian bakery shoppes
where they put away the cream at three;   225
three years of coming too late for anything
(so laugh; you've got a dirty mind);
thirty years of trying to say to St. Francis
Ex-say-vee-ur
'Frank, I love you; don't get shook'   230
and him trembling like some kind of crazy spastic.
   [he reflects]
Maybe we should start a corporation.
Christ!
(Sometimes you can't tell   235
if they're cursing or blessing)
Stick with me, baby,

and you'll wear mink. Or mourning.
   [he threatens]
Or your face,   240
your own for once,
borne before you like a mask
confusing the hell out of everybody
and when it drops
they'll, all of them, know your absolute control.   245
   [he wonders]
I never thought you had control
and now I see
   [he smiles]
that was the problem . . . thinking. Excuse me.   250
The kids have come
and I've lost my place.
   [he is confused]
At first,
when you're first back, everything   255
is . . .
   [he gropes]
         . . . I almost said
you love me.

David Henderson   Sketches of Harlem

It was Tiny's habit
To go down to the GREAT WHITE WAY
Without understanding the subway ride.

   2
The man asked Bubba to sign
A petition for more fallout shelters.   5
All Bubba wanted to know was
Which way the bomb was coming—
From Washington Heights
Or Sutton Place.

   3
The boy arrived from Mississippi   10
And got a room on Seventh Avenue the same day.
Right away he wrote to Mama:
  "Dear Ma,
   I got up here safely.
   I got me a room in Harlem   15
   and everything is all right."

   4
Black small boy asking Mama
Why the sun shines at night
And she answering that it

Ain't shining at all.   20
"That's a moon."

8 *Washington Heights:* a middle-class, largely Jewish area of New York City, just to the northwest of Harlem.   9 *Sutton Place:* an expensive apartment–residential area of New York City, southeast of Harlem.

Glossary
of Poetical
and Critical
Terms

---

accent The emphasis or stress placed on a poetic syllable; the Greek thesis, or downbeat. An unaccented syllable is the arsis, or upbeat.

accentual verse Verse having a regular number of accents in each line, regardless of placement. Frequent in Anglo-Saxon poetry.

acrostic A poem in which the first letters of each line form a word or pattern. See also *telestich*.

adonic A two-foot meter consisting of a dactyl and a spondee.

Alcaic A lyric meter consisting of four strophes of four lines with four accents in each line.

Alexandrine An iambic hexameter line with caesura after the third iamb.

allegory See *fourfold interpretation*.

alliteration Repetition of similar sounds (usually consonants) at the beginning of words.

ambiguity That which conveys more than one meaning. Its use may be accidental or intentional; it may yield undesirable meanings or relevant nuances which lead to richer interpretation.

amphibrach (or *Cretic*) See *foot*.

amphimacer See *foot*.

Anacreontic A poem concerned with wine and women. Its

four-line stanza rhymes *abab* or *aabb;* each line consists of three trochees plus an additional stressed syllable.

anacrusis   The addition of one or two unaccented syllables at the beginning of a poetic line.

anagoge   See *fourfold interpretation.*

analogue   Something similar to something else, such as two narratives which are not directly related as to source.

anapest   See *foot.*

anaphora   Repetition of a word or phrase at the beginning of a poetic line.

antibacchius   See *foot.*

antispast   See *foot.*

antistrophe   The stanza sung by the Greek chorus as it returns across the stage. See *ode.*

antithesis   Balance and contrast.

Apollonian   The element which suggests moderation, order, and social conformity. It transcends the bodily and sensual. It is associated with classicism and contrasted with the Dionysian element.

apostrophe   Address of something as animate being or of someone absent as though he were present.

archetype   The original pattern from which all things derive. Carl Jung argued the existence of a collective unconscious in men's minds, consisting of numerous experiences (birth, death, perceptions of rising and falling, etc.), and these are reflected in dreams and myths, and thus in literature.

architectonics   Unified structural design of a poem.

arsis   See *accent.*

Asclepiad, Lesser   A classical meter:

$$ --/ -\smile\smile-/ -\smile\smile-/ \ \smile. \ / $$

Asclepiad, Greater   A classical meter:

$$ --/ -\smile\smile-/ -\smile\smile-/ -\smile\smile-/ \ \smile\, . $$

assonance   In words close together, identical vowel sounds but with different following consonants.

aubade   A lyric associated with dawn.

aube   A lyric expressing the woman's regret that dawn is coming and that she and her lover must part.

bacchius   See *foot.*

ballad   A traditional or popular story transmitted in song. It is therefore impersonal in tone and may have abrupt transitions in narrative, when lines have been omitted over the years. The *ballad stanza* is a quatrain of alternating lines of iambic tetrameter and iambic trimeter; the trimeter lines rhyme.

ballade   Frequently a poem of three eight-line stanzas, rhyming *ababbcbC,* and a four-line envoi, rhyming *bcbC.* There are only three rhymes employed, the last line of each stanza and the envoi constituting a refrain.

baroque   An ornate style which almost obscures order or pattern; such literature shows balance but also strain. Compare *mannerism.*

beata ille   See *topiary poem.*

blank verse   Unrhymed iambic pentameter.

burlesque An imitation which aims at amusing through exaggeration of a mannerism or a fault.

caesura A rhythmic break in the verse line; formerly the term was used only when a break occurred within a metrical foot.

canzone A lyric poem usually of several stanzas of fourteen lines plus a commiato (or envoi); the two parts of each stanza are linked by an identical rhyme of the last line of the fronte and the first line of the sirima.

carpe diem A motif counseling enjoyment of one's opportunities and emphasizing the transiency of life. Similar is the motif of *carpe rosam* in which a rose symbolizes present beauty or youth.

catachresis Deliberate misuse of words whereby meanings are twisted or seemingly incompatible (e.g., "blind mouths").

catalexis Omission of one or more final unaccented syllables.

chiasmus A crossover of words, phrases, or sound so that the first part is balanced by inversion of the words of the second part (e.g., "Of married Maid, and Virgin Mother born").

choriambus See *foot*.

classic That attitude which prefers the probable, unified, and static. Older literary models and "nature" (i.e., human nature) are imitated. Opposed to romantic.

concrete poem A nonverbal poem creating a picture of an idea or emotion by the placement of letters on the page.

closed couplet A heroic couplet (two rhyming lines of iambic pentameter) containing a complete thought often with antithesis between the lines.

complaint A lyric poem in which a lover bemoans his loved one's indifference.

conceit A metaphor which is considered extreme or particularly striking. The metaphysical conceit was usually novel and often furnished an image integral to the unity of the poem.

consonance In words close together, identical consonant sounds but with different preceding vowel sounds.

couplet Two successive verse lines which are equivalent in meter and/or which rhyme.

dactyl See *foot*.

dead metaphor One which has lost its figurative value (e.g., the *foot* of a hill).

débat A medieval literary form in which two speakers dispute a topic.

decasyllablic A ten-syllable line of verse, often preferred as a description of a blank verse line rather than iambic pentameter.

decorum A tenet of style that requires that propriety must not be violated. Involved are words, metaphors, tone, and character; style must be appropriate to speaker, subject, occasion, and audience.

diaeresis The break in a poetic line when the end of a metrical foot coincides with the end of a word.

diction   Choice of words, phraseology.

dimeter   A two-foot line of verse.

Dionysian   The element which suggests excess, frenzy, and self-assertion, and which explores new ideas. It emphasizes the bodily and sensual. It is associated with romanticism and contrasted with the Apollonian element.

dirge   A short elegy lamenting a death.

discordia concors   An image yoking generally dissimilar things together on the basis of proposed points of similarity. The image suggests that something can be understood through examination of its opposite.

dissociation of sensibility   The separation of intellect and feeling such as T. S. Eliot argued arose in poetry of the later seventeenth century and after.

distich   Two lines of verse which are similar in structure.

dithyramb   An emotional choral hymn in honor of Dionysius, god of wine. It became any wild or emotional song.

doggerel   Crude and usually humorous verse with irregular meter and strained rhyme.

donnee   The assumption upon which a literary work proceeds; a basic idea which shapes an action.

dramatic monologue   A poem spoken by a single fictional character to himself or to someone else (or a group) whose presence can be discerned.

echo verse   A poem in which the final syllables of each line (or a number of lines) are restated with different meanings.

eclogue   A pastoral poem in which one or more shepherds speak.

elegiac stanza   An iambic pentameter quatrain rhyming *abab*.

elegy   A poem originally in alternating lines of dactylic hexameter and dactylic pentameter (the elegiac couplet). In English poetry it is often represented by iambic pentameter rhyming couplets. Themes are love or praise of living or dead, and therefore mournful contemplation or funeral lament. As funeral lament it was often a pastoral (or eclogue).

elision   The omission or slurring of part of a word ("ne'er").

emblematic verse   A poem accompanied by a drawing (an emblem) whose significance is interpreted; it is often allegoric. See also *shaped verse*.

empathy   Projection of the reader to assume the pathos of the author or characters of the poem.

end rhyme   That which occurs at the end of poetic lines.

end-stopped line   That which requires a definite pause in rhythm and meaning at its termination.

enjambment   The running over of one line into the next because closely related words appear in both lines; a run-on line.

envoi   A concluding stanza of a poem, dedicating the poem to someone, or a poem of farewell.

epic   A long narrative poem, often divided into discrete sections, with a heroic figure and employing a number of conventions. It usually begins *in medias res* (i.e., in the midst of the full narrative); it is built on long similes and stock epithets; it includes scenes of warfare and epic games; and it involves gods and their intervention in man's life. The style is high (elevated and elaborate). Its subject matter is usually legendary and historically significant.

epigram A short poem, often witty, presenting a pointed idea tersely.

epistle A letter; the verse epistle is a poem couched in the form of a letter. It is epideictic (complimentary) and/or paranectic (instructive).

epitaph A burial inscription.

epithalamion A lyric poem, usually joyous and ceremonial, in honor of a bride and/or bridegroom. It praises marriage and a particular marriage.

epitrite See *foot*.

epode The stanza sung by a Greek chorus when standing still. See *ode*.

epyllion A short epic poem with emphasis on the pictorial; equated with idyll.

falling meter Meter in which unaccented syllables appear at the end of the poetic feet (as trochaic or dactylic verse).

feminine ending A verse line whose final syllable is unaccented.

feminine rhyme A verse line whose final two syllables rhyme.

figurative language Words and phrases which have meanings beyond their surface or literal meaning. A trope (or figure of speech) suggests such meanings through connotations, through relationships created between words or ideas, through ambiguity, or through suggestive associations. See also *vehicle*.

flyting A quarrelsome exchange of words.

foot A metric unit of one or more syllables.

Two Syllables		Three Syllables		Four Syllables	
iamb	˘ —	amphibrach	˘ — ˘	antispast	˘ — — ˘
pyrrhic	˘ ˘	amphimacer	— ˘ —	choriambus	— ˘ ˘ —
spondee	— —	anapest	˘ ˘ —	epitrite (three longs and one short in any combination)	
trochee	— ˘	antibacchius	— — ˘		
		bacchius	˘ — —	paeon (three shorts and one long in any combination)	
		dactyl	— ˘ ˘		
		molossus	— — —	proceleusmaticus	˘ ˘ ˘ ˘
		tribrach	˘ ˘ ˘		

form Structural pattern or arrangement of content; genre.

fourfold interpretation The literal, allegoric, tropological (moral) and anagogic interpretations of a work. Allegory presents meaning metaphorically; characters and actions are symbols of abstract qualities or ideas. There is an equivalency between symbol and its metaphoric meaning. Narrative is often present as is moral significance. Tropology also presents meaning metaphorically, but the interpretation is a coherent statement of a moral conclusion or principle. There are no simple equivalencies. The interpretation arises primarily from the actions and words of the characters. Anagoge too presents meaning metaphorically, but the interpretation is mystical or spiritual, leading to an upbuoying of the spirit and a universal vision. The interpretation emerges primarily from the words of the characters; often Christ and his doctrines figure in the interpretation.

fourteener A line of seven iambs.

free verse (or *vers libre*) Verse thta does nto follow a fixed metrical pattern; the unit is the stanza.

georgic A poem treating rural life, particularly the labor of farming.

glyconic A classical meter: $\_\_/\_\cup\cup\_/\cup\_.$

haiku A Japanese verse form of seventeen syllables, arranged in three lines of five, seven, and five syllables.

hemistich A half line of poetry, preceding or following the caesura.

hendecasyllabic (*Phalaecean*) A verse line of eleven syllables.

heptameter A verse line of seven feet.

heroic couplet See *closed couplet*.

hexameter A verse line of six feet.

hiatus A pause caused by two consecutive similar sounds (e.g., "till life falters").

hieroglyphic A general term encompassing emblematic, patterned, or shaped verse; a poem which presents a symbol by its line positioning and arrangement.

Homeric simile A lengthy simile which includes a number of parallels between the likened things.

hovering stress A stress equally divided between two adjacent syllables.

Hudibrastic verse Doggerel in iambic tetrameter couplets used for mock-heroic purposes.

hymn A song in praise of God or heroes, usually sung by a chorus.

hyperbole An exaggerated, extravagant, or flowery metaphor. Also called overstatement.

hypermeter An additional unstressed syllable (or more) at the beginning or end of a line.

iamb See *foot*.

ictus A poetical accent.

idyll A short picturesque poem, usually pastoral; sometimes an *epyllion*.

image An impression or picture engaging one of the senses so as to suggest further meaning or sensations. Imagery is a series of similar images throughout a literary work or within a section of the work; if these images are directly related to one another (and particularly when concentrated), they constitute an image cluster.

Imagist One of a group of poets (c. 1912 and later) who

disavowed "poetic" language and subjects and who presented details in a concentrated concrete image.

imitation (mimesis) Re-creation of a form (e.g., heroic action) in a substance (e.g., a poem) which is not natural for it; it thus reflected the original without being identical in substance (e.g., actual movement). Also, a loose copy of another poem.

intentional fallacy The alleged error of interpreting a poem according to the author's intention, which is seldom really known.

inversion A foot substituted for another with reversed accents; e.g., a trochee for an iamb (_ ◡ / ◡ _).

invocation A prayer for help or inspiration; often addressed to a deity.

ionic A classical meter: _ _ / ◡ ◡ (*a majore*); ◡ ◡ / _ _ (*a minore*).

irony A disparity between what is said and what is meant, or between what is intended and what is achieved. Verbal irony exists when the statement is negated or modified by implication within the statement. Socratic irony exists when ignorance or humility is assumed in order to confute. Sophoclean irony exists when the reader is aware of the outcome of an action or statement although the doer or speaker expects something quite different.

kenning A compound metaphor standing for a single noun.

lai A short narrative to be sung to musical accompaniment.

leonine rhyme Rhyme of the word preceding the caesura with the last word of the line.

litotes A form of understatement which affirms an idea by denying its opposite (e.g., "no mean accomplishment").

logaoedic A classical meter combining various feet (e.g., dactyls and trochees).

lyric Originally, a poem to be sung; now a short poem, expressing emotion or meditation.

macaronic verse Verse containing a mixture of languages or words resembling foreign words.

madrigal A short lyric to be sung by several unaccompanied voices; frequently pastoral.

mannerism Excessive adherence to peculiarities of style. Conventions appear in distorted or unusual form, and patterns are altered in the course of their use.

Marinism Flamboyant mannerism, almost baroque.

metaphor A direct comparison by identification of two dissimilar things.

metaphysical poetry The usual designation for the poetry of John Donne and his followers (both in the seventeenth and the twentieth centuries). It implies far-fetched conceits, colloquial style, intellectualism and ingenuity, some obscurity, and the yoking of opposites.

meter The pattern of metrical feet in a line or stanza.

metonymy The use of one word for an associated word (e.g., "deep" for ocean).

mimesis See *imitation*.

mixed metaphor   A combination of two different metaphors; the effect is often humorous.

mock epic (*mock heroic*).   An amusing work that treats a trivial theme in a lofty style; comic effect lies in the disparity between them.

molossus   See *foot*.

monody   A lament by a single person; see *elegy*.

monometer   A verse line of one foot.

monomyth   The myth of Christ, or of death (falling) and resurrection (rising). See *myth*.

motif   A recurrent word, phrase, situation, object, or idea.

myth   A broad, basic image that informs life and gives it philosophic meaning. Any idea, true or false, which is generally accepted and which helps to explain something otherwise inexplicable. As mythology, a narrative of the origins of life and/or of the deeds of superhuman beings.

mythopoeic   Creating or employing myth as the underlying structural or referential basis for a poem.

narrative   A story, a running account of a series of events.

neoclassic   The attitude that older authors (especially those of Greece and Rome) are superior and are therefore to serve as models. See *classic* for full definition.

objective correlative   That by which an author expresses an emotion through a set of objects, a situation, or a chain of events so that the emotion is evoked in the reader.

occasional poem   A poem written for a particular occasion or event.

octave   The first eight lines of a sonnet.

octosyllabic   A line of eight syllables.

ode   A song in honor of gods or heroes, originally; a lyric, usually long. The Pindaric ode consists of several stanzas, each stanza containing a strophe, an antistrophe, and an epode. Lines are of uneven length as are each of the three parts. The Horatian ode, celebrating love or patriotism, consisted of several four-line stanzas. The irregular ode developed in England as a series of stanzas of varying lengths and of varying line lengths, supposedly similar to the Pindaric. A type of Horatian ode also developed consisting of several stanzas of the same length and line pattern. The English ode is a single stanza (seldom two) that is irregular in line length and pattern.

onomatopoeia   The use of words whose pronunciation resembles the sound of that object or idea being named.

ottava rima   An eight-line stanza of iambic pentameter, rhyming *abababcc*.

oxymoron   A yoking of two seemingly contradictory words or ideas (e.g., "the burning lake").

paean   An ode invoking Apollo as god of medicine; later a hymn of praise or joy.

paeon   See *foot*.

paradox   Usually a statement or situation that seems self-contradictory, or one that presents an insoluble problem.

parody   An amusing composition that imitates the style of another work.

pastoral   A poem dealing with shepherds, literally or figuratively.

pathetic fallacy   The assignment of human feelings to inanimate things.

pathos   The quality that evokes sympathy or sorrow or pity; suffering, experienced by the passive and innocent; strong emotional feeling.

pentameter   A verse line of five feet.

persona   The character in a literary work who is not the author, but who supplies the voice relating the work. A persona evidences an attitude toward his subject, himself, and his audience.

personification   The assigning of human characteristics to abstract ideas or inanimate objects

Petrarchan   See *sonnet.*

Phalaecean   See *hendecasyllabic.*

Pherecratean   A classical meter: $\breve{\times} = / - \smile \smile / \_ \breve{\smile}$.

poulter's measure   A rhyming couplet of iambic hexameter and iambic septameter.

proceleusmaticus   See *foot.*

pruning poem   A poem which uses in successive lines the last word of a previous line, but with part of that word cut off; e.g., the respective use of "Adam," "dam," and "am" at the ends of three successive lines, etc.

proem   A short introduction to a poem. See also *invocation.*

prosody   Generally equivalent to *versification;* it stresses technical aspects.

pyrrhic   See *foot.*

pythiambic   A classical meter consisting of couplets of dactylic hexameter and iambic trimeter.

quantitative verse   Verse dependent upon the length of time required for pronunciation of a syllable; the number of long sounds (accents) depends on the meter, but the number of syllables is immaterial. For the most part, syllables are long if their vowels are long or if they end with a consonant (a closed syllable); syllables are short if their vowels are short or if they end with a vowel sound (an open syllable).

quatrain   Any four-line stanza.

refrain   Words, phrases, or lines repeated as intervals throughout the poem.

rhyme   The repetition of similar sounds in words occupying similar positions within a poem (usually at the ends of lines). Eye rhyme occurs when the words look alike but do not sound alike (e.g., "tough," "though").

rhyme royal   A stanza of seven lines of iambic pentameter, rhyming *aababbcc.*

rhythm   Repetition of the rise and fall of verse sound; the pattern thus established.

rime riche   Rhyme of the same words or homonyms.

rising meter   Rhythm created by an accent's falling on the last syllable of a foot.

rococo   A style employing extreme ornateness and curvilinear patterns; symmetry is frequent.

romantic   That attitude which prefers the improbable, varied, and dynamic. Attributes are deep emotion, originality, spontaneity, and individualistic qualities of the author. Opposed to classic.

rondeau   A verse form of thirteen to fifteen lines with eight syllables per line, employing two rhymes. Specific rhyme words are not repeated, and a shorter refrain, derived from the opening phrase, appears at the middle and end.

rondel   A verse form of thirteen lines, employing two rhymes. Some lines may be repeated in various positions, and a fourteenth line may repeat the second refrain.

roundelay   Used for any verse form accompanied by music and using a refrain.

run-on line   See *enjambment*.

sapphic   A classical meter of four lines, consisting of three eleven-syllable lines and a fourth five-syllable line.

satire   Ridicule or criticism of human folly, leading to contempt or amusement. There is probably less intent to reform than is usually stated by critics. Menippean satire is generally philosophic and moral, and attacks pretension. Horatian satire is gentle and attacks foibles. Juvenalian satire is bitter and attacks vices.

scansion   Analysis of poetic pattern of accents, feet, and meter.

sentimental   Generally a pejorative term indicating an excess of tender emotion or disproportionate amount of sentiment. Evil is denied or overlooked, for man is assumed to be innately good; forgiveness is tenderly given, primarily through expectation that the offending person has been reformed.

septenary   A line of seven feet.

sestet   The last six lines of a sonnet.

sestina   A verse form of six unrhymed six-line stanzas, with each stanza using the same terminal words arranged in varying (but fixed) patterns; a three-line envoi repeats the six words in medial and terminal positions. Pattern: 1, 2, 3, 4, 5, 6; 6, 1, 5, 2, 4, 3; 3, 6, 4, 1, 2, 5; 5, 3, 2, 6, 1, 4; 4, 5, 1, 3, 6, 2; 2, 4, 6, 5, 3, 1; 2-5, 4-3, 6-1.

shaped verse   A verse form which creates an image of the subject or meaning of the poem (such as George Herbert's "Easter Wings"). It may suggest an idea (such as the idea of falling by having parts of the verse line descend) or meaning through eye-movement (such as "Mile-" at the end of one line and "End Green" at the beginning of the next in Milton's *Tetrachordon* sonnet). See also *emblematic verse* and *hieroglyphic*.

simile   A direct comparison between two unlike things; introduced by "like" or "as."

skeltonics   A poem of irregular short verse lines with two or three accents per line.

slant rhyme   Rhyming of words with similar rather than identical consonant or vowel sounds.

sonnet   A fourteen-line verse form (although the term is used for some longer or shorter poems) in iambic pentameter, usually dealing with love or the brevity of life, but since Milton, also dealing with patriotic, moral, or philosophic themes. The Petrarchan or Italian sonnet has an octave (setting forth the background or premise) and a sestet (setting forth the resolution). Its rhyme scheme is *abba, abba, cdd, ccd* (or *cde, cde*); other variations are possible in the sestet. The sestet is also known as the volta, or turn. The Shakespearean or English sonnet consists of three quatrains (the first two setting forth the background or premise, and the third giving the resolution) and a couplet (summarizing the conclusion epigrammatically). Its rhyme scheme is often *abab, cdcd, efef, gg,* but variations are frequent. The Spenserian sonnet reduces the break between the second and third quatrains. The Miltonic sonnet, basically Petrarchan, often shifts the turn to a medial position (e.g., in line eight or line nine), and thus creates a more unbroken form.

Spenserian stanza   A nine-line stanza of eight iambic pentameter lines, rhyming *ababbcbc,* and one alexandrine using the *c* rhyme.

spondee   See *foot.*

sprung rhythm   A verse rhythm dependent upon the number of accents rather than syllables in each line; an accent begins the line, but accents may be followed by other accented syllables or by one to four unaccented syllables.

stanza   A repeated division of a poem, usually unified in thought and form.

stock response   A reader's stereotyped reaction to some element within the poem.

stress   See *accent.*

strophe   The stanza sung by the Greek chorus as it moves across the stage away from the chorus. See *ode.*

submerged metaphor   That in which both terms are not stated although the identification is clear.

style   Mode of expression, implying the author's attitude toward his subject and his reader. It depends on the words, images, or ideas presented, the ways in which they are presented, including devices of expression, and the tone which is established. Classically certain standards of style were expected according to genre and decorum. For example, the high (or grand) style was correct for epic; the middle (or mean) style was proper for lyrics such as the ode; and the low (or plain) style was appropriate for satire or pastoral.

syllabic verse   Verse measured by the number of syllables in each line.

symbol   Something that stands for something else; equivalencies are involved. The symbol is concrete and real, but it or its qualities reveal the abstract or invisible world. A symbolist is one who expresses the unknown world through a series of symbols drawn from life experience.

synaeresis   The blending of two consecutive vowels, normally distinct, into one syllable (e.g., "sweet" as one syllable). Compare *elision* and *synalepha*.

synalepha   Omission of the first vowel sound when two vowels are contiguous or their fusion (e.g., "to other" as "tother").

syncope   Omission of letters or syllables from the middle of a word.

synecdoche   Use of a part to represent the whole (e.g., "five dollars a head").

synesthesia   The blending of several sense reactions into a single image.

tanka   A Japanese verse form of thirty-one syllables in five lines, arranged as five, seven, five, seven, and seven syllables.

tail rhyme   Rhyming of short lines when alternating with longer lines.

telestich   A poem in which the last letters of each line form a word or pattern. See also *acrostic*.

tenor   The real subject of a metaphor or symbol; it is that which the *vehicle* (which see) represents.

tension   The relation set up between seemingly opposed elements; for example, the differences in rhythm created by rhyme on the one hand and overflowing thought on the other, or by image and the thought it suggests.

tercet   A three-line stanza.

terza rima   An interlocking rhyme scheme in tercets and ending in a rhymed couplet: *aba, bcb, cdc, . . .*

tetrameter   A verse line of four feet.

texture   The quality of a poem through the study of its imagery, meter, symbols, sound, etc., as opposed to larger issues of design or structure.

thesis   See *accent*.

threnody   A funeral lament; less formal and shorter than the elegy.

tone   The attitude of the author toward his subject and his reader as inferred by the reader.

topiary poem   A poem describing a garden (archetypally Eden); it employs the *beata ille* (or *beata vir*) theme (the happy man). Also used for *shaped verse*.

topographical poem   A poem praising a particular place (such as a noble's estate) or one in which the author surveys a geographic area (as Pope's *Windsor Forest*); often it is a vehicle for critical comment.

topos   (plural *topoi*)   A place or occasion which supplies an organizing or structural principle for a poem.

transferred epithet   An adjective joined to a noun that it does not logically modify (e.g., "bleeding war").

travesty   A poem treating a lofty theme in trivial terms.

tribrach   See *foot*.

trimeter   A verse line of three feet.

triolet   A verse of eight lines in which the first line is used three times. There are only two rhymes, and the second line also recurs as a refrain.

triplet A three-line stanza.

tristich A three-line stanza, constituting a full poem.

trochee See *foot*.

trope See *figurative language*.

truncation See *catalexis*.

type A person or thing regarded as a symbol of someone or something else; specifically the prefiguring in the Old Testament of persons and events in the New Testament. Now used generally regardless of time though with religious significance.

typology The theory of types, particularly of the prefiguring of Christ.

ubi sunt A motif emphasizing the transiency of life and human glory ("where are they?" that once were beautiful or powerful).

understatement A statement that says less than it implies; the opposite of hyperbole.

unity Coherence where all parts work together and jointly contribute to the whole. Organic unity implies that no part is separable from another without fundamental damage.

vehicle The figurative subject of a metaphor or symbol; it is a concrete, familiar symbol. See *tenor*.

vers de société Graceful, light, sophisticated lyric poetry; it does not employ satire or broad humor.

vers libre See *free verse*.

versification The study of verse, meter, and form.

villanelle A verse form consisting of five three-line stanzas and one four-line stanza. Only two rhymes are used, and the first and last lines of the first stanza each appear three times more in successive stanzas.

virelay An indefinite verse form which varies in number of lines per stanza and in the number of stanzas. Usually it employs two rhymes only and a refrain; if more rhymes are introduced, the new rhyme is picked up in the following stanza, and a return to the *a* rhyme completes the poem.

voice See *persona*.

zeugma The use of a word to modify or govern two words although it makes sense with only one.

Author,
Title,
and First-line
Index

———————